The GOLF COURSE Guide TO THE BRITISH ISLES

The GOLF COURSE Guide TO THE BRITISH ISLES

BY DONALD STEEL OF THE SUNDAY TELEGRAPH

PUBLISHED BY COLLINS
WITH THE
Daily Telegraph

First published 1968
Seventh revised edition 1986
Reprinted 1986

Maps drawn by Kazia Kram and Michael Shand and revised by Terry Andrews

ISBN 0 00 434159 7

Phototypeset by Presentia Art, Horsham
Printed in Great Britain by Redwood Burn, Trowbridge

Contents

Foreword

It is almost twenty years since the first edition of the Golf Course Guide was published. In that period, something like a million new golfers have taken up the game in Great Britain and Ireland; so you might say that the need for a catalogue of courses is greater than ever.

If they haven't already done so, now is the time for new golfers to go in search of the incomparable variety of courses which lie within these shores. Golf is so much more fortunate than other sports where one football pitch, tennis court or swimming pool is much the same as another. They lack the aesthetic delights that mean so much to golfers, good and bad.

For the seventh edition, the Guide has undergone something of a facelift – a new compact look with a new sample of essays and a novel miscellany of design oddities, although the purpose of the Guide is still the same. It allows readers to know where they will be welcome and how much a round might cost. And it also provides help in getting to the courses.

I see from the first edition in 1968 that 18 holes at Ganton cost £1 while a weekly ticket at Turnberry set you back 50 shillings. Nowadays, a new golf ball costs something in between. The pound in your pocket is not what it was but it certainly hasn't checked the surge in the popularity of the game and I hope that, in its own way, this Guide will add to that popularity.

Finally, my grateful thanks to club secretaries for filling in our forms and for supplying the information. Without them there would be no Guide.

Donald Steel
March 1986.

Golf Courses and their Design Oddities

There is a modern belief that all championship courses must have a par of 72, contain four par 5s and four par 3s, and be not less than 7000 yards long. It is as crazy a notion as maintaining that all loaves of bread should be the same size and shape. Choice is a matter of personal taste. However, the chief fault, where courses are concerned, lies in the overworked and misused word 'championship'.

A definition of a championship course is one on which a championship has been played. Not will be, may be, or should have been – and not just a tournament either. A common phrase describing new courses is 'championship standard'; but who decides? On the other hand, it can be argued that the Wiltshire Girls championship is as much a championship as the US Open and that it is misleading to apply the same cachet.

To some extent that is true, but every course in the world, indeed every hole on every course, is different and it is the lack of any set pattern in their layout which makes them so. For example, the Old course at St Andrews, the most famous of all, has only two par 5s and two par 3s; and you play seven holes before reaching the first short hole. Some longish courses have no par 5s. Many courses begin or end with a short hole. A few begin **and** end with a short hole; others may have a total of five or six. The Red course at the Berkshire is made up of six threes, six fours and six fives.

Largely to illustrate these inconsistencies, and largely for my own amusement, I have prepared a list of some of the courses covered by this Guide which may help to explode a few myths. It is not claimed to be a complete list and readers may wish to prepare their own categories next time they are flying the Atlantic, tossing and turning at night, under the hair dryer or bored with a lecture.

18-hole courses over 5800 yards beginning with a par 3

Royal Lytham and St Annes, Royal Mid-Surrey, Berkshire (Blue), Liphook, Hayling Island, Addington, Southport and Ainsdale, West Cornwall, Longcliffe, Ashburnham, Churston, Huntercombe, Purley Downs, Meyrick Park, City of Derry, Peebles, Dartford, West Bowling, Wearside, Llandudno (Maesdu), Livingston, Royal Norwich, Skips, Colville Park, Houldsworth, Llanymynech, Whitchurch (Cardiff), Withington, Knole Park.

18-hole courses over 5800 yards ending with a par 3

Berkshire (Red), Moor Park (High), Royal St David's, St Pierre, Killarney, Lindrick, Sandy Lodge, Goodwood, Piltdown, Sandiway, Parkstone, Chelmsford, Boyce Hill, Brora, Kirkcaldy, Dunwood Manor, Nottingham City, Glamorganshire (Penarth), Mount Oswald, Airdrie, Downes Crediton, Dougalston, Dunstable Downs, Erewash Valley, Louth, Saffron Walden, Fortrose and Rosemarkie, Sickleholme, Bremhill Park, Cold Ashby, Ellesmere, Ashford (Kent), Milford Haven, Alloa, Carlyon Bay, West Lothian, Royal Eastbourne, Howley Hall, Northcliffe, Wallsend, Barnard Castle, Kilsyth Lennox, Chapel-en-le-Frith, Worksop, Hoebridge, Padeswood and Buckley, Stoke by Nayland (both courses), Breightmet, Great Barr, Dewsbury, Wetherby, Tredegar Park, Courtown, Bandon, Cawder, Prestwick St Nicholas, Old Padeswood, Ryton, Langley Park, Royal Guernsey.

18-hole courses beginning and ending with a par 3.
Hawick, Didsbury, Bingley St Ives, , Southwold, Bearsted.

18-hole course with four consecutive par 3s
Clober

18-hole courses with three consecutive par 3s
Chipstead, Callander, Ilfracombe, Betws-y-coed (twice)

18-hole courses over 5800 yards with consecutive par 3s
Cruden Bay, Machrihanish, West Sussex, Sandy Lodge, Elgin, Brancepeth Castle, Stoneham, North Oxford, Potters Bar, Haywards Heath, Glamorganshire (Penarth), Consett and District, Birr, Barnard Castle, Erewash Valley, Bandon, Royal Jersey, Knott End, Linlithgow, Harburn, Tain, Waterlooville, Tredegar Park, Kidderminster, Royal Epping Forest, Brough, Burntisland, Royal Eastbourne, Balmoral, Willesley Park, Bishop Auckland.

Courses over 6000 yards with more than five par 3s
Berkshire (Red) (6), Sandy Lodge (6), Darlington (6).

18-hole courses with less than three par 3s
St Andrews (Old), Elie.

Courses over 6,000 yards with no par 5s
Aldeburgh, Elie.

Courses where first short hole comes at the 9th Blyth, Royal Cromer, Torquay, Maryport, Breightmet, Bremhill Park, **8th** St Andrews (Old), Ratho Park, Sand Moor, Royal Eastbourne, Shandon Park, Blainroe, West Kent, **7th** Wells, Western Gailes, Cork (Little Island), Great Lever and Farnworth, Shifnal.

Courses where last short hole comes at 10th
Furness, **11th** St Andrews (Old), Elie, **12th** Royal Dublin, Bishop Auckland, Bishop's Stortford, Woodhall Spa and Royal Lytham and St Annes.

Open, Amateur or national championship courses with only two par 5s
St Andrews (Old), Turnberry, Southerness, Royal Aberdeen, Royal Dornoch, Prestwick, Western Gailes, Ganton, Moortown, Royal St George's, Sunningdale (Old).

Courses with three successive par 5s
Bishop Auckland (2nd to 4th), West Berkshire (13th to 15th), Sutton Coldfield (5th to 7th), Cleckheaton and District (6th to 8th), Whitburn (7th to 9th), Monmouthshire (6th to 8th).

Courses over 7000 yards West Berkshire, The Belfry (Brabazon), Thorpe Wood, West Malling.

Holes under 100 yards Erewash Valley (4th, 89 yds), Bridport and West Dorset (2nd, 93 yds), Dun Laoghaire (7th, 95 yds), Ilfracombe (4th, 81 yds).

Publisher's note

For easy reference the country has been divided into 28 areas and each area has been given an identifying letter from A to Z, then AA and BB. Within these areas the courses are arranged alphabetically and numbered, starting from 1 in each new area. There is a map at the start of each section which shows the location of the golf courses within that section identified by the number given to each course. The outline map opposite shows the 28 areas within the book and the index at the back of the book (page 301) lists each golf course and gives its identifying letter and number for any reference in case of doubt.

All the information in this book has been compiled with the help of club secretaries. Information on subjects such as green fees is liable to change quickly and the publishers would welcome letters from club secretaries or golfers finding any discrepancy between details given in the guide and their own experiences. It should be noted that many green fees are subject to V.A.T. and that weekend rates usually apply on public holidays also.

The distribution of golf courses into grouped county areas has generally been done on the basis of the address. This has resulted in some courses, particularly around London and other major cities, being included in 'wrong' areas. Reference to the index will clear up any confusion and show the identifying letter and number under which each course is located.

Area Map Reference

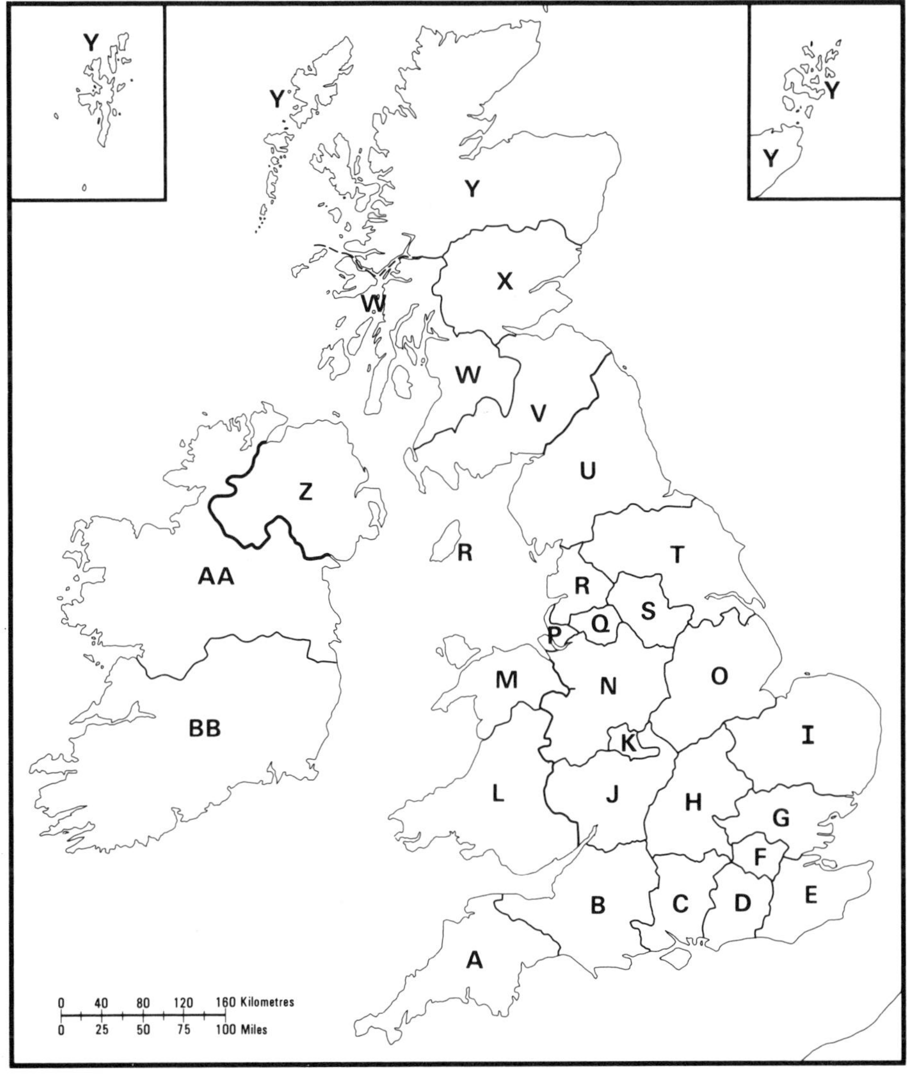

A Cornwall, Devon and Channel Islands

Everybody has heard of Westward Ho! but not everyone who ought to has played there. Modern championships at national level have passed it by more on the grounds of its inaccessibility and a lack of accommodation than any lack of quality as a test of golf. Westward Ho! is the oldest seaside course in England and, as such, is worthy of special recognition.

It is no ordinary place. In fact, a visit there is something of a pilgrimage. It was at the Royal North Devon Club that Horace Hutchinson and J.H. Taylor learned their golf and it is interesting that, on leaving school at the age of 11, one of Taylor's first jobs was as a boot boy in the home of Horace Hutchinson's father. Later, Taylor became one of the world's leading players and ended his days as President of the Club. He described the view from his cottage in Northam as 'the finest in Christendom'.

It may be thought that much has changed in over 120 years of the Club's history but Westward Ho! was a design of nature and nowhere, except perhaps St Andrews or Prestwick, is there a more natural setting for the game.

One of its charms is that nobody has attempted to up-date it and, in the memorable match played to celebrate the Club's centenary in 1964, Max Faulkner and Christy O'Connor looked thoroughly at home wearing the costume and using the equipment familiar to Taylor in his early days.

The area abounds in splendid holiday golf and there is much rewarding exploring to be done. In talking about Saunton, Westward Ho!'s distinguished neighbour across the water, one has to use the most exalted terms. It is the finest course in the south-west, one of the finest in the country – an Open championship course in any other region.

It has hosted several notable occasions but it is also a paradise for botanists, bird watchers and, when the sun shines, bathers. The beach, fringed by the golfing dunes, is superb and, as such, is ideal for a short stay or simply as a stopping place en route for Cornwall.

The journey over the county border into Cornwall is much easier to attempt in the imagination than on crowded summer roads. Cornwall has many pleasant courses including St Enodoc, Trevose, a wonderful holiday centre immensely popular with families, Bude, Newquay, Lelant and Carlyon Bay.

Most have a seaside setting, but for lovers of inland golf there is little better than the Manor House Hotel course at Moretonhampstead on the edge of Dartmoor in Devon, especially the treacherous charm of the first nine holes. With a fine hotel right on the doorstep there is no urge to move far, but the East Devon Club at Budleigh Salterton is excellent and praise, too, for Thurlestone, Torquay and Churston with its lovely views of Torbay.

The Jersey courses are well known to me, Royal Jersey and La Moye making a splendid foil for each other, La Moye on its western headland and Royal Jersey much closer to sea level at the other end of the island.

With nine holes at St Clements, Jersey is better served numerically than Guernsey but Royal Guernsey, described elsewhere, is highly popular. My late partner, Frank Pennink, was responsible for the nine holes on Alderney and was very pleased with the way they turned out, a view supported by many who have sampled their charm.

A1 Alderney

☎ Alderney (048 182) 2835
Routes des Carriers, Alderney, Channel Islands.
1 mile E of St Annes.
Undulating seaside course.
9 holes, 2528 yards, S.S.S.32
Double rounds for 18 S.S.S.65
Course designed by Frank Pennink.
Visitors: welcome at all times, except competition days.
Green fees: weekdays £6 per day, weekends and Bank Holidays £7; 1 week £28, 2 weeks £42, 3 weeks £63, 4 weeks £63
Society meetings: catered for on weekdays by arrangement and weekends for special events.
Catering: bar food served on weekdays; Sun lunch; special parties or lunches by arrangement.
Hotels: Devereux House; Sea View.

A2 Axe Cliff

☎ Seaton (0297) 20499
Axmouth, Seaton, Devon, EX12 4AB
Off A35, 1 mile from Seaton.
Undulating seaside course.
18 holes, 5000 yards, S.S.S.64
Club founded in 1892
Visitors: welcome Mon to Sat.
Green fees: weekdays £5.50; Sat and Bank Holidays £6.
Catering: snacks and meals available
Hotels: Hawkes Hyde; Bay.

A3 Bigbury

☎ Bigbury (054 881) 557 and 207
Bigbury-on-Sea, Kingsbridge, Devon, TQ7 4BB
Take A379 Plymouth to Kingsbridge road; turn right 2 miles from Modbury at Harraton Cross, signposted Bigbury-on-Sea. Golf Club is a further 5 miles from here.
Undulating seaside course.
18 holes, 6038 yards, S.S.S.69
Course designed by J.H. Taylor.
Club founded in 1926.
Visitors: welcome all week
Green fees: weekdays £7 per day, weekends £8 per day.
Society meetings: welcome by arrangement on weekdays and some weekends.
Catering: full catering and bar facilities.
Hotels: Bigbury Farmhouse, Bigbury; Seagulls, Bigbury-on-Sea; Thurlestone, Thurlestone, Kingsbridge.

A4 Bude and N Cornwall

☎ Bude (0288) 2006 Sec. and Steward, 3635 Pro.
Burn View, Bude, Cornwall, EX23 8DA.
A39, 1 minute from Bude town centre.
Seaside links course.
18 holes, 6202 yards, S.S.S.70
Course designed by Tom Dunn.
Club founded in 1890.
Visitors: welcome, but very busy in July and Aug.
Green fees: Mon to Sat £6.50 per day, Sun and Bank Holidays £8 per day; £25 per week, £40 per fortnight.
Society meetings: welcome
Catering: by arrangement
Hotels: numerous good hotels in area.

A5 Budock Vean

☎ Falmouth (0326) 250288
Mawnan Smith, Falmouth, Cornwall, TR11 5LG
On main road between Falmouth and Helston, 7 miles from Helston.
Undulating parkland course.
9 holes, 5222 yards, S.S.S.65.
Course designed by James Braid, D, Cook and P.H. Whiteside
Club founded in 1932.
Visitors: welcome any time.
Green fees: weekdays £5 per day, weekends and Bank Holidays £8 (£4 with member).
Society meetings: catered for all year on application, except Sun.
Catering: snacks, lunches and table d'hôte or à la carte dinner.
Hotels: Budock Vean.

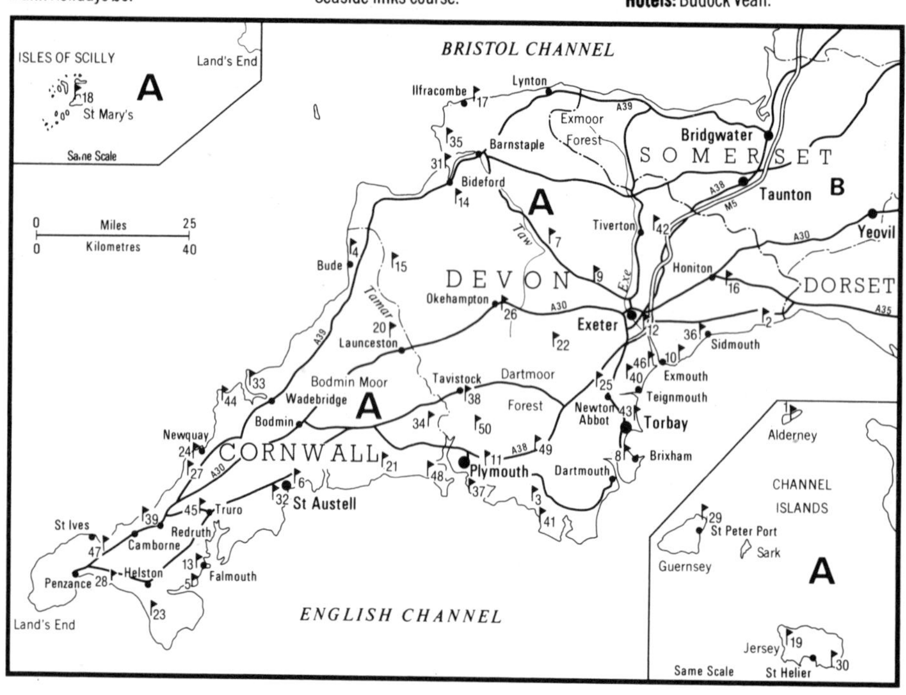

A6 Carlyon Bay Hotel

☎ Par (072 681) 2304
Carlyon Bay, St. Austell, Cornwall, PL25 3RD
Main Plymouth to Truro road 1 mile W. of St Blazey.
Clifftop/parkland course.
18 holes, 6400 yards, S.S.S.71
Course designed by Hamilton Stutt.
Club founded in 1926.
Visitors: welcome but tee off times between 8.30 am and 12 noon reserved for Hotel guests.
Green fees: weekdays £7.50, weekends £9, £5 if with a member.
Society meetings: Societies welcome.
Catering: bar snacks and meals available.
Hotels: Carlyon Bay.

A7 Chulmleigh

☎(0769) 80519
Leigh Road, Chulmleigh, North Devon, EX18 7BL.
1 mile off A377 midway between Exeter and Barnstaple.
Meadowland course.
18 holes, 1440 yards, S.S.S.54
Course designed by J.W.D. Goodban OBE
Club founded in 1975
Visitors: welcome
Green fees: £1.50 per round or day.
Society meetings: catered for on weekdays.
Catering: by arrangement.
Hotels: Fox and Hounds, Eggesford, nr Chulmleigh.

A8 Churston

☎ Churston (0803) 842751 Sec. 842128 Clubhouse, 842894 Pro.
Churston, nr Brixham, Devon.
On A379 3 miles from Paignton.
Downland course.
18 holes, 6201 yards, S.S.S.70
Course designed by H.S. Colt.
Club founded in 1890.
Visitors: members of recognised golf clubs only, proof required.
Green fees: on application.
Society meetings: by arrangement.
Catering: available each day during summer; opening hours depend on time of year.
Hotels: numerous good hotels in area.

A9 Downes Crediton

☎ Crediton (036 32) 3991
Hookway, Crediton, Devon, EX17 3PT
Off A377 Exeter – Crediton road 8 miles NW of Exeter. Turn off at Crediton railway station.
Parkland course.
18 holes, 5973 yards, S.S.S.70
Club founded in 1976
Visitors: welcome on weekdays
Green fees: weekends £8, weekdays £6.
Society meetings: catered for on application.
Catering: lunches and evening meals served.
Hotels: Ship, Crediton.

A10 East Devon

☎ Budleigh Salterton (03954) 3370
North View Rd, Budleigh Salterton, Devon.
5 miles E of Exmouth on A376.
Heathland seaside course.
18 holes, 6214 yards, S.S.S.70
Club founded in 1903
Visitors: welcome but advisable to contact to confirm.
Green fees: weekdays £8.50 per day, weekends £10.
Society meetings: arrange through Sec.
Catering: lunches every day except Mon; evening meals by prior arrangement.
Hotels: Southlands; Rosemullion.

A11 Elfordleigh G & CC

☎ Plymouth (0752) 336428
Plympton, Plymouth, Devon, PL7 5EB
Off A38. 5 miles NE of Plymouth.

Undulating parkland course.
S.S.S.67
Course designed by J.H. Taylor
Club founded in 1932.
Visitors: welcome except on competition days.
Green fees: weekdays £4, weekends and Bank Holidays £5.
Society meetings: weekdays by arrangement.
Catering: lunches and evening meals including bar snacks.
Hotels: Elfordleigh.

A12 Exeter G & CC

☎ Topsham (039 287) 4139
Countess Wear, Exeter, Devon, EX2 7AE.
On A377 to Exmouth.
Parkland course.
18 holes, 6055 yards, S.S.S.69
Course designed by James Braid
Visitors: welcome weekdays
Green fees: £9 per day weekdays (£5 with member), £10 Sat.
Society meetings: Thurs only.
Catering: lunches and snacks every day.
Hotels: Moat House, Countess Wear, Exeter.

A13 Falmouth

☎ Falmouth (0326) 311262
Swanpool Rd, Falmouth, Cornwall, TR11 3BQ
1 mile W of Swanpool Beach, Falmouth.
Seaside parkland course.
18 holes, 5581 yards, S.S.S.67
Club founded in 1928
Visitors: welcome.
Green fees: weekdays £6 per round or £8 per day, weekends and Bank Holidays £7 per round or £8 per day, weekly ticket £28.
Catering: meals or bar snacks all day.
Hotels: Denmere Manor; Royal Duchy; St Michaels; Greenlawns; Heudon; Somerdale.

A14 Great Torrington

☎ Bideford (023 72) 72792
Weare Trees, Torrington, North Devon. EX38 7EZ
1 mile N of Torrington on Wear Gifford road.
Undulating commonland course.
9 holes, 4418 yards, S.S.S.62
Club founded in 1932.
Visitors: welcome except for Sun mornings.
Green fees: weekdays £3, weekends and Bank Holidays £4.
Society meetings: by arrangement.
Catering: by prior arrangement.
Hotels: Castle Hill, Torrington.

A15 Holsworthy

☎ Holsworthy (0409) 2531 Sec.
Holsworthy, N. Devon.
1½ miles W of Holsworthy on A3072.
Parkland course.
18 holes, 5894 yards, S.S.S.68
Club founded in 1937.
Visitors: welcome midweek and some weekends.
Green fees: £5 per day.
Society meetings: small societies catered for.
Catering: snacks available at lunchtime.

A16 Honiton

☎ Honiton (0404) 44422 Sec, 2943 Pro.
Middlehills, Honiton, Devon, EX14 8RT.
2 miles S of Honiton.
Parkland course.
18 holes, 5236 yards, S.S.S.66
18 holes, 5900 yards, S.S.S.68 (as from June 86).
Club founded in 1896.
Visitors: members of a recognised Golf Club welcome any time except prior reservation for competition.
Green fees: weekdays £6.50 per day, weekends and Bank Holidays £9 per day.
Society meetings: limited number catered for usually on Thurs.
Catering: lunch, high tea and dinner, except Sun.
Hotels: Dolphin; Angel; Deer Park.

A17 Ilfracombe
☎Ilfracombe (0271) 62176
Hele Bay, Ilfracombe, North Devon.
On A399 Ilfracombe to Combe Martin road, 2 miles from Ilfracombe.
Undulating course.
18 holes, 5857 yards, S.S.S.68 (white tees)
18 holes, 5679 yards, S.S.S.67 (yellow tees)
Club founded in 1888.
Visitors: welcome.
Green fees: £7 per day or round; £21 for 5 days; £36 for 10 days; Juniors half-price.
Society meetings: bookings taken (green fee reduction on numbers over 15).
Catering: bar snacks except Mon.
Hotels: Lee Bay; Grangewood; Abbeydale; Collingdale; all in Ilfracombe.

A18 Isles of Scilly
☎Scillonia (0720) 22692
St Mary's, Isles of Scilly, TR21 0NF
1 mile from Hugh Town on St Mary's.
Moorland course.
9 holes, 5974 yards, S.S.S.69
Course designed by Dr Brushfield.
Club founded in 1904.
Visitors: welcome on weekdays and Sat.
Green fees: £5 per day (£2.50 with a member).
Catering: lunches and meals served except Mon when only snacks available.
Hotels: Godolphin; Tregarthen's; Star Castle; Atlantic.

A19 La Moye
☎Jersey (0534) 43401
La Moye, Jersey.
From Airport, follow main road, turning right at main traffic lights at junction. Sign indicating the club will be seen on right-hand side of road about a mile down.
Links course.
18 holes, 6673 yards, S.S.S.72 (white tees)
18 holes, 6362 yards, S.S.S.70 (yellow tees)
Club founded in 1902.
Visitors: with membership card.
Green fees: weekdays £13 per day; weekends and Bank Holidays £15 per day.
Society meetings: as arranged.
Catering: full catering facilities.
Hotels: Mermaid, St Peter; Atlantic, St Brelade.

A20 Launceston
☎Launceston (0566) 3442
St Stephens, Launceston, Cornwall.
Take Bude road from Launceston, 1 mile N of town turn left opposite St Stephens church. Club is 300 yards on right.
Undulating parkland course.
18 holes, 6409 yards, S.S.S.71
Course designed by Hamilton Stutt.
Club founded in 1927.
Visitors: welcome.
Green fees: £6 per day or round.
Society meetings: welcome.
Catering: meals served.
Hotels: White Hart, Launceston; Arundel Arms, Lifton.

A21 Looe Bin Down
☎Widegates (050 34) 247
Widegates, Looe, Cornwall.
Midway between Liskeard and Looe.
Moorland Meadowland course.
18 holes, 5875 yards, S.S.S.68
Course designed by Harry Vardon.
Club founded in 1934.
Visitors: welcome anytime.
Green fees: £7 per day.
Society meetings: by arrangement.
Catering: bar snacks during licensed hours; meals by arrangement.
Hotels: Snooty Fox, Widegates; Hannafort Point, Looe; Webbs, Liskeard.

A22 Manor House Hotel
☎Moretonhampstead (0647) 40355
Moretonh'td, Newton Abbot, TQ13 8RE.
12 miles from Exeter and Newton Abbot on

Princetown road.
Parkland course.
18 holes, 6016 yards, S.S.S.69
Course designed by J.W. Abercrombie.
Visitors: welcome.
Green fees: weekdays £9, weekends and Bank Holidays £9.50; free to residents.
Society meetings: by prior arrangement.
Catering: full facilities.
Hotels: Manor House.

A23 Mullion

☎Mullion (0326) 240685
Cury, Helston, Cornwall.
5 miles from Helston on A3083 Lizard road.
Undulating course.
18 holes, 5610 yards, S.S.S.67
Visitors: welcome except on competition days, Sun mornings or Sat afternoons.
Green fees: weekdays £4 per round, £5.50 per day; weekends £6.50 per day.
Society meetings: by arrangement.
Catering: meals served except Tues.
Hotels: Polurrion, Mullion; Mullion Cove, Mullion.

A24 Newquay

☎Newquay (063 73) 4354 and 2091
Tower Road, Newquay, TR17 1LT.
½ mile from town centre in the direction of Fistral beach.
Seaside course.
18 holes, 6140 yards, S.S.S.69
Course designed by H.S. Colt.
Club founded in 1891.
Visitors: welcome at all times.
Green fees: £7.50 per round, £9.50 per day, £30 per week.
Society meetings: welcome weekdays.
Catering: lunches served except Mon.
Hotels: Brecon Court; Bristol; Atlantic; Golf View; all in Newquay.

A25 Newton Abbot (Stover)

☎Newton Abbot (0626) 2460
Bovey Rd, Newton Abbot, S Devon. TQ12 6QQ.
On A382 Newton Abbot to Bovey Tracey rd, N of Newton Abbot.
Parkland course.
18 holes, 5724 yards, S.S.S.68
Course redesigned by James Braid in 1931.
Club founded in 1899.
Visitors: welcome but restrictions on Tues and Sun.
Green fees: weekdays £8, weekends £9 per day.
Society meetings: mainly Thurs.
Catering: lunches served daily; evening meals by arrangement except Mon and Sun.
Hotels: Globe, Newton Abbot; Buckland Hall, Buckland-in-the-Moor, Ashburton; Cookshayes, Moretonhampstead.

A26 Okehampton

☎Okehampton (0837) 2113
Okehampton, Devon, EX20 1EF.
Take A30 to Okehampton town centre from where the club is clearly signposted. Turn towards Dartmoor at the traffic lights, take the third right then the right fork and club is second on the right; the name is on the entrance post.
Undulating moorland course.
18 holes, 5307 yards, S.S.S.67
Club founded in 1913.
Visitors: welcome but no athletes shorts, ankle socks or denim may be worn.
Green fees: weekdays £5 per day or round (£4 with member), £6 on Sat (£5 with member).
Society meetings: welcome by prior arrangement; £4 per person if number 12 or more.
Catering: full lunches served; other meals by arrangement.
Hotels: White Hart, Okehampton; Manor, Fowley Cross, Okehampton; Oxenham Arms, South Zeal, Okehampton.

A27 Perranporth

☎Perranporth (0872) 573701 and 572454
Budnick Hill, Perranporth, TR6 0AB.
A3075 from Newquay then B3285. Club is on fringe of town adjacent to beach.
Links course.
18 holes, 6208 yards, S.S.S.71
Course designed by James Braid.
Club founded in 1927.
Visitors: welcome weekdays and weekends.
Green fees: on application.
Society meetings: offered reduced rates, but must book in advance.
Catering: full meals and bar snacks every day.
Hotels: Ponsmere; Beach Dunes; Promenade; the Club also has own caravan site for golfers and families.

A28 Praa Sands

☎Penzance (0736) 763445
Germoe Crossroads, Penzance, Cornwall. T20 9RB
Off A394, halfway between Helston and Penzance.
Parkland course.
9 holes, 4036 yards, S.S.S.60
Club founded in May 1971.
Visitors: welcome except Fri from 5 pm and Sun morning.
Green fees: £5 per day or round (£2.50 with member).
Society meetings: welcome by prior arrangement.
Catering: breakfast, lunch and dinner.
Hotels: Praa Sands; Lesceave Cliff; Mount Haven; Mount Prospect.

A29 Royal Guernsey

☎Guernsey (0481) 47022
L'Ancresse, Vale, Guernsey, Channel Is.
3 miles from St Peter Port.
Seaside course.
18 holes, 6143 yards, S.S.S.70
Course designed by Mackenzie Ross.
Club founded in 1890.
Visitors: welcome on weekdays with proof of membership of own club.
Green fees: £7 per round, £9 per day, £30 per week, £45 per 2 weeks.
Society meetings: welcome weekdays.
Catering: lunches served daily; evening meals on Tues, Thurs, Fri and Sat.
Hotels: Pembroke, L'Ancresse, Vale; L'Ancresse Lodge, L'Ancresse, Vale.

A30 Royal Jersey

☎Jersey (0534) Sec 54416, 51042 Steward and members
Grouville, Jersey, Channel Islands.
4 miles E of St Helier on road to Gorey.
Seaside course.
18 holes, 6097 yards, S.S.S.69
Club founded in 1878.
Visitors: welcome weekdays after 10 am, weekends and Bank Holidays after 2.30 pm (BST)or 12.30 (whites).
Green fees: weekdays £13 per day, weekends and Bank Holidays £20 per day.
Society meetings: small parties only.
Catering: full facilities by prior arrangement with Steward.
Hotels: Beachcomber, Grouville; Grouville Bay.

A31 Royal North Devon

☎Bideford (023 72) 73824 Clubhouse, 73817 Sec.
Westward Ho! Bideford, Devon, EX39 1HD
From Northam village take the road down Bone Hill past the P.O., keeping left. The club house is visible as you come down the hill.
Links course.
18 holes, 6644 yards, S.S.S.72
Course laid out by Tom Morris.
Club founded in 1864.
Green fees: weekdays £7 per round or day, weekends £8 per round or day.
Society meetings: welcome.
Catering: every day except Mon.
Hotels: Durrant House, Heywood Rd, Northam; Culloden House, Westward Ho!

Royal Guernsey

One of Royal Guernsey's most celebrated claims to fame is that it was the first course Henry Cotton ever saw. He used to be taken for walks over it by his mother, herself a Guernsey woman, although the family had moved to London by the time Cotton was four years old. So the course was denied added lustre by being, in part, responsible for the golfing development of the great man, but for almost a century it has served the needs of local golfers and hundreds of visitors alike.

There have been two or three versions of the layout, the most recent caused principally by the occupation of the Germans whose idea of bunkers consisted of solid stone rather than sand. The difficulty of demolishing these emplacements means they survive as reminders of darker days, but golfers have never been easily suppressed and L'Ancresse Common on the island's northern shores has maintained the defiant spirit and noble traditions of Channel Island golf to perfection.

It has a seaside flavour with a variety of spectacular views of beach, bathers and boats although there is no hint of dunes. The major hazard on the front nine is a dense crop of gorse which makes accurate driving an integral part of success, together with the more unusual feature of Guernsey cows munching at intervals along the rough with an air of relaxed contentment that is the envy of players. Under Guernsey law they must be tethered, which may be to spare them the fate of the young bullock in a field near Headingley GC which, as the **Golfer's Handbook** used to relate, was found on slaughter to have had 56 golf balls in its five stomachs.

Royal Guernsey's first hole, curving round the hill in front of the clubhouse, makes a pleasant start even if the pitch to a small green must be precisely struck. The 2nd immediately calls for higher skills. It recalls the story of a newcomer to Walton Heath playing one foggy morning and enquiring of James Braid, with whom he was paired, the line on a certain hole. 'It's on the spire of yon' church', replied Braid. 'You canna see it this morning but that's the line.' Well, the line on the 2nd from the back tee is on Vale Church and there is little room for error. A narrow ribbon of fairway fringes the gorse on the left and the first sight of the sea on the right in the shape of Grand Havre, but the labyrinth of gorse weaves an ever more constant pattern all the way to the turn, notably at the 9th, the hardest hole of all, at 460 yards.

Before that point is reached, the 4th is not much shorter although the 6th, the only par five on the first nine, and the 5th and 8th introduce welcome variety of length. The second nine, running at right angles to the first, makes a fine study in the shapes of its greens, the downhill approach to a sunken 10th contrasting with the new 12th, the raised 13th and the clever angling of the 14th – the second par 5.

The 14th green is the limit of the course in an easterly direction and the 15th and 16th, running parallel to the best example of Guernsey's beaches, head for home – the 15th in the form of an excellent two shotter. The 17th, in a slight dogleg, climbs the hill while the short 18th, plunging down again, completes the circuit which combines so many admirable qualities. It tests the good players without plaguing the weak, giving enjoyment to all in a setting that, seen at its best, is a glorious place to play. What more could you ask?

A32 St Austell

☎St Austell (0726) 74756 Sec, 72649 Clubhouse.
Tregongeeves Lane, St Austell, Cornwall, PL26 7DS.
On A390 St Austell – Truro rd 1 mile W of St Austell. The Tregongeeves Lane junction is clearly signposted just below the St Mewan school.
Heathland/parkland course.
18 holes, 5875 yards, S.S.S.68
Club founded in 1913.
Visitors: welcome with reservation, must be club members and hold handicap certificates.
Green fees: weekdays £6 per round or day, weekends and Bank Holidays £7 per round or day.
Society meetings: catered for with reduction in green fees.
Catering: full service.
Hotels: numerous hotels in area.

A33 St Enodoc

☎Trebetherick (020 886) 3216
Rock, Wadebridge, Cornwall, PL27 6LB
From Wadebridge take B3314 Port Isaac rd for 3 miles and then turn left to Rock.
Links course.
18 holes, 6188 yards, S.S.S.70
18 holes, 4151 yards, S.S.S.61 (short course)
Course designed by James Braid.
Club founded in 1890.
Visitors: welcome on most days, but it is advisable to telephone.Handicap certificate 24 or below required for main course.
Green fees: main course £9.50 per day, short course £6 per day.
Society meetings: welcome on w'kdays, except Fri, except in April, July and Aug.
Catering: lunches except Fri.
Hotels: numerous good hotels in area.

A34 St Mellion CC

☎Liskeard (0579) 50101
St Mellion, Saltash, Cornwall. PL12 6SD
3 miles S of Callington on A388.
Parkland course.
18 holes, 5759 yards, S.S.S.68
Jack Nicklaus International Course due to open summer 1986.
Course designed by J.Hamilton Stutt.
Club founded in 1976.
Visitors: welcome on weekdays.
Green fees: £10 per round mid-week.
Society meetings: catered weekdays.
Catering: meals and snacks daily.
Hotels: St Mellion.

A35 Saunton

☎Braunton (0271) 812436
Saunton, nr Braunton, N.Devon, EX33 1LG.
On B3231 from Braunton to Croyde, 7 miles from Barnstaple.
Traditional links course.
East 18 holes, 6703 yards, S.S.S.73
West 18 holes, 6322 yards, S.S.S.71
E course designed by Herbert Fowler
W course designed by Frank Pennink
Club founded in 1897.
Visitors: welcome.
Green fees: £8 per day on W course; £10 per day on E course (championship course).
Society meetings: welcome but should contact Manager.
Catering: full catering available all day.
Hotels: Saunton Sands, Saunton; Preston House, Saunton.

A36 Sidmouth

☎Sidmouth (0395) 3451 Sec, 3023 Clubhouse.
Peak Hill, Cotmaton Rd, Sidmouth, EX10 8SZ.
Take Exeter Station Rd, to Woodlands Hotel, then turn right on Cotmaton Rd.
Undulating parkland course.
18 holes, 5188 yards, S.S.S.66
Club founded in 1898.
Visitors: welcome.
Green fees: weekday £6, weekends and Bank Holidays £7.
Society meetings: welcome.
Catering: meals served except Tues.
Hotels: numerous in Sidmouth.

A37 Staddon Heights

☎Plymouth (0752) 42475
Staddon Heights, Plymstock, Plymouth, Devon. PL9 9SP.
Leave Plymouth city on the Plymstock Rd. Clubhouse is 5 miles S of city near Royal Navy aerial towers.
Links course.
18 holes, 5861 yards, S.S.S.68
Club founded in 1903.
Visitors: welcome on weekdays but some restrictions at weekends due to club competitions.
Green fees: weekdays £6 per day (£3 with member), weekends £7 per day (£3.50 with member).
Society meetings: welcome weekdays.
Catering: available every day.
Hotels: Highlands, Plymstock.

A38 Tavistock

☎Tavistock (0822) 2049
Down Rd, Tavistock, Devon, PL19 9AQ
Take the Whitchurch Rd, turning into Down Rd and onto Whitchurch Down.
Moorland course.
18 holes, 6250 yards, S.S.S.70
Club founded in 1891.
Visitors: welcome, but telephone in advance.
Green fees: weekends and Bank Holidays £8 day (£4 with member), weekdays £6 per day (£3 with member).
Society meetings: by arrangement.
Catering: lunches, bar snacks, and evening meals every day.
Hotels: Bedford, Tavistock; Moorland Links, Yelverton; Arundel Arms, Lifton.

A39 Tehidy Park

☎Portreath (0209) 842208
Camborne, Cornwall, TR14 0HH.
Off A30 2 miles NE of Camborne on the Portreath rd.
Parkland course.
18 holes, 6222 yards, S.S.S.70
Club founded in 1922.
Visitors: welcome by arrangement.
Green fees: weekdays £8 per day, weekends £12 per day.
Society meetings: by arrangement.
Catering: lunchtime bar snacks or running buffet; evening à la carte.
Hotels: Pendarves Lodge and Tyacks, Camborne; Glencoe, Gwithian; Penventon, Redruth.

A40 Teignmouth

☎Teignmouth (062 67) 4194 Sec, 3614 Clubhouse, 2894 Pro.
Exeter Rd, Teignmouth, Devon, TQ14 9NY.
2 miles from Teignmouth on B3192 to Exeter. 900 feet above Teignmouth, on Haldon Moor.
Moorland course.
18 holes, 6142 yards, S.S.S.69
Course designed by Dr Mackenzie.
Club founded in 1924.
Visitors: welcome, but must be members of a golf club or have a handicap certificate.
Green fees: weekdays £8 per day, weekends £9 per day, with member.
Society meetings: prior booking for weekdays.
Catering: full catering service every day.
Hotels: Venn Farm, Teignmouth; Cockhaven Manor, Bishopsteignton; Combe Bank, Landscore Rd, Teignmouth.

A41 Thurlestone

☎Kingsbridge (0548) 560405
Thurlestone, nr Kingsbridge, S Devon, TQ7 3NZ.
Take Thurlestone turning from A379 Plymouth to Salcombe rd. Club situated 4 miles S of Kingsbridge.
Downland course.
18 holes, 6337 yards, Par 71, S.S.S.70
Club founded in 1897.
Visitors: only members of recognised golf club or those in possession of a current

handicap certificate.
Green fees: on application.
Society meetings: no.
Catering: normally available all day.
Hotels: Thurlestone; Fursey Close; Charnwood Guest House. All in Thurlestone.

A42 Tiverton

☎Tiverton (0884) 252187
Post Hill, Tiverton, Devon, EX16 4NE
5 miles from junction 27 on M5 towards Tiverton on A373. Take 1st exit left on dual carriageway through Samford Peverell – Halberton.
Parkland/meadowland course.
18 holes, 6227 yards, Par 71, S.S.S.70
Course designed by James Braid.
Club founded in 1932.
Visitors: member of golf clubs welcome, but should telephone in advance.
Green fees: weekdays £7 per day, weekends £8.50 per day.
Society meetings: by arrangement.
Catering: available most days.
Hotels: Greenhead Lands, Samford Peverell; Tiverton.

A43 Torquay

☎Torquay (0803) 37471
Petitor Rd, St Marychurch, Torquay, TQ1 4QF.
N of Torquay on A379 Teignmouth Rd, on the outskirts of the town.
Parkland course.
18 holes, 6251 yards, S.S.S.70
Club founded in 1910.
Visitors: welcome if members of recognised golf clubs.
Green fees: weekdays £7.50 per day (£5.50 with member); weekends and Bank Holidays £8.50 (£6.50 with member).
Society meetings: on weekdays.
Catering: meals and snacks served. Except Mon.
Hotels: numerous good hotels in area.

A44 Trevose CC

☎Padstow (0841) 520208
Constantine Bay, Padstow, Cornwall, PL28 8JB.
4 miles W of Padstow off B3276.
Seaside links course.
18 holes, 6608 yards, S.S.S.72
9 holes, 1357 yards.
Course designed by Colt.
Club founded in 1925.
Visitors: welcome anytime but handicap certificate required. Restrictions for 3 and 4 ball matches.
Green fees: daily £7.50 – £9.50, weekly £30 – £42, Fortnightly £38 – £52, prices varying according to season.
Society meetings: welcome, except during summer school holidays.
Catering: all meals available (except during staff holidays in winter months).
Hotels: Treglos; Polmark; plus own self-catering accommodation.

A45 Truro

☎Truro (0872) 78684
Treliske, Truro, Cornwall, TR1 3LG.
1½ miles W of Truro on A390. Course signposted just off roundabout.
Undulating parkland course.
18 holes, 5347 yards, S.S.S.66
Course designed by Colt, Alison and Morrison.
Club founded in 1937.
Visitors: welcome subject to competitions.
Green fees: weekdays £7 per day (£3.50 with member), weekends and Bank Holidays £9 (£4.50 with member).
Society meetings: welcome weekdays.
Catering: lunches and evening meals every day.
Hotels: Brookdale, Carlton, Truro; Green Lawns, Falmouth.

A46 Warren

☎Dawlish (0626) 862255
Dawlish Warren, Dawlish, Devon, EX7 0NF.

Take A379 from Exeter to Dawlish Warren.
Links course.
18 holes, 5968 yards, S.S.S.69
Club founded in 1892.
Visitors: welcome on weekdays.
Green fees: weekdays £5.50, weekends £7 (£4 with member).
Society meetings: weekdays by arrangement with Sec.
Catering: bar snacks all week; meals served except Mon.
Hotels: Langstone Cliff, Dawlish Warren, Dawlish.

A47 West Cornwall

☎Penzance (0736) 753401
Lelant, St Ives, Cornwall, TR26 3DZ.
A30 to Hayle, then A3074 to St Ives.
Seaside course.
18 holes, 5839 yards, S.S.S.68
Club founded in 1889.
Visitors: welcome with handicap certificate.
Green fees: weekdays £7 per round, £8 per day; weekends £9 per round, £12 per day; weekly £30.
Catering: lunches and teas available; evening meals by arrangement, full à la carte menu.
Hotels: Badger, Lelant; Hendra's, Carbis Bay, St Ives.

A48 Whitsand Bay Hotel

☎St Germans (0503) 30418
Portwrinkle, Crafthole, Torpoint, Cornwall.
On B3274 6 miles SW of Torpoint.
Clifftop course.
18 holes, 5367 yards, S.S.S.67
Course designed by William Fernie.
Club founded in 1905.
Visitors: welcome at all times.
Green fees: weekends and Bank Holidays £7, weekdays £6.
Society meetings: arrangement with Sec.
Catering: arrangement with Steward and Stewardess.
Hotels: Whitsand Bay; Finnygook Inn.

A49 Wrangaton

☎South Brent (036 47) 3229
Wrangaton, South Brent, S Devon, TQ10 9HJ.
Turn off A38 between South Brent and Bittaford at Wrangaton P.O.
Moorland course.
9 holes, 5790 yards. S.S.S.68
Club founded in 1895.
Visitors: welcome weekdays and Sat.
Green fees: weekdays £4, Sun and Bank Holidays £5.
Society meetings: weekdays only.
Catering: snacks at lunchtime.
Hotels: The Stagecoach, Wrangaton.

A50 Yelverton

☎Yelverton (0822) 852824
Golf Links Rd, Yelverton, Devon, PL29 6BN.
8 miles N of Plymouth and 5 miles S of Tavistock on A386.
Moorland course.
18 holes, 6350 yards, S.S.S.70
Course designed by Herbert Fowler.
Club founded in 1904.
Visitors: welcome weekdays and weekend afternoons.
Green fees: weekdays £7 per day (£5 with member), weekends £9 per day (£6 with member).
Society meetings: welcome weekdays.
Catering: lunches except Tues; bar snacks available during bar hours.
Hotels: Moorland Links, Yelverton.

B Somerset, Dorset, Wiltshire and Avon

When the question of golfing holidays is discussed, this is not a region to which everyone inclines. However the Bournemouth area alone is bristling with fine courses and those who aren't familiar with them should immediately mend their ways. Ferndown, Parkstone and Broadstone stand comparison with any of the sand and heather courses in Surrey and, if a shade less demanding, can be a shade more enjoyable for some as a result.

They are in easy reach of each other while Bournemouth can also boast two of the finest public courses in the world, Meyrick Park and Queen's Park (Boscombe), the sterner of the two, with a touch of switchback in its make-up. Both have housed national professional events and nobody should be deterred from playing either on account of their 'public' label.

On the other side of Poole Harbour and commanding some of the best views anywhere is Isle of Purbeck, which should form part of any holiday itinerary; but a little further west and north the more pastoral setting of Sherborne is a scenic match for it. Sherborne is a delightful place to play and is a convenient halfway house for travellers bound for Somerset where Burnham and Berrow is undoubtedly worth the trip.

Here you find a links of challenge and charm, a stage chosen for many a championship and equally popular with the women as well as the men. J.H. Taylor described it as one of the most sporting courses conceivable, with large sandhills and small greens, paying it the ultimate accolade of helping to hone the mashie play for which he was famous.

Weston-super-Mare is another pleasant course and whilst Bath and Bristol aren't exactly renowned for their golf, Mendip, Lansdown, Long Ashton and Bristol and Clifton shouldn't be overlooked. Wiltshire is one of the least endowed golfing counties but Tidworth Garrison, open to the winds blowing across Salisbury Plain, is a lovely spot with fairways that soak up the heaviest rains.

B1 Ashley Woods

☎ Blandford (994) 52253
Wimborne Rd, Blandford, Dorset, DT11 9HN.
From Blandford 1 mile S along B3082 Wimborne Rd.
Undulating meadowland course.
9 holes, 6227 yards, S.S.S.70
Club founded in 1936.
Visitors: welcome.
Green fees: weekdays £6.50, weekends and Bank Holidays £10.
Society meetings: can be arranged on weekdays.
Catering: lunches served except Mon.
Hotels: numerous good hotels in area.

B2 Bath

☎ Bath (0225) 25182
Sham Castle, North Rd, Bath, BA2 6JG
Take A36 Bath to Warminster rd, turn up North Rd and club is about 800 yds on left; 1½ miles SE of Bath.
Downland course.
18 holes, 6369 yards, S.S.S.70
Club founded in 1880.
Visitors: welcome with hand. certs.
Green fees: weekdays £7, weekends £8; £5 with member at any time.
Society meetings: welcome Wed and Fri.
Catering: full catering facilities except Thurs when only bar snacks available.
Hotels: Francis, Queens Square, Bath; Dukes, 53/54 Great Pulteney St, Bath; Redcar, Henrietta St, Bath.

B3 Boscombe

☎ Bournemouth (0202) 36198
Queens Park, Bournemouth.
Proceed along Wessex Way and turn R at the Queens Park Club roundabout.
Undulating
18 holes, 6505 yards, S.S.S.72
Club founded in 1905.
Visitors: welcome on weekdays. Bookings direct or by telephone.
Green fees: £5.50 per round.
Society meetings: bookings to the Parks Department, Town Hall, Bournemouth.
Catering: lunches and teas available.
Hotels: all Bournemouth hotels within easy reach.

B4 Brean

☎ Brean Down (027875) 467 or 359
Coast Rd, Brean, Burnham-on-Sea, Somerset TA8 2RF
4½ miles off M5, Junction 22 following signs for Brean, Leisure Centre on right.
Moorland/meadowland course.
14 holes, 5470 yards, S.S.S.67
Club founded in 1973.
Visitors: welcome every day except Sun; on Sun welcome with member after 10 am and afternoon without member.
Green fees: weekdays £4 (£3 with member), weekends £6 (£5 with member).
Society meetings: welcome.
Catering: full facilities at adjoining Leisure Centre.
Hotels: Dunstan House,

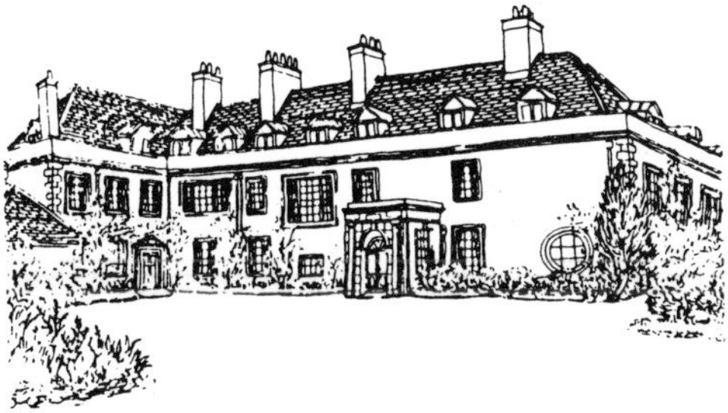

W A L E S
Newport
Cardiff
BRISTOL CHANNEL
Bristol
Swindon
Chippenham
Marlborough
Bath
Weston-super-Mare
A V O N
Mendip Hills
Devizes
WILTSHIRE
Salisbury Plain
Frome
Warminster
Wells
Minehead
Quantock Hills
Bridgwater
S O M E R S E T
Taunton
Salisbury
HAMPSHIRE
Yeovil
D E V O N
Blandford Forum
D O R S E T
Exeter
Lyme Regis
Dorchester
Poole
Christchurch
Bournemouth
Wareham
Weymouth
Bill of Portland
0 Miles 20
0 Kilometres 30

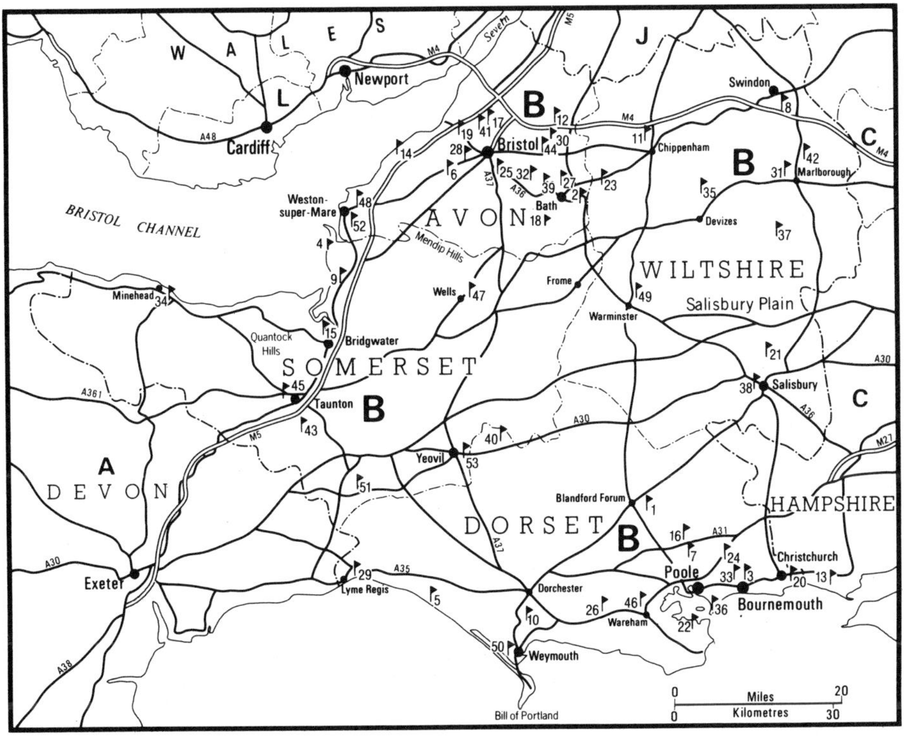

Burnham-on-Sea; Royal Clarence, Burnham-on-Sea.

B5 Bridport & W Dorset

☎ Bridport (0308) 22597
East Cliff, West Bay, Bridport, Dorset DT6 4EP
Off A35, 1½ miles S of Bridport on B3157.
Seaside course.
18 holes, 5246 yards, S.S.S.66
Club founded in 1891.
Visitors: welcome.
Green fees: weekdays 1 April to 31 Oct £7, 1 Nov to 31 Mar £4; weekends and Bank Holidays 1 April to 31 Oct £8, 1 Nov to 31 Mar £5.
Society meetings: welcome.
Catering: full range except Mon; bar open every day.
Hotels: Haddon House; Bridport Arms.

B6 Bristol & Clifton

☎ Bristol (0272) 393474
Failand, Bristol BS8 3TH
Junction 19 off M5; 4 miles along A369 to Bristol turn R at traffic lights, then further 1½ miles.
Parkland course.
18 holes, 6294 yards, S.S.S.70
Club founded in 1891.
Visitors: welcome on weekdays and at weekends between 11am and 12.30pm.
Green fees: on application.
Society meetings: on application.
Catering: lunch and afternoon tea every day, evenings by arrangement.
Hotels: Birkdale; Redwood Lodge; Avon Gorge.

B7 Broadstone

☎ Broadstone (0202) 692595
Wentworth Drive, Off Station Approach, Broadstone, Dorset.
Off A349 halfway between Wimborne and Poole.
Heathland course.
18 holes, 6129 yards, S.S.S.70
Course designed by George Dunn and H.S. Colt.
Club founded in 1898.
Visitors: by prior arrangement with Sec.
Green fees: weekdays £10 per round, £13 per day; weekends £12 per round, £15 per day.
Society meetings: by prior arrangement with Sec.
Catering: full catering service preferably by prior arrangement with the Sec.
Hotels: numerous good hotels in area.

B8 Broome Manor

☎ Swindon (0793) 32403
Pipers Way, Swindon, Wilts, SN3 1RG
2 miles from Junction 15 off M4 to Swindon.
Public parkland course.
18 holes, 6359 yards, S.S.S.70
9 holes, 5610 yards, S.S.S.67
Course designed by Hawtree & Son.
Club founded in 1976.
Visitors: welcome.
Green fees: 18 hole weekdays £3.50, weekends £3.95; 9 hole weekdays £2, weekends £2.40.
Society meetings: welcome, max. 40.
Catering: full catering always available
Hotels: Crest; Goddard Arms; Post House.

B9 Burnham & Berrow

☎ Burnham-on-Sea (0278) 785760 Sec, 783137 Clubhouse.
St Christopher's Way, Burnham-on-Sea, Somerset TA8 2PE
Junction 22 off M5, 1 mile N of Burnham-on-Sea.
Links course.
18 holes, 6550 yards, S.S.S.72
9 holes, 6327 yards.
Club founded in 1890.
Visitors: welcome, but should ring in advance.
Green fees: weekdays £9, weekends and Bank Holidays £11.
Society meetings: by arrangement.
Catering: available daily from 11 am to 6 pm; if arranged in advance, available outside these hours, including breakfast.
Hotels: Dunstan House, Love Lane, Burnham-on-Sea; Battleborough Grange, Bristol Rd, Brent Knoll; Cloisters Guest House, 94 Berrow Rd, Burnham-on-Sea; Pine Grange, 27 Berrow Rd, Burnham-on-Sea.

B10 Came Down

☎ Upwey (030 581) 2531
Came Down, Dorchester, Dorset DT2 8NR
2 miles S of Dorchester off A354.
Undulating downland course.
18 holes, 6152 yards, S.S.S.70
Course designed by J.H. Taylor.
Club founded in 1890.
Visitors: welcome; restricted at weekends.
Green fees: £7 per day (£5.50 with member).
Society meetings: welcome by appointment on weekdays.
Catering: lunches and teas available daily.
Hotels: Kings Arms, Dorchester.

B11 Chippenham

☎ Chippenham (0249) 652040 Sec, 655519 Pro.
Malmesbury Rd. Chippenham, Wilts SN15 5LT
Junction 17 off M4 1 mile from town centre on A429.
Meadowland course.
18 holes, 5540 yards, S.S.S.67
Club founded 1896.
Visitors: welcome on weekdays; at weekends by reservation.
Green fees: weekdays £7, weekends and Bank Holidays £9; reductions with member.
Society meetings: welcome on Tue, Thurs and Fri.
Catering: full service except Mon when snacks available.
Hotels: Old Bell, Malmesbury; Angel, Chippenham.

B12 Chipping Sodbury

☎ Chipping Sodbury (0454) 319042
Chipping Sodbury, Bristol BS17 6PU
Leave M4 at Exit 18 and M5 at Exit 14; from Chipping Sodbury take Wickwar Rd, first turn on R.
Parkland course.
18 holes, 6912 yards, S.S.S.73
9 holes, 3076 yards.
Course designed by Fred Hawtree.
Visitors: welcome, but after 12 noon on Sun.
Green fees: weekdays £7, weekends and Bank Holidays £8; reduction with member.
Society meetings: welcome by arrangement on weekdays.
Catering: meals served.
Hotels: Moda; Cross Hands; The Poplars.

B13 Christchurch

☎ Christchurch (0202) 473817
Iford Bridge Golf Course, Iford, Christchurch, Dorset.
Off A35, then signposted.
9 holes, 4824 yards, S.S.S. Club founded in 1977.
Visitors: welcome.
Green fees: weekends £3, weekdays £2.60.
Society meetings: by arrangement with local Council.
Catering: bar facilities and snacks served.
Hotels: many good hotels in area.

B14 Clevedon

☎ Clevedon (0272) 874057 Sec, 874704 Pro, 873140 Steward
Castle Rd, Clevedon, Avon BS21 7AA
Leave M5 at Junction 19, follow signs to Clevedon, on outskirts of Clevedon turn R

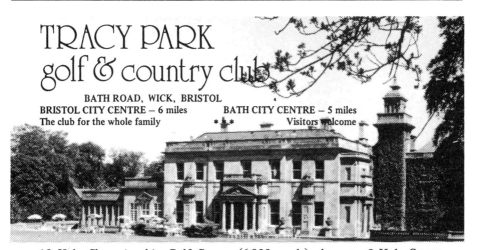

into Holly Lane, at top of hill turn R into private lane to golf club and castle.
Undulating parkland course.
18 holes, 5835 yards, S.S.S.69
Club founded in 1898.
Visitors: welcome, must be members of recognised golf club with handicap; weekends best after 11 am.
Green fees: weekdays £7 (£3.50 with member), weekends £10 (£5 with member).
Society meetings: only by arrangement with Sec.
Catering: full catering except Tues when only snacks available.
Hotels: Walton Park, Wellington Terrace, Clevedon; Highcliffe, Wellington Terrace, Clevedon; Royal Pier, Marine Parade, Clevedon.

B15 Enmore Park

☎ Spaxton (027 867) 481
Enmore, Bridgwater, Somerset TA5 2AN
3 miles W of Bridgwater on Spaxton Rd.
Undulating parkland course.
18 holes, 6443 yards, S.S.S.71
Course designed by A.R. Bradbeer.
Club founded in 1932.
Visitors: welcome.
Green fees: weekdays £7 (£5 with member), weekends £8.50 (£6.50 with member).
Society meetings: catered for on weekdays except Wed, early booking advised.
Catering: available except Mon.
Hotels: Walnut Tree, North Petherton; Old Vicarage, Bridgwater.

B16 Ferndown

☎ Ferndown (0202) 874602
119 Golf Links Rd, Ferndown, Dorset, BH22 8BU
A31 to Tricketts Cross.
Heathland links course.
18 holes, 6442 yards, S.S.S.71
Course designed by Harold Hilton.
Club founded in 1913.
Visitors: welcome with handicap certificate or letter of introduction.
Green fees: £15 old course (£7 new course).
Society meetings: welcome on Mon, Wed and Fri only.
Catering: full service available.
Hotels: The Dormy; Coach House.

B17 Filton

☎ Bristol (0272) 694169
Golf Course Lane, Filton, Bristol, BS12 7QS
From Almondsbury Interchange (M4/5) take A38 towards Bristol, after 2 miles turn R at roundabout and R at traffic lights.
Parkland course.
18 holes, 6025 yards, S.S.S.69
Club founded in 1909.
Visitors: welcome on weekdays.
Green fees: £7 per day.
Society meetings: accepted on weekdays when course is free.
Catering: full catering available.
Hotels: Crest, Hambrook.

B18 Fosseway

☎ Midsomer Norton (0761) 412214
Charlton Lane, Midsomer Norton, Bath, Somerset BA3 4BD
Off A367 S of Bath, through Radstock and turn L at Charlton roundabout.
Parkland course.
9 holes, 8492 yards, S.S.S.61
Club founded in 1969.
Visitors: welcome except Sun morning and Wed after 5 pm.
Green fees: Mon, Tues, Thurs and Fri £3.50 per day; Wed (up to 5pm) £3 per morning, £2 per afternoon; Saturday and Bank Holidays £4.50; Sun (after 1pm) £3.
Society meetings: No.
Catering: bar meals and full à la Carte restaurant available.
Hotels: Court, Emborough and Guest Houses in area.

B19 Henbury

☎ Bristol (0272) 500044
Henbury Hill, Westbury-on-Trym, Bristol BS10 7QB
Junction 17 off M5, 2 to 3 minutes to club.
Parkland course.
18 holes, 6039 yards, S.S.S.70
Club founded in 1891.
Visitors: welcome weekdays.
Green fees: weekdays £7.50 (£5 with member), weekends and Bank Holidays £8 (£5 with member).
Society meetings: catered for on Tues and Fri by arrangement.
Catering: full range available.
Hotels: Ship, Alveston, Bristol.

B20 Highcliffe Castle

☎ Highcliffe (042 52) 72953
107 Lymington Rd, Highcliffe on Sea, Dorset. BH23 4LA
A35 to Hinton Admiral, follow signpost to Highcliffe, approx 1 mile. On A337 3 miles E of Christchurch.
Seaside course.
18 holes, 4732 yards, S.S.S.63
Club founded in 1913.
Visitors: welcome providing members of recognised golf clubs.
Green fees: weekdays £4 (£3 with member), weekends and Bank Holidays £9 (£7 with member).
Society meetings: welcome, please give plenty of time to arrange.
Catering: full catering, except Tues.
Hotels: Chewton Glen, Highcliffe; Red House, Barton on Sea.

B21 High Post

☎ Middle Woodford (072273)356
Great Durnford, Salisbury, Wilts.
Halfway between Salisbury and Amesbury on the A345.
Downland course.
18 holes, 6267 yards, S.S.S.70
Club founded in 1922.
Visitors: welcome.
Green fees: £8
Society meetings: catered for on weekdays.
Catering: full catering facilities.
Hotels: numerous good hotels in area.

B22 Isle of Purbeck

☎ Studland (092 944) 361
Studland, Dorset, BH19 3AB
Between Studland and Swanage, on B3351, overlooking Poole Harbour and Bournemouth.
Undulating heathland course.
18 holes, 6248 yards, S.S.S.71
9 holes, 2022 yards, S.S.S.30
Course designed by H.S. Colt.
Club founded in 1892.
Visitors: welcome.
Green fees: 18 hole weekdays £10, weekends and Bank Holidays £11.50; 9 hole £5.50 per day.
Society meetings: welcome.
Catering: lunches and evening meals.
Hotels: Knoll House, Studland; Pines, Swanage; Manor House, Studland.

B23 Kingsdown

☎ Box (0225) 742530
Kingsdown, Corsham, Wilts. SN14 9BS
Turn off A4 onto A363, turn L at Crown Inn 250 yds, uphill for 2 miles.
Heathland course.
18 holes, 6265 yards, S.S.S.70
Club founded in 1880.
Visitors: with handicaps are welcome except on competition days.
Green fees: weekdays £7.50 (£3.50 with member); weekends £9 (£4 with member).
Society meetings: by prior arrangement, maximum 45.
Catering: simple catering always available.

Hotels: Stage Coach, Corsham; Beaufort, Bath.

B24 Knighton Heath

☎ Bournemouth (0202) 572633
Francis Avenue, Bournemouth, Dorset BH11 8NX
On main A348 Poole to Ringwood road, 4 miles N of Bournemouth: signposted at Wallisdown roundabout.
Heathland course.
18 holes, 6206 yards, S.S.S.70
Club founded in 1976.
Visitors: welcome after 9.30 am with handicap certificate.
Green fees: weekdays £10, weekends and Bank Holidays £12.
Society meetings: by arrangement Wed to Fri.
Catering: available except Mon and Tues.
Hotels: numerous good hotels in area.

B25 Knowle

☎ Bristol (0272) 770660
Fairway, Brislington, Bristol BS4 5DF
3 miles S of city centre on the A4 to junction with West Town Lane, entrance on left 800 yds along West Town Lane.
Parkland course.,
18 holes, 6016 yards, S.S.S.69
Course designed by Hawtree and Taylor.
Club founded in 1905.
Visitors: weekdays unrestricted, weekends with member; proof of membership of recognised club required.
Green fees: weekdays £7, weekends and Bank Holidays £9, weekly ticket £20.
Society meetings: welcome Thurs only.
Catering: full catering facilities.
Hotels: numerous good hotels in area.

B26 Lakey Hill

☎ Bere Regis (0929) 471776
Hyde, Wareham, Dorset BH20 7NT
3 miles W of Wareham off Worgret Rd.
Meadowland course.
18 holes, 6146 yards, S.S.S.69
Course designed by Brian Bamford.
Club founded in 1978.
Visitors: welcome.
Green fees: weekdays £8 per day (£4 with member), weekends £10 per day (£5 with member).
Society meetings: welcome weekdays.
Catering: lunches served every day.
Hotels: Springfield, Stoborough.

B27 Lansdown

☎ Bath (0225) 22138 or 25007
Lansdown, Bath BA1 9BT
Junction 18 off M4, next to Bath Racecourse.
Parkland course.
72 holes, 6267 yards, S.S.S.70
Course designed by C.K. Cotton
Club founded in 1894.
Visitors: welcome
Green fees: weekdays £8 per day, weekends and Bank Holidays £9 per round.
Society meetings: welcome preferably Wed to Fri.
Catering: available every day.
Hotels: Lansdown Grove; Francis.

B28 Long Ashton

☎ Bristol (0272) 392316
Long Ashton, Bristol BS18 9DW
Leave M5 at Junction 19, take A369 to Bristol, turn R into B3129 at traffic lights and then L onto B3128. Club is ½m on R.
Undulating, moorland/ parkland course.
18 holes, 6051 yards, S.S.S.70
Course designed by Hawtree and Taylor
Club founded in 1893.
Visitors: welcome but must have a current handicap.
Green fees: weekdays £9, weekends and Bank Holidays £11.
Society meetings: normally on Wed.
Catering: full catering available daily.
Hotels: Redwood Lodge, Failand.

B29 Lyme Regis

☎ Lyme Regis (029 74) 2043
Timber Hill, Lyme Regis, Dorset DT7 3HQ
Off A3052 Charmouth Rd 1 mile E of town.
Undulating meadowland course.
18 holes, 6123 yards, S.S.S.70
Club founded in 1894.
Visitors: welcome on weekdays and after 11.30 am most Sun.
Green fees: weekdays and weekends £7.50 (£5 with member); £6 if staying at certain hotels.
Society meetings: catered for on weekdays and Sat.
Catering: full service except on Mon.
Hotels: Alexandra, Lyme Regis; Buena Vista, Lyme Regis; Mariners, Lyme Regis; Fairwater Head, Hawkchurch; Devon, Uplyme; Queens Arms, Charmouth; Fernhill, Charmouth; Newhaven, Lyme Regis.

B30 Mangotsfield

☎ Bristol (0272) 565501
Carsons Rd, Mangotsfield, Bristol.
M32 - leave junction Filton/Dawnend. Follow sign for Dawnend and Mangotsfield.
Hilly meadowland course.
Club founded in 1970/77
Visitors: welcome.
Green fees: weekdays £6, weekends £7.
Society meetings: by arrangement with Manager.
Catering: meals served.
Hotels: The Linden, High St, Kingswood.

B31 Marlborough

☎ Marlborough (0672) 52147
The Common, Marlborough, Wilts SN8 1DU
¾ mile from town centre on A345 to Swindon.
Downland course.
18 holes, 6440 yards, S.S.S.71
Club founded in 1888.
Visitors: welcome on weekdays and weekends except on competition days.
Green fees: weekdays £6 per day or round (£4 with member), weekends £8 per day or round (£5 with member)
Society meetings: welcome Tues and Thurs, and on Mon and Fri for small groups of 12.
Catering: meals served daily, restricted service on Mon and Fri.
Hotels: Castle and Ball; Ivy House; Savernake Forest.

B32 Mendip

☎ Oakhill (0749) 840570 Sec, 840793 Pro
Gurney Slade, Bath, Avon BA3 4UT
3 miles N of Shepton Mallet, just off A37.
Undulating downland course.
18 holes, 5958 yards, S.S.S.69
Course designed by Vardon and Pennink.
Club founded in 1908.
Green fees: weekdays £6.50 (£4 with member), weekends £8 (£5 with member). Juniors ½ price weekdays.
Society meetings: welcome, particularly on Thurs and Fri.
Catering: snacks, lunches and dinners available Tues to Sun.
Hotels: Charlton House, Shepton Mallet; Glen, Evercreech; Mendip Lodge, Frome.

B33 Meyrick Park

☎ Bournemouth (0202) 290871 Bookings, 529513 Sec.
Central Drive, Bournemouth, Dorset BH2 6LQ
10 minutes walk from town centre.
Parkland course.
18 holes, 5878 yards, S.S.S.69
Course designed by Tom Dunn.
Club founded in 1894.
Visitors: municipal course open to public.

Green fees: £5.50 per round.
Society meetings: welcome; contact Recreation Officer, Town Hall for details.
Catering: café open weekdays; bar open usual hours.
Hotels: numerous good hotels in area.

B34 Minehead & W Somerset

☎ Minehead (0643) 2057
The Warren, Minehead, Somerset
TA24 5SJ
E end of sea front.
Links course.
18 holes, 6130 yards, S.S.S.69
Course designed by Johnny Alan.
Club founded in 1882.
Visitors: welcome.
Society meetings: by prior arrangement with Sec.
Catering: meals by prior arrangement with Steward, snacks always available.
Hotels: York; Wyndcott; Northcliff.

B35 North Wilts

☎ Cannings (038 086) 627
Bishops Cannings, Devizes, Wilts
SN10 2LP
1 mile from the A4 at Calne.
Downland course.
18 holes, 6450 yards, S.S.S.71
Club founded in 1890.
Visitors: welcome.
Green fees: weekdays £7, weekends £8.
Society meetings: welcome by prior arrangement.
Catering: full catering facilities available.
Hotels: Bear, Devizes; Lansdowne Strand, Calne.

B36 Parkstone

☎ Parkstone (0202) 707138
Links Rd, Parkstone, Poole, Dorset
BH14 9JU
A35 Bournemouth to Poole road; turn S at St Osmonds Church
Undulating heathland course.
18 holes, 6250 yards, S.S.S.70
Course designed by Willie Park.
Club founded in 1910.
Visitors: welcome weekdays 9.30 am – 12.30 pm and 2-4 pm limited at weekends with handicap. Advance booking recommended.
Green fees: weekdays £10 per round, £14 per day; weekends £12 per round, £15 per day.
Society meetings: as for visitors
Catering: lunches and snacks available; dinners if booked.
Hotels: numerous good hotels in area.

B37 RAF Upavon

☎ Stonehenge (0980) 630787
Asst. Sec.
RAF Upavon, Pewsey, Wilts SN9 6BE
2 miles SE of Upavon village on A342.
Undulating downland course.
9 holes, 5116 metres, S.S.S.67
Visitors: welcome on weekdays and with member at weekends.
Green fees: £4 per day (payable at Guardroom)
Society meetings: welcome on weekdays, maximum 32.
Catering: by special arrangement.
Hotels: Antelope, Upavon.

B38 Salisbury & S Wiltshire

☎ Salisbury (0722) 742645 Sec.
Netherhampton, Salisbury, Wilts
SP2 8PR
On A3094 2 miles fron Salisbury and from Wilton.
Parkland course.
9 holes, 4848 yards, S.S.S.64
18 holes, 6189 yards, S.S.S.70
Course designed by J.H. Taylor
Club founded in 1888.
Visitors: welcome.
Green fees: weekdays £7 per day (£3.50 with member), weekends and Bank Holidays £8 per day (£4.50 with member).
Society meetings: welcome by arrangement.
Catering: full catering facilities.
Hotels: Rose and Crown, Harnham Rd, Salisbury; Pembroke Arms, Wilton, Salisbury.

B39 Saltford

☎ Saltford (02217) 3220
Saltford, Bristol
Off A4 between Bath and Bristol.
Meadowland course.
18 holes, 6081 yards, S.S.S.69
Visitors: welcome.
Green fees: weekdays £7 (£4 with member), weekends £9 (£5 with member), juniors £3.
Society meetings: Thurs by arrangement.
Catering: meals served daily.
Hotels: Grange, Keynsham; Crown, Saltford.

B40 Sherborne

☎ Sherborne (0963) 814431
Higher Clatcombe, Sherborne, Dorset
DT9 4RN
1 mile N of Sherborne off B3145 to Wincanton
Parkland course.
18 holes, 5600/ 5800 yards, S.S.S.67/68
Course designed by James Braid.
Club founded in 1894.
Visitors: welcome but not before 10 am except by special arrangement, handicap or club affiliation cert. req'd.
Green fees: weekdays £7 per day, weekends and Bank Holidays £10 p. d.
Society meetings: weekdays by arrangement.
Catering: full range of snacks and meals.
Hotels: Post House, Sherborne; Queens Arms, Corton Denham; The Bear, Wincanton; Holbrook House.

B41 Shirehampton Park

☎ Avonmouth (0272) 823059
Clubhouse, 822083 Sec.
Park Hill, Shirehampton, Bristol
BS11 0UL
1½ miles from Junction 18 on M5, B4018 through village of Shirehampton
Undulating parkland course.
18 holes, 5493 yards, S.S.S.67
Club founded in 1907.
Visitors: welcome on weekdays and weekends with member.
Green fees: £7.
Society meetings: Mon only by arrangement.
Catering: full catering on weekdays.
Hotels: numerous good hotels in area.

B42 Swindon

☎ Ogbourne St George (067 284) 327
Ogbourne St George, Marlborough, Wilts
SN8 1TB
Junction 15 off M4, on A345 to Marlborough.
Undulating course.
18 holes, 6226 yards, S.S.S.70
Course designed by Taylor, Hawtree and Cotton.
Club founded in 1929.
Visitors: welcome on weekdays, restricted at weekends.
Green fees: weekdays £8.50 per day (£5 with member), weekends and Bank Holidays £9 per day (£5.50 with member).
Society meetings: welcome on weekdays.
Catering: full service every day.
Hotels: Crest, Swindon; Aylesbury Arms, Marlborough.

B43 Taunton & Pickeridge

☎ Blagdon Hill (082 342) 240
Corfe, Taunton TA3 7BY
Take B3170, 4 miles S of Taunton, pass

Sherborne

Sherborne belongs to that category of courses that provides the right degree of testing quality without, in any way, impairing the enjoyment of a round in an incomparable setting – views, on a good day, spanning two or three counties. Taking the road up the hill out of a town famous for its abbey and its schools, you reach the club down a narrow country lane. Before the club's founding in 1894, the whole area was part of the fertile agricultural plain that surrounds it, but the second nine in particular covers some gently rolling land of which Harry Colt would undoubtedly have approved.

He believed that undulations and hummocks are of great value through the green as they provide difficult stances and lies, without which no golf course can be deemed to be perfect. There never will be the perfect course because it all depends, as Professor Joad used to say, on what you mean by perfect. However, there is a pleasant contrast at Sherborne between the first ten holes on one side of the road and the last eight on the other.

Judged from the first six holes, Sherborne suggests a non-stop assault with woods and long irons. The first nine is, in fact, more than 800 yards longer than the second although that does not necessarily mean that the second nine is any easier in relation to par. What it does mean is that the first six holes, which include three par 5s, hold the key to a good score, the 1st and 3rd being notably good par 4s.

It is easy enough though to have your card in tatters almost before you have started. There is plenty of scope for going out of bounds with an opening drive to a fairway which tapers cleverly to ensure that the further you hit the ball, the straighter you have to be. Control is essential, too, with the second shot to the 2nd, doglegging round the practice ground, while the 3rd and 4th, running up and back, are two of the best holes.

The 5th is the first of an excellent batch of short holes which vary in length and character, as all good short holes should, the 5th being perhaps the finest and the 7th the most daunting. In between, the par 5, 6th, demands a well positioned drive to allow a flat stance for what is most likely to be a long second; and the second, too, requires both care and thought in order to leave the easiest pitch when the pin is tucked away at the back of the green.

Nothing less than the most truly-hit tee shot will suffice at the 7th but there is a little respite at the 8th and 9th which epitomise the compact nature of the layout on a limited acreage. It accommodates one more hole, the third par 3, before crossing back and passing the clubhouse and on down the excellent 459-yard 11th where the sloping terrain demands that, to hold both fairway and green, there is a very definite, if narrow, line to adopt.

It is from the tee that the full panorama of the view unfolds, an unmistakable slice of England at its greenest and best. There are other chances to stand and stare but not until the business in hand is complete and the ridge up the 18th fairway has been safely scaled.

In the meantime, the tiny 12th is not to be taken lightly. It is an admirable illustration that short holes don't have to be 200 yards to give a sense of achievement at hitting the green; and, though of modest length also, the 13th and 14th, one up and one back down again, permit little error in judging the pitches comprising the second shots.

The 15th has much in common with the 7th, a tee shot with the emphasis on carry, while the drive at the 16th must be well flighted to clear the trees guarding the wooded menace on the right. It may be wiser to take the safer line to the left and to rub shoulders with those turning back up the 17th with its hopes of a birdie. But, by now, thoughts are focused on negotiating the final slope to the 18th.

This is done preferably with a drive and crisp iron but, for those flagging physically and in spirit, the sight of the clubhouse has the same effect as an oasis in the desert and it's no mirage. It has splendid reviving powers and if, on reflection, your golf is best forgotten, look not on the dark side. A further glimpse at the scenic splendour will promptly persuade you that it has been amply worthwhile.

through Corfe village, then take first L.
Undulating course.
18 holes, 5927 yards, S.S.S.68
Club founded in 1892.
Visitors: welcome weekdays by arrangement, handicap cert. req'd.
Green fees: weekdays £7, weekends £9.
Society meetings: catered for by arrangement on weekdays except Tues.
Catering: lunch and evening meals available.
Hotels: County, Taunton; Castle, Taunton.

B44 Tracy Park G & C C

☎ Abson (027 582) 2251
Bath Rd, Wick, Bristol BS15 5RN
Junction 18 off M4, S on A46 for 4 miles, R on A420 for 2 miles.
Parkland course.
18 holes, 6800 yards, S.S.S.73
9 holes, 5200 yards.
Course designed by Grant Aitken.
Club founded in June 1975.
Visitors: welcome; normal format is 9 holes in morning and 18 holes in afternoon.
Green fees: weekdays £8 per day, weekends and Bank Holidays £10 p. d.
Society meetings: welcome.
Catering: full catering facilities.
Hotels: Lansdown Grove, Bath; Beaufort, Bath; Holiday Inn, Bristol.

B45 Vivary

☎ Taunton (0823) 73875
Taunton, Somerset.
In centre of Taunton.
Parkland course.
18 holes, 4620 yards, S.S.S.62
Visitors: welcome, except after 4.30 pm Wed.
Green fees: £2.50 off peak times, £3.50 peak times.
Society meetings: welcome with prior booking.
Hotels: County, Castle.

B46 Wareham

☎ Wareham (092 95) 54156 members, 54147 Sec.
Sandford Rd, Wareham, Dorset BH20 4DH
A351 from Poole, 8 miles from Poole.
Undulating meadowland course.
9 holes, 2453 yards, S.S.S.64
18 hole course due by 1989.
Club founded in 1926.
Visitors: welcome most days with some restrictions at weekends.
Green fees: £5 per player day/ round.
Society meetings: no.
Catering: bar snacks available.
Hotels: numerous good hotels in area.

B47 Wells (Somerset)

☎ Wells (0749) 72868
East Horrington Rd, Wells, Somerset BA5 3DS
1½ miles from city centre off B3139.
Meadowland/ parkland course.
18 holes, 5288 yards, S.S.S.66
Club founded in 1895.
Visitors: welcome on weekdays.
Green fees: weekdays £4.50 (£3.50 with member), weekends and Bank Holidays £6 (£5 with member).
Society meetings: welcome on weekdays by arrangement.
Catering: meals and snacks served except Mon.
Hotels: Swan, Sadler St.

B48 Weston-Super-Mare

☎ Weston-s-Mare (0934) 21360
Uphill Rd North, Weston-super-Mare, Avon BS23 4NQ
M5 or A370 from Bristol
Seaside course.
18 holes, 6225 yards, S.S.S.70
Course designed by T. Dunn.
Visitors: welcome.
Green fees: weekdays £6.90, weekends £8.50.
Society meetings: by arrangement.
Catering: snacks and meals daily.
Hotels: Royal Pier; Grand Atlantic; Beachlands.

B49 West Wilts

☎ Warminster (0985) 212702
Elm Hill, Warminster, Wilts BA12 0AU
A350 towards Westbury, on edge of town.
Downland course.
18 holes, 5701 yards, S.S.S.68
Club founded in 1891.
Visitors: welcome on weekdays, weekends by arrangement.
Green fees: weekdays £7.50, weekends £9.
Society meetings: bookings taken Wed, Thur and Fri.
Catering: available except Mon and Tue evenings.
Hotels: Old Bell, Warminster; Farmer, Warminster.

B50 Weymouth

☎ Weymouth (0305) 773981
Links Rd, Westham, Weymouth, Dorset DT4 0PF
Off main Dorchester rd via Radipole Ln.
Seaside course,
18 holes, 5760 yards, S.S.S.17
Visitors: welcome.
Green fees: weekdays £4.50, weekends £6 per round.
Society meetings: welcome.
Catering: snacks and meals available.
Hotels: Lupins; Burlington; Gresham.

B51 **Windwhistle**
☎ Winsham (046 030) 231
Cricket St Thomas, Chard, Somerset TA20 4DG
On the A30 5m from Crewkerne, 3m from Chard, opposite wildlife park.
Parkland course.
11 holes, 6055 yards, S.S.S.69
Course designed by James Braid and J.H. Taylor.
Club founded in 1933.
Visitors: welcome but advisable to telephone in advance.
Green fees: weekdays £4.50, weekends and Bank Holidays £6.
Society meetings: by appointment only.
Catering: available except Sun.
Hotels: Shrubbery, Ilminster; George, Chard.

B52 **Worlebury**
☎ Weston-super-Mare (0934) 23214 Clubhouse, 25789 Sec.
Worlebury Hill Rd, Weston-super-Mare, Avon BS22 9SX
Off A370 from Bristol, 2½ miles from Weston-super-Mare.
Seaside meadowland course.
18 holes, 5945 yards, S.S.S.68
Course designed by Harry Vardon.
Club founded in 1909.
Visitors: welcome on weekdays.
Green fees: weekdays £7 (£4 with member), weekends £10 (£6 with member).
Society meetings: catered for on weekdays.
Catering: snacks, lunches and evening meals available.
Hotels: Grand Atlantic, Beachland.

B53 **Yeovil**
☎ Yeovil (0935) 75949 Clubhouse, 22965 Sec.
Sherborne Rd, Yeovil, Somerset BA21 5BW
1 mile E of Yeovil on A30 Yeovil to Sherborne Rd.
Undulating parkland course.
18 holes, 6139 yards, S.S.S.69
Course designed by Fowler and Alison
Club founded in 1919.
Visitors: welcome.
Green fees: weekdays £7, weekends £8.50
Society meetings: weekdays by arrangement.
Catering: full catering except Mon.
Hotels: Manor, Henford, Yeovil; Three Choughs, Henford, Yeovil; Mermaid, High Street; Pen Mill.

C Hampshire, Berkshire, Isle of Wight

For the purposes of competitive county golf, Hampshire includes the Isle of Wight and also the Channel Islands (see section A). It is a county of great significance and variety when considering its courses. It also claims Hayling Island to add to that variety and where better to start a brief summary of Hampshire's delights? The championship qualities of Hayling, on the edge of the Solent, has a nautical air, giving it undoubted distinction while its seaside character contrasts nicely with the mainland clubs.

My pick of these would be North Hants (Fleet), Blackmoor and Liphook, a noble trinity that exemplify the best of inland golf, a continuation of the rich seam of heather, sand, pine and silver birch running westwards from Surrey and Berkshire. It is hard to know which to put first, all demanding close acquaintance and affection, but a word, too, for the Army GC (Aldershot), Stoneham and Brokenhurst Manor on the edge of the New Forest.

Brokenhurst is a real favourite of mine but, as this section takes in Berkshire as well, let us retrace our steps and pay our respects, reverent respects, to the Red and Blue courses at the Berkshire, East Berks, very much in the same mould, Swinley Forest, a hallowed retreat, and Sunningdale, although in terms of playing qualification Sunningdale is more in Surrey than Berkshire.

On the matter of golf in the Isle of Wight, I have to rely on entirely favourable hearsay.

C1 Alresford
☎ Alresford (096 272) 3153
Cheriton Rd, Alresford, Hants SO24 0PN
1 mile S of Alresford town.
Undulating parkland course.
9 holes, 5992 yards, S.S.S.69
Course designed by Frank Pennink.
Club founded in 1890.
Visitors: welcome weekdays and after 11 am weekends.
Green fees: weekdays £5, weekends £10.
Society meetings: welcome but ring Alresford 3746 to make arrangements.
Catering: available except Mon; ring Alresford 3067 for Steward.
Hotels: Swan, Alresford.

C2 Alton
☎ Alton (0420) 82042
Old Odiham Rd, Alton, Hants. GU34 4BU
On A32 out of Alton towards Odiham, after 2 miles turn R at Golden Pot Public House, take next R immediately and club is ½ mile on R.
Undulating meadowland course.
9 holes, 5699 yards, S.S.S.67
Club founded in 1908.
Visitors: welcome except on competition days when course is closed until 5.30 pm.
Green fees: weekdays £5, weekends and Bank Holidays £8.50.
Society meetings: societies between 16 and 30 players welcome on weekdays by prior arrangement.
Catering: snacks usually available; full catering by prior arrangement.
Hotels: Swan, High St, Alton; Alton House, Normandy St, Alton.

C3 Ampfield Par 3
☎ Braishfield (0794) 68480 Pro, 68750
Winchester Rd, Ampfield, Romsey, Hants SO5 9BQ
On A31 2½ miles W of Hursley village, next door to White Horse Public House.
Parkland course.
18 holes, 2478 yards, S.S.S.53
Course designed by Henry Cotton MBE.
Club founded in 1963.
Visitors: welcome but advisable to telephone first to avoid busy times.
Green fees: weekdays £3.30 per round, £4.60 per day; weekends and Bank Holidays £5.50 per round, £7.70 per day.
Society meetings: small societies welcome weekdays by prior arrangement.
Catering: light meals and snacks.
Hotels: Potters Heron Motor, Ampfield; White Horse, Romsey.

C4 Andover
☎ Andover (0264) 58040
Winchester Rd, Andover, Hants SP10 2EF
Just off A303 on Andover by-pass, entrance to club about 500 yards after leaving A303.
Downland course.
9 holes, 5933 yards, S.S.S.68
Club founded in 1907.
Visitors: welcome except Sun am, Bank Holidays and competition days.
Green fees: weekdays £5 (£3 with member), weekends and Bank Holidays £6 (£4 with member).
Society meetings:welcome weekdays.
Catering: lunches and dinners available.
Hotels: White Hart, Bridge St, Andover; Danebury, High St, Andover.

C5 Army
☎ Farnborough (0232) 540638 Sec, 541104 Clubhouse, 547232 Pro.
Laffans Rd, Aldershot, Hants GU11 2HF
A325 to Queens Hotel, follow signs to club.
Heathland course.
18 holes, 6533 yards, S.S.S.71
Course designed by Frank Pennink.
Club founded in 1883.

Visitors: welcome on Mon, Thurs and Fri; at weekends guests of members only.
Green fees: £8 per round, £11 per day.
Society meetings: welcome Mon, Thurs and Fri.
Catering: available 11 am to 5 pm.
Hotels: Queens.

C6 Barton-on-Sea

☎ New Milton (0425) 615308
Marine Drive, Barton-on-Sea, New Milton, Hants BH25 7BY
Off A337 at the extreme E end of Marine Drive at Barton.
Seaside course.
18 holes, 5565 yards, S.S.S.67
Course designed by S. Colt.
Club founded in 1898.
Visitors: welcome weekdays after 8.30 am and weekends and Bank Holidays after 11.15 am; advisable to ring to ascertain programme for day.
Green fees: weekdays £9 per day or round, weekends and Bank Holidays £12.
Society meetings: societies 12 and over on Mon, Wed and Fri accepted.
Catering: snacks and teas available, evening catering for societies by arrangement.
Hotels: Chewton Glen, New Milton; Red House, Barton-on-Sea; Old Coastguard.

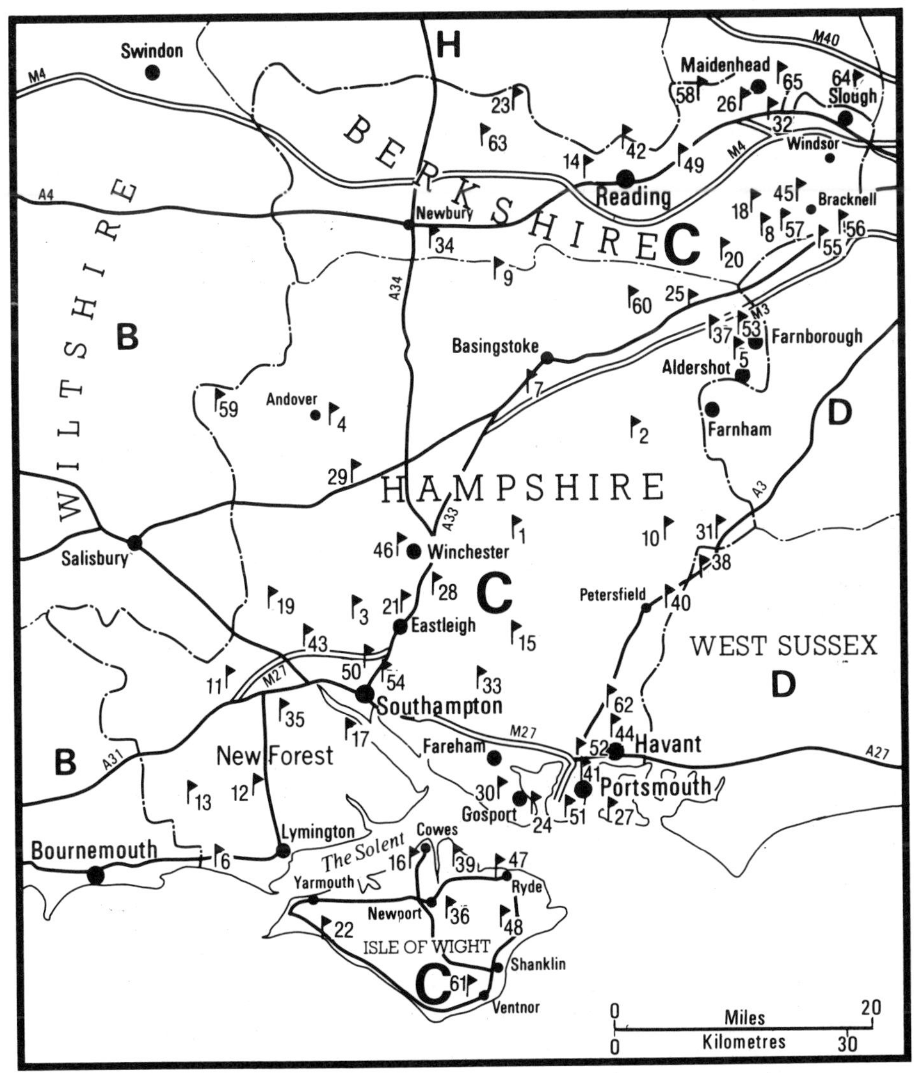

C7 Basingstoke
☎ Basingstoke (0256) 465990
Kempshott Park, Basingstoke, Hants RG23 7LL
On A30 3 miles W of Basingstoke.
Parkland course.
18 holes, 6253 yards, S.S.S.70
Club founded in 1927.
Visitors: welcome on weekdays and at weekends if playing with a member.
Green fees: £8 per round or £10 per day.
Society meetings: catered for on Wed and Thurs.
Catering: lunches served except Mon.
Hotels: Beach Arms, Oakley.

C8 Berkshire
☎ Ascot (0990) 21496/5
Swinley Rd, Ascot, Berks SL5 8AY
Situated on A332 between Ascot and Bagshot.
Heathland course,
36 holes.
Course designed by Fowler.
Club founded in 1928.
Visitors: weekdays only on request.
Green fees: £11.50 per round, £17 for 2 rounds.
Society meetings: weekdays on request to Sec.
Catering: lunches served except Mon.
Hotels: Berystede, Ascot; Truketess, Bagshot; Royal Foresters, Winkfield Row.

C9 Bishopswood
☎ Tadley (073 56) 5213
Bishopswood Lane, Tadley, Basingstoke, Hants RG26 6AT
6 miles N of Basingstoke, off A340 W of Tadley.
9 holes, 3237 yards, S.S.S.71
Course designed by Blake and Phillips.
Club founded in 1976.
Visitors: welcome except on club competition days.
Green fees: 18 holes weekdays £4, weekends £5; 9 holes weekdays £2.30, weekends £3.
Society meetings: welcome by arrangement on weekdays.
Catering: snacks and light meals only.
Hotels: numerous good hotels in area.

C10 Blackmoor
☎ Bordon (042 03) 2775
Golf Lane, White Hill, Bordon, Hants GU35 9EH
Off A325 between Farnham and Petersfield, turn into Firgrove Rd at Whitehill Crossroads.
Parkland/heathland course.
18 holes, 6213 yards, S.S.S.70
Course designed by H.S. Colt.
Club founded in 1913.
Visitors: welcome on weekdays and by arrangement at weekends, with handicap certificate.
Green fees: weekdays £11 (£6.50 after 2 pm), weekends £13.50 (£8.50 after 2 pm); half-price with member.
Society meetings: weekdays only.
Catering: full catering service available.
Hotels: Prince of Wales, Whitehill; Silver Birch, Greatham; The Queens, Selborne; New Inn, Kingsley.

C11 Bramshaw
☎ Southampton (0703) 813433
Brook, Lyndhurst, Hants SO4 7HE
Exit from M27 (Cadnam) and B3078 for 1m.
Manor course, parkland; forest course, undulating.
Manor 18 holes, 6233 yards, S.S.S.70
Forest 18 holes, 5774 yards, S.S.S.68
Club founded in 1880.
Visitors: welcome, but after 10 am at weekends.
Green fees: on application.
Society meetings: societies welcome weekdays only.
Catering: full catering available.
Hotels: Bell Inn.

C12 Brokenhurst Manor
☎ Lymington (0590) 23332
Sway Rd, Brockenhurst, Hants SO4 7SG
1 mile outside Brockenhurst village on Sway Rd, 5 miles from Lymington.
Parkland course.
18 holes, 6216 yards, S.S.S.70
Course designed by H.S. Colt.
Club opened for play in 1917.
Visitors: welcome with handicap certificate; advance booking by telephone advisable.
Green fees: weekdays £10, weekends £14; half-price with member.
Society meetings: catered for on Thurs.
Catering: full catering facilities.
Hotels: Balmer Lawn; Careys Manor; Cloud; all in Brockenhurst.

C13 Burley
☎ Burley (042 53) 2431
Burley, Ringwood, Hants BH24 4BB
A31 from Ringwood, turn R at Picket Post, through Burley St and Burley; club on L at top of hill.
Undulating moorland course.
9 holes, 6140 yards, S.S.S.69
Club founded in 1905.
Visitors: welcome.
Green fees: weekdays £5, weekends £6; half-price with member.
Society meetings: none.
Catering: no catering facilities.
Hotels: White Buck, Bisterne Close, Burley; Burley Manor; Moorhill House, Burley.

C14 Calcot Park
☎ Reading (0734) 27124
Bath Rd, Calcot, Reading, RG3 5RN
From Junction 12 on M4 take A4 to Reading for 1 mile.
Parkland course.
18 holes, 6283 yards, S.S.S.70
Club founded in 1930.
Visitors: welcome weekdays only, except Bank Holidays.
Green fees: £10 per visit.
Society meetings: catered for on Tues, Thurs and Fri.
Catering: lunches served except Mon.
Hotels: Calcot, Bath Rd, Calcot; Gatehouse, Bath Rd, Reading.

C15 Corhampton
☎ Droxford (0489) 877279
Sheeps Pond Lane, Droxford, Southampton, Hants SO3 1QZ
Right off A32 at Corhampton on B3057 for 1 mile.
Downland course.
18 holes, 6088 yards, S.S.S.69
Club founded in 1890.
Visitors: welcome on weekdays and with member at weekends and Bank Holidays.
Green fees: weekdays £8 per day or round (£4.50 with member), weekends and Bank Holidays £5.50 with m. o.
Society meetings: catered for on Mon and Thurs.
Catering: luncnes, teas and dinners served except Tues.
Hotels: Little Uplands Country Guest House, Droxford.

C16 Cowes
☎ Cowes (0983) 292303
Crossfield Ave, Cowes PO31 8HN
Make for Cowes High School, the course is at the far end of the school playing field.
Parkland course.
9 holes, 2940 yards, S.S.S.68
Club founded in 1908.
Visitors: welcome by arrangement.
Green fees: £5 per day or round, weekly

ticket £20.
Society meetings: no.
Catering: bar snacks on weekdays from 11.30 am to 13.30 pm except Sun.
Hotels: Fountain, High St, Cowes.

C17 Dibden
☎ Southampton (0703) 845596
Dibden, Southampton, Hants SO4 5TB
Follow Hythe sign at Dibden roundabout on A326, course entrance ½ mile at bottom of hill on right hand side.
18 holes, 6206 yards, S.S.S.70
Course designed by Hamilton Stutt.
Visitors: welcome.
Green fees: weekends £4.20 per round, weekdays £3 per round.
Society meetings: by arrangement with Pro.
Catering: full catering available.
Hotels: numerous hotels in Southampton.

C18 Downshire
☎ Bracknell (0344) 424066
Easthampstead Park, Wokingham, Berks RG11 3DH
M3 or M4 to Bracknell, then follow signs, 2 miles from Bracknell.
Parkland course.
18 holes, 6382 yards, S.S.S.70
Course designed by F. Hawtree.
Club founded in 1973.
Visitors: welcome every day.
Green fees: £4.20 per round.
Society meetings:welcome by arrangement.
Catering: bar and cafeteria facilities available.
Hotels: Ladbroke Mercury, Bracknell; St Annes Manor, Wokingham.

C19 Dunwood Manor
☎ Romsey (0794) 40549
Shootash Hill, Romsey, Hants SO5 0GF
Off A27 Romsey to Salisbury rd, after 2 miles turn R at Shootash crossroads into Danes Rd, club is on left.
Undulating parkland course.
18 holes, 5959 yards, S.S.S.69
Visitors: welcome weekdays.
Green fees: weekdays £6 per round, £7.50 per day; weekends £8.50; £30 per week.
Society meetings: welcome weekdays by arrangement.
Catering: snack menu available every lunchtime; evening meals by arrangement with Stewardess.
Hotels: numerous hotels in area.

C20 East Berkshire
☎ Crowthorne (0344) 772041
Ravenswood Ave, Crowthorne, Berks RG11 6BD
SW of Bracknell on A3095 and B3348.
Heathland course.
18 holes, 6315 yards, S.S.S.70
Course designed by P. Paxton.
Club founded in 1903.
Visitors: welcome on weekdays.
Green fees: weekdays £12 per day (£6 with member).
Society meetings: catered for on weekdays.
Catering: lunches and snacks every day.
Hotels: Waterloo.

C21 Fleming Park
☎ Eastleigh (0703) 612797 Pro, 619692 Catering
Magpie Lane, Eastleigh, Hants SO5 PLH
A27/M27, turn off at Eastleigh sign, 1 mile to course.
Parkland course.
18 holes, 4402 yards, S.S.S.62
Club founded in 1973.
Visitors: welcome, useful to phone in advance.
Green fees: 18 holes weekdays £3, weekends and Bank Holidays £4.20; 9 holes afternoon weekdays £1.70, weekends and Bank Holidays £2.60.
Society meetings: by arrangement with David Miller, Pro.
Catering: bar snacks and meals available.
Hotels: Crest, Leigh Rd.

C22 Freshwater Bay
☎ Freshwater (0983) 752955
Afton Down, Freshwater Bay, Isle of Wight PO40 9TZ
2 miles from Yarmouth on A3055 overlooking Freshwater Bay.
Seaside, downland course.
18 holes, 5628 yards, S.S.S.68
Club founded in 1893.
Visitors: welcome at all times.
Green fees: weekdays £6 per round or day, weekends £7 per round or day.
Society meetings: catered for on weekdays and weekends by arrangement.
Catering: light refreshments only.
Hotels: Albion, Freshwater Bay; Saunders, Freshwater Bay; Nodes Garden, Totland.

C23 Goring & Streatley
☎ Goring-on-Thames (0491) 872688
Rectory Rd, Streatley-on-Thames, Berks RG8 9QA
On A329 10 miles NW of Reading.
Parkland course.
18 holes, 6255 yards, S.S.S.70
Club founded in 1890.
Visitors: welcome weekdays.
Green fees: £10 per day.
Society meetings: catered for on weekdays only, ring for details.
Catering: full restaurant service.
Hotels: Beetle and Wedge.

C24 Gosport & Stokes Bay
☎ Gosport (0705) 581625 Steward, 52794 Sec.
Military Rd, Haslar, Gosport.
On A32 6 miles S of Fareham.
Seaside course.
9 holes, 5806 yards, S.S.S.68
Club founded in 1885.

Visitors: welcome except Sun mornings and Ladies Day on Thurs.
Green fees: £5 per day.
Society meetings: only small society meetings welcome.
Catering: bar snacks available; other meals to order.
Hotels: Anglesey,Crescent Rd, Gosport.

C25 Hartley Wintney

☎ Hartley Wintney (025 126) 2214 Club, 4211 Sec, 3779 Pro.
London Rd, Hartley Wintney, Hants RG27 8PT
On A30 8 miles NE of Basingstoke.
Parkland course.
9 holes, 6082 yards, S.S.S.69
Club founded in 1891.
Visitors: welcome but with restrictions on Wed, weekends and Bank Holidays.
Green fees: weekdays £5.50 per round, £8.50 per day; weekends and Bank Holidays £7.50 per round, £12.50 per day.
Society meetings: catered for on Tues and Thurs.
Catering: snacks and lunches available.
Hotels: Lismoyne, Fleet; The Lamb, London Rd, Hartley Wintney.

C26 Hawthorn Hill

☎ Maidenhead (0628) 75588
Drift Rd, Nr. Maidenhead, Berks.
Leave M4 going W at exit 8/9. Take the A330 towards Bracknell for 2½ miles. Course on right. Course 1 mile from ICI Research Centre at Jealotts Hill.
Undulating parkland.
18 holes, 6212 yards, S.S.S.70
Course designed by Clive D. Smith.
Club founded in 1985.
Visitors: welcome.
Green fees: 18 hole £5 (weekdays), £6 (weekends and Bank Holidays); 9 hole £2.80 (weekdays), £3.40 (weekends and Bank Holidays).
Society meetings: by arrangement.
Catering: bar snacks, lunches and dinners available.
Hotels: nearby in Maidenhead, Windsor, Bracknell, Reading and Ascot.

C27 Hayling

☎ Hayling Island (0705) 464446
Ferry Rd, Hayling Island, Hants PO11 0BX
5 miles S of Havant off M27 to A3023, situated at W end of the seafront.
Seaside course.
18 holes, 6489 yards, S.S.S.71
Course designed by J. Simpson.
Club founded in 1883.
Visitors: welcome if members of recognised golf club holding handicap certificate.
Green fees: weekdays £8.50, weekends and Bank Holidays £11.50.
Society meetings: accepted through application to Sec.
Catering: available every day, meals by arrangement with resident caterer.
Hotels: Newtown House, Manor Rd, Hayling Island.

C28 Hockley

☎ Twyford (0962) 713165
Twyford, Winchester, Hants SO21 1PL
2 miles S of Winchester on A333.
Downland course.
18 holes, 6260 yards, S.S.S.70
Course designed by James Braid.
Club founded in 1915.
Visitors: welcome weekdays, and at weekends with member or by arrangement with Sec.
Green fees: weekdays £9 (£3.50 with member), weekends and Bank Holidays £11 (£5 with member).
Society meetings: catered for on weekdays except Tues or Fri.
Catering: lunches served.
Hotels: Wessex, Winchester.

C29 Leckford & Longstock

☎ Andover (0264) 810710
Leckford, Stockbridge, Hants.
2½ miles N of Stockbridge on Andover rd.
Downland course.
9 holes, S.S.S.71
Course designed by John Morrison.
Visitors: invitation only.
Society meetings: no.
Catering: none.
Hotels: Grosvenor, Stockbridge.

C30 Lee-on-the-Solent

☎ Lee-on-the-Solent (0705) 551170
Brune Lane, Lee-on-the-Solent, Hants PO13 9HP
3 miles S of Fareham.
Meadowland course.
18 holes, 6022 yards, S.S.S.69
Club founded in 1905.
Visitors: welcome on weekdays.
Green fees: weekdays £6.50 per round, £7.50 per day (£3.25 per round, £3.75 per day with member). Weekends and Bank Holidays with member £3.75 per round, £4.25 per day.
Society meetings: catered for on Thurs.
Catering: lunches and snacks served except Mon.
Hotels: Belle Vue, Marine Parade E, Lee-on-the-Solent.

C31 Liphook

☎ Liphook (0428) 723271
Wheatsheaf Enclosure, Liphook, Hants GU30 7EH
1 mile S of Liphook on A3.
Heathland course.
18 holes, 6207 yards, S.S.S.70
Course designed by Arthur Groome.
Club founded in 1922.
Visitors: welcome by prior arrangement, except Sun am.
Green fees: weekdays £9 per round, £14 per day; weekends £15.
Society meetings: welcome by arrangement.
Catering: full meals by previous booking. Snacks always available.
Hotels: Georgian, Haslemere; Angel, Midhurst; Spread Eagle, Midhurst.

C32 Maidenhead

☎ Maidenhead (0628) 24693 Sec, 24067 Pro Shop.
Shoppenhangers Rd, Maidenhead, Berks SL6 2PZ
Off A308, adjacent to Maidenhead Railway Station.
Parkland course.
18 holes, 6344 yards, S.S.S.70
Club founded in 1896.
Visitors: welcome during week, except Tues; advisable to telephone beforehand.
Green fees: £11 (£5.50 with member).
Society meetings: either Wed or Thur, maximum 30.
Catering:full catering facilities.
Hotels: Crest, Shoppenhangers Rd, Maidenhead.

C33 Meon Valley G & C C

☎Wickham (0329) 833455
Sandy Lane, Shedfield, Southampton SO3 2HQ
On A334 8 miles E of Southampton between Botley and Wickham.
Parkland course.
18 holes, 6519 yards, S.S.S.71
Course designed by Hamilton Stutt.
Club founded in 1978.
Visitors:welcome.
Green fees:£10.
Society meetings:by arrangement; residents only at weekends.
Catering:meals and snacks available.
Hotels: Meon Valley.

C34 Newbury & Crookham

☎Newbury (0635) 40035
Bury's Bank Rd, Greenham, Newbury, Berks RG15 8BZ
2 miles SE of Newbury off A34.
Parkland course.
18 holes, 5880 yards, S.S.S.68
Course designed by J.H. Turner.
Club founded in 1873.
Visitors:weekdays no restrictions, weekends with members only.

Liphook

For most golfers charm is a more important quality in a course than challenge. Liphook is the type which combines the two in equal measure. 6207 yards is not long these days but matching the par of 70 is another matter when the heather and trees, the hallmark of the best Surrey and Hampshire courses, place such a premium on controlled shot-making.

You can certainly appreciate the lovely setting rather more when you keep straight, the countryside possessing more normal contouring than the valleys, plateaux and gulleys that characterise the land surrounding the Devil's Punchbowl at **Hindhead** just up the Portsmouth Road. It is a road that, when the club was founded in 1922, was very much more peaceful than it is now. Crossing it in order to get to the 15th tee is quite a task for weary limbs but, in terms of golf course architecture, Liphook has rightly been hailed as an example for the connoisseur.

My late senior partner, Ken Cotton, was always singing its praises but the remarkable part of the story is that its designer, A.C.M. Croome, was first and foremost a schoolmaster. Liphook was the only new course for which he was entirely responsible. Jack Neville keeps him notable company in this regard, Neville's lone masterpiece being Pebble Beach. However, it was ill health rather than lack of demand that prevented Croome pursuing the final chapter of a working life that had more variety than most.

In addition to being a housemaster at Radley College, he wrote about cricket and golf for several newspapers, both games at which he excelled himself. He was founder member of the Oxford and Cambridge Golfing Society, donating the Croome Shield for annual competition among College pairs at the President's Putter, and was a regular competitor in the Amateur and other championships.

It was while he was writing that he formed a lasting friendship with J.F. Abercromby, the designer of Addington, among others, who persuaded him to join forces in the firm of Fowler, Abercromby, Simpson and Croome – as elite a quartet as anyone could muster. At first, Croome's role was primarily on the administrative and publicity side, but inside every golfer is a golf course architect clamouring to get out. Croome did so and Liphook was the expression of his talents.

His creation obeys the dictum that there is a right and a wrong way to play every hole, a golfer having to plan his strategy and then supply the shots to match. The position of the clubhouse was changed after World War II, calling for a new first and last hole, the work of John Morrison whose plan was to provide a fine, long short hole to get players moving.

No clubhouse gets a better view of its 1st and 18th holes but, apart from the difficulty of the opening tee shot, Liphook is quick to let golfers know what is expected of them. There are three par 4s of well over 400 yards in the first six holes, the 4th, High View, being particularly demanding. It leads to the first crossing of the busy road and on to the first of the three par 5s where some individual thorn trees are a feature of the drive.

The 6th, with its little grassy hollow behind the green, doubles back on the 5th, the attractive short 7th starting the section of ten holes on the other side of the railway. The railway is not the feature it is on some courses although the 7th and 8th run roughly parallel to it. The 9th, 438 yards, another demanding 4, prompts a long, uphill second over a road and a heathery dell but the 10th offers a more inviting drive even if a ditch lurks on the approach to the green.

A large central bunker dominates the short 11th in a visual sense, the 12th, Forest Mere, completing the long par 4s and invariably not without a victim or two. A nice downhill drive and a slightly uphill second gives the longer hitters a chance of a birdie at the 13th, and, for those negotiating the dogleg successfully, a good pitch can do the same at the 14th.

Then it is a deep breath and a mad dash to the 15th where the drive takes us up over a steep ridge with the temptation to cut off more than is good for us. The 16th is the reverse of the 15th, a quarry and the corner of a wood awaiting any poorly struck or mis-directed second. The walk to the 17th is a last reminder of the Portsmouth Road which explains in part the club's traditionally strong links with the Navy; but the 17th's tee shot across a diagonal, corrugated bank of gorse and heather makes the fifth and last short hole difficult to judge, a further instance of Liphook's reputation that it is not just nautical men all at sea.

Green fees:£9 per day or round.
Society meetings:by arrangement on Wed, Thurs and Fri.
Catering:full catering by arrangement, except Mon.
Hotels: Chequers, Newbury.

C35 New Forest

☎ Lyndhurst (042 128) 2450 or 2752
Lyndhurst, Hants SO4 7BU
NE of Lyndhurst on the A35.
Heathland course.
18 holes, 5748 yards, S.S.S.68
Course designed by Peter Swann.
Club founded in 1888.
Visitors: welcome Mon to Sat, and Sun after 1.30 pm.
Green fees: £4 per round or day.
Society meetings: welcome Mon to Sat.
Catering: service available 11 am to 5 pm
Hotels: Crown; Lyndhurst Park.

C36 Newport

☎ Newport (0983) 525076
St George's Down, Newport, Isle of Wight PO30 3BA
A3056 Newport to Sandown rd ½ mile from Newport.
Downland course.
9 holes, 2852 yards, S.S.S.68
Club founded in 1896.
Visitors: welcome.
Green fees: weekdays £4, weekends and Bank Holidays afternoon £6.
Catering: snack meals available.
Hotels: numerous good hotels in area.

C37 North Hants

☎ Fleet (0252) 6443
Minley Rd, Fleet, Hants GU13 8RE
½ mile N of Fleet Station on B3013.
Heathland course.
18 holes, 6257 yards, S.S.S.70
Visitors: welcome on weekdays, please phone first.
Green fees: £8 per round, £12.80 per day.
Society meetings: catered for on Tues and Wed.
Catering: snacks, lunches and dinners available.
Hotels: Lismoyne, Church Rd, Fleet; Oaklea Guest House, Hook, Hants.

C38 Old Thorns

☎ Liphook (0428) 724555
London Kosaido G. & C.C., Longmoor Rd, Liphook, Hants GU30 7PE
On A3 into Liphook, at mini-roundabout go down B2131 for about 1 mile until sign on lefthand side saying London Kosaido G.C.; turn up this lane and go right to end.
18 holes, S.S.S.72
Course designed by Commander Harris, adapted by Peter Alliss and Dave Thomas.
Club founded in 1982.
Visitors: welcome.
Green fees: £10 per round, £15 per day, £5 per round after 4 pm.
Society meetings: welcome.
Catering: full à la carte menu and Japanese restaurant.
Hotels: Old Thorns.

C39 Osborne

☎ (0593) 295421
Osborne, East Cowes, Isle of Wight PO32 67X
A3052 Newport to E Cowes Rd, situated in the grounds of Osborne House.
Parkland course.
9 holes, 6285 yards, S.S.S.70
Club founded in 1903.
Visitors: welcome except Tues 11.30 – 2.30 pm and Sun before 12 pm.
Green fees: weekdays £6 per day, weekends £6.50 per day.
Society meetings: weekdays only.
Catering: none.
Hotels: Crossway, Crossway, E Cowes.

C40 Petersfield

☎ Petersfield (0730) 63725 or 62386
The Heath, Petersfield, Hants GU31 4EJ
A3 to town centre, then Heath Rd to course.
Heath and meadowland course.
18 holes, 5751 yards, S.S.S.68
Club founded in 1881.
Visitors: welcome.
Green fees: weekdays £6 per round, £9 per day; weekends £8 per round, £12 per day.
Catering: bar snacks available.
Hotels: White Hart; Concorde.

C41 Portsmouth

☎ Portsmouth (0705) 372210 Pro.
Crookhorn Lane, Widley, Portsmouth, Hants PO7 5QL
Located on the hills overlooking Portsmouth Harbour on the N of the city, within 1 mile of both the A3 and A3M.
Undulating parkland course.
18 holes, 6259 yards, S.S.S.70
Club founded in 1926.
Visitors: welcome; bookable at weekends.
Green fees: weekdays £3, weekends and Bank Holidays £4.
Society meetings: as arranged with Pro.
Catering: full restaurant facilities.
Hotels: Holiday Inn; Post House, Hayling Island; Bear, Havant; Red Willows, Widley.

C42 Reading

☎ Reading (0734) 472909
Kidmore End Rd, Emmer Green, Reading, Berks RG4 8SG
2 miles N of Reading off Peppard Rd (B481).
Parkland course.
18 holes, 6011 yards, S.S.S.69
Club founded in 1910.
Visitors: welcome on weekdays.
Green fees: £10 per day.
Society meetings: arrangement with Sec.
Catering: all meals served except Mon.
Hotels: Caversham Bridge, Reading; Remada, Reading; White Hart, Sonning.

C43 Romsey

☎ Southampton (0703) 732218
Nursling, Southampton SO1 9XW
Junction of M271 and A3057 N of Southampton.
Undulating woodland course.
18 holes, 5752 yards, S.S.S.68
Course designed by Charles Lawrie.
Club founded in 1925.
Visitors: weekdays only.
Green fees: £7 per day, £5 per round.
Society meetings: catered for on weekdays only, phone for reductions.
Catering: full catering except Thurs.
Hotels: New Forest Motel, White Horse, Romsey; Anglesea Road, Shirley, Southampton.

C44 Rowlands Castle

☎ Rowlands Castle (070 541) 2784 or 2216
Links Lane, Rowlands Castle, Hants PO9 6AE
3 miles N of Havant off B2149
Parkland course.
18 holes, 6627 yards, S.S.S.72
18 holes, 6381 yards, S.S.S.70
Club founded in 1902.
Visitors: welcome every day but ring Rowlands Castle 2785 to confirm at weekends.
Green fees: £7.50 per round or day.
Society meetings: catered for on weekdays, except Wed.
Catering: full catering service everyday until 6 pm.
Hotels: Bear, Havant; Brookfield, Emsworth.

C45 Royal Ascot

☎ Ascot (0990) 25175
Winkfield Rd, Ascot, Berks SL5 7LJ
In centre of Royal Ascot racecourse.
Heathland/ moorland course.
18 holes, 5653 yards, S.S.S.67
Course designed by J.H. Taylor
Club founded in 1887
Visitors: welcome on weekdays.
Green fees: weekdays £7 or £11 all day (£4.50 with member), weekends and

Sunningdale (New)

When you talk of Fortnum and Mason, Morecambe and Wise, Darby and Joan or Brighton and Hove, there is no suggestion that one name is mightier than the other. With golf courses, mention of Old and New tends to imply the opposite. Old Prestwick, the Old courses at St Andrews, Sunningdale or Walton Heath possess a seniority and a hallowed ring that is impossible to deny.

As a rule, club golfers deplore change although they invariably express their dislike without even considering the implications. When a New or second course is added, blind loyalty allows it to be tolerated rather than cherished. Few go to St Andrews to play the New if they can play the Old. Much the same applies to Walton Heath and Sunningdale but, whilst believing firmly that a day's golf isn't complete without a round on each, my preference at Sunningdale is marginally for the New, chosen by the English Golf Union to house the 1986 Brabazon Trophy.

The most lamented New course was that at Addington which fell victim to a housing scheme after the last war. There were some who maintained that J.F. Abercromby only built it to prove that the land could be drained but it was laid out in the same bracken, heather and silver birch country that lends Sunningdale its glory.

When the Roberts brothers founded Sunningdale at the turn of the century, the whole area right out to Chobham Common and beyond was a barren, treeless wilderness. Whereas the Old has become more or less enclosed, the New has retained its original character. Its density of heather is decidedly thicker and envelops the ball with relish when a slightly stray shot drifts on the wind.

In the Youths championship of 1983, played in stiff winds over hard ground, the degree of control necessary was far greater than it would have been on its more celebrated neighbour. Out by the 4th, 6th and 8th, there is little protection or comfort. Just the forlorn feeling that only a succession of stoutly hit drives and second shots will keep a good score intact.

It was over the New course that Gary Player first came to the public eye in this country, his victory in the Dunlop tournament of 1956 climaxing a titanic struggle with Arthur Lees, the local professional who, for years, played both courses better and more consistently than anyone has ever done. The New, like the Old, demands that the drives are well positioned in order to achieve the best angle and line for the second shots, accuracy being the greater virtue than power.

The opening drive, for instance, has to be up the left in order not to sacrifice length by seeing it running sideways down the slope. The tee shot at the 2nd, the first of five short holes, has little margin for error when the pin is tucked on the top shelf of a tapering green. The penalties for missing many of the greens on the New can be quite alarming and this is undoubtedly one of its defences. The other is that on many of the holes, there is a temptation to bite off more than you can chew with drives involving longish carries on holes which curve rather than run straight.

The 3rd has caught countless in this manner, the 7th, 11th, 12th and 15th running it a close second. One of the hardest par 4s is the 4th with the last part of a long second uphill; but the most spectacular hole, both in appearance and in a playing sense, is the par 5 6th. It weaves a serpentine path through a minefield of heather, making it difficult to know whether to attack or play safe. Both approaches have their drawbacks.

An extension of the hole and a modified green are one of several changes made in the last twenty years or so, although the biggest improvement surrounds the 8th, a short second to an unusual green being replaced by a long iron that has to be inch perfect to hold a new green. The 9th, despite a blind drive over a ridge to a fairway that plunges as soon as the guide post is cleared, is a second shot hole and nothing but the best serves at the short 10th, very often a wood even for the strongest.

Wind direction dictates how hard the homeward holes play. The New has enormous variety in the shots it demands especially on the last eight. For those without yardage charts, which in any case can be a doubtful blessing, judgement of distance is a problem. On the 12th and 15th, this is largely because the greens are above the level of the fairway although on the short 14th, a classic hole, the angling of the green reduces the size of the landing area.

On the long 13th, the problem is more of getting approaches to stop on a green running away from you while on the 16th the threat of out of bounds lurks. It is an elegant hazard in the shape of landscaped gardens but out of bounds all the same. The 17th, the last of the par 3s, is another difficult green to hit, and, if the 18th offers the chance of a finishing birdie, the drive must be as truly hit as any.

Bank Holidays £6 with member.
Society meetings: welcome.
Catering: available all week by arrangement.
Hotels: Forresters; Berystede.

C46 Royal Winchester
☎ Winchester (0962) 52462
Sarum Rd, Winchester, Hants SO22 5QE
Leave Winchester on Romsey Rd.
Downland course.
18 holes, 6218 yards, S.S.S.70
Course designed by H.S. Colt and A.P. Taylor.
Club founded in 1888.
Visitors: welcome on weekdays especially members of other golf clubs, who may be asked to produce a handicap certificate. At weekends and Bank Holidays must be introduced by and play with member.
Green fees: weekdays £9 per round or day.
Society meetings: welcome normally on Mon and Wed only.
Catering: facilities available most days.
Hotels: Chantry Mead, Bereweeke Ave, Winchester; Southgate, Southgate St, Winchester; Wessex, Paternoster Row, Winchester.

C47 Ryde
☎ Ryde (0983) 614809
Binstead Rd, Ryde, Isle of Wight PO33 3NF
Main Ryde to Newport road.
Parkland course.
9 holes, 5200 yards, S.S.S.66
Club founded in 1921.
Visitors: welcome except Wed afternoons and Sun mornings.
Green fees: weekdays £6, weekends £7.50.
Catering: meals and snacks served.
Hotels: Yelfs.

C48 Shanklin & Sandown
☎ Shanklin (0983) 403217
The Fairway, Sandown, I of W PO36 9PR
On A3055 nr Sandown station.
Seaside course.
18 holes, 6000 yards, S.S.S.69
Club founded in 1900.
Visitors: welcome.
Green fees: weekdays £8, weekends £10; 5 day £30, 7 day £40, 14 day £55.
Society meetings: catered for on weekdays.
Catering: lunches and snacks served daily, evening meals by arrangement.

C49 Sonning
☎ Reading (0734) 693332
Duffield Rd, Sonning-on-Thames, Berks RG5 4RJ
A4 Maidenhead/ Reading road, behind Readingensians Rugby Ground.
Parkland course.
18 holes, 6310 yards, S.S.S.70
Club founded in 1914.
Visitors: welcome weekdays with handicap certificate.
Green fees: rates on application.
Society meetings: welcome by prior arrangement.
Catering: full service available.
Hotels: White Hart, Sonning-on-Thames.

C50 Southampton
☎ Southampton (0703) 760373
Golf Course Rd, Bassett, Southampton, Hants.
N end of city, off Bassett Ave, halfway between Chilworth roundabout and Winchester Rd roundabout.
Parkland municipal course.
18 holes, 5683 metrres, S.S.S.70
9 holes, 2185 metres.
Club founded in 1935.
Visitors: welcome.
Green fees: 9 holes weekdays £1.50, weekends £2.40; 18 hole weekdays £3, weekends £4.80.
Society meetings: by arrangement with Council Municipal Golf Course Manager.
Catering: breakfasts, lunches and bar snacks available.
Hotels: Albany, The Ave, Southampton; Bassett, Bassett.

C51 Southsea
☎ Portsmouth (0705) 660945
The Mansion, Great Salterns, Eastern Rd, Portsmouth PO3 6QB
2 miles off M27/ A27/ A3 on E road into Portsmouth.
Meadowland municipal course.
18 holes, 5900 yards, S.S.S.68
Club founded in 1926.
Visitors: welcome.
Green fees: weekdays £3, weekends £3.80.
Society meetings: by arrangement with Portsmouth City Council.
Catering: none available.
Hotels: numerous good hotels in area.

C52 Southwick Park
☎ Cosham (0705) 380131
Pinsley Drive, Southwick, Fareham, Hants PO17 6EL

A333 7 miles N of Portsmouth, follow signs to HMS Dryad.
Parkland course.
18 holes, 5855 yards, S.S.S.68
Course designed by Charles Lawrie.
Club founded in 1977.
Visitors: welcome weekday mornings.
Green fees: weekdays Royal Navy Personnel £2.85 per round, visitors £5.50 per round (£3.75 with member); weekends Royal Navy Personnel £3.60 per round, visitors with member £4.75 per round.
Society meetings: catered for on Tues.
Catering: bar snacks available.
Hotels: Holiday Inn, Cosham; Roundabout, Fareham.

C53 Southwood
☎ Farnborough (0252) 548700
Ively Rd, Cove, Farnborough, Hants GU14 0LJ
1 mile W of A325 Farnborough.
Parkland public course.
9 holes, 2263 yards, S.S.S.31
Course designed by John D. Harris.
Club founded in 1977.
Visitors: welcome, bookable at weekends.
Green fees: summer rate £2.10 (OAP £1.10).
Society meetings: weekdays.
Catering: bar snacks, teas and lunches available.
Hotels: Queens, Lynchford Rd, Farnborough.

C54 Stoneham
☎ Southampton (0703) 768151, 769272 Sec.
Bassett Green Rd, Bassett, Southampton, SO2 3NE
From A33 turn left at Chilworth roundabout, ½ mile on left side of A27.
Heather, parkland course.
18 holes, 6310 yards, S.S.S.70
Course designed by Willie Park.
Club founded in 1908.
Visitors: welcome any time, advisable to telephone in advance.
Green fees: weekdays £8 per day or round, weekends and Bank Holidays £10 per day or round.
Society meetings: welcome Mon, Thurs and Fri by arrangement.
Catering: snack lunches except Sun; teas available every day; lunches by order.
Hotels: Polygon; Post House; Wessex; Albany.

C55 Sunningdale
☎ Ascot (0990) 21681
Ridgemount Rd, Sunningdale, Ascot SL5 9RW
Ridgemount Rd is 50 yards W of Sunningdale Railway Station crossing on the A30.
Heathland course.
old: 18 holes, 6341 yards, S.S.S.70
new: 18 holes, 6676 yards, S.S.S.72
Course designed by Willie Park.
Club founded in 1902.
Visitors: welcome on weekdays by introduction and with members at weekends and Bank Holidays.
Green fees: £25 per day.
Society meetings: welcome Tues and Thurs by arrangement.
Catering: full luncheon service except Mon; other catering by arrangement.
Hotels: Berystede, Ascot; Pennyhill Park, Bagshot.

C56 Sunningdale Ladies'
☎ Ascot (0990) 20507
Cross Rd, Sunningdale, Berks SL5 9RX
Second turning left on A30 going W from Sunningdale level crossing.
Heathland course.
18 holes, 3622 yards, S.S.S.60
Club founded in 1905.
Visitors: welcome by arrangement with Sec.
Green fees: weekdays £7 (£4 with member), weekends and Bank Holidays £9 (£5 with member); men by arrangement with Sec.
Society meetings: by arrangement with Sec.
Catering: light lunches and teas daily.
Hotels: Berystede, Bagshot Rd, Sunninghill.

C57 Swinley Forest
☎ Ascot (0990) 20197
Coronation Rd, South Ascot, Berks SL5 9LE
1½ miles from Ascot Station, through S Ascot village, right into Coronation Rd and fourth right to club.
Undulating course.
18 holes, 6001 yards, S.S.S.69
Course designed by H. S. Colt.
Club founded in 1909.
Visitors: welcome only by invitation of member.
Green fees: not available.
Society meetings: apply to Sec.
Catering: lunches served.
Hotels: Berystede, Ascot; Royal Foresters, Ascot.

C58 Temple
☎ Littlewick Green (062 882) 4248
Henley Rd, Hurley, Maidenhead, Berks SL6 5LH
A423 Maidenhead to Henley from M4.
Undulating parkland course.
18 holes, 6200 yards, S.S.S.70
Course designed by Willie Park.
Club founded in 1910.
Visitors: welcome on weekdays.
Green fees: £14 per day, £12 per ½ day; £5 with member.
Society meetings: catered for on Tues to Fri (incl).
Catering: lunches or evening meals (10 persons or more) served except Mon.
Hotels: Ye Olde Bell, Hurley; Compleat Angler, Marlow; Euro Crest, Maidenhead.

C59 Tidworth Garrison
☎ Stonehenge (0980) 42301
Bulford Rd, Tidworth, Hants. SP9 7AF
A338 to Tidworth, then 1 mile along Bulford Rd from bus station.
Downland course.
18 holes, 5990 yards, S.S.S.69
Club founded in 1908.
Visitors: welcome, prior telephone call advisable.
Green fees: £7 per round or day.
Society meetings: welcome by prior arrangement.
Catering: lunches and teas available daily; dinner by prior arrangement. Snacks only on Mon.
Hotels: Antrobus Arms, Amesbury.

C60 Tylney Park
☎ Hook (025 672) 2079
Rotherwick, Basingstoke, Hants
Off A30 at Nately Scures, follow signs for Rotherwick: approx 1½ miles.
Parkland course.
18 holes, 6138 yards, S.S.S.70
Course designed by W. Wiltshire.
Visitors: welcome.
Green fees: weekdays £7 (£4 with member), weekends £8.50 (£5 with member).
Society meetings: welcome Mon to Fri.
Catering: meals served.
Hotels: Raven Hook

C61 Ventnor
☎ Ventnor (0983) 853326
Steephill Down Rd, Ventnor, Isle of Wight.
A3055 to Ventnor, course on downs above town.
Undulating downland course.
9 holes, 5772 yards, S.S.S.68
Club founded in 1892.
Visitors: welcome except on Sun mornings and Bank Holidays.
Green fees: weekdays £3, weekends £4 (£2 with member).
Society meetings: none.
Catering: bar only.
Hotels: Llynfi, Spring Hill, Ventnor; Macracarpa, Mitchell Ave, Ventnor.

C62 Waterlooville

☎ Portsmouth (0705) 263388
Idsworth Rd, Cowplain, Portsmouth PO8 8BD
Off A3 in Cowplain, 5 miles N of Portsmouth.
Parkland course.
18 holes, 6647 yards, S.S.S. White tees 72, yellow tees 70.
Club founded in 1907.
Visitors: welcome on weekdays.
Green fees: £7 per round or day (£3.50 with member).
Society meetings: catered for on Thurs only.
Catering: full catering is available.
Hotels: Holiday Inn, Cosham; Post House, Hayling Island; The Bear, Havant.

C63 West Berks

☎ Chaddleworth (048 82) 574
Chaddleworth, Newbury, Berks
Off M4 at Junction 14, A338 towards Wantage, first right turn for 1 mile, follow signs to RAF Welford.
Downland course.
18 holes, 7053 yards, S.S.S.74
Club founded in 1978.
Visitors: welcome.
Green fees: weekdays £5.75, weekends and Bank Holidays £6.75.
Society meetings: welcome.
Catering: full service available.
Hotels: numerous good hotels in area.

C64 Wexham Park

☎ Fulmer (028 16) 3271
Wexham St, Wexham, Slough, Berks SL3 6ND
2 miles from Slough towards Gerrards Cross, follow signs to Wexham Park Hospital and club is ½ mile further on.
Parkland course.
18 holes, 5424 yards, S.S.S.67
Course designed by Emil Lawrence and David Morgan.
Club founded in 1976.
Visitors: welcome.
Green fees: weekdays £3.20 (9 holes £2.20), weekends £4.60 (9 holes £2.80).
Society meetings: welcome.
Catering: full service available.
Hotels: Bull, Gerrards Cross.

C65 Winter Hill

☎ Bourne End (062 85) 27613
Grange Lane, Cookham, Maidenhead, Berks SL6 9RP
4 miles from Maidenhead via M4; 6 miles from M40 via Marlow.
Parkland course.
18 holes, 6432 yards, S.S.S.71
Course designed by Charles Lawrie.
Club founded in 1976.
Visitors: welcome daily, although after 12 noon weekends without handicap cert.
Green fees: weekdays £9, weekends £10; £5 per round Mon, Wed and Fri in Dec, Jan and Feb.
Society meetings: Wed preferred.
Catering: meals and snacks available.
Hotels: Eurocrest, Maidenhead and High Wycombe; Compleat Angler, Marlow.

D Surrey and West Sussex

Surrey is a county which is more richly endowed with fine golf courses than any other. Its richness is, in many ways, a freak of nature because the discovery in the early part of the century of what is generally called the sand and heather belt led to a rapid increase in the population of inland courses.

It was land, what is more, that had a poor agricultural value, although the building of golf courses soon led to an explosion of house building as everyone, not just golfers, found that the fashionable and desirable thing was to own a lovely garden running down to a green fairway. It has formed the basis of much fortune making in property development in all corners of the world but the pioneer was T.A. Roberts, founder of Sunningdale, who as agent of St John's College, Cambridge, more than earned his agent's fee by planning many of the houses that adorn part of both courses.

Sunningdale was open for play (the Old course, at any rate) in 1902 but the oldest of the heathery courses is Woking, still one of the best. It is not as formidable as Sunningdale, Walton Heath and, more recently, Wentworth but it heads the list of those where interest and enjoyment are paramount. There are now so many of them that it is impossible to class them in any sort of order of precedence so I will list them alphabetically for the sheer pleasure of doing so: Addington, Burhill, Camberley Heath, Coombe Hill, Hankley Common, New Zealand, St George's Hill, Sunningdale and then the welter of Ws, Walton Heath, Wentworth, West Byfleet, West Hill, Woking and Worplesdon. Given nice weather and good condition of the courses, it would be impossible not to enjoy a day's golf on any of them; Surrey golf is full of variety and contrast.

For lovers of parkland golf, there is Royal Mid-Surrey, Roehampton, RAC and Tandridge. Effingham and Guildford proclaim the best of golf on chalky downland while Farnham and West Surrey have parts that are heathery and parts that are a mixture of parkland and downland.

I have led this section on Surrey but West Sussex has much to offer, not least West Sussex GC itself at Pulborough which is every bit as good as anything in Surrey and far more beautiful. In terms of setting, there is nothing much better than Goodwood while Cowdray Park at Midhurst has its admirers. For the rest, there is Selsey, Bognor, Littlehampton and Ham Manor, working east along the coast, while Worthing is another fine example of downland golf and Hill Barn, its neighbour, a splendid municipal course on which several fully-fledged professional tournaments have been held.

D1 Addington

☎ 01-777 6057
205 Shirley Church Rd. Croydon, Surrey CR0 5AB
2½ miles from E Croydon station.
Heathland course.
18 holes, 6242 yards, S.S.S.71
Course designed by J.F. Abercromby.
Club founded in 1914.
Visitors: welcome on weekdays only.
Green fees: £10.
Society meetings: only by advance booking.
Catering: meals served.
Hotels: numerous good hotels in Croydon.

D2 Addington Court

☎ 01-657 0281/ 2/ 3
Featherbed Lane, Addington, Croydon, Surrey CR0 9AA
2 miles E of Croydon, leave B261 at Addington village.
Undulating public courses.
Championship 18 holes, 5577 yards, S.S.S.67
Falconwood 18 holes, 5513 yards, S.S.S.67
Course designed by F. Hawtree Snr.
Club founded in 1933.
Visitors: welcome.
Green fees: summer – Championship £4.80, Falconwood £3.80; reduced rates from Nov to March.
Society meetings: welcome on weekdays.
Catering: full catering.
Hotels: Selsdon Park, Selsdon; The Aerodrome, Purley Way, Croydon; Central, 3 South Park Hill Rd, Croydon.

D3 Addington Palace

☎ 01-654 3061
Gravel Hill, Addington Park, Croydon, Surrey CR0 5BB
2 miles from E Croydon station.

Parkland course.
18 holes, 6262 yards, S.S.S.71
Club founded in 1923.
Visitors: welcome on weekdays and with member at weekends or Bank Holidays.
Green fees: weekdays £11 per round or day (with member £5 per round or day), weekends £6 per round or day with member only.
Society meetings: catered for on Tues, Wed or Fri and on Thurs afternoons.
Catering: snacks and meals during day, except Mon.
Hotels: Selsdon Park; Holiday Inn, Croydon.

D4 Banstead Downs
☎ 01-642 2284
Burdon Lane, Belmont, Sutton, Surrey SM2 7DD
100 yards E of junction of A216 and B2230.
Downland course.
18 holes, 6150 yards, S.S.S.69
Club founded in 1890.
Visitors: welcome with letter of introduction on weekdays, Saturdays; Bank Holidays and Sunday mornings with member only.
Green fees: weekdays £10, afternoon £7, Sundays £10 afternoon; ½ price with member.
Society meetings: by arrangement.
Catering: 11 am – 6 pm, dinner by arrangement.
Hotels: Thatched House, Cheam; Drift Bridge, Epsom.

D5 Betchworth Park
☎ Dorking (0306) 882052 Sec, 884334 Pro.
Reigate Rd, Dorking, Surrey RH4 1NZ
1 mile E of Dorking on A25 to Reigate, entrance opposite horticultural gardens.
Parkland course.
18 holes, 6266 yards, S.S.S.70
Club founded in 1913.
Visitors: welcome weekdays except Tues and Wed mornings; restricted at weekends, subject to club events.
Green fees: weekdays £10 per day, weekends £13.50 per day.
Society meetings: catered for all day Mon and Thurs and Tues and Wed pm
Catering: lunches and teas served.
Hotels: Burford Bridge, Box Hill, Dorking; White Horse, Dorking; Punchbowl, Dorking.

D6 Bognor Regis
☎ Bognor Regis (0243) 821929
Downview Rd, Felpham, Bognor Regis, Sussex PO22 8JD
A259 Littlehampton to Bognor Road, turn right at traffic lights at Felpham, 2 miles short of Bognor Regis.
Parkland course.
18 holes, 6238 yards, S.S.S.70
Club founded in 1892.
Visitors: welcome with handicap certificate; weekends from April to Oct with member only.
Green fees: weekdays £8, weekends £10.
Society meetings: restricted, by arrangement only.
Catering: meals served by arrangement.
Hotels: Royal Norfolk, Bognor Regis; Beach, Littlehampton.

D7 Bramley
☎ Guildford (0483) 892696 Sec.
Bramley, Guildford, Surrey GU5 0AL
Situated 4 miles S of Guildford on A281 Guildford to Horsham road, between the villages of Shalford and Bramley.
Parkland course.
18 holes, 5910 yards, S.S.S.68
Course designed by Charles Mayo and redesigned by James Braid.
Club founded in 1913.
Visitors: welcome on weekdays and with member at weekends.
Green fees: £7.50 per round (£3.50 with member), £9.50 per day (£4.50 with member).
Society meetings: welcome on weekdays by prior arrangement.
Catering: snacks and meals available during bar opening hours.
Hotels: Bramley Grange, Bramley.

D8 Burhill
☎ Walton-on-Thames (0932) 227345
Walton-on-Thames, Surrey KT12 4BL
Off A3 on A245 towards Byfleet, right into Seven Hills Rd and again into Burwood Rd, entrance is second on right.
Parkland course.
18 holes, 6224 yards, S.S.S.70
Course designed by H.S. Colt.
Club founded in 1907.
Visitors: weekdays only by arrangement.
Green fees: £16 (£11 after noon).
Society meetings: accepted on Wed, Thurs or Fri.
Catering: meals and snacks served.
Hotels: Seven Hills, Cobham; Oatlands Park, Weybridge.

D9 Camberley Heath
☎ Camberley (0276) 23258
Golf Drive, Camberley, Surrey GU15 1JG
On A325 S of Camberley, near M3 Exit 4, follow signs to Frimley and Bagshot.
Undulating heathland course.
18 holes, 6402 yards, S.S.S.71
Course designed by H.S. Colt.
Club founded in 1913.
Visitors: welcome, but must have handicap certificate from recognised golf club and should telephone for tee reservation.
Green fees: weekdays £14 per day, £10 per round.
Society meetings: by arrangement.
Catering: meals and snacks served.
Hotels: good hotels in area.

D10 Chessington
☎ 01-391 0948
Garrison Lane, Chessington, Surrey KT9 2LW
Opposite Chessington South station, very near to Chessington Zoo.
Parkland course.
9 holes, 1655 yards, S.S.S.30
Course designed by Patrick Tallack PGA.
Club founded in 1983.
Visitors: welcome.
Green fees: £2 for 9 holes.
Society meetings: welcome.
Catering: full catering facilities available.
Hotels: Seven Hills, Cobham; Oatlands Park, Weybridge.

D11 Chipstead
☎ Downland (073 75) 55781
How Lane, Coulsdon, Surrey CR3 3PR
Follow signs to Chipstead from A217.
Parkland course.
18 holes, 5454 yards, S.S.S.67
Club founded in 1906.
Visitors: welcome on weekdays.
Green fees: £10 (£8 after 2 pm).
Society meetings: catered for Tues afternoons and all day Thurs.
Catering: lunches served except Mon.
Hotels: numerous hotels in area.

D12 Coombe Hill
☎ 01-942 2284
Golf Club Drive, Kingston Hill, Surrey KT2 7DG
¼ mile W of A3.
Parkland course.
18 holes, 6286 yards, S.S.S.71
Course designed by Abercromby.
Club founded in 1911.
Visitors: by appointment only.
Green fees: weekdays £18, weekends £25.
Society meetings: welcome weekdays.
Catering: lunches served every day.
Hotels: Seven Hills; Richmond Hill.

D13 Coombe Wood

☎ 01-942 0388
George Rd, Kingston Hill, Surrey KT2 7NS
1 mile N of Kingston-on-Thames, off Kingston Hill.
Parkland course.
18 holes, 5210 yards, S.S.S.66
Course designed by T. Williamson.
Club founded in 1904.
Visitors: weekdays only.
Green fees: £10 per round, £11 per day.
Society meetings: welcome Wed, Thurs.
Hotels: Antoinette, Beaufort Rd, Kingston-on-Thames.

D14 Copthorne

☎ 0342 (712508)
Bovers Arms Rd, Copthorne, Crawley, West Sussex RH10 3LL
On A264, 4 miles W of Crawley.
Heathland course.
18 holes, 6505 yards, S.S.S.71
Course designed by James Braid.
Visitors: welcome weekdays, with member only at weekends.
Green fees: £10 per round, £12 per day.
Society meetings: Thursday and Friday by arrangement.
Catering: bar snacks; meals by arrangement.
Hotels: Copthorne.

D15 Cottesmore

☎ Crawley (0293) 28256
Buchan Hill, Pease Pottage, Crawley, Sussex RH11 9AT
Last turn off M23 S to Pease Pottage, 1 mile down Horsham Road from Pease Pottage on right hand side.
Undulating meadowland course.
Old course 18 holes, 6100 yards, S.S.S.70
New course 18 holes, 5500 yards, S.S.S.68
Course designed by M.D. Rogerson.
Club founded in 1975.
Visitors: welcome.
Green fees: Old course weekends £12, weekdays £8; New course weekends and weekdays £8.

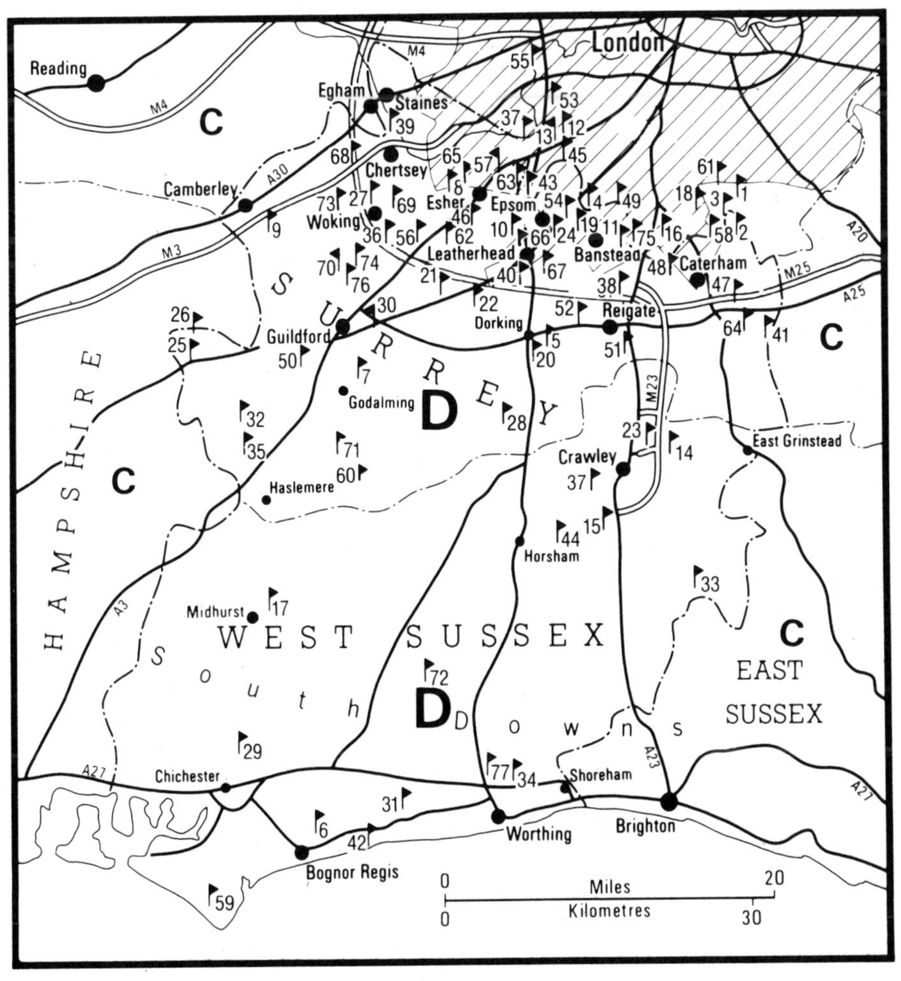

Society meetings: welcome by arrangement.
Catering: meals and snacks served.
Hotels: Cottesmore Country Club.

D16 Coulsdon Court

☎ 01-668 0414
Coulsdon Rd, Coulsdon, Surrey CR3 2LL
Just off A23, 2 miles S of Croydon, 2 miles N of M25 and M23.
Parkland course.
18 holes, 6030 yards, S.S.S.68
Course designed by H.S. Colt.
Club founded in 1926.
Visitors: welcome.
Green fees: weekdays £4, weekends and Bank Holidays £6; reductions for Juniors and OAPs.
Society meetings: welcome on weekdays but only with full catering.
Catering: full restaurant facilities Tues to Sat evenings; full menu every lunchtime.
Hotels: Pickard, Brighton Rd, Burgh Heath; Aerodrome, Purley Way, Croydon.

D17 Cowdray Park

☎ Midhurst (073 081) 3599 Sec, 2091 Pro.
Midhurst, W. Sussex GU29 0BB
Situated about 1 mile E of Midhurst on A272.
Parkland course.
18 holes, 5972 yards, S.S.S.70
Club founded in 1920.
Visitors: welcome.
Green fees: weekdays £8, weekends and Bank Holidays £10; half price with member; Juniors £1.
Society meetings: catered for on weekdays except Fri and Tues.
Catering: bar snacks daily, evening meals by arrangement.
Hotels: Angel, Midhurst; Spread Eagle, Midhurst.

D18 Croham Hurst

☎ 01-657 2075
Croham Rd, South Croydon, Surrey CR2 7HJ
On A23 ½ mile from South Croydon station, on road to Selsdon, on right.
Parkland course.
18 holes, 6274 yards, S.S.S.70
Course designed by Hawtree and Sons.
Club founded in 1911.
Visitors: welcome, telephone Pro (01-657 7705) prior to visit.
Green fees: £14 per day or round.
Society meetings: welcome by arrangement, booking 1 year in advance.
Catering: Lunches served except Mon.
Hotels: Selsdon Park; Aerodrome.

D19 Cuddington

☎ 01-393 0952
Banstead Rd, Banstead, Surrey SM7 1RD
200 yds from Banstead station.
Parkland course.
18 holes, 6282 yards, S.S.S.70
Club founded in 1929.
Visitors: welcome, providing accompanied by handicap certificate or letter of introduction.
Green fees: weekdays £12 per round or day, weekends £16 after 4 pm summer or 3 pm winter.
Society meetings: catered for on Thurs.
Catering: meals and snacks served.
Hotels: Pickard; Driftbridge.

D20 Dorking

☎ Dorking (0306) 886917
Chart Park, Dorking, Surrey RH5 4BX
A24, 1 mile S of Dorking.
Undulating parkland course.
9 holes, 5120 yards, S.S.S.65
Course designed by James Braid.
Club founded in 1897.
Visitors: welcome weekdays, members only weekends and Bank holidays, Ladies Day Wed morn.
Green fees: weekdays £5, evenings £3.50, £3 with member.
Society meetings: by arrangement.
Catering: snacks served weekdays, meals weekends only.
Hotels: Burford Bridge; White Horse; Punch Bowl.

D21 Drift

☎ East Horsley (048 65) 4641
The Drift, East Horsley, Surrey KT24 5HD
Turn off A3 onto B2039 signposted East Horsley, 2 miles.
Woodland course.
18 holes, 6404 yards, S.S.S.71
Club founded in 1975.
Visitors: welcome on weekdays.
Green fees: £8 per round, £11 per day.
Society meetings: welcome weekdays.
Catering: bar snacks available every day and evening meals except Mon; lunches available by arrangement.
Hotels: Thatchers, East Horsley.

D22 Effingham

☎ Bookham (0372) 52203
Guildford Rd, Effingham, Surrey KT24 5PZ
On A246 8 miles E of Guildford.
Downland course.
18 holes, 6488 yards, S.S.S.71
Course designed by H.S. Colt.
Club founded in 1927.
Visitors: welcome on weekdays by prior arrangement.
Green fees: £15 per day (£10 after noon).
Society meetings: welcome on Wed, Thurs and Fri.
Catering: snacks, lunches and teas served; evening meals by arrangement.
Hotels: Thatchers, East Horsley; Preston Cross, Bookham; Bookham Grange, Bookham.

D23 Effingham Park

☎ Copthorne (0342) 716528
Copthorne, Sussex RH10 3EU
Easy access from M23.
Parkland course.
9 holes, 1750 yards, S.S.S.30
Club founded in 1980.
Visitors: welcome except on Sun mornings before 10.30 am.
Green fees: 9 holes – weekdays £3, weekends £4; 18 holes – weekdays £4.50, weekends £5.
Society meetings: welcome on weekdays.
Catering: light refreshments available.
Hotels: Copthorne, Copthorne, Sussex.

D24 Epsom

☎ Epsom (037 27) 23363 Members & Steward, 21666 Sec.
Longdown Lane, Epsom, Surrey KT17 4JR
¼ mile N of Epsom Downs station.
Downland course.
18 holes, 5725 yards, S.S.S.68
Club founded in 1889.
Visitors: welcome on weekdays from 8 am, except Tues when 12.30 pm, weekends only after 11 am.
Green fees: weekdays £5.50 per round, £7.50 per day; weekends £6 per round, £7.50 per day; after 5 pm £4 per round.
Society meetings: catered for on Wed and Fri, maximum 32.
Catering: no regular catering. Sandwiches and snacks available if ordered before 11 am.
Hotels: Driftbridge.

D25 Farnham

☎ Runfold (025 18) 2109
The Sands, Farnham, Surrey GU10 1PX
1 mile E of Farnham on A31, turning to The Sands, signposted.
Parkland/ heathland course.
18 holes, 6313 yards, S.S.S.70
Club founded in 1896.
Visitors: welcome weekdays with handicap certificate; guests of members only at weekends.
Green fees: weekdays £8 per round, £10.50 per day.
Society meetings: welcome by arrangement weekdays.
Catering: full catering available on request.
Hotels: Hogs Back; Bush; Mitre; Bishops Table.

D26 Farnham Park

☎ Farnham (0252) 715216
Folly Hill, Farnham, Surrey.
¾ mile N of Farnham, next to castle in Farnham park.
Par 3 parkland course.
9 holes, 1163 yards, S.S.S.54

A golfer's paradise. On the course... and off.

Free Golf Clinic
Saturdays 3 – 4 pm.

At **Selsdon Park**, we now have just about everything you need to help you unwind. Within our Tropical Leisure Complex we have an attractive pool, jacuzzi, steam bath, sauna, squash courts, mini gym and much more.

There are also inviting bars, a renowned restaurant and a Saturday Dinner Dance. Full size snooker tables. Hard and grass tennis courts. Croquet. Riding (extra). And from May to September an open-air heated pool.

But what makes Selsdon Park so special is our championship golf course, free to residents. 18 holes, 5854 metres. Where you can learn to swing better than ever before with the help of our resident professional Bill Mitchell. You may even see our tournament professional Christine Langford on the course.

Come for a week or a perfect weekend. We're close to central London – just half an hour away, yet beautifully situated in two hundred acres amidst the Surrey Hills.

All rooms with private bathroom and colour TV. Plus everything else for your comfort.

SELSDON PARK HOTEL
DIAMOND JUBILEE
1925 1985

WEEKLY/Full Board	WEEKEND/Demi-Pension
From £41 per person per day 7 days or more	From £35 per person per day 2 or 3 nights

Based on twin occupancy. Single or superior accommodation attracts a supplementary charge. Reductions of up to 50% for children.

For your free colour brochure write to Mr. G. C. Aust.

SELSDON PARK HOTEL
★★★★
Sanderstead, South Croydon, Surrey.
Telephone: 01-657 8811. Telex: 945003
Britain's Largest Proprietor-owned Hotel

Goodwood

From the top of Trundle Hill, an impregnable fortress in Roman times, the view takes the breath away. As well as picking out all the coastal landmarks from Worthing to Portsmouth, the inland splendour offers contrast at all points of the compass. It is no wonder that descriptions of the racecourse are always wrapped in superlatives. Although not enjoying quite such an elevated view of things, Goodwood's golfers are seldom unaware of the surroundings in which they play.

Unless the wind is blowing you off your feet or low cloud descends like a veil, Goodwood stimulates. It is true that the course needs a bit of wind to give it necessary bite (which does not?) but one of the game's most priceless assets is to get you away from the rigours of everyday life. Goodwood does that in abundant measure.

Some of the holes would win no prizes in a design contest. I believe that applies to all downland courses, which vary alarmingly according to ground and air conditions. A hole that is a drive and pitch one day can be two woods the next, but a change in Goodwood's character is not entirely dependent on the elements. Four holes, the 3rd to the 6th, in the valley in the lee of Trundle Hill, offer a more sheltered interlude and there is some surprise when the visitor finds himself grappling with a tree-lined finish for the last two holes on the other side of the road.

Coming from Chichester, it is possible to drive past the clubhouse without knowing that it is a clubhouse and there is a longish walk to the first tee. Coming from the direction of Havant, on the other hand, bunkers and guide posts can be spotted a long way off. The 1st is a reasonably gentle opener, a par 5 within the scope of most, although to get home in two the drive has to be well placed and the second shot bold enough to skirt the corner of the wood which forms the dogleg. The 2nd offers an inviting drive but then comes the first variation. Downhill short holes are always appealing and the 3rd introduces us to a loop in which positional play is all important.

The left is the side to be on the 4th and 5th from the tee, the 6th offering a definite chance of a birdie. This is just as well because the climb up to the 7th reveals the hardest par 4 on the course at 470 yards with a wind against more often than not.

A pleasant second shot to a well guarded green at the 9th brings us back to the vicinity of the clubhouse and then it is about turn down the 10th where two large bunkers dominate the drive. There is a chance to survey the scene from the 11th tee but it is too exciting a hole to be distracted for long. A par 5 with a downhill drive and an uphill second is the herald to three holes round an attractive wood.

The wood flanks the second part of the 11th and the short 12th which provides a demanding target but it is even more a peril at the 319-yard 13th, the drive having to be threaded between the trees on the right and the threat of out of bounds on the left. There is a real pastoral flavour about this part of the course which continues with the stronger players flexing their muscles to get home in two at the par 5 14th – if wary of the dew pond awaiting a pushed second.

The 15th, a longish 4, follows the opposite direction to the 11th and is a splendid foil to the 16th, a short par 4 like the 6th. A small glade of pines on the left of the green is the main feature but there is nothing to suggest what follows on the other side of the road. There is a definite enclosed look about the 17th and several ways of straying from the straight and narrow. The rough is fiercer than anywhere else and the trees are old and well established.

Pheasant calls may soften the pain of failing to match par on the last of the 5s but Goodwood is one of those courses ending with a short hole and there is the added lure of the welcome of the clubhouse built in characteristic Sussex flint.

Course designed by Henry Cotton.
Club founded in 1963.
Visitors: open to public at all times.
Green fees: weekdays £1.40 per round, weekends £1.60 per round.
Society meetings: none.
Catering: light snacks served.
Hotels: Bush, Farnham.

D27 Foxhills

☎ Ottershaw (093 287) 2050.
Stonehill Rd, Ottershaw, Surrey KT16 0EL
Off A320 at Otter Public House, turn right and right again into Foxhills Rd.
Heathland courses.
Chertsey 18 holes, 6658 yards, S.S.S.72
Longcross 18 holes, 6406 yards, S.S.S.71
Course designed by F. Hawtree.
Club founded in 1978.
Visitors: welcome Mon to Fri.
Green fees: £10 for 18 holes, £14 for 36 holes.
Society meetings: welcome Mon to Fri, minimum 20.
Catering: lunches available every day in clubhouse; dinners served in Manor House except Sun and Mon.
Hotels: numerous good hotels in area.

D28 Gatton Manor

☎ Oakwood Hill (030 679) 555
Ockley, Dorking, Surrey RH5 5PQ
A29 1½ miles SW of Ockley.
Undulating parkland course.
18 holes, 6145 to 6902 yards, S.S.S.69-73
Course designed by D.B. and D.G. Heath.
Club founded in 1969.
Visitors: welcome except Sun mornings.
Green fees: weekdays £10 per day, £7 per round; weekends £12 per day, £8 per round.
Society meetings: catered for on weekdays.
Catering: meals and snacks served.
Hotels: Gatton Manor.

D29 Goodwood

☎ Chichester (0243) 774968
Goodwood, Chichester, West Sussex PO18 0PN
On A266 5 miles N of Chichester.
Downland/ parkland course.
18 holes, 6370 yards, S.S.S.70
Course designed by James Braid.
Club founded in 1891.
Visitors: welcome on weekdays and at weekends when competitions are not being held.
Green fees: weekdays £8 per day, weekends and Bank Holidays £11 per day.
Society meetings: welcome weekdays.
Catering: lunches served except Mon and Sun.
Hotels: Goodwood Park, Waterbeach, Chichester; Dolphin and Anchor, Chichester; Chichester Lodge, Chichester.

D30 Guildford

☎ Guildford (0483) 63941
High Path Rd, Merrow, Guildford, Surrey GU1 2HI
2 miles E of Guildford on A246.
Downland course.
18 holes, 6080 yards, S.S.S.70
Course designed by James Braid.
Club founded in 1886.
Visitors: welcome on weekdays; weekends with member only.
Green fees: £6.50 per round, £10 per day, Juniors £3 with member only.
Society meetings: welcome by arrangement.
Catering: bar snacks, restaurant by arrangement.
Hotels: Angel; White Horse, Guildford; Cleverdale, Epsom.

D31 Ham Manor

☎ Rustington (0903) 783288
Angmering, W. Sussex BN16 4JE
3 miles E of Littlehampton.
Gently undulating parkland course.
18 holes, 6216 yards, S.S.S.70
Course designed by H.S. Colt.
Club founded in 1936.
Visitors: welcome on weekdays and at weekends with reservation.
Green fees: weekdays £9, weekends £13.
Society meetings: welcome on weekdays except Mon.
Catering: lunches served except Mon.
Hotels: numerous good hotels in area.

D32 Hankley Common

☎ Frensham (025 125) 2493
Tilford Rd, Tilford, Farnham, Surrey GU10 2DD
4 miles SW of Farnham, take road to Hindhead over railway crossing, fork right to Tilford.
Heathland course.

18 holes, 6403 yards, S.S.S.71
Course designed by James Braid.
Club founded in 1895.
Visitors: welcome on weekdays and by arrangement with Sec at weekends and Bank holidays; must have a bona fide handicap and be member of recognised golf club.
Green fees: weekdays £12, weekends and Bank Holidays £15.
Society meetings: on Tues and Wed.
Catering: always available.
Hotels: Frensham Pond, Frensham; Pride of the Valley, Churt; The Bush, Farnham.

D33 Haywards Heath

☎ Haywards Heath (0444) 414457
High Beech Lane, Haywards Heath, W. Sussex RG16 1SL
N of Haywards Heath, Nr, Lindfield.
Parkland course.
18 holes, 6202 yards, S.S.S.70
Club founded in 1922.
Visitors: welcome.
Green fees: weekdays £8, weekends and Bank Holidays £10.
Society meetings: on Wed and Thurs.
Catering: lunch available, other catering by arrangement.
Hotels: Birch, Haywards Heath; Hilton Park, Haywards Heath; Ockenden Manor.

D34 Hill Barn

☎ Worthing (0903) 37301
Hill Barn Lane, Worthing, Sussex BN14 9QE
NE of Worthing off Upper Brighton road to Excess roundabout.
Downland municipal course.
18 holes, 6224 yards, S.S.S.70
Club founded in 1935.
Visitors: welcome.
Green fees: weekdays £5 per round, weekends £6 per round.
Society meetings: welcome.
Catering: meals served.
Hotels: Chatsworth; Beach.

D35 Hindhead

☎ Hindhead (042 873) 4614
Churt Rd, Hindhead, Surrey GU26 6HX
1½ miles N of Hindhead on A287.
Heathland course.
18 holes, 6349 yards, S.S.S.70
Club founded in 1904.
Visitors: welcome weekdays and at weekends after noon.
Green fees: weekdays £10 (£5 with member), weekends and Bank Holidays £13 (£6 with member).
Society meetings: welcome on Wed, Thurs
Catering: lunches served daily; dinner for societies only in excess of 20 players.
Hotels: Devil's Punch Bowl, Hindhead; Pride of the Valley, Churt.

D36 Hoebridge

☎ Woking (048 62) 22611
Old Woking Rd, Old Woking, Surrey GU22 8JH
On B382 Old Woking road between Old Woking and West Byfleet.
Meadowland course.
Main 18 holes, 6587 yards, S.S.S.72
Par 3 18 holes, 2289 yards.
Course designed by John Jacobs.
Club founded in June 1982.
Visitors: welcome.
Green fees: Main £5 per round, £3.10 for 9 holes; Par 3 £3 per round, £1.90 for 9 holes.
Society meetings: welcome weekdays.
Catering: meals and snacks served.
Hotels: Northfleet, Woking.

D37 Home Park

☎ 01-977 2423
Hampton Wick, Kingston-upon-Thames, Surrey KT1 4AD
From Kingston over Kingston Bridge, at roundabout turn left, 50 yds on left through iron gates at Old Kings Head Public House, straight road to club.
Parkland course.
18 holes, 6519 yards, S.S.S.71
Club founded in 1895.
Visitors: welcome on non comp. days.
Green fees: weekdays £6 per day, weekends £8 per day.
Society meetings: minimum 20 catered for on weekdays.
Catering: meals and snacks served daily.
Hotels: Antoinette, Beaufort Rd, Kingston-upon-Thames.

D38 Kingswood (Surrey)

☎ Mogador (0737) 832188
Sandy Lane, Kingswood, Tadworth, Surrey.
4 miles S of Sutton on A217.
Parkland course.
18 holes, 6821 yards, S.S.S.73
Course designed by James Braid.
Club founded in 1928.
Visitors: welcome weekdays and after 3 pm at weekends or Bank Holidays.
Green fees: weekdays £12 (£8 with member), weekends and Bank Holidays £15 (£9 with member).
Society meetings: by arrangement.
Catering: full catering available including dinner.
Hotels: Bridge, Reigate; Piccard Motel, Banstead.

D39 Laleham

☎ Chertsey (093 28) 64211
Chertsey, Surrey KT16 8RP
A320 between Staines and Chertsey, opposite Thorpe Water Park.
Parkland course.
18 holes, 6203 yards, S.S.S.70
Club founded in 1907.
Visitors: welcome on weekdays or with member at weekends.
Green fees: £6.50 per round, £8.75 per day.
Society meetings: welcome on Mon, Tues and Wed.
Catering: all day catering available.
Hotels: Runnymede, Egham; Thames Lodge, Staines.

D40 Leatherhead

☎ Oxshott (037 284) 3966
Kingston Rd, Leatherhead, Surrey KT22 0DP
Off M25.
Parkland course.
18 holes, 6069 yards, S.S.S.69
Club founded in 1901.
Visitors: welcome weekdays with handicap certificate.
Green fees: £10 per round, £12 per day.
Society meetings: catered for.
Catering: full catering.
Hotels: The Non Bull, Leatherhead.

D41 Limpsfield Chart

☎ Limpsfield Chart (088 388) 2106
Limpsfield, Oxted, Surrey RH8 0SL
On A25 between Oxted and Westerham. East from Oxted over traffic lights 300 yds on right.
Parkland course.
9 holes, 5718 yards, S.S.S.68
Club founded in 1889.
Visitors: welcome Mon, Tues, Wed and Fri.
Green fees: £6 for 18 holes.
Society meetings: can be arranged
Catering: meals served.
Hotels: Kings Arms, Westerham; White Hart, Brastead.

D42 Littlehampton

☎ Littlehampton (0903) 717170
170 Rope Walk, Riverside, Littlehampton, W. Sussex BN17 5DL
From Littlehampton take the road to Bognor Regis. After crossing the bridge over the river take the first turn to the left. This turn is marked To Golf Club, signs to Clubhouse.
Meadowland/ links course.
18 holes, 5621 yards, S.S.S.70
Club founded in 1889.
Visitors: welcome, except for novices; reasonable dress on course and in clubhouse.
Green fees: weekdays £8 per day, £6 after 5 pm; weekends and Bank Holidays £10 per day after 1 pm, £7 after 5 pm.
Society meetings: welcome by arrangement.
Catering: all meals served; groups must book.
Hotels: Beach, Littlehampton; Bailifscourt, Climping.

D43 Malden
☎ 01-942 0654
Traps Lane, New Malden, Surrey KT3 4RS
½ mile from New Malden railway station.
Parkland course.
18 holes, 6315 yards, S.S.S.70
Club founded in 1897.
Visitors: welcome on weekdays only.
Green fees: £11; £7 after 2.30 pm.
Society meetings: by arrangement on weekdays.
Catering: lunches and teas served daily except Mon.
Hotels: numerous good hotels in area.

D44 Mannings Heath
☎ Horsham (0403) 66217 Sec, 65224 Club.
Goldings Lane, Mannings Heath, W. Sussex RH13 6JU
3 miles SE of Horsham on A281; 4 miles from M25, exit at Pease Pottage or Handcross.
Undulating parkland course.
18 holes, 6402 yards, S.S.S.71
Club founded in 1908.
Visitors: welcome weekdays, preferably by prior arrangement.
Green fees: weekdays £9.
Society meetings: catered for on Tues, Wed and Fri only.
Catering: full catering available, except Mon.
Hotels: Kings Head, Carfax, Horsham; Cisswood, Lower Beeding, Horsham.

D45 Mitcham
☎ 01-648 1508
Carshalton Rd, Mitcham Junction, Surrey CR4 4HN
A237 off A23, by Mitcham Junction station.
Meadowland course.
18 holes, 5935 yards, S.S.S.68
Club founded in 1894.
Visitors: welcome; restricted at weekends.
Green fees: weekdays £4, weekends and Bank Holidays £5.
Society meetings: welcome on weekdays.
Catering: meals served.
Hotels: numerous hotels in area.

D46 Moore Place
☎ Esher (0372) 63533
Portsmouth Rd, Esher, Surrey KT10 9LN
On A3 Portsmouth rd, ½ mile from centre of Esher towards Cobham.
Undulating parkland course.
9 holes, 1756 yards
Course designed by R. Tobin.
Club founded in 1977.
Visitors: welcome.
Green fees: weekdays £1.70 for 9 holes, weekends £2.25 for 9 holes.
Catering: large Berni Inn restaurant attached to course.
Hotels: Greyhound, Hampton Court Rd, Hampton Court.

D47 North Downs
☎ Woldingham (088 385) 2057/ 3298/ 3004
Northdown Rd, Woldingham, Surrey CR3 7AA
Woldingham Rd at roundabout on A22 at N end of Caterham by-pass.
Undulating course.
18 holes, 5787 yards, S.S.S.68
18 holes, 5517 yards, S.S.S.67
Club founded in 1899.
Visitors: welcome.
Green fees: on application.
Society meetings: on application.
Catering: bar lunches available; meals by arrangement.
Hotels: numerous hotels in area.

D48 Oaks Sport Centre
☎ 01-643 8363
Woodmansterne Rd, Carshalton, Surrey.
Off B280 S of Carshalton.
Meadowland course.
18 holes, 5745 yards, S.S.S.68
9 holes, 1590 yards, S.S.S.29
Visitors: welcome.
Green fees: weekdays £3.50: weekends £4.50; reduced rates Juniors and OAPs. 9 holes, weekdays £1.50, weekends £1.80.
Society meetings: welcome.
Catering: meals served.
Hotels: Greyhound; Carshalton.

D49 Purley Downs
☎ 01-657 8347 Sec, 1231 Steward.
106 Purley Downs Rd, Purley, Surrey CR2 0RB
Off A233 between Purley and Croydon stations, past Volkswagen Building and first left.
Downland course.
18 holes, 6243 yards, S.S.S.70
Club founded in 1890.
Visitors: welcome on weekdays.
Green fees: £12.
Society meetings: welcome weekdays by arrangement.
Catering: lunch, tea and dinner served.
Hotels: numerous good hotels in area.

D50 Puttenham
☎ Guildford (0483) 810498
Puttenham, Guildford, Surrey GU3 1AL
Just off A31 Farnham to Guildford road (Hogs Back), 4 miles S of Guildford.
Heathland course.
18 holes, 5367 yards, S.S.S.66
Club founded in 1894.
Visitors: welcome on weekdays and with member only at weekends and Bank Holidays.
Green fees: £8 per day or round.
Society meetings: catered for on Wed and Thurs.
Catering: full service available.
Hotels: Hogs Back, Farnham; Crawford House, Guildford.

D51 Redhill & Reigate
☎ Reigate (073 72) 44626 Clubhouse, 40777 Sec, 44433 Pro.
Clarence Lodge, Pendleton Rd, Redhill, Surrey RH1 6LB
1 mile S of Reigate (A217), at traffic lights turn left (A2044), in ¼ mile turn left into Pendleton Rd.
Moorland course.
18 holes, 5193 yards, S.S.S.65
Course designed by James Braid.
Club founded in 1887.
Visitors: welcome but no play at weekends or Bank Holidays before 10.30 am; no play Sun afternoons between 1 June and 30 Sept.
Green fees: weekdays £4 (£3 with member), weekends £5 (£4 with member).
Society meetings: catered for on weekdays.
Catering: by arrangement with Steward.
Hotels: numerous hotels in area.

D52 Reigate Heath
☎ Reigate (073 72) 42610
Reigate Heath, Reigate RH2 8QR
½ mile S of A25 on W of Reigate.
Heathland course.
9 holes, 5554 yards, S.S.S.67
Club founded in 1895.
Visitors: welcome, but it is advisable to telephone in advance; Sun with members only.
Green fees: weekdays £7 per round, £9 per day; Sat £9 per round, £12 per day.
Society meetings: welcome on Wed and Thurs.
Catering: available every day except Mon.
Hotels: Cranleigh, West St, Reigate.

D53 Richmond
☎ 01-940 4351 or 1463
Sudbrook Park, Richmond, Surrey TW10 7AS
On A307 1 mile S of Richmond, look for Sudbrook Lane on left.
Parkland course.
18 holes, 5965 yards, S.S.S.69
Club founded in 1891.
Visitors: welcome on weekdays and at weekends by prior arrangement.
Green fees: weekdays £14.50, weekends £17.50.
Society meetings: welcome Tues and Thurs from mid-March until late Oct.

Catering: bar snacks available every day; lunches must be ordered before 10 am.
Hotels: Petersham; Richmond Gate.

D54 RAC C C
☎ Ashtead (03722) 76311
Woodcote Park, Epsom, Surrey KT18 7EW
A24, 1¾ miles from Epsom.
Parkland course.
Coronation 18 holes, 5520 yards, S.S.S.67
Old 18 holes, 6672 yards, S.S.S.72
Club founded in 1913.
Visitors: welcome by introduction only.
Green fees: on request.
Society meetings: on request.
Catering: full service available for members and guests only.
Hotels: numerous hotels in area.

D55 Royal Mid-Surrey
☎ 01-940 1894
Old Deer Park, Richmond, Surrey TW9 2SB
250 yards from Richmond roundabout on A316, entrance by Richmond Athletic Ground.
Parkland course.
Inner 18 holes, 5544 yards, S.S.S.67
Outer 18 holes, 6052 yards, S.S.S.70
Club founded in 1892.
Visitors: welcome, provided members of recognised Club with current handicap; special permission from Sec at weekends.
Green fees: weekdays £15 per round or day, weekends £20.
Society meetings: catered for Tues to Fri.
Catering: lunches and snacks served except Mon.
Hotels: Richmond Hill; Richmond Gate.

D56 St George's Hill
☎ Weybridge (0932) 42406
St George's Hill, Weybridge, Surrey KT13 0NL
B374 from station towards Cobham, ½ mile on left.
Heathland course.
18 holes, 3305 yards, S.S.S.72
Course designed by H.S. Colt.
Club founded in 1913.
Visitors: welcome but must book tee time in advance.
Green fees: £20 and £14.
Society meetings: catered for Wed-Fri.
Catering: full lunch restaurant and bar snacks served.
Hotels: numerous good hotels in area.

D57 Sandown Park
☎ Esher (0372) 65921 or 63340
More Lane, Esher, Surrey KT10 8AN
About 1 mile from Esher station, in centre of Sandown Park racecourse, off Portsmouth Rd.
Meadowland course.
9 holes, 2829 yards, S.S.S.67
Course designed by John Jacobs and Harold Bowpitt.
Club founded in 1969.
Visitors: welcome; on weekend mornings course must be booked.
Green fees: weekdays £2 per round, weekends £2.80 per round.
Society meetings: none.
Catering: full service available every day.
Hotels: Seven Hills, Cobham; The Haven, Thames Ditton.

D58 Selsdon Park Hotel
☎ 01-657 8811
Sanderstead, S. Croydon, Surrey CR2 8YA
B275 from Croydon, B268 at Selsdon.
Parkland course.
18 holes, 6402 yards, S.S.S.71
Course designed by J.H. Taylor.
Club founded in 1930.
Visitors: welcome; contact Pro at first tee.
Green fees: weekdays £9, Sat £15, Sun and Bank Holidays £17.
Society meetings: welcome by prior arrangement.
Catering: full service available.
Hotels: Selsdon Park.

D59 Selsey
☎ Selsey (0243) 602203
Golf Links Lane, Selsey, Chichester, W. Sussex PO20 9DR
On B2145, 7 miles S of Chichester.
Seaside course.
9 holes, 5730 yards, S.S.S.67
Club founded in 1909.
Visitors: welcome if members of recognised club.
Green fees: weekdays £5.50 per round, weekends £7 per round, except pm £6 per round, Bank Holidays £9 per day.
Society meetings: small societies welcome.
Catering: lunches and snacks served.

D60 Shillinglee Park
☎ Haslemere (0428) 53237
Chiddingfold, Godalming, Surrey GU8 4TA
Off A283, 2 miles S of Chiddingfold.
Undulating parkland course.
9 holes, 2500 yards, S.S.S.63
Course designed by Roger Mace.
Club founded in 1980.
Visitors: welcome at all times, booking essential at weekends.
Green fees: £2.50 for 9 holes, £4.25 per day; Juniors and OAPs £1.75 for 9 holes, £2.50 per day.
Society meetings: welcome.
Catering: full catering service as from April 1986.
Hotels: Crown Inn, Chiddingfold.

D61 Shirley Park
☎ 01-654 1143
Addiscombe Rd, Croydon CR0 7LB
1 mile from E Croydon station.
Parkland course.
18 holes, 6210 yards, S.S.S.70
Club founded in 1939
Visitors: welcome on weekdays without reservation.
Green fees: £11 per day or round.
Society meetings: catered for daily except Wed.
Catering: lunch and tea served daily.
Hotels: Airport, Croydon.

D62 Silvermere
☎ Cobham (0932) 66007
Redhill Rd, Cobham, Surrey.
Redhill road leaves A245 mid-way between Cobham and Byfleet.
Woodland/ parkland/ meadowland.
18 holes, 6333 yards, S.S.S.Unconfirmed
Visitors: welcome.
Green fees: weekdays £4.50, weekends and Bank Holidays £6.
Society meetings: welcome on weekdays, maximum 100.
Catering: bar and restaurant.
Hotels: Seven Hills.

D63 Surbiton
☎ 01-398 3101
Woodstock Lane, Chessington, Surrey KT9 1UG
2 miles E of Esher, off A3 at Ace of Spades roundabout.
Parkland course.
18 holes, 6211 yards, S.S.S.70
Club founded in 1896.
Visitors: welcome with reservation.
Green fees: £10 per person.
Society meetings: catered for.
Catering: full catering facilities.
Hotels: Haven, Portsmouth Rd, Esher.

D64 Tandridge
☎ Oxted (088 33) 2274
Oxted, Surrey RH8 9NQ
Off A25 by Oxted, 2 miles E of Godstone Junction 6 from M25.
Parkland course.
18 holes, 6260 yards, S.S.S.70
Club founded in 1923.
Visitors: welcome on Mon, Wed and Thurs only unless with member.
Green fees: £13 per day.

Society meetings: catered for on Mon, Wed and Thurs.
Catering: lunches every day except Tues.
Hotels: Hoskins Arms, Oxted.

D65 Thames Ditton & Esher

☎ 01-398 1551
Scilly Isles, Portsmouth Rd, Esher, Surrey.
Off A3 by Scilly Isles roundabout.
Parkland course.
9 holes, 5415 yards, S.S.S.65
Club founded in 1892.
Visitors: welcome on weekdays and during afternoons at weekends.
Green fees: weekdays £4, weekends £5.
Society meetings: welcome by arrangement, maximum 40.
Catering: light snacks available; carvery by arrangement.
Hotels: Richmond Hill; Petersham.

D66 Tyrrells Wood

☎ Leatherhead (0372) 376025
Tyrrells Wood, Leatherhead, Surrey KT22 8QP
Turn off Leatherhead by-pass at sign to Tyrrells Wood, after 1¼ mile turn right, Clubhouse is ¾ mile on right.
Undulating parkland course.
18 holes, 6219 yards, S.S.S.70
Course designed by James Braid.
Club founded in 1922.
Visitors: welcome on weekdays and after noon at weekends, advisable to phone first.
Green fees: weekdays £11.50, weekends £18.
Society meetings: catered for on weekdays.
Catering: lunches and snacks served daily.
Hotels: New Bull Hotel, Leatherhead; Burford Bridge Hotel, Dorking.

D67 Walton Heath

☎ Tadworth (073 781) 2060
Tadworth, Surrey KT20 7TP
Leave M25 at Exit 8, follow A217 towards London, turn left onto B2032, turning for golf club about 1 mile on right.
Heathland course.
Old 18 holes, 6813 yards, S.S.S.73
New 18 holes, 6659 yards, S.S.S.72
Course designed by Herbert Fowler.
Club founded in 1904.
Visitors: welcome on weekdays, only by previous arrangement.
Green fees: £16.50; £11.50 after 11.30 am.
Society meetings: catered for on weekdays.
Catering: lunches and teas served daily.
Hotels: numerous good hotels in area.

D68 Wentworth

☎ Wentworth (099 04) 2201
Virginia Water, Surrey GU25 4LS
On the A30 between Egham and Sunningdale
West 18 holes, 6945 yards, S.S.S.74
East 18 holes, 6176 yards, S.S.S.70
9 holes, 1731 yards, S.S.S.30
Course designed by H.S. Colt.
Club founded in 1924.
Visitors: welcome on weekdays, bookings in advance.
Green fees: £24.
Society meetings: welcome on Tues, Wed and Thurs, maximum 120.
Catering: lunches and dinners served for parties of 25 to 200.
Hotels: Royal Berkshire, Runnymede.

D69 West Byfleet

☎ Byfleet (093 23) 45230, 43433 Sec.
Sheerwater Rd, West Byfleet, Surrey KT14 6AA
On A245 about ¾ mile W of West Byfleet.
Heathland/parkland course.
18 holes, 6211 yards, S.S.S.70
Course designed by Cuthbert Butchart.
Club founded in 1904.
Visitors:welcome weekdays only.
Green fees: £12.50 per round or day.
Society meetings: by arrangement on Tues and Wed only.
Catering: snacks, lunches and teas served; evening meals by arrangement; lunches only on Sun.
Hotels: Seven Hills, Seven Hills Rd, Cobham; Wheatsheaf, Chobham Rd, Woking.

D70 West Hill

☎ Brookwood (048 62) 4365
Bagshot Rd, Brookwood, Surrey GU22 0BH
On A322 which connects Guildford to Bagshot, club entrance next to railway bridge at Brookwood.
Moorland course.
18 holes, 6307 yards, S.S.S.70
Course designed by W. Park and J. White.
Club founded in 1909.
Visitors: weekdays only.
Green fees: £10 per round, £15 per day.
Society meetings: weekdays only.
Catering: meals to order; snacks always available.
Hotels: Brookwood, Brookwood; Worplesdon Place, Worplesdon.

D71 West Surrey

☎ Godalming (048 68) 21275
Enton Green, Godalming GU8 5AG
1½ miles from Milford traffic lights on A3, ½ mile from Milford station.
Parkland course.
18 holes, 62 yards, S.S.S.70
Course designed by Herbert Fowler.
Club founded in 1910.
Visitors: welcome subject to availability provided member of golf club.
Green fees: £12.65 per day, £9.20 per round.
Society meetings: catered for on weekdays only.
Catering: full catering available.
Hotels: Inn on the Lake, Godalming; Meads, Meadrow, Godalming.

D72 West Sussex

☎ Pulborough (079 82) 2563
Pulborough, W. Sussex RH20 2EN
1½ miles E of Pulborough on A283.
Heathland course.
18 holes, 6156 yards, S.S.S.70
Course designed by Guy Campbell, Cecil Hutchison and Col S.U. Hotchkin
Club founded in 1930.
Visitors: welcome by prior arrangement, with handicap certificate.
Green fees: weekdays £10, weekends and Bank Holidays £12.
Society meetings: welcome, normally Wed and Thurs.
Catering: full lunch, snacks and tea daily, evening catering for societies by arrangement.
Hotels: Roundabout, Monkmead Lane, West Chiltington; Abingworth Hall, Thakeham, Storrington.

D73 Windlemere

☎ Chobham (09905) 8727
Windlesham Rd, West End, Woking, Surrey GU24 9QL
Take A322 from Bagshot towards Guildford. Turn left on A319 towards Chobham. Course is on left opposite the Gordon Boys' School.
Gently undulating parkland.
9 holes, 2673 yards, S.S.S.33
Course designed by Clive D. Smith.
Club founded in 1978.
Visitors: open to the public upon payment of green fees.
Green fees: 18 hole weekdays £4.60, weekends and Bank Holidays £5.50; 9 hole weekdays £2.50, weekends and Bank Holidays £3.20.
Society meetings: as arranged with Pro at Club.
Catering: bar snacks always available.
Hotels: are to be found in the neighbouring towns of Woking (5 miles), Ascot (5 miles), Bracknell (8 miles), Camberley (4 miles).

West Hill

For cricketers, mention of the three Ws conjures up memories of the great West Indians, Frank Worrell, Everton Weekes and Clyde Walcott. Down in Surrey, however, golfers recognise the three Ws as West Hill, Woking and Worplesdon.

They are an attractive trinity of courses where, if a few large houses and trees didn't block the way, it would be perfectly possible to play from one to the other two with a few stout strokes.

An enviable fixture list at Cambridge took me to all three in early spring for three years in a row and great fun it was. Later, there came participation in the mixed foursomes at Worplesdon and the Alba Trophy at Woking but I had known West Hill from the days when my brother and I took turns to partner my father in the Fathers and Sons, a tournament whose popularity is as strong as ever.

Coming from a course where there was a little more latitude from the tee, West Hill always seemed alarmingly narrow, particularly as, in common with most of Surrey's best courses, the fairways are lined with trees and heather. Young golfers have to learn the hard way that discretion is the better part of long hitting valour.

Control is the first requirement but the thing which has always impressed me about West Hill is the architectural balance it displays. You are as likely to use all fourteen clubs in your bag as anywhere; and there is a definite emphasis on positional play.

This may have something to do with the fact that the club was founded by a woman, Mrs Geoffrey Lubbock. Anyone bold enough to have done such a thing because they were unable to find anywhere to play on a Sunday around the turn of the century may well have insisted that the design bore the ladies primarily in mind. On the other hand, I would give the credit to Willie Park, architect of Sunningdale's Old course a few years earlier, and Jack White, Sunningdale's first professional, for doing no more than good architects should.

Anyway, they certainly proved they meant business straightaway, a broad ditch adding devilment to the second shot to the 1st and running on to broaden out and do much the same at the par 5 3rd with its drive over a heathery ridge alongside the busy railway line to Bournemouth.

The 2nd, parallel to the 1st, is the first of many admirably testing par 4s and the 4th the first of five short holes which vary both in length and direction. The 5th and 6th involve drives up long slopes but two of my favourite holes are the 8th and 10th, the 8th with the ideal drive down the left and the 10th where the temptation to play away from the out of bounds on the left is easily and frequently overdone.

At the 11th, both drive and second shot have to carry thick belts of heather although the 12th, in spite of the tricky contouring of its green, offers the chance of a birdie. Contrast to the short 13th is found at the 15th, one of the best examples of long short holes, but it is all part of what amounts to a stern finish.

Ability to shape the drive is an advantage at the 14th; two good shots are needed at the 16th and there are all sorts of ways of turning a five into a six at the 17th. Then, finally, the 18th has out of bounds awaiting a hook, heather and scrub to the right and a large bunker to be surmounted before reaching the green in front of the clubhouse.

It is reached not without relief but with the feeling that all worthwhile achievement involves a mixture of risk and judgement plus the urge, for those whose achievement was modest or whose judgement was poor, to try again.

D74 **Woking**
☎ Woking (048 62) 60053
Pond Rd, Hook Heath, Woking, Surrey GU22 0JZ
Just S of first road bridge over railway, W of Woking station (Woking-Brookwood line), take Hollybank Rd. Then immediately right into Golf Club Rd and right at end to clubhouse. Avoid Woking town centre.
Heathland course.
18 holes, 6322 yards, S.S.S.70
Course designed by Tom Dunn,
Club founded in 1892.
Visitors: welcome on weekdays by prior arrangement.
Green fees: weekdays £11 per round, £17.50 per day.
Society meetings: welcome by prior arrangement.
Catering: lunches available at club if booked before 10.30 am.
Hotels: Mayford Manor, Guildford Rd, Mayford; Glen House, St Johns Hill Rd, Woking.

D75 **Woodcote Park**
☎ 01-660 2577
Meadow Hill, Bridle Way, Coulsdon, Surrey CR3 2QQ
Situated at the far end of Meadow Hill, which is off Smitham Bottom Lane, Purley, main road from Wallington to Coulsdon.
Slightly undulating parkland course.
18 holes, 6624 yards, S.S.S.71
Club founded in 1912.
Visitors: welcome on weekdays and with member at weekends or Bank Holidays.
Green fees: £9 per day or round.
Society meetings: accepted on Mon, Tues afternoons, Wed and Thurs.
Catering: snacks served all day; lunches for societies and Sun.
Hotels: Aerodrome, Purley Way, Croydon.

D76 **Worplesdon**
☎ Brookwood (048 67) 2277 Sec, 3287 Pro.
Heath House Rd, Woking, Surrey GU22 0RA
Leave Guildford on A322 to Bagshot, after 4 miles turn right into Heath House Rd.
Heathland course.
18 holes, 6422 yards, S.S.S.71
Course designed by J.F. Abercromby.
Club founded in 1908.
Visitors: welcome weekdays.
Green fees: £17 per day, £12 per round.
Society meetings: catered for most weekdays during season.
Catering: snacks and meals served.
Hotels: Worplesdon Place, Worplesdon.

D77 **Worthing**
☎ Worthing (0903) 60801
Links Rd. Worthing, W. Sussex BN14 9QZ
At top of hill on A27 ¼ mile E of Offington roundabout at junction with A24 London road.
Downland course.
Lower 18 holes, 6477 yards, S.S.S.71
Upper 18 holes, 5243 yards, S.S.S.66
Course designed by H.S. Colt.
Club founded in 1906.
Visitors: welcome on weekdays.
Green fees: weekdays £8, weekends and Bank Holidays £12.
Society meetings: catered for on weekdays except Tues.
Catering: lunches served except Mon when only snacks available.
Hotels: Chatsworth, Steyne Gardens, Worthing; Findon Manor, Findon, W. Sussex.

E Kent and East Sussex

Kent and East Sussex combine just about the full range of courses to be found in this country. There are the seaside championship links of Rye, Littlestone, Deal, Sandwich and Princes. Fine examples of parkland golf are provided by Knole Park, Wildernesse and Sundridge Park. Crowborough Beacon and Seaford extol the virtues of golf on the Downs. Royal Ashdown is part moorland, part downland and part heathery heath while Pyecombe and Piltdown, also a bit of a mixture, epitomise the glories of the type of clubs and courses found only in Britain.

On the subject of Rye, my pen is always liable to run away with me and has done often enough in the past not to warrant a repeat. Maybe, at times, it has been at the expense of Littlestone which is good enough to test the best but better known as an ideal holiday course. The finish is particularly good and there is a joyous feeling of escape that so many golfers prize. This becomes increasingly apparent from whichever direction Littlestone is approached. It wouldn't be stretching a point too far, in fact, to say Littlestone is the type of course that makes it the town's main attraction.

Taking the winding coast road from Rye, the county boundary is crossed; but, before straying too far into Kent, a word for the Brighton courses, notably the Dyke, for Cooden Beach and Seaford from whose elevated perch it is possible to enjoy some glorious views. Beachy Head is one landmark although that is along the coast towards Eastbourne and Royal Eastbourne the course close to Henry Longhurst's prep school. Longhurst claims his eye was repeatedly attracted by the silhouette of golfers when he should have been getting on with his work.

Royal Ashdown Forest is another course with magnificent views but the surroundings in no way supersede the challenge of the golf which everyone admires. It is a course, Piltdown is another, where there are no sand bunkers. Its defences are sure enough without them, although the most famous course in Kent, Royal St George's, boasts some of the biggest bunkers to be seen in England.

There is little to mistake this stretch of coast for the Garden of England, North Foreland sharing a certain bleak beauty with its famous neighbours. You have to go west of Canterbury to see the hop gardens, the orchards and the green fields, but the best and most valuable regions for agriculture are rarely noted for golf and you have to head for London before the golfing instincts become more satisfied.

Sevenoaks has Knole Park and Wildernesse which are splendid, Rochester and Cobham is pleasant while West Kent, Langley Park and Sundridge Park are well worth breaking a journey for 18 holes.

E1 Ashdown Forest Hotel

☎ Forest Row (034 282) 2010
Chapel Lane, Forest Row, E. Sussex RH18 5BB
3 miles S of East Grinstead on A22 in village of Forest Row, left on B2110, Chapel Lane fourth on right.
Heathland/ woodland course.
18 holes, 5433 yards, S.S.S.67
Visitors: welcome every day, advisable to phone at weekends.
Green fees: weekdays £9 per day, £6 per round, 'Twilight' ticket £3; weekends and Bank Holidays £10 per day, £7 per round, 'Twilight' ticket £4.
Society meetings: societies of up to 80 catered for every day.
Catering: breakfasts, lunches, dinners and bar snacks served.
Hotels: Ashdown Forest.

E2 Ashford (Kent)

☎ Ashford (0233) 20180
Sandyhurst Lane, Ashford, Kent TN25 4NT
Off A20, 1½ miles N of Ashford.
Undulating heathland course.
18 holes, 6246 yards, S.S.S.70
Club founded in 1903.
Visitors: welcome except weekend and Bank Holiday mornings.
Green fees: weekdays £9, weekends £12.50.
Society meetings: welcome by arrangement on weekdays.
Catering: full catering service except Mon.
Hotels: Eastwell Manor, Eastwell Park, Ashford; Croft, Canterbury Rd, Ashford.

E3 Barnehurst
☎ Crayford (0322) 523746
Mayplace Rd. East, Barnehurst, Kent DA7 6JU
To Bexleyheath Clock Tower then on to Mayplace Rd. East, golf club on left.
Moorland course.
9 holes, 5320 yards, S.S.S.66
Club founded in 1903.
Visitors: welcome Mon, Wed and Fri.
Green fees: on application.
Society meetings: none.
Catering: bar snacks served; lunches can be arranged with Stewardess.
Hotels: Crest, Bexley.

E4 Bearsted
☎ Maidstone (0622) 38198 Sec, 38389 Club.
Ware St, Bearsted, Maidstone, Kent ME14 4PQ
3 miles E of Maidstone on A2011, near Bearsted station.
Undulating course.
18 holes, 6253 yards, S.S.S.70
Club founded in 1895.
Visitors: welcome on weekdays if member of recognised golf club with hand. cert.; at weekends with member only.
Green fees: £7 per round, £10 per day.
Society meetings: welcome Tues to Fri by arrangement with Sec.
Catering: lunches and evening meals by arrangement.
Hotels: Great Danes, Ashford Rd, Hollingbourne.

E5 Beckenham Place Park
☎ 01-650 2292
Beckenham Hill Rd, Beckenham, Kent BR3 2BP
1 mile from Catford going towards Bromley, right at Homebase.
Parkland course.
18 holes, 5722 yards, S.S.S.68
Club founded in 1932.
Visitors: welcome.
Green fees: weekdays £3.20 per round, weekends £4.50 per round.
Society meètings: none.
Catering: meals and snacks served.
Hotels: Bromley Court.

E6 Bexleyheath
☎ 01-303 6951
Mount Drive, Mount Rd, Bexleyheath, Kent DA6 8JS
1 mile from Bexleyheath station.
Undulating course.
9 holes, 5239 yards, S.S.S.66
Club founded in 1907.
Visitors: welcome weekdays.
Green fees: £5 per round.
Society meetings: by arrangement.
Catering: meals available.
Hotels: Crest, Southwold Rd, Bexley, Kent.

E7 Brighton & Hove
☎ Brighton (0273) 556482
Dyke Rd, Brighton, E.Sussex BN1 8YJ
N of Brighton Centre, 2½ miles up Dyke Rd on left side.
Downland course.
9 holes, 5722 yards, S.S.S.68
Course designed by Captain J.E.H. Gelston.
Club founded in 1887.
Visitors: welcome all week; phone to confirm course availability.
Green fees: Mon to Sat 18 holes £8, 9 holes £5; Sun and Bank Holidays 18 holes £10, 9 holes £6.
Society meetings: by arrangement.
Catering: snacks and full meal by arrangement.
Hotels: Old Ship, Brighton; Courtlands; Langfords, Hove.

E8 Bromley
☎ 01-462 7014
Magpie Hall Lane, Bromley, Kent BR2 8JF
A21, 2 miles S of Bromley.
Parkland course.
9 holes, 2507 yards, S.S.S.69

Visitors: welcome.
Green fees: weekdays 9 holes £1.75, weekends £3, Juniors £1.10.
Society meetings: welcome.
Catering: snacks available.

E9 Broome Park G & CC

☎ Canterbury (0227) 831701
Barham, Canterbury, Kent CT4 6QX
Off M2 onto A2 then Folkestone Rd A260, 700 yards on right hand side, 8 miles from Canterbury.
Parkland course.
18 holes, 6606 yards, S.S.S.72
Course designed by Donald Steel.
Club founded in 1980.
Visitors: welcome Mon to Sat.
Green fees: £8 per round, £14 per day.
Society meetings: welcome.
Catering: breakfasts, lunches, snacks and dinners served.
Hotels: numerous good hotels in Canterbury, Dover and Folkestone.

E10 Canterbury

☎ Canterbury (0227) 453532
Scotland Hills, Canterbury, Kent CT1 1TW
A257 1 mile from Canterbury.
Parkland course.
18 holes, 6209 yards, S.S.S.70
Course designed by H.S. Colt.
Club founded in 1927.
Visitors: welcome on weekdays.
Green fees: weekdays £8 per round, £12 per day; Sat £10 per round, £14.50 per day; Sun afternoon £13.50 per round; reductions if playing with member.
Society meetings: catered for on Tues and Thurs.
Catering: lunches and evening meals served except Sun and Mon when only lunches available.
Hotels: Ebury; Canterbury; Victoria; Ersham Lodge.

E11 Cherry Lodge

☎ Biggin Hill (0959) 72550
Jail Lane, Biggin Hill, Kent TN16 3AX
Off A233 S of RAF station.
Undulating downland course.
18 holes, 6908 yards, S.S.S.74
Course designed by John Day.
Club founded in 1969.
Visitors: welcome weekdays.
Green fees: £11.50 per day, £7.50 per round.
Society meetings: by arrangement.
Catering: lunches, a la carte evening.
Hotels: Kings Arms, Westerham; Bromley Court, Bromley.

E12 Chestfield

☎ Chestfield (022 779) 2365 Sec, 2243 Clubhouse, 3563 Pro
Chestfield Rd, Whitstable, Kent CT5 3LU
½ mile off Thanet Way (Chestfield roundabout).
Parkland seaside course.
18 holes, 6080 yards, S.S.S.69
Club founded in 1924.
Visitors: welcome.
Green fees: weekdays £5.50 per round, £8 per day; weekends £7 per round, £10 per day.
Society meetings: welcome weekdays only by arrangement.
Catering: snacks served; club restaurant available for meals with advance notice.
Hotels: Marine, Tankerton, Whitstable.

E13 Chislehurst

☎ 01-467 2782
Camden Park Rd, Chislehurst, Kent BR7 5HJ
½ mile from Chislehurst station, on A222 to Bromley.
Parkland course.
18 holes, 5128 yards, S.S.S.65
Club founded in 1894.
Visitors: welcome on weekdays and with member only at weekends.
Green fees: £10 per day (£4 with member).
Society meetings: welcome weekdays for limited number.
Catering: coffee, lunch and tea served daily; other meals by arrangement.
Hotels: numerous hotels in area.

E14 Cobtree Manor

☎ Maidstone (0622) 53276
Maidstone, Kent
M2 or M20 and then A229 turn off. Club is on A229.
Parkland course.
18 holes, 5701 yards, S.S.S.68
Club founded in 1984.
Visitors: welcome (Municipal course).
Green fees: £3.30 weekdays, £5 weekends.
Society meetings: no.
Catering: bar food available, evening meals by arrangement.
Hotels: Great Danes; Crest.

E15 Cooden Beach

☎ Cooden (0959) 2040
Coodensea Rd, Cooden, E. Sussex.
A259 Eastbourne to Hastings road, follow 'Cooden Beach' sign at Little Common roundabout.
Seaside parkland course.
20 holes, 6411 yards, S.S.S.71
Visitors: welcome.
Green fees: weekdays £9, weekends £10 (subject to review).
Society meetings: weekdays only.
Catering: lunches served except Mon.
Hotels: Cooden Beach adjacent.

E16 Cranbrook

☎ Cranbrook (0580) 718233 or 712934
Benenden Rd, Cranbrook, Kent TN17 4AL
14 miles S of Maidstone, A229 to Sissinghurst, 1¼ miles from Sissinghurst on Benenden Rd.
Parkland course.
18 holes, 6128 yards, S.S.S.70
Course designed by John D. Harris.
Club founded in 1969.
Visitors: welcome except on major competition days.
Green fees: weekdays £6 (£5 with member), weekends and Bank Holidays £9 (£7 with member).
Society meetings: welcome weekdays.
Catering: lunches, dinners and snacks available daily.
Hotels: Willesley, Cranbrook; George, Cranbrook; Kennel Holt, Cranbrook.

E17 Cray Valley

☎ Orpington (0689) 37909 Pro, 31927 Clubhouse.
Sandy Lane, St. Paul's Cray, Orpington, Kent.
A20 to Ruxley roundabout, junction with A223.
Undulating meadowland course.
18 holes, 5624 yards, S.S.S.67
9 hole Beginner's course.
Course designed by S. Barrow.
Club founded in 1970.
Visitors: welcome on weekdays; weekends by prior arrangement.
Green fees: weekdays £4.50, weekends and Bank Holidays £5.50.
Society meetings: welcome weekdays by arrangement.
Catering: snack meals and lunches available; evening meals by arrangement.
Hotels: numerous good hotels in area.

E18 Crowborough Beacon

☎ Crowborough (089 26) 61511
Beacon Rd, Crowborough, E. Sussex TN6 1UJ
8 miles S of Tunbridge Wells on A26.
Heathland course.
18 holes, 6304 yards, S.S.S.70
Club founded in 1895.
Visitors: welcome by prior arrangement and with handicap certificates.
Green fees: on application.

Society meetings: catered for on Mon, Tues and Wed only.
Catering: full service available except Thurs.
Hotels: Crest, Beacon Rd, Crowborough.

E19 Dale Hill

☎ Ticehurst (0580) 200112
Ticehurst, Wadhurst, E. Sussex TN5 7DQ
Turn off A21 at Flimwell, on B2087 towards Ticehurst.
Parkland/ meadowland course.
18 holes, 6035 yards, S.S.S.69
Club founded in 1973.
Visitors: welcome.
Green fees: weekdays £7, weekends £8.
Society meetings: welcome.
Catering: full catering facilities.
Hotels: Tudor Arms, Hawkhurst; Spindlewood, Walcrouch.

E20 Darenth Valley

☎ Otford (095 92) 2944
Station Rd, Shoreham, Kent TN15 7SA
Along A225 Sevenoaks to Dartford road, 4 miles N of Sevenoaks.
Meadowland course.
18 holes, 6356 yards, S.S.S.71
Course designed by R. Tempest.
Club founded in 1973.
Visitors: welcome, bookings advisable at weekends.
Green fees: weekdays £4 per round, weekends £6 per round.
Society meetings: welcome except Sun.
Catering: lunches and bar snacks served except Tues or Sun evening.
Hotels: Emma, Dunton Green.

E21 Dartford

☎ Dartford (0322) 26455
Dartford Heath, Dartford, Kent DA1 2TN
Situated on Dartford Heath, 2 miles from Dartford town centre.
Heathland course.
18 holes, 5914 yards, S.S.S.68
Club founded in 1897
Visitors: welcome weekdays if member of recognised golf club or with member and at weekends only with member.
Green fees: weekdays £10 (£5 with member).
Society meetings: catered for on Fri only; booking well in advance.
Catering: snacks available; lunches by arrangement; evening meals on Wed and Fri by arrangement.
Hotels: Royal Bull; Victoria.

E22 Deangate Ridge

☎ Medway (0634) 251180
Hoo, Rochester, Kent ME3 8RZ
A228 from Rochester to Isle of Grain, then take road signed to Deangate Ridge, 4 miles NE of Rochester.
Parkland municipal course.
18 holes, 6300 yards, S.S.S.70
Course designed by Fred Hawtree.
Club founded in 1972.
Visitors: welcome weekdays; bookings may be made at weekends.
Green fees: weekdays £2.80, weekends £4.
Society meetings: accepted.
Catering: full catering facilities.
Hotels: Crest, Rochester; Inn on the Lake, Shorne, Rochester.

E23 Dyke

☎ Poynings (9856) 296
Dyke Rd. Brighton, Sussex BN1 8YJ
Situated on the Downs, 4½ miles N of Brighton, take Dyke Rd from Brighton.
Downland course.
18 holes, 6519 yards, S.S.S.71
Club founded in 1910.
Visitors: welcome, except Sun mornings.
Green fees: weekdays £10 per day, weekends and Bank Holidays £12 per day.
Society meetings: catered for on weekdays.
Catering: meals and snacks served.
Hotels: Eaton, Hove; Courtlands, Hove.

E24 Eastbourne Downs

☎ Eastbourne (0323) 20827
East Dean Rd, Eastbourne, E. Sussex BN20 8ES
On A259 W of Eastbourne.
Downland course.
18 holes, 6684 yards, S.S.S.72
Course designed by J.H. Taylor.
Club founded in 1908.
Visitors: welcome.
Green fees: weekdays £6 per round, weekends £7.50 per round.
Society meetings: welcome by arrangement.
Catering: snacks, lunches except Mon and Tues.
Hotels: Cavendish; Lansdowne; Grand; Queens.

E25 East Brighton

☎ Brighton (0273) 604838
Roedean Rd, Brighton, E. Sussex BN2 5RA
Follow A259 E from Brighton town centre and turn left opposite Brighton Marina.
Downland course.
18 holes, 6291 yards, S.S.S.72
Club founded in 1892.
Visitors: welcome, telephone in advance.
Green fees: weekdays, weekends and Bank Holidays £8 (£4 after 4 pm); half-price with member.
Society meetings: catered for on weekdays and occasionally on Sat.
Catering: lunches and bar snacks daily except Mon; breakfast or dinner with 24 hours notice.
Hotels: Old Ship; Grand; Metropole; Royal Crescent; Queens; Royal Albion.

E26 Edenbridge G & CC

☎ Edenbridge (0732) 865097
Crouch House Rd, Edenbridge, Kent TN8 5LQ
Travelling N through Edenbridge High St turn left into Stangrove Rd (30 yards before Edenbridge Town railway station), at end of road turn right, course will be found a short distance on left.
Undulating meadowland course.
18 holes, 6635 yards, S.S.S.72
Club founded in 1970.
Visitors: welcome.
Green fees: weekdays £4.50, weekends and Bank Holidays £6.
Society meetings: welcome weekdays.
Catering: lunches served.
Hotels: Wonham, Eastbourne Rd, South Godstone.

E27 Faversham

☎ Eastling (079 589) 251
Belmont Park, Faversham, Kent ME13 0HB
Leave M2 at Junction 6, take A251 to Faversham, follow A2 to Sittingbourne for ½ mile, turn left at Brogdale Rd, and follow golf club signs.
Parkland course.
18 holes, 5979 yards, S.S.S.69
Club founded in 1902.
Visitors: welcome except at weekends, on Bank Holidays and between 20th Dec and 6th Jan.
Green fees: £10 per day, £6 per round.
Society meetings: welcome Wed, Thurs and Fri.
Catering: lunches and evening meals.
Hotels: The Ship, Faversham.

E28 Gillingham

☎ Medway (0634) 53017 Sec, 55862 Pro, 50999 Bar.
Woodlands Rd, Gillingham, Kent ME7 2BX
On A2 at Gillingham, about 2 miles from M2, turn off to Gillingham.
Meadowland course.
18 holes, 5863 yards, S.S.S.68
Course designed by James Braid.
Club founded in 1908.
Visitors: welcome on weekdays by arrangement if member of golf club.
Green fees: weekdays £7 per round, £10 per day (£4 per round, £6 per day with

member); weekends only with member £4 per round, £6 per day.
Society meetings: by arrangement on Mon, Tues, Wed and Fri.
Catering: lunches or evening meals served.
Hotels: Park, Nelson Rd, Gillingham.

E29 Hastings

☎ Hastings (0424) 52981 or 52977
Battle Rd, St. Leonards-on-sea, E. Sussex.
A2100 from Battle to Hastings, 3 miles NW of Hastings.
Undulating parkland course.
18 holes, 6073 yards, S.S.S.70
Course designed by Frank Pennink.
Club founded in 1973.
Visitors: welcome.
Green fees: weekdays £4.50, weekends £5.
Society meetings: welcome weekdays.
Catering: meals served.
Hotels: Beauport Park.

E30 Hawkhurst

☎ Hawkhurst (058 05) 2396
High St, Hawkhurst, Cranbrook, Kent TN18 4JS
On A268, 2 miles from A21 at Flimwell, ½ mile from junction with A229.
Undulating parkland course.
9 holes, 5769 yards, S.S.S.68
Course designed by Rex Baldock.
Club founded in 1968.
Visitors: welcome at all times except Sun mornings.
Green fees: weekdays £5 (£3 with member), weekends and Bank Holidays £7 (£5 with member).
Society meetings: welcome weekdays.
Catering: bar snacks only except by advance arrangement.
Hotels: Royal Oak, Hawkhurst.

E31 Herne Bay

☎ Herne Bay (0227) 373964
Eddington, Herne Bay, Kent CT6 7PG
Take Thanet Way to Herne Bay, near railway station.
Parkland course.
18 holes, 5403 yards, S.S.S.66
Club founded in 1920.
Visitors: welcome at all times, but some restrictions at weekends and Bank Holidays.
Green fees: weekdays £7 per round, £9 per day; weekends and Bank Holidays £8 per round, £10.50 per day.
Society meetings: welcome any time.
Catering: full facilities at club; prior notice required by Steward for full meals.
Hotels: numerous good hotels in area.

E32 High Elms

☎ Farnborough (0689) 58175
High Elms Rd, Downe, Kent.
5 miles out of Bromley off the A21 to Sevenoaks.
Parkland course.
18 holes, 6210 yards, S.S.S.70
Course designed by Fred Hawtree.
Club founded in 1969.
Visitors: welcome at any time.
Green fees: weekdays £3.50, weekends and Bank Holidays £6.
Society meetings: by arrangement.
Catering: bar facilities.
Hotels: Bromley Court, Bromley Hill, Bromley, Kent.

E33 Highwoods

☎ Bexhill (0424) 212625 or 216277
Ellerslie Lane, Bexhill-on-Sea, E. Sussex TN39 4LJ
Off A259 from Eastbourne or Hastings, 2 miles from Bexhill; from Battle A269 via Ninfield, turn right in Sidley.
Undulating parkland course.
18 holes, 6218 yards, S.S.S.70
Course designed by J.H. Taylor.
Club founded in 1925.
Visitors: welcome with handicap certificate; restricted times for four balls.
Green fees: weekdays £9, weekends and Bank Holidays £10.

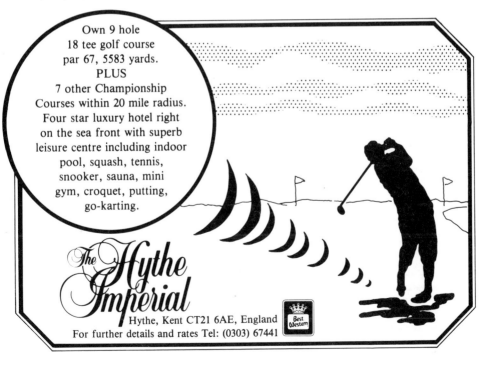

Society meetings: catered for on Wed and Thurs by arrangement.
Catering: snacks available every day; lunch by prior arrangement except Mon.
Hotels: Granville; Cooden Beach; Moor Hall.

E34 Hollingbury Park
☎ Brighton (0273) 552010
Ditchling Rd, Brighton, Sussex BN1 7HS
1 mile from Brighton, A23 to Brighton town centre, turn left at one way, up hill to top, turn left, 200 yds on right.
Undulating downland course.
18 holes, 6502 yards, S.S.S.71
Club founded in 1909.
Visitors: welcome any time.
Green fees: £4.25 per round, £5.20 per day.
Society meetings: welcome weekdays.
Catering: snacks and meals till 5 pm, later meals served.
Hotels: numerous good hotels in Brighton.

E35 Holtye
☎ Cowden (034 286) 635
Holtye Common, Cowden, Edenbridge, Kent TN8 7ED
On A264 between East Grinstead and Tunbridge Wells, 5 miles from East Grinstead.
Heathland course.
9 holes, 5289 yards, S.S.S.66
Club founded in 1892.
Visitors: welcome weekdays and afternoons at weekends; unless with a member, advisable to phone prior to visit.
Green fees: weekdays £6 (£4 with member), weekends and Bank Holidays £9 (£5 with member).
Society meetings: by appointment.
Catering: light snacks served; bar available most lunchtimes; full meals by arrangement for societies.
Hotels: Spa, Tunbridge Wells; Felbridge, East Grinstead.

E36 Hythe Imperial
☎ Hythe (0303) 67441 Hotel, 67554 Sec.
Princes Parade, Hythe, Kent CT21 6AE
Turn off M20 to Hythe, to E end of seafront.
Seaside course.
2 x 9 holes, 5583 yards, S.S.S.67
Club reformed in 1955.
Visitors: welcome, weekends usually busy.
Green fees: weekdays £6 (£5 with member), weekends £8.50 (£6 with member).
Society meetings: small groups catered for by arrangement.
Catering: snacks and meals available.
Hotels: Imperial.

E37 Knole Park
☎ Sevenoaks (0732) 452150 Sec, 451740 Pro, 452709 Steward.
Seal Hollow Rd, Sevenoaks, Kent TN15 0HJ
½m W of Seal is Seal Hollow Rd leading to Sevenoaks, approx 1m up Seal Hollow Rd.
Parkland course.
18 holes, 6249 yards, S.S.S.70
Course designed by Fowler, Abercromby, Simpson and Croome.
Club founded in 1924.
Visitors: welcome on weekdays with hand. cert., should telephone in advance.
Green fees: £10 per round, £14 for 2 rounds.
Society meetings: welcome, but must book 12 months in advance and all members must have handicaps.
Catering: bar snacks served; meals by arrangement.
Hotels: Sevenoaks Park.

E38 Lamberhurst
☎ Lamberhurst (0892) 890241
Church Rd, Lamberhurst, Kent TN3 8DT
On A21 S from Tunbridge Wells, entrance to course immediately left on outskirts of Lamberhurst village.
Undulating parkland course.
18 holes, 6277 yards, S.S.S.70
Course designed by Frank Pennink.
Club founded in 1920.
Visitors: welcome any day but after 12 noon at weekends and Bank Holidays unless accompanied by member.
Green fees: weekdays £9, weekends £12.50.
Society meetings: catered for on Tues, Wed and Thurs only.
Catering: lunch, dinner and snacks served except Mon when sandwiches only available.
Hotels: Star and Eagle, Goudhurst.

E39 Langley Park
☎ 01-658 6849
Barnfield Wood Rd, Beckenham, Kent BR3 2SZ
At lights near Bromley South station turn into Westmoreland Rd, clubhouse 1¾ miles on left.
Gently undulating parkland course.
18 holes, 6488 yards, S.S.S.71
Course designed by J.H. Taylor.
Club founded in 1910.
Visitors: welcome on weekdays with introduction or handicap certificate.
Green fees: £10 per round, £12 per day; half-price with member.
Society meetings: by arrangement
Catering: lunches and snacks weekdays.
Hotels: Bromley Court.

E40 Leeds Castle
☎ Hollingbourne (062 780) 467
Maidstone, Kent.
M20 from Maidstone towards Ashford, onto A20 at Hollingbourne, after 1½ miles turn right into Broomfield Rd, entrance 50 yards on the right.
Parkland course.
9 holes, 18 tees, S.S.S.69
Course opened in 1924.
Visitors: welcome, but telephone first.
Green fees: 9 holes £3.50, 18 holes, £5.50; reductions for OAPs and Juniors at certain times.
Society meetings: welcome by prior arrangement.
Catering: meals served by arrangement.
Hotels: Great Danes, Hollingbourne, Maidstone, Kent.

E41 Lewes
☎ Lewes (0273) 3074 or 3245
Chapel Hill, Lewes, Sussex.
On A27 Lewes to Eastbourne road opposite junction of Cliffe High St and South St.
Downland course.
18 holes, 5951 yards, S.S.S.69
Club founded in 1896.
Visitors: welcome.
Green fees: weekdays £5.50 per day, weekends £7.50 per day.
Society meetings: welcome weekdays except Wed and weekends after 10.30 am.
Catering: light snacks and full catering for societies available.
Hotels: White Hart, Lewes.

E42 Littlestone
☎ New Romney (0679) 63355
St. Andrews Rd, Littlestone, New Romney, Kent TN28 8RB
A20 to Ashford, B2070 to New Romney, 1 mile from New Romney.
Seaside links course.
18 holes, 6417 yards, S.S.S.71
9 holes, 1998 yards, S.S.S.32
Course designed by Laidlaw Purves.
Club founded in 1888.
Visitors: welcome every day including weekends by arrangement with Sec.
Green fees: details on application.
Society meetings: welcome every day including weekends by arrangement.
Catering: every day except Tues.
Hotels: Stade Court, Hythe; Broadacre, New Romney; Blue Dolphins, New Romney.

E43 Lullingstone Park
☎ Knockholt (0959) 34542 Pro, 34517 Restaurant.
Park Gate, Chelsfield, Orpington, Kent.
A20 to Swanley, then B258 Daltons Rd, to Park Gate.

Leeds Castle

There is something awe-inspiring about playing golf against a backcloth of castles. At Harlech, the castle is 'monarch of all she surveys'. It would be quite easy to follow those playing over Royal St David's from its ramparts with a keen eye or good telescope, and at Dunstanburgh, on the north-east coast, ancient walls are a dominant, if more derelict, feature of a charming course. Brancepeth Castle is another notable example, and air travellers on the approach to London's Heathrow may have noticed, with much less golfing envy, the few holes within the confines of Windsor Castle.

However there is nothing to compare with the delightful surroundings of Leeds Castle, which is in the green heartland of Kent and not the West Riding of Yorkshire.

A more cryptic view is that it is all so beautiful, it is a pity to spoil things by playing golf, but if you hit lucky on a nice, quiet day, you can look upon it as all part of gracious living on your own private estate. There is a welcome peace and spaciousness about the park and its magnificent trees that calls to mind St Pierre, another historic setting where the old Manor House stored the crown jewels during the Battle of Agincourt.

A tour of Leeds Castle is a history lesson in itself but the nine holes make it difficult to concentrate on the task in hand. Nowhere else that I know does an elegant moat form such an appealing water hazard as black swans and other rare birds glide lazily over it dodging wayward balls. The one criticism I have, in fact, is that the best comes in the first two holes.

The 1st, between a large tree and the reeds bordering the moat, is a superb hole in any context. At 441 yards with a glorious drive and a long second to a green slightly above you, is as hard a four as you will find; but the 2nd provides definite options, a death or glory stroke across the clear waters of the moat or the dry land route in easy stages. A really long drive will get you home, or so you are inclined to think. The 300 yards may not have been measured as the crow flies or, in the environment of Leeds, some exotic goose, but whatever glory or disaster befalls you, the remaining seven holes are more pastoral.

After a long walk to the tee, the 3rd launches on the only par 5, the second part of the hole being nicer than the first. There is an invitation to open the shoulders as, indeed, there is at the 4th, a modest length dogleg to the right over a high bunker. The small greens have been thoughtfully constructed and add considerably to both the pleasure and the challenge. The 5th, the first short hole, is a case in point, the left and front guarded by a couple of bunkers, the right fringed by a sharp slope the bottom of which leaves an awkward pitch.

The 6th calls for a firm drive up over a brow and a well judged second to a green amid a stand of pines. The 7th, with a tee almost backing on to the busy A20, a mile or so from the southern end of the M20, is a right angle dogleg to the left with another excellent green, but after playing the short 8th along a ridge, the 9th, it must be said, is a rival to the 1st.

An invitingly downhill well hit drive leaves a second to be lined up on one of the towers of the castle, a subtle swale bordering the green making club selection awkward for the better players; but one beauty of a nine hole course is that there is always a second time around. You may not improve given another chance. Ignorance can be bliss where golf is concerned but you will never be disappointed. My guess is that Leeds Castle will feature large on your list of return fixtures.

Parkland municipal course.
9 holes, 2432 yards
18 holes, 6674 yards, S.S.S.72
Course designed by Fred Hawtree.
Club founded in 1923.
Visitors: welcome.
Green fees: 18 holes weekdays £3.50 (OAP £2), weekends £5; 9 holes weekdays £2 (OAP £1), weekends £3 (OAP £2).
Society meetings: by arrangement
Catering: meals by arrangement.
Hotels: Bull, Swanley.

E44 Mid-Kent

☎ Gravesend (0474) 68035
Singlewell Rd, Gravesend, Kent DA11 7RB
A2 S of Gravesend, turn off at Tollgate Moathouse Hotel.
Parkland course.
18 holes, 6221 yards, S.S.S.70
Course designed by Frank Pennink.
Club founded in 1909.
Visitors: welcome on weekdays and weekends with member except on comp. days; must have hand. cert.
Green fees: £5 per round, £9 per day.
Society meetings: welcome on Tues, maximum 70 and Thurs, maximum 16.
Catering: snacks, lunches and teas served; dinner by prior arrangement.
Hotels: Tollgate, Gravesend; Inn on the Lake, Cobham.

E45 Nevill

☎ Tunbridge Wells (0892) 25818
Benhall Mill Rd, Tunbridge Wells, Kent TN2 5JW
Turn into Forest Rd from A267 out of Tunbridge Wels.
Parkland/heathland course.
18 holes, 6336 yards, S.S.S.70
Course designed by C.K. Cotton.
Club founded in 1914.
Visitors: welcome weekdays and with member at weekends; handicap certificates required.
Green fees: weekdays £10 per day, weekends and Bank Holidays £12 per day.
Society meetings: welcome.
Catering: meals and bar snacks served.
Hotels: Spa, Tunbridge Wells; Calverley, Tunbridge Wells.

E46 North Foreland

☎ Thanet (0843) 62140
Convent Rd, Broadstairs, Kent CT10 3PU
1½ miles from Broadstairs station.
Seaside, downland course.
18 holes, 6382 yards, S.S.S.70
Course designed by Fowler and Simpson.
Club founded in 1903.
Visitors: welcome all day on weekdays; weekends and Bank Holidays only in afternoons. Handicap certificates must be produced.
Green fees: summer weekdays £8 per round, £10 per day; weekends £10 per round, £12.50 per day; Winter weekdays £6.50 per round, £10 per day; weekends £9 per round, £12.50 per day.
Society meetings: welcome weekdays by arrangement with Sec with hand. certs.
Catering: bar snacks, lunches and teas available daily; evening meals by arrangement with Caterer.
Hotels: Castle Keep, Kingsgate Castle, Broadstairs; Fayreness, Marine Drive, Kingsgate, Broadstairs; Royal Albion, Albion St, Broadstairs.

E47 Peacehaven

☎ Newhaven (0273) 514049 or 512571
Brighton Rd, Newhaven, Sussex BN9 9UH
On A259 1 mile W of Newhaven.
Undulating downland course.
9 holes, 5007 yards, S.S.S.65
Club founded in 1895.
Visitors: welcome weekdays and weekends after 11.00 am except on competition days.
Green fees: weekdays £4.25 for 18 holes, £2.50 for 9 holes; weekends £5.50, £5.75 per day.
Society meetings: Tues to Fri, max. 30.
Catering: lunches can be ordered except Mon and Tues; bar snacks at all times.
Hotels: Peacehaven; Old Ship, Brighton.

E48 Piltdown

☎ Newick (082 572) 2033
Piltdown, Uckfield, E. Sussex TN22 3XB
2½ miles W of Uckfield, between A272 and B2102.
Undulating moorland course.
18 holes, 6059 yards, S.S.S.69
Course designed by Jack Rowe, G.M. Dodd and Frank Pennink.
Club founded in 1904.
Visitors: welcome but must be members of recognised golf club; before 1 pm on Sun and Bank Holidays must play with member.
Green fees: £9.50 per round or per day (£4.25 with member).
Society meetings: welcome weekdays.
Catering: daily by prior arrangement.
Hotels: Maidens Head, Uckfield; Roebuck, Wytch Cross.

E49 Poult Wood

☎ Tonbridge (0732) 364039 Pro
Higham Lane, Tonbridge, Kent.
2 miles N of Tonbridge off A227.
Parkland course.
18 holes, 5569 yards, S.S.S.67
Course designed by Fred Hawtree.
Club founded in 1974.
Visitors: welcome.
Green fees: weekdays £2.75 per round, weekends £4 per round.
Society meetings: on weekdays only.
Catering: full catering available.
Hotels: Rose and Crown, High St, Tonbridge.

E50 Princes

☎ Sandwich (0304) 611118
Sandwich Bay, Sandwich, Kent CT13 9QB

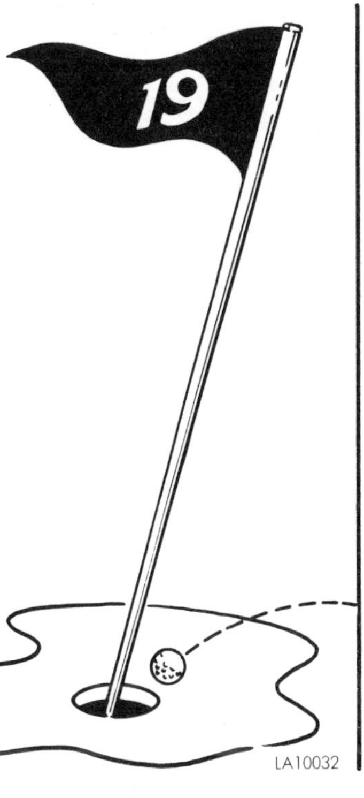

3m from Sandwich through town centre.
Seaside links course.
9 holes, 6690 yards
Course designed by J.S.F. Morrison and Sir Guy Campbell.
Club founded in 1904.
Visitors: welcome.
Green fees: weekdays £9 per round, weekends and Bank Holidays £11 per round.
Society meetings: welcome, special offers, Oct - March.
Catering: full meals available.
Hotels: in Sandwich, Dover, Ramsgate; on course hotel anticipated in 1986.

E51 Pyecombe

☎ Hassocks (079 18) 5372 Sec, 4176 Steward.
Clayton Hill, Pyecombe, Sussex BN4 7FF
On A273, ½ mile from junction with A23 at Pyecombe, 5 to 6 miles N of Brighton.
Downland course.
18 holes, 6201 yards, S.S.S.70
Club founded in 1894.
Visitors: welcome on weekdays after 9.15 am, Sat after 10.30 am and Sun after 11.00 am.
Green fees: weekdays £6, weekends £8.
Society meetings: bookings accepted for Mon, Wed and Thurs.
Catering: lunches, afternoon teas and evening meals served (can be booked by ringing Hassocks 3338).
Hotels: Hassocks, Hassocks.

E52 Rochester & Cobham Park

☎ Shorne (047 482) 3411
Park Pale by Rochester, Kent ME2 3UI
Situated on A2, turn left on to B2009 and follow signs to clubhouse.
Undulating parkland course.
18 holes, S.S.S.71
Club founded in 1892.
Visitors: welcome on weekdays but must be accompanied by member at weekends.
Green fees: weekdays £10 per round, £14 per day.
Society meetings: catered for on Tues and Thurs.
Catering: snacks, lunches and dinner.
Hotels: Inn on the Lake; Leather Bottle, Cobham.

E53 Royal Ashdown Forest

☎ Forest Row (034 282) 2018
Chapel Lane, Forest Row, Sussex RH18 5LR
A22 E. Grinstead to Eastbourne road, 4½ miles S of E. Grinstead turn left in Forest Row opposite church onto B2110, after ½ mile turn right into Chapel Lane, top of hill turn left, over heath to clubhouse.
Undulating moorland course.
18 holes, 6439 yards, S.S.S.71
Club founded in 1888.
Visitors: welcome, preferably by prior arrangement with Sec.
Green fees: weekdays £11.50, weekends and Bank Holidays £12.50.
Society meetings: by arrangement on weekdays except Tues.
Catering: snacks always available; order hot lunches in advance.
Hotels: Ashdown Forest; Brambletye.

E54 Royal Cinque Ports

☎ Deal (0304) 374007
Golf Rd, Deal, Kent CT14 6RF
Go to N of seafront at Deal.
Seaside links course.
Medal 18 holes, 6409 yards, S.S.S.71
Club founded in 1892.
Visitors: welcome with golf handicap and letter of introduction.
Green fees: weekdays £16 per day, weekends £18 per day.
Society meetings: by arrangement
Catering: full service available.
Hotels: Bell, Sandwich; Royal, Deal.

E55 Royal Eastbourne

☎ Eastbourne (0323) 29738 Sec, 30412 Steward & members
Paradise Drive, Eastbourne, Sussex BN20 8BP
½ mile from Town Hall.

Royal Cinque Ports, Deal

Nowhere in Britain, indeed nowhere in the world, do three Open championship courses lie in such close proximity as Prince's, Sandwich and Deal. You can chip a ball from Prince's to Sandwich and you could almost drive a ball from Sandwich onto the furthest reaches of Deal if it were not for the line of buildings that once included the late lamented Guilford Hotel.

Nowadays, only Sandwich, re-instated in 1981, meets all the demands imposed by a modern Open, the old version of Prince's being largely demolished during the last war; but no course has remained more untouched by the years than Deal or, to give it its proper title, the Royal Cinque Ports GC.

The sea has done its best on three occasions to sweep it away, large areas being devastated by floods swept in on angry tides. The most recent invasion was 1978 but it resulted in a gigantic exercise to strengthen the sea wall which is now thought to be man enough to repulse everything the elements can throw at it.

Like many championship links, Deal was no doubt more formidable in the days of the gutty ball and hickory shafts, the hummocky nature of the ground on many fairways being considerably easier to negotiate with a steel shaft and modern ball.

Its last Open was in 1920 when George Duncan profited from Abe Mitchell's spectacular collapse on the final day, but the tournament that keeps Deal in the forefront of the public eye is the Haford Hewitt whose participating legions descend every April to put themselves through a process of friendly torture.

The drama invariably unfolds on the 18th and 19th and, for that reason, they are the best remembered holes. The 1st is innocent enough as a first hole in spite of the stream in front of the green, the chance of driving out of bounds or of burying a hook in the clumps of rushes. However, as the 19th, its cloak is far more sinister. The fairway seems to shrink in width and the stream casts some hypnotic power over those who seem to have all strength and co-ordination drained from their hands.

The 2nd, a stern two-shooter, is the sort of hole you could only find on a British seaside links, a label even more applicable to the 3rd. There are two or three enormous hollows between twin sandhills and the green.

The 4th, Sandy Parlour, is the first of three short holes which make as good a set as you will find, each calling for a different shot with a different club in a different direction. David Blair thought enormously highly of them and was very much what one might term a Deal man, as was Leonard Crawley. Their shotmaking powers were well suited to controlling the ball in moderate winds that for ordinary folk make the fives many and the fours few.

From the 2nd to the 7th, you get used to the wind from the same quarter except for the pitch to the 6th – a stroke that catches many by surprise. First time players on the course never expect to find the green where it is.

The 9th, 10th and 11th are excellent fours, running largely at right angles to the rest of the holes particularly the finish which is easy or difficult according to the wind. The 12th is another old-fashioned shaped green while the 16th and 17th also have their own distinctive contours. The 16th, in fact, is perched up like a gun turret, the steep, guardian bank frequently killing off a long second seeking a birdie four.

On the 17th, the problem for the second shot is finding a predictable landing area but at the 18th the only recommended way of hitting a flat, plateau green is carrying the shot all the way. Here again, the stream crossing the fairway claims its haul of balls although there is less excuse for causing a ripple than on the 1st. Bernard Darwin wrote many moons ago that Deal consists of plenty of 'fine, straight-ahead, long-hitting golf'. It still does.

Undulating downland course.
18 holes, 6084 yards, S.S.S.69
9 holes 2147 yards, S.S.S.61
Club founded in 1887.
Visitors: welcome.
Green fees: 18 holes weekdays £8.50, weekends £9.50; 9 holes £6.
Society meetings: catered for except at weekends.
Catering: full facilities except on Mon.
Hotels: Grand; Lansdowne; Queens; Hydro; Cavendish.

E56 Royal St George's

☎ Sandwich (0304) 613090
Sandwich, Kent CT13 9PB
1 mile from Sandwich to Sandwich Bay, turn left at district sign of Worth for clubhouse.
Links course.
Medal 18 holes, 6534 yards, S.S.S.72
Championship 18 holes, 6857 yards, S.S.S.74
Course designed by Laidlaw Purvis.
Club founded in 1887.
Visitors: weekdays with introduction from club Sec; handicap limit of 18.
Green fees: on application.
Society meetings: welcome weekdays.
Catering: lunches served.
Hotels: Bell, Sandwich; Royal, Deal.

E57 Ruxley

☎ Orpington (0689) 71490
Sandy Lane, St Paul's Cray, Orpington, Kent.
A20 to Ruxley roundabout, into Sandy Lane.
Undulating parkland public course.
18 holes, 4964 yards, S.S.S.65
Club founded in 1973.
Visitors: welcome on weekdays from 7 am and at weekends after 11.30 am.
Green fees: weekdays £4, weekends £5.50.
Society meetings: welcome.
Catering: breakfasts and lunches served daily; evening meals Fri and Sat.
Hotels: Crest, Bexley, Kent.

E58 Rye

☎ Camber 241
Camber, Rye, E. Sussex.
A259 from Rye, then Camber road to Lydd.
Links course.
18 holes, 6301 yards, S.S.S.72
Course designed by H.S. Colt.
Visitors: welcome if introduced by, or playing with, member.
Green fees: weekdays £7 per day, £3 per round (£4 per day with member); weekends £10 per day, £5 per round, (£6 per day with member).
Society meetings: by arrangement.
Catering: lunch and tea served.
Hotels: in Rye.

E59 St Augustine's

☎ Thanet (0843) 590333 Sec, 590222 Pro.
Cottington Rd, Cliffsend, Ramsgate, Kent CT12 5JN
B2048 Ramsgate to Sandwich rd, turn right at Hoverport, left at Viking Caravan Club, right at Post Office, entrance at railway bridge.
Parkland course.
18 holes, 5138 yards, S.S.S.65
Course designed by Tom Vardon.
Club founded in 1907.
Visitors: welcome on showing hand. cert.
Green fees: weekdays £8, weekends and Bank Holidays £10.
Society meetings: welcome weekdays.
Catering: full catering except on Mon.
Hotels: Castle Keep, Kingsgate, Broadstairs; San Clu, East Cliff Promenade, Ramsgate.

E60 Seaford

☎ Seaford (0323) 892442
East Blatchington, Seaford, E. Sussex BN25 2JD
Off A259 N of Seaford.
Downland course.
18 holes, 6241 yards, S.S.S.70
Course designed by J.H. Taylor.
Club founded in 1887.
Visitors: welcome weekdays after 9.30 am and weekends after 1.00 pm; telephone in advance.
Green fees: £12 per day or round.
Society meetings: welcome after 9.30 am by prior arrangement.
Catering: lunch, tea and dinner available.
Hotels: Dormy House on course.

E61 Seaford Head

☎ Seaford (0323) 894843
Southdown Rd, Seaford, E. Sussex BN25 4JS
S of A259, 12 miles from Brighton, 8 miles from Eastbourne.
Seaside course.
18 holes, 5348 metres, S.S.S.68
Course designed by Thomsons of Felixstowe (1887).
Club founded in 1907.
Visitors: welcome.
Green fees: weekdays £4.20 per round, £6.30 for 2 rounds; weekends £5.30 per round, £7.40 for 2 rounds.
Society meetings: welcome.
Catering: light snacks and bar facilities
Hotels: Seaford Head, Chyngton Rd, Seaford; Victoria Sea, Esplanade, Seaford.

E62 Sene Valley

☎ Folkestone (0303) 68514
Sene, Folkestone, Kent.
A20 from Ashford or from Folkestone; club is signposted from A20 between Ashford and Folkestone.
Undulating downland course.
18 holes, 6320 yards, S.S.S.70
Course designed by Henry Cotton.
Club founded in 1888.
Visitors: welcome but advisable to phone to check availability.
Green fees: on application.
Society meetings: welcome by arrangement with Manager.
Catering: available daily, except Mon.
Hotels: Imperial, Hythe; Burlington.

E63 Sheerness

☎ Sheerness (0795) 662585
Power Station Rd, Sheerness, Kent ME12 3AE
9 miles from Sittingbourne on A249.
Seaside course.
18 holes, 6500 yards, S.S.S.71
Club founded in 1906.
Visitors: welcome, except Sun when must be guest of member.
Green fees: weekdays £6, weekends £8.
Society meetings: weekdays preferred.
Catering: full catering service.
Hotels: Seaview, Broadway, Sheerness; Royal, Broadway, Sheerness.

E64 Shortlands

☎ 01-658 0301
Meadow Rd, Shortlands, Kent BR2 0PB
½ mile from Shortlands station.
Meadowland course.
9 holes, 5261 yards, S.S.S.66
Visitors: only with members.
Society meetings: none.
Catering: by arrangement.
Hotels: Bromley Court.

E65 Sidcup

☎ 01-300 2150
7 Hurst Rd, Sidcup, Kent DA15 9AE
A222 off A2, 400 yds N of Sidcup railway station.
Parkland course.
9 holes, 5692 yards, S.S.S.67
Course designed by James Braid & H. Myrtle.
Club founded in 1891.
Visitors: welcome on weekdays and with member at weekends.
Green fees: weekdays £5.
Society meetings: welcome on weekdays, subject to prior arrangement.
Catering: meals and snacks served Mon.
Hotels: numerous hotels in area.

E66 Sittingbourne & Milton Regis

☎ Newington (0795) 842261
Wormdale, Newington, Sittingbourne, Kent ME9 7PX
1 mile N of Exit 5 off M2 on A249.
Undulating course.
18 holes, 6121 yards, S.S.S.69
Course designed by Harry Hunter.
Club founded in 1929.
Visitors: welcome on weekdays.
Green fees: weekdays £8 per round, £11 for 2 rounds; Sat and Bank Holidays £10 per round, £15 for 2 rounds.
Society meetings: catered for on Tues and Thurs.
Catering: meals served except Mon.
Hotels: Coniston, Sittingbourne.

E67 Sundridge Park

☎ 01-460 0278
Garden Rd, Bromley, Kent BR1 3LU
5 mins walk from Sundridge Park station.
Parkland courses
East 18 holes, 6148 yards, S.S.S.71
West 18 holes, 5708 yards, S.S.S.69
Course designed by James Braid & Jack Randall
Club founded in 1901.
Visitors: welcome on weekdays and with member at weekends.
Green fees: £12 per round, £15 per day.
Society meetings: welcome weekdays only. Special arrangements for Tues (Ladies Day) and weekends.
Catering: lunches, teas and bar snacks; evening meals by arrangement.
Hotels: Bromley Court, Bromley, Kent.

E68 Tenterden

☎ Tenterden (058 06) 3987
Woodchurch Rd. Tenterden, Kent.
1 mile E of Tenterden on B2067.
Undulating parkland course.
9 holes, 5119 yards, S.S.S.65
Visitors: welcome except Sun mornings.
Green fees: weekdays £5, weekends and Bank Holidays £7.
Society meetings: by arrangement.
Catering: light meals served; other catering by arrangement.
Hotels: Vine Inn, White Lion.

E69 Tunbridge Wells

☎ Tunbridge Wells (0892) 23034
Langton Rd, Tunbridge Wells.
Adjacent to Spa Garage & Hotel.
Undulating course.
9 holes, 4684 yards, S.S.S.62
Club founded in 1889.
Visitors: welcome weekdays only.
Green fees: £5.75.
Society meetings: by arrangement.
Catering: Tues – Sun, lunch and dinners.
Hotels: Spa; Wellington; Royal Wells.

E70 Walmer & Kingsdown

☎ Deal (0304) 373256
The Leas, Kingsdown, Deal, Kent CT14 8ER
Off A258, 2½ miles S of Deal.
Undulating meadowland course.
18 holes, 6451 yards, S.S.S.71
Course designed by James Braid.
Club founded in 1909.
Visitors: welcome on weekdays and after 11 am at weekends.
Green fees: weekdays £9, weekends and Bank Holidays £10.
Society meetings: welcome, but must book in advance.
Catering: full catering available; for parties or societies book in advance.
Hotels: Royal, Deal; Clarendon, Deal; Guildford House, Deal; Dover Moat House.

E71 Waterhall

☎ Brighton (0273) 508658
Mill Rd, Brighton, E. Sussex BN1 8YN
W of the town, 5 miles from centre, towards Devils Dyke.
Hilly downland course.
18 holes, 5615 yards, S.S.S.68
Visitors: welcome on weekdays.
Green fees: weekdays £5.25.
Society meetings: welcome weekdays.
Catering: catering available except Tues.
Hotels: Norfolk Continental; Preston Continental.

E72 Westgate & Birchington

☎ Thanet (0843) 31115
Domneva Rd, Westgate-on-sea, Kent.
On A28, ¼ mile from Westgate station.
Seaside links course.
18 holes, 4926 yards, S.S.S.64
Club founded in c.1923.
Visitors: welcome if members of recognised club.
Green fees: weekdays £5, weekends and Bank Holidays £6.
Society meetings: by arrangement.
Catering: by arrangement.
Hotels: Edgewater; Iveyside.

E73 West Hove

☎ Brighton (0273) 419738
369 Old Shoreham Rd, Hove, Sussex
N of Portslade stn., junction with A272.
Downland course.
18 holes, 6130 yards, S.S.S.69
Course designed by James Braid.
Club founded in 1910.
Visitors: welcome weekdays all day and weekend afternoons.
Green fees: weekdays £8, weekends £10.
Society meetings: catered for weekdays.
Catering: available daily except Mon.
Hotels: numerous good hotels in area.

E74 West Kent

☎ Farnborough (0689) 51323
West Hill, Downe, Orpington, Kent BR6 7JJ
A21 to Orpington, head for Downe village.
Undulating meadowland course.
18 holes, 6392 yards, S.S.S.70
Club founded in 1916.
Visitors: welcome on weekdays with hand. cert. or letter of introduction and at weekends if guest of member.
Green fees: £13 per day.
Society meetings: by arrangement.
Catering: full catering by arrangement; bar snacks and meals at all times.
Hotels: Continental, Court, Bromley.

E75 West Malling

☎ Maidstone (0732) 844785 Sec, 844795 Enquiries, 844022 Pro.
London Rd, Addington, Maidstone, Kent.
A20 from London, turn left at Greenaway Hotel, 8 miles NW of Maidstone.
Parkland course.
18 holes, 7029 yards, S.S.S.73
Club founded in 1971-72.
Visitors: welcome.
Green fees: weekdays £7.50 per round, £10 per day; weekends after 11.30 am £10 per round, £12 per day.
Society meetings: by arrangement.
Catering: meals and snacks served.
Hotels: Greenaway; Post House; Larkfield.

E76 Whitstable & Seasalter

☎ Whitstable (0227) 272020
Collingwood Rd, Whitstable, Kent CT51 1EB
From A299 Thanet Way turn off at Long Reach roundabout and drive down Borstal Hill, pass under railway bridge, take second left into Nelson Rd and second left again along unmade road.
Seaside links course.
18 holes, 5276 yards, S.S.S.63
Club founded in 1914.
Visitors: welcome on weekdays, but only with member at weekends.
Green fees: £5 per round (£2.50 with member).
Society meetings: welcome on agreed dates, preferably Fri by arrangement with Club Sec.
Catering: bar snacks available.
Hotels: Marine, Marine Parade, Whitstable.

E77 Wildernesse

☎ Sevenoaks (0732) 61199 Sec, 61527 Pro, 61526 Club.
Seal, Sevenoaks, Kent.
On A25 from Sevenoaks to Maidstone, turn right at sign in village of Seal.

Parkland course.
18 holes, S.S.S.72
Visitors: weekdays only by appointment with official club handicap.
Green fees: £14 per day, £10 per round.
Society meetings: by arrangement with Sec.
Catering: full lunch served daily.
Hotels: Post House, Wrotham; Royal Oak, Sevenoaks; Sevenoaks Park, Sevenoaks.

E78 Willingdon

☎ Eastbourne (0323) 32383
Southdown Rd, Eastbourne, E. Sussex
BN20 9BU
½ mile N of Eastbourne off A22.
Downland course.
18 holes, 6049 yards, S.S.S.69
Course designed by J.H. Taylor; modernised by Dr Mackenzie (1925)
Club founded in 1898.
Visitors: welcome on weekdays.
Green fees: weekdays £9 per day (£5.50 with member); weekends £10 per day (£7 with member).
Society meetings: welcome weekdays.
Catering: lunches available except Mon.
Hotels: Grand; Queens; Lansdowne.

E79 Woodlands Manor

☎ Otford (095 92) 3806
Tinkerpot Lane, Sevenoaks, Kent
TN15 6AB
Off A20 at Portobello Inn, West Kingsdown, or A225, 4 miles NE of Sevenoaks.
Undulating parkland course.
18 holes, 5858 yards, S.S.S.68 (summer)
Club founded in 1928.
Visitors: welcome weekdays; weekends after 1 pm, with a handicap certificate.
Green fees: on request.
Society meetings: welcome.
Catering: meals served.
Hotels: Brands Hatch Place, Fawkham.

E80 Wrotham Heath

☎ Borough Green (0732) 884800
Seven Mile Lane, Comp, Sevenoaks, Kent
TN15 8QZ
Off A20 1 mile S of Wrotham Heath.
Undulating parkland course.
9 holes, 5823 yards, S.S.S.68
Club founded in 1906.
Visitors: welcome on weekdays with handicap certificate.
Green fees: £7,50 per round, £10 per day.
Society meetings: welcome.
Catering: lunches and dinners available by arrangement with Steward.
Hotels: Post House, Wrotham Heath.

F Greater London

Anyone writing about London courses in the early part of this century would have found a very different picture from that existing today. Almost thirty have fallen victim to the city's spread including Hanger Hill, West Drayton, Neasden, Acton, Harrow, Northwick Park, Clapham Common, Ranelagh (Barnes), Tooting Bec and Streatham. But there has been the odd addition in recent years. One on the site of the old Heston Aerodrome is a case in point while another is planned not far away on reclaimed land.

With so many suburban settings, Greater London, and Middlesex in particular, can hardly be classed as a centre for holiday golf. Soil foundations, which nobody can do anything about, tend to be on the heavy side but there is much for which to be thankful and, if you live in London, it is far easier to regard golf courses as havens of retreat than if you live surrounded by green fields.

Hampstead, Hendon, Highgate, much of it laid out on top of a reservoir, and Mill Hill are as close as any to the centre of the capital but there are courses further out which, when they were designed, were very much on the edge of the country. Ashford Manor and Northwood are good examples, Northwood earning two pages in Bernard Darwin's, "The Golf Courses of Great Britain", a rare compliment.

By way of introduction, he remarked that 'Northwood is the best course on which to be taken ill, if you must be ill, since it is there that half the doctors in London play. But there is nothing in the golf to make you feel ill, since especially in dry weather, it is very attractive'. Having lived in the neighbourhood for years and played against Middlesex there, I can vouch that its attraction lives on, but I remember other county battles at West Middlesex, Ashford Manor, Hendon and Fulwell.

Enfield, Crews Hill and Bush Hill Park are situated a mile or two apart in North Middlesex and, if I mention Hillingdon and Harefield Place, it is on the understandable grounds of sentiment that they were the first golf courses I ever saw. I used to cycle for piano lessons down Vine Lane in Hillingdon, stopping to look over the fence at golfers putting on the green nearest to the road, but Greater London (why can't it still be Middlesex?) takes in many famous names, notably Royal Blackheath, Royal Wimbledon, Royal Epping Forest and Wimbledon Common. I am also reminded that it includes Sandy Lodge and South Herts but, having played against Hertfordshire on both, no amount of so called boundary reorganisation can convince me that they are in anything other than Hertfordshire.

F1 Airlinks

☎ 01-561 1418
Southall Lane, Hounslow, Middx TW5 9PE
Off M4 at Junction 3 onto A312 and A4020.
Meadowland/parkland course.
18 holes, 5883 yards, S.S.S.69
Course designed by P. Alliss & D. Thomas.
Club founded in Jan 1984.
Visitors: welcome.
Green fees: weekends and Bank Holidays £5, weekdays £4.
Society meetings: welcome weekdays.
Catering: bar and snack facilities.
Hotels: all London Airport hotels in vicinity.

F2 Aquarius

☎ 01-693 1626
Marmora Rd, Honor Oak, London SE22.
Off Forest Hill Rd.
9 holes, 5034 yards, S.S.S.65
Club founded in 1912.
Visitors: welcome with member only.
Society meetings: none.
Catering: limited service available.
Hotels: numerous good hotels in London.

F3 Ashford Manor

☎ Ashford (078 42) 52049
Fordbridge Rd, Ashford, Middx TW15 3RT
Staines by-pass A308, 2m E of Staines.
Parkland course.
18 holes, 6343 yards, S.S.S.70
Club founded in 1898.
Visitors: welcome on weekdays but must be member of recognised golf club; at weekends only by prior arrangement.
Green fees: weekdays £10, weekends £12.
Society meetings: catered for on weekdays.
Catering: lunch daily except Mon; high tea daily.
Hotels: many hotels in area.

F4 Brent Valley

☎ 01-567 1287
Church Rd, Cuckoo Lane, Hanwell, London W5.
A4020 Uxbridge Rd, Hanwell, on to Church Rd by Brent Lodge Animal Centre.
Meadowland course.
18 holes, 5440 yards, S.S.S.66
Visitors: welcome, booking can be made.
Green fees: weekdays £3.10 (evening £1.80), weekends £4.60 (evening £2.40); £4.40 per round.
Society meetings: contact P. Warner or Pro.
Catering: normally every day.

F5 Bush Hill Park

☎ 01-360 5738
Bush Hill Rd, Winchmore Hill, London N21 2BU
½ mile S of Enfield town.
Parkland course.
18 holes, 5809 yards, S.S.S.68
Club founded in 1895.
Visitors: welcome on weekdays but at weekends only with member.
Green fees: £9 per day.
Society meetings: catered for except on Mon, Wed and weekends.
Catering: full catering by arrangement.
Hotels: Royal Chace, Enfield.

F6 Crews Hill

☎ 01-363 6674
Cattlegate Rd, Crews Hill, Enfield, Middx EN2 8AZ
Off A1005 Enfield to Potters Bar rd into East Lodge Lane, turn right into Cattlegate Rd.
Parkland course.
18 holes, 6230 yards, S.S.S.70
Club founded in 1921.
Visitors: weekends and Bank Holidays only with member; members of recognised golf clubs welcome on weekdays.
Green fees: information on request.
Society meetings: catered for by advance booking.
Catering: lunches served except Mon.
Hotels: Royal Chace Hotel, The Ridgeway, Enfield, Middx.

F7 Dulwich & Sydenham Hill

☎ 01-693 3961
Grange Lane, College Rd, London SE21 7LH
Off S Circular road at Dulwich College and College Rd.
Parkland course.

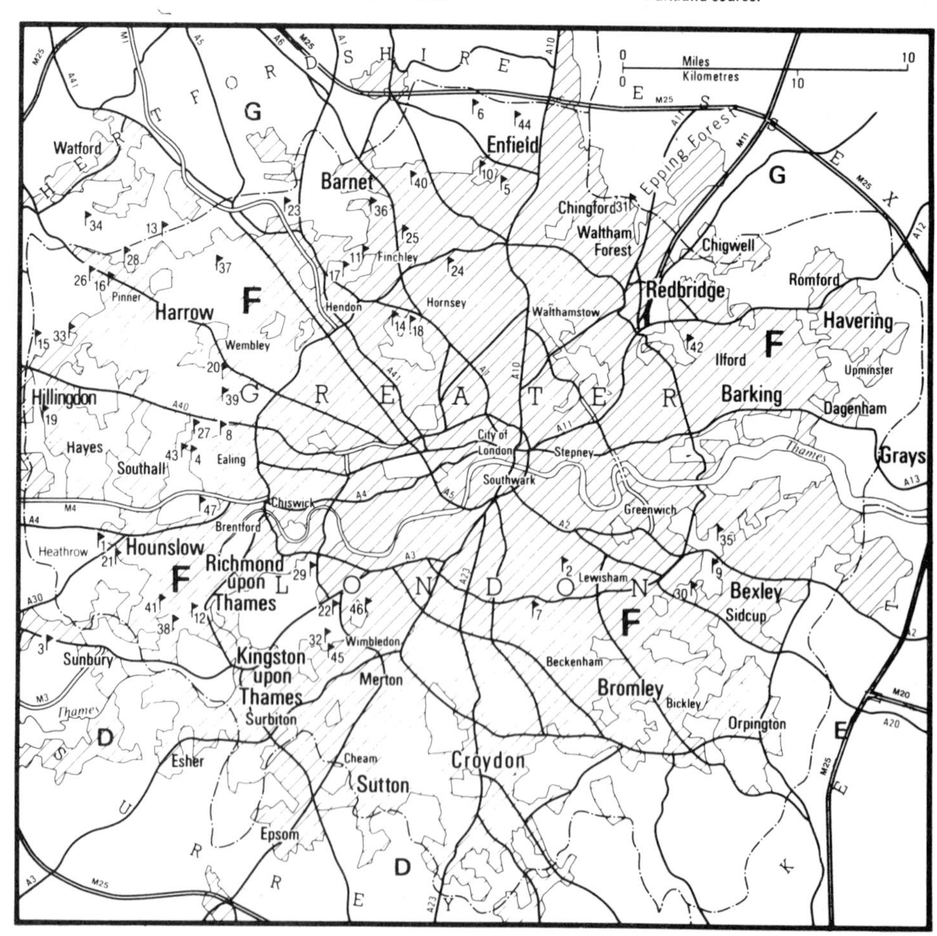

18 holes, 6051 yards, S.S.S.69
Club founded in 1894
Visitors: welcome on weekdays only with introduction.
Green fees: £11 per round or day.
Society meetings: weekdays except Tues.
Catering: snacks available every day, dinners and lunches served on Wed and Sat only.
Hotels: Queens, Crystal Palace.

F8 Ealing
☎ 01-997 0937
Perivale Lane, Greenford, Middx UB6 8SS
Off A40 W opposite Hoover factory.
Parkland course.
18 holes, 6216 yards, S.S.S.70
Club founded in 1907.
Visitors: welcome weekdays only by prior arrangement.
Green fees: £9.50.
Society meetings: by arrangement.
Catering: full catering available.

F9 Eltham Warren
☎ 01-850 1166
Bexley Rd, Eltham, London SE9 2PE
Continuation of Eltham High St, ½ mile E.
Parkland course.
9 holes, 5840 yards, S.S.S.68
Club founded in 1890.
Visitors: welcome weekdays with handicap certificate.
Green fees: £7 (£3 with member).
Society meetings: welcome weekdays.
Catering: lunches and evening meals served by arrangement.
Hotels: in London.

F10 Enfield
☎ 01-363 3970
Old Park Rd S, Enfield, Middx EN2 7DA
1 mile NE of Enfield, near Enfield Chase railway station.
Parkland course.
18 holes, 6137 yards, S.S.S.70
Course designed by James Braid.
Club founded in 1984.
Visitors: welcome on weekdays, 24 hours notice, with handicap and if member of another club.
Green fees: £8 per day.
Society meetings: weekdays only.
Catering: meals available every day.
Hotels: Royal Chace, The Ridgeway, Enfield; Enfield, Bycullah Rd, Enfield.

F11 Finchley
☎ 01-346 2436
Nether Court, Erith Lane, Mill Hill, London NW7 1PU
Nearest main junction is A1 and A41, Mill Hill East underground station five minutes walk.
Parkland course.
18 holes, 6411 yards, S.S.S.71
Course designed by James Braid.
Club founded in 1929.
Visitors: welcome most times during week and afternoon at weekends, by arrangement with Pro (01-346 5086).
Green fees: weekdays £9 per round, weekends £14.
Society meetings: welcome Wed and Fri by arrangement.
Catering: snacks and meals except Mon.
Hotels: Hendon Hall, Ashley Lane, Hendon.

F12 Fulwell
☎ 01-977 2733
Wellington Rd, Hampton Hill, Middx TW12 1JY
2 miles S of Twickenham on A311, opposite Fulwell station.
Meadowland course.

18 holes, 6490 yards, S.S.S.71
Course designed by D. Morrison.
Club founded in 1904.
Visitors: welcome on weekdays and with introduction of member at weekends.
Green fees: weekdays £12, weekends £13.
Society meetings: catered for Wed to Fri, bookings well in advance.
Catering: lunches and teas except Mon.
Hotels: Cardinal Wolsey, Hampton Court.

F13 Grimsdyke

☎ 01-428 4539
Oxhey Lane, Hatch End, Pinner, Middx HA5 4AL
2 miles W of Harrow, A4008.
Parkland course.
18 holes, 5598 yards, S.S.S.67
Course designed by James Braid.
Club founded in 1910.
Visitors: welcome on weekdays and with member at weekends.
Green fees: £8 per round, £10 per day.
Society meetings: welcome on weekdays.
Catering: full catering except Mon.
Hotels: Grimsdyke.

F14 Hampstead

☎ 01-455 7089
Winnington Rd, Hampstead, London N2 0TU
A41 from Highgate village, 1 mile down Hampstead Lane; course adjacent to Spaniards Inn.
Undulating parkland course.
9 holes, 5812 (18) yards, S.S.S.68
Club founded in 1893.
Visitors: welcome on weekdays, prior booking with Pro requested; restricted times at weekends.
Green fees: weekdays £10 per round (18 holes), £12.50 per day; weekends and Bank Holidays £15 per round (18 holes), £20 per day.
Society meetings: none.
Catering: luncheon by prior booking with Stewardess (01-455 7421); snacks always available.
Hotels: La Gaffe, Heath St, Hampstead; Central, Golders Green.

F15 Harefield Place

☎ Uxbridge (0895) 31169
The Drive, Harefield Place, Uxbridge, Middx UB10 9PA
2 miles N of Uxbridge.
Public parkland course.
18 holes, 5711 yards, S.S.S.68
Visitors: by arrangement with London Borough of Hillingdon.
Green fees: weekdays £3.90, weekends £4.20.
Society meetings: by arrangement with London Borough of Hillingdon.
Catering: full catering facilities.
Hotels: Master Brewer, Hillingdon.

F16 Haste Hill

☎ Northwood (65) 26485
The Drive, Northwood, Middx HA6 1HN
On A404.
Parkland course.
18 holes, 5787 yards, S.S.S.68
Club founded in 1930.
Visitors: welcome.
Green fees: weekdays £2.90, weekends £4.30.
Society meetings: welcome by arrangement.
Catering: meals served daily.

F17 Hendon

☎ 01-346 6023
Off Sanders Lane, Mill Hill, London NW7 1DG
To Hendon Central take Queens Rd through Brent St, continue to roundabout, take first exit on left, club is ½ mile on left in Devonshire Rd.
Parkland course.
18 holes, 6241 yards, S.S.S.70
Club founded in 1901.
Visitors: welcome on weekdays; must book at weekends.
Green fees: weekdays £8.50 per round, £12 per day; weekends £15.
Society meetings: welcome but should book several months in advance.
Catering: meals served.
Hotels: Hendon Hall.

F18 Highgate

☎ 01-340 3745
Denewood Rd, London N6 4AH
Off Hampstead Lane near Renwood House, turn into Sheldon Ave then first left into Denewood Rd.
Parkland course.
18 holes, 5964 yards, S.S.S.69
Club founded in 1904.
Visitors: welcome on weekdays.
Green fees: weekdays £9 per round, £15 per day.
Society meetings: welcome on weekdays except Wed mornings.
Catering: lunch, snacks and teas served.
Hotels: numerous hotels in London.

F19 Hillingdon

☎ Uxbridge (0895) 33956 Sec, 51980 Pro, 39810 Members.
18 Dorset Way, Hillingdon, Middx UB10 0JR
Turn off A40 to Uxbridge, past RAF Station, up Hillingdon Hill to left turn at Vine Public House into Vine Lane, club gates ¾ mile on left.
Undulating parkland course.
9 holes, 5459 yards, S.S.S.67
Course designed by Harry Woods & Chas. E. Stevens.
Club founded in 1892.
Visitors: welcome with introduction of member if have handicap certificate or are a member of recognised golf club; at weekends and Bank Holidays after 12.30 pm only with member.
Green fees: £9 per day, £7 per part day.
Society meetings: welcome with 3 months notice on Mon, Tues and Fri.
Catering: snacks available, meals by arrangement.
Hotels: Old Cottage, Royal Lane, Hillingdon; Woodlands Guest House, 84 Long Lane, Ickenham; Master Brewer, A40.

F20 Horsenden Hill

☎ 01-902 4555
Woodland Rise, Greenford, Middx UB6 0RD
Signposted off Whitton Ave E.
Undulating parkland course.
9 holes, 3236 yards, S.S.S.56
Club founded in 1935.
Visitors: welcome.
Green fees: weekdays £1.55 per round (Junior/OAP 80p per round), weekends £2.20 per round (Junior/OAP £1.10 per round).
Society meetings: none.
Catering: snacks available; restaurant meals by arrangement.
Hotels: numerous hotels in area.

F21 Hounslow Heath

☎ 01-570 5271
Staines Rd, Hounslow, Middx.
On main road from Hounslow town to Bedfont, on left hand side.
Parkland course.
18 holes, 5820 yards, S.S.S.68
Course designed by Fraser Middleton.
Club founded in 1979.
Visitors: all welcome; bookings may be made at weekends.
Green fees: weekdays £3.10, weekends £3.95.
Society meetings: no.
Catering: snacks always available.
Hotels: Hounslow.

F22 London Scottish

☎ 01-788 0135
Windmill Enclosure, Wimbledon Common, London SW19 5NQ
2 miles from Wimbledon railway station.
Parkland course.

18 holes, 5436 yards, S.S.S.67
Club founded in 1865.
Visitors: welcome on weekdays, except Bank Holidays.
Green fees: £5 per round.
Society meetings: none.
Catering: lunches served and evening meals if ordered except on Mon.
Hotels: numerous hotels in London.

F23 Mill Hill
☎ 01-959 2339
100 Barnet Way, Mill Hill, London NW7 3AL
On A1, ½ mile N of Apex Corner, 1 mile S of Stirling Corner.
Parkland course.
18 holes, 6286 yards, S.S.S.70
Club founded in 1925.
Visitors: welcome on weekdays.
Green fees: weekdays £9.
Society meetings: arranged on Mon, Wed and Fri.
Catering: lunches served daily.
Hotels: numerous hotels in London.

F24 Muswell Hill
☎ 01-888 1764 Sec, 8046 Pro.
Rhodes Ave, Wood Green, London N22 4UT
1 mile from Bounds Green tube station, 1½ miles from N Circular Road.
Undulating course.
18 holes, 6470 yards, S.S.S.71
Club founded in 1893.
Visitors: welcome; weekdays unrestricted, weekends bookings only.
Green fees: weekdays £10, £7.50 after 3 pm, weekends £11.
Society meetings: catered for weekdays only.
Catering: snacks and society meals served.
Hotels: numerous hotels in London.

F25 North Middlesex
☎ 01-445 1604
Friern Barnet Lane, Whetstone, London N20.
A1000 5 miles N of Finchley.
Undulating parkland course.
18 holes, 5611 yards, S.S.S.67
Club founded in 1928.
Visitors: welcome if members of recognised club.
Green fees: weekdays £8 (with member £3.50), weekends £12 (with member £5).
Society meetings: welcome except Mon.
Catering: lunches served except Mon.

F26 Northwood
☎ Northwood (65) 25329
Rickmansworth Rd, Northwood HA6 2QW
On main road between Northwood Hills and Rickmansworth A404.
Parkland course.
18 holes, 6230 yards, S.S.S.70
6464 yards, S.S.S.71
Club founded in 1891.
Visitors: welcome on weekdays.
Green fees: £8.50 per round, £12.50 per day.
Society meetings: catered for Mon, Thurs and Fri; minimum 25 for evening meal.
Catering: full catering daily.
Hotels: Tudor Lodge, Eastcote; Long Island, Rickmansworth.

F27 Perivale Park
☎ 01-578 1693
Ruislip Rd. East, Greenford, Middx.
On Ruislip Rd. East between Greenford and Perivale.
Parkland course.
9 holes, 2667 yards, S.S.S.65 (men) 67 (women).
Visitors: welcome.
Green fees: weekdays £1.55, weekends £2.20.
Society meetings: welcome.
Catering: snacks served.
Hotels: Kenton, Hanger Hill.

F28 Pinner Hill
☎ 01-866 0963
South View Rd, Pinner Hill, Middx HA5 3YA
Off A404 at Northwood Hills roundabout.
Parkland course.
18 holes, 6293 yards, S.S.S.70
Course designed by J.H. Taylor.
Club founded in 1928.
Visitors: welcome on weekdays.
Green fees: Mon, Tues and Fri £9, Wed, Thurs £2.40, Sat £12.
Society meetings: welcome except Wed, Thurs.
Catering: lunches and teas served.

F29 Roehampton
☎ 01-876 1621
Roehampton Lane, London SW15 5LR
Off A306 bottom of Roehampton Lane.
Parkland course.
18 holes, 6011 yards, S.S.S.69
Club founded in 1901.
Visitors: welcome with member only.
Green fees: weekdays £7, weekends £9.
Society meetings: societies of up to 36 players accepted on weekdays if introduced by member.
Catering: lunch and tea every day.
Hotels: numerous good hotels in London.

F30 Royal Blackheath
☎ 01-850 1795
Court Rd, Eltham, London SE9 5AF
5 minutes walk from Mottingham station.
Parkland course.
18 holes, 6200 yards, S.S.S.70
Course designed by James Braid.
Club founded in 1608.
Visitors: welcome with introduction.
Green fees: £16 per day.
Society meetings: welcome by arrangement.
Catering: restaurant available.
Hotels: numerous hotels in London.

F31 Royal Epping Forest
☎ 01-529 6407 Club, 2195 Sec.
Forest Approach, Chingford, London E4 7AZ
300 yds S of Chingford railway station.
Parkland course.
18 holes, 6220 yards, S.S.S.70
Club founded in 1888.
Visitors: private club playing on public course.
Green fees: weekdays £3.05, weekends £4.60.
Society meetings: no.
Catering: for club members only.

F32 Royal Wimbledon
☎ 01-946 2125
29 Camp Rd, Wimbledon SW19 4UW
¾ mile W of War Memorial in Wimbledon village.
Parkland course.
18 holes, 6300 yards, S.S.S.70
Club founded in 1865.
Visitors: by prior arrangement with Sec.
Green fees: weekdays £15 per day (£8 with member).
Society meetings: weekdays only.
Catering: snacks and lunches available on certain days.
Hotels: numerous good hotels in area.

F33 Ruislip
☎ Ruislip 38081 or 38835 Pro.
Ickenham Rd, Ruislip, Middx
1 mile N of A40, Hillingdon.
Parkland course.
18 holes, 5500 yards, S.S.S.68
Course designed by Sandy Herd.
Club founded in 1936.
Visitors: welcome without reservation every day including weekends.
Green fees: weekdays £2.90, weekends £3.60.
Society meetings: by arrangement with Steward or Pro.
Catering: breakfast, lunches and snacks
Hotels: Master Brewer, Western Ave., Hillingdon.

F34 Sandy Lodge
☎ Northwood (65) 25429
Sandy Lodge Lane, Northwood, Middx HA6 2JD
2 miles S of Watford and 2 miles N of Northwood, immediately adjoining Moor Park station, Metropolitan line. Take A4125 from Northwood to Watford, left

into Sandy Lodge Lane.
Links course.
18 holes, 6340 yards, S.S.S.70
Course designed by Harry Vardon.
Club founded in 1910.
Visitors: weekdays only by arrangement; at weekends with member only.
Green fees: £14 per day, £10 per round.
Society meetings: welcome on weekdays by arrangement with Sec.
Catering: snacks available every day; lunches and dinners by arrangement.
Hotels: Grimsdyke, Grimsdyke; Bell House, Beaconsfield; Ladbroke Mercury, Watford.

F35 Shooters Hill
☎ 01-854 6368
'Lowood,' Eaglesfield Rd, London SE18 3DA
Off Shooters Hill.
Parkland course.
18 holes, 5718 yards, S.S.S.68
Club founded in 1903.
Visitors: members of other golf clubs only, unless playing with member.
Green fees: weekdays £9 per round, £12.50 all day (with member £4.50 per round, £7.50 per day); weekends with member only £4.50 per round, £7.50 per day.
Society meetings: welcome on Tues and Thurs only.
Catering: lunches daily by arrangement.
Hotels: Clarendon, Blackheath.

F36 South Herts
☎ 01-445 2035
Links Drive, Totteridge, London N20 8QU
400 yds from A1000 at Whetstone to Totteridge Lane then 400 yds to Links Drive.
Parkland course.
18 holes, 6432 yards, S.S.S.71
Course designed by Harry Vardon.
Club founded in 1899.
Visitors: weekdays only (Tues Ladies Day).
Green fees: £9 per round, £12 per day.
Society meetings: catered for on Wed, Thurs and Fri.
Catering: lunches, snacks and teas served, except Mon when only snacks.
Hotels: Crest, South Mimms.

F37 Stanmore.
☎ 01-954 2599 Sec, 2646 Pro.
Gordon Ave, Stanmore, Middx HA7 2RL
Entrance off Gordon Ave, via Old Church Lane.
Undulating parkland course.
18 holes, 5815 yards, S.S.S.68
Club founded in 1893.
Visitors: welcome on weekdays; open to public on Mon and Fri.
Green fees: Tues to Thurs £7.50 per round, £10 per day; Mon and Fri (public days) £2.40 per round, £3.90 per day; weekends £5 with member.
Society meetings: Wed and Thurs only by prior arrangement.
Catering: lunches available except Mon.
Hotels: Grimsdyke.

F38 Strawberry Hill
☎ 01-894 1246
Wellesley Rd, Twickenham, Middx.
Adjacent to Strawberry Hill station.
Parkland course.
9 holes, 2381 yards, S.S.S.62
Course designed by J.H. Taylor.
Club founded in 1900.
Visitors: welcome on weekdays and with member at weekends or Bank Holidays.
Green fees: £6 for 18 holes.
Society meetings: not accepted.
Catering: hot snacks and sandwiches available at bar.

F39 Sudbury
☎ 01-902 3713
Bridgewater Rd, Wembley, Middx HA0 1AL
Junction of A4005 and A4090, Sudbury Town (Piccadilly Line) 5 minutes walk.
Undulating parkland course.
18 holes, 6282 yards, S.S.S.70
Club founded in 1920.
Visitors: welcome on weekdays.
Green fees: weekdays £9.50 (£5 with member), weekends and Bank Holidays £13 (£6.50 with member).
Society meetings: catered for on weekdays and by arrangement.
Catering: lunches served except Mon.
Hotels: Harrow, 12/22 Pinner Rd, Harrow; Hindes, 8 Hindes Rd, Harrow; King's Head, 88 High St, Harrow.

F40 Trent Park
☎ 01-366 7432
Bramley Rd, Southgate, London N14
Opposite Oakwood tube station (Piccadilly Line).
Parkland course.
18 holes, 5971 yards, S.S.S.69
Club founded in 1974.
Visitors: welcome every day but advisable to book at weekends.
Green fees: weekdays £2.40, weekends £3.90.
Society meetings: always welcome.
Catering: snacks always available; meals by prior arrangement.
Hotels: Royal Chace, Ridgeway, Enfield; West Lodge, Cockfosters Rd, Cockfosters.

F41 Twickenham
☎ 01-979 0032 Pro, 892 5579 Sec.
Staines Rd, Twickenham, Middx.
On A305 near Hope and Anchor roundabout.
Municipal commonland course.
9 holes, 6014 yards, S.S.S.69
Course designed by Charles Lawrie
Club founded in 1977.
Visitors: welcome.
Green fees: weekdays £3, weekends £4.80.
Society meetings: welcome by arrangement with Pro, Mr. A. Tickle.
Catering: fully licensed bar; snacks and cooked meals to order.
Hotels: Richmond Gate, Richmond.

F42 Wanstead
☎ 01-989 3938
Overton Drive, Wanstead, London E11 2LW
Off A12 at Wanstead station, right into 'The Green,' into St Mary's Ave, left at T-junction at St Mary's Church.
Parkland course.
18 holes, 6211 yards, S.S.S.70
Club founded in 1893.
Visitors: welcome on weekdays with prior arrangement.
Green fees: £8 per round, £10 per day.
Society meetings: welcome by arrangement weekdays only.
Catering: meals served.
Hotels: Sir Alfred Hitchcock, 147 Whipps Cross Rd, Leytonstone; Prince Regent, Woodford Bridge.

F43 West Middlesex
☎ 01-574 3450 Sec, 1800 Pro.
Greenford Rd, Southall, Middx UB1 3EE
A40 from Central London to Greenford, take left exit off roundabout, 2 miles straight down road.
Undulating parkland course.
18 holes, 6242 yards, S.S.S.70
Course designed by James Braid.
Club founded in 1890.
Visitors: welcome on weekdays; Mon and Wed are Public days.
Green fees: Mon and Wed £4 per round; Tues, Thurs and Fri £8 per round; weekends only after 4 pm £8.
Society meetings: can be booked only on Tues, Thurs and Fri.
Catering: hot and cold snacks available all week; 3 course meals should be booked in advance.
Hotels: Canarvan, Ealing Common; Osterley, Great West Rd, Osterley.

F44 Whitewebbs
☎ 01-363 4458
Beggars Hollow, Clay Hill, Enfield, Middx.
1 mile N of Enfield.
Parkland course.
18 holes, 5881 yards, S.S.S.68
Club founded in 1932.
Visitors: welcome.

Green fees: weekdays £3.15, weekends £4.20.
Society meetings: by arrangement.
Catering: meals served.
Hotels: West Lodge; Royal Chace.

F45 Wimbledon Common

☎ 01-946 7571 Sec, 0294 Pro.
Camp Rd, Wimbledon Common SW19 4UW
1 mile NW of War Memorial, past Fox and Grapes on right in Camp Rd.
Moorland course.
18 holes, 5486 yards, S.S.S.67
Course designed by Tom and Willie Dunn.
Club founded in 1908.
Visitors: welcome on weekdays.
Green fees: £4 per round, £6 per day.
Society meetings: accepted if sponsored by club members only.
Catering: light meals available.
Hotels: numerous hotels in Wimbledon.

F46 Wimbledon Park

☎ 01-946 1002
Home Park Rd, Wimbledon Park, London SW19 7HR
250 yds from Wimbledon Park station (District Line).
Parkland course.
18 holes, 5456 yards, S.S.S.67
Club founded in 1889.
Visitors: welcome on weekdays and some weekends after 3 pm (ring Pro 01-946 4053).
Green fees: £8 per round, £12 per day.
Society meetings: catered for on weekdays only.
Catering: full facilities except Mon.
Hotels: numerous hotels in London.

F47 Wyke Green

☎ 01-560 8777
Syon Lane, Osterley, Isleworth, Middx TW7 5PT
Golf club located in Syon Lane, off the A4 N of Gillette Corner.
Parkland course.
18 holes, 6242 yards, S.S.S.70
Course designed by W.H. Tate.
Club founded in 1928.
Visitors: welcome with handicap; advisable to telephone first.
Green fees: weekdays £10 per round, Sat after 10 am and Sun after 3 pm £15 p. r.
Society meetings: catered for on Tues and Thurs by arrangement.
Catering: snacks and meals available.
Hotels: Osterley, Great West Rd, Hounslow, Middx.

G Essex and Hertfordshire

Michael Bonallack was raised on the courses of Essex which is recommendation enough for any county. Thorpe Hall was his home club although he is an honorary member of many more, all inclined to regard him as one of their own. Thorndon Park, Chelmsford and Orsett are perhaps the pick of the courses in Essex with Frinton lending a touch of the seaside to emphasise how far its limits extend from the chimes of Bow Bells. However, the majority serve some of the most densely populated areas around the capital.

Romford, Ilford, Chingford, Chigwell, Wanstead and West Essex are the best examples, Romford once being the club of James Braid. Essex is liberally served with public courses, Epping Forest even having the prefix 'Royal'. There are nine in all making Essex fourth in the league table behind Lancashire, Yorkshire and Middlesex in the provision made to municipal golfers. The two courses at Hainault Forest are as busy as any and there are others at Basildon, Belhus Park, Southend and Thurrock.

For a relatively small county, Hertfordshire can boast more than forty courses, most of them of the parkland variety although Berkhamsted, one of the best known, certainly cannot be so categorised. On a ridge of the Chilterns, it is a natural, old-fashioned common ideal for golf and testing enough to have no need for sand bunkers. Ashridge, a near neighbour, is defined as a parkland course but it is not so obvious a candidate as Moor Park, Porters Park or West Herts which is situated in Cassiobury Park, Watford.

Professional tournaments and a much photographed clubhouse account for Moor Park's reputation, handsome trees and undulating ground making the High an acknowledged test, while Sandy Lodge, on the other side of the Metropolitan Line, is very much on a par. There is a West Herts, South Herts, East Herts and Mid-Herts, making it something of a puzzle why there is no North Herts to complete the set; but the county can claim eight or nine new courses in the last twenty years or so including a new home for East Herts. Three of the best courses are Hadley Wood, Harpenden and Brookmans Park.

G1 **Abridge G & CC**
☎ Stapleford (04028) 396
Stapleford Tawney, Abridge, Essex RM4 1ST
M11 from London Exit 5 via Abridge; from N. M11 exit 7 via Epping.
Parkland course.
18 holes, 6703 yards, S.S.S.72
Course designed by Henry Cotton.
Club founded in 1964.
Visitors: welcome except Sun.
Green fees: on request.
Society meetings: welcome on Mon and Wed.
Catering: meals served.
Hotels: Tree Tops; Bell; The Cock; all in Epping.

G2 **Aldenham G & CC**
☎ Radlett (092 76) 7775 or 7889
Radlett Rd. Aldenham, Watford, Herts.
Junction 5 on M1, follow A41 toward London, turn off at Ladbroke Hotel towards Radlett, 30 minutes by car from Marble Arch.
Undulating course.
18 holes, 6445 yards, S.S.S.71
Club founded in 1975.
Visitors: welcome on weekdays and after 1 pm at weekends.
Green fees: weekdays £8 per round, weekends £15 per round.
Society meetings: tailored to individual requirements.
Catering: public restaurant and bar.
Hotels: Ladbroke; Spiders Web.

G3 **Arkley**
☎ 01-449 0394 or 440 8473 Pro.
Rowley Green Rd, Barnet, Herts EN5 3HL
Off A1 at Stirling Corner to A411, signposted at Rowley Lane on left.
Parkland course.
2 x 9 holes, 6045 yards, S.S.S.69
Club founded in 1909.
Visitors: welcome on weekdays and with member at weekends.
Green fees: £7.50 per day, £4 per round (£3 with member).
Society meetings: by arrangement on Wed and Thurs preferably.
Catering: lunches served except Mon and evening meals by arrangement.
Hotels: Thatched Barn.

G4 **Ashridge**
☎ Little Gaddesden (044 284) 2244
Little Gaddesden, Berkhamsted, Herts HP4 1LY

A41 to Berkhamsted, turn right at Northchurch on B4506.
Parkland course.
18 holes, 6508 yards, S.S.S.71
Course designed by Sir Guy Campbell, Col Hotchkin and Cecil Hutchison.
Club founded in 1932.
Visitors: on application.
Green fees: on application.
Society meetings: catered for on weekdays from March to Oct.
Catering: full lunch available except Mon.
Hotels: Bell Inn, Aston Clinton; Aubrey Park, Redbourn.

G5 Basildon

☎ Basildon (0268) 3297
Clay Hill Lane, Basildon, Essex.
From A127 through Basildon to Kingswood roundabout; from A13 turn left at Five Bells roundabout to Kingswood roundabout.
Undulating parkland course.
18 holes, 6122 yards, S.S.S.69
Course designed by Frank Pennink.
Club founded in 1966.
Visitors: welcome every day.
Green fees: weekdays £4.20, weekends £8.
Society meetings: welcome weekdays.
Catering: snacks available.
Hotels: Crest, Basildon.

G6 Batchwood Hall

☎ St Albans (0727) 52101
Batchwood Drive, St Albans.
NW corner of town.
Parkland course.
18 holes, 6463 yards, S.S.S.71
Club founded in 1935.
Visitors: welcome without reservation.
Green fees: weekdays £3.60, weekends £4.80.
Society meetings: not catered for.
Catering: none.
Hotels: numerous hotels in area.

G7 Belfairs Park

☎ Southend on Sea (0702) 525345 or 520322
Eastwood Rd. N, Leigh-on-Sea, Essex SS9 4LR
Please note that the club is private but plays on the undernoted public course.
Parkland public course.
18 holes, S.S.S.68

G8 Belhus Park

☎ South Ockendon (0708) 854260
Belhus Park, South Ockendon, Essex RM15 4QR
A13 to Aveley, Essex.
Parkland course.
18 holes, 5900 yards, S.S.S.68
Course designed by Cotton (C.K.), Pennink, Lawrie & Partners.
Visitors: welcome.
Green fees: weekdays £2, weekends £4.50.
Society meetings: by arrangement.
Catering: bar and restaurant.
Hotels: Royal, Purfleet; Europa, North Stifford; Old Plough House, Bulphan.

G9 Bentley

☎ Coxtie Green (0277) 73179
Ongar Rd, Brentwood, Essex CM15 9SS
4 miles from Brentwood on A128 to Ongar.
Parkland course.
18 holes, 6766 yards, S.S.S.72
Course designed by Alec Swan.
Club founded in 1972.
Visitors: welcome on weekdays.
Green fees: £8 per round, £10 per day.
Society meetings: welcome on weekdays.
Catering: lunches and light snacks available.
Hotels: Post House, Brentwood.

G10 Berkhamsted

☎ Berkhamsted (044 27) 3730 or 5832 Sec.
The Common, Berkhamsted, Herts HP4 2QB
Take Junction 8 off M1 into Hemel Hempstead, at roundabout take Leighton Buzzard road, after about 3 miles take Potters End turn and follow road to club.
Heathland course.
18 holes, 6546 yards, S.S.S.72
Course designed by G.H. Gowring (1890/2, Founder), 1912 C.J. Gilbert with advice from Harry Colt, 1927 course extension with advice from James Braid.
Club founded in 1890.
Visitors: welcome except on competition days; advisable to telephone in advance.
Green fees: weekdays £8 for 1 round, £12 for 2 rounds; weekends and Bank holidays £15 for 1 or 2 rounds.
Society meetings: catered for usually on Wed and Fri.
Catering: meals available every day except Mon.
Hotels: Swan, Berkhamsted; Post House, Hemel Hempstead; Rose and Crown, Tring; Hamberlins, Northchurch.

G11 Birch Grove

☎ Layer dela Haye (0206) 34276
Layer Rd, Colchester CO2 0HS
2 miles S of town.
Meadowland course.
9 holes, 2828 yards, S.S.S.54
Club founded in 1970.
Visitors: welcome.
Green fees: £3.
Catering: lunches and snacks served.
Hotels: many good hotels in area.

G12 Bishop's Stortford

☎ Bishop's Stortford (0279) 54715
Dunhow Rd, Bishop's Stortford, Herts CM23 5HP
Exit 8 from M11, follow signs to town centre/hospital, golf course is on left next to Nags Head on E edge of town.
Parkland course.
18 holes, 6440 yards, S.S.S.71
Club founded in 1910.
Visitors: welcome on weekdays and with member at weekends.
Green fees: £10 per day, £8 per round.
Society meetings: welcome, max. 40.
Catering: bar snacks available every day; restaurant and bar meals except Mon.
Hotels: Foxley.

G13 Boxmoor

☎ Hemel Hempstead (0442) 42434
18 Box Lane, Hemel Hempstead, Herts.
¾ mile from Hemel Hempstead station on A41.
Undulating parkland course.
9 holes, 4854 yards, S.S.S.64
Club founded in 1890.
Visitors: welcome without reservation except Sun.
Green fees: weekdays £3, Sat £4.
Society meetings: welcome with 4 weeks' notice.
Catering: limited service available.
Hotels: numerous in area.

G14 Boyce Hill

☎ South Benfleet (037 45) 3625
Vicarage Hill, South Benfleet, Essex SS7 1PD
7 miles W of Southend-on-Sea, A127 to Rayleigh Weir (3 miles from course), A13 to Victoria House Corner (1m from course).
Undulating parkland course.
18 holes, 5377 yards, S.S.S.68
Course re-designed by James Braid.
Club founded in 1922.
Visitors: welcome Mon and Wed all day, Tues afternoons only.
Green fees: £10 per round.
Society meetings: on Thurs only.
Catering: service throughout day.
Hotels: numerous hotels in area.

G15 Braintree

☎ Braintree (0376) 24117

Kings Lane, Stisted, Braintree, Essex CM7 8DA
1½ miles NE of Braintree on A120.
Parkland course.
18 holes, 6026 yards, S.S.S.69
Course designed by Hawtree and Son.
Visitors: welcome except Sun; Sat with handicap certificate.
Green fees: weekdays £7.40 per round, £9.80 per day; weekends £10 per round, £20 per day.
Society meetings: welcome by arrangement on Mon, Wed and Thurs (Tues is Ladies Day).
Catering: meals served.
Hotels: White Hart, Braintree.

G16 Brickendon Grange

☎ Bayford (099 286) 258
Brickendon, Nr. Hertford, Herts SG13 8PD
3 miles S of Hertford near Bayford station.
Undulating parkland course.
18 holes, 6315 yards, S.S.S.70
Course designed by C.K. Cotton.
Club founded in 1968.
Visitors: welcome on weekdays.
Green fees: £10 per round.
Society meetings: welcome weekdays.
Catering: snack lunches served.
Hotels: numerous good hotels in area.

G17 Brookmans Park

☎ Potters Bar (0707) 52487
Golf Club Rd, Hatfield, Herts AL9 7AT
On Hatfield Rd, A1000 1 mile N of Potters Bar, 3 miles S of Hatfield.
Parkland course.
18 holes, 6438 yards, S.S.S.70
Club founded in 1930.
Visitors: welcome weekdays and at weekends with member and handicap certificate.
Green fees: £11 per day, £9 per round, £6 after 4 pm.
Society meetings: accepted on Wed, Thurs and Fri.
Catering: snacks served at lunchtime; evening meals available only for societies.
Hotels: Royal Chace, The Ridgeway, Enfield; West Lodge Park, Hadley Wood, Barnet; Ponsbourne, Newgate Street Village, Hertford.

G18 Bunsay Downs

☎ Danbury (024 541) 2648 or 2369 Members
Little Baddow Rd, Woodham Walter, Nr Maldon, Essex.
Leave A414 at Danbury (signposted Woodham Walter), course is ½ mile to W of village.
Gently undulating meadowland course.
9 holes, 2913 yards, S.S.S.68
Club founded in 1982.
Visitors: welcome.
Green fees: £3 for 9 holes, £4 for 18 holes.
Society meetings: welcome.
Catering: breakfast, lunch and evening meals available from 10 am (8 am weekends) to 10 pm.
Hotels: many good hotels in Chelmsford and Maldon.

G19 Burnham-on-Crouch

☎ Maldon (0621) 782282
Ferry Rd, Creeksea, Burnham-on-Crouch, Essex CM0 8PQ
1¼ miles W of Creeksea.
Undulating meadowland course.
9 holes, 5350 yards, S.S.S.68
Club founded in 1918.
Visitors: welcome but not on weekend mornings.
Green fees: weekdays £7, weekends £9.
Society meetings: catered for mainly Wed (Ladies Day Thurs).
Catering: bar snacks available except Mon; evening meals by arrangement.
Hotels: White Harte, The Quay, Burnham-on-Crouch.

G20 Bushey G & Squash C

☎ 01-950 2283
High St, Bushey, Herts.
On A411 1½ miles M1/A411.
Private parkland course.
9 holes, 3000 yards, S.S.S.69
Course designed by Donald Steel, Cotton (C.K.), Pennink, Lawrie & Partners Ltd.
Club founded in 1980.
Visitors: welcome, except Wed.
Green fees: weekdays £6, weekends £8.
Society meetings: by arrangement, limited numbers.
Catering: meals served.
Hotels: Ladbroke Mercury; Spiders Web; both on A41.

G21 Bushey Hall

☎ Watford (0923) 25802
Bushev Hall Drive, Bushey, Herts WD2 2EP

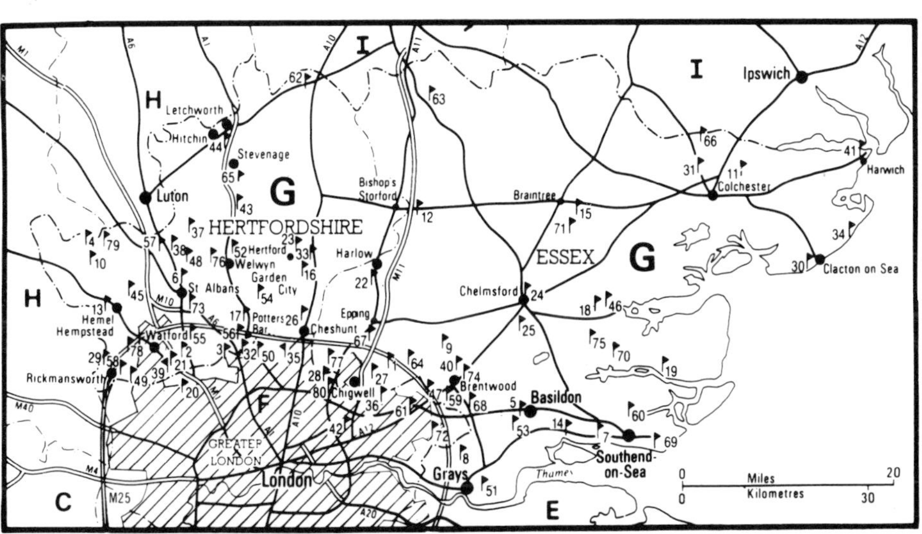

1 mile SE Watford.
Undulating parkland course.
18 holes, 6071 yards, S.S.S.69
Club founded in 1886.
Visitors: welcome on weekdays.
Green fees: on application.
Society meetings: catered for on weekdays, except Wed.
Catering: full service available.
Hotels: numerous hotels in London area.

G22 Canons Brook
☎ Harlow (0279) 21482
Elizabeth Way, Harlow, Essex CM19 5BE
M11 to Harlow, Edinburgh Way then Elizabeth Way.
Parkland course.
18 holes, 6462 yards, S.S.S.72
Course designed by Henry Cotton.
Club founded in 1963.
Visitors: welcome on weekdays.
Green fees: £8 per round or day.
Society meetings: welcome on weekdays; may be booked.
Catering: service from Tues to Sat.
Hotels: Churchgate; Moat House.

G23 Chadwell Springs
☎ Ware (0920) 3647
Hertford Rd, Ware, Herts SG12 9LE
On A119 halfway between Hertford and Ware.
Parkland course.
9 holes, 3209 yards, S.S.S.71
Course designed by J.H. Taylor.
Club founded in 1975.
Visitors: welcome weekdays, weekends after noon (subject to competition times).
Green fees: weekdays £6 (£5 with member), weekends £9 (£6 with member).
Society meetings: welcome on weekdays.
Catering: meals served.
Hotels: Salisbury Arms, Hertford; Cannons, Ware.

G24 Channels
☎ Chelmsford (0245) 440005
Belsteads Farm Lane, Little Waltham, Chelmsford, Essex CM3 3PT
Undulating course.
18 holes, 6100 yards, S.S.S.69
Course designed by Cotton, Pennink, Lawrie and Partners.
Club founded in 1974.
Visitors: welcome on weekdays, but phone Pro, Ian Sinclair (0245 441056), in advance. No jeans or collarless shirts.
Green fees: on application.
Society meetings: welcome by arrangement with Sec, S.M.Everitt.
Catering: meals and snacks available.
Hotels: South Lodge, Chelmsford.

G25 Chelmsford
☎ Chelmsford (0245) 56483
Widford Rd, Chelmsford, Essex CM2 9AP
A12 to Wood St roundabout, Chelmsford, turn right (from London) and right again.
Undulating parkland course.
18 holes, 5912 yards, S.S.S.68
Club founded in 1892.
Visitors: welcome on weekdays if members of recognised club, weekends with member only.
Green fees: on application.
Society meetings: by arrangement.
Catering: bar snacks and lunches daily except Mon; dinners Fri and Sat only.
Hotels: South Lodge; Miami.

G26 Cheshunt
☎ Waltham Cross (0992) 24009
Park Lane, Cheshunt, Herts EN7 6QD
A10 to Cheshunt, then signposted.
Parkland course.
18 holes, 6608 yards, S.S.S.71
Club founded in 1976.
Visitors: welcome on weekdays and by arrangement at weekends.
Green fees: weekdays £2.90, weekends £4.20.
Society meetings: catered for any time by arrangement.
Catering: cafeteria service all day.

G27 Chigwell
☎ 01-500 2059
High Rd, Chigwell, Essex IG7 5DH
On A113, 13½ miles NE of London.
Parkland course.
18 holes, 6279 yards, S.S.S.71
Club founded in 1925.
Visitors: welcome weekdays with reservation and letter of introduction.
Green fees: £9 per round, £11 per day, £5 with member.
Society meetings: by arrangement.
Catering: lunches and teas served.
Hotels: Roebuck, Buckhurst Hill.

G28 Chingford
☎ 01-529 5708
Bury Rd, Chingford, London E4.
Off Station Rd.
Parkland course.
18 holes, 6309 yards, S.S.S.69
Course designed by James Braid.
Club founded in 1888.
Visitors: welcome. Red outer garment must be worn.
Green fees: weekdays £3.05 per round, weekends £4.60 per round, Mon - Fri £1.35 for OAPs (10.00-15.00 hrs).
Society meetings: by appointment.
Catering: snacks, no bar.

G29 Chorleywood
☎ Chorleywood (092 78) 2009
Common Rd, Chorleywood.
Clubhouse close to Chorleywood station and Sportsman Hotel.
Parkland course.
9 holes, 5676 yards, S.S.S.67
Club founded in 1890.
Visitors: welcome but advisable to phone.
Green fees: weekdays £5, weekends £6.
Society meetings: by arrangement.
Catering: snacks normally available and meals by arrangement.
Hotels: Sportsman, Chorleywood.

G30 Clacton-on-Sea
☎ Clacton-on-Sea (0255) 421919
West Rd, Clacton-on-Sea, Essex CO15 1AJ
On A133 16 miles from Colchester, 1 mile W of pier next to old Butlins Holiday Camp.
Undulating seaside course.
18 holes, 6217 yards, S.S.S.70
Course designed by Jack White.
Club founded in 1892.
Visitors: welcome on weekdays and weekends, with reservations.
Green fees: weekdays £7 per round, £9 per day; weekends and Bank Holidays £10; half-price with member.
Society meetings: welcome weekdays.
Catering: available except Mon.
Hotels: Royal; Esplanade; Glengarry; all on Marine Parade East.

G31 Colchester
☎ Colchester (0206) 853396 Sec.
Braiswick, Colchester, Essex CO4 5AU
¾ mile up Bergholt Rd from Colchester North station.
Parkland course.
18 holes, 6319 yards, S.S.S.70
Course designed by James Braid.
Club founded in 1909.
Visitors: welcome on weekdays but ring first; at weekends only with member.
Green fees: £7 per round, £10 per day.
Society meetings: limited number of society meetings usually on Thurs.
Catering: lunches and early evening meals available (book before playing).
Hotels: George, High St, Colchester; Marks Tey, Marks Tey, Colchester.

G32 Dyrham Park
☎ 01-440 3361
Galley Lane, Barnet, Herts.
2 miles outside Barnet near Arkley, off A1.
Parkland course.

18 holes, 6369 yards, S.S.S.70
Visitors: with member only.
Society meetings: by arrangement.
Catering: restaurant.

G33 East Herts

☎ Ware (0920) 821981 or 821978 Sec.
Hamels Park, Buntingford, Herts SG9 9NA
A10 between Buntingford and Ware, ¼ mile N of Puckeridge roundabout.
Parkland course.
18 holes, 6449 yards, S.S.S.71
Club founded in 1898.
Visitors: welcome on weekdays.
Green fees: £9.50 per round, £11.50 per day.
Society meetings: catered for on Mon, Wed, Thurs and Fri.
Catering: meals served.
Hotels: Canons, Ware.

G34 Frinton

☎ Frinton (025 56) 4618
Esplanade, Frinton-on-Sea, Essex CO13 9EP
A133 Colchester to Weeley village, B1033 to Frinton and turn right at seafront.
Seaside course.
18 holes, 6259 yards, S.S.S.70
Course designed by Tom Dunn.
Club founded in 1896.
Visitors: welcome.
Green fees: weekdays £8 per round, £10 per day; weekends after 11 am £9 per day.
Society meetings: by arrangement.
Catering: full service available.
Hotels: Maplin; Rock; Glencoe.

G35 Hadley Wood

☎ 01-499 4328
Beech Hill, Barnet, Herts EN4 0JJ
From M25 take A111 towards Cockfosters, third turning right into Beech Hill, entrance 400 yds on left.
Parkland course.
18 holes, 6473 yards, S.S.S.71
Course designed by Alister Mackenzie.
Club founded in 1921.
Visitors: welcome on weekdays with handicap certificate or letter from own club Sec.
Green fees: weekdays £11 for 1 round, £14 for 2 rounds, £6 after 5 pm (with member £5.50 for 1 round, £6.50 for 2 rounds, £2 after 5 pm); weekends with member £6 for 1 round, £7 for 2 rounds, £3 after 5 pm; Junior £1.50.
Society meetings: catered for on Wed, Thurs and Fri.
Catering: Available except Mon, advisable to telephone in season.
Hotels: W. Lodge Pk, Cockfosters Rd, Barnet.

G36 Hainault Forest

☎ 01-500 2097
Chigwell Row, Hainault, Essex.
On A127 12 miles from Central London.
Parkland course.
18 holes, 5754 yards, S.S.S.67
18 holes, 6445 yards, S.S.S.71
Club founded in 1912.
Visitors: public course.
Green fees: weekdays £2.40, weekends £3.90.
Catering: meals served.
Hotels: Valentine, Gants Hill.

G37 Harpenden

☎ Harpenden (058 27) 2580
Hammonds End, Redbourn Lane, Harpenden, Herts AL5 2AX
Off A1081 4 miles N of St Albans on B487
Parkland course.
18 holes, 6363 yards, S.S.S.70
Visitors: welcome on weekdays only
Green fees: £8 per round, £10 per day (£4 per round with member).
Society meetings: catered for on weekdays except Thurs.
Catering: by arrangement.
Hotels: Moathouse; Gleneagles.

G38 Harpenden Common

☎ Harpenden (058 27) 5959
East Common, Harpenden, Herts AL5 1BL
Off A6 4 miles from St Albans on B487.
Commonland course.
18 holes, 5613 yards, S.S.S.67
Club founded in 1931.
Visitors: welcome on weekdays and by invitation at weekends.
Green fees: £6 per round, £8.50 per day.
Society meetings: catered for on Thurs and Fri.
Catering: lunches and snacks available; dinner by arrangement.
Hotels: Mote House, Harpenden; Glen Eagles, Harpenden.

G39 Hartsbourne G & C C

☎ 01-950 1133
Hartsbourne Ave, Bushey Heath, Herts WD2 1JW
Turn S off A411 at entrance to Bushey Heath village 5 miles SE of Watford.
Parkland course.
18 holes, 6305 yards, S.S.S.70
9 holes, 5432 yards, S.S.S.70
Club founded in 1946.
Visitors: accompanied by member only.
Green fees: not applicable.
Society meetings: welcome Wed and Fri.
Catering: lunches except Mon and Fri.
Hotels: Spiders Web; Ladbroke Mercury; both on A41.

G40 Hartswood

☎ Brentwood (0277) 21850 Sec.
King Georges Playing Fields, Ingrave Rd, Brentwood, Essex.
1 miles S of Brentwood on A128.
Municipal parkland course.
18 holes, 6160 yards, S.S.S.69
Club founded in 1964.
Visitors: welcome.
Green fees: weekdays £3 per round, weekends £4.60 per round.
Society meetings: welcome weekdays by arrangement.
Catering: full catering every day.
Hotels: Post House, Brentwood.

G41 Harwich & Dovercourt

☎ Harwich (0255) 503616
Station Rd, Parkeston, Harwich, Essex CO12 4NZ
A120 towards Parkeston Quay, after last roundabout 200 yards on left.
Meadowland course.
9 holes, 5692 yards, S.S.S.68
Club founded in 1903.
Visitors: welcome.
Green fees: £6.50 (£4 with member).
Society meetings: welcome by arrangement.
Catering: bar snacks or full catering as required.
Hotels: Cliff, Dovercourt; Towers, Dovercourt.

G42 Ilford

☎ 01-554 2930
291 Wanstead Park Rd, Ilford, Essex IG1 3TR
½ mile from Ilford railway station.
Parkland course.
18 holes, 5414 yards, S.S.S.68
Club founded in 1906.
Visitors: welcome on weekdays; restricted at weekends.
Green fees: weekdays £6 per round, £9 per day; weekends £8 per round.
Society meetings: catered for on Mon, Wed and Fri.
Catering: lunches served every day; dinners only on Thurs and Sat.

G43 Knebworth

☎ Stevenage (0438) 812752
Deards End Lane, Knebworth, Herts SG3 6NL
1 mile S of Stevenage on B197.
Parkland course.
18 holes, 6440 yards, S.S.S.71
Club founded in 1908.
Visitors: welcome on weekdays and with member at weekends and Bank Holidays.
Green fees: £11 per day, £8.50 per round.
Society meetings: catered for on Mon, Tues and Thurs only.
Catering: meals available from 10.30 am to 9.30 pm on weekdays and from 11.30 am to 5.30 pm at weekends.
Hotels: Roebuck, Stevenage; Heath Lodge, Welwyn.

G44 Letchworth

☎ Letchworth (0462) 683203
Letchworth Lane, Letchworth, Herts SG6 3NQ
2 miles from A1(M), near village of Willian, adjacent to Letchworth Hall Hotel.
Parkland course.
18 holes, 6082 yards, S.S.S.69
Course re-designed by Harry Vardon.
Club founded in 1905.
Visitors: welcome on weekdays.
Green fees: weekdays £7.50 per round, (£3.50 with member), £10 per day (£6 with member).
Society meetings: catered for on Wed, Thurs and Fri.
Catering: lunches served except Mon.
Hotels: Letchworth Hall; Greenlawns; Butterfield House, Baldock.

G45 Little Hay

☎ Hemel Hempstead 833798
Hemel Hempstead, Herts.
Off A41 at Box Lane traffic lights.
Meadowland course.
18 holes, 6610 yards, S.S.S.72
Course designed by Hawtree and Son.
Club founded in 1977.
Visitors: welcome.
Green fees: weekdays £2.75, weekends £4.
Society meetings: by arrangement.
Catering: from Jan 86, full meal facilities.
Hotels: Bobsleigh.

G46 Maldon

☎ Maldon (0621) 53212
Beeleigh, Langford, Maldon, Essex CM9 7SS
2 miles NW of Maldon on B1019, turn off at the Essex Waterworks in Langford.
Meadowland course.
9 holes, 6197 yards, S.S.S.69
Club founded in 1891.
Visitors: welcome on weekdays.
Green fees: £5 for 18 holes, £7 per day.
Society meetings: welcome by appointment.
Catering: only available for societies and meetings by arrangement.
Hotels: Blue Boar, Maldon.

G47 Maylands G & C C

☎ Ingrebourne (040 23) 73080
Colchester Rd, Harold Park, Romford, Essex RM3 0AZ
On A12 between Romford and Brentwood.
Undulating parkland course.
18 holes, 6182 yards, S.S.S.69 (Ladies S.S.S.72)
Course designed by Colt, Alison, Morrison & Williams.
Club founded in 1936.
Visitors: welcome if members of other clubs with introduction.
Green fees: £8 per round, £10 per day.
Society meetings: by arrangement on weekdays only.
Catering: meals and snacks every day.
Hotels: Moat House, Post House.

G48 Mid-Herts

☎ Wheathampstead (058 283) 2242 Sec, 3385 Steward, 3118 Pro.
Gustard Wood, Wheathampstead, St Albans, Herts AL4 8RS
On B651 6 miles N of St Albans
Heathland/parkland course.
18 holes, 6094 yards, S.S.S.69
Club founded in 1893.
Visitors: welcome on weekdays only with reservation.
Green fees: £10 per day, £7 per round.
Society meetings: by arrangement.
Catering: lunch and dinner served Tues to Sat.
Hotels: St Michaels Manor, Fish Pool St, St Albans, Herts.

G49 Moor Park

☎ Rickmansworth (0923) 773146
Moor Park Mansion, Moor Park, Rickmansworth, WD3 1QN.
Situated on A404 between Rickmansworth and Northwood, ¾ mile from Moor Park station.
Parkland course.
High 18 holes, 6713 yards, S.S.S.72
West 18 holes, 5815 yards, S.S.S.68
High-championship tees 6903 yards, S.S.S.73
Course designed by H.S. Colt.
Club founded in 1923.
Visitors: welcome with 24 hours notice.
Green fees: on request.
Society meetings: accepted on Mon, Tues, Wed and Fri.
Catering: snacks and meals served.
Hotels: Grimsdyke, Harrow Weald; Sportsman, Chorleywood; Bellhouse, Gerrards Cross.

G50 Old Fold Manor

☎ 01-440 9185
Hadley Green, Barnet, Herts.
On Potters Bar road, ¼ mile from Barnet.
Parkland course.
18 holes, 6449 yards, S.S.S.71
Club founded in 1910.
Visitors: welcome on weekdays, with member only at weekends.
Green fees: £10 per day.
Society meetings: welcome Thurs only.
Catering: meals served except Mon and Wed.

G51 Orsett

☎ (0375) 891 352
Brentwood Rd, Orsett, Essex
On A128 400 yds from A13.
Heathland course.
18 holes, 6622 yards, S.S.S.72
Course designed by James Braid.
Visitors: welcome weekdays.
Green fees: £8 per round, £10 per day.
Society meetings: by arrangement.
Catering: meals served daily.
Hotels: Plough; Orsett Hall.

G52 Panshanger
☎ Welwyn Garden City (0707) 333350
Herns Lane, Welwyn Garden City, Herts.
Off B1000 close to A1, 1 mile NE of town.
Undulating parkland course.
18 holes, 6538 yards, S.S.S.70
Club founded in 1976.
Visitors: welcome.
Green fees: weekdays £3, weekends £4.
Society meetings: book through Pro.
Catering: lunches served daily.

G53 Pipps Hill
☎ Basildon (0268) 23456
Aquatels Recreation Centre, Cranes Farm Rd, Basildon, Essex.
On A127 or A13.
Meadowland course.
9 holes, 2829 yards, S.S.S.67
Visitors: welcome.
Green fees: weekdays £2.50, weekends £4.
Society meetings: welcome on weekdays.
Catering: meals served.
Hotels: Essex Centre.

G54 PL London
☎ Potters Bar (0707) 42624 or 42626
Bedwell Park, Essendon, Hatfield, Herts AL9 6JA
A1000 from Potters Bar, B158 towards Essendon.
Undulating parkland course.
18 holes, 6878 yards, S.S.S.73
Course designed by Fred Hawtree Senior.
Club founded in 1976.
Visitors: welcome.
Green fees: weekdays £4.70, weekends and Bank Holidays £7.50.
Society meetings: welcome.
Catering: bar snacks at lunchtime.
Hotels: numerous hotels in area.

G55 Porters Park
☎ Radlett (092 76) 6262 Club, 4127 Sec.
Shenley Hill, Radlett, Herts WD7 7AZ
Turn off A5 to Shenley road at railway station, ½ mile to top of hill, club on bend of road.
Undulating parkland course.
18 holes, 6313 yards, S.S.S.70
Club founded in early 1890s – 1899 at present site.
Visitors: welcome weekdays with introduction or by arrangement and at weekends and Bank Holidays with member.
Green fees: £8.50 per round, £12 per day.
Society meetings: catered for on Wed and Thurs only.
Catering: available by arrangement with Chef (092 76 6262).
Hotels: Red Lion, Radlett; Noke, St Albans.

G56 Potters Bar
☎ Potters Bar (0707) 52020
Darkes Lane, Potters Bar, Herts EN6 1DE
A1000 N of Barnet, Tesco opposite entrance to club.
Undulating parkland course.
18 holes, 6273 yards, S.S.S.70
Club founded in 1923.
Visitors: welcome on weekdays, except Wed mornings, and with member at weekends; advisable to phone in advance.
Green fees: £10 per round.
Society meetings: accepted, details on application.
Catering: full service all day; restricted menu on Mon and Fri.
Hotels: Crest, South Mimms; St Michael's Manor, St Albans.

G57 Redbourn
☎ Redbourn (058 285) 3493
Kingsbourne Green Lane, Redbourn, Herts AL3 7AQ
S off M1 at junction 9 on to A5, turn left, 1 mile down Luton Lane.
Parkland course.
18 holes, 6407 yards, S.S.S.71
9 holes, 1361 yards, Par 27 (public course).
Visitors: welcome on weekdays.
Green fees: £6 (18 hole course), £3.50 (9 hole course).
Society meetings: by arrangement.
Catering: bar snacks and restaurant.
Hotels: Aubrey Park.

G58 Rickmansworth
☎ Rickmansworth (0923) 773163 Clubhouse, 775278 Pro Shop.
Moor Lane, Rickmansworth, Herts.
A4145, 2 miles S of town.
Undulating municipal parkland course.
18 holes, 4412 yards, S.S.S.62
Club founded in 1944/5
Visitors: welcome.
Green fees: weekdays £3, weekends and Bank Holidays £4.30.
Society meetings: by arrangement with Steward.
Catering: hot meals served all day.
Hotels: numerous hotels in area.

G59 Risebridge
☎ Romford (0277) 41429
Risebridge Chase, Lower Bedfords Rd, Romford, Essex.
2 miles from Gallows Corner and Romford station.
Parkland course (also pitch & putt).
18 holes, 5237 yards, S.S.S.70
Visitors: welcome – bookings for weekends.
Green fees: weekdays £2.80, weekends £4.30.
Society meetings: by arrangement.
Catering: snacks daily.
Hotels: Brentwood Post House.

G60 Rochford Hundred
☎ Southend (0702) 544302
Rochford Hall, Hall Rd, Rochford, Essex SS4 1NW
Off Rochford to Southend road adjacent to airport; 4 miles N of Southend.
Parkland course.
18 holes, 6255 yards, S.S.S.69
Course designed by James Braid.
Club founded in 1893.
Visitors: welcome on weekdays and with member only at weekends.
Green fees: £10 per day, £8 per round.
Society meetings: by arrangement on Wed or Thurs.
Catering: lunches only Mon to Fri.
Hotels: Airport, Aviation Way.

G61 Romford
☎ Romford (0277) 40986
Heath Drive, Gidea Park, Romford, Essex RM2 5QB
1½ miles from Romford town centre, off A12.
Parkland course.
18 holes, S.S.S.70
Course designed by James Braid.
Club founded in 1894.
Visitors: welcome on weekdays only if member of golf club.
Green fees: £8 per round, £11 per day.
Society meetings: catered for on Mon, Tues, Thurs or Fri.
Catering: meals served.
Hotels: Ladbroke Mercury, Southend Rd, Romford; Post House, Brentwood; Moat House, Brentwood.

G62 Royston
☎ Royston (0763) 42696
Baldock Rd, Royston, Herts SG8 5BG
Situated on the A505 on outskirts of town to E, actual golf course on Therfield Heath.
Undulating heathland course.
18 holes, 6032 yards, S.S.S.69
Club founded in 1892.
Visitors: welcome.
Green fees: weekdays £7, weekends £9.
Society meetings: welcome on weekdays.
Catering: bar snacks and lunches.
Hotels: Banyers Hotel, Melbourn St, Royston; Old Bull, Market Hill, Royston.

G63 Saffron Walden
☎ Saffron Walden (0799) 22786

Windmill Hill, Saffron Walden, Essex CB10 1BX
Take B184 from Stumps Cross roundabout on M11 (Junction 9), entrance just before entering town.
Parkland course.
18 holes, 6608 yards, S.S.S.72
Club founded in 1919.
Visitors: welcome on weekdays but only with member at weekends and Bank Holidays.
Green fees: £10.
Society meetings: on certain Mon, Wed, Thurs and occasional Fri.
Catering: lunches available every weekday; evening meals for societies.
Hotels: Saffron.

G64 Skips
☎ Ingrebourne (040 23) 48234
Horsemanside, Tysea Hill, Stapleford Abbotts, Essex RM4 1JU
B175 to Stapleford Abbotts, left up Tysea Hill.
Meadowland course.
18 holes, 6146 yards, S.S.S.71
Course designed by Cotton, Pennink, Lawrie and Partners.
Club founded in 1972.
Visitors: welcome at all times.
Green fees: weekdays £1.50 for 9 holes, £2 for 18 holes; weekends and Bank Holidays £2 for 9 holes, £3 for 18 holes.
Society meetings: none.
Catering: no catering.
Hotels: Post House, Brentwood.

G65 Stevenage
☎ Shephall (043 888) 424
Aston Lane, Aston, Stevenage, Herts SG2 7EL
On to A602 to Hertford from A1, course signposted about 1½ miles.
Parkland/meadowland course.
18 holes, 6451 yards, S.S.S.71
Course designed by John Jacobs.
Club founded in 1980.
Visitors: welcome every day, but necessary to book at weekends.
Green fees: weekdays £2.75, weekends £4.
Society meetings: welcome weekdays.
Catering: full meals and bar snacks.
Hotels: Roebuck.

G66 Stoke-by-Nayland
☎ Nayland (0206) 262836
Keepers Lane, Leavenheath, Colchester, Essex CO6 4PZ
A134 from Colchester for 7 miles, turn off onto B1068 to Stoke-by-Nayland.
Undulating meadowland course.
18 holes, 6471 yards, S.S.S.71
18 holes, 6498 yards, S.S.S.71
Club founded in 1972.
Visitors: welcome weekdays and weekends (after 10 am); phone at weekends to check availability.
Green fees: weekdays £6.50 per round, £10 per day; weekends £8 per round, £12 per day.
Society meetings: catered for mainly on weekdays.
Catering: full catering available; large groups by arrangement.
Hotels: numerous hotels in Colchester or Sudbury.

G67 Theydon Bois
☎ Theydon Bois (0378) 3054
Theydon Rd, Epping, Essex CM16 4EH
On A11 1 mile S of Epping.
Undulating woodland course.
18 holes, 5472 yards, S.S.S.68
Club founded in 1898.
Visitors: welcome on weekdays.
Green fees: £8 per round or per day.
Society meetings: catered for on Mon, Tues and Wed.
Catering: by arrangement.
Hotels: Post House, Bell Common, Epping.

G68 Thorndon Park
☎ Brentwood (0277) 811666
Ingrave, Brentwood, Essex CM13 3RH
2 miles SE of Brentwood on A128.
Parkland course.
18 holes, 6455 yards, S.S.S.71
Club founded in 1920.
Visitors: welcome on weekdays and with member at weekends.
Green fees: weekdays £9 per round, £13 per day.
Society meetings: catered for on Tues and Fri.
Catering: meals served on weekdays except Mon.
Hotels: Post House, Brentwood.

G69 Thorpe Hall
☎ Southend-on-Sea (0702) 582050 or 582205 Sec.
Thorpe Hall Ave, Thorpe Bay, Essex SS1 3AT
Thorpe Hall Ave joins the seafront, about 2 miles E of Southend Pier.
Parkland/meadowland course.
18 holes, 6259 yards, S.S.S.71
Club founded in 1907.
Visitors: welcome on weekdays.
Green fees: weekdays £13 per day or round, weekend afternoons £13 per round.
Society meetings: catered for on Wed and Fri only.
Catering: lunches served except Mon.
Hotels: Roslin, Thorpe Esplanade, Thorpe Bay; Ilfracombe House, Wilson Rd, Southend-on-Sea; West Park, Park Rd, Westcliff-on-Sea.

G70 Three Rivers G & C C
☎ Maldon (0621) 828631
Stow Rd, Purleigh, Nr Chelmsford, Essex CM3 6RR
From London A127 to A130 to A132, on B1012 from Chelmsford (10 miles); A12 to A130 to A132.
Parkland course.
Kings course 18 holes, 6609 yards, S.S.S.72
Queens course 9 holes x 2, 2142 yards, Par 54.
Course designed by Fred Hawtree.
Club founded in 1973.
Visitors: weekdays & p.m. weekends with member only restricted according to competitions.
Green fees: weekdays £8.50 (£6 with member), weekends £10 (£9 with member).
Society meetings: Tues and Thurs preferred. Other days by arrangement.
Catering: at all times.
Hotels: Three Rivers G & C.C.

G71 Towerlands
☎ Braintree (0376) 26802
Panfield Rd, Braintree, Essex CM7 5BJ
Course on B1053 out of Braintree.
Undulating meadowland course.
9 holes, 2698 yards, S.S.S.66
Course designed by George R. Shiels.
Club founded on 1st July, 1985.
Visitors: welcome.
Green fees: weekdays £5, weekends and Bank Holidays £7.
Society meetings: welcome.
Catering: full restaurant and bar
Hotels: White Hart, Braintree; Foley House, High Garrett, Braintree.

G72 Upminster
☎ Upminster (86) 22788
114 Hall Lane, Upminster, Essex.
A127 towards Southend.
Parkland course.
18 holes, 5926 yards, S.S.S.68
Club founded in 1927.
Visitors: welcome weekdays if members of a recognised club.
Green fees: £8 per round, £12 per day.
Society meetings: by arrangement.
Catering: meals served except Mon.
Hotels: Ladbroke, Upminster; Post House, Brentwood.

G73 Verulam
☎ St Albans (0727) 53327
London Rd, St Albans, Herts AL1 1TG
A6 to St Albans.
Parkland course.
18 holes, 6836 yards, S.S.S.71
Visitors: welcome weekdays with

members only at weekends.
Green fees: Mon £5 per round, £8 per day, Tues – Fri £8 per round, £10 per day.
Society meetings: by arrangement.
Catering: meals by arrangement except Mon.
Hotels: Peahen; Red Lion; Sopwell House; The Haven.

G74 Warley Park

☎ Brentwood (0277) 224891
Magpie Lane, Little Warley, Brentwood, CM13 3DX
Off M25 junction 29 A127 Southend - immediately left Gt. Warley, left, 1st right, left into Magpie Lane (6 mins from M25).
Undulating parkland course.
27 holes (3 x 9) played 1-2, 1-3; 2.3.
Course designed by R. Plumbridge.
Club founded in 1975.
Visitors: welcome with handicap certificate.
Green fees: £11.50 per round, £15 per day.
Society meetings: welcome by arrangement.
Catering: 1st class restaurant.
Hotels: New World; Post House.

G75 Warren

☎ Danbury (024 541) 3258 or 4662
Woodham Walter, Maldon, Essex CM9 6RW
A414 6 miles E of Chelmsford towards Maldon.
Undulating parkland course.
18 holes, 6211 yards, S.S.S.70
Club founded in 1934.
Visitors: welcome on weekdays.
Green fees: £9 per round, £11 per day; half-price with member.
Society meetings: catered for on Mon, Tues, Thurs and Fri.
Catering: full service available.
Hotels: Pontlands Park, Great Baddow; Blue Boar, Maldon.

G76 Welwyn Garden City

☎ Welwyn Garden City (0707) 325243
Mannicotts, High Oaks Rd, Welwyn Garden City, Herts AL8 7BP
Off N at Stanborough, follow B197 to town centre.
Undulating parkland course.
18 holes, 6200 yards, S.S.S.69
Course designed by Hawtree and Son.
Club founded in 1922.
Visitors: welcome on weekdays.
Green fees: £10 per day, £8 per round
Society meetings: welcome on Mon, Wed, Thurs and Fri.
Catering: lunches and snacks served except Mon.
Hotels: Crest, Welwyn Garden City; Garden, Welwyn Garden City.

G77 West Essex

☎ 01-529 4367 Pro, 7558 Sec, 1029 Steward.
Bury Rd, Sewardstunkbury, Chingford London E4 7QL
Off A11, ¾ mile from Chingford station.
Parkland course.
18 holes, 6342 yards, S.S.S.70
Course designed by James Braid.
Club founded in 1900.
Visitors: welcome on weekdays only, except Tues before 10.30 am and Thur after 12 noon.
Green fees: £9 per round.
Society meetings: welcome, book in advance.
Catering: full catering.
Hotels: Royal Forest.

G78 West Herts

☎ Watford (0923) 36484
Cassiobury Park, Watford, Herts
WD1 7SL
2 miles from Watford on A412.
Parkland course.
18 holes, 6488 yards, S.S.S.71
Course designed by Tom Morris & Harry Vardon.
Visitors: welcome weekdays, weekends with member only.
Green fees: £9.50 per round, £13 per day, £5 per day with member.
Society meetings: welcome Wed and Fri
Catering: lunches and teas served except Mon.
Hotels: Caledonian; Southern Cross.

G79 Whipsnade Park

☎ Little Gaddesden (044 284) 2330 or 2331
Studham Lane, Dagnall, Herts HP4 1RH
Off M1 at Junction 9 between villages of Dagnall and Studham.
Parkland course.
18 holes, 6800 yards, S.S.S.72
Club founded in 1974.
Visitors: welcome on weekdays.
Green fees: £7 per round, £10 per day; weekends £14.
Society meetings: welcome on weekdays.
Catering: snacks and meals except Mon.
Hotels: Post House, Hemel Hempstead; Moat House, Markyate, Herts.

G80 Woodford

☎ 01-504 0553
2 Sunset Ave, Woodford Green, Essex
IG8 0ST
A11 to Woodford Green, near Castle Public House.
Parkland course.
9 holes, 5806 yards, S.S.S.68
Club founded in 1890.
Visitors: welcome on weekdays, except Tue and Thurs mornings and with member only at weekends.
Green fees: £5 per round, £6 per day.
Society meetings: by arrangement.
Catering: snacks served and meals by arrangement.
Hotels: Castle; Packfords.

H Buckinghamshire, Bedfordshire, Oxfordshire, Northamptonshire

From Stoke Poges and Denham in the south to Woburn in the north, Buckinghamshire is full of good and enjoyable places to play. Beaconsfield, Burnham Beeches, Ellesborough, Harewood Downs and Gerrards Cross are further examples, although it is impossible for me not to link Berkshire and Oxfordshire with Buckinghamshire, as the men's county team does.

Huntercombe, Frilford Heath, Burford and Tadmarton Heath are obvious favourites in Oxfordshire but, for the geographical purposes of this Guide, Buckinghamshire and Oxfordshire are grouped with Northamptonshire and Bedfordshire, the latter with only about a dozen courses from which to draw their county teams.

Dunstable Downs and John O'Gaunt are two I can strongly recommend and, when crossing into Northamptonshire, the same goes for the Northamptonshire County Club at Church Brampton with its collection of excellent par 4s. Delapre Golf Complex has an assortment of attractions including a driving range, par 3 and pitch and putt courses to supplement a full 18 holes.

However, a word for the public courses in the area covered. Farnham Park near Slough, Abbey Hill at Milton Keynes, Windmill Hill at Bletchley, Mowsbury at Bedford and Stockwood Park at Luton are way above average.

H1 Abbey Hill
☎ Milton Keynes (0908) 563845
Monks Way, Stony Stratford, Milton Keynes.
1 mile S of Stony Stratford.
Meadowland course.
18 holes, 6505 yards, S.S.S.70
Club founded in 1975.
Visitors: welcome weekdays, weekends with reservation.
Green fees: weekdays £3, weekends £4.20.
Society meetings: by arrangement.

H2 Aspley Guise & Woburn Sands
☎ Milton Keynes (0908) 583596
West Hill, Aspley Guise, Milton Keynes MK17 8DX
2 miles S of M1 Junction 13, half-way between Aspley Guise and Woburn Sands.
Parkland course.
18 holes, 6115 yards, S.S.S.70
Course designed by Sandy Herd.
Club founded in 1914.
Visitors: welcome on weekdays with handicap certificate.
Green fees: weekdays £8 per round or day (£3.50 with member), weekends £3.50 with member.
Society meetings: catered for on Wed and Fri.
Catering: full catering facilities Tues to Sun evenings inclusive.
Hotels: Bedford Arms, Woburn.

H3 Badgemore Park
☎ Henley-on-Thames (0491) 572206 Sec, 574175 Pro.
Henley-on-Thames, Oxon RG9 4NR
Leave the M4 at Junction 8/9 on Henley and Oxford spur, over the river into Henley, straight through the town (leaving the Town Hall on right), after ¾ mile course on right hand side.
Parkland course.
18 holes, 6112 yards, S.S.S.69
Course designed by Bob Sandow.
Club founded in July 1972.
Visitors: welcome on weekdays.
Green fees: on application.
Society meetings: large or small parties welcome by arrangement on weekdays.
Catering: full range of bar snacks available daily.
Hotels: Red Lion; Sydney House.

H4 Beaconsfield
☎ Beaconsfield (049 46) 6545
Seer Green, Beaconsfield, Bucks HP9 2UR
Off M40 onto A355 Amersham Rd, right at Jordans sign, adjacent to Seer Green/Jordans railway halt.
Parkland course.
18 holes, 6469 yards, S.S.S.71
Course designed by H.S. Colt.
Club founded in 1914.
Visitors: welcome weekdays.
Green fees: £12 per day or round.
Society meetings: catered for on Tues and Wed.
Catering: snacks served.
Hotels: Bell House, Gerrards Cross; The Bull, Gerrards Cross.

H5 Bedford & County
☎ Bedford (0234) 52617
Green Lane, Clapham, Beds MK41 6ET
Off A6 N of Bedford before Clapham village.
Parkland course.
18 holes, 6347 yards, S.S.S.70
Club founded in 1912.
Visitors: welcome on weekdays and with member at weekends.
Green fees: £7 per round, £9 per day.
Society meetings: welcome Tues, Thurs and Fri.
Catering: full catering facilities.
Hotels: Woodlands Manor, Green Lane, Clapham; De Parys, De Parys Ave, Bedford.

H6 Bedfordshire
☎ Bedford (0234) 61669
Bromham Rd, Biddenham, Bedford MK40 4AF

1½ miles from town centre on A428, NW of town boundary.
Parkland course.
18 holes, 6172 yards, S.S.S.69
Club founded in 1891.
Visitors: welcome on weekdays and by appointment at weekends.
Green fees: weekdays £6 per round, £8 per day; weekends £10 per round, £12 per day;
Society meetings: catered for on weekdays.
Catering: luncheons served every day.
Hotels: Moat House; Woodlands; De Parys Guest House.

H7 Bremhill Park

☎ Shrivenham (0793) 782946
Shrivenham, Swindon, Wilts SN6 8HH
A420 Swindon to Oxford road 6 miles from Swindon, leave by-pass for Shrivenham, club on E boundary of village.
Parkland course.
18 holes, 6040 yards, S.S.S.71
Course designed by D. Wright.
Club founded in 1968.
Visitors: welcome at any time, advance booking on Sun.
Green fees: weekdays £4 (£3.30 with member), weekends and Bank Holidays £6.50 (£4.50 with member).
Society meetings: catered for.
Catering: light snacks and meals served.
Hotels: Crest, Swindon; South Marston and C.C., South Marston, Swindon.

H8 Buckingham

☎ Buckingham (0280) 815566
Tingewick Rd, Buckingham MK18 4AE
2 miles from Buckingham on A421 towards Oxford.
Undulating parkland course.
18 holes, 6082 yards, S.S.S.69
Club founded in 1914.
Visitors: welcome weekdays and with member at weekends.
Green fees: weekdays £10 per round or per day.
Society meetings: catered for given adequate notice, weekdays only.
Catering: snacks and meals available.
Hotels: White Hart, Buckingham; Swan and Castle, Buckingham.

H9 Burford

☎ Burford (099 382) 2583
Burford, Oxon OX8 4J8
19 miles W of Oxford at junction of A40 and A361, at Burford roundabout.
Parkland course.
18 holes, 6405 yards, S.S.S.71
Club founded in 1936.
Visitors: by arrangement.
Green fees: weekdays £9, weekends £14.
Society meetings: by arrangement.
Catering: full service available.
Hotels: over 12 hotels within 1 mile of course.

H10 Burnham Beeches

☎ Burnham (062 86) 61448 Sec, 61661 Pro.
Green Lane, Burnham, Bucks SL1 8EG
Take M40 to Beaconsfield turn off, follow signs to Slough, turn right and follow Burnham signs (not Burnham Beeches) to Green Lane.
Parkland course.
18 holes, 6415 yards, S.S.S.70
Club founded in 1891.
Visitors: welcome weekdays.
Green fees: £12 per round, £14.50 per day.
Society meetings: catered for on Thurs and Fri.
Catering: full service every day.
Hotels: Burnham Beeches; Grovefield.

H11 Cainhoe Wood G & CC

☎ Silsoe (0525) 60800
Beadlow, Shefford, Beds.
On A507 between Silsoe and Shefford, 1½ miles W of Shefford.
Parkland course.
18 holes, 9 holes.
Club founded in 1970.
Visitors: welcome weekdays and with handicaps at weekends. Smart casual dress at all times.
Green fees: 18 holes weekdays £6, weekends £8; 9 holes (twice) weekdays £4, weekends £6.
Society meetings: fully catered for Mon to Sat.
Catering: full catering available.
Hotels: Cainhoe Wood Lodge.

H12 Cherwell Edge

☎ Banbury (0295) 711591
Chacombe, Banbury,. Oxon.
3 miles E of Banbury, A442 to Northampton.
Public parkland course.
18 holes, 5322 metres, S.S.S.68
Course designed by Richard Davies.
Club founded in 1983.
Visitors: welcome every day.
Green fees: weekdays 9 holes £1.70, 18 holes £2.80; weekends and Bank Holidays 9 holes £2.40, 18 holes £3.70; special rates for OAPs and Juniors.
Society meetings: welcome every day by arrangement with Manager, R. Davies.
Catering: snacks and meals served.
Hotels: Crest, Banbury; Thatched House, Sulgrave, Banbury.

H13 Chesham & Ley Hill

☎ Chesham (0494) 784541
Ley Hill, Chesham, Bucks HP5 1UZ
A41, left at Boxmoor, to Bovingdon and follow signs.
Heathland course.
9 holes, 5147 yards, S.S.S.65
Club founded in 1919.
Visitors: welcome weekdays except Tues and Fri after 1 pm; weekends with member only.
Green fees: £4.50 for 18 holes, £2.50 with member.
Society meetings: by arrangement with committee.
Catering: light meals and snacks except Mon.
Hotels: at Chesham.

H14 Chesterton

☎ Bicester (0869) 241204
Chesterton, Bicester, Oxon OX6 8TE
From Oxford take Northampton Rd, then Chesterton sign at Weston-on-the-Green for 1 mile.
Meadowland course.
18 holes, 6520 yards, S.S.S.71
Course designed by R.R. Stagg.
Club founded in 1973/4.
Visitors: welcome; no ladies before noon on Sun.
Green fees: weekdays £7 per day, weekends and Bank Holidays £10 per day.
Society meetings: catered for on weekdays by arrangement.
Catering: bar snacks and restaurant available.
Hotels: Weston Manor, Weston-on-the-Green; Jersey Arms, Middleton Stoney.

H15 Chipping Norton

☎ Chipping Norton (0608) 2383
Southcombe, Chipping Norton, Oxon.
½ mile S of town centre on London road or junction of A34/A44 on left.
Parkland course.
9 holes, 6142 yards, S.S.S.69
Visitors: welcome on weekdays.
Green fees: £6.50 per round or day.
Society meetings: welcome on Mon, Tues or Wed only, maximum 30.
Catering: full catering available.
Hotels: The Fox; The Crown.

H16 City of Coventry (Brandon Wood)

☎ Coventry (0203) 543141
Brandon Lane, Brandon, Coventry.

On A45 6 miles S of Coventry, 120 yds S of London Rd roundabout.
Parkland course.
18 holes, 6530 yards, S.S.S.71
Course designed by Frank Pennink
Visitors: welcome.
Green fees: £3.50 per round.
Society meetings: welcome but must book.
Catering: meals served every day.
Hotels: Brandon Hall.

H17 **Cold Ashby**
☎ Northampton (0604) 740548 or 740099 Pro.
Cold Ashby, Northampton NN6 7EP
5 miles E of Junction 18 M1, just off A50 Northampton to Leicester road.
Undulating meadowland course.
18 holes, 5898 yards, S.S.S.69
Club founded in 1973.
Visitors: welcome weekdays and after 10.30 am at weekends.
Green fees: weekdays £5.50 per round, £6.75 per day; weekends £6.50 per round, £7.50 per day.
Society meetings: catered for on weekdays and at restricted times at weekends.
Catering: full range of bar snacks and restaurant meals available.
Hotels: Post House, Crick, Northampton; Pytchley, West Maddon, Northampton; Moat House, Silver St, Northampton.

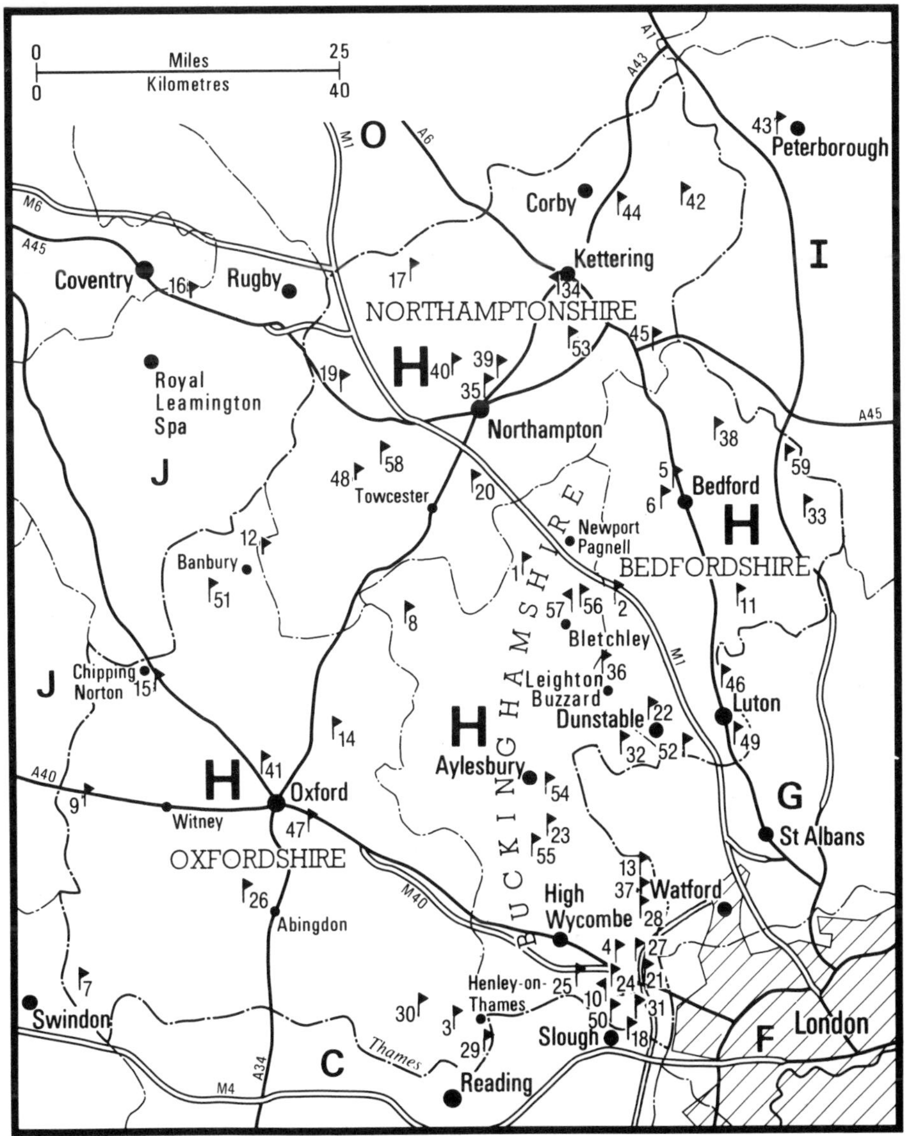

H18 Datchet

☎ Slough (0753) 43887
Buccleuch Rd, Datchet, Slough, Berks SL3 5BP
2 miles from Slough and Windsor, easy access from M4.
Parkland course.
9 holes, 5978 yards, S.S.S.69
Club founded in 1890.
Visitors: welcome on weekdays before 3 pm.
Green fees: £7 per round, £10 per day.
Society meetings: small societies welcome on Tues only.
Catering: bar snacks available.
Hotels: The Manor, Datchet.

H19 Daventry & District

☎ Daventry (0327) 702829
Norton Rd, Daventry, Northants NN11 4AA
1 mile N of town, course next to BBC Station.
Undulating meadowland course.
9 holes, 5582 yards, S.S.S.67
Club founded in early 1920.
Visitors: welcome, except before 11 am on Sun.
Green fees: weekdays £4 (£2.50 with member), weekends £5 (£3 with member).
Society meetings: for details contact Pro.
Catering: arranged for societies only.
Hotels: John-O'Gaunt, Daventry; Wheatsheaf, Daventry.

H20 Delapre Park

☎ Northampton (0604) 63957 or 64036
Eagle Drive, Nene Valley Way, Northampton NN4 0DU
3 miles from Junction 15 M1 on A508.
Parkland public course.
18 holes, 6293 yards, S.S.S.70
Course designed by J. Jacobs and J. Corby.
Club founded in 1976.
Visitors: welcome.
Green fees: weekdays £3.50, weekends £4.50.
Society meetings: welcome on most days, applications in writing.
Catering: catering daily 9 am to 9.30 pm.
Hotels: New Swallow (1986), Eagle Drive; Westone Moathouse, Weston Favell.

H21 Denham

☎ Uxbridge (0895) 832022
Tilehouse Lane, Denham, Bucks UB9 5DE
Leave M40 at Uxbridge/Gerrards Cross turn off, take A40 towards Gerrards Cross, turn right onto A412 towards Watford and take second turning left to club.
Parkland course.
18 holes, 6439 yards, S.S.S.71
Course designed by H.S. Colt.
Club founded in 1910.
Visitors: welcome Mon to Thurs with introduction; book in advance.
Green fees: £16 per day, £10 per round.
Society meetings: catered for on Tues, Wed and Thurs.
Catering: available every day.
Hotels: Bull; Bellhouse, Gerrards Cross.

H22 Dunstable Downs

☎ Dunstable (0582) 604472
Whipsnade Rd, Dunstable, Beds LU6 2WB
2 miles from Dunstable on Whipsnade road, left at third mini-roundabout.
Downland course.
18 holes, 6184 yards, S.S.S.70
Club founded in 1907.
Visitors: welcome on weekdays and with member at weekends.
Green fees: weekdays £7.50 per round, £10 per day; reduction with member.
Society meetings: catered for on Tues, Thurs and Fri.
Catering: full catering service except all day Mon and Wed afternoons.
Hotels: Old Palace Lodge, Dunstable; Kitts Inn, High St. N, Dunstable.

H23 Ellesborough

☎ Wendover (0296) 622375
Butlers Cross, Aylesbury, Bucks HP17 0TZ
1 mile W of Wendover on B4010.
Undulating downland course.
18 holes, 6203 yards, S.S.S.70
Course designed by James Braid.
Club founded in 1906.
Visitors: welcome on weekdays with handicap certificate.
Green fees: £12 per day.
Society meetings: welcome on Wed and Thurs, maximum 40.
Catering: lunches and snacks available except Mon.
Hotels: Bellmore, Stoke Mandeville; Bernard Arms, Princes Risborough; Halfway House; Red Lion, Wendover.

H24 Farnham Park

☎ Farnham Common (9764) 3332 Pro, 3335 Catering.
Park Rd, Stoke Poges, Bucks
Turn off A4 at Slough, take Farnham road at Farnham Royal roundabout, proceed about ½ mile, turn right and the course is on your left.
Parkland municipal course.
18 holes, 4864 yards, S.S.S.68
Visitors: welcome.
Green fees: weekdays £3, weekends £4.20; OAP 5 days £2, 9 holes £1.20.
Society meetings: welcome, max. 36.
Catering: lunches served daily.
Hotels: numerous good hotels in area.

H25 Flackwell Heath

☎ Bourne End (062 85) 20929 Sec, 20027 Clubhouse.
Treadaway Rd, Flackwell Heath, High Wycombe, Bucks HP10 9PE
Off A40 High Wycombe to Beaconsfield road at Loudwater roundabout, up Treadaway Hill, on left before apex of hill into Treadaway Rd.
Undulating course.
18 holes, 6150 yards, S.S.S.69
Club founded in 1904.
Visitors: welcome with introduction by member and on production of handicap certificate or letter of introduction from own golf club.
Green fees: £10 per day or round (£4 with member).
Society meetings: smaller societies up to 36 welcome.
Catering: full service Wed to Sun and restricted service on Mon and Tues
Hotels: Crest, Crest Rd, Handycross, High Wycombe; Falcon, High St, High Wycombe; Drake Court, 141 London Rd, High Wycombe.

H26 Frilford Heath

☎ Frilford Heath (0865) 390428
Frilford Heath, Abingdon, Oxon OX13 5NW
A338 Oxford to Wantage road, 3 miles W of Abingdon.
Wooded heathland course.
18 holes, 6768 yards, S.S.S.73
18 holes, 6006 yards, S.S.S.69
Course designed by J.H. Taylor and C.K. Cotton.
Club founded in 1908.
Visitors: welcome on weekdays but at weekends by prior arrangement.
Green fees: weekdays £13 (£7.50 with member), weekends £18.50 (£9.50 with member).
Society meetings: catered for by previous arrangement only.
Catering: cooked meals by prior arrangement, snacks at any time.
Hotels: Dog House, Frilford Heath; Crown and Thistle, Abingdon.

H27 Gerrards Cross

☎ Gerrards Cross (0753) 883263
Chalfont Park, Gerrards Cross, Bucks SL9 0QA
Leave A40 by A413, continue to first roundabout (approx 1 mile) and leave by third exit onto private road.
Parkland course.

18 holes, 6031 yards, S.S.S.69
Course designed by Len Holland.
Club founded in 1922.
Visitors: welcome on weekdays and after 3 pm at weekends and Bank Holidays; please telephone in advance and bring handicap certificate.
Green fees: weekdays £12 per round or day up to 3 pm, £8 after 3 pm; weekends and Bank Holidays £15 after 3 pm.
Society meetings: welcome on Wed afternoon and all day on Thurs and Fri.
Catering: bar snacks available and lunches by arrangement.
Hotels: Bull, Gerrards Cross; Greyhound Inn, Chalfont St Peter; Bellhouse, Beaconsfield.

H28 Harewood Downs

☎ Little Chalfont (024 04) 2184
Cokes Lane, Chalfont St Giles, Bucks HP8 4TA
Off A413 2 miles short of Amersham.
Parkland course.
18 holes, 5958 yards, S.S.S.69
Club founded in 1907.
Visitors: welcome on weekdays.
Green fees: £9 per round, £11 per day.
Society meetings: welcome weekdays.
Catering: meals and snacks every day; limited service on Mon.
Hotels: Crown, Amersham; Greyhound, Chalfont St Peter.

H29 Henley

☎ Henley (0491) 575742 sec.
Harpsden, Henley-on-Thames, Oxon RG9 4HG
M4 to Junction 9 Reading, follow A4155 to Caversham/Henley, turn left to Harpsden village 1 mile before reaching Henley, clubhouse on left.
Parkland course.
18 holes, 6130 yards, S.S.S.69
Course designed by James Braid.
Club founded in 1908.
Visitors: welcome on weekdays and with members at weekends.
Green fees: weekdays £10 per round, £12 per day.
Society meetings: catered for on Wed and Thurs.
Catering: arrangements to be made with Steward.
Hotels: Red Lion, Hart St; Elizabethan, Station Rd.

H30 Huntercombe

☎ Nettlebed (0491) 641207
Nuffield, Henley-on-Thames, Oxon RG9 5SL
A423, 6 miles from Henley towards Oxford.
Woodland/heathland course.
18 holes, 6223 yards, S.S.S.70
Course designed by Willie Park Junior.
Club founded in 1902.
Visitors: welcome with prior notice (4 balls not allowed).
Green fees: weekdays £11 per day, weekends after 10.30 am £15.
Society meetings: catered for on Tues and Thurs only.
Catering: by arrangement.
Hotels: White Hart, Nettlebed, Henley-on-Thames.

H31 Iver

☎ Slough (0753) 655615
Hollow Hill Lane, Langley Park Rd, Iver, Bucks SL0 0JJ
Nr. Langley Station, Slough.
Parkland course.
9 holes, 6214 yards, S.S.S.70
Course designed by David Morgan.
Club founded in 1984.
Visitors: always welcome.
Green fees: weekdays £3.20 (9 holes £2.20), weekends £4.60 (9 holes £2.80).
Society meetings: welcome.
Catering: meals always available.
Hotels: Holiday Inn, Langley.

H32 Ivinghoe

☎ Cheddington (0296) 668696
Wellcroft, Ivinghoe, Leighton Buzzard, Beds LU7 9EP
In Ivinghoe village, 4 miles from Tring and 6 miles from Dunstable.
Meadowland course.
9 holes, S.S.S.62
Course designed by R. Garrad & Sons.
Club founded in 1967.
Visitors: welcome, after 8 am at weekends and 9 am on weekdays.
Green fees: weekdays £3 for 18 holes, £3.50 per day; weekends £3.50 for 18 holes, £4 per day.
Catering: meals served except Mon.
Hotels: Rose and Crown, Tring.

H33 John O'Gaunt

☎ Potton (0767) 260360
Sutton Park, Sandy, Beds SG19 2LY
On B1040 Biggleswade ($2\frac{1}{2}$ m) to Potton ($\frac{1}{2}$ m) road.
Undulating parkland courses.
John O'Gaunt 18 holes, 6505 yards, S.S.S.71
Carthagena 18 holes, 5882 yards, S.S.S.68
Visitors: welcome all week.
Green fees: weekdays £10 per day, weekends £14.
Society meetings: welcome weekdays.
Catering: lunches and evening meals daily, except Sun evenings.
Hotels: Stratton House, Biggleswade; Rose and Crown, Potton.

H34 Kettering

☎ Kettering (0536) 512074 Clubhouse, 511104 Sec, 81014 Pro.
Headlands, Kettering, Northants NN15 6XA
Headlands joins Bowling Green Rd, on which are the Council Offices, continue along Headlands for about $\frac{1}{2}$ mile, past

the Fire Station on the left, and golf club is over railway bridge on the right.
Meadowland course.
18 holes, 6035 yards, S.S.S.69
Club founded in 1891.
Visitors: welcome on weekdays and with member at weekends.
Green fees: £8.50 per day (with member £4.50 per day).
Society meetings: on Wed only.
Catering: bar snacks served and meals by arrangement except Mon.
Hotels: George, Sheep St, Kettering; Royal, High St, Kettering.

H35 Kingsthorpe

☎ Northampton (0604) 719602 or 711173
Kingsley Rd, Northampton NN2 3BU
2 miles from town centre, off A508.
Parkland course.
18 holes, 6006 yards, S.S.S.69
Visitors: welcome on weekdays.
Green fees: weekdays £8, (with member £3).
Society meetings: catered for on weekdays.
Catering: full catering facilities available.
Hotels: Northampton Moat House.

H36 Leighton Buzzard

☎ Leighton Buzzard (0525) 373811
Plantation Rd, Leighton Buzzard, Beds LU7 7JF
1 mile N of Leighton Buzzard off A418, take left fork at Stag Inn.
Parkland course.
18 holes, 5454 yards, S.S.S.69
Club founded in 1925.
Visitors: welcome on weekdays and with member at weekends.
Green fees: £9 per round, £11 per day (with member £5 per round, £6 per day).
Society meetings: catered for except Mon, Tues and at weekends.
Catering: full service available except Mon and Tues, when snacks only served.
Hotels: Swan, Market Sq, Leighton Buzzard; Sandhouse, Watling St, Heath Reach.

H37 Little Chalfont

☎ Little Chalfont (024 04) 4877
Lodge Lane, Little Chalfont, Bucks.
200 yds from A404 at Little Chalfont.
Undulating parkland course.
Course re-designed by James Dunne.
Club founded in 1980.
Visitors: welcome at all times.
Green fees: weekdays £4, weekends and Bank Holidays £6.
Society meetings: welcome.
Catering: lunches served daily; evening meals by arrangement.
Hotels: The Sportsman, Chorleywood.

H38 Mowsbury

☎ Bedford (0234) 771041 or 771042
Cleat Hill, Kimbolton Rd, Bedford MK41 8DQ
On Kimbolton road from Bedford, 2 miles N of city centre.
Parkland municipal course.
18 holes, 6514 yards, S.S.S.71
Club founded in 1965.
Visitors: welcome.
Green fees: on application.
Society meetings: on application to Amenities Dept, Bedford Town Hall.
Catering: snacks and meals available.
Hotels: numerous good hotels in area.

H39 Northampton

☎ Northampton (0604) 711054
Kettering Rd, Northampton NN3 1AA
NE of town centre on A43.
Meadowland course.
18 holes, 6002 yards, S.S.S.69
Club founded in 1893.
Visitors: welcome on weekdays and with member only at weekends.
Green fees: £8 per round or day.
Society meetings: catered for on Mon, Thurs or Fri.
Catering: meals available except Tues.
Hotels: Northampton Moat House, Silver St, Northampton; Westone Moat House, Weston Favell, Northampton.

H40 Northamptonshire County

☎ Northampton (0604) 843025
Golf Lane, Church Brampton, Northampton NN6 8AZ
Off A50 Northampton to Leicester road, 4½ miles from Northampton.
Undulating heathland/parkland course.
18 holes, 6503 yards, S.S.S.71
Course designed by H.S. Colt.
Club founded in 1909.
Visitors: welcome with hand. cert. or member; advisable to book in advance.
Green fees: weekdays £10, weekends £12 (£4 with member).
Society meetings: welcome on Wed and for smaller parties on Thurs or Mon, provided no fixtures.
Catering: snacks available and evening meals by arrangement.
Hotels: Moat House, Northampton; Red Lion Inn, East Haddon; Post House, Crick.

H41 North Oxford

☎ Oxford (0865) 54924
Banbury Rd, Oxford
Situated between Summertown and Kidlington, 2½ miles N of city centre.
Parkland course.
18 holes, 5485 yards, S.S.S.67
Club founded in 1921.
Visitors: welcome, but after 10.30 am at weekends.
Green fees: weekdays £10, weekends £20.
Society meetings: catered for on Wed, Thurs and Fri.
Catering: meals and snacks served.
Hotels: Randolph, Oxford.

H42 Oundle

☎ Oundle (0832) 73267
Benefield Rd, Oundle, Peterborough, Cambs PE8 4EZ
On A427 Oundle to Corby road, 1 mile from Oundle.
Undulating course.
18 holes, 5507 yards, S.S.S.67
Club founded in 1893.
Visitors: welcome on weekdays.
Green fees: weekends £8 (£5 with member), weekdays £6 (£4 with member).
Society meetings: welcome except at weekends.
Catering: full catering service available.
Hotels: Talbot, Oundle; Bridge, Thrapston.

H43 Peterborough Milton

☎ Castor (073 121) 489
Milton Ferry, Peterborough PE6 7AG
On A47 4 miles W of Peterborough.
Parkland course.
18 holes, 6431 yards, S.S.S.71
Course designed by James Braid.
Club founded in June 1938.
Visitors: weekdays only by prior arrangement with Sec.
Green fees: £9 per round.
Society meetings: weekdays only by prior arrangement with Sec.
Catering: full catering except Mon.
Hotels: Haycock Inn, Wansford, Peterborough; Moat House, Thorpe Wood, Peterborough.

H44 Priors Hall

☎ Corby (0536) 60756
Stamford Rd, Weldon, Northants.
A43 Corby to Stamford Rd 2 miles E of Weldon.
Parkland course.
18 holes, 6677 yards, S.S.S.72
Club founded in 1965.
Visitors: unlimited.

Green fees: £2.25 weekdays, £3.30 weekends.
Society meetings: welcome weekdays.
Catering: snacks and meals.
Hotels: Grosvenor, George St, Corby.

H45 Rushden & District

☎ Rushden (0933) 312581
Kimbolton Rd, Chelveston, Wellingborough, Northants NN9 8LB
On A45 2 miles E of Higham Ferrers.
Undulating meadowland course.
9 holes, 6300 yards, S.S.S.71
Club founded in 1921.
Visitors: welcome on weekdays except Wed afternoon and with member at weekends.
Green fees: £6 (£4 with member).
Society meetings: welcome weekdays.
Catering: by request.
Hotels: Westward, Rushden; Queen Victoria, Rushden; Green Dragon, Higham Ferrers.

H46 South Bedfordshire

☎ Luton (0582) 591500
Warden Hill Rd, Luton, Beds
Take A6 N from Luton, course 2½ miles from centre of Luton.
Undulating course.
18 holes, 6342 yards, S.S.S.70
9 holes, S.S.S.64
Club founded in 1892.
Visitors: welcome on weekdays without reservation except Tues (Ladies Day); at weekends handicap certificate from affiliated golf club required.
Green fees: weekdays £8 per day, £6 per round; weekends £10 per round; 9 hole £4 per 18 hole round.
Society meetings: welcome by arrangement except Mon or Tues.
Catering: snacks available and meals by arrangement except Mon.
Hotels: Strathmore; Crest; Culverdene

H47 Southfield

☎ Oxford (0865) 242158
Hill Top Rd, Oxford OX4 1PF
Cowley Rd, Southfield Rd, then right into Hill Top Rd; situated between Headington and Cowley.
Undulating parkland course.
18 holes, 6230 yards, S.S.S.70
Course designed by James Braid.
Club founded in 1920.
Visitors: welcome on weekdays, except Bank Holidays.
Green fees: weekdays £9 (£5 with member).
Society meetings: welcome weekdays.
Catering: available every day except Mon.
Hotels: Randolph, Beaumont St, Oxford; Moat House, Wolvercote, Oxford.

H48 Staverton Park

☎ Daventry (0327) 705911
Staverton. Daventry, Northants NN11 6JT
On A425 Daventry to Leamington road, 1 mile S of Daventry.
Undulating meadowland course.
18 holes, 6634 yards, S.S.S.72
Course designed by Com. John Harris.
Club founded in 1978.
Visitors: welcome.
Green fees: weekdays £8 per day, weekends and Bank Holidays £10 per day.
Society meetings: welcome every day except Sun.
Catering: full catering at all times.
Hotels: John O'Gaunt, Daventry; Wheatsheaf, Daventry.

H49 Stockwood Park

☎ Luton (0582) 413704 Pro, 23612 Sec.
Stockwood Park, London Rd, Luton, Beds.
Junction 10 off the M1, turn left towards town centre, then left at first set of traffic lights into Stockwood Park.

Tadmarton, a testing time in the gorse

It is natural, I suppose, that golf clubs should develop a stronger individual character than clubs of other kinds, and in this country where there is such a variety of courses it is not surprising that this impression is more marked than anywhere else in the world.

At the older championship links – St Andrews, Prestwick, Royal St George's, Westward Ho! and so on – there is an atmosphere that is at once distinguishable from all the others, but the same applies to many less celebrated clubs upon which the public gaze is seldom directed. When I was invited to play at Tadmarton Heath in North Oxfordshire, this fact was quickly confirmed.

Perhaps my feelings were influenced by having achieved the perfect escape from the general confusion of Christmas week; or maybe the drive from Banbury Cross through the neighbouring countryside formed an unusually romantic introduction to the golf, but much respected opinion had told me that Tadmarton Heath – one of only seven clubs in the county – had many fine qualities. If it is a course that Roger Wethered saw fit to play as often as he could, it is surely one that is good enough for most of us.

In an age when there is so much emphasis on power and stretching holes to limits for which they were not designed, it was encouraging to see from a glance at the card that Tadmarton measured below 6,000 yards, but in this case bare details were deceptive. In winds that never miss those exposed parts it must frequently seem to play about twice its normal length.

As a course it has what may conveniently be described as a split personality; the first nine holes are open and the second nine possess a characteristic commonly associated with heathland golf – a profusion of gorse which makes some of the fairways alarmingly narrow.

As this tests a player's nerve at a critical point in the round, it is as well that there should have been temptation earlier to open the shoulders, but for all the latitude that may be allowed, there are many splendidly demanding second shots – particularly those at the 1st, 2nd, 4th, 6th and 9th – which can only be negotiated successfully from drives that have been strategically placed.

The first seven holes do not stray far from the clubhouse, the short 7th – with its attractive shot over the waters of the Holy Well which are said to provide a cure for rheumatism – bringing some danger to its walls and windows. But the fun really begins when the 9th turns away alongside the road by the gate and the short 10th (114 yds) induces a tremble or two at the prospect of seeing more of the prominent bunker and the intervening gorse than of the freely undulating green.

Gorse again dominates the drive over the distant ridge at the 11th and the cleverly angled second at the 14th, where a slice off the tee is not to be recommended, but the 15th (288 yds) and the 17th (365 yds), despite their innocent length, are the two holes where the slightest deviation from the fairway inevitably decrees a prickly fate.

Although the 18th immediately provides relief on the right, the staunchest of hopes may already have been destroyed, though even that need be no cause for discontent.

All around the scene is one of simple beauty and tranquillity. The whirl of traffic is far away, and ahead, in the warmth of the old Cotswold stone clubhouse that was converted from a farmhouse, lies the assurance that all thoughts of golf can, if necessary, be dulled – though not, let me hasten to add, the urge to try again.

Meadowland course.
18 holes, 5964 yards, S.S.S.69
Club founded in 1971.
Visitors: welcome at all times.
Green fees: weekdays £2.80, weekends and Bank Holidays £4.20.
Society meetings: welcome on weekdays
Catering: meals and snacks
Hotels: Strathmore, Luton; Eurocrest, Dunstable Rd.

H50 Stoke Poges

☎ Slough (0973) 26385
Stoke Park, Park Rd, Stoke Poges, Slough, Bucks SL2 4PG
Off A4 at Slough into Stoke Poges Lane then 1½ miles on left.
Parkland course.
18 holes, 6654 yards, S.S.S.72
Course designed by H.S. Colt.
Club founded in 1908.
Visitors: welcome on weekdays, except Bank Holidays, with handicap certificate.
Green fees: weekdays £12 per day, £8 per round (with member £5 per round or day); weekends with member £8 per round or per day.
Society meetings: welcome on Wed for small groups or Thurs and Fri for medium to large groups, by arrangement.
Catering: lunches available on weekdays except Mon.
Hotels: New Grovefield, Burnham; Ethorpe, Gerrards Cross; Burnham Beeches, Burnham; Holiday Inn, Langley; Bellhouse, Beaconsfield; Bull, Gerrards Cross.

H51 Tadmarton Heath

☎ Hook Norton (0608) 737278
Wiggington, Banbury, Oxon OX15 5HL
5 miles W of Banbury off B4035 Shipston on Stour road.
Heathland course.
18 holes, 5917 yards, S.S.S.69
Course designed by Major C.K. Hutchison.
Club founded in 1922.
Visitors: welcome on weekdays by appointment and with member at weekends.
Green fees: £12 per day, £9 per round; half-price with member.
Society meetings: welcome on Tues, Wed and Fri, maximum 36.
Catering: meals and snacks except Mon.
Hotels: Olde School, Bloxham, Banbury; Banbury Moat House, Oxford Rd, Banbury.

H52 Tilsworth

☎ Leighton Buzzard (0525) 210721
Dunstable Rd, Tilsworth, Leighton Buzzard, Bedfordshire.
On A5, 1 mile N of Dunstable.
Parkland course.
9 holes, 5443 yards, S.S.S.67
Club founded in 1974.
Visitors: welcome except on Sun before noon.
Green fees: weekdays £2, weekends and Bank Holidays £4.
Catering: lunches served.

H53 Wellingborough

☎ Wellingborough (0933) 677324 Sec, 678752 Pro.
Harrowden Hall, Great Harrowden, Wellingborough, Northants NN9 5AD
2 miles N of Wellingborough on A509 to Kettering, turn right (signposted to Finedon) at church.
Parkland course.
18 holes, 6604 yards, S.S.S.72
Course designed by Hawtree & Son.
Club founded in 1893.
Visitors: welcome on weekdays, except on Tues between 12 and 2.30 pm, and with

The Duchess Takes Her Bow

When the idea of golf at Woburn was first conceived, the Dukes and Duchess courses were planned and cleared together. As events turned out, the Duchess was delayed while the Dukes earned immediate praise, but now the Duchess forms a twin attraction that has few equals.

In terms of character, the two courses have much in common, arising from the same dense forest in which it was virtually impossible six or seven years ago to see more than ten yards ahead. The massive tree felling operation was the biggest ever undertaken on a new course in Britain but from the moment in the summer of 1979 when 18 holes on the Duchess were open for play, a remarkable story was complete.

Work only began on its construction in the summer of 1978, and in May 1979, after the severest winter for many years, half of it was not yet sown. Yet by October of that year all 18 holes were being played. Adjustments to the shape and levels of greens were made to mould with the natural contours, thus avoiding regular, artificial patterns. This was achieved by the club's own greenkeeping staff who wrought wonders. They were not alone in believing that it would have been impossible to have found a finer piece of land for an inland course in Britain; or that you could not improve upon the arrangement whereby a course is built by those who subsequently have to look after it.

Having seen the development of both Dukes and Duchess from the start, my main concern is that it might have blurred my judgement. However, that is a risk I have to take when describing a course which forms a nice contrast to its neighbour. Now the course has seen several professional tournaments and filmed matches as well as the English Amateur strokeplay championship for the Brabazon Trophy.

The Duchess is not as long, nor does it have the spectacular rises and falls that mark the beginning of the Dukes, but it is a supreme test of the art of control, manoeuvrability and varied shotmaking.

The enjoyment of the Duchess lies in an ideal balance of its holes. There is contrast in the par fives; the short holes vary nicely in length and there is a good mixture of par fours from a drive and pitch to two full shots. The 1st gives a good first impression, the distant green on an elusive plateau being reached only with a well struck second from a tumbling fairway.

In four holes, in fact, there is all the variation you can have. The 2nd, a par 3, needs a shot through the eye of a needle; the 3rd calls for a straight drive and well judged pitch over a belt of heather and the 4th, a left hand dogleg, is a par 5 where there are plenty of ways of taking six.

The 5th green in its alcove of giant beech is the first on the other side of the lane leading down to Bow Brickhill Church while the 6th, changing direction yet again, rewards positional play more than most par fives.

It is a rare feature that no two consecutive holes follow the same direction and the short 7th twists back over the ancient earth-works that make an excellent golfing landmark. Next comes the 8th, a classic dogleg to a three level green, and then the turn is reached by way of the 9th green which, like the 10th tee, needed enormous build-up.

Over the brow at the 10th, the chief hazard is the angled green, but the 11th, 12th and 13th all have distinctive markings, the 13th occupying a natural little punchbowl. From there it is over the road again with two spanking two shot holes for the experts and two three shot holes for the rest.

There is no doubt that the finish is

demanding but the 16th and 17th offer scenic relief, if nothing else; and by then the 18th is the only obstacle, though a tough one, between you and the non-golfing delights which Woburn has to offer. Swimming, tennis and squash await those with the fitness and energy to tackle them but a relaxing drink will be the comfort that most seek. In which case, you can look out on a sylvan setting of peace and tranquillity; and ponder whether golf has anything better to offer.

member only at weekends.
Green fees: £8 per round, £11 per day.
Society meetings: welcome on Mon, Wed, Thurs and Fri.
Catering: snacks and meals available.
Hotels: The Hind, Sheep St, Wellingborough.

H54 **Weston Turville**
☎ Aylesbury (0296) 24084
New Rd, Weston Turville, Aylesbury, Bucks HP22 5QT
A41 or A312, situated 2 miles from Aylesbury town centre between Aston Clinton and Wendover.
Parkland course.
13 holes, 6782 yards, S.S.S.72
Club founded in 1973.
Visitors: welcome except Sun morning.
Green fees: weekdays £4.50 for 18 holes, weekends and Bank Holidays £5.75 for 18 holes.
Society meetings: by arrangement.
Catering: lunches served.
Hotels: Bell, Aston Clinton; Five Bells, Weston Turville.

H55 **Whiteleaf**
☎ Princes Risborough (084 44) 3097
Whiteleaf, Aylesbury, Bucks.
1½ miles from Princes Risborough on Aylesbury Rd, turn right for Whiteleaf.
Undulating course.
9 holes, 5391 yards, S.S.S.66
Club founded in 1904.
Visitors: welcome on weekdays.
Green fees: £6 for 18 holes, £9 for 36 holes.
Society meetings: welcome but must write for details.
Catering: meals and snacks available except Mon; lunch and dinner until 9 pm on Tues and Fri.
Hotels: George and Dragon, High St, Princes Risborough; Bernard Arms, Great Kimble, Aylesbury; Thatchers, Thame.

H56 **Windmill Hill**
☎ Milton Keynes (0908) 648149
Tattenhoe Lane, Bletchley, Milton Keynes, Bucks MK3 7RB
M1 exit 13 A421 join H8 turn off at sign for Windmill Hill golf course.
Meadowland course.
18 holes, 6773 yards, S.S.S.72
Course designed by Henry Cotton.
Club founded in 1972.

Visitors: welcome at all times.
Green fees: weekdays £3, weekends £4.20.
Society meetings: catered for all day on Mon, Wed, Thurs and Fri and on Sat pm.
Catering: meals and snacks served except Tues lunchtime.
Hotels: Bedford Arms, Woburn; Holt, Aspley Guise; Shenley, Shenley.

H57 Woburn G & C C

☎ Milton Keynes (0908) 70756
Bow Brickhill, Milton Keynes MK17 9LJ
Junction 13 off M1, into Woburn Sands, turn left for Woburn, after ½ mile turn right at sign.
Dukes 18 holes, 6883 yards, S.S.S.74
Duchess 18 holes, 6616 yards, S.S.S.72
Course designed by Charles Lawrie.
Club founded in 1976.
Visitors: by arrangement only on completion of booking form.
Green fees: in season, unless with member, prices are offered inclusive day; details on application.
Society meetings: by arrangement.
Catering: snacks and meals served.
Hotels: Bedford Arms, Woburn; and numerous others in area.

H58 Woodlands

☎ Preston Capes (032 736) 291
Woodlands Vale, Farthingstone, Towcester, Northants NN12 8MA
Junction 16 off M1, W off A5 between Weedon and Towcester, 3 miles from Weedon.
Undulating parkland course.
18 holes, 6330 yards, S.S.S.71
Course designed by M. Gallagher.
Club founded in 1974.
Visitors: welcome at all times.
Green fees: weekdays £6, weekends £8
Society meetings: catered for at all times, by arrangement.
Catering: full services available.
Hotels: Crossroads, Weedon; Globe, Weedon; Saracens, Towcester.

H59 Wyboston Lakes

☎ Huntingdon (0480) 212501
Wyboston Lakes, Wyboston, Beds.
Off A1 and A45, 1 mile S of St Neots.
Parkland course.
18 holes, 5310 yards, S.S.S.69
Course designed by Neil Oackden.
Club founded in 1980/81.
Visitors: welcome every day.
Green fees: weekdays 18 holes £3, 9 holes £1.50; weekends 18 holes £4, 9 holes £2.50.
Society meetings: welcome Mon to Fri.
Catering: full catering service.
Hotels: motel to be built on site.

I Suffolk, Norfolk and Cambridgeshire

In a book published in 1910, Bernard Darwin devoted as big a chapter to East Anglian courses as to almost any. He wrote with obvious warmth about them, hardly surprising since he first began to play the game at Felixstowe. One of the charms of reading his descriptions of clubs in Norfolk and Suffolk is that time seems to have brought little change. Nearly all are still recognisable.

Without becoming out-dated, they have retained their charm and natural features. In still conditions, few could examine fully the skills of modern professionals, but in the winds that so often plague balance and nerve, they are a formidable challenge, exemplifying the best traditions of British golf.

Where else in the world is there a course comparable to Brancaster? Here is the very essence of a seaside links; a long, narrow strip of land with the holes going out hugging the huge salt marsh and those coming home flirting with the dunes guarding the shore. The ground plays fast enough to make old men rub their hands, the greens hold only the truest of pitches and there are good, old-fashioned sleeper bunkers.

There are six courses in Norfolk and Suffolk which naturally divide themselves into three groups of near neighbours: Brancaster (Royal West Norfolk) and Hunstanton, Royal Cromer and Sheringham, Aldeburgh and Thorpeness.

Having dealt with Brancaster, we must pay our respects to Hunstanton, the only modern day championship course in the area. I take no part in the arguments about the respective merits of the two. It is a good thing that they are different and I enjoy a day's golf at one as much as the other.

My memories of Cromer and Sheringham are largely boyhood ones and I cannot now remember the individual holes too clearly except for the 18th at Sheringham which is by the railway or, at least, was before the days of Dr Beeching. Golfers find it particularly hard to forgive him this particular closure since it was the source of Joyce Wethered's oft-quoted remark, "What train?"

Although both are hard by the sea, the turf is not like that at Brancaster; it is more downland in character. The names of Aldeburgh and Thorpeness are usually linked because of their proximity on the Suffolk coast although they are, in fact, surprisingly different: Thorpeness, with a good deal of heather, reminds one more of the Surrey heathland while Aldeburgh, a mile or so inland, is set on nice, light soil amid a thickish network of gorse. Whether there is too much gorse will depend on the accuracy of your driving. Not far from Aldeburgh is Woodbridge, a Club which, like Yarmouth and Felixstowe, has celebrated its centenary and offers excellent golf.

For the connoisseur, Royal Worlington and Newmarket, the little nine hole course on which generations of Cambridge golfers have sharpened up their skills, is an absolute must.

It is hard when courses have sentimental attachments to view them critically but Worlington is an architectural masterpiece, laid out on the smallest of acreages yet supplying an expansive challenge of which nobody ever tires.

On account of Worlington's fame, some of the other courses in the neighbourhood are frequently overlooked; but Thetford, a few miles up the road to Norwich, is always worth a visit while in Norwich itself lies Royal Norwich and the modern complex of Barnham Broom, the handiwork of Frank Pennink.

Gog Magog is the best in Cambridgeshire but I can recommend St Neots, Ely and Cambridgeshire Hotel from first hand.

11 Aldeburgh

☎ Aldeburgh (072 885) 2890
Saxmundham Rd, Aldeburgh, Suffolk IP15 5PE
6 miles E of A12 midway between Ipswich and Lowestoft.
Heathland course.
18 holes, 6330 yards, S.S.S.71
9 holes, 4228 yards, S.S.S.64
Club founded in 1884.
Visitors: welcome on weekdays and weekends by arrangement with Sec.
Green fees: on application.
Society meetings: welcome by arrangement with Sec.
Catering: lunches served.
Hotels: Wentworth; White Lion; Brudenell; Uplands; all in Aldeburgh.

12 Barnham Broom G & CC

☎ Norwich (060 545) 393
Norwich, Norfolk NR9 4DD
Off A47 8 miles SW of Norwich.
Meadowland course.
18 holes, 6603 yards, S.S.S.72
Course designed by Frank Pennink.
Club founded in 1977.
Visitors: welcome with evidence of golf club membership.
Green fees: on application.
Society meetings: welcome, maximum 100, by arrangement.
Catering: snacks and meals served.
Hotels: Barnham Broom.

13 Beccles

☎ Beccles (0502) 712244 Clubhouse, 712479 Sec.
The Common, Beccles, Suffolk
1 mile off A146, 9 miles W of Lowestoft.
Heathland course.
9 holes, 2696 yards, S.S.S.67
Club founded in 1899.
Visitors: welcome, only with member on Sun morning.
Green fees: weekends and Bank Holidays £5.50, weekdays £4.50.
Society meetings: none.
Catering: light refreshments at weekends.
Hotels: Kings Head, Beccles; Waveney House, Beccles.

14 Bungay & Waveney Valley

☎ Bungay (0986) 2337
Outney Common, Bungay, Suffolk NR35 1DS
A143 Bury St Edmunds to Great Yarmouth road, about ½ mile from town centre.
Moorland course.
18 holes, 6000 yards, S.S.S.68
Course designed by James Braid.
Club founded in 1889.
Visitors: welcome on weekdays and with member at weekends.
Green fees: weekdays £7 per round or day (at weekends £3.50 with member).
Society meetings: welcome by arrangement.
Catering: lunches and meals available except Mon.
Hotels: Swan, Harleston; Waveney, Beccles.

15 Bury St Edmunds

☎ Bury St Edmunds (0284) 5979
Tuthill, Bury St Edmunds, Suffolk IP28 6LG
Off A45 2 miles W of Bury St Edmunds onto B1106.
Undulating parkland course.
18 holes, 6615 yards, S.S.S.72
Course designed by Ted Ray.
Club founded in 1924.
Visitors: welcome; at weekends not before 10 am and with handicap certificate.
Green fees: weekdays £8 per day, weekends and Bank Holidays £12 per day; half-price with member.
Society meetings: welcome weekdays.
Catering: lunches served except Sun; dinner by arrangement.
Hotels: Angel; Suffolk; Everards; all in Bury St Edmunds.

16 Cambridgeshire Moat House Hotel

☎ Crafts Hill (0954) 80555
Bar Hill, Cambs CB3 8EU
Adjacent to A604, 4 miles NW of Cambridge.
Undulating parkland course.
18 holes, 6734 yards, S.S.S.72
Club founded in 1974.
Visitors: welcome at most times, restricted at weekends; prior telephone call suggested.
Green fees: weekdays £8 per round or day, weekends and Bank Holidays £10.50 per round or day.
Society meetings: welcome by prior arrangement.
Catering: full restaurant or lunchtime bar meals.
Hotels: Cambridgeshire Moat House.

17 Cretingham

☎ Earl Soham (072 882) 275
Cretingham, Woodbridge, Suffolk IP13 7BA
2 miles from A1120 at Earl Soham.
Meadowland course.
9 holes, 1955 yards, S.S.S.30
Club founded in 1984.
Visitors: welcome but advisable to phone at weekends.
Green fees: £3.
Society meetings: by arrangement with Sec.
Catering: full range of meals including dinner.
Hotels: bed and breakfast available on premises; Crown, Framlingham; Seckford Hall.

18 Dereham

☎ Dereham (0362) 3122
Quebec Rd, Dereham, Norfolk NR19 2DS
Take B1105 from Dereham.
Parkland course.
9 holes, 6225 yards, S.S.S.70
Club founded in 1934.
Visitors: welcome with hand. cert.
Green fees: weekdays £5, weekends £6.50.
Society meetings: by arrangement.
Catering: by arrangement.
Hotels: Phoenix; George; Kings Head.

19 Diss

☎ Diss (0379) 2847
Stuston, Diss, Norfolk.
Halfway between Norwich and Ipswich, 2 miles W of A140 (turn at Scole).
Commonland course.
9 holes, 5900 yards, S.S.S.68
Club founded in 1903.
Visitors: welcome weekdays before 4 pm and weekends after 4 pm in summer; no restrictions between Oct and March.
Green fees: weekdays £5 per day, weekends £6 per day; half-price with member.
Society meetings: welcome weekdays.
Catering: all meals served except Sun and Mon.
Hotels: Brome Grange; Park; Scole Inn.

110 Eaton

☎ Norwich (0603) 51686
Newmarket Rd, Norwich NR4 6SF
Take right exit off A11 into Sunningdale, signposted.
Undulating course.
18 holes, 6074 yards, S.S.S.69
Club founded in 1908.
Visitors: welcome if members of recognised club with hand. cert.
Green fees: weekdays £8, weekends £10, half fee with a member.
Society meetings: limited.
Catering: lunches served, dinner by arrangement.
Hotels: Annesley, Newmarket Rd, Norwich; Arlington, Newmarket Rd.

111 Ely City

☎ Ely (0353) 2751
Cambridge Rd, Ely, Cambs CB7 4HX
On A10, outskirts of Ely going towards Cambridge.
Parkland course.
18 holes, 6686 yards, S.S.S.72
Course designed by Henry Cotton.
Club founded in 1962.
Visitors: welcome without reservation on weekdays; handicap certificate required at weekends, unless with member.
Green fees: weekdays £8 per day, weekends and Bank Holidays £12 per day.
Society meetings: welcome weekdays.
Catering: bar snacks, lunches, afternoon teas and dinners available.
Hotels: Nyton House; Lamb; Fenland Lodge.

112 Eynesbury Hardwicke

☎ Huntingdon (0480) 215153
Eynesbury Hardwicke, St Neots, Cambridgeshire PE19 4XN
3 miles E of A1 through St Neots.
Undulating meadowland course.
18 holes, 6214 yards, S.S.S.71
Club founded in 1976.
Visitors: welcome weekdays and weekends.
Green fees: weekdays £5 (£3 with member), weekends £8 (£5 with member).
Society meetings: welcome weekdays.
Catering: food available during bar hours.
Hotels: The Rocket, St Neots.

113 Fakenham

☎ Fakenham (0328) 2867
Sports Centre, The Race Course, Fakenham, Norfolk.
B1146 from Dereham or A1067 from Norwich.
Parkland course.
9 holes, 5879 yards, S.S.S.68
Course designed by Charles Lawrie.
Club founded in 1981.
Visitors: welcome.
Green fees: weekdays £5, weekends £7.50.
Society meetings: by arrangement.
Catering: pending.
Hotels: Crown; Limes.

114 Felixstowe Ferry

☎ Felixstowe (0394) 286834
Ferry Rd, Felixstowe, Suffolk IP11 9RY
A45 to Felixstowe, avoid turning right off A45, follow signs to Yachting Centre.
Links course.
18 holes, 6042 yards, S.S.S.70
Course designed by Henry Cotton & Sir Guy Campbell.
Club founded in 1880.
Visitors: welcome.
Green fees: weekdays £7 per day, weekends and Bank Holidays £10.
Society meetings: welcome all year, not Thurs, by arrangement with Sec.
Catering: lunches and evening meals ordered before play.
Hotels: Marlborough, Sea Rd, Felixstowe; Orwell Moat House, Hamilton Rd, Felixstowe; 2 flats at club.

115 Flempton

☎ Culford (028 484) 291
Flempton, Bury St Edmunds, Suffolk.
4 miles NE of Bury St Edmunds on A1101 to Mildenhall.
Breckland course.
9 holes, 6050 yards, S.S.S.69
Course designed by J.H. Taylor.
Club founded in 1895.
Visitors: welcome on weekdays and with member at weekends and Bank Holidays.
Green fees: £8 per round, £10 per day (£4.50 with member).
Society meetings: not encouraged.

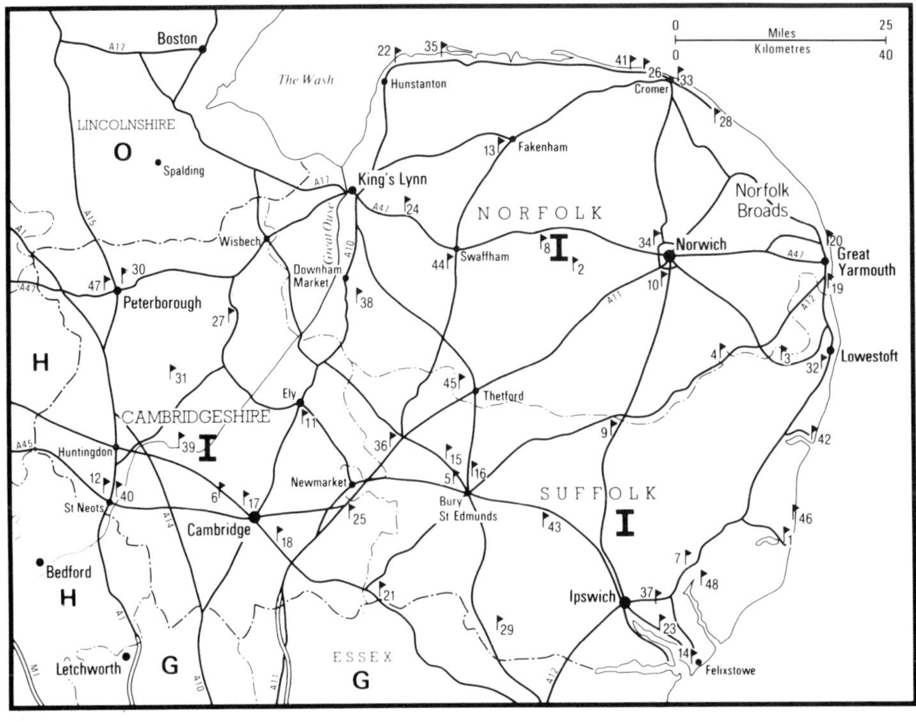

Aldeburgh

Whether Aldeburgh is more famous for its golf or its music depends where your interests lie. For some, there are presumably divided loyalties but golf unquestionably was there first and in 1984 Aldeburgh became the fourth club in East Anglia to celebrate its centenary.

In many little towns in Britain made famous by their courses, there are constant reminders of the modern world. Prestwick, the home of championship golf, and Troon resound to giant airliners; Sandwich has its distant cooling towers and the sight and noise of hovercraft. Golfers at St Andrews are faced by a skyline increasingly dotted with buildings neither royal nor ancient and even the Honourable Company of Edinburgh Golfers now have their first fairway overlooked by houses. Aldeburgh is one notable exception. All is as recognisable as it was when six good men and true first realised the potential of some attractive heathland for golf.

Like most heathland, it is liberally sprinkled with gorse which, if lending an undeniably natural look, highlights the course's demands. In expressing his fondness for Aldeburgh, Bernard Darwin qualified his remarks; 'though now and again when I am sore and spiky from sitting in gorse bushes, and hot and tired from searching for my ball, I could wish there was just a little less gorse'. I rather fancy there is more gorse now than there was then but it remains a neat way of saying that you must keep straight.

Although everyone likes to see the ball hit long distances, and envies those who can, control is the most prized of Aldeburgh's golfing virtues. 6,330 yards is a relatively modest length by today's standards but, measured against a par of 68 which contains not a single five, good scoring is a tall order. Nine par fours over 400 yards put the problem in a nutshell.

Its championship qualities have been more freely acknowledged by the ladies than the men. The English Ladies' championship has been staged there on four occasions although this may be explained by the fact that the club has always given the ladies equal rights and that lady golfers, generally speaking, cope better with tight courses.

Aldeburgh does not extend her favours lightly but there is nothing misleading or unfair either. A glance around from the first tee shows exactly what is in store both in terms of golfing requirements and in the gentle rise and fall of the land that adds such a pleasant feature. Those well familiar with the surroundings can picture at will the view from the 5th or 6th with the waters of the River Alde shining behind a little row of fir trees. Known as Little Japan because of resemblance to a Japanese landscape, it typifies a tranquil scene which, despite the nearness of the sea, oozes pastoral delights.

After the first two holes have broken the golfer in as sympathetically as Aldeburgh can, the 3rd, slightly uphill before turning nicely left, raises the pitch an octave with the first of the outstanding two-shotters. You will travel a long way and not find four better short holes, the first of which, the 4th, is the next obstacle. Encircled by a large, horseshoe-shaped sleepered bunker, it is within the compass of all although, when the hole is cut at the back on the right, it is a brave player who attacks the flag.

The 5th takes you away with a fine sweep to the westernmost point; the 6th, a sharp dogleg round some mighty trees, does an about-turn while the 7th, where you have to dice with a central fairway bunker, is another excellent four with a downhill approach to the green.

In keeping with all good 9ths,

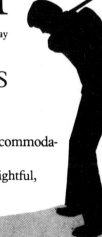

Aldeburgh's returns to the clubhouse, a hole given extra renown by having been the scene of Bernard Darwin's final shot in a notable playing career. On the other hand, not recorded is his accompanying remark which all who knew him will readily understand, 'now I can retire gracefully from this unspeakable game'.

However, the temptation to go on is great – the lure of the 10th and 11th with more than their share of bunkers, the cracking short par four 12th and two contrasting fours to follow. The 15th and 17th, particularly the latter, are further examples of beautiful short holes but the 17th is preceded and followed by two more stouter than stout fours. Few will be able to boast a total of eight strokes or better for them even under favourable conditions but Aldeburgh does not have to be conquered to be enjoyed. It is reward enough to have come and seen.

Catering: by arrangement before play.
Hotels: Suffolk, Bury St Edmunds; Bull, Barton Mills, Bury St Edmunds; Bell, Mildenhall, Bury St Edmunds.

116 Fornham Park

☎ Bury St Edmunds (0284) 63426
Fornham St Martin, Bury St Edmunds, Suffolk
Off A45 at Bury St Edmunds or off A134 Bury – Thetford at Culford Rd, Fornham St Martin.
18 holes, 6079 yards, S.S.S.69
Club founded in 1976.
Visitors: welcome.
Green fees: weekdays £5, weekends £8.
Society meetings: welcome.
Catering: lunches served, dinners served Tues – Sat.
Hotels: Suffolk; Angel, Bury St Edmunds.

117 Girton

☎ Cambridge (0223) 276169
Dodford Lane, Girton, Cambs CB3 0QE
3 miles N of Cambridge A604
Flat open course.
18 holes, 5927 yards, S.S.S.68
Club founded in 1936.
Visitors: welcome on weekdays only.
Green fees: £7 per day.
Society meetings: welcome on weekdays.
Catering: meals and snacks served except Mon.
Hotels: Post House, Impington.

118 Gog Magog

☎ Cambridge (0223) 247626
Shelford Bottom, Cambridge CB2 4AB
2 miles S of Cambridge on A1307 Colchester road.
Undulating course.
18 holes, 6386 yards, S.S.S.70
9 holes, 5532 yards, S.S.S.68
Club founded in 1901.
Visitors: welcome weekdays with introduction by member or hand. cert.
Society meetings: welcome on Tues and Thurs only.
Catering: lunches served daily.
Hotels: University Arms; Garden House; Gonville.

119 Gorleston

☎ Great Yarmouth (0493) 661911
Warren Rd, Gorleston, Great Yarmouth, Norfolk NR31 6JT
Off A12 Yarmouth to Lowestoft road, Yarmouth end of dual carriageway, follow signs down Links Rd to Squash Club, club entrance 200 yards on left, Warren Rd.
Seaside course.
18 holes, 6279 yards, S.S.S.70
Club founded in 1906.
Visitors: welcome if members of recognised club (Ladies Day Wed).
Green fees: weekdays £7, weekends and Bank Holidays £8.50, weekly £24.
Society meetings: welcome.
Catering: full service except Mon.
Hotels: numerous hotels in Great Yarmouth.

120 Great Yarmouth & Caister

☎ Great Yarmouth (0493) 728699
Beach House, Caister-on-Sea, Great Yarmouth, Norfolk NR31 6JT
About 1 mile N of Great Yarmouth on A149 take right turn at roundabout, turn right into signposted lane almost immediately after roundabout.
Seaside links course.
18 holes, 6235 yards, S.S.S.70
Club founded in 1882.
Visitors: welcome, advisable to telephone in advance.
Green fees: weekdays £6.50 per day, Sun after 11.30 am £8.50 per day; weekly and fortnightly tickets on request.
Society meetings: welcome by arrangement.
Catering: coffee, lunch and evening meals always available.
Hotels: Carlton; Cavendish; Hamilton; Ocean Edge; Sandringham; Windyshore; all in Great Yarmouth.

121 Haverhill

☎ Haverhill (0440) 61951
Coupals Rd, Haverhill, Suffolk.
A604 from Cambridge, ½ mile SE of Haverhill, turn right into Coupals Rd after passing Snooker Club.
Parkland course.
9 holes, 5680 yards, S.S.S.68
Course designed by J. Frew.
Visitors: welcome except Sun mornings and competition days.
Green fees: weekdays £6 (£3.50 with member), weekends £7 (£4.50 with member).
Society meetings: weekdays only.
Catering: bar available but no catering.
Hotels: Woodlands.

122 Hunstanton

☎ Hunstanton (048 53) 2811
Golf Course Rd, Old Hunstanton, Norfolk PE36 6JQ
Off A149 in Old Hunstanton (signposted to club), 1 mile NE of Hunstanton.
Links course.
18 holes, 6670 yards, S.S.S.72
Club founded in 1891.
Visitors: welcome every day provided have handicap at another club.
Green fees: weekdays £11, weekends and Bank holidays £16; reduced rates after 4 pm and in winter.
Society meetings: catered for every day except Bank Holiday weekends.
Catering: bar snacks available every day, full meals by prior arrangement.
Hotels: Lodge, Old Hunstanton; Titchwell Manor, Titchwell; Le Strange Arms, Old Hunstanton.

123 Ipswich

☎ Ipswich (0473) 78941
Purdis Heath, Bucklesham Rd, Ipswich,

A short drive to the sea and a long list of pros — What's the link?

The link is Hunstanton Golf Club, the only championship course in Norfolk and some of the finest seaside golf you'll find in Britain.

At Hunstanton you'll follow in the footsteps of leading professionals and amateurs. The immaculate greens and wide, sweeping fairways offer an exciting challenge to low and high handicaps alike.

Enjoy the views over the Wash. The sea air keeps us frost-free and the sandy soil allows play in the wettest weather.

No wonder that Hunstanton was voted one of the top courses in Britain.

Pay us a visit soon. You'll be sure of a warm welcome.

Hunstanton Golf Club Old Hunstanton, Norfolk PE36 6JQ
tel: Hunstanton (04853) 2811

Recommended Hotels
Congham Hall Country House Hotel tel: Hillington 600250
Le Strange Arms Hotel tel: Hunstanton 2810
Lodge Hotel tel: Hunstanton 2896

SPECIAL BREAKS? TRY THE LINKS.

FULLY LICENCED

FREE GOLF

CHILDRENS GAMES ROOM

If you enjoy Golf you'll love the Links Country Park Hotel and Golf Club.

Situated on the beautiful North Norfolk coastline, the Hotel is the ideal centre from which to combine a few rounds of Golf with a taste of unspoilt Norfolk.

Special weekend Breaks run throughout the season, simply contact the Hotel for current Special Breaks on offer.

AA & RAC ★ ★ ★

The Links Country Park Hotel & Golf Club

WEST RUNTON·NORFOLK

West Runton, Cromer, Norfolk, NR27 9QH
Telephone: West Runton (026 375) 691

Suffolk IP3 8UQ
3 miles E of Ipswich off A45, at roundabout by St Augustine's Church turn into Bucklesham Rd.
Heathland course.
18 holes, 6405 yards, S.S.S.71
9 holes, 3860 yards, S.S.S.59
Course designed by James Braid with Hawtree & Taylor.
Club founded in 1928.
Visitors: welcome to 9 hole course any time, and to 18 hole course by arrangement.
Green fees: 18 holes weekdays £10 per day, £6 per round; weekends £12 per day, £8 per round; 9 holes £3 per day or round.
Society meetings: on weekdays.
Catering: full service of meals and snacks available.
Hotels: numerous hotels in area.

124 King's Lynn
☎ Castle Rising (055 387) 654
Castle Rising, King's Lynn, Norfolk PE31 6BD
On A149 from King's Lynn to Hunstanton, at Castle Rising sign turn left, about ¾ mile on left hand side.
Parkland course.
18 holes, 6552 yards, S.S.S.71
Course designed by Alliss & Thomas.
Club founded in 1923.
Visitors: welcome on weekdays.
Green fees: weekdays £10 (£7.50 with member), weekends and Bank Holidays £14 (£8 with member).
Society meetings: catered for on weekdays, except Tues.
Catering: lunches served on weekdays.
Hotels: Dukes Head, Tuesday Market, King's Lynn; Red Cat, North Wootton, King's Lynn.

125 Links
☎ Newmarket (0638) 663000 Sec, 662395 Pro, 662708 Clubhouse.
Cambridge Rd, Newmarket, Suffolk.
1 mile S of Newmarket High St.
Undulating parkland course.
18 holes, 6402 yards, S.S.S.71
Club founded in 1908.
Visitors: welcome except on Sun before 11.30 am unless playing with member.
Green fees: weekdays £8 per round, £10 per day; weekends and Bank Holidays £10 per round, £12 per day.
Society meetings: by arrangement on Tues, Wed and Thurs.
Catering: full service available.
Hotels: Rutland, Newmarket High St; White Hart, Newmarket High St.

126 Links Country Park
☎ West Runton (026 375) 691
West Runton, Norfolk NR27 9QH
In West Runton village 2 miles from Sheringham, turn for railway station, over the bridge 100 yds on left.
Undulating downland course.
9 holes, 4814 yards, S.S.S.64
Visitors: welcome.
Green fees: weekdays £5 per day, weekends £6 per day.
Society meetings: catered for on weekdays and some weekends.
Catering: meals and snacks served.
Hotels: Links Country Park.

127 March
☎ March (035 42) 52364
Frogs Abbey, Grange Rd, March, Cambs.
A141, W off March by-pass, signposted.
Parkland course.
9 holes, 6300 yards, S.S.S.70
Club founded in 1922.
Visitors: welcome on weekdays only.
Green fees: £7.
Society meetings: no facilities.
Catering: no facilities.
Hotels: Griffin; White Horse.

128 Mundesley
☎ Mundesley (0263) 720095
Links Rd, Mundesley, Norwich, Norfolk NR11 8ES
Turn off the Mundesley to Cromer road by Mundesley Church, signposted as you enter the village.
Undulating course.
9 holes, 5376 yards, S.S.S.66
Course designed in part by Harry Vardon.
Club founded in 1903.
Visitors: welcome except on Wed from 12.30 am to 3.30 pm and Sun from 8 am to 11 am.
Green fees: weekdays £6 per day, weekends and Bank Holidays £7 per day.
Society meetings: by arrangement with Sec.
Catering: available every day except Tues.
Hotels: Manor, Mundesley; Royal, Mundesley.

129 Newton Green
☎ Sudbury (0787) 77501
Newton Green, Sudbury, Suffolk
On A134, 3 miles E of Sudbury.
Moorland course.
9 holes, 5442 yards, S.S.S.66
Club founded in 1908.
Visitors: welcome on weekdays, weekends with member only.
Green fees: £6 per day.
Society meetings: by arrangement.
Catering: snacks available.
Hotels: Saracen's Head.

130 Orton Wood
☎ Peterborough (0733) 237478
Ham Lane, Peterborough PE2 0UU
On A625 Peterborough to Windle road, 2 miles W of Peterborough at entrance to Ferry Meadows Country Park.
12 holes. (18 holes April 1987)
Course designed by Dennis Fitton & Roger Fitton.
Visitors: welcome, advisable to book starting times.
Green fees: weekends and Bank Holidays £3.25; weekdays men £2.15, ladies £1.75, Juniors and OAPs £1.20.
Society meetings: no.
Catering: catering at Granary adjacent to clubhouse during opening hours.
Hotels: Moat House.

131 Ramsey
☎ Ramsey (0487) 812600
4 Abbey Terrace, Ramsey, Huntingdon, Cambs PE17 1DD
12 miles SE of Peterborough, off B1040.
Parkland course.
18 holes, 6136 yards, S.S.S.70
Club founded in 1965.
Visitors: welcome at any time.
Green fees: weekdays £7, weekends and Bank Holidays £10.
Society meetings: welcome weekdays.
Catering: full catering facilities.
Hotels: St Ives, Huntingdon.

132 Rookery Park
☎ Lowestoft (0502) 60380 Sec, 4009 Steward.
Beccles Rd, Carlton Colville, Lowestoft NR33 8HJ
On A146 2 miles W of Lowestoft.
Parkland course.
18 holes, 6650 yards, S.S.S.72
Course designed by Charles Lawrie.
Club founded in 1975.
Visitors: welcome all year.
Green fees: weekdays £7 per day, weekends £9 (£4 with member).
Society meetings: Mon, Wed and Fri.
Catering: full catering facilities.
Hotels: Victoria; Oulton; Wherry; Royal St George; Hedley House.

133 Royal Cromer
☎ Cromer (0263) 512884
145 Overstrand Rd, Cromer, Norfolk NR27 0JH
1 mile E of Cromer on B1159, main coast road, adjoins Cromer lighthouse.
Undulating seaside course.
18 holes, 6508 yards, S.S.S.71
Course designed by James Braid.
Club founded in 1888.
Visitors: accepted weekdays and after 11 am most weekends.
Green fees: weekdays £8 per day, weekends and Bank Holidays £10 per day.
Society meetings: accepted on weekdays.
Catering: daily, but limited on Tues.
Hotels: Cliftonville, Cromer; Cliff House.

134 **Royal Norwich**
☎ Norwich (0603) 49928
Drayton High Rd, Hellesdon, Norwich NR6 5AH
500 yds down A1067 Fakenham road from ring road.
Parkland/heathland course.
18 holes, 6603 yards, S.S.S.72
Club founded in 1893.
Visitors: welcome on weekdays if members of golf club with handicap, and at weekends with member.
Green fees: weekdays £10 per round or day, weekends £12 per round or day; half-price with member.
Society meetings: by arrangement.
Catering: snacks and lunches available; evening meals by arrangement.
Hotels: Lenwade House; Norwich.

135 **Royal West Norfolk**
☎ Brancaster (0485) 210223
Brancaster, King's Lynn, Norfolk PE31 8AX
7 miles E of Hunstanton on B124, take Beach Rd from Brancaster village to club.
Seaside links course.
18 holes, 6428 yards, S.S.S.71
Course designed by Holcombe Ingleby.
Club founded in 1892.
Visitors: welcome, except at weekends in July, Aug and Sept when must play with member.
Green fees: weekdays £10, weekends £13.50.
Society meetings: small societies by arrangement.
Catering: snacks daily and lunches by arrangement.
Hotels: The Manor, Titchwell; The Lodge, Old Hunstanton; Tolcarne, Hunstanton; Le Strange Arms, Old Hunstanton; Caley Hall, Old Hunstanton.

136 **Royal Worlington & Newmarket**
☎ Mildenhall (0638) 712216
Worlington, Bury St Edmunds, Suffolk IP28 8SD
7 miles NE of Newmarket, A45 then A11 to Freckenham, turn left to Worlington.
Links course.
9 holes, 3105 yards, S.S.S.70
Course designed by H.S. Colt.
Club founded in 1893.
Visitors: welcome on weekdays.
Green fees: £11 (£5.50 with member).
Society meetings: by arrangement on weekdays.
Catering: lunches served.
Hotels: Bull, Barton Mills; Bell.

137 **Rushmere**
☎ Ipswich (0473) 75648 Sec, 77109 Steward and members, 78076 Pro.
Rushmere Heath, Ipswich, IP4 5QQ
Off A12 just E of Ipswich, at junction of A12 and A45 turn into Glenavon Rd and follow signs.
Undulating heathland course.
18 holes, 6287 yards, S.S.S.70
Club founded in 1896.
Visitors: welcome every day, but only after 10.30 at weekends and Bank Holidays.
Green fees: weekdays £6 per round, £7.50 per day; weekends and Bank Holidays £8 per round or day.
Society meetings: welcome by arrangement with Sec.
Catering: full catering service.
Hotels: Marlborough, Henley Rd, Ipswich; Graham Court, Anglesea Rd, Ipswich.

138 **Ryston Park**
☎ Downham Market (036 63) 383834 or 382133
Denver, Downham Market, Norfolk PE38 0HH
On A10 just before turning to village of Denver, 1 mile S of Downham Market.
Parkland course.
9 holes, 6292 yards, S.S.S.70
Club founded in 1933.
Visitors: welcome, except weekends and Bank Holidays.
Green fees: at present £8 guests: one per member; not weekends. Juniors £4 with adult visitor; £2 with adult member.
Society meetings: by arrangement.
Catering: by arrangement.
Hotels: in Downham Market.

139 **St Ives**
☎ St Ives (0480) 68392
Westwood Rd, St Ives, Cambs PE17 4RS
B1040 off A45.
Parkland course.
9 holes, 6052 yards, S.S.S.69
Club founded in 1923.
Visitors: welcome.
Green fees: weekdays £7, weekends £9.
Society meetings: welcome.
Catering: bar snacks available; other meals by arrangement.
Hotels: numerous hotels in area.

140 **St Neots**
☎ Huntingdon (0480) 72363 Sec, 74311 Club
Crosshall Rd, St Neots, Huntingdon, Cambs PE19 4AE
On A45 1½ miles W of St Neots off A1.
Parkland/meadowland course.
18 holes, 6027 yards, S.S.S.69
Course designed by Harry Vardon.
Club founded in 1890.
Visitors: welcome any day, but on Sun before 11 am with member only.
Green fees: weekdays £8 per day, weekends and Bank Holidays £10 per day.
Society meetings: welcome except Sat, Sun and Mon; no start before 9 am.
Catering: full service in Clubhouse.
Hotels: Stephensons Rocket, Crosshall Rd, St Neots; Kings Head, South St, St Neots.

141 **Sheringham**
☎ Sheringham (0263) 823488
Weybourne Rd, Sheringham, Norfolk NR26 8HG
½ mile W of Sheringham on A149.
Seaside course.
18 holes, 6430 yards, S.S.S.71
Club founded in 1891.
Visitors: welcome with handicap certificate.
Green fees: weekdays £9, weekends £11.
Society meetings: welcome on weekdays by arrangement.
Catering: full catering available.
Hotels: Dormy House.

142 **Southwold**
☎ Southwold (0502) 723234 Clubhouse, 723248 Sec.
The Common, Southwold, Suffolk IP18 6TB
From A12 follow A1095 signposted Southwold, turn right at Kings Head Hotel, proceed across Common, golf club about ½ mile on right hand side.
Commonland course.
9 holes, 6001 yards, S.S.S.69
Club founded in 1884.
Visitors: welcome except on comp. days.
Green fees: weekdays £6 per day, weekends and Bank Holidays £7 per day.
Society meetings: by arrangement.
Catering: bar and lunches available; evening meals by arrangement.
Hotels: a number of hotels in Southwold.

143 **Stowmarket**
☎ Rattlesden (044 93) 473 Sec, 392 Pro.
Lower Rd, Onehouse, Stowmarket, Suffolk IP14 3DA
2½ miles SW of Stowmarket, off B115.
Parkland course.
18 holes, 6119 yards, S.S.S.69
Club reformed in 1962.
Visitors: welcome, but advisable to check availability of course.
Green fees: weekdays £6.50 per round, £8.50 per day; weekends and Bank Holidays £9 per round, £12 per day.
Society meetings: catered for on Tues, Wed afternoon, Thurs and Fri; prices and menus on application.
Catering: full service daily except Mon when bar snacks only.
Hotels: Cedars, Needham Rd, Stowmarket; The Limes, Needham Market.

144 **Swaffham**
☎ Swaffham (0760) 21611
Cley Rd, Swaffham, Norfolk PE37 8AE
1 mile out of town on Cockley Cley road, signposted in town market place.

Moorland course.
9 holes, 6252 yards, S.S.S.70
Club founded in 1922.
Visitors: welcome at all times; with member only Sat and Sun mornings.
Green fees: £6 per day (£4 with member).
Society meetings: small societies (20) only during week.
Catering: meals available by arrangement with Steward.
Hotels: George, Swaffham.

145 Thetford

☎ Thetford (0842) 2258 Clubhouse, 2169 Sec.
Brandon Rd, Thetford, Norfolk IP24 3NE
1¼ miles NW of A11 on B1107 to Brandon.
Heathland course.
18 holes, 6499 yards, S.S.S.71
Course designed by C.H. Mayo.
Club founded in 1912.
Visitors: welcome on weekdays and by arrangement at weekends, with club handicap.
Green fees: weekdays £7.50, weekends £9.
Society meetings: catered for on weekdays only, excluding Tues.
Catering: full facilities except Tue.
Hotels: Bell, Thetford; Anchor, Thetford; Thomas Paine, Thetford.

146 Thorpeness

☎ Aldeburgh (072 885) 2176
Thorpeness, Suffolk IP16 4NH
Leave A12 at Saxmundham, on to B119, then B1353.
Moorland course.
18 holes, 6241 yards, S.S.S.71
Course designed by James Braid.
Club founded in 1923.
Visitors: welcome.
Green fees: weekdays £8 per round, £11 per day; weekends £10 p. r., £13 p. d.
Society meetings: catered for on weekdays.
Catering: full catering facilities.
Hotels: Thorpeness Golf Club.

147 Thorpe Wood

☎ Peterborough (0733) 267701
Nene Parkway, Peterborough PE3 6SE
On A47 to Leicester 2 miles W of Peterborough, next to Moat House Hotel.
Parkland course.
18 holes, 7086 yards, S.S.S.74
Course designed by Peter Alliss & Dave Thomas.
Club founded in 1976.
Visitors: welcome, advisable to book starting times.
Green fees: weekends and Bank Holidays £4.25; weekdays men £3, ladies £2.75, Juniors and OAPs £1.90.
Society meetings: by arrangement up to a year in advance.
Catering: lunches and snacks available, other catering by arrangement.
Hotels: Moat House.

148 Woodbridge

☎ Woodbridge (039 43) 2038
Bromeswell Heath, Woodbridge, Suffolk IP12 2PF
2 miles E of Woodbridge through village of Melton onto B1084.
Heathland course.
18 holes, 6314 yards, S.S.S.70
Club founded in 1893.
Visitors: welcome; advisable to check availability of course.
Green fees: weekdays £9 per round, £12 per day; weekends and Bank Holidays £12 per round, £15 per day; 9 holes weekdays £6 per day, weekends and Bank Holidays £8.
Society meetings: welcome by arrangement with Sec.
Catering: snacks available every day and full meals by arrangement.
Hotels: Melton Grange, Woodbridge; Seckford Hall, Woodbridge; Bull, Woodbridge; Crown, Woodbridge.

J Warwickshire, Herefordshire, Worcestershire and Gloucestershire

Although the four counties cover considerable acreage, they are not heavily populated with golf courses. However, Worcestershire, Herefordshire and Gloucestershire can claim many courses with commanding views; Kington on Bradnor Hill in Herefordshire is the highest course in England.

Broadway, Cotswold Hills and Gloucester Golf and Country Club are other examples but Blackwell is a course of definite charm and challenge; the Worcestershire club, over a hundred years old, is in the heart of Elgar country; Tewkesbury is part of the St Pierre/Telford/Meon Valley stable and the Welcombe Hotel at Stratford-upon-Avon is another to combine good golf with a first rate hotel.

Closer to Birmingham, Copt Heath, Olton, Forest of Arden, Edgbaston, Moor Hall and Moseley offer a nice way to escape from the city. Then, of course, there's the Belfry, scene of the heart warming European victory in the 1985 Ryder Cup.

J1 Atherstone
☎ Atherstone (082 77) 3110 or 4579
The Outwoods, Atherstone, Warwicks CV9 2RL
Coleshill Rd out of Atherstone, ½ mile on left approached by private road.
Undulating parkland course.
11 holes, 6239 yards, S.S.S.70
Club founded in 1894.
Visitors: welcome on weekdays.
Green fees: weekdays £6 (£3 with member), weekends and Bank Holidays £4 with member.
Society meetings: catered for on weekdays by prior appointment.
Catering: full service except Tues.
Hotels: Red Lion, Atherstone; Three Tuns, Atherstone.

J2 Belmont
☎ Belmont (0432) 277445
Belmont House, Belmont, Hereford HR2 9SA
2 miles S of Hereford on Abergavenny Rd, A465.
18 holes, 6766 yards, S.S.S.72
Course designed by R. Sandow.
Club founded on 30th May 1983.
Visitors: welcome.
Green fees: weekdays £5.75 per day, weekends £7.50 per day.
Society meetings: welcome by arrangement.
Catering: full catering available.
Hotels: apply for our list.

J3 Blackwell
☎ 021-445 1994
Blackwell, Bromsgrove, Worc B60 1PY
3 miles E of Bromsgrove, from Blackwell village centre, along Station Rd and under railway bridge, club entrance on left after 40 yds.
Parkland course.
18 holes, 6128 yards, S.S.S.71
Club founded in 1893.
Visitors: welcome on weekdays but advisable to check by telephone first because of large society commitment.
Green fees: £11 per day (with member £2.50 per day); Juniors £4 per day.
Society meetings: accepted on Wed or Thurs and on Fri for smaller groups.
Catering: morning coffee, lunches and evening meals available if prior notice given.
Hotels: numerous hotels in area.

J4 Broadway
☎ Broadway (0386) 853683
Willersey Hill, Broadway, Worc. WR12 7LG
1¼ miles E of Broadway off A44.
Undulating course.
18 holes, 6211 yards, S.S.S.70
Club founded in 1896.
Visitors: welcome with handicap certificate; telephone enquiries advisable.
Green fees: weekdays £8, weekends and Bank Holidays £10.
Society meetings: limited number on Wed, Thurs and Fri only.
Catering: full facilities except Mon; booking advisable especially at weekends.
Hotels: Dormy House, Willersey Hill, Broadway; Noel Arms, High St, Chipping Campden.

J5 Churchill & Blakedown
☎ Kidderminster (0562) 700200
Churchill Lane, Blakedown, Kidderminster, Worc DY10 3NB
Off A456 3 miles NE of Kidderminster, turn under railway viaduct in the village of Blakedown.
Hilly, meadowland course.
9 holes, 5399 yards, S.S.S.67
Club founded in 1926.
Visitors: welcome, but at weekends and on Bank Holidays only with member.
Green fees: £5 per day (£2.50 with member).
Society meetings: by arrangement with Sec.
Catering: lunches and evening meals served except Mon.
Hotels: Gainsborough, Kidderminster; Talbot, Stourbridge.

J6 Cirencester
☎ Cirencester (0285) 2465
Cheltenham Rd, Bagendon, Cirencester, Glos GL7 7BH
Adjoins A435 Cirencester to Cheltenham road, 1½ miles from Cirencester.

Undulating course.
18 holes, 6100 yards, S.S.S.69
Course designed by James Braid.
Club founded in 1893.
Visitors: welcome at all times.
Green fees: weekdays £8 (£4 with member), weekends and Bank Holidays £10 (£5 with member).
Society meetings: catered for on Tues, Wed and Fri.
Catering: lunches and evening meals except Mon in summer and Tues in winter.
Hotels: Kings Head, Market Place; Stratton House, Gloucester Rd; Fleece, Market Place; all in Cirencester.

J7 Cleeve Hill Municipal

☎ Bishop Cleeve (0242 67) 2592
Cheltenham, Glos GL52 3PW
Approx 6 miles N from M5, 4 miles N of Cheltenham off A46.
Undulating heathland course.
18 holes, 6217 yards, S.S.S.70
Visitors: welcome.
Green fees: £3.50 weekdays, £4.50 weekends, £1.50 OAPs.
Society meetings: welcome by arrangement.
Catering: restaurant facilities.
Hotels: Malvern View; De La Bere; Cleeve Hill.

J8 Cotswold Hills

☎ Cheltenham (0242) 515264 Sec, 515263 Pro.
Ullenwood, Cheltenham, Glos GL53 9QT
3 miles S of Cheltenham, between A436 and B4070.
Undulating course.
18 holes, 6716 yards, S.S.S.72
Course designed by M.D. Little.
Club founded in 1902.
Visitors: members of recognised clubs welcome.
Green fees: weekdays £6 per round, £7.50 per day; weekends and Bank Holidays £9 per round, £11 per day.
Society meetings: welcome on Wed, Thurs and Fri.
Catering: bar snacks, lunches and dinners except Mon when sandwiches available.
Hotels: Crest.

J9 Droitwich G & C C

☎ Droitwich (0905) 770129 Steward, 770207 Pro, 774344 Sec.
Ford Lane, Droitwich WR9 0BQ
Junction 5 off M5, A38 to Droitwich, take first right, 1 mile N of town.
Undulating meadowland course.
18 holes, 6036 yards, S.S.S.69
Club founded in 1897.
Visitors: welcome on weekdays and with member at weekends and Bank Holidays.
Green fees: £8.
Society meetings: catered for on Wed and Fri.
Catering: snacks and restaurant facilities available.
Hotels: Chateau Impney; Raven; St Andrews.

J10 Evesham

☎ Evesham (0386) 869395 Clubhouse & Pro, 552373 Sec.
Evesham Rd, Fladbury Cross, Pershore, Worcs WR10 2QS
On B4084 3 miles from Evesham.
Parkland course.
9 holes, 6418 yards, S.S.S.71
Club founded in 1894.
Visitors: welcome with handicap certificate on weekdays between 8 am and dusk except for competition days, or weekends only permitted if playing with member.
Green fees: £7 per day or round (£3 with member).
Society meetings: only by arrangement, max. 24.
Catering: snacks and sandwiches served during bar hours; full meals strictly by prior arrangement.
Hotels: Avonside, Wyre Piddle; Angel, Pershore; Evesham, Evesham; Park View, Evesham.

J11 Gloucester G & C C

☎ Gloucester (0452) 25653
Robinswood Hill, Gloucester GL4 9EA
2 miles S of Gloucester city centre on B4073 to Painswick.
Parkland course.
18 holes, 6135 yards,
Course designed by Donald Steel.
Club founded in 1976.
Visitors: welcome any time; telephone Gloucester 411331 for availability.
Green fees: weekdays £6 per round, weekends £8.
Society meetings: welcome all year.
Catering: snacks served at clubhouse and meals available at hotel.
Hotels: Gloucester Hotel and C.C..

J12 Habberley

☎ Kidderminster (0562) 745756
Habberley, Kidderminster, Worc DY11 5RG
3m N of Kidderminster on Trimpley Rd.
Hilly parkland course.
9 holes, 5104 yards, S.S.S.69
Club founded in 1924.
Visitors: welcome on weekdays if member of recognised club.
Green fees: £5 per day.
Society meetings: welcome by arrangement.
Catering: by prior notice.
Hotels: Gainsborough, Kidderminster; Swan, Stourport.

J13 Herefordshire

☎ Hereford (0432) 71219
Ravens Causeway, Wormsley, Hereford HR4 8LY
Turn left off B4110 at Three Elms Inn, 6 miles NW of Hereford on road to Weobley.
Undulating parkland course.
18 holes, 6036 yards, S.S.S.69
Club founded in 1898.
Visitors: welcome.
Green fees: weekdays £6, weekends and Bank Holidays £7.
Society meetings: by prior arrangement on most days; but limited to small number at certain weekends.
Catering: available on request, but limited on Mon.
Hotels: Red Lion, Weobley; Priory, Stretton Sugwas.

J14 Kenilworth

☎ Kenilworth (0926) 58517
Crew Lane, Kenilworth, Warwickshire CV8 2EA
A429 Kenilworth road, then via Common Lane, Knowle Hill and Crew Lane to clubhouse.
Undulating course.
18 holes, 6408 yards, S.S.S.71
Club founded in 1887.
Visitors: welcome every day; advisable ring Pro beforehand (Kenilworth 512732).
Green fees: weekdays £9, weekends £12.
Society meetings: apply in writing, bookings preferred on Wed but other days accepted.
Catering: full catering daily; advisable to contact Stewardess (Kenilworth 54038).
Hotels: De Montford; Avonside; Chesford Grange.

J15 Kidderminster

☎ Kidderminster (0562) 2303
Russell Rd, Kidderminster, Worc.
The course is signposted off A449 and is within 1 mile of town centre.
Parkland course.
18 holes, 5659 yards, S.S.S.69
Club founded in 1909.
Visitors: welcome on weekdays only.
Green fees: £8.65 per day.
Society meetings: welcome by prior arrangement usually Thurs.
Catering: full catering except Mon.
Hotels: several in town and nearby.

J16 Kington Herefordshire

☎ Kington (0544) 230340
Bradnor Hill, Kington, Herefordshire.
On B4355, 1 mile N of Kington.
Moorland course; highest 18 hole course in England and Wales.
18 holes, 5830 yards, S.S.S.68
Course designed by C.K. Hutchison.
Club founded in 1926.
Visitors: welcome if from other

recognised club.
Green fees: weekdays £4.50 per day, weekends and Bank Holidays £6.
Society meetings: welcome, especially on weekdays.
Catering: full service available.
Hotels: Beacon, Bradnor Hill; Burton, Kington; Swan, Kington.

J17 Leamington & County

☎ Leamington Spa (0926) 28014 or 20298
Golf Lane, Whitnash, Leamington Spa, Warwickshire CV31 2QA
2 miles S of town centre, off A452.
Undulating parkland course.
18 holes, 6430 yards, S.S.S.71
Course designed by H.S. Colt.
Club founded in 1908.
Visitors: welcome on weekdays.
Green fees: £8 per round, £11 per day.
Society meetings: by prior arrangement.
Catering: luncheons, teas, evening meals and snacks served except Mon.
Hotels: numerous hotels in Cheltenham.

J18 Leominster

☎ Leominster (0568) 2863
Ford Bridge, Leominster, Herefordshire
On A49, 4 miles S of Leominster.
Undulating meadowland course.
9 holes, 5249 yards, S.S.S.66
Club founded in 1967.
Visitors: welcome.
Green fees: weekdays £5 (£2 with member), weekends and Bank Holidays £6.50 (£3 with member).
Society meetings: catered for on weekdays, except Mon.
Catering: full catering except Mon.
Hotels: Talbot, Leominster; Royal Oak, Leominster.

J19 Lilley Brook

☎ Cheltenham (0242) 526785
Cirencester Rd, Charlton Kings, Cheltenham, Glos GL53 8EG
2 miles from centre of Cheltenham on the Cheltenham to Cirencester road, A435.
Parkland course.
18 holes, 6226 yards, S.S.S.70
Club founded in 1922.
Visitors: welcome on weekdays and weekends by appointment.
Green fees: weekdays £7.50 per day, £6 per round; weekends £12.50 per day, £10 per round.
Society meetings: by appointment.
Catering: all meals available; advance notice requested.
Hotels: numerous good hotels

J20 Little Lakes

☎ Bewdley (0299) 403650
Lye Head, Rock, Bewdley, Worc DY12 2UU
A456 2 miles W of Bewdley, turn left at Greenhouse and Garden Centre, proceed for ½ mile.
Undulating parkland course.

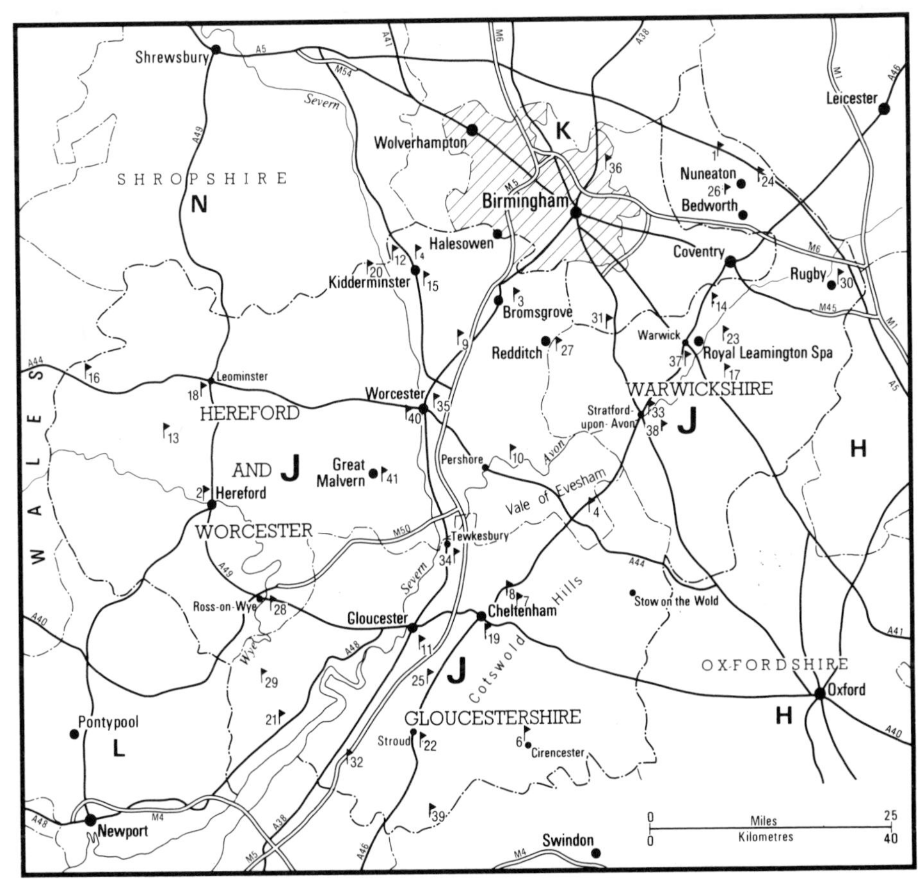

9 holes, 6204 yards, S.S.S.71
Club founded in 1975.
Visitors: welcome.
Green fees: weekdays £3, £2; weekends £4, £2.50.
Society meetings: welcome on weekdays and at selected weekends.
Catering: lunches and bar snacks available most days.
Hotels: Gainsborough House, Kidderminster; George, Bewdley; Mount Olympus, Stourport.

J21 Lydney
☎ Dean (0594) 42614
Lakeside Ave, Lydney, Glos.
Entering Lydney on A48 from Gloucester, turn left at bottom of Highfield Hill and look for Lakeside Ave, 7th turning on left.
Parkland course.
9 holes, 5382 yards, S.S.S.66
Club founded in 1912.
Visitors: welcome on weekdays and with member at weekends.
Green fees: £5.
Society meetings: by arrangement with Hon Sec. (Dean 43940).
Catering: none.
Hotels: Feathers, Lydney.

J22 Minchinhampton
☎ Nailsworth (045 383) 3866
New Course, Minchinhampton, Stroud, Glos GL6 9BE
Leave M5 at Junction 13, 5m E of Stroud on Minchinhampton to Avening rd.
Meadowland course.
18 holes, 6675 yards, S.S.S.72
New course designed by F.W. Hawtree.
Club formed in 1889.
Visitors: welcome at all times subject to availability of course.
Green fees: weekdays £7.30, weekends £8.50 (£4 with member).
Society meetings: welcome subject to handicap certs. and availability.
Catering: available at all times.
Hotels: Bear of Rodborough, Rodborough Common; Burleigh Court, Burleigh, Stroud; Amberley Inn, Amberley, Stroud; Hare and Hounds, Westonbirt, Tetbury.

J23 Newbold Comyn
☎ Leamington Spa (0926) 21157
Newbold Terrace East, Leamington Spa, Warwicks.
Off B4099 Willes Rd, centrally located.
Parkland course.
18 holes, 6259 yards, S.S.S.70
Club formed in 1973.
Visitors: welcome.
Green fees: weekdays £2.80, weekends £3.50.
Society meetings: no.
Catering: bar and restaurant facilities.
Hotels: Crown; Manor.

J24 Nuneaton
☎ Nuneaton (0203) 347810
Golf Drive, Whitestone, Nuneaton, Warwicks CV11 6QF
Leave M6 at Junction 3 on A444, 2 miles S of Nuneaton.
Undulating meadowland course.
18 holes, 6368 yards, S.S.S.71
Club formed in 1906.
Visitors: welcome on weekdays and at weekends, if playing with member.
Green fees: £8 per day (£3.45 playing with member); if over 65 and playing with member £2.30.
Society meetings: welcome on Wed and Fri.
Catering: full catering service available.
Hotels: Long Shoot, Long Shoot, Nuneaton; Chase, Higham Lane, Nuneaton.

J25 Painswick
☎ Painswick (0452) 812180
Painswick Beacon, Painswick, Stroud, Glos.
1 mile N of Painswick village on A46.
Commonland course.
18 holes, 4780 yards, S.S.S.64
Club formed in 1891.
Visitors: welcome weekdays and with member at weekends.
Green fees: weekdays £3.50, weekends £5.
Society meetings: by arrangement.
Catering: bar snacks available at lunchtime and in the evening.
Hotels: Painswick, Painswick; Falcon, Painswick; Tara, Upton-St-Leonards.

J26 Purley Chase
☎ Chapel End (0203) 395348
Ridge Lane, Atherstone, Nuneaton, Warwicks CV10 0RB
4 miles from Nuneaton off B4114 Nuneaton to Birmingham Rd (turn right at Pipers Lane).
Meadowland course.
18 holes, 6604 yards, S.S.S.71
Course designed by B. Tomlinson
Club formed in 1980.
Visitors: welcome on weekdays; weekends afternoons only.
Green fees: weekdays and weekends £6 per round (£4 with member); £9 per day (£6 with member); Juniors and Colts £2.50 per round, £4 per day.
Society meetings: welcome weekdays and some weekend afternoons.
Catering: full catering available daily.
Hotels: Chase, Higham Lane, Nuneaton; Longshoot, Watling St, Nuneaton.

J27 Redditch
☎ Redditch (0527) 43309
Lower Grinsty, Green Lane, Callow Hill, Redditch, Worc B97 5JP
On A441 3 miles from town centre.
Undulating parkland/wooded course.
18 holes, 6671 yards, S.S.S.72
Course designed by F. Pennink, C.K. Cotton & Partners.
Club formed in 1913.
Visitors: members of recognised golf club welcome on weekdays and with member at weekends.
Green fees: £6 plus VAT (with member £2 plus VAT).
Society meetings: accepted; fees on application.
Catering: full service except Mon.
Hotels: Southcrest, Mount Pleasant.

J28 Ross-on-Wye
☎ Gorsley (098 982) 267 Office, 457 Club, 439 Pro.
Two Park, Gorsley, Ross-on-Wye, Herefords HR9 7UT
On B4421, 100 yards from Junction 3 off M50.
Parkland course.
18 holes, 6500 yards, S.S.S.73
Course designed by C.K. Cotton.
Visitors: welcome, telephone Pro Gorsley 439 before travel. Wide wheel trolleys only, ticket and tee after bar opens 4.30 pm.
Green fees: weekdays £8.50, weekends £9.50.
Society meetings: by arrangement.
Catering: full catering except Mon.
Hotels: Chase, Ross-on-Wye; Royal, Ross-on-Wye.

J29 Royal Forest of Dean
☎ Dean (0594) 32583/33262
Lords Hill, Coleford, Glos GL16 8BD
M5, M50 4 miles Monmouth, 8 miles Ross, M4 8 miles Chepstow.
Parkland course.
18 holes, 5519 yards, S.S.S.67
Course designed by John Day.
Club formed in 1972.
Visitors: welcome every day (must book at weekends).
Green fees: weekdays £5, weekends £6.
Society meetings: catered for on weekdays, special package available.
Catering: full meals available (tennis, swimming and bowling in summer).
Hotels: own 32 bedroom (Bell's) on course.

J30 Rugby
☎ Rugby (0788) 2306 or 75134 Pro.
Clifton Rd, Rugby CV21 3RD
On Rugby to Market Harborough road, on right just past railway bridge as leaving town.
Parkland course.
18 holes, 5457 yards, S.S.S.67
Club formed in 1891.
Visitors: welcome on weekdays and with

member at weekends and Bank Holidays.
Green fees: £6.50 per round or day.
Society meetings: catered for on weekdays by arrangement with match Sec (0788 814164).
Hotels: Three Horse Shoes, Sheep St, Rugby; Moathouse, Crick.

J31 Shirley
☎ 021-744 6001
Stratford Rd, Solihull, W Midlands.
On A34, 7 miles S of Birmingham.
Parkland course.
18 holes, 6445 yards, S.S.S.71
Visitors: welcome.
Green fees: weekdays £9.20, weekends £11.
Society meetings: by arrangement.
Catering: meals served except Mon.
Hotels: St John's; George, Solihull.

J32 Stinchcombe Hill
☎ Dursley (0453) 2015
Stinchcombe Hill, Dursley, Glos GL11 6AQ
1 mile along narrow lane (signposted) off A4135 Tetbury to Dursley road OR approach direct from Dursley town centre ½ mile up hill past bus station.
Meadowland, downland course.
18 holes, 5710 yards, S.S.S.68
Club founded in 1889
Visitors: welcome any day but after 10.30 am at weekends and Bank Holidays only with members; prior booking advised.
Green fees: weekdays £7, weekends and Bank Holidays £8 (with member £5). reduced from 1 Nov to 31 March.
Society meetings: catered for usually on Wed, other days by arrangement.
Catering: full catering service and bar.
Hotels: Berkeley Arms, Berkeley; Hare and Hounds, Westonbirt; Prince of Wales, Berkeley; Newport Towers, Newport; Swan, Wotton-under-Edge.

J33 Stratford-upon-Avon
☎ Stratford-upon-Avon (0789) 205749
Tiddington Rd, Stratford-upon-Avon, Warwicks CV37 7BA
½m from river bridge on B4089
Parkland course.
18 holes, 6309 yards, S.S.S.70
Club formed in 1894 (1928 on present site).
Visitors: welcome on weekdays by arrangement.
Green fees: £8 currently.
Society meetings: Tues and Thurs by arrangement.
Catering: snacks and meals available.
Hotels: in area.

J34 Tewkesbury Park Hotel
☎ Tewkesbury (0684) 295405
Lincoln Green Lane, Tewkesbury GL20 7DN
½ mile S of town on A38, 3 miles from Junction 9 off M5.
Parkland course.
18 holes, 6533/6197 yards, S.S.S.71/69
Course designed by Frank Pennink.
Club formed in 1976.
Visitors: welcome with handicap cert.
Green fees: weekdays £8, weekends £9; half-price with member.
Society meetings: welcome.
Catering: snacks and meals available.
Hotels: Tewkesbury Park.

J35 Tolladine
☎ Worcester (0905) 21074
Tolladine Rd, Worcester WR4 9BA
Leave M5 at Junction 6 Warndon about 1 mile from city centre.
Meadowland course.
9 holes, 5630 yards, S.S.S.67
Club formed in 1898.
Visitors: welcome on weekdays and with member at weekends or Bank Holidays.
Green fees: weekdays £6 (with member £3), weekends £3.70.
Society meetings: by arrangement with Sec.
Catering: light snacks available.
Hotels: Gifford; Star.

J36 Walmley
☎ 021-373 0029
Brooks Rd, Wylde Green, Sutton Coldfield, W Midlands B72 1HR
6 miles N of Birmingham, turn off

Birmingham to Sutton Coldfield road $\frac{1}{4}$ mile N of Chester road (Yenton Pub), right into Greenhill Rd, Brooks Rd continues from this.
Parkland course.
18 holes, 6340 yards, S.S.S.70
Club formed in 1902.
Visitors: welcome on weekdays.
Green fees: £9 (with member £3.25 weekdays, £3.75 weekends and Bank Holidays).
Society meetings: welcome weekdays.
Catering: full catering available except Mon when only bar snacks available.
Hotels: Penns Hall.

J37 Warwick

☎ Warwick (0926) 494316
The Racecourse, Warwick CV34 6HW
Centre of Warwick Racecourse.
Meadowland course.
9 holes, 2682 yards, S.S.S.66
Course designed by D.G. Dunkley.
Club formed in 1886.
Visitors: welcome except race days.
Green fees: weekdays £1.40 for 9 holes, weekends £1.70 for 9 holes.
Society meetings: welcome on weekdays only.
Catering: bar available but no food.
Hotels: Woolpack; Warwick Arms.

J38 Welcombe Hotel

☎ Stratford-upon-Avon (0789) 295252
Warwick Rd, Stratford-upon-Avon, Warwicks CV37 0NR
$1\frac{1}{2}$ miles from Stratford on A34 to Warwick.
Parkland course.
18 holes, 6202 yards, S.S.S.70
Course designed by T.J. McAuley.
Club formed in 1980.
Visitors: welcome on weekdays and with handicap certificate at weekends; phone booking advisable.
Green fees: weekdays £9.50, weekends and Bank Holidays £10.50; half-price with member; residents £7.50.
Society meetings: welcome on weekdays and on weekend afternoons.
Catering: snacks and meals available.
Hotels: Welcombe.

J39 Westonbirt

☎ Tetbury (0666) 242
Tetbury, Glos GL8 8QP
Turn off A433 3 miles SW of Tetbury, through Westonbirt village, take turning opposite Westonbirt Arboretum entrance.
Parkland course.
9 holes, 4504 yards, S.S.S.62
Course designed by Monty Hearn.
Visitors: welcome.
Green fees: weekdays £3 per day, weekends £3 per round.
Society meetings: by arrangement.
Catering: available at Holford Arms.
Hotels: Hare and Hounds, Westonbirt.

J40 Worcester G & C C

☎ Worcester (0905) 422555
Boughton Park, Worcester WR2 4EZ
$1\frac{1}{2}$ miles from town centre on Bransford road, a few yards from the Portobello Inn, follow the signs for Hereford.
Parkland course.
18 holes, 5890 yards, S.S.S.68
Course designed by Dr. A. Mackenzie.
Club formed in 1927.
Visitors: welcome on weekdays and with member at weekends, handicap certificate required.
Green fees: £10 per day or round.
Society meetings: by prior arrangement.
Catering: snacks available and meals by arrangement, except Mon.
Hotels: Giffard; Star.

J41 Worcestershire

☎ Malvern (068 45) 5992 Sec, 3905 Stewards, 64428 Pro.
Wood Farm, Malvern Wells, Worc WR14 4PP
2 miles S of Great Malvern, turn off A449 onto B4209, follow signs.
Meadowland/parkland course.
18 holes, 6430 yards, S.S.S.71
Club formed in 1879.
Visitors: welcome on weekdays and after 10 am at weekends.
Green fees: weekdays £8.50 (£4 with member), weekends £10.50 (£5 with member).
Society meetings: catered for on Thurs, Fri or Tues afternoons by preference.
Catering: full service except Mon.
Hotels: Cottage in the Wood; Foley Arms.

K Birmingham, West Midlands

K1 Belfry
☎ Curdworth (0675) 70301
Lichfield Rd, Wishaw, N Warwicks B76 9PR
M6 Junction 4, follow signs to Lichfield along A446, sited at the apex of A4091 to Tamworth and A446 to Lichfield.
Parkland course. Championship courses.
Brabazon 18 holes, 6975 yards, S.S.S.72
Derby 18 holes, 6077 yards, S.S.S.70
Course designed by Peter Alliss & Dave Thomas.
Club founded in 1977.
Visitors: welcome at all times, but prior reservation is recommended.
Green fees: Brabazon weekdays £11.50 per round, weekends £13.50 per round; Derby weekdays £7.50, weekends £9.50.
Society meetings: welcome, but advance reservation is essential.
Catering: meals and snacks available.
Hotels: Belfry.

K2 Bloxwich
☎ Bloxwich (0922) 405724
Stafford Rd, Bloxwich, Walsall, W Midlands WS3 3PQ
A34, 4 miles N of Walsall centre.
Parkland course.
18 holes, 6286 yards, S.S.S.70
Course designed by J. Sixsmith.
Club founded in 1924.
Visitors: welcome on weekdays and with member at weekends.
Green fees: weekdays £8.
Society meetings: catered for on weekdays by arrangement.
Catering: bar lunches, teas and evening meals by arrangement except Mon.
Hotels: Baron's Court; Crest; County; Royal.

K3 Boldmere
☎ 021-354 3379
Monmouth Drive, Sutton Coldfield, W Midlands.
A452 Chester road, 6 miles NE of Birmingham city centre.
Parkland course.
18 holes, 4408 yards, S.S.S.62
Club founded around 1935.
Visitors: welcome on weekdays.
Green fees: £3.50.
Society meetings: catered for on weekdays by arrangement.
Catering: licensed restaurant available.
Hotels: Penns Hall, Sutton Coldfield; Parson and Clarke.

K4 Calderfields
☎ Walsall (0922) 640540 or 32243
Aldridge Rd, Walsall, W Midlands.
Take Junction 7 M6, entrance next to Dilke Arms on Aldridge road A454.
Parkland course.
18 holes, 6636 yards, S.S.S.72
Course designed by Roy Winter.
Club founded in 1981.
Visitors: welcome.
Green fees: weekdays £3.50, weekends £4.
Society meetings: welcome.
Catering: meals and snacks served.
Hotels: Crest, Walsall; Post House, Walsall.

K5 Cocks Moor Woods
☎ 021-444 3584
Alcester Rd. South, Kings Heath, Birmingham B14 6ER
On A435, near city boundary.
Parkland course.
18 holes, 5888 yards, S.S.S.68
Club founded in 1924.
Visitors: welcome.
Green fees: weekdays £3.20, weekends £3.50.
Society meetings: by arrangement.
Catering: snacks served.
Hotels: in Birmingham.

K6 Copt Heath
☎ Knowle (056 45) 2650
Warwick Rd, Knowle, Solihull, W Midlands B93 9LN
On A41 ¼ mile S of Junction 5 with M42.
Parkland course.
18 holes, 6504 yards, S.S.S.71
Course designed by H. Vardon.
Club founded in 1910.
Visitors: only members of recognised golf clubs with official club handicap are welcome.
Green fees: £11 per round, £13.75 per day.
Society meetings: welcome on Wed and Thurs only, by arrangement with Sec.
Catering: full catering except Mon.
Hotels: Greswolde.

K7 Coventry
☎ Coventry (0203) 414152
Finham Park, Coventry CV3 6PJ
2 miles S of Coventry on A444 Stoneleigh to Leamington Spa road.
Parkland course.
18 holes, 6613 yards, S.S.S.72
Club founded in 1887.
Visitors: welcome with handicap certificate on weekdays and with member at weekends.
Green fees: £10 per day.
Society meetings: catered for on Wed and Thurs only.
Catering: full service available except Mon when snacks only served.
Hotels: De Vere, Coventry; Leofric, Coventry; Post House, Coventry.

K8 Dartmouth
☎ 021-588 2131
Vale St, West Bromwich, W Midlands B71 4DW
West Bromwich to Walsall road, right at Churchfield, behind Churchfield High School.
Undulating meadowland course.
9 holes, 6060 yards, S.S.S.69
Club founded in 1910.
Visitors: welcome on weekdays.
Green fees: weekdays £4 + VAT (£2 + VAT with member), weekends and Bank Holidays with member only £3 + VAT. 5 day M £3 + VAT.
Society meetings: catered for on weekdays by advance booking.
Catering: lunches served except Tues.
Hotels: Moat, West Bromwich; Post House, Great Barr.

K9 Druids Heath
☎ Aldridge (0922) 55595
Stonnall Rd, Aldridge, W Midlands W59 8JZ
Off A452 6 miles NW of Sutton Coldfield.
Undulating course.
18 holes, 6914 yards, S.S.S.73
Club founded in 1974.
Visitors: welcome on weekdays and with member at weekends.
Green fees: weekdays £8.05, weekends £9.20.
Society meetings: details on request.
Catering: bar snacks and full catering for society meetings available.
Hotels: Fairlawns; Baron Court.

K10 Dudley
☎ Dudley (0384) 53719
Turners Hill, Rowley Regis, Warley, W Midlands B65 9DP
1 mile S of town centre.
Undulating course.
18 holes, 5715 yards, S.S.S.67

Club founded in 1966.
Visitors: welcome.
Green fees: £6.
Society meetings: by arrangement.
Catering: meals served.
Hotels: Station, Dudley.

K11 Edgbaston

☎ 021-454 1736
Church Rd, Edgbaston, Birmingham B15 3TB
A38 1 mile from Five Ways in Birmingham city centre, entrance to clubhouse is next door to Edgbaston Old Church.
Parkland course.
18 holes, 6118 yards, S.S.S.69
Course designed by H.S. Colt.
Club founded in 1896.
Visitors: welcome at all times.
Green fees: weekdays £9.50 – £11, weekends and Bank Holidays £15.
Society meetings: catered for on weekdays by prior arrangement.
Catering: lunches daily and other meals by arrangement.
Hotels: numerous good hotels in Birmingham.

K12 Forest of Arden G & CC

☎ Meriden (0676) 22118
Maxstoke Lane, Meriden, Coventry, Warwickshire CV7 7HR
10 miles NW of Coventry off A45; 2½ miles E of Birmingham International Airport.
Parkland course.
18 holes, 6962 yards, S.S.S.73
9 holes, 1890 yards.
Club founded in 1970.
Visitors: welcome on weekdays and with member at weekends.
Green fees: 18 hole £8.50 per round, £10.50 per day; 9 hole £4 per day.
Society meetings: welcome by arrangement.
Catering: snacks and full meals available all day.
Hotels: Manor, Meriden; Haigs, Balsall Common.

K13 Fulford Heath

☎ Wythall (0564) 822806
Tanners Green Lane, Wythall, Birmingham B47 6BH
1 mile from main Alcester road, signposted to Tanners Green.
Meadowland course.
18 holes, 6216 yards, S.S.S.70
Club founded in 1934.
Visitors: welcome on weekdays and weekends, by arrangement with Sec.
Green fees: £7.
Society meetings: catered for on Tues and Thurs only.
Catering: full service except Mon.

K14 Gay Hill

☎ 021-430 8544
Alcester Rd, Hollywood, Birmingham B47 5PP
On A435, 7 miles from city centre.
Meadowland course.
18 holes, 6500 yards, S.S.S.71
Club founded in 1921.
Visitors: welcome on weekdays.
Green fees: £10 (without member).
Society meetings: Thurs only.
Catering: meals available.
Hotels: in Birmingham & Solihull.

K15 Grange

☎ Coventry (0203) 451465
Copsewood, Coventry, W Midlands CV3 1HS
2½ miles from Coventry centre on Binley Rd, A428.
Meadowland course.
9 holes, 6002 yards, S.S.S.69
Club founded in 1924.
Visitors: welcome on weekdays except evenings.
Green fees: £6 per day, £4 per round.
Society meetings: by arrangement on weekdays only.
Catering: none.
Hotels: numerous hotels in area.

K16 Great Barr

☎ 021-357 1232
Chapel Lane, Great Barr, Birmingham B43 7BA
Adjacent to Exit 7 off M6, 6 miles NW of Birmingham.
Meadowland course.
18 holes, 6545 yards, S.S.S.72
Club founded in 1961.
Visitors: welcome on weekdays.
Green fees: weekdays £7.
Society meetings: welcome on Tues and Thurs by arrangement.
Catering: snacks, lunches and dinners by arrangement.
Hotels: Post House, Great Barr.

K17 Halesowen

☎ 021-501 3606
The Leasowes, Halesowen, W Midlands B62 8QF
Exit Junction 3 off M5, to Kidderminster, then to Halesowen.
Parkland course.
18 holes, 5673 yards, S.S.S.68
Club founded in 1908.
Visitors: welcome on weekdays only.
Green fees: £8 per day.
Society meetings: to be arranged with Sec.
Catering: lunches and dinners served Tues to Fri.
Hotels: numerous hotels in Birmingham.

K18 Handsworth

☎ 021-554 0599
11 Sunningdale Close, Handsworth Wood, Handsworth, Birmingham B20 1NP
3 miles NW of city centre off A41, 1 mile from M6.
Parkland course.
18 holes, 6312 yards, S.S.S.70
Club founded in 1895.
Visitors: welcome but with members only at weekends and Bank Holidays.
Green fees: £8.50 (£3 with member).
Society meetings: by prior arrangement.
Catering: lunch and dinner except Mon.
Hotels: Moat House, West Bromwich; Post House, Great Barr, Birmingham; Barr, Great Barr, Birmingham.

K19 Harborne

☎ 021-427 1728
40 Tennal Rd, Birmingham B32 2JE
Via Harborne village and War Lane, SW of Birmingham.
Undulating parkland/moorland course.
18 holes, 6300 yards, S.S.S.70
Course designed by H.S. Colt.
Club founded in 1893.
Visitors: welcome on weekdays and with member at weekends.
Green fees: £9 (£3 with member).
Society meetings: catered for on Wed, Thurs and Fri.
Catering: catering available Tues to Fri.
Hotels: Lambert Court, Hagley Rd; Strathallan, Hagley Rd; Plough and Harrow, Harley Rd; Apollo, Harley Rd.

K20 Harborne Church Farm

☎ 021-427 1204
Vicarage Rd, Harborne, Birmingham B17 0SN
From Birmingham, via Broad St, Harborne Rd and War Lane to Vicarage Rd.
Parkland municipal course.
9 holes, 4514 yards, S.S.S.62
Club founded in 1926.
Visitors: welcome.
Green fees: weekdays £2, weekends £3.
Society meetings: no.
Catering: snacks and meals in café.
Hotels: numerous hotels in Birmingham.

K21 Hatchford Brook

☎ 021-743 9821
Coventry Rd, Sheldon, Birmingham B26 3PY
Almost on city boundary adjacent to Airport, on main A45 Coventry road.
Parkland course.
18 holes, 6164 yards, S.S.S.69
Club founded in 1969.
Visitors: all welcome.
Green fees: £3.75 per round.
Society meetings: not catered for.
Catering: canteen facilities while course open.
Hotels: numerous good hotels in NEC and Airport complex.

K22 Hearsall

☎ Coventry (0203) 713470
Beechwood Ave, Coventry CV5 6DF
Just off A45.
Parkland course.
18 holes, 5951 yards, S.S.S.69
Club founded in 1824.
Visitors: welcome any time except at weekends and on Wed after 3 pm when with member only.
Green fees: weekdays £9 per day, weekends and Bank Holidays £10.
Society meetings: on application to Sec.
Catering: full service available.
Hotels: numerous hotels in Coventry.

K23 Hill Top

☎ 021-554 4463
Park Lane, Handsworth Wood, Birmingham 20.
Parkland course.
18 holes, 6200 yards, S.S.S.69
Club founded in 1980.
Visitors: welcome.
Green fees: £3.20 weekdays, £3.50 weekends.
Society meetings: none.
Catering: cafeteria open daily.
Hotels: Post House, Walsall.

K24 Himley Hall

☎ Wombourne (0902) 895207
Log Cabin, Himley Hall Park, Dudley, W Midlands DY3 4DF
From A449 Wolverhampton to Kidderminster road turn at traffic lights signposted Dudley onto B4176, then turn into Himley Hall Park on left.
Parkland course.
18 holes, 6107 yards, S.S.S.69
9 holes, 3090 yards.
Course designed by W.G. Cox & D.A. Baker.
Club founded in 1980.
Visitors: welcome.
Green fees: weekdays 9 holes £1.75, weekends £2.20; 18 holes weekdays £2.65, weekends £3.30.
Society meetings: catered for by arrangement.
Catering: tea, coffee and snacks available.
Hotels: Himley House; Summerhill, Kingswinford.

K25 Kings Norton

☎ Wythall (0564) 826706
Brockhill Lane, Weatheroak, Alvechurch, Birmingham B48 7ED
8 miles from centre of Birmingham between A435 and A441.
Parkland course (3 loops of 9) 27 holes.
Blue 9 holes, 3567 yards,
Red 9 holes, 3497 yards,
Yellow 9 holes, 3294 yards, S.S.S.72
Also 12 hole Par 3 course.
Course designed by F. Hawtree & Son.
Club founded in 1892.
Visitors: welcome on weekdays and with member at weekends.
Green fees: £7.50 per day (£3.50 with member).
Society meetings: welcome Mon to Fri.
Catering: meals served except Mon.
Hotels: St John's, Solihull; George, Solihull; Chateau Impney, Droitwich.

K26 Ladbrook Park

☎ Tanworth-in-Arden (056 44) 2264
Poolhead Lane, Tanworth-in-Arden,

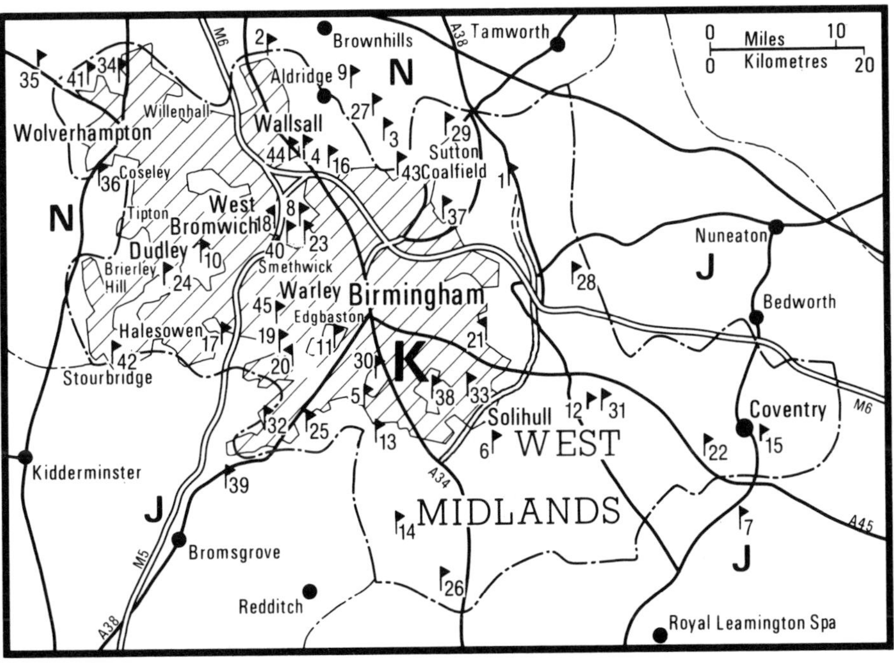

Solihull B94 5ED
A4023 4 miles from Hockley Heath.
Undulating parkland course.
18 holes, 6407 yards, S.S.S.71
Course designed by H.S. Colt.
Club founded in 1908.
Visitors: welcome on weekdays and with member at weekends.
Green fees: £9.50.
Society meetings: by arrangement with Sec Mrs G.P. Taylor.
Catering: lunches, afternoon teas and booked evening meals, except Mon.
Hotels: Yew Trees, Henley-in-Arden; White Swan, Henley-in- Arden; St John's, Solihull; George, Solihull.

K27 Little Aston

☎ 021-353 2066
Streetly, Sutton Coldfield B74 3AN
3 miles N of Sutton Coldfield in Little Aston Park
Parkland course.
18 holes, 6724 yards, S.S.S.73
Course designed by Harry Vardon.
Club founded in 1908.
Visitors: welcome on weekdays by prior arrangement.
Green fees: weekdays £13 per day.
Society meetings: catered for on weekdays.
Catering: meals available except Mon.
Hotels: Fairlawns, Little Aston Rd, Aldridge, Walsall.

K28 Maxstoke Park

☎ Coleshill (0675) 64915
Castle Lane, Coleshill, Birmingham B46 2RD
Junction 4 off M6, A446 to Coleshill, take B4114-6 to Atherstone for 2 miles, right turn into Castle Lane, course in Maxstoke Castle grounds.
Parkland course.
18 holes, 6437 yards, S.S.S.71
Course designed by Ortree.
Club founded in 1896.
Visitors: welcome on weekdays.
Green fees: £10 per day, £7 per round.
Society meetings: catered for on Tues and Thurs by prior arrangement.
Catering: lunches served except Mon.
Hotels: Swan, Coleshill; Manor, Meriden; Post House & Allesley, Allesley, Coventry.

K29 Moor Hall

☎ 021-308 6130
Moor Hall Park, Sutton Coldfield, W Midlands B75 6LN
2 miles from Sutton Coldfield on Tamworth road A453.
Parkland course.
18 holes, 6249 yards, S.S.S.70
Club founded in 1932.
Visitors: welcome on weekdays only.
Green fees: £10 (£2.50 with member).
Society meetings: catered for on Tues and Wed only.
Catering: full service except Mon.
Hotels: Moor Hall; Penns Hall.

K30 Moseley

☎ 021-444 2115
Springfield Rd, Kings Heath, Birmingham B14 7DX
On Birmingham ring road, ½ mile E of Alcester Rd.
Parkland course.
18 holes, 6227 yards, S.S.S.70
Club founded in 1892.
Visitors: welcome with member or by introduction.
Green fees: £8.50.
Society meetings: welcome normally on Thurs by arrangement.
Catering: lunches and dinners available daily except Mon.
Hotels: numerous hotels in Birmingham.

K31 North Warwickshire

☎ Meriden (0676) 22259
Hampton Lane, Meriden, W Midlands CV7 7LL
6 miles N of Coventry on A45.
Parkland course.
9 holes, 3181 yards, S.S.S.70
Club founded in 1894.
Visitors: welcome on weekdays, except Thurs (Ladies Day), and with member only at weekends.
Green fees: £6 per 18 holes.
Society meetings: by arrangement.
Catering: not available.
Hotels: Manor, Meriden; Post House, Allesley, Coventry.

K32 North Worcestershire

☎ 021-475 1047
Frankley Beeches Rd, Northfield, Birmingham B31 5LP
Main A38 road to Northfield, turn up Frankley Beeches Rd, then third road on left brings you straight to club.
Meadowland course.
18 holes, 5919 yards, S.S.S.69
Course designed by James Braid.
Club founded in 1907.
Visitors: welcome on weekdays and with members at weekends or Bank Holidays.
Green fees: £8 plus VAT.
Society meetings: welcome any day except Fri.
Catering: full catering facilities at club.
Hotels: Alexander, Bunbury Rd, Northfield; Bunbury, Bunbury Rd, Northfield.

K33 Olton

☎ 021-705 1083
Mirfield Rd, Solihull, W Midlands B91 1JH
7 miles S of Birmingham off A41
Parkland course.
18 holes, 6229 yards, S.S.S.71
Visitors: welcome on weekdays and with member at weekends.
Green fees: £8.50.
Society meetings: by arrangement.
Catering: lunch by arrangement except Mon.
Hotels: St John's, Solihull; George, Solihull.

K34 Oxley Park

☎ Wolverhampton (0902) 25445
Bushbury, Wolverhampton WV10 6DE
Off A449, 1 mile N of Wolverhampton
Parkland course.
18 holes, 6153 yards, S.S.S.69
Visitors: welcome, booking advisable at weekends.
Green fees: weekdays £7.50, weekends £9.
Society meetings: Wed by arrangement.
Catering: bar lunches available, meals on request.
Hotels: Mount; Ravensholt; Park Hall.

K35 Patshull Park

☎ Pattingham (0902) 700100
Burnhill Green, Wolverhampton, W Midlands WV6 7HR
Exit 3 from M54 to Albrighton then signposted Patshull.
Parkland course.
18 holes, 6460 yards, S.S.S.71
Course designed by John Jacobs.
Visitors: welcome weekdays or weekends.
Green fees: weekdays £7, weekends £8.
Society meetings: welcome weekdays and limited number at weekends.
Catering: meals and snacks in hotel.
Hotels: own hotel adjacent.

K36 Penn

☎ Wolverhampton (0902) 341142
Penn Common, Penn, Wolverhampton, W Midlands WV4 5JN
2 miles SW of Wolverhampton off A449.
Heathland course.
18 holes, 6449 yards, S.S.S.71

Club founded in 1908.
Visitors: welcome on weekdays and with member at weekends or Bank Holidays.
Green fees: weekdays £6.
Society meetings: welcome weekdays.
Catering: lunches served except Sun and Mon.
Hotels: Park Hall, Goldthorn Park, Wolverhampton; Goldthorn, Penn Rd, Wolverhampton.

K37 Pype Hayes
☎ 021-351 1014
Eachelhurst Rd, Walmley, Sutton Coldfield, W Midlands B76 8EP
Off M6 at Spaghetti Junction, onto Tyburn Rd, 1 mile to Eaglehurst Rd.
Parkland course.
18 holes, 5811 yards, S.S.S.68
Club founded in 1932.
Visitors: by arrangement with Pro.
Green fees: weekdays £3.20, weekends £3.50.
Society meetings: by arrangement with Pro.
Catering: meals available every day.
Hotels: Sutton Court, 66 Lichfield Rd, Sutton Coldfield.

K38 Robin Hood
☎ 021-706 0061
St Bernards Rd, Solihull, W Midlands B92 7DJ
From Olton station (6 miles S of Birmingham on A41) travel NE up St Bernards Rd for 1 mile, drive to clubhouse on right hand side.
Parkland course.
18 holes, 6609 yards, S.S.S.72
Course designed by H.S. Colt.
Club founded in 1893.
Visitors: welcome on weekdays, excluding Tues mornings and Bank Holidays.
Green fees: weekdays £9.50 (£3 with member).
Society meetings: as for visitors.
Catering: bar snacks available Tues to Fri, evening meals and special requirements by arrangement.
Hotels: George, The Square, Solihull; St Johns Swallow, Warwick Rd, Solihull.

K39 Rose Hill
☎ 021-453 3159
Lickey Hills, Rednal, Birmingham.
M5, exit 4, on city boundary.
Parkland course.
18 holes, 6010 yards, S.S.S.69
Course designed by Carl Bretherton.
Club founded in 1927.
Visitors: welcome.
Green fees: weekdays 18 holes £3.20, 9 holes £2.15; weekends 18 holes £3.50, 9 holes £2.40.
Society meetings: by arrangement.
Catering: snacks served.
Hotels: Rose and Crown.

K40 Sandwell Park
☎ 021-553 4637
Birmingham Rd, West Bromwich, W Midlands B71 4JJ
Junction 1 off M5, ¼ mile from West Bromwich Albion Football Ground.
Parkland, links course.
18 holes, 6470 yards, S.S.S.72
Club founded in 1897.
Visitors: welcome on weekdays only.
Green fees: £8 per round, £10 per day.
Society meetings: welcome weekdays.
Catering: full catering available, except Mon.
Hotels: West Bromwich Moat House.

K41 South Staffordshire
☎ Wolverhampton (0902) 751065
Danescourt Rd, Tettenhall, Wolverhampton WV6 9BQ
3 miles W of Wolverhampton town centre, on A41 to Telford.
Parkland course.

18 holes, 6538 yards, S.S.S.71
Course designed by H.S. Colt.
Club founded in 1893.
Visitors: welcome on weekdays and with member at weekends.
Green fees: £8 per round, £10 per day.
Society meetings: welcome weekdays.
Catering: available on weekdays for visitors and societies.
Hotels: Mount, Tettenhall Wood; Connaught, Tettenhall Rd, Wolverhampton.

K42 Stourbridge

☎ Stourbridge (0384) 395566
Worcester Lane, Pedmore, Stourbridge DY8 2RB
2 miles from Stourbridge town centre on Worcester road.
Parkland course.
18 holes, 6178 yards, S.S.S.69
Club founded in 1892.
Visitors: welcome on weekdays, except Wed before 4 pm, and with member at weekends and Bank Holidays.
Green fees: £8.50 per round or day (£3 with member).
Society meetings: Tues only.
Catering: lunches and evening meals served except Sun and Mon.
Hotels: Pedmore House, Stourbridge.

K43 Sutton Coldfield

☎ 021-353 9633
110 Thornhill Rd, Streetly, Sutton Coldfield B74 3ER
Located 9 miles NE of Birmingham on B4138 road, nearest motorway access is Junction 6 of the M6.
Heathland course.
18 holes, 6541 yards, S.S.S.71
Course re-designed by Dr Mackenzie.
Club founded in 1889.
Visitors: welcome on weekdays and on non-comp. weekends, Ladies Day is Tues.
Green fees: weekdays £8.50 (£3 with member), weekends £10.
Society meetings: Written requests required for parties of 12 or more.
Catering: bar snacks, lunches and evening meals available.
Hotels: Parson and Clerk, Chester Rd, Streetly; Fairlawns, Little Aston Rd, Aldridge; Sutton Court, 66 Lichfield Rd, Sutton Coldfield.

K44 Walsall

☎ Walsall (0922) 613512
The Broadway, Walsall, W Midlands WS1 3EY
1 mile S of Walsall centre, 400 yards from the Crest Motel.
Parkland/meadowland course.
18 holes, 6232 yards, S.S.S.70
Club founded in 1907.
Visitors: welcome on weekdays, but must be with member at weekends.
Green fees: £8.50 (£3.50 with member).
Society meetings: society and company days welcome.
Catering: full service at all times.
Hotels: Crest; Post House; County.

K45 Warley

☎ 021-429 2440
Lightwoods Hill, Warley, W Midlands.
Off A456 4½ miles W of centre of Birmingham, behind Dog Public House.
Parkland course.
9 holes, 2606 yards, S.S.S.64
Visitors: welcome on weekdays.
Green fees: £3 for 18 holes.
Society meetings: not catered for.
Catering: available from 9 am to 4 pm in summer.
Hotels: many on the main Hagley Rd.

L South Wales

Twenty years or so ago, golfers bound for Porthcawl and Southerndown took a rather more circuitous route than they do today although there was little except the lovely countryside to make them tarry. In a golfing sense, this was remote territory and even now Herefordshire has fewer courses than almost any other county in Britain; but in the building explosion of the sixties, Ken Cotton created St Pierre in an old deer park outside Chepstow. At the same time Ross-on-Wye forsook its original nine hole home, and its sheep, for something quite exceptional.

Both clubs always strike a chord with me because they were the first new courses I ever saw built and there could not have been a better or more contrasting initiation. Ross-on-Wye, carved out of rough woodland, still stands as one of the major constructional feats in Britain in modern times. St Pierre is a fine example of a country club, nestling as it does almost within the shadow of the Severn Bridge in the neighbouring county of Monmouthshire.

For around £9,000, the old park at St Pierre, with its many huge trees which have stood for hundreds of years, was converted into a course which its architect modestly maintained made itself. Golfers quickly got to hear of its reputation and its owner and founder, Bill Graham, a man of energy and vision, established one of the most thriving clubs within the historic walls of the old manor house.

The facilities on offer, which include a splendid second course, squash and badminton, are a great tribute to Graham and it was no time at all before St Pierre, so accessible from all parts, was in demand for professional tournaments, notably the old Dunlop Masters; and in 1980 it was honoured by the LGU staging the Curtis Cup there.

From the Severn Bridge, it is possible to be teeing-off at Royal Porthcawl within the hour or sampling the delights of Southerndown on its more lofty perch overlooking acres of undeveloped dune land.

Porthcawl and Southerndown are well enough known not to need anything in the way of recommendation; they are as delightful in their separate ways as is the Newport Club at Rogerstone. The city of Cardiff has a number of clubs and there have been two recent additions at Monmouth and Belmont, Hereford.

L1 Aberdare

☎ Aberdare (0685) 871188
Abernant, Aberdare, Mid Glam CF44 0RY
Through town centre of Aberdare past the General Hospital, ½ mile from town centre.
Meadowland course.
18 holes, 5875 yards, S.S.S.69
Club founded in 1921.
Visitors: welcome at all times.
Green fees: weekdays £5, weekends and Bank Holidays £6.
Society meetings: dates available on application to Sec.
Catering: full à la carte menu and bar snacks available.
Hotels: Black Lion, Aberdare; Baverstocks, Merthyr Tydfil.

L2 Aberystwyth

☎ Aberystwyth (0970) 615104
Brynymor, Aberystwyth, Dyfed
N end of promenade immediately behind sea front hotels, access road adjacent to Cliff Railway, 1 mile from town centre.
Undulating meadowland course.
18 holes, 5735 yards, S.S.S.68
Course designed by Harry Vardon.
Club founded in 1911.
Visitors: welcome.
Green fees: weekdays £6 per day, weekends and Bank Holidays £7.
Society meetings: welcome by arrangement.
Catering: full catering facilities.
Hotels: Belle View Royal, Promenade; Court Royale, Eastgate; Bay, Promenade; Sea Bank, Promenade.

L3 Ashburnham

☎ Burry Port (055 46) 2269 Sec, 2466 Club.
Cliffe Terrace, Burry Port, Dyfed SA16 0HN
9 miles from Llanelli exit on M4, 4 miles from Llanelli on A484.
Championship links course.
18 holes, 7016 yards, S.S.S.74
18 holes, 6646 yards, S.S.S.73/74
Club founded in 1894.
Visitors: welcome on weekdays.
Green fees: weekdays £8 (£6 with member), weekends and Bank Holidays £12 (£10 with member).
Society meetings: welcome weekdays.
Catering: full service except Mon.
Hotels: Ashburnham, Pembrey; Stradley Park, Llanelli; Stepney, Llanelli; Diplomat, Llanelli.

L4 Bargoed

☎ Bargoed (0443) 830143

Heolddu, Bargoed, Mid Glam.
15 miles from Cardiff on A469. Turn left opposite Gwerthonor Hotel; 2nd left at Heolddu Leisure centre.
Undulating parkland course.
18 holes, 6012 yards, S.S.S.70
Visitors: welcome on weekdays, weekends with member only.
Green fees: weekdays £6.50 (£5 with member), weekends £5.
Society meetings: weekdays by arrangement.
Catering: snacks and meals served.
Hotels: Maes Manor, Blackwood.

L5 Blackwood

☎ Blackwood (0495) 223152
Cwmgelli, Blackwood, Gwent.
¾m N of Blackwood on A4048 Tredegar rd.
Meadowland course.
9 holes, 5304 yards, S.S.S.66
Club founded in 1914
Visitors: welcome at all times.
Green fees: weekdays £4, weekends and Bank Holidays £5; ½ price with member.
Society meetings: catered for on weekdays by arrangement.
Catering: golf societies only by arrangement.
Hotels: Maes Manor, Blackwood; Plas Inn, Gordon Rd, Blackwood.

L6 Borth & Ynyslas

☎ Borth (097 081) 202
Borth, Dyfed AY24 5JS
7 miles N of Aberystwyth.
Seaside links course.
18 holes, 6094 yards, S.S.S.70
Club founded in 1885.
Visitors: members welcome.
Green fees: weekdays £6 per day, Ladies £5 per day; weekends and Bank Holidays, July and Aug Men £7 per day, Ladies £6 per day.
Society meetings: by written application to Sec.
Catering: by arrangement with Stewardess.
Hotels: Grand; Golf; Railway; Cliff Haven; all in Borth.

L7 Brecon

☎ Brecon (0874) 2004
Newton Park, Llanfaes, Brecon, Powys LD3 8PA
300 yds from roundabout on by pass S of town.
Meadowland course.
9 holes, 5218 yards, S.S.S.66
Club founded in 1902.
Visitors: welcome.
Green fees: weekdays £3, weekends £4.
Society meetings: by application only.
Catering: no.
Hotels: Bishop's Meadow; Castle of Brecon; Wellington.

L8 Brynhill

☎ Barry (0446) 720277 Sec, 735061 Clubhouse.
Port Rd, Barry, S Glam.
A48 to Culverhouse Cross from Cardiff, then road to Barry, golf club on Port Rd near Colcot Arms Hotel.
Undulating meadowland course.
18 holes, 5511 metres, S.S.S.69
Course designed by G.K. Cotton.
Club founded in 1921.
Visitors: welcome, but with member only on Sun.
Green fees: weekdays £7 (£4 with member), weekends £9 (£6.50 with member).
Society meetings: welcome.
Catering: lunches and dinners, except Mon; book in advance with Stewardess.
Hotels: Barry; International; Mount Sorrel.

L9 Bryn Meadows G & CC

☎ Blackwood (0495) 225590 or 227276
The Bryn, Hengoed, Mid Glam CF8 7SM
A469 15 miles from Cardiff, turn up lane opposite filling station near Crown Hotel.
Parkland course.
18 holes, 5963 yards, S.S.S.69
Course designed by E. Jefferies & B. Mayo.
Club founded in 1973.
Visitors: welcome on weekdays.
Green fees: weekdays £5.50 (£4.50 with member), weekends £8 (£6.50 with member), weekly ticket £23 (£18 with member).
Society meetings: welcome weekdays.
Catering: bar snacks available from Mon to Sat; à la carte meals served from Tues to Sat.
Hotels: Bryn Meadows.

L10 Builth Wells

☎ Builth Wells (0982) 553296
Builth Wells, Powys LD2 3NN
A483 immediately W of Builth Wells.
Parkland course.
18 holes, 5458 yards, S.S.S.67
Club founded in 1923.
Visitors: welcome.
Green fees: from £6 per day.
Society meetings: welcome.
Catering: full service available.
Hotels: Lake, Llangammarch Wells; Lion, Builth Wells; Llanfair, Church St, Builth Wells.

L11 Caerphilly

☎ Caerphilly (0222) 883481
Pencapel, Mountain Rd, Caerphilly, Mid Glam CF8 1HJ
10 minutes from Caerphilly railway and bus stns, 7 miles from Cardiff on A469.
Undulating course.
14 holes, 6063 yards, S.S.S.71
Club founded in 1906.
Visitors: welcome on weekdays and with member at weekends.
Green fees: £7 per round (£4.50 with member).
Society meetings: welcome weekdays.
Catering: full catering facilities.
Hotels: Greenhill, Mountain Rd; Mount, Mountain Rd.

L12 Cardiff

☎ Cardiff (0222) 753320 Sec, 753067 Clubhouse, 754772 Pro.
Sherborne Ave, Cyncoed, Cardiff, S Glam CF2 6SJ
Take A48M off the M4, 3 miles to Pentwyn exit, take industrial road for 2 miles to village, turn left at roundabout and again left at Spar Shop, club 150 yards.
Undulating parkland course.
18 holes, 6016 yards, S.S.S.70
Club founded in 1921.
Visitors: welcome weekdays, with member at weekends, advisable to phone first.
Green fees: £8.50 per day.
Society meetings: catered for on Thurs between April and Oct.
Catering: lunches, evening meals and bar snacks available Mon to Sat.
Hotels: Post House; Inn on the Avenue.

L13 Cardigan

☎ Cardigan (0239) 612035
Gwbert-on-Sea, Cardigan, Dyfed SA43 1PR
3 miles NW of Cardigan, take left fork at Cardigan Cenotaph at N end of town.
Seaside meadowland course.
18 holes, 6207 yards, S.S.S.70
Visitors: welcome at any time.
Green fees: weekdays £6 (£5 with member), weekends and Bank Holidays £7 (£6 with member).
Society meetings: welcome by arrangement with Sec.
Catering: bar snacks and lunches every day except Mon; evening meals by arrangement with Steward.
Hotels: Cliff, Gwbert; Anchor, Gwbert; Black Lion, Cardigan; Angel, Cardigan.

L14 Carmarthen

☎ Conwyl Elfed (0267) 214

Blaenycoed Rd, Carmarthen, Dyfed SA33 6EH
4 miles NW of Carmarthen.
Undulating course.
18 holes, 6212 yards, S.S.S.71
Visitors: welcome.
Green fees: weekdays £5.50, weekends and Bank Holidays £6.50.
Society meetings: welcome by arrangement.
Catering: facilities available except Wed.
Hotels: numerous good hotels in Carmarthen.

L15 Cilgwyn

☎ Llangybi (0570) 45 286
Llangybi, Lampeter, Dyfed SA48 8NN
4 miles NE of Lampeter on A485 in village of Llangybi.
Parkland course.
9 holes, 5318 yards, S.S.S.67
Course designed by Robert Sandow.
Club founded in 1905.
Visitors: welcome.
Green fees: weekdays £5, weekends £6.50; reduction with member.
Society meetings: catered for throughout year.
Catering: restaurant and bar meals available Tues to Sun.
Hotels: Black Lion, High St, Lampeter; Falcondale, Lampeter.

L16 Clyne

☎ Swansea (0792) 401989
Owls Lodge Lane, Mayals, Blackpyl, Swansea SA3 3DR
Coast rd from Swansea to Blackpyl (3 miles); turn right into Mayals Rd.
Moorland course.
18 holes, 6267 yards, S.S.S.71
Course designed by H.S. Colt.
Visitors: welcome.
Green fees: weekdays £7, weekends £8.
Society meetings: Wed and Fri by arrangement.
Catering: meals served, except Mon.
Hotels: Dragon, Swansea; Osbourne, Langland Bay.

L17 Cradoc

☎ Brecon (0874) 3658
Penoyre Park, Cradoc, Brecon, Powys LD3 9LP
2 miles N of Brecon on B4520
Parkland course.
18 holes, 6318 yards, S.S.S.71
Course designed by C.K. Cotton.
Club founded in 1968.
Visitors: welcome at all times, but

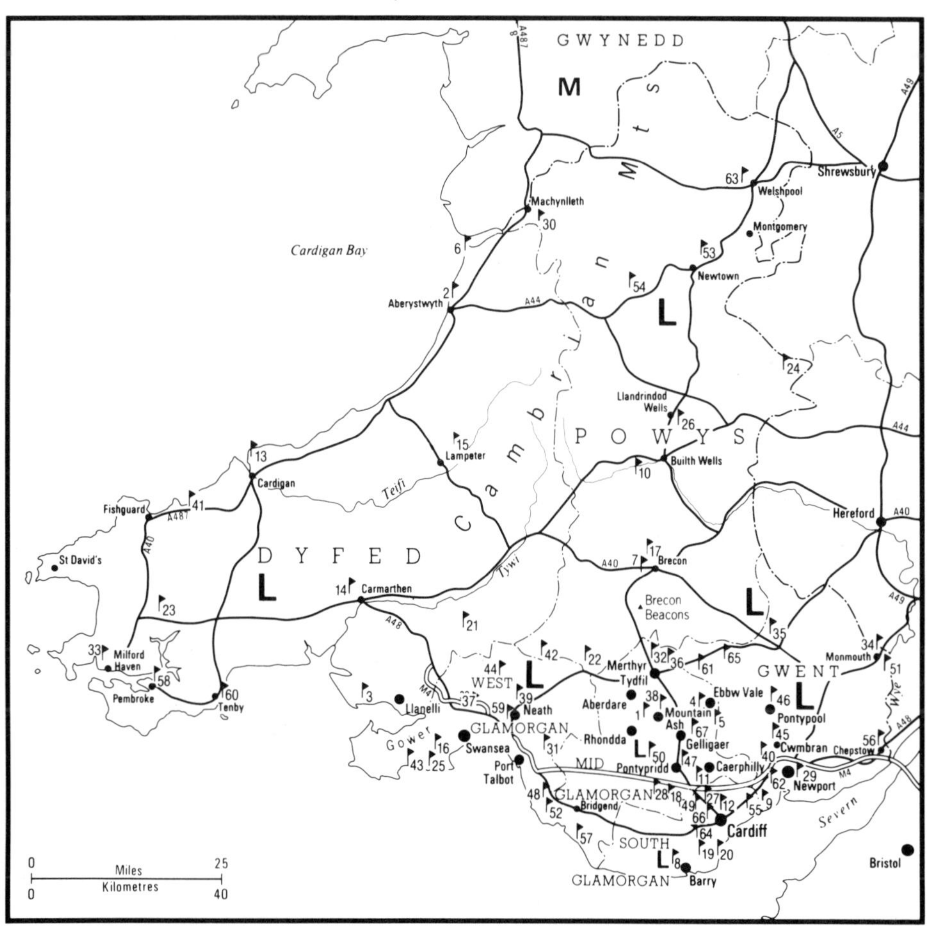

advisable to book with John Stuples, Pro.
Green fees: weekdays £5.50 per day, weekends £8 per day.
Society meetings: catered for on weekdays and at weekends.
Catering: lunches and evening meals served except Mon.
Hotels: Nythfa House, Brecon; Bishops Meadow, Brecon; Wellington, Brecon; Mountains, Libarys, Brecon.

L18 Creigiau

☎ Pentyrch (0222) 890263
Creigiau, Cardiff, S Glam CF4 8NN
4 miles NW of Cardiff towards Llantrisant.
Parkland course.
18 holes, 5736 yards, S.S.S.68
Club founded in 1921.
Visitors: welcome weekdays only.
Green fees: £7 per day (£3.50 with member).
Society meetings: by prior arrangement with Sec/Manager.
Catering: full service except Mon.
Hotels: numerous good hotels in Cardiff.

L19 Dinas Powis

☎ Dinas Powis (0222) 512727
Old Highwalls, Dinas Powis, S Glam CF6 4AJ
On A4055 Cardiff to Barry road.
Parkland course.
18 holes, 5151 yards, S.S.S.66
Club founded in 1914.
Visitors: welcome.
Green fees: weekdays £7, weekends £9.
Society meetings: welcome.
Catering: full catering available.
Hotels: Star, Station Rd, Dinas Powis.

L20 Glamorganshire

☎ Penarth (0222) 701185
Lavernock Rd, Penarth, S Glam CF6 2UP
Take Junction 33 off M4, join A4160 and then A4267 which passes the golf club.
Parkland course.
18 holes, 6150 yards, S.S.S.70
Club founded in 1890.
Green fees: weekdays £7.50, weekends and Bank Holidays £10.
Society meetings: welcome weekdays.
Catering: available at club, preferable to make arrangements in advance.
Hotels: numerous hotels in Cardiff and Barry.

L21 Glynhir

☎ Llandybie (0269) 850472
Glynhir Rd, Llandybie, Ammanford, Dyfed SA18 2TF
1¼ miles from Ammanford on A483 Llandybie road, turn right up Glynhir Rd and continue for almost 2 miles to club.
Undulating parkland/meadowland course.
18 holes, 6090 yards, S.S.S.70
Course designed by F.W. Hawtree.
Club founded in 1964.
Visitors: welcome, but some restriction at weekends.
Green fees: winter (1 Nov to 31 March) weekdays £3, weekends £5; summer (1 April to 31 Oct) weekdays £6, weekends £8.
Society meetings: welcome on weekdays and limited number at weekends.
Catering: full catering facilities.
Hotels: The Mill at Glynhir, Glynhir Rd, Llandybie, Ammanford, Dyfed. This adjoins the course. Cawdon, Llandeilo, Dyfed; Wernolau, Ammanford, Dyfed.

L22 Glynneath

☎ Glynneath (0639) 720452
Penycraig, Pontneathvaughan, Neath, W Glam SA11 5UG
On A4109 10 miles N of Neath.
Hillside course.
12 holes, 5385 yards, S.S.S.67
Club founded in 1931.
Visitors: welcome.
Green fees: weekdays £2.50, weekends £5.
Society meetings: welcome weekdays.
Catering: by arrangement.
Hotels: Plas-y-Felin, Pontwalby, Glynneath.

L23 Haverfordwest

☎ Haverfordwest (0437) 3565
Arnolds Down, Narberth Rd, Haverfordwest, Dyfed SA61 1JB
A40 Carmarthen to Haverfordwest, on right hand side of A40, 1 mile from town.
Undulating meadowland course.
18 holes, 5908 yards, S.S.S.70
Club founded in 1910.
Visitors: welcome.
Green fees: weekdays £5.50, weekends £7.50.
Society meetings: catered for on weekdays and at weekends.
Catering: lunches served except Tues.
Hotels: Mariners, Haverfordwest; County, Haverfordwest; Little Haven, Little Haven; Broad Haven, Broad Haven.

L24 Knighton

☎ Knighton (0547) 528646
The Ffrydd, Knighton, Powys LD7 1EF
½ mile S of Knighton.
Undulating course.
9 holes, 5600 yards, S.S.S.66
Course designed by Harry Vardon.
Club founded in 1913.
Visitors: welcome.
Green fees: weekdays and Sat £3, Sun £5.
Society meetings: no.
Catering: planned by April 1986.
Hotels: Norton Arms, Knighton; Red Lion, Knighton.

L25 Langland Bay

☎ Swansea (0792) 66023
Langland Bay, Swansea, W Glam SA3 4QR
M4 to Swansea, 6 miles W.
Seaside parkland course.
18 holes, 5827 yards, S.S.S.69
Club founded in 1904.
Visitors: welcome, if member of recognised golf club.
Green fees: weekdays £8, weekends and Bank Holidays £9.
Society meetings: welcome if booked in advance, maximum 40.
Catering: bar meals available; cooked meals to be ordered before playing.
Hotels: Osborne, Langland Bay; Caswell Bay, Caswell Bay, Swansea.

L26 Llandrindod Wells

☎ Llandrindod Wells (0597) 2010
Llandrindod Wells, Powys.
Signposted from A483, ½ mile E of town, above lake.
Mountain course.
18 holes, 5749 yards, S.S.S.68
Course designed by Harry Vardon.
Club founded in 1907.
Visitors: welcome at all times.
Green fees: £6 per day.
Society meetings: catered for at all times by prior arrangement .
Catering: lunches and snacks served by arrangement with Steward.
Hotels: Metropole; Commodore, Glen Usk.

L27 Llanishen

☎ Cardiff (0222) 755078
Cwm, Lisvane, Cardiff CF4 5UD
5 miles to N of Cardiff city centre, 1½ miles N of Llanishen church via Heol Hir.
Parkland course.
18 holes, 5296 yards, S.S.S.66
Club founded in 1905.
Visitors: welcome on weekdays, but weekends only with member.
Green fees: £7.
Society meetings: catered for on Thurs, with advance booking.
Catering: full dining facilities available.
Hotels: Phoenix, Llanishen; Cedars.

L28 **Llantrisant & Pontyclun**
☎ Llantrisant (0443) 222148
Lanelay Rd, Talbot Green, Pontyclun, Mid Glam CF7 8HZ
On A4119 10 miles from Cardiff.
Parkland course.
12 holes, 5712 yards, S.S.S.68
Club founded in 1927.
Visitors: welcome on weekdays.
Green fees: £7 (£4 with member).
Society meetings: welcome weekdays.
Catering: lunches served in week; dinner by arrangement.
Hotels: Heronstone, Bridgend; New Inn, Pontypridd; City Inn, Llansannor.

L29 **Llanwern**
☎ Newport (0633) 412029
Golf House, Tenyson Ave, Llanwern, Gwent NP6 2DY
Leave M4 at Junction 24, after ¼ mile turn left into Llanwern village.
Meadowland course.
18 holes, 6202 yards, S.S.S.70
9 holes, 5674 yards.
Club founded in 1928.
Visitors: welcome on weekdays (jacket and tie to be worn in evenings).
Green fees: £8 per day.
Society meetings: by arrangement.
Catering: full facilities available.
Hotels: Ladbroke Mercury.

L30 **Machynlleth**
☎ Machynlleth (0654) 2000
Newtown Rd, Machynlleth, Powys.
½ mile from Machynlleth on A489 to Newtown.
Undulating course.
9 holes, 5734 yards, S.S.S.67
Course designed by James Braid.
Club founded in 1907.
Green fees: weekdays £4, weekends and Bank Holidays £4.50.
Society meetings: not catered for.
Catering: no facilities for catering.
Hotels: Wynstan, Machynlleth; Plas Dolgudg, Machynlleth.

L31 **Maesteg**
☎ Maesteg (0656) 732037
Mount Pleasant, Neath Rd, Maesteg, Mid Glam.
Adjacent to main Maesteg to Port Talbot road.
Moorland course.
18 holes, 5845 yards, S.S.S.69
Club founded in 1912.
Visitors: welcome.
Society meetings: agreement.
Catering: lunches and evening meals.
Hotels: hotels in area.

L32 **Merthyr Tydfil**
☎ Merthyr Tydfil (0685) 3308
Cilsanws, Cefn Coed, Merthyr Tydfil, Mid Glam.
Off the Heads of the Valley road A465 at Cefn Coed.
Mountain course.
9 holes, 5794 yards, S.S.S.68
Club founded in 1908.
Visitors: welcome.
Green fees: weekdays £3, weekends £5.
Society meetings: welcome weekdays.
Catering: snacks and bar meals served.
Hotels: Baverstocks; Tregenna.

L33 **Milford Haven**
☎ Milford Haven (064 62) 2368
Woodbine House, Hubberston. Milford Haven.
Clubhouse situated ¾ mile from town centre to W.
Meadowland course.
18 holes, 6158 yards, S.S.S.70
Course designed by D. Snell.
Visitors: welcome at all times.
Green fees: £5 for day.
Society meetings: by arrangement.
Catering: meals and snacks available at most times.
Hotels: Little Haven, Little Haven; Sir Benfro, Herbrandston, Milford Haven.

L34 **Monmouth**
☎ Monmouth (0600) 2212
Leasebrook Lane, Monmouth, Gwent.
1 mile along A40 Monmouth to Ross road.
Parkland course.
9 holes, 5454 yards, S.S.S.66
Club founded in 1921.
Visitors: welcome at all times except Sun mornings.
Green fees: weekdays £5 per day, weekends and Bank Holidays £7 per day.
Society meetings: welcome by arrangement.
Catering: meals served except Mon.
Hotels: Leasebrook CTR; Kings Head.

L35 **Monmouthshire**
☎ Abergavenny (0873) 3171 Club, 2606 Sec, 2532 Pro.
Llanfoist, Abergavenny, Gwent NP7 9HE
M4 to Newport then A4042, take road to Llanfoist between Llanfoist and Llanellen.
Meadowland course.
18 holes, 6045 yards, S.S.S.69
Course designed by James Braid.
Club founded in 1892.
Visitors: welcome on weekdays and with member at weekends.
Green fees: weekdays £7.50, weekends and Bank Holidays £11.
Society meetings: by arrangement on Mon and Fri only.
Catering: full catering except on Tues when only bar snacks available.
Hotels: Angel, Abergavenny; Llanwenarth Arms.

L36 **Morlais Castle**
☎ Merthyr (0685) 2822
Pant, Dowlais, Merthyr Tydfil, Mid Glam CF48 2UY
Follow signs for Brecon Mountain Railway.
Moorland course.
9 holes, 3129 yards, S.S.S.70.
Club founded in 1900.
Visitors: welcome except on Sat afternoons.
Green fees: £4 (£3 with member).
Catering: lunches or evening meals served every day.
Hotels: Castle, Merthyr Tydfil; Baverstocks, Swansea Rd, Merthyr Tydfil.

L37 **Morriston**
☎ Swansea (0792) 71079, 72335 Pro, 796528 Sec.
160 Clasemont Rd, Morriston, Swansea, West Glam SA6 6AJ
3 miles N of Swansea city centre on A4067, then ½ mile W along A40.
Parkland course.
18 holes, 5722 yards, S.S.S.68
Club founded in 1919.
Visitors: welcome but advisable to contact Sec during summer.
Green fees: weekdays £5 plus VAT, weekends and Bank Holidays £6 plus VAT; 25% reduction with member.
Society meetings: by arrangement.
Catering: lunches or snacks served most days except Mon.
Hotels: Dragon; Dolphin.

L38 **Mountain Ash**
☎ Mountain Ash (0443) 472265
Cefnpennar, Mountain Ash, Mid Glam CF45 4ES
A470 to Abercynon, then A4059 to Mountain Ash.
Mountain course.
18 holes, 5485 yards, S.S.S.68
Club founded in 1908.
Visitors: welcome.
Green fees: weekdays £5.50, weekends and Bank Holidays £7.50.
Society meetings: by arrangement.
Catering: available every day except Mon.
Hotels: Baverstock's, Aberdare; Thorne, Abercynon.

L39 **Neath**
☎ Neath (0639) 3615
Cadoxton, Neath, West Glam SA10 7AH
3 miles from Neath, opposite Cadexton Church.

Mountain course.
18 holes, 6436 yards, S.S.S.72
Course designed by James Braid.
Club founded in 1934.
Visitors: welcome.
Green fees: weekdays £5, weekends and Bank Holidays £6.
Society meetings: welcome, apply in writing to Sec.
Catering: service from bar snacks to à la carte meals available, except Mon.
Hotels: Glynclydach.

L40 Newport

☎ Newport (0633) 892643
Great Oak, Rogerstone, Newport, Gwent NR1 6FX
From M4 junction 27 take B4691 (signposted Highcross), after 1¼ miles turn right at Vixen Garage.
Undulating parkland course.
18 holes, 6370 yards, S.S.S.71
Club founded in 1903.
Visitors: welcome on weekdays and with member at weekends.
Green fees: weekdays £8.50 (£4.50 with member), weekends and Bank Holidays £11 (£5.50 with member).
Society meetings: catered for on Wed, Thurs and Fri.
Catering: lunches and dinners by arrangement, except Tues.
Hotels: Harris, Chepstow Rd, Newport.

L41 Newport (Pembs)

☎ Newport (0239) 820244
Newport, Dyfed SA42 0NR
Follow signs to Newport Sands from Newport.
Seaside course.
9 holes, 6178 yards (for 18), S.S.S.69
Club founded in 1925.
Visitors: welcome.
Green fees: £5.50.
Society meetings: by arrangement.
Catering: snacks served.
Hotels: Golden Lion, Newport; Fishguard

L42 Palleg

☎ Glantawe (0639) 842524
Palleg Rd, Lower Cwmtwrch, Swansea
15 miles N of Swansea on Brecon road A4067, turn left at Aubrey Arms roundabout, course is 1 mile from here.
Undulating meadowland/moorland course.
9 holes, 3260 yards, S.S.S.72
Course designed by C.K. Cotton.
Club founded in 1930.
Visitors: welcome except during major competitions.
Green fees: weekdays £3, weekends £5; half-price with member.
Society meetings: welcome except on Bank Holidays.
Catering: by arrangement, except Mon.
Hotels: Ganafon; Abercrave Inn.

L43 Pennard

☎ Bishopton (044 128) 3131
2 Southgate Rd, Southgate, Swansea, West Glam SA3 2BT
8 miles W of Swansea on B4436.
Undulating seaside course.
18 holes, 6266 yards, S.S.S.71
Club founded in 1908.
Visitors: welcome.
Green fees: weekdays £7, weekends and Bank Holidays £8.
Society meetings: welcome including most weekends.
Catering: bar snacks available; lunches and evening meals by arrangement.
Hotels: numerous hotels in Swansea.

L44 Pontardawe

☎ Pontardawe (0792) 863.18
Cefn Llan, Pontardawe, Swansea.
4 miles N of M4 on A4067.
Meadowland course.
18 holes, 6061 yards, S.S.S.69
Club founded in 1924.
Visitors: welcome.
Green fees: weekdays £4.50, weekends £7.
Society meetings: weekdays and Sun by arrangement.
Catering: meals served, except Mon.
Hotels: Glanafon County, Pontardawe.

L45 Pontnewydd

☎ Cwmbran (063 33) 2170
West Pontnewydd, Cwmbran, Gwent NP4 4AR
Follow signs for West Pontnewydd or Upper Cwmbran, 2 miles N of Cwmbran.
Meadowland course.
10 holes, S.S.S.67
Club founded in 1875.
Visitors: welcome on weekdays, and with member at weekends or Bank Holidays.
Green fees: £6.
Catering: meals available lunchtime and evening except Mon.
Hotels: Parkway Cwmbran; Cwmbran Centre; Somerton; Commodore.

L46 Pontypool

☎ Pontypool (049 55) 3655
Trevethin, Pontypool, Gwent NP4 8DJ
1 mile N of town centre.
Undulating parkland, moorland course.
18 holes, 6058 yards, S.S.S.69
Club founded in 1903.
Visitors: welcome, advisable to phone at weekends.
Green fees: weekdays £6 per day, weekends and Bank Holidays £7 per day.
Society meetings: welcome except Sat.
Catering: full service available every day.
Hotels: Commodore; Conifers.

L47 Pontypridd

☎ Pontypridd (0443) 402359
Ty-Gwyn, The Common, Pontypridd, Mid Glam.
9 miles from Cardiff, take A470 N to Pontypridd and Merthyr
Undulating mountain course.
18 holes, 5420 yards, S.S.S.68
Course designed by Bradbeer.
Club founded in 1905.
Visitors: welcome.
Green fees: weekdays £4.50 (£3.50 with member), weekends and Bank Holidays £5.50.
Society meetings: welcome weekdays.
Catering: meals available during licensing hours, except Thurs.
Hotels: any hotels in Cardiff.

L48 Pyle & Kenfig

☎ Porthcawl (065 671) 3093
Wawn-y-Mer, Kenfig, Mid Glam CF33 4PU
Leave M4 at Junction 37, follow Porthcawl
Seaside links course.
18 holes, 6640 yards, S.S.S.73
Club founded in 1922.
Visitors: welcome on weekdays and with member only on Sun and Bank Holidays.
Green fees: £8 per round or day (£5 with member).
Society meetings: welcome.
Catering: meals and bar snacks
Hotels: Maid of Sker, Nottage; Rose and Crown, Nottage; Fairways; Atlantic; Seabank; all 3 in West Drive, Porthcawl.

L49 Radyr

☎ Radyr (0222) 842408 Manager, 842476 Pro, 842442 Members.
Drysgol Rd, Radyr, Cardiff CF4 8BS
Off A470 at Taffs Well.
Parkland course.
18 holes, 6031 yards, S.S.S.70 Summer
18 holes, 5616 yards, S.S.S.68 Winter
Club founded in 1902.
Visitors: welcome (proof of handicap may be asked for).
Green fees: weekdays £8, weekends £10.
Society meetings: catered for on Wed and Fri.
Catering: meals served except Thurs.
Hotels: numerous hotels in Cardiff.

L50 Rhondda

☎ Tonypandy (0443) 433204
Pontygwaitn, Ferndale, Rhondda, Mid

Glam CF43 3PW
On Cardiff to Rhondda rd 3m from Porth.
Mountain top course.
18 holes, 6428 yards, S.S.S.70
Club founded in 1904/1910.
Visitors: welcome, Sat and Sun am with member.
Green fees: £6.
Society meetings: by arrangement.
Catering: meals except Mon, preferably ordered before play.
Hotels: Dunraven; Gordon.

L51 The Rolls of Monmouth

☎ Monmouth (0600) 5353
The Hendre, Monmouth, Gwent MP5 4HG
3¼ miles W of Monmouth on B4233 (Abergavenny Rd).
Undulating parkland course.
18 holes, 6723 yards, S.S.S.72
Course designed by Urbis Planning Design Group.
Club founded in 1982.
Visitors: welcome any time.
Green fees: £10.50 per day (£7.50 with member).
Society meetings: welcome any day.
Catering: full catering or snacks
Hotels: King's Head, Monmouth; Priory, Skenfrith; Pilgrim, Much Birch.

L52 Royal Porthcawl

☎ Porthcawl (065 671) 2251
Porthcawl, Mid Glam CF36 3UW
Leave M4 at Junction 37 winding through A4283 to reach Porthcawl via South Cornelly and Nottage.
Heathland, downland course.
Championship course 18 holes, 6605 yards, S.S.S.74
Course designed by Charles Gibson
Club founded in 1891.
Visitors: welcome with introduction of member or club Sec.
Green fees: weekdays £10, weekends and Bank Holidays £12.
Society meetings: by arrangement.
Catering: lunches and teas available; evening meals by arrangement.
Hotels: Atlantic; Seabank; Fairways; Maid of Sker; Seaways.

L53 St Giles

☎ Newtown (0686) 25844
Pool Rd, Newtown, Powys SY16 3AJ
1 mile to E of Newtown on main Welshpool to Newtown road, A483.
Undulating parkland course.
9 holes, 5864 yards, S.S.S.68
Club founded around 1910.
Visitors: welcome at all times.
Green fees: weekdays £4 per day, weekends and Bank Holidays £5 per day.
Society meetings: catered for with advance booking.
Catering: lunches, evening meals and snacks served except Mon.
Hotels: Elephant and Castle, Newtown; Bear, Newtown; Dolforwyn Hall, Caersws.

L54 St Idloes

☎ Llanidloes (055 12) 2559
Pen-Rhallt, Llanidloes, Powys
Off A492 to A407 for 1 mile.
Hillside, slightly undulating course.
9 holes, 5320 yards, S.S.S.66
Visitors: welcome.
Green fees: weekdays £3, weekends £4, weekly £12.
Society meetings: by appointment.
Catering: by appointment.
Hotels: Lloyds; Trewythen Arms.

L55 St Mellons

☎ Castleton (0633) 680408 Sec, 680101 Pro, 680401 Club.
St Mellons, Cardiff, Gwent CF3 8XS
On A48 between Newport and Cardiff on left, follow yellow sign for St Mellons C.C.
Parkland course.
18 holes, 6250 yards, S.S.S.70
Visitors: welcome on weekdays and with member at weekends.
Green fees: £8 per day.
Society meetings: by arrangement
Catering: meals served.
Hotels: Wentloog Castle; St Mellons C.C.

L56 St Pierre G & C C

☎ Chepstow (029 12) 5261
St Pierre Park, Chepstow, Gwent NP6 6YA
On A48, 1 mile from Chepstow roundabout.
Old course, parkland; new course, meadowland.
Old 18 holes, 6619 yards, S.S.S.72
New 18 holes, 5757 yards, S.S.S.69
Old Course designed by C.K. Cotton, New by Bill Cox.
Club founded in 1964.
Visitors: welcome with reservation.
Green fees: weekdays old course £13, new £9, both £17; weekends, old course £16, new £11, both £18.50.
Society meetings: welcome weekdays.
Catering: 2 restaurants and coffee shop.
Hotels: available at club.

L57 Southerndown

☎ Southerndown (0656) 880326 Club, 880476 Office.
Ewenny, Bridgend, Mid Glam CF35 5BT
4 miles from Bridgend on A48 from Cardiff to Swansea, in Ogmore-by-Sea; turn off at Pelican Inn.
Downland course.
18 holes, 6615 yards, S.S.S.73
Club founded in 1905.
Visitors: welcome except for Bank Holidays.
Green fees: weekdays £7.50 (£4 with member), weekends £11 (£6 with member).
Society meetings: catered for normally on Tues and Thurs.
Catering: lunches served except Mon.
Hotels: Sealawns, Ogmore-by-Sea; Craig-yr-Eos, Ogmore-by Sea.

L58 South Pembrokeshire

☎ Pembroke (0646) 683817
Defensible Barracks, Pembroke Dock, Dyfed.
1½ miles S of Hobbs Point at W end of A477, ½ from Pembroke Dock.
Seaside parkland course.
9 holes, 5804 yards, S.S.S.69
Club founded in 1969.
Visitors: welcome at any times.
Green fees: £4 per day (Juniors £2), weekly (Mon to Fri) £10.
Society meetings: by arrangement
Catering: full catering available.
Hotels: Cleddau Bridge, Pembroke Dock; Bush, Pembroke Dock.

L59 Swansea Bay

☎ Skewen (0792) 814153
Jersey Marine, Neath, West Glam SA10 6JP
Just off main A48 road between Neath and Swansea.
Links course.
18 holes, 6302 yards, S.S.S.70
Club founded in 1892.
Visitors: welcome.
Green fees: weekdays £5 (£4 with member), weekends and Bank Holidays £6.50 (£5.50 with member).
Society meetings: catered for.
Catering: meals served except on Wed.
Hotels: Dragon, Kingsway, Swansea.

L60 Tenby

☎ Tenby (0834) 2978
The Burrows, Tenby, Dyfed SA70 7NP
A40 from Carmarthen to St Clears, then A477 on W of Tenby town centre.
Links course.
18 holes, 6232 yards, S.S.S.71
Club founded in 1888.
Visitors: welcome.
Green fees: weekdays £7.50 per day, weekends and Bank Holidays £8.50 per day (reduced rates Oct 1 to March 31); reductions for Juniors.
Society meetings: catered for.
Catering: snacks available during bar hours, other meals by arrangement.
Hotels: Kinloch Court; Royal Lion.

L61 **Tredegar & Rhymney**
☎ Rhymney (0685) 840743
Cwmtysswg, Rhymney, Mid Glam.
B4256 1½ miles from Rhymney
Undulating mountain course.
9 holes, 2865 yards, S.S.S.67
Club founded in 1921.
Visitors: welcome.
Green fees: £4 (£2 with member).
Society meetings: welcome weekdays.
Catering: by arrangement
Hotels: Castle, Castle St, Tredegar.

L62 **Tredegar Park**
☎ Newport (0633) 894433
Bassaleg Rd, Newport, Gwent NP9 3PX
Leave M4 at Junction 27, to Newport, first right in Western Ave.
Parkland course.
18 holes, 6044 yards, S.S.S.70
Course designed by James Braid.
Club founded in 1912.
Visitors: welcome on production of own club membership card or handicap
Green fees: weekdays £8, weekends and Bank Holidays £10.
Society meetings: welcome weekdays.
Catering: lunches and evening meals served except Mon.
Hotels: Celtic Manor, The Coldra, Newport; Westgate, Commercial St.

L63 **Welshpool**
☎ Castle Caereinion (0938) 249, 337 Sec.
Y Golfa, Welshpool, Powys.
4 miles from Welshpool on A458.
Mountain course.
18 holes, 5708 yards, S.S.S.69
Course designed by James Braid.
Club founded in 1922.
Visitors: welcome.
Green fees: £4, £5, subject to review.
Society meetings: welcome by arrangement.
Catering: meals except Mon.
Hotels: Royal Oak.

L64 **Wenvoe Castle**
☎ Cardiff (0222) 594371 Sec, 593649 Pro.
Wenvoe, Cardiff CF5 6BE
A48 W from Cardiff, left after 3 miles onto A4050, course 2 miles on right.
Parkland course.
18 holes, 6411 yards, S.S.S.71
Club founded in 1936.
Visitors: welcome with member or on production of recognised club card.
Society meetings: catered for on Mon, Thurs and Fri.
Catering: lunch and dinners available except Tues.
Hotels: several in Cardiff.

L65 **West Monmouthshire**
☎ Brynmawr (0495) 310233
Pond Rd, Nantyglo, Gwent NP3 4JX
Turn off A467 at Dunlop Semtex Ltd, signposted.
Mountain course.
18 holes, 6097 yards, S.S.S.69
Club founded in 1909.
Visitors: welcome.
Green fees: weekdays £4, weekends and Bank Holidays £5.
Society meetings: welcome.
Catering: full service available.
Hotels: Griffin, Brynmawr.

L66 **Whitchurch**
☎ Cardiff (0222) 620985
Pantmawr Rd, Whitchurch, Cardiff, S Glam CF4 6XD
Off M4 at Exit 32, 500 yds S on A470, filter left at lights to meet club entrance.
Parkland course.
18 holes, 6245 yards, S.S.S.70
Course re-designed by James Braid (1934).
Club founded in 1915.
Visitors: full members of golf clubs with current handicap welcome.
Green fees: weekdays £8 per day, weekends and Bank Holidays £10.
Society meetings: catered for on Thurs,

minimum 24.
Catering: full service available every day.
Hotels: Cedars, Llanishen, Cardiff.

L67 **Whitehall**
☎ Abercynon (0443) 740245
Nelson, Treharris, Mid Glam.
Take Treharris and Nelson exit at roundabout on A470, turn right and head S for ¼ mile, take first left turning up Mountain Rd.
Mountain course.
9 holes, 5750 yards, S.S.S.68
Club founded in 1922.
Visitors: welcome on weekdays and with member at weekends.
Green fees: weekdays £3, weekends £5.
Society meetings: no.
Catering: lunches and dinners served by arrangement.
Hotels: Castle, Merthyr.

M North Wales

M1 Aberdovey

☎ Aberdovey (0654) 72210
Aberdovey, Gwynedd LL35 0RT
On A493, adjoining Aberdovey station.
Championship links course.
18 holes, 6456 yards, S.S.S.71
Course designed by James Braid.
Club founded in 1892.
Visitors: welcome.
Green fees: weekdays £8.50 per day, weekends £10.
Society meetings: by arrangement.
Catering: full meal service.
Hotels: Trefeddian, Aberdovey; Plaspenhelyg, Aberdovey; Bodfor, Aberdovey.

M2 Abergele & Pensarn

☎ Abergele (0745) 824034
Tan-y-Goppa Rd, Abergele, Clwyd.
Through the market town of Abergele from A55, turn left after passing through town in direction of Llanddulas.
Parkland course.
18 holes, 6086 yards, S.S.S.69
Course designed by Hawtree and Son.
Club founded in 1910.
Visitors: welcome.
Green fees: weekdays £6, weekends £8.
Society meetings: welcome weekdays.
Catering: snacks, lunches, table d'hôte and à la carte meals available.
Hotels: Yo, Colwyn Bay; Kinmel Manor, Abergele; Rhos Abbey, Rhos-on-Sea.

M3 Abersoch

☎ Abersoch (075881) 2622
Pwllheli, Gwynedd LL53 7EY
6 miles from Pwllheli; beyond village turn left into Golf Rd.
Links course.
9 holes, 5792 yards, S.S.S.68
Course designed by Harry Vardon.
Club founded in 1910.
Visitors: welcome.
Green fees: on application.
Society meetings: by arrangement.
Catering: meals served.
Hotels: Egryn; Wylsa; Riverside.

M4 Anglesey

☎ Rhosneigr (0407) 810219
Station Rd, Rhosneigr, Gwynedd LL64 5QT
Left off A5 about 8 miles from Holyhead.
Seaside course.
18 holes, 5573 metres, S.S.S.69
Club founded in 1911.
Visitors: welcome.
Green fees: weekdays £5, weekends £6.
Society meetings: by arrangement.
Catering: meals served.
Hotels: Maelog Lake; Rhoslan.

M5 Bala

☎ Bala (0678) 520359
Penlan, Bala, Gwynedd LL23 7SR
A494, first right out of Bala for Dolgellau towards lake.
Mountainous course.
10 holes, 4934 yards, S.S.S.64
Club founded in 1928.
Visitors: welcome.
Green fees: weekdays £5 per day, weekends and Bank Holidays £7.
Society meetings: none.
Catering: by arrangement only.
Hotels: White Lion Royal, High St, Bala; Pras Coch, High St, Bala.

M6 Baron Hill

☎ Beaumaris (0248) 810231
Beaumaris, Gwynedd LL58 8YN
Signposted from Beaumaris, ¾ mile from town centre.

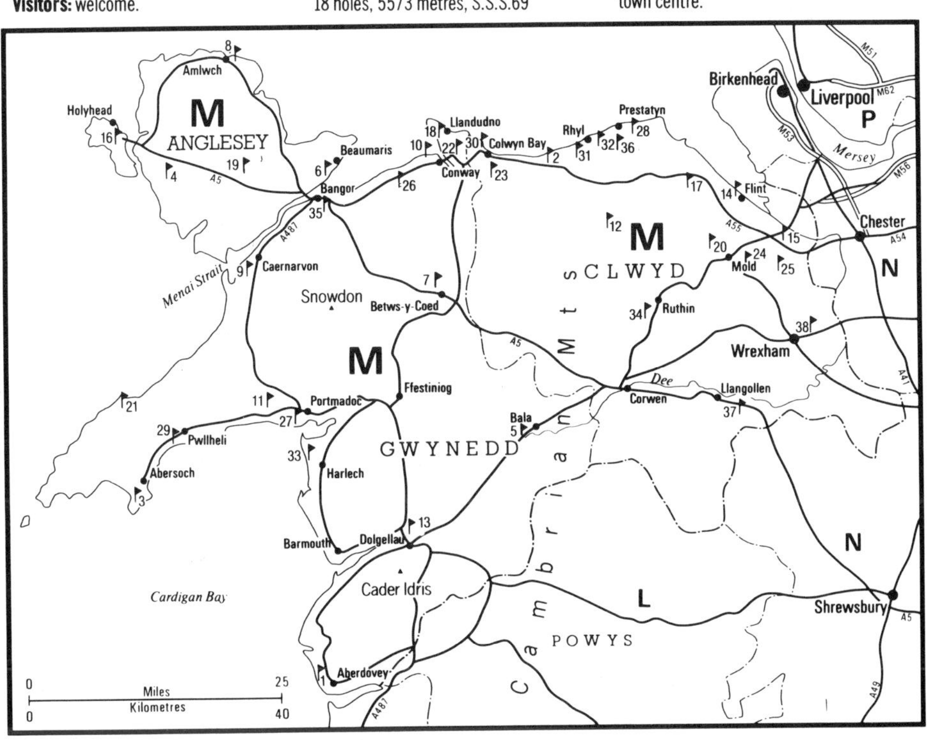

Undulating seaside course.
9 holes, 5564 yards, S.S.S.67
Club founded in 1895.
Visitors: welcome.
Green fees: weekdays £5, weekends and Bank holidays £6; weekly ticket £20.
Society meetings: welcome on application to Hon Sec.
Catering: light snacks and sandwiches.
Hotels: Henllys Hall, Beaumaris; Bulkeley Arms, Beaumaris; Bishopgate House, Beaumaris; Liverpool Arms, Beaumaris.

M7 Betws-y-Coed
☎ Betws-y-Coed (069 02) 556
Betws-y-Coed, Gwynedd.
Just off main A5 road in the middle of village of Betws-y-Coed.
Parkland course.
18 holes, 4996 yards, S.S.S.64
Club founded in 1974.
Visitors: welcome.
Green fees: weekdays £5, weekends and Bank Holidays £7.
Society meetings: welcome.
Catering: lunches, coffee and evening meals served.
Hotels: large number of first class hotels and boarding houses in the village.

M8 Bull Bay
☎ Amlwch (0407) 830213
Bull Bay Rd, Amlwch, Anglesey LL68 9RY
A5025 15 miles from Menai Bridge.
Undulating seaside course.
18 holes, 6160 yards, S.S.S.70
Course designed by Herbert Fowler.
Club founded in 1913.
Visitors: welcome.
Green fees: April to Oct weekdays £5, weekends £7, Nov to March £3 per day.
Society meetings: welcome.
Catering: bar snacks and meals served except Tues.
Hotels: Bull Bay; Trecastell; Gadlys.

M9 Caernarfon
☎ Caernarfon (0284) 3783
Llanfaglan, Caernarfon, Gwynedd
2½ miles S of town along the Menai Straits.
Parkland course.
18 holes, 5859 yards, S.S.S.69
Club founded in 1908.
Visitors: welcome.
Green fees: £5 per day.
Society meetings: by arrangement.
Catering: snacks available.
Hotels: Royal; The Stables, Llanwnda; Black Bay; Menai Caravan Park.

M10 Conwy (Caernarvonshire)
☎ Conwy (049 263) 2423 Sec, 3400 Club, 3225 Pro.
Morfa, Conwy, Gwynedd.
From Conwy, A55 to Bangor, down Morfa Drive over cattle grid, clubhouse 300 yards on left.
Championship links course.
18 holes, 6901 yards, S.S.S.73
Club founded in 1890.
Visitors: welcome except on major competition days.
Green fees: weekdays £6.50, weekends and Bank Holidays £8, weekly (5 days) £19.50.
Society meetings: by arrangement.
Catering: full catering except Tues.
Hotels: Bryn Cregin Garden, Deganwy; Castle, High St, Conwy; Park Hall, Bangor Rd, Conwy.

M11 Criccieth
☎ Criccieth (076 671) 2154
Ednyfed Hill, Criccieth, Gwynedd
A497, 4 miles from Portmadoc, turn right past Memorial Hall, ½ mile up hill.
Undulating hilltop course.
18 holes, 5787 yards, S.S.S.68
Club founded around 1904.
Visitors: welcome.
Green fees: £5.
Society meetings: welcome.
Catering: meals and snacks served by arrangement with Steward.
Hotels: George IV.

M12 Denbigh
☎ Denbigh (074 571) 4159 (coin box)
Henllan Rd, Denbigh, Clwyd
B5382 Denbigh to Henllan road, 1 mile out of Denbigh.
Undulating parkland course.
18 holes, 5650 yards, S.S.S.67.
Club founded in 1923.
Visitors: welcome.
Green fees: weekdays £5, weekends and Bank Holidays £7.
Society meetings: welcome, write to Match Sec.
Catering: by written application.
Hotels: Bryn Morfydd, Llanrhaeadr, Denbigh; Bull, Denbigh; Oriel House, St Asaph.

M13 Dolgellau
☎ Dolgellau (0341) 422603
Pencefn Rd, Dolgellau, Gwynedd LL40 1SL
Turn off the town by-pass onto the old A494 road, turn right 25 yds past top of main bridge, signposted from there on. Approx. ½ mile from town centre.
Parkland course.
Course played twice with alternate tees.
9 holes, 4662 yards, S.S.S.62
Club founded in 1911.
Visitors: welcome.
Green fees: £6 per day including weekends. £25 per week. Green fees reviewed in April.
Society meetings: catered for – must be booked with Steward.
Catering: bar and catering facilities available.
Hotels: Royal Ship; Golden Lion Royal.

M14 Flint
☎ Flint (035 26) 2327
Cornist Park, Flint, Clwyd CH6 5HJ
About 1 mile from A548 coast road, turn right at Town Hall, follow signs to Cornist Park.
Parkland course.
9 holes, 5829 yards, S.S.S.68
Club founded in 1966.
Visitors: welcome on weekdays and with member at weekends.
Green fees: £2.50 per day.
Society meetings: welcome on weekdays by arrangement.
Catering: available if previously ordered.
Hotels: Springfield; Pentre Halkyh.

M15 Hawarden
☎ Hawarden (0244) 531447
Groomsdale Lane, Hawarden, Deeside, Clwyd CH5 3EH
A55 9 miles W of Chester, first left after Hawarden station.
Parkland course.
9 holes, 5735 yards, S.S.S.68
Club founded in 1911.
Visitors: welcome on weekdays, with member only.
Green fees: £2.
Society meetings: by arrangement only.
Catering: full service available.
Hotels: numerous good hotels in Chester.

M16 Holyhead
☎ Holyhead (0407) 3279
Trearddur Bay, Anglesey, Gwynedd LL65 2YG
Follow A5 from Bangor, turn left at Valley traffic lights, through Trearddur Bay, on right hand side.
Undulating course.
18 holes, 5540 metres, S.S.S.70
Club founded in 1920.
Visitors: welcome.
Green fees: weekdays £7, weekends and Bank Holidays £8.
Society meetings: welcome.
Catering: lunch, tea and dinner served.
Hotels: Beach; Trearddur; Dormy House.

M17 Holywell
☎ Holywell (0352) 710040
Brynford, Holywell, Clwyd.
Turn left at traffic lights on A55 from Chester at Holywell, then proceed 1 mile to crossroads, turn right at Brynford, signpost to Pantasaph.
Moorland course.
9 holes, 6484 yards, S.S.S.71

Club founded in 1906.
Visitors: welcome except on comp. days.
Green fees: weekdays £4, weekends £5.
Society meetings: catered for on weekdays.
Catering: lunch and evening meals served if booked in advance.
Hotels: Miners Arms; Fielding Arms.

M18 Llandudno

☎ Llandudno (0492) 76450
Hospital Rd, Llandudno, Gwynedd LL30 1HU
Alongside the main Llandudno Hospital, approximately 1 mile from town centre.
Seaside parkland course.
18 holes, 6513 yards, S.S.S.72
Course designed by Tom Jones.
Club founded in 1915.
Visitors: welcome any day provided member of recognised golf club.
Green fees: weekdays £6.50 per day (£2 with member), weekly (5 days) £25; weekends and Bank Holidays £7.50 (£2 with member).
Society meetings: catered for by arrangement with Sec.
Catering: lunches and evening meals served except Mon.
Hotels: numerous good hotels in area.

M19 Llangefni (Public)

☎ Llangefni (0248) 722193
Llangefni, Anglesey, N Wales.
A5 to Llangefni.
9 holes, 2000 yards, S.S.S.28
Course designed by Hawtree & Son.
Club founded in 1983.
Visitors: welcome, hire clubs available.
Green fees: £1.15 per round weekdays, £1.70 weekends (½ price for OAPs and Juniors).
Society meetings: none.
Catering: none.
Hotels: Bull, Llangefni.

M20 Mold

☎ Mold (0352) 740318
Pantymwyn, Mold, Clwyd.
3 miles from Mold; leave on the Denbigh road, turn left at the Clegg Arms, turn right at the T-junction and club is 2½ miles on left.
Undulating parkland course.
18 holes, 5521 yards, S.S.S.67
Club founded in 1909.
Visitors: welcome.
Green fees: weekdays £4 per day, weekends and Bank Holidays £6 per day.
Society meetings: welcome by arrangement.
Catering: bar snacks at any time; full catering by arrangement.
Hotels: Bryn Howell, Mold; Dolphin, Mold; Chequers, Northop.

M21 Nefyn & District

☎ Nefyn (0758) 720218
Morfa Nefyn, Pwllheli, Gwynedd LL53 6DA
1 mile W of Nefyn.
Seaside course.
18 holes, 6335 yards, S.S.S.71
Club founded in 1907.
Visitors: members of recognised golf clubs welcome.
Green fees: weekdays £6.50, weekends and Bank Holidays £8.
Society meetings: by prior arrangement with Sec.
Catering: full facilities available.
Hotels: Caeau Capel; Woodlands Hall; Linksway; Erw Goch.

M22 North Wales

☎ Llandudno (0492) 75325
Bryniau Rd, West Shore, Llandudno, Gwynedd
½ mile from town centre.
Seaside links course.
18 holes, 6132 yards, S.S.S.69
Club founded in 1890.
Visitors: welcome.
Green fees: weekdays £7, weekends £8, weekly ticket (Mon to Fri) £25.
Society meetings: catered for all year.
Catering: full catering daily except Tues.
Hotels: numerous good hotels in area.

M23 Old Colwyn

☎ Colwyn Bay (0492) 515581
Woodland Ave, Old Colwyn, Clwyd LL29 9NL
200 yards off A55 in Old Colwyn, turn into Boddelwyddan Ave between chapel and M and K Garage.
Undulating meadowland course.
9 holes, 5800 yards, S.S.S.66
Club founded in 1907.
Visitors: welcome except on Sat afternoons and on Tues and Wed evenings.
Green fees: weekdays £3, weekends and Bank Holidays £4; ½ price with member.
Society meetings: by arrangement except Sat.
Catering: dinner available on weekdays and lunch or dinner at weekends by arrangement with Stewardess.
Hotels: Lyndale; 70°.

M24 Old Padeswood

☎ Buckley (0244) 547401
Station Rd, Padeswood, Mold, Clwyd CH7 4JL
2½ miles S of Mold, 8 miles W of Chester on A5118.
Meadowland course.
18 holes, 6728 yards, S.S.S.72
Course designed by Arthur Joseph.
Club founded in 1933.
Visitors: welcome on weekdays and at weekends, except on competition days.
Green fees: weekdays £5 (£4 with member), weekends and Bank Holidays £6 (£5 with member).
Society meetings: welcome by arrangement.
Catering: bar snacks available and meals for groups by arrangement.
Hotels: Bryn Awel, Denbigh Rd, Mold.

M25 Padeswood & Buckley

☎ Buckley (0244) 542537 Office, 543636 Pro and Members
The Caia, Station Lane, Padeswood, Mold Clwyd CH7 4JD
Off A5118, 3 miles E of Mold, 2 miles S of Buckley; 2nd club on right.
Parkland/meadowland course.
18 holes.
Club founded in 1933.
Visitors: welcome on weekdays before 9 am until 4.30 pm; on Sun permission of Captain required in advance.
Green fees: weekdays £5 (£2.50 with member), weekends £7.50 (£5 with member), Juniors half-price.
Society meetings: welcome weekdays.
Catering: snacks, lunches and evening meals except Mon and Tues.
Hotels: The Druid; The Arches; Chequers.

M26 Penmaenmawr

☎ Penmaenmawr (0492) 623330
Conway Old Rd, Penmaenmawr, Gwynedd LL34 6RD
Main A55 from Conway to Penmaenmawr turn left at Mountain View Hotel along Conway Old Rd for 1 mile.
Undulating parkland course.
9 holes, 5031 yards, S.S.S.65
Club founded in 1910.
Visitors: welcome.
Green fees: weekdays £3.50 per day (£2 with member), weekends and Bank Holidays £6; £15 for 1 week, £27 for 2 weeks, £37 for 4 weeks.
Society meetings: welcome.
Catering: meals and snacks to order.
Hotels: Sychnant Pass, Conway; Mountain View, Penmaenmawr.

M27 Portmadoc

☎ Portmadoc (0776) 2037
Morfa Bychan, Portmadoc, Gwynedd LL49 9UU
1½ miles from Portmadoc, take road to Morfa Bychan.
Seaside course.
18 holes, 5838 yards, S.S.S.68
Visitors: welcome.
Green fees: weekdays £5, weekends £6.
Society meetings: by arrangement.
Catering: meals and snacks served.
Hotels: Royal Sportsman; Tyddyn Llwyn.

M28 Prestatyn

☎ Prestatyn (0745) 4320
Marine Rd East, Prestatyn, Clwyd

Follow A548 coast road to Prestatyn, cross railway bridge and turn right at Pontins Prestatyn Sands.
Seaside course.
18 holes, 6713 yards, S.S.S.72
Course designed by S. Collins.
Club founded in 1905.
Visitors: welcome daily except Sat.
Green fees: weekdays £6, weekends and Bank Holidays £8, half-price with member.
Society meetings: welcome on weekdays and Sun.
Catering: full service available.
Hotels: Grand; Bryn Gwalia, Gronant Rd, Prestatyn.

M29 Pwllheli

☎ Pwllheli (0758) 612520
Golf Rd, Pwllheli, Gwynedd LL53 5PS
Turn into Cardiff Rd in town centre; bear right at first fork.
Seaside parkland course.
18 holes, 6110 yards, S.S.S.69
Club founded in 1900.
Visitors: welcome.
Green fees: on application.
Society meetings: welcome.
Catering: full catering service.
Hotels: Bron Eifion Country House, Criccieth; Tower, Pwllheli; Riverside, Abersoch.

M30 Rhos-on-Sea

☎ Llandudno (0492) 49100 or 49641
Penrhyn Bay, Llandudno, Gwynedd LL30 3PU
Between Colwyn Bay and Llandudno on promenade.
Undulating seaside course.
18 holes, 6064 yards, S.S.S.69
Club founded in 1899.
Visitors: welcome.
Green fees: on application.
Society meetings: welcome.
Catering: on request.
Hotels: residential (on site)

M31 Rhuddlan

☎ Rhuddlan (0745) 590217
Meliden Rd, Rhuddlan, Clwyd.
On A525, 1 mile S of Rhyl.
Parkland course.
18 holes, 6045 yards, S.S.S.69
Club founded in 1930.
Visitors: welcome.
Green fees: Mon to Sat £6, Sun and Bank Holidays £8; half-price with member.
Society meetings: welcome, except Tues or at weekends from April to Sept.
Catering: lunches and dinners served except Mon.
Hotels: numerous hotels in Rhyl.

M32 Rhyl

☎ Rhyl (0745) 53171
Coast Rd, Rhyl, Clwyd.
1 mile from station on A548 to Prestatyn.
Seaside course.
9 holes, 6057 yards, S.S.S.69
Club founded in 1890.
Visitors: welcome.
Green fees: weekdays £3.50, weekends £4.50.
Society meetings: by arrangement.
Catering: bar snacks, lunches served except Mon.
Hotels: Westminster; Marina; Grange.

M33 Royal St David's

☎ Harlech (0766) 780203 Club, 780361 Sec.
Harlech, Gwynedd LL46 2UB
Between Barmouth and Portmadoc, on A496.
Seaside course.
18 holes, 6495 yards, S.S.S.72
Club founded in 1894.
Visitors: by arrangement with Sec or Pro.
Green fees: weekdays £8 per day, weekends and Bank Holidays £11 per day.
Society meetings: by arrangement with Sec or Pro.
Catering: meals served.
Hotels: St Davids, Harlech; Maes-y-Nevadd, Talsarnau, Harlech.

M34 Ruthin Pwllglas

☎ Ruthin (082 42) 2296
Ruthin Pwllglas, Ruthin, Clwyd.
2½ miles S of Ruthin in A494, right fork before Pwllglas village.
Parkland/moorland course.
9 holes, 5306 yards, S.S.S.66
Course designed by David Lloyd Rees.
Club founded in 1906.
Visitors: welcome.
Green fees: weekdays £3.50 (£2.50 with member), weekends and Bank Holidays £5 (£4 with member).
Society meetings: on application.
Catering: none.
Hotels: Ruthin Castle.

M35 St Deiniol

☎ Bangor (0248) 353098
Bangor, Gwynedd LL57 1PX
Off A5 on E outskirts of Bangor, at top of Beach Rd, overlooking Penrhyn Harbour, turn left and immediately left again up a hill, golf club signposted.
Undulating parkland course.
18 holes, 5545 yards, S.S.S.67
Course designed by James Braid.
Club founded in 1906.
Visitors: welcome at all times.
Green fees: weekdays £4 (£2 with member), weekends £5 (£2.50 with member).
Society meetings: catered for mainly on weekdays but by special arrangement at weekends.
Catering: lunches and bar snacks available during bar hours.
Hotels: British, Bangor; Castle, Bangor.

M36 St Melyd

☎ Prestatyn (074 56) 4405 or 88858 Pro.
The Paddock, Prestatyn LL19 9NB
Situated between Prestatyn and Meliden village on main road A547.
Undulating meadowland course.
9 holes, 5805 yards, S.S.S.68
Club founded in 1922.
Visitors: welcome on weekdays.
Green fees: weekdays £5 per day, weekends £6 per day; half-price for Juniors.
Society meetings: always welcome but subject to prior arrangement.
Catering: full service except Tues.
Hotels: Pontins Holiday Village; Grand; Nant Hall; Bryn Gwalia.

M37 Vale of Llangollen

☎ Llangollen (0978) 860040
Llangollen, Clwyd LL20 7PR
On A5 1 mile S of Llangollen.
Parkland course.
18 holes, 6617 yards, S.S.S.72
Visitors: welcome.
Green fees: weekdays £6.50, weekends and Bank Holidays £8.
Society meetings: catered for.
Catering: full catering available.
Hotels: Hand; Bryn Howel; Royal; Tyn y Wern; all in Llangollen.

M38 Wrexham

☎ Wrexham (0978) 364268, 261033 or 351476
Holt Rd, Wrexham, Clwyd LL13 9SB
Situated on A534 2 miles E of Wrexham.
Undulating sandy course.
18 holes, 6137 yards, S.S.S.69
Course designed by James Braid.
Club founded in 1907.
Visitors: welcome except on competition days.
Green fees: on request.
Society meetings: catered for on Mon and Fri.
Catering: full service daily except Thurs.
Hotels: Cross Lanes, Marchwiel, Wrexham; Holt Lodge, Holt Rd., Wrexham; Wynstay, Wrexham.

N Cheshire, Staffordshire, Shropshire, Derbyshire

This is a section offering a mighty contrast in the golf. Apart from the seaside tradition of Royal Liverpool, the oldest club by far in Cheshire (or should it be Wirral or Merseyside?), Cheshire is largely flat, green and leafy. Derbyshire, on the other hand, undulates considerably. Shropshire is perhaps a mixture of the two while Staffordshire contains more attraction than you might expect of a county with an industrial heart.

Of the courses on the Wirral peninsula, Royal Liverpool takes pride of place. Wallasey, home of Dr Frank Stableford and his points system, has some fine, bold dunes while Caldy enjoys some holes along the shores of the Dee Estuary with marvellous views of North Wales.

To the east of Chester, I can speak highly of Delamere Forest and Sandiway and, crossing over the M6, a round at Mere, Wilmslow or Prestbury is always rewarding. Before the days of the M6, the journey to Hoylake took you up close to Shrewsbury with thought of a round at Hawkstone Park which has earned extra notoriety by producing an Open champion in Sandy Lyle. With a fine hotel to accompany two 18 hole courses, it is one of the best courses in Shropshire. Staffordshire were a playing force in the land a few years ago, their players owing their prowess to playing on courses like Little Aston, Whittington Barracks, Beau Desert and Trentham.

Players in Derbyshire are not quite so lucky. I fear my knowledge of golf there is not as complete as it should be, but I can speak well of Burton-on-Trent and Matlock, and I hear good things of Kedleston Park, Cavendish and Sickleholme.

N1 Alderley Edge

☎ Wilmslow (0625) 585583
Brook Lane, Alderley Edge, Cheshire SK9 7RU
From Alderley Edge, turn left off A34 opposite Tower Garage, towards Mobberley/Knutsford
Undulating parkland course.
9 holes, 5839 yards, S.S.S.68
Course designed by T.G. Renouf
Club founded in 1907.
Visitors: welcome except on Tues and Sat.
Green fees: weekdays £6.50, (£3 with member), weekends and Bank Holidays £8 (£4 with member).
Society meetings: welcome Thurs only.
Catering: available except Mon.
Hotels: De Trafford Arms, Alderley Edge; Mottram Hall, Mottram St Andrew.

N2 Alfreton

☎ Alfreton (0773) 832070
Highfields, Wingfield Rd, Oakerthorpe, Derbys DE5 7DH
Take the Matlock road out of Alfreton, about ¾ mile.
Parkland course.
9 holes, 5012 yards, S.S.S.65
Club founded in 1893.
Visitors: welcome Tues to Fri; with member only weekends and Mon.
Green fees: £6 per round, £7.50 per day.
Society meetings: welcome.
Catering: meals served except Mon.
Hotels: Swallow, South Normanton.

N3 Allestree Park

☎ Derby (0332) 550616
Allestree Hall, Allestree, Derby.
Leave Derby on A6, 4 miles from city centre, signposted Allestree Park.
Undulating parkland course.
18 holes, 5749 yards, S.S.S.68
Club founded in 1940.
Visitors: welcome at all times, except for competition Sun mornings.
Green fees: weekdays £3 per round, weekends £3.50 per round.
Society meetings: welcome.
Catering: available by prior arrangement.
Hotels: Clovelly, Kedleston Rd, Derby.

N4 Ashbourne

☎ Ashbourne (0335) 42078
Clifton, Ashbourne, Derbyshire.
1 mile S of Ashbourne on A515 to Sudbury and Lichfield.
Undulating parkland course.
9 holes, 5359 yards, S.S.S.66
Course designed by Frank Pennink.
Club founded in 1910.
Visitors: welcome on weekdays; ring in advance for availability at weekends.
Green fees: weekdays £3, Sun and Bank Holidays £5.
Society meetings: small parties welcome.
Catering: by arrangement with Steward.
Hotels: Cock Inn, Clifton; Clifton Hall, Clifton; Green March, Ashbourne.

N5 Astbury

☎ Congleton (0260) 272772
Peel Lane, Astbury, Congleton, Cheshire CW12 4RE
On the outskirts of Congleton, reached by leaving A34 Congleton to Newcastle road at Astbury village.

Meadowland course.
18 holes, 6269 yards, S.S.S.70
Club founded in 1925.
Visitors: members of recognised golf clubs welcome.
Green fees: £7 per day.
Society meetings: catered for on Thurs only by arrangement.
Catering: by arrangement except Tues.
Hotels: Bulls Head, Mill St, Congleton; Lion and Swan, Swan Bank, Congleton.

N6 Bakewell

☎ Bakewell (062 981) 2307
Station Rd, Bakewell, Derbys DE4 1GB
¾ mile from Bakewell Square cross bridge over River Wye on A619 Sheffield to Chesterfield road, left up Station Rd and after a third of a mile turn right before Industrial Estate.
Hilly parkland course.
9 holes, 4808 yards, S.S.S.64
Course designed by George Low.
Club founded in 1899.
Visitors: welcome, with some restrictions on Sun mornings.
Green fees: weekdays £6 (£3 with member), weekends and Bank Holidays £10 (£5 with member).
Society meetings: catered for on weekdays, by arrangement.
Catering: meals served except Mon (Oct 1 to March 31) or Tues (April 1 to Sept 30).
Hotels: Rutland Arms, The Square, Bakewell.

N7 Beau Desert

☎ Hednesford (054 38) 2626 or 2492 Pro.
Hazel Slade, Hednesford, Cannock, Staffs WS12 5PT
Take A460 from Cannock through Hednesford, right at traffic lights, signposted Hazel Slade, and next left.
Moorland course.
18 holes, 6285 yards, S.S.S.71
Club founded in 1921.
Visitors: welcome but check with Pro at weekends.
Green fees: weekdays £9, weekends £12.
Society meetings: welcome weekdays.
Catering: full catering facilities.
Hotels: Cedar Tree, Rugeley.

N8 Birchwood

☎ Padgate (0925) 818819
Kelvin Close, Risley, Warrington, Cheshire.
M62, junction 11; follow A574 for Risley/Birchwood (entrance opposite Data-General).
Parkland course.
18 holes, 6666 yards, S.S.S.72
Course designed by T.J. McAuley.
Club founded in 1979.
Visitors: welcome.
Green fees: weekdays £7, weekends £10.
Society meetings: welcome (restricted times).
Catering: full meals available.

N9 Branston

☎ Burton-on-Trent (0283) 43207
Burton Rd, Branston, Burton-on-Trent DE14 3DP
Take A5121 off the A38 towards Burton-on-Trent, pass church on right, over railway bridge, pass petrol station on right, entrance to club 200 yards on right.
Undulating course.
18 holes, 6458 yards, S.S.S.71
Club founded in 1976.
Visitors: welcome any time; booking necessary at weekends.
Green fees: weekdays £6.50 per day, weekends £7.50 per day.
Society meetings: weekdays only.
Catering: lunch served except Mon; evening meals by arrangement.
Hotels: Riverside, Branston.

N10 Breadsall Priory G & CC

☎ Derby (0332) 832235
Moor Rd, Morley, Derby.
3 miles NE of Derby off A61, towards Breadsall, turn left into Rectory Lane and right onto Moor Rd.
Undulating parkland course.
18 holes, 6402 yards, S.S.S.71
Course designed by David Cox, John Flanders and Richard Lambert.
Club founded in 1977.
Visitors: welcome by appointment.
Green fees: weekdays £7.50, weekends and Bank Holidays £10.
Society meetings: welcome by appointment.
Catering: full bar and catering services.
Hotels: Breadsall Priory.

N11 Bridgnorth

☎ Bridgnorth (0742) 3315
Stanley Lane, Bridgnorth, Shropshire WV16 4SF
Through High St, along Broseley Rd for some 400 yards, right into Stanley Ln.
Parkland course.
18 holes, 6673 yards, S.S.S.72
Club founded in 1889.
Visitors: welcome.
Green fees: weekdays £7, weekends £9.
Society meetings: welcome weekdays.
Catering: snacks, lunches and dinners served except Mon.
Hotels: Falcon; Parlors Hall; Croft; Commercial.

N12 Brocton Hall

☎ Stafford (0785) 662627
Brocton, Stafford ST17 0TH
4 miles S of Stafford on A34, turn left at crossroads signposted Brocton, club entrance 300 yards on left.
Parkland course.
18 holes, 6095 yards, S.S.S.69
Course designed by Harry Vardon.
Club founded in 1923.
Visitors: members of recognised golf club with handicap certificate welcome.
Green fees: weekdays £9, weekends and Bank Holidays £10.50.
Society meetings: catered for on Tues and Thurs, if members of recognised golf club with handicap certificate.
Catering: luncheons and evening meals available by reservation with Caterers.
Hotels: Tillington Hall, Eccleshall Rd, Stafford.

N13 Burslem

☎ Stoke-on-Trent (0782) 87006
Wood Farm, High Lane, Tunstall.
2 miles N of Hanley, sit. on High Lane.
Moorland course.
11 holes, 5584 yards, S.S.S.67
Club founded in 1907.
Visitors: welcome on weekdays and with member on Sat.
Green fees: £5 (£2 with member), Bank Holidays £6.
Society meetings: by application.
Catering: meals by prior arrangement with Steward.
Hotels: Grand, Hanley; George, Burslem.

N14 Burton-on-Trent

☎ Burton-on-Trent (0283) 44551 Office, 68708 Clubhouse
43 Ashby Rd East, Burton-on-Trent DE15 0PS
A50 from Burton to Ashby 3 miles.
Meadowland course.
18 holes, 6555 yards, S.S.S.71
Club founded in 1894.
Visitors: welcome on weekdays and with member at weekends or Bank Holidays.
Green fees: weekdays £8.50 (£3 with member), weekends and Bank Holidays £10.50.
Society meetings: welcome on weekdays.
Catering: snacks available except Mon and à la carte meals on request.
Hotels: Stanhope Arms, Ashby Rd, Burton-on-Trent.

N15 **Buxton & High Peak**
☎ Buxton (0298) 3453
Fairfield, Buxton, Derbys.
1 mile from Buxton station on A6.
Meadowland course.
18 holes, 5954 yards, S.S.S.69
Club founded in 1887.
Visitors: welcome.
Green fees: weekdays £8, weekends £10.
Society meetings: by arrangement.
Catering: meals served.
Hotels: Hawthorn Farm Guest House; St Anne's; Palace, Buxton.

N16 **Cavendish**
☎ Buxton (0298) 3494 or 5052 Pro.
Gadley Lane, Buxton, Derbys SK17 6XD
¾ mile from town centre going W on A53 St John's Rd to Leek, right on Carlisle Rd, then left on Watford Rd.
Parkland/downland course.
18 holes, 5815 yards, S.S.S.68
Course designed by Dr Alistair Mackenzie.
Club founded in 1925.
Visitors: welcome.
Green fees: weekdays £6, weekends £8; half-price with member.
Society meetings: catered for on weekdays and some weekends by arrangement with Pro.
Catering: snacks available at all times and meals by prior arrangement.
Hotels: Lee Wood; Buckingham; Portland; Egerton.

N17 **Chapel-en-le-Frith**
☎ Chapel (0298) 812118 Clubhouse, 813943 Sec.
The Cockyard, Manchester Rd, Chapel-en-le-Frith, Stockport, Cheshire SK12 6UH
A6 from Stockport through Disley and Whaley Bridge turn left at second set of traffic lights in Whaley Bridge and continue on A6 for 2 miles, club is on left side of A6, almost opposite Hanging Gate Public House.
Meadowland course.
18 holes, 6065 yards, S.S.S.69
Club founded in 1906.
Visitors: welcome.
Green fees: weekdays £5.50 (£3 with member), weekends and Bank Holidays £6.50 (£3 with member).
Society meetings: welcome but only by prior arrangement.
Catering: morning coffee, light lunches and dinners served.
Hotels: Leewood, Manchester Rd, Buxton; St Annes, The Crescent, Buxton; Palace, Palace Rd, Buxton.

N18 **Chester**
☎ Chester (0244) 677760
Curzon Park North, Chester CH4 8AR
1 mile from centre of Chester, off A55,

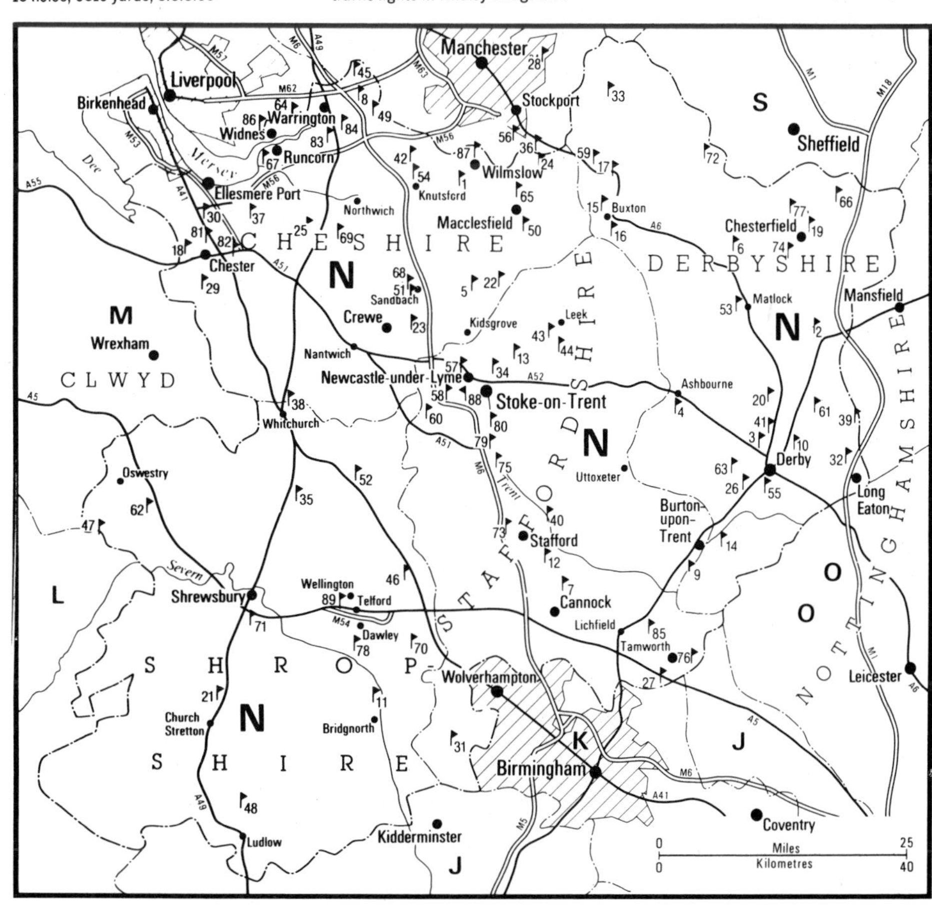

course located behind Chester Racecourse.
Parkland course.
18 holes, 6487 yards, S.S.S.71
Club founded in 1901.
Visitors: by arrangement.
Green fees: weekdays £7, weekends £8.50.
Society meetings: by arrangement.
Catering: full catering facilities.
Hotels: Grosvenor, Chester; Pied Bull, Chester.

N19 Chesterfield

☎ Chesterfield (0246) 79256
Walton, Chesterfield, Derbyshire S42 7LA
2m from town centre on Matlock rd A632.
Parkland course.
18 holes, 6326 yards, S.S.S.70
Club founded in 1909.
Visitors: welcome on weekdays.
Green fees: weekdays £7.50 per round, £10 per day (£2 with member).
Society meetings: catered for on weekdays if booked in advance.
Catering: lunches and dinners every day.
Hotels: Chesterfield, Corporation St; Portland, West Bars.

N20 Chevin

☎ Derby (0332) 841864
Golf Lane, Duffield, Derby DE6 4EE
5 miles N of Derby on A6.
Undulating parkland/moorland course.
18 holes, 6043 yards, S.S.S.69
Club founded in 1894.
Visitors: welcome on weekdays and with member at weekends.
Green fees: £9 per round or day.
Society meetings: welcome except Mon.
Catering: meals served except Mon.
Hotels: Kedleston; Strutt Arms, Milford.

N21 Church Stretton

☎ Church Stretton (0694) 722281
Trevor Hill, Church Stretton, Shropshire SY6 7AA
½ mile off A49 W of town.
Undulating moorland course.
18 holes, 5008 yards, S.S.S.65
Course designed by James Braid.
Club founded in 1898.
Visitors: welcome except on competition days, usually Sun in season.
Green fees: weekdays £4, weekends £6.
Society meetings: by arrangement with Hon Sec (0694 722633)
Catering: by arrangement.
Hotels: Denehurst, Shrewsbury Rd; Sandford, Watling St; Longmynd, Cunnery Rd.

N22 Congleton

☎ Congleton (0260) 273540
Biddulph Rd, Congleton, Cheshire SW12 3LZ
1 mile SE of Congleton Station on main Congleton to Biddulph road A527.
Parkland course.
9 holes, 5055 yards, S.S.S.65
Club founded in 1898.
Visitors: welcome except Sun morning and Sat afternoon; ring for details of competition weekends.
Society meetings: welcome on Mon by prior arrangement.
Catering: snacks and meals to order.
Hotels: Lion and Swan, Congleton; Bulls Head, Congleton.

N23 Crewe

☎ Crewe (0270) 585032 Pro, 584099 Sec, 584227 Steward.
Fields Rd, Haslington, Crewe, Cheshire CW1 1TB
1 mile S of A534 at Haslington, between Crewe and Sandbach.
Parkland/meadowland course.
18 holes, 6277 yards, S.S.S.70
Club founded in 1911.
Visitors: welcome on weekdays (Ladies Day Thurs) and with member at weekends.
Green fees: £8 per day, £7 after 12.30 (£3 with member).
Society meetings: by prior arrangement on Tues.
Catering: bar snacks, lunches and dinners served.
Hotels: Crewe Arms, Crewe; Saxon Cross, Sandbach; Lamb, Nantwich.

N24 Davenport

☎ Stockport (0625) 877321 Clubhouse, 877319 Pro.
Worth Hall, Middlewood Rd, Higher Poynton, Stockport SK12 1TS
From Stockport take A6 to Rising Sun at Hazel Grove, then take A523 Macclesfield road, at Poynton traffic lights turn left into Park Lane, club is approx. 1½m.
Undulating parkland course.
18 holes, 6006 yards, S.S.S.69
Course designed by Fraser Middleton.
Club founded in 1913.
Visitors: welcome except Sun before 10 am; on Wed and Sat (competition days) by arrangement with Pro.
Green fees: weekdays £8 per day, weekends £10 per day, half-price with member.
Society meetings: welcome on Thurs or Tues by arrangement with Sec.
Catering: full catering available, but prior notice must be given to Steward.
Hotels: Alma Lodge, Stockport.

N25 Delamere Forest

☎ Sandway (0606) 882807
Station Rd, Delamere, Northwich, Cheshire CW8 2JE
From A556 Manchester to Chester road take B5152 towards Frodsum; the lane to club is on right, approximately 1 mile from A556, immediately by Delamere station.
Undulating heathland course.
18 holes, 6287 yards, S.S.S.70
Course designed by Herbert Fowler.
Club founded in 1910.
Visitors: welcome (2 balls only at weekends).
Green fees: weekdays £8, weekends £10.
Society meetings: large parties, maximum 76, catered for on Tues and Thurs; small parties catered for on Wed.
Catering: bar snacks available and other meals by arrangement except Fri.
Hotels: Oaklands, Weaverham; Hartford Hall, Northwich; Woodpecker, Northwich; Swan, Tarporley.

N26 Derby

☎ Derby (0332) 766323
Shakespeare St, Sinfin, Derby DE2 9HD
1 mile off A5111 at Normanton.
Parkland municipal course.
18 holes, 6183 yards, S.S.S.69
Club founded in 1923.
Visitors: welcome.
Green fees: weekdays £2.50, weekends and Bank Holidays £3.30.
Society meetings: catered for by arrangement on weekdays.
Catering: meals available every day.
Hotels: numerous hotels in Derby.

N27 Drayton Park

☎ Tamworth (0827) 251139 Club, 251478 Pro.
Drayton Park, Tamworth, Staffs B78 3TN
2 miles S of Tamworth on A4091.
Parkland course.
18 holes, 6240 yards, S.S.S.71
Course designed by James Braid.
Club founded in 1897.
Visitors: welcome on weekdays only, booking required.
Green fees: as applicable.
Society meetings: established and bona fide Societies welcome on Tues and Thurs.
Catering: full catering facilities available, advance booking for Societies.
Hotels: Gungate, Tamworth.

N28 Dukinfield

☎ 061-338 2340
Yew Tree Lane, Dukinfield, Cheshire SK16 5DF
From Ashton Rd 1 mile then right into Yew Tree Lane, club 1 mile on right, on hill behind Senior Service Factory.
Hillside course.
18 holes, 5544 yards, S.S.S.67
Club founded in 1913.
Visitors: welcome on weekdays except Wed afternoons.
Green fees: £6 (£3 with member).
Society meetings: by arrangement with Sec.
Catering: meals by prior arrangement with Stewardess except Mon.
Hotels: York House, Ashton-under-Lyne.

N29 Eaton

☎ Chester (0244) 674385
Eaton Park, Eccleston, Chester.
About 2 miles S of Chester on A483 Wrexham road.
Parkland course.
18 holes, 6446 yards, S.S.S.71
Visitors: welcome on weekdays by arrangement.
Green fees: weekdays £8 (£4 with member), weekends £10 (£5 with member).
Society meetings: welcome weekdays.
Catering: lunches served except Mon.
Hotels: Grosvenor, Chester; Post House, Wrexham Rd, Chester.

N30 Ellesmere

☎ 061-790 2122
Clubhouse, 790 8591 Pro.
Old Clough Lane, Worsley, Manchester M28 5HZ
5 miles W of Manchester, on A580, adjacent to Junction 14 on M62.
Undulating parkland course.
18 holes, 5957 yards, S.S.S.69
Club founded in 1913.
Visitors: members of recognised golf club welcome by arrangement with Pro, except during club competitions.
Green fees: weekdays £6.50 (£2.75 with member), weekends and Bank Holidays £7.50 (£3.25 with member).
Society meetings: catered for on weekdays; apply in writing to Hon Sec.
Catering: facilities available at all times, by prior arrangement with Steward's wife.
Hotels: numerous hotels in Manchester.

N31 Enville

☎ Kinver (0384) 872074 Sec and Manager, 872551 Club, 872585 Pro.
Highgate Common, Enville, Stourbridge, W Midlands DY7 5BN
Off A458 Bridgnorth road, past Fox Inn and turn right to Halfpenny Green airport.
Moorland course
Highgate 18 holes, 6541 yards, S.S.S.72
Ledge 18 holes, 6207 yards, S.S.S.70
Club founded in 1935.
Visitors: welcome on weekdays and with member at weekends.
Green fees: £10 per day (£3.50 with member).
Society meetings: by arrangement a year in advance if poss. weekdays only.
Catering: full catering except Mon.
Hotels: Anchor, Kinver.

N32 Erewash Valley

☎ Ilkeston (0602) 322984
Stanton-by-Dale, Ilkeston, Derbys.
From M1 Junction 25 follow signs to Stanton Ironworks Co. Ltd., through Sandiacre.
Meadowland/parkland course.
18 holes, 6444 yards, S.S.S.72
Club founded in 1905.
Visitors: welcome on weekdays.
Green fees: weekdays £7.50 per day (£3 with member), weekends and Bank Holidays £9 per day (£4 with member).
Society meetings: welcome by arrangement.
Catering: lunches served; dinners by arrangement with Steward.
Hotels: Post House, Sandiacre; Novotel, Sandiacre.

N33 Glossop & District

☎ Glossop (045 74) 3117
Hurst Lane, off Sheffield Rd, Glossop, Derbys SK13 8RH
1 mile out of town on A57 Sheffield road.
Moorland course.
11 holes, 5726 yards, S.S.S.68
Club founded in 1895.
Visitors: welcome.
Green fees: £5 per round.
Society meetings: welcome.
Catering: meals served by arrangement.
Hotels: Hurst Lee Guest House.

N34 Greenway Hall

☎ Stockton Brook (0782) 503158
Stockton Brook, Stoke-on-Trent ST9 9LI
Off A53 Stoke to Leek road, approximately 5 miles from Stoke.
Meadowland course.
18 holes, 5676 yards, S.S.S.67
Club founded in 1908.
Visitors: welcome with member only.
Green fees: £4.
Society meetings: by appointment only.
Catering: by prior arrangement with Steward.
Hotels: many good hotels in area.

N35 Hawkstone Park Hotel

☎ Lee Brockhurst (093 924) 611
Weston, Shrewsbury SY4 5UY
Junction 4 M54, easy access M6.
Parkland courses 2 x 18 hole.
Hawkstone 18 holes, 6203 yards, S.S.S.71
Weston 18 holes, 5063 yards, S.S.S.66
Visitors: welcome.
Green fees: from £6.
Society meetings: minimum 12 persons, from £5.50.
Catering: snacks and full meals.
Hotels: own hotel on premises.

N36 Hazel Grove

☎ 061-483 3217 Clubhouse, 7272 Pro.
Buxton Rd, Hazel Grove, Stockport, Cheshire SK7 6LU
Buxton Rd is on A6.
Moorland course.
18 holes, 6300 yards, S.S.S.70.
Visitors: welcome except on comp. days.
Green fees: weekdays £8, weekends £10.
Society meetings: catered for on Thurs and Fri.
Catering: meals served except Mon.
Hotels: numerous hotels in area.

N37 Helsby

☎ Helsby (092 82) 2021
Towers Lane, Helsby, Warrington, Cheshire WA6 0JB
Junction 14 off M56 to Helsby, turn into Primrose Ln, first right into Towers Ln.
Parkland course.
18 holes, 6262 yards, S.S.S.70
Course designed by James Braid.
Club founded in 1902.
Visitors: welcome on weekdays.
Green fees: £10 per day, £8 per round.
Society meetings: catered for on Mon and Thurs only.
Catering: full service except Tues.
Hotels: Grosvenor, Chester; Queens, Chester.

N38 Hill Valley G & C C

☎ Whitchurch (0948) 3584
Terrick Rd, Whitchurch, Shropshire SY13 4JZ
Off A49, 1 mile from centre of Whitchurch, signposted.
Undulating parkland course.

18 holes, 6050 yards, S.S.S.69
Course designed by P. Alliss & D. Thomas.
Club founded in 1975.
Visitors: welcome.
Green fees: weekdays £7 per day, weekends and Bank Holidays £9.
Society meetings: welcome.
Catering: snacks, lunches and dinners available every day.
Hotels: Terrick Hall.

N39 Ilkeston Borough
☎ Ilkeston (0602) 320304 Sec
Peewit, West End Drive, Ilkeston, Derbys.
½ mile W of Ilkeston market place.
Meadowland municipal course.
9 holes, 4000 yards, S.S.S.60
Club founded in 1929.
Visitors: welcome.
Green fees: £2.15 per round.
Society meetings: welcome.
Catering: not available.
Hotels: Rutland, Bath St, Ilkeston.

N40 Ingestre Park
☎ Weston (0889) 270061
Ingestre, Weston, Stafford ST18 0RE
5 miles E of Stafford, via Great or Little Haywood, off A51.
Undulating meadowland course.
18 holes, 6376 yards, S.S.S.70
Club founded in 1977.
Visitors: welcome daily, but at weekends only with member.
Green fees: £7 per day; less with member.
Society meetings: by arrangement with Sec except Mon or Bank Holidays.
Catering: full catering daily except Mon.
Hotels: numerous good hotels in Stafford.

N41 Kedleston Park
☎ Derby (0332) 840035
Kedleston, Quarndon, Derby DE6 4JD
Follow RAC signs to Kedleston Hall, 4 miles N of Derby off A5111.
Parkland course.
18 holes, 6636 yards, S.S.S.72
Course designed by James Braid.
Club founded in 1946.
Visitors: welcome weekdays and with member at weekends (only spiked golf shoes to be worn).
Green fees: £12 per day, £9.50 per round.
Society meetings: welcome weekdays.
Catering: full meals every day.
Hotels: Kedleston.

N42 Knutsford
☎ Knutsford (0565) 4610
Mereheath Lane, Knutsford.
2 miles from Junction 19 on M6, make for Knutsford entrance to Tatton Park club a few yards on right down Mereheath Ln.
Parkland course.
9 holes, 6288 yards, S.S.S.70
Club founded in 1891.
Visitors: welcome on weekdays by arrangement with Hon Sec.
Green fees: weekdays £8 (£1.25 with member), weekends and Bank Holidays £10 (£1.75 with member).
Society meetings: catered for on certain weekdays mainly Thurs.
Catering: by arrangement with Steward.
Hotels: George, Knutsford; Angel, Knutsford; Cottons, Knutsford; Rose and Crown, Knutsford; Swan, Bucklow Hill

N43 Leek
☎ Leek (0538) 385889
Birchall, Cheadle Rd, Leek, Staffs ST13 5RE
¾ mile S of Leek on A520
Moorland course.
18 holes, 6229 yards, S.S.S.70
Club founded in 1892.
Visitors: welcome on weekdays.
Green fees: weekdays £9 (£5 with member), weekends £12 (£6 with member).
Society meetings: mainly on Wed.
Catering: lunch and dinner Tues to Sat.
Hotels: Three Horse Shoes.

N44 Leek Westwood
☎ Leek (0538) 382651
Newcastle Rd, Leek, Staffs ST13 7AA
½ mile W of Leek on A53.
Moorland course.
9 holes, 5567 yards, S.S.S.67
Visitors: welcome on weekdays.
Green fees: £5 (£2 with member).
Society meetings: by arrangement.
Catering: by arrangement.
Hotels: Jester, Leek.

N45 Leigh
☎ Culcheth (092 576) 2943
Kenyon Hall, Broseley Lane, Culcheth, Warrington WA3 4BG
5 minutes from Culcheth village centre.
Parkland course.
18 holes, 5853 yards, S.S.S.68
Club founded in 1906.
Visitors: welcome by arrangement.
Green fees: weekdays £6.50, weekends £7.50.
Society meetings: catered for on Tues.
Catering: lunches served except Mon.
Hotels: Greyhound, Warrington Rd, Leigh; George and Dragon, Warrington Rd, Glazebury.

N46 Lilleshall Hall
☎ Telford (0952) 603840 or 604776
Lilleshall, Newport, Shropshire TF10 9AS
About 5 miles from Newport turn off A41 into Sheriffhales Rd, 2 miles later turn right into Abbey Rd.
Parkland course.
18 holes, 5891 yards, S.S.S.68
Course designed by H.S. Colt.
Club founded in 1937.
Visitors: welcome on weekdays and with member at weekends.
Green fees: weekdays £7.50 per day (£3 with member), weekends £5 with member.
Society meetings: by prior arrangement.
Catering: full facilities every day until 6.30 pm; snacks available during bar opening hours.
Hotels: Royal Victoria, St Mary's St, Newport.

N47 Llanymynech
☎ Llanymynech (0691) 830542
Pant, Oswestry, Shropshire SY10 8LB
1 mile W of A483 Welshpool to Oswestry road and 6 miles S of Oswestry, turn by Cross Guns Inn, signposted to club in village of Pant.
Upland course.
18 holes, 6114 yards, S.S.S.69
Club founded in 1933.
Visitors: welcome mainly on weekdays.
Green fees: weekdays £5.50, weekends and Bank Holidays £7.50.
Society meetings: welcome mainly on weekdays.
Catering: meals served except Mon.
Hotels: Wynnstay, Oswestry.

N48 Ludlow
☎ Bromfield (058 477) 285
Bromfield, Ludlow, Shropshire SY8 2BT
Take A49 Ludlow to Shrewsbury road, turn right 2 miles out of Ludlow, signposted.
Parkland course.
18 holes, 6239 yards, S.S.S.70
Club founded in 1889.
Visitors: always welcome.
Green fees: weekdays £7 per day (£2.60 with member), weekends and Bank Holidays £9 (£3.25 with member).
Society meetings: welcome on weekdays, write for details.
Catering: snacks and meals available by arrangement.
Hotels: Overton Grange, Ludlow Rd, Ludlow; Angel, Broad St, Ludlow; Feathers, Bull Ring, Ludlow.

N49 Lymm
☎ Lymm (092 575) 5020
Whitbarrow Rd, Lymm, Cheshire WA13 9AM
5 miles SE of Warrington.
Parkland course.
18 holes, 6319 yards, S.S.S.70
Club founded in 1907.
Visitors: welcome.
Green fees: weekdays £8 (£4 with member), weekends and Bank Holidays

£10 (£5 with member).
Society meetings: usually on Wed.
Catering: meals available.
Hotels: Lymm; Statham Lodge; Dingle.

N50 Macclesfield

☎ Macclesfield (0625) 23227
The Hollins, Macclesfield, Cheshire SK11 7EA
Off Windmill St in Macclesfield (A527 Macclesfield to Leek road).
Hilly course.
9 holes, 5974 yards, S.S.S.69
Club founded in 1889.
Visitors: welcome on weekdays.
Green fees: weekdays £5 (£3 with member), weekends and Bank Holidays £6 (£4 with member).
Catering: lunches served except Tues.
Hotels: Ellesmere, Buxton Rd, Macclesfield.

N51 Malkins Bank

☎ Sandbach (093 67) 5931
Betchton Rd, Sandbach, Cheshire.
1½ miles from Junction 17 off M6.
Parkland municipal course.
18 holes, 6071 yards, S.S.S.69
Course designed by Hawtree and Son.
Club founded in 1980.
Visitors: welcome at all times.
Green fees: weekdays £2.60, weekends £3.25.
Society meetings: welcome.
Catering: meals and snacks served.
Hotels: Old Hall, Sandbach.

N52 Market Drayton

☎ Market Drayton (0630) 2266
Sutton, Market Drayton, Shropshire
1½ miles S of town.
Undulating meadowland course.
11 holes, 6265 yards, S.S.S.69
Club founded in 1912.
Visitors: welcome, except Sun with member only.
Green fees: weekdays £5, weekends £6.
Society meetings: welcome on weekdays, max 30.
Catering: meals served by arrangement.
Hotels: Royal Victoria, Newport; Corbet Arms, Market Drayton.

N53 Matlock

☎ Matlock (0629) 2191
Chesterfield Rd, Matlock, Derbyshire DE4 5LF
On A632 Matlock to Chesterfield Road, 1½ miles out of Matlock.
Moorland/parkland course.
18 holes, 5871 yards, S.S.S.68
Club founded in 1907.
Visitors: welcome on weekdays.
Green fees: weekdays £7.50 per day (£3.50 with member), weekends £10 (£5 with member).
Society meetings: welcome weekdays.
Catering: lunches served except Mon.
Hotels: New Bath, Matlock Bath; Peacock, Rowsley, Bakewell.

N54 Mere G & C C

☎ Bucklow Hill (0565) 830155
Chester Rd, Mere, Knutsford, Cheshire WA16 6LJ
From Junction 19 off M6 take A556 for 2 miles, from Junction 7 off M55 take A556 past Swan at Bucklow Hill.
Parkland course.
18 holes, 6723 yards, S.S.S.72
Course designed by George Duncan & James Braid.
Club founded in 1934.
Visitors: welcome only by arrangement with Pro.
Green fees: Mon, Tues and Thurs £15, weekends and Bank Holidays £20.
Society meetings: catered for by arrangement on Mon, Tues and Thurs.
Catering: meals and snacks available.
Hotels: Swan, Bucklow Hill; Cottons, Knutsford.

N55 Mickleover
☎ Derby (0332) 513339 Steward, 518662 Pro.
Uttoxeter Rd, Mickleover, Derby.
3 miles W of Derby, take A516 out of Derby, join B5020 to Mickleover.
Meadowland course.
18 holes, 5621 yards, S.S.S.67
Club founded in 1923.
Visitors: by arrangement with Pro.
Green fees: weekdays £8, weekends and Bank Holidays £10.
Society meetings: welcome Mon and Thurs.
Catering: snacks, lunches and evening meals served except Tues.
Hotels: Crest.

N56 Mirrlees
☎ 061-449 9513 Hon Sec.
Bramhall Moor Lane, Hazel Grove, Stockport SK7 5AH
From Stockport follow A6 to Hazel Grove, turn right into New Moor Lane, course is ¼ mile on right hand side.
Parkland course.
9 holes, 6102 yards, S.S.S.69
Club formed in 1925.
Visitors: welcome with member only.
Green fees: £3 per round, £4 per day.
Society meetings: none.
Catering: bar snacks available.
Hotels: numerous good hotels in area.

N57 Newcastle
☎ Newcastle (0782) 618526 Pro, 617006 Sec.
Whitmore Rd, Newcastle under Lyme, Staffs ST5 2QB
1½ miles from Newcastle under Lyme.
Parkland course.
18 holes, 6450 yards, S.S.S.71
Club formed in 1910.
Visitors: welcome on weekdays.
Green fees: £10 (£3.50 with member).
Society meetings: catered for on Mon, Wed and Thurs.
Catering: bar snacks, lunches and evening meals served.
Hotels: Post House, Clayton; Borough Arms, Newcastle under Lyme.

N58 Newcastle under Lyme
☎ Newcastle (0782) 617006 Sec, 618526 Pro, 616583 Steward.
Whitmore Rd, Newcastle, Staffs ST5 2QB
Off M6 at Junction 15 onto A519, then A525 for 2 miles.
Parkland course.
18 holes, 6450 yards, S.S.S.71
Club formed in 1910.
Visitors: welcome on Mon, Wed and Thurs.
Green fees: £8 per day (£3.50 with member).
Society meetings: catered for on Mon, Wed and Thurs.
Catering: bar snacks or meals available as required.
Hotels: Staffordshire Post House; Borough Arms, Newcastle.

N59 New Mills
☎ New Mills (0663) 43485
Shaw Marsh, New Mills, Stockport, Cheshire.
Take St Mary Rd from centre of New Mills, about ¾ mile.
Moorland course.
9 holes, 5707 yards, S.S.S.68
Club formed in 1907.
Visitors: welcome on weekdays and Sat morning, except competition days.
Green fees: weekdays £5 per day, Sat £6.
Society meetings: welcome on weekdays by arrangement with Sec.
Catering: snacks and meals available.
Hotels: Pack Horse and Sportsman, Hayfield; Moorside, Disley.

N60 Onneley
☎ Stoke-on-Trent (0782) 750577
Onneley, Crewe, Cheshire CW3 5QF
1 mile from Woore on A51 to Newcastle.
Undulating meadowland course.
9 holes, 5584 yards, S.S.S.67
Club formed in 1967.
Visitors: welcome on weekdays and with member on Sat.
Green fees: weekdays £4 (£2 with member).
Society meetings: welcome weekdays.
Catering: by arrangement prior to visit.
Hotels: numerous hotels in area.

N61 Ormonde Fields G & C C
☎ Ripley (0773) 42987 Pro, 44157 Club.
Nottingham Rd, Codnor, Ripley, Derbys DE5 9RL
Off M1 at Junction 26, take A610 towards Ripley for about 2 miles.
Undulating course.
18 holes, 6007 yards, S.S.S.69
Club formed in 1906.
Visitors: welcome at any time during the week and by arrangement with Sec at weekends.
Green fees: weekdays £5 per day, weekends £7 per day.
Society meetings: welcome at any time by arrangement.
Catering: Full catering facilities available, from bar snacks to full meals.
Hotels: Sun Inn, Eastwood; Novatel, Stapleford; Post House, Stapleford.

N62 Oswestry
☎ Queens Head (069 188) 221 or 535
Aston Park, Oswestry, Shropshire SY11 4JJ
NW of Shrewsbury, just off A5, 2 miles from Oswestry.
Parkland course.
18 holes, 6046 yards, S.S.S.69
Course designed by James Braid.
Club formed in 1930.
Visitors: welcome.
Green fees: weekdays £6 (£2.50 with member), weekends £8 (£3 with member).
Society meetings: catered for on Wed and Fri by application.
Catering: snacks available every day and meals if ordered in advance.
Hotels: Wynstay, Oswestry; Lion, Shrewsbury.

N63 Pastures
☎ Derby (0332) 513921 extn 317
Pastures Hospital, Mickleover, Derby DE3 2DQ
On A516 4 miles W of Derby.
Undulating meadowland course.
9 holes, 5005 yards, S.S.S.64
Course designed by Frank Pennink.
Club formed in 1969.
Visitors: welcome with member only.
Green fees: weekdays £3 (Juniors under 18 50p), weekends and Bank Holidays £4 (Juniors under 18 £1).
Society meetings: weekdays by special arrangement.
Catering: no catering except for societies.
Hotels: Crest, Littleover, Derby.

N64 Poulton Park
☎ Padgate (0925) 812034
Dig Lane, Cinnamon Brow, Warrington.
Off A574, turn into Crab Lane, 3 miles from Warrington.
Meadowland course.
9 holes, 2756 yards, S.S.S.67
Club formed in 1978.
Visitors: welcome on weekdays (Ladies Day Tues) but only late afternoon at weekends.
Green fees: weekdays £5, weekends £6.50.
Society meetings: by arrangement
Catering: meals and snacks except Mon.
Hotels: good hotels in area.

N65 Prestbury
☎ Prestbury (0625) 82824
Macclesfield Rd, Prestbury, Cheshire SK10 4BJ
2 miles NW of Macclesfield on Macclesfield Rd leaving Prestbury village.
Undulating meadowland course.
18 holes, 6359 yards, S.S.S.71
Course designed by Colt & Morrison.
Club formed in 1921.

Visitors: welcome on weekdays and with member at weekends; advisable to phone in advance.
Green fees: £10 per day or round (£5 with member).
Society meetings: welcome Thurs only.
Catering: lunches, dinners and bar snacks served except Mon.
Hotels: Edge, Alderley Edge; Mottram Hall, Mottram St Andrews.

N66 Renishaw Park
☎ Eckington (0246) 432044
Station Rd, Renishaw, Sheffield S31 9UZ
Junction 30 off M1, take the sign for Eckington, club approximately 1½ miles on the right.
Parkland course.
18 holes, 6253 yards, S.S.S.70
Course designed by R. Sitwell.
Club formed in 1911.
Visitors: welcome on weekdays; ring club for dress code.
Green fees: weekdays £6.50 per round, £7 per day.
Society meetings: none.
Catering: full catering available with 24 hours notice.
Hotels: Sitwell Arms; Mosborough Hall.

N67 Runcorn
☎ Runcorn (092 85) 72909 or 74214 Sec.
Clifton Rd, Runcorn, Cheshire WA7 4SU
Signposted The Heath off A557.
High parkland course.
18 holes, 6008 yards, S.S.S.69
Club formed in 1909.
Visitors: welcome on weekdays (Ladies Day Tues).
Green fees: weekdays £6, weekends and Bank Holidays £8.
Society meetings: by advance arrangement on weekdays except Tues.
Catering: snacks and meals served by arrangement.
Hotels: Crest, Beechwood, Runcorn; Lord Daresbury, Daresbury, Warrington.

N68 Sandbach
☎ Sandbach (093 67) 2117
117 Middlewich Rd, Sandbach, Cheshire CW11 9EA
1m N of town centre on A50 Middlewich Rd.
Meadowland course.
Club formed in 1921.
Visitors: welcome on weekdays except Tues in summer.
Green fees: £6.50 per day or round.
Society meetings: by arrangement with Sec, by Dec 31 of previous year.
Catering: meals and snacks available except Mon and Thurs.
Hotels: Saxon Cross; Old Hall; Wheatsheaf; all in Sandbach.

N69 Sandiway
☎ Sandiway (0606) 883247
Chester Rd, Sandiway, Northwick, Cheshire CW8 2DJ
On A556 14 miles E of Chester, 4 miles from Northwich.
Undulating parkland course.
18 holes, 6435 yards, S.S.S.72
Course designed by Ted Ray.
Club formed in 1921.
Visitors: welcome on weekdays and certain weekends with letter of introduction.
Green fees: weekdays £10.50, weekends and Bank Holidays £13.50.
Society meetings: catered for on Tues.
Catering: meals served every day by arrangement.
Hotels: Hartford Hall, Northwich; Oaklands, Weaverham.

N70 Shifnal
☎ Telford (0952) 460330 or 460457 Pro
Decker Hill, Shifnal, Shropshire TF11 8QL
On B4379 1 mile from Shifnal.
Parkland course.
18 holes, 6422 yards, S.S.S.71
Course designed by Frank Pennink.
Club formed in 1929.
Green fees: £6.50 per day.
Society meetings: catered for on weekdays except Thurs.
Catering: full catering service.
Hotels: Park House, Shifnal; Old Bell, Shifnal.

N71 Shrewsbury
☎ Shrewsbury (074 372) 2976
Condover, Shropshire.
4 miles SW of Shrewsbury, follow signs for Condover and golf club.
Meadowland course.
18 holes, 6229 yards, S.S.S.70
Course designed by C.K. Cotton, Pennink, Lawrie and Partners.
Club formed in 1890.
Visitors: welcome if members of recognised club.
Green fees: weekdays £6.50, weekends £8.50 (£3 all week with member).
Society meetings: by arrangement.
Catering: meals served except Mon.
Hotels: in Shrewsbury.

N72 Sickleholme
☎ Hope Valley (0433) 51306
Bamford, Sheffield S30 2BH
On A625, 14 miles W of Sheffield, near Marquis of Granby.
Hillside meadowland course.
18 holes, 6064 yards, S.S.S.69
Club formed in 1898.
Visitors: welcome, except Wed mornings.
Green fees: weekdays £7.50, weekends £8.50.
Society meetings: welcome weekdays.
Catering: catering facilities available every day but limited on Fri.
Hotels: Rising Sun, Bamford; George, Hathersage; Maynard Arms, Grindleford.

N73 Stafford Castle
☎ Stafford (0785) 3821
Newport Rd, Stafford
½ mile from Stafford main street.
Meadowland course.
9 holes, 6347 yards, S.S.S.70
Club formed in 1907.
Visitors: welcome weekdays.
Green fees: £4.50.
Society meetings: by prior arrangement.
Catering: bar meals available daily, others by arrangement except Mon.
Hotels: Swan, Stafford; Tillington Hall, Stafford; Vine, Stafford.

N74 Stanedge
☎ Chesterfield (0246) 566156
Walton Hay Farm, Walton, Chesterfield, Derbys S45 0LW
5 miles SW of Chesterfield, at top of long hill on A632, turn on to B5057; In leading to club is 300yds W of Red Lion Inn.
Undulating moorland course.
9 holes, 4867 yards, S.S.S.64
Club formed in 1931.
Visitors: welcome weekday mornings and with member weekday afternoons, Sat or Bank Holidays; no visitors on Sun.
Green fees: weekdays £4 (£3 with member), Sat and Bank Holidays £4.50.
Society meetings: welcome on weekdays subject to prior arrangement.
Catering: only available for parties by prior arrangement.
Hotels: Chesterfield; Portland; Glen Stuart; all in Chesterfield.

N75 Stone
☎ Stone (0785) 813103
Filleybrooks, Stone, Staffs ST15 0NB
½ mile N of Stone on A34 next to Wayfarer Hotel.
Meadowland course.
9 holes, 6272 yards, S.S.S.70
Club formed in 1923.
Visitors: welcome on weekdays and with member at weekends or Bank Holidays.
Green fees: £6 (with member £2).
Society meetings: welcome weekdays.
Catering: lunches and dinners served by arrangement except Mon.
Hotels: Crown, Stone; Stonehouse, Stone.

N76 Tamworth
☎ Tamworth (0827) 53850
Eagle Drive, Tamworth, Staffs B77 4EG
Off B5000 Tamworth to Polesworth road, signposted from Railway Arches at Tamworth roundabout.

Undulating moorland course.
18 holes, 6691 yards, S.S.S.72
Club formed in 1975.
Visitors: welcome.
Green fees: £3.
Society meetings: welcome on weekdays only, maximum 30.
Catering: bar snacks available during opening hours.
Hotels: Castle, Tamworth; Shrubberies, Victoria Rd, Tamworth.

N77 Tapton Park
☎ Chesterfield (0246) 73887
Murray House, Crow Lane, Chesterfield.
½ mile from Chesterfield station.
Parkland course.
18 holes, 6048 yards, S.S.S.69
Visitors: by arrangement with Pro J. Delaney.
Green fees: weekdays £2.25, weekends £2.75.
Society meetings: by arrangement.
Catering: full bar and catering facilities.
Hotels: Chesterfield.

N78 Telford Hotel G & C C
☎ Telford (0952) 585642 or 586052
Great Hay, Telford, Shropshire TF7 4DT
Off A442 at Sutton Hill, S of Telford.
Undulating meadowland course.
18 holes, 6228 yards, S.S.S.70
Visitors: welcome, advisable to check availability.
Green fees: weekdays £7.50, weekends and Bank Holidays £12.
Society meetings: welcome weekdays.
Catering: full facilities available.
Hotels: Telford Golf & C.C.

N79 Trentham
☎ Stoke-on-Trent (0782) 658109 Sec, 642347 Club
14 Barlaston Old Rd, Trentham, Stoke-on-Trent ST4 8HB
3 miles S of Newcastle under Lyme on A34, turn at the Trentham roundabout onto A5035 to Uttoxeter, take first turning on right by National Westminster Bank, club is immediately on right.
Parkland course.
18 holes, 6523 yards, S.S.S.71
Club formed in 1895.
Visitors: on weekdays except Tues.
Green fees: weekdays £10 (£2.50 with member), weekends £13 (£2.50 with member).
Society meetings: welcome weekdays.
Catering: lunches and bar snacks available on weekdays; dinner served if booked in advance.
Hotels: Crown, Stone; Clayton Lodge, Clayton, Newcastle.

N80 Trentham Park
☎ Stoke-on-Trent (0782) 658800 Sec, 642125 Pro
Trentham Park, Trentham, Stoke-on-Trent ST4 8AE
4 miles S of Newcastle under Lyme on A34, 1 mile from Junction 15 on M6.
Parkland course.
18 holes, 6403 yards, S.S.S.71
Club formed in 1880.
Visitors: welcome.
Green fees: weekdays £8, weekends £10.
Society meetings: catered for on Wed and Fri.
Catering: meals served except Mon.
Hotels: Clayton Lodge, Clayton, Newcastle; Post House, Clayton Rd, Newcastle.

N81 Upton-by-Chester
☎ Chester (0244) 381183
Upton Lane, Upton-by-Chester, Chester CH2 1EE
1½ miles N of Chester off Liverpool Road.
Parkland course.
18 holes, 5875 yards, S.S.S.68
Club formed in 1934.
Visitors: welcome.
Green fees: weekdays £7, weekends and Bank Holidays £10.
Society meetings: welcome weekdays.
Catering: meals available every day.
Hotels: many in Chester and nearby.

N82 Vicars Cross
☎ Chester (0244) 335174
Tarvin Rd, Littleton, Chester CH3 7HN
A51 2 miles E of Chester.
Meadowland course.
18 holes, 5804 yards, S.S.S.68
Course designed by E. Parr.
Club formed in May 1939.
Visitors: welcome but ring to check availability.
Green fees: weekdays £6 per round, £9 per day; weekends and Bank Holidays £7.50 per round, £10 per day.
Society meetings: on Mon and Thurs.
Catering: bar snacks available; lunch and evening meals by arrangement.
Hotels: Royal Oak, Hoole Rd, Chester; Queen, City Rd, Chester.

N83 Walton Hall
☎ Warrington (0925) 66775
Warrington Rd, Higher Walton, Warrington WA4 5LU
4 miles from Warrington along A56, ½ mile from M56.
Undulating parkland course.
18 holes, 6801 yards, S.S.S.73
Club formed in 1972.
Visitors: welcome.
Green fees: weekdays £2.40, weekends and Bank Holidays £3.25.
Society meetings: catered for by appointment.
Catering: bar snacks available during licensed hours and meals available by arrangement with Steward.
Hotels: Lord Daresbury.

N84 Warrington
☎ Warrington (0925) 65431 Pro, 61775 Sec
London Rd, Appleton, Warrington, Cheshire WA4 5HR
On A49 from M56 or S on A49 through town, 3 miles S of Warrington.
Undulating parkland course.
Long 18 holes, 6217 yards, S.S.S.70
Short 18 holes, 5890 yards, S.S.S.68
Course designed by James Braid.
Club formed in 1902.
Visitors: welcome.
Green fees: weekdays £8.50, weekends and Bank Holidays £11.50.
Society meetings: welcome by arrangement; on Wed over 30, on Thurs up to 30.
Catering: meals and snacks available except Mon.
Hotels: Hill Cliffe Hydro; Old Vicarage.

N85 Whittington Barracks
☎ Whittington (0543) 432212 Clubhouse, 432261 Pro, 432317 Sec.
Tamworth Rd, Lichfield WS14 9PW
On A51 2½ miles from Lichfield station.
Moorland course.
18 holes, 6457 yards, S.S.S.71
Club formed in 1886.
Visitors: welcome on weekdays and with member at weekends.
Green fees: £10.
Society meetings: welcome on Wed and Thurs only.
Catering: facilities at club except Mon.
Hotels: George, Bird St, Lichfield; Little Barrow, Beacon St, Lichfield; Swan, Bird St, Lichfield.

N86 Widnes
☎ 051-424 2995
Highfield Rd, Widnes, Cheshire
Near town centre.
Parkland course.
18 holes, 5688 yards, S.S.S.67
Club formed in 1923/4
Visitors: welcome on weekdays.
Green fees: £6 per round, £8 per day.
Society meetings: welcome weekdays, except Tues.
Catering: meals served by arrangement.
Hotels: Hillcrest.

N87 **Wilmslow**
☎ Mobberley (056 587) 2148
Great Warford, Mobberley, Knutsford, Cheshire WA16 7AY
2 miles from Wilmslow on B5085.
Parkland course.
18 holes, 6500 yards, S.S.S.71
Club formed in 1889.
Visitors: welcome every day except Wed before 2 pm; advisable to ring in advance.
Green fees: weekdays £11, weekends and Bank Holidays £14.
Society meetings: catered for on Tues and Thurs.
Catering: bar snacks available during opening hours; meals by arrangement.
Hotels: Edge, Macclesfield Rd, Alderley Edge; Mottram Hall, Mottram St Andrew, Prestbury; Belfry, Handforth, Wilmslow.

N88 **Wolstanton**
☎ Stoke-on-Trent (0782) 622413 Sec, 616995 Clubhouse.
Dimsdale Old Hall, Hassam Parade, Newcastle-under-Lyme, Staffs ST5 9DR
1½ miles NW of Newcastle under Lyme on A34, turn off at Lymelight Hotel into Dimsdale Parade, then first right into Hassam Parade.
Meadowland/parkland course.
18 holes, 5807 yards, S.S.S.68
Club formed in 1925.
Visitors: welcome on weekdays.
Green fees: weekdays £5.50 (£2.50 with member).
Society meetings: welcome Mon and Fri.
Catering: lunches served except Fri.
Hotels: Crest.

N89 **Wrekin**
☎ Telford (0952) 44032
Ercall Woods, Wellington, Telford TF6 5BX
M54 onto A5, take Golf Links Lane off A5.
Parkland course.
18 holes, 5699 yards, S.S.S.67
Club formed in 1902.
Visitors: welcome.
Green fees: £5.75 per round or day.
Society meetings: welcome.
Catering: meals by arrangement.
Hotels: Charlton; Buckatree.

O Nottinghamshire, Leicestershire, Lincolnshire

There are few inland courses to match the Notts GC (Hollinwell), or Woodhall Spa in Lincolnshire, both places where a round never disappoints. They are the pick of their respective counties although Sherwood Forest and Coxmoor are near neighbours of Hollinwell that can be highly recommended.

Newark, Worksop, Stanton-on-the-Wolds and Oxton have their admirers, too, and, driving from Newark into Lincolnshire, the Lincoln Club at Torksey is a good stopping point. Further south, Burghley Park at Stamford enjoys stately surroundings and Luffenham Heath is as fine an example of heathland golf as you will find.

In the north, Market Rasen is very pleasant while Seacroft at Skegness is a notable seaside links in contrast to the heart of Leicestershire which is parkland in character. Rothley Park and the Leicestershire club are perhaps the best and Longcliffe and the nine holes at Charnwood Forest extol the virtues more of heathland.

O1 Beeston Fields

☎ Nottingham (0602) 257062
Beeston Fields, Nottingham NG9 3DD
Off A52 4 miles W of Nottingham, 4 miles from M1 Exit 25.
Parkland course.
18 holes, 6404 yards, S.S.S.71
Course designed by Tom Williamson.
Club formed in 1923.
Visitors: welcome.
Green fees: weekdays £7.50 (£3 with member), weekends £9.
Society meetings: catered for on Mon and Wed.
Catering: catering facilities available.
Hotels: Brackley House, Beeston; Albany, Strathdon; Post House.

O2 Belton Park

☎ Grantham (0476) 67399 or 63355
Belton Lane, Londonthorpe Rd, Grantham, Lincs NG31 9SH
A607 from Grantham signposted to Sleaford and Lincoln, turn right at traffic lights at Park signposted Londonthorpe, golf club is 1 mile on left.
Parkland courses.
Brownlow 9 holes, 6412 yards, S.S.S.71
Ancaster 9 holes, 6101 yards, S.S.S.69
Belmont 9 holes, 5857 yards, S.S.S.68
Course designed by Dave Thomas & Peter Alliss.
Club formed in 1892.
Visitors: welcome with handicap; telephone for availability.
Green fees: weekdays £8 (£4 with member), weekends and Bank Holidays £12 (£5 with member).
Society meetings: catered for on weekdays only with advance booking.
Catering: restaurant service every day.
Hotels: George; Angel and Royal; King's; Avenue; Garden; all in Grantham.

O3 Birstall

☎ Leicester (0533) 674322
Station Rd, Birstall, Leicester LE4 3BB
3 miles N of town just off A6.
Parkland course.
18 holes, 6203 yards, S.S.S.70
Visitors: welcome weekdays except Tues.
Green fees: £8.
Society meetings: on Wed and Fri.
Catering: full catering except Mon.
Hotels: Goscote.

O4 Blankney

☎ Metheringham (0526) 20263
Blankney, Lincoln, Lincs LN4 3AZ
On B1188 10 miles from Lincoln, 1 mile past Metheringham.
Parkland course.
18 holes, 6232 yards, S.S.S.70
Course designed by Lt Col Hotchkin.
Club formed in 1903.
Visitors: welcome on weekdays; at weekends reservations through Pro Shop.
Green fees: weekdays £6 per round or day (£4 with member), weekends £8 (£6 with member).
Society meetings: catered for on weekdays except Tues.
Catering: bar snacks, lunches and evening meals served.
Hotels: Moor Lodge, Branston; Golf, Woodham Spa; Eastgate, Lincoln.

O5 Boston

☎ Boston (0205) 62306 Clubhouse, 50589 Sec.
Cowbridge, Horncastle Rd, Boston, Lincs PE22 7EL
2 miles N of Boston on B1183, look for sign on right when crossing first bridge.
Parkland/moorland course.
18 holes, 5795 yards, S.S.S.68
Course designed by B.S. Cooper and extended by Donald Steel.
Club formed in 1962.
Visitors: welcome.
Green fees: weekdays £5.50, weekends and Bank Holidays £7.50.
Society meetings: welcome weekdays.
Catering: full catering facilities except Wed when only bar snacks available.
Hotels: White Hart, Bridge Food, Boston; New England, Wide Bargate, Boston.

O6 Bulwell Forest

☎ Nottingham (0602) 278008
Hucknall Rd, Bulwell, Nottingham NG6 9LQ
4 miles N of city centre, follow signs for Bulwell or Hucknall, 3 miles from M1 Junction 26.
Moorland course.

18 holes, 5572 yards, S.S.S.67
Club formed in 1902.
Visitors: welcome.
Green fees: £2.70 per round.
Society meetings: by arrangement.
Catering: by arrangement.
Hotels: Savoy; Royal.

07 Burghley Park

☎ Stamford (0780) 53789
St Martins Without, Stamford, Lincs PE9 3JX
Leave A1 at roundabout S of town, course entrance is first gateway on the right, 1 mile S of Stamford.
Parkland course.
18 holes, 6236 yards, S.S.S.70
Club formed in 1890.
Visitors: welcome on weekdays and at weekends by prior arrangement with Pro Shop (Stamford 62100).
Green fees: weekdays £7 per day, weekends £8 per day.
Society meetings: catered for on weekdays only, maximum 40.
Catering: full catering service, except Tues, from 11 am to 7 pm, later by arrangement.
Hotels: George of Stamford; Lady Annes; Crown.

08 Carholme

☎ Lincoln (0522) 23725
Carholme Rd, Lincoln LN1 1SE
On A57, 1 mile from city centre.
Parkland course.
18 holes, 6086 yards, S.S.S.69
Visitors: welcome on weekdays and Sat.
Green fees: weekdays £4.50 (£3 with member), weekends and Bank Holidays £6 (£4.50 with member).
Society meetings: welcome weekdays.
Catering: lunches served except Mon.
Hotels: numerous good hotels in Lincoln.

09 Charnwood Forest

☎ Woodhouse Eaves (0509) 890259
Breakback Lane, Woodhouse Eaves, Loughborough, Leics.
B591 off A6 at Quomdon, follow signs to Woodhouse Eaves, 3 miles SE.

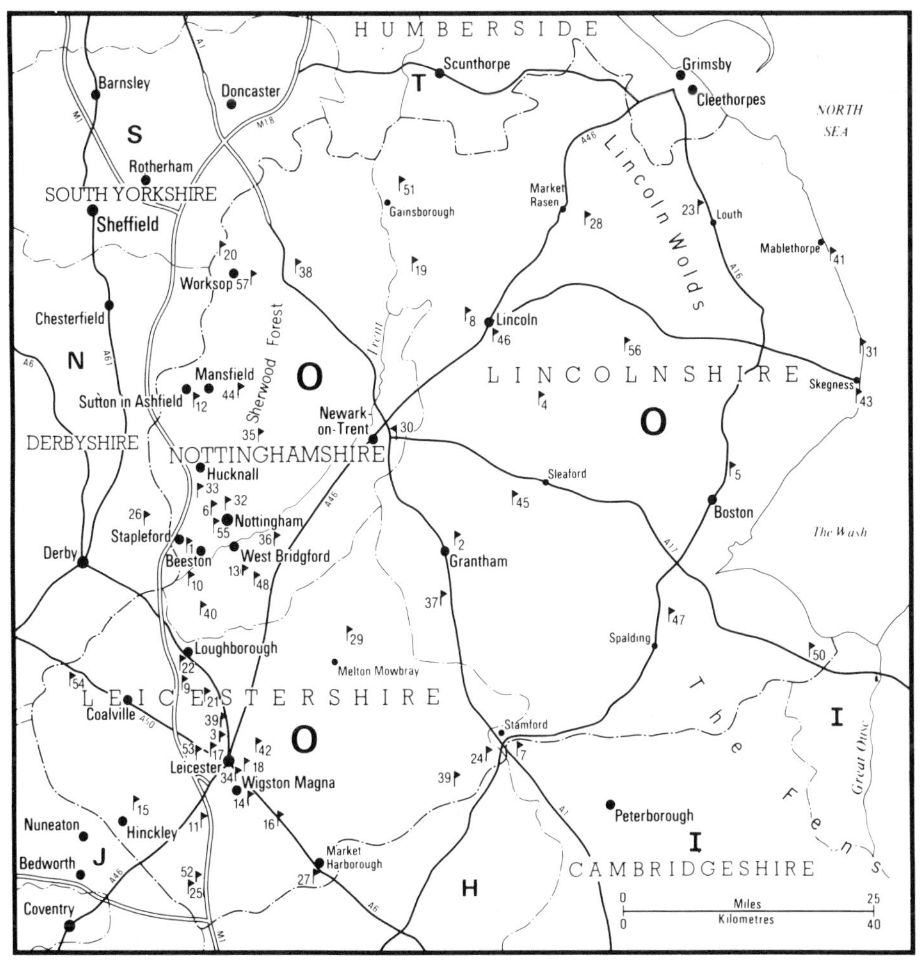

Undulating course.
9 holes, 6202 yards, S.S.S.70
Club formed in 1891.
Visitors: welcome.
Green fees: weekdays £7, weekends £8.
Society meetings: by arrangement.
Catering: full catering except Mon and Thurs when limited service available.
Hotels: Bulls Head, Woodhouse Eaves; Crow, Loughborough.

O10 Chilwell Manor

☎ Nottingham (0602) 257050 or 258958
Meadow Lane, Chilwell, Nottingham NG9 6AE
4 miles W of Nottingham, near Beeston, on A6005.
Parkland course.
18 holes, 6379 yards, S.S.S.69
Club formed in 1906.
Visitors: welcome with reservations, restricted at certain busy times.
Green fees: weekdays £8, weekends and Bank Holidays £10.
Society meetings: limited number of dates for larger parties; smaller parties of 12 or under welcome by arrangement.
Catering: full catering by arrangement.
Hotels: Post House, Sandiacre; Novotel (UK) Ltd., Bostocks Lane, Long Eaton.

O11 Cosby

☎ Leicester (0533) 864759
Chapel Lane, Cosby, Leics.
A46 or A426 S out of Leicester, in Cosby village take Broughton Rd.
Parkland course.
18 holes, 6270 yards, S.S.S.70
Club formed in 1895.
Visitors: welcome on weekdays and with member at weekends.
Green fees: £7 per day (£3 with member).
Society meetings: by arrangement.
Catering: meals served except Mon.
Hotels: Charnwood, Narborough; Four Seasons, Narborough.

O12 Coxmoor

☎ Mansfield (0623) 559878
Coxmoor Rd, Sutton-in-Ashfield, Notts NG17 5LF
On A611 2 miles SW of Mansfield, 5 miles from M1, Exit 27.
Heathland course.
18 holes, 6501 yards, S.S.S.72
Club formed in 1913.
Visitors: welcome (Tues Ladies Day).
Green fees: £9 per day.
Society meetings: by arrangement.
Catering: meals served.
Hotels: Midland.

O13 Edwalton Municipal

☎ Nottingham (0602) 234775
Edwalton Village, Nottingham
Left off A606 from Nottingham at Edwalton Hall Hotel.
Parkland course.
Main 9 holes, 3336 yards, S.S.S.36
Par 3 9 holes, 1592 yards, S.S.S.27
Course designed by Frank Pennink.
Course opened in 1981.
Visitors: welcome.
Green fees: Main weekdays £1.60, weekends £2; Par 3 weekdays £1, weekends £1.50.
Society meetings: catered for on weekdays.
Catering: lunches and evening meals.
Hotels: Edwalton Hall.

O14 Glen Gorse

☎ Leicester (0533) 714159 Sec, 712226 Clubhouse, 713748 Pro.
Glen Rd, Oadby, Leicester LE2 4RF
Follow main road A6 towards Market Harborough, club on right hand side just past Oadby.
Parkland course.
18 holes, 6641 yards, S.S.S.72
Club formed in 1933.
Visitors: welcome on weekdays and with member only at weekends or Bank Holidays.
Green fees: £8 per day.
Society meetings: welcome weekdays.
Catering: lunches and evening meals served except Mon.
Hotels: Post House, Leicester; Moat House, Oadby; Yew's, Great Glen.

O15 Hinckley

☎ Hinckley (0455) 615124
Leicester Rd, Hinckley, Leics LE10 3DR
NE boundary of Hinckley on A47.
Parkland course.
18 holes, 6578 yards, S.S.S.71
Club formed in 1894.
Visitors: welcome on weekdays and with member at weekends.
Green fees: £7 per round, £9 per day (with member £3 per round, £5 per day).
Society meetings: welcome on weekdays except Tues.
Catering: meals available except Mon.
Hotels: Island, Watling St, Hinckley.

O16 Kibworth

☎ Kibworth (053 753) 2301
Weir Rd, Kibworth Beauchamp, Leics LE8 0LP
8 miles SE of Leicester on A6.
Meadowland course.
18 holes, 6282 yards, S.S.S.70
Club formed in 1900.
Visitors: welcome on weekdays, weekends with member only.
Green fees: weekdays £7 (£3.50 with member), £2.50 juniors with member.
Society meetings: welcome Wed, Thurs, Fri by arrangement.
Catering: meals and snacks.
Hotels: Angel, Market Harborough; Hermitage, Oadby; Coach & Horses, Kibworth.

O17 Kirby Muxloe

☎ Leicester (0533) 393457 Sec, 392813 Pro, 393107 Clubhouse.
Station Rd, Kirby Muxloe, Leicester LE9 9EN
On A47 3 miles W of Leicester.
Parkland course.
18 holes, 6303 yards, S.S.S.70
Club founded in 1910.
Visitors: welcome on weekdays before 3.45 pm and with Captain's permission at weekends.
Green fees: weekdays £8 (£3 with member), weekends £10.
Society meetings: catered for on Wed and with restrictions on Thurs or Fri.
Catering: meals served except Sun and Mon, teas served on Sun.
Hotels: Moat House, Hinckley Rd, Leicester Forest East; Old Tudor Rectory, Glenfield, Leicester.

O18 Leicestershire

☎ Leicester (0533) 738825
Evington Lane, Leicester LE5 6DJ
Make for Evington village in SE district of Leicester, 2 miles from city centre.
Parkland course.
18 holes, 6312 yards, S.S.S.70
Club formed in 1891.
Visitors: welcome.
Green fees: weekdays £10 (£3 with member), weekends and Bank Holidays £11.
Society meetings: welcome on weekdays by prior arrangement.
Catering: lunches and teas daily.
Hotels: Daval; Rowans; Thornwood; Stanfre House; Gordon Lodge; all on London Rd A6.

O19 Lincoln

☎ Torksey (042 771) 210
Torksey, Lincoln LN1 2EG
Off A156, 12 miles NW of Lincoln.
Undulating meadowland course.
18 holes, 6400 yards, S.S.S.70
Club formed in 1891.
Visitors: welcome, with reservation and letter of introduction.

Green fees: weekdays £6 per round, £8.50 per day; weekends £8.50 per round, £12.50 per day.
Society meetings: weekdays by arrangement.
Catering: meals served by arrangement.
Hotels: White Hart; Grand, Lincoln.

020 Lindrick

☎ Worksop (0909) 475820
Lindrick, Worksop, Notts S81 8BH
On A57, 4 miles W of Worksop.
Heathland course.
36 holes, 6613 yards, S.S.S.72
Club formed in 1891.
Visitors: welcome with reservation.
Green fees: weekdays £15 per round, £17 per day, weekends £15 per round, £20 per day.
Society meetings: weekdays by arrangement.
Catering: snacks available and meals by arrangement.
Hotels: Crown, Bawtry; Ye Olde Bell, Retford.

021 Lingdale

☎ Woodhouse Eaves (0509) 890035 Clubhouse, 890703 Sec.
Joe Moores Lane, Woodhouse Eaves, Leics LE12 8TF
5 miles S of Loughborough on B5330.
Undulating parkland course.
9 holes, 3057 metres, S.S.S.72
Course designed by D.W. Tucker.
Club formed in 1967.
Visitors: welcome on weekdays and some weekends.
Green fees: weekdays £6 (£3 with member), weekends £8 (£4 with member).
Society meetings: welcome weekdays.
Catering: lunches and dinners served except Mon.
Hotels: De Montfort, Leicester Rd, Loughborough.

022 Longcliffe

☎ Loughborough (0509) 239129 Sec, 231450 Pro.
Snell's Nook Lane, Nampantan, Loughborough, Leics LE11 3YA
Adjacent to M1 motorway, leave M1 at Junction 23 and follow A512 towards Loughborough, within ¼ mile turn right into Snells Nook Lane, golf course is ¾ mile on right.
Undulating heathland course.
18 holes, 6485 yards, S.S.S.71
Club formed in 1905.
Visitors: welcome on weekdays.
Green fees: weekdays £10 per round or day (£3 with member), weekends and Bank Holidays £3 with member only.
Society meetings: welcome weekdays.
Catering: bar snacks, lunches and evening meals available except Mon.
Hotels: Kings Head, High St, Loughborough; Cedars, Cedar Rd, Loughborough; Forest Rise, Forest Rd, Loughborough.

023 Louth

☎ Louth (0507) 603681
Crowtree Lane, Louth, Lincs LN11 9LJ
From Lincoln or Gainsborough turn right at Trout Farm on outskirts of Louth, from Sleaford turn left by the Grammar School, course is situated in Hubbard Hills 1 mile outside of Louth.
Undulating meadowland course.
18 holes, 6502 yards, S.S.S.71
Club formed in 1965.
Visitors: welcome at any time.
Green fees: weekdays £6 per round, £8 per day, weekends £8 per round.

Society meetings: welcome weekdays.
Catering: full catering facilities.
Hotels: Withcall House; Rockery Farm.

024 Luffenham Heath

☎ Stamford (0780) 720205
Ketton, Stamford, Lincs PE9 3UU
6 miles SW of Stamford on A6121 by Fosters Bridge, off A47 at Morcott onto A6121.
Undulating heathland course.
18 holes, 6254 yards, S.S.S.70
Course designed by James Braid.
Club formed in 1911.
Visitors: by prior arrangement.
Green fees: weekdays £10, weekends and Bank Holidays £15.
Society meetings: welcome weekdays.
Catering: light lunches and teas available; meals by arrangement.
Hotels: George, Stamford; Falcon, Uppingham.

025 Lutterworth

☎ Lutterworth (045 55) 2532
Rugby Rd, Lutterworth, Leics LE17 5HN
½ mile from M1, Exit 20 on A4114.
Undulating course.
15 holes, 5734 yards, S.S.S.68
Club formed in 1904.
Visitors: welcome on weekdays and with member at weekends.
Green fees: £5 per round, £6.50 per day.
Society meetings: catered for Mon to Fri.
Catering: full catering except Sun.
Hotels: Denbigh Arms, Lutterworth.

026 Mapperley

☎ Nottingham (0602) 265611
Central Ave, Mapperley Plains, Nottingham NG3 5RH
From Nottingham take Woodborough Rd, Central Ave is about 4 miles NE of Nottingham, turn right at Speeds (Volvo) Garage.
Hilly meadowland course.
18 holes, 6224 yards, S.S.S.70
Club founded about 1905.
Visitors: welcome.
Green fees: weekdays £6.50, weekends £7.50.
Society meetings: welcome weekdays.
Catering: lunch and evening meals served except Wed, when only snacks available.
Hotels: many hotels around Nottingham.

027 Market Harborough

☎ Market Harborough (0858) 63684
Oxendon Rd, Market Harborough, Leics.
1m S of town on A508 Northampton rd.
Parkland course.
9 holes, 6080 yards, S.S.S.69
Club formed in 1898.
Visitors: welcome on weekdays and with member on Sat.
Green fees: £5 (£2.50 with member).
Society meetings: only by arrangement 6 months in advance.
Catering: none available.
Hotels: Three Swans, High St, Market Harborough.

028 Market Rasen & District

☎ Market Rasen (0673) 842416
Legsby Rd, Market Rasen, Lincs LN8 3DZ
B1202 off A46, 1 mile S of racecourse.
Moorland course.
18 holes, 6031 yards, S.S.S.69
Club formed in 1922.
Visitors: welcome on weekdays.
Green fees: £6.50 per day.
Society meetings: welcome Tues or Fri.
Catering: meals served.
Hotels: Gordon Arms, The Chase.

029 Melton Mowbray

☎ Melton Mowbray (0664) 62118
Waltham Rd, Thorpe Arnold, Melton Mowbray, Leics LE14 4SD
On A609 between Melton Mowbray and Grantham, 2 miles NE of Melton Mowbray.
Undulating course.
9 holes, 6168 yards, S.S.S.69
Visitors: welcome.
Green fees: weekdays £5, weekends £7.
Society meetings: by arrangement on weekdays.
Catering: bar meals available.
Hotels: George, Melton Mowbray; Harborough, Melton Mowbray.

030 Newark

☎ Fenton Claypole (063 684) 282, 492 or 241
Coddington, Newark, Notts NG24 2QX
4 miles E of Newark on A17 toward Sleaford; off A1 1 mile E of Coddington
Parkland course.
18 holes, 6486 yards, S.S.S.71
Club formed in 1901.
Visitors: welcome.
Green fees: weekdays £8 per day or round, weekends and Bank Holidays £10 per day or round.
Society meetings: by arrangement on weekdays.
Catering: bar snacks and meals by prior arrangement except Fri.
Hotels: Robin Hood, Newark.

031 North Shore

☎ Skegness (0754) 3298
North Shore Rd, Skegness, Lincs PE25 1DN
1 mile N of town on Seaward side of Ingoldmells Rd.
Links/parkland course.
18 holes, 6010 yards, S.S.S.69
Course designed by James Braid.
Club formed in 1910.
Visitors: welcome if members of bona fide golf club with handicap.
Green fees: weekdays £7 per round or day, weekends and Bank Holidays £8 per round or day.
Society meetings: by arrangement.
Catering: meals and snacks available.
Hotels: North Shore.

032 Nottingham City

☎ Nottingham (0602) 278021
Lawton Drive, Bulwell, Nottingham NG6 8BL
2 miles off M1 at Junction 26.
Parkland municipal course.
18 holes, 6120 yards, S.S.S.70
Club formed in 1910.
Visitors: welcome on weekdays and by booking at weekends.
Society meetings: welcome on weekdays except Fri.
Catering: meals served.
Hotels: numerous hotels in Nottingham.

033 Nottinghamshire

☎ Mansfield (0623) 753225
Hollinwell, Derby Rd, Kirkby-in-Ashfield, Notts NG17 7QR
Leave M1 at Junction 27, then 2 miles N on A611.
Undulating moorland course.
18 holes, 7020 yards, S.S.S.74
Course designed by Willie Park.
Club formed in 1887.
Visitors: welcome on weekdays and with member at weekends, by prior arrangement.
Green fees: on application.
Society meetings: welcome.
Catering: full catering every day.
Hotels: Swallow.

034 Oadby

☎ Leicester (0533) 709052
Leicester Rd, Oadby, Leicester LE2 4AB
On A6 S of Leicester, just outside city limits.
Moorland course.
18 holes, 6228 yards, S.S.S.70
Club formed in 1975.
Visitors: welcome.
Green fees: weekdays £2.10 (OAPs and Juniors £1.60), weekends £2.65 (OAPs and Juniors £2).
Society meetings: on application to Oadby and Wigston Borough Council, Station Rd, Wigston, Leics.
Catering: on application to Steward.
Hotels: numerous hotels in Leicester.

035 Oxton
☎ Nottingham (0602) 653545
Oaks Lane, Oxton, Southwell, Notts NG25 0RH
On A614 Doncaster road between Arnold and Ollerton.
Meadowland course.
18 holes, 5681 metres, S.S.S.72
Course designed by Pennink.
Club formed in 1965.
Visitors: welcome but should make reservation at weekends.
Green fees: weekdays £4.50 per round, £7.50 per day; weekends and Bank Holidays £5.75 per round, £9.50 per day; reductions if under 16 or over 60.
Society meetings: welcome.
Catering: lunches and bar snacks.
Hotels: Springfield, Epperstone; Swallow, Ollerton; Savoy, Nottingham.

036 Radcliffe-on-Trent
☎ Radcliffe-on-Trent (060 73) 3000 Sec, 2396 Pro
Cropwell Rd, Radcliffe on Trent, Notts NG12 2JH
Off A52 Nottingham to Grantham road, 7 miles W of Nottingham.
Undulating parkland course.
18 holes, 6434 yards, S.S.S.71
Course re-designed by Frank Pennink.
Club formed in 1909.
Visitors: welcome on weekdays.
Green fees: weekdays £7.50 (£4 with member), weekends and Bank Holidays £9.50 (£6 with member).
Society meetings: welcome weekdays.
Catering: lunches and evening meals served.
Hotels: numerous hotels in Nottingham and West Bridgeford.

037 Retford
☎ Retford (0777) 703733
Ordsall, Retford, Notts
S off A620.
Woodland course.
9 holes, 5697 metres, S.S.S.70
Visitors: welcome on weekdays, with members only at weekends.
Green fees: weekdays £5 (£2 with member), weekends £3 (with member only).
Catering: full meal facilities.
Hotels: West Retford; Ye Olde Bell, Barnby Moor.

038 Rothley Park
☎ Leicester (0533) 302019 Clubhouse, 302809 Sec, 303023 Pro.
Westfield Lane, Rothley, Leicester LE7 7LH
6 miles N of Leicester, W of A6.
Parkland course.
18 holes, 6487 yards, S.S.S.71
Club founded in 1912.
Visitors: welcome but must be member of recognised golf club with handicap.
Green fees: weekdays £9 per person, weekends and Bank Holidays £12 per person.
Society meetings: apply to Sec.
Catering: full catering except Mon.
Hotels: Rothley Court, Westfield Lane, Rothley.

039 RAF North Luffenham
☎ Stamford (0780) 720041 ext 313.
North Luffenham, Oakham, Leics LE15 8RL
Follow signposts for RAF North Luffenham from A606, station is close to Rutland Water.
Meadowland course.
18 holes, 5629 yards, S.S.S.66
Club founded in 1975.
Visitors: welcome; all visitors are requested to book in at main guardroom.
Green fees: £2.50 (£2 with member), OAPs and Juniors £1.
Society meetings: by arrangement with Sec.
Catering: by arrangement with Sec.
Hotels: George, Stamford; Crown, Oakham.

040 Rushcliffe
☎ East Leake (050 982) 2959
Stocking Lane, East Leake, Loughborough, Leics LE12 5RL
Off M1 at Junction 24, follow signs to Nottingham, then Gotham and East Leake.
Undulating parkland course.
18 holes, 6057 yards, S.S.S.69
Club founded in 1911.
Visitors: welcome, but Tues is Ladies Day.
Green fees: weekdays £7 per day, weekends and Bank Holidays £10.
Society meetings: welcome on weekdays only; if over 16 must be booked before Jan.
Catering: bar snacks and meals served.
Hotels: numerous good hotels in area.

041 Sandilands
☎ Sutton-on-Sea (0521) 41432
Roman Bank, Sandilands, Sutton-on-Sea, Mablethorpe, Lincs LN12 2RJ
4 miles S of Mablethorpe on A52 coast road, course runs next to sea wall.
Seaside course.
18 holes, 5995 yards, S.S.S.69
Club founded in 1901.
Visitors: welcome.
Green fees: weekdays £7 per day, £6 per round; weekends and Bank Holidays £8 per day, £7 per round; reduction with member.
Society meetings: welcome.
Catering: snacks and light meals.
Hotels: Grange; Links.

042 Scraptoft
☎ Leicester (0533) 419000
Beeby Rd, Scraptoft, Leicester LE7 9SJ
Turn off A47 main Leicester to Peterborough road to Scraptoft at Thurnby.
Meadowland course.
18 holes, 6146 yards, S.S.S.69
Visitors: welcome.
Green fees: weekdays £7 per day, weekends and Bank Holidays £9 per day.
Society meetings: welcome.
Catering: meals served except Mon.
Hotels: White House, Scraptoft; Grand.

043 Seacroft
☎ Skegness (0754) 3020
Seacroft, Skegness, Lincs PE25 3AU
1 mile S of Skegness alongside road to Gibraltar Rd Bird Sanctuary.
Moderately undulating seaside links course.
18 holes, 6478 yards, S.S.S.71
Club founded in 1895.
Visitors: welcome.
Green fees: weekdays £6 per round, £8 per day; weekends and Bank Holidays £8 per round, £10 per day.
Society meetings: by arrangement.
Catering: available on prior booking.
Hotels: Vine, Vine Rd, Seacroft; Crown, Drummond Rd, Seacroft; Links, Drummond Rd, Seacroft.

044 Sherwood Forest
☎ Mansfield (0602) 26689
Eakring Rd, Mansfield, Notts NG18 3EW
On A617 2½ miles SE of Mansfield.
Wooded heathland course.
18 holes, 6709 yards, S.S.S.73
18 holes, 6281 yards, S.S.S.70
Course designed by James Braid.
Club founded in 1911/12.
Visitors: welcome on Mon, Thurs and Fri, otherwise by arrangement with Sec.
Green fees: weekdays £10 per day, weekends £14.
Society meetings: welcome by arrangement with Sec.
Catering: meals served.
Hotels: Swallow; Pine Lodge, 281 Nottingham Rd, Mansfield; Midland, Midland Place, Mansfield.

045 Sleaford
☎ South Rauceby (052 98) 273
South Rauceby, Sleaford, Lincs NG34 8PL
On A153 Sleaford to Grantham road, 2 miles W of Sleaford.

Heathland course.
18 holes, 6443 yards, S.S.S.71
Course designed by James Braid.
Club founded in 1905.
Visitors: welcome.
Green fees: weekdays £7 (with member £3.50), weekends £9 (with member £4.50).
Society meetings: welcome on weekdays.
Catering: full catering except Mon.
Hotels: The Mallards, Eastgate, Sleaford; Lion, Northgate, Sleaford.

046 Southcliffe & Canwick

☎ Lincoln (0522) 22166
Canwick Park, Washingborough Rd, Lincoln LN4 1EF
2 miles E of city centre.
Parkland course.
18 holes, 6257 yards, S.S.S.70
Course designed by F. Hawtree.
Club founded in 1900.
Visitors: welcome at most times.
Green fees: £5.50 (£4 with member).
Society meetings: welcome weekdays.
Catering: lunches and evening meals served except Mon.
Hotels: Eastgate Post House; Washingborough Hall.

047 Spalding

☎ Surfleet (077 585) 234
Surfleet, Spalding, Lincs PE11 4DG
4 miles N of Spalding off A16.
Meadowland course.
18 holes, 5782 yards, S.S.S.68
Visitors: members of recognised club welcome.
Green fees: weekdays £6, weekends and Bank Holidays £8; £26 per week.
Society meetings: welcome Thurs only.
Catering: by arrangement with Stewardess.
Hotels: numerous hotels in Spalding.

048 Stanton-on-the-Wolds

☎ Plumtree (060 237) 2006
Stanton-on-the-Wolds, Keyworth, Notts NG12 5AH
Off A606 at Blue Star Garage 8 miles SE of Nottingham.
Meadowland course.
18 holes, 6379 yards, S.S.S.70
Course designed by Tom Williamson.
Club founded in 1906.
Visitors: welcome by arrangement with Pro, K. Fear (Plumtree 2390).
Green fees: £8 per round, £10 per day.
Society meetings: by arrangement with Sec, H.G. Gray FCA.
Catering: meals by arrangement with Steward.
Hotels: Edwalton.

049 Stoke Rochford

☎ Great Ponton (047 683) 275
Stoke Rochford, Grantham, Lincs.
Off A1 5 miles S of Grantham, entrance at Roadhog service station.
Parkland course.
18 holes, 6204 yards, S.S.S.70
Course designed by C. Turner.
Club founded in 1926.
Visitors: welcome on weekdays and after 10.30 am at weekends or Bank Holidays.
Society meetings: catered for by arrangement on weekdays.
Catering: meals served.
Hotels: The George; Angel and Royal; White Hart; Shirley Croft; all in Grantham.

050 Sutton Bridge

☎ Holbeach (0406) 350323
New Rd, Sutton Bridge, Spalding, Lincs
On A17 10 miles W of Kings Lynn.
Parkland course.
9 holes, 5850 yards, S.S.S.68
Club founded in 1914.
Visitors: welcome on weekdays, except competition days, and with member at weekend; handicap certificate required.
Green fees: £6.
Society meetings: limited number catered for.
Catering: meals served except Mon.
Hotels: Bridge, Sutton Bridge.

051 Thonock

☎ Gainsborough (0427) 2278
Thonock, Gainsborough, Lincs.
1 mile E of town centre.
Parkland course.
18 holes, 5824 yards, S.S.S.68
Visitors: welcome, wise to ring first.
Green fees: £4.25 weekdays, £6 weekends.
Society meetings: welcome on weekdays by arrangement.
Catering: meals served except Tues.

052 Ullesthorpe

☎ Leire (0455) 209023 or 202361
Frolesworth Rd, Ullesthorpe, Lutterworth, Leics.
B577 off A5 to Claybrooke and Ullesthorpe, follow signs to course.
Meadowland course.
18 holes, 6048 yards, S.S.S.70
Visitors: welcome.
Green fees: weekdays £5.50, weekends and Bank Holidays £7.
Society meetings: welcome, details on application.
Catering: bar snacks and restaurant.
Hotels: Island, Watling St, Hinckley; Denbigh Arms, Lutterworth.

053 Western Park

☎ Leicester (0533) 872339
Scudmore Rd, Braunstonefrith, Leicester LE3 1UQ
Off A47, 2 miles W of city centre.
Parkland course.
18 holes,
Course designed by F.W. Hawtree.
Club founded in c 1900.
Visitors: welcome on weekdays, weekends by reservation.
Green fees: £2.20 weekdays, £3.20 weekends.
Society meetings: by arrangement.
Catering: restaurant and bar.
Hotels: Europa Lodge; Post House.

054 Willesley Park

☎ Ashby-de-la-Zouch (0530) 414596
Tamworth Rd, Ashby-de-la-Zouch, Leics LE6 5PF
On A453, approximately 1½ miles from centre of Ashby-de-la-Zouch S towards Tamworth.
Undulating parkland/heathland course.
18 holes, 6310 yards, S.S.S.70
Club founded in 1920.
Visitors: welcome if members of recognised club (Ladies Day Tues).
Green fees: weekdays £8 per round, £10 per day; weekends and Bank Holidays £9 per round, £11 per day.
Society meetings: welcome by arrangement.
Catering: full catering except Mon.
Hotels: Royal; Measham Inn.

055 Wollaton Park

☎ Nottingham (0602) 787574
Wollaton Park, Nottingham NG8 1BT
Parkland course.
18 holes, 6494 yards, S.S.S.71
Club founded in 1927.
Visitors: welcome except Wed (Ladies Day).
Green fees: weekdays £7.50 per round, £10.50 per day; weekends and Bank Holidays £9.50 per round, £13.50 per day.
Society meetings: catered for on Tues and Fri only.
Catering: meals available every day, by prior arrangement at weekends.
Hotels: variety of hotels in Nottingham.

056 Woodhall Spa

☎ Woodhall Spa (0526) 52511
The Broadway, Woodhall Spa, Lincs LN10 6PU
On B1191, 6 miles SW of Horncastle, 18 miles SE of Lincoln, 18 miles NE of Sleaford.
Heathland course.
18 holes, 6866 yards, S.S.S.73
Course designed by Col. S.V. Hotchkin.

Club founded in 1906.
Visitors: welcome any day, but prior arrangement essential.
Green fees: weekdays £9 per round, £11 per day; weekends £10 per round, £12 per day.
Society meetings: welcome any day, but prior arrangement essential.
Catering: full catering always available.
Hotels: Golf; Petwood; Dower House; Spa.

057 **Worksop**
☎ Worksop (0909) 477731
Windmill Lane, Worksop, Notts S80 2SQ
On S of town, from town centre approach via Lowtown St and Netherton Rd, course is adjacent to Worksop College.
Sandy heathland course.
18 holes, 6651 yards, S.S.S.72
Club founded in 1914.
Visitors: welcome, advisable to ring first.
Green fees: weekdays £8 per day, £6 per round; weekends and Bank Holidays £8 per round.
Society meetings: by arrangement on weekdays.
Catering: full catering available.
Hotels: Ye Old Bell, Barnby Moor, Retford; Van Dykes, Chesterfield Rd, Worksop.

P Merseyside

P1 Allerton Municipal

☎ 051-428 1046
Allerton, Liverpool 18
From city centre on Allerton Rd.
Undulating parkland course.
9 holes, S.S.S.34
18 holes, 5081 yards, S.S.S.67
Visitors: welcome.
Green fees: 9 holes £1, 18 holes £1.50; OAPs and Juniors half-price.
Catering: snacks served.
Hotels: in Liverpool.

P2 Arrowe Park

☎ 051-677 1527
Arrowe Park, Woodchurch, Birkenhead, Merseyside
3 miles from town centre, take Borough Rd, Woodchurch Rd and then opposite Landicon Cemetery.
Public parkland course.
18 holes, 6377 yards, S.S.S.70
Club founded in 1932.
Visitors: welcome, phone Pro first to find state of tee.
Green fees: £2.60 per round.
Society meetings: arrange with Pro.
Catering: no catering facilities.

P3 Bidston

☎ 051-638 3412
Scoresby Rd, Leasowe, Wirral, Merseyside L46 1QQ
A551 from Wallasey, ¾ mile.
Parkland course.
18 holes, 6207 yards, S.S.S.70
Club founded in 1913.
Visitors: welcome.
Green fees: weekdays £5.25 (£2.60 with member), weekends £9 (£4.35 with member).
Society meetings: welcome weekdays.
Catering: full catering facilities.
Hotels: Leasowe Castle.

P4 Bootle

☎ 051-928 6196
Dunnings Bridge Rd, Bootle, Merseyside L30 2PP
A565, 5 miles from Liverpool.
Seaside/links course.
18 holes, 6362 yards, S.S.S.70
Course designed by F. Stephens.
Club founded in 1934.
Visitors: welcome.
Green fees: weekdays £2.20, weekends £3.30.
Society meetings: by arrangement.
Catering: meals served.
Hotels: Park, Netherton.

P5 Bowring

☎ 051-489 1901
Bowring Park, Roby Rd, Huyton, Liverpool L36 4HD
4½ miles from city centre.
Parkland course.
9 holes, 2500 yards, S.S.S.66
Club founded in c.1911.
Visitors: welcome.
Green fees: £1.50, OAPs and Juniors 75p.
Hotels: Edenhurst (adjacent).

P6 Brackenwood

☎ 051-608 3093
Bracken Lane, Bebington, Wirral, Merseyside
Off M56 at Junction 4, signposted.
Parkland course.
18 holes, 6285 yards, S.S.S.70
Club founded in 1885.
Visitors: welcome.
Green fees: £2.60.
Society meetings: by arrangement.
Catering: pending.
Hotels: in area.

P7 Bromborough

☎ 051-334 2155
Raby Hall Rd, Bromborough, Wirral, Merseyside L63 0NW
½ mile from Bromborough station, ¾ mile from A41 Birkenhead to Chester road.
Parkland course.
18 holes, 6650 yards, S.S.S.73
Club founded in 1904.
Visitors: welcome on weekdays; advisable to book with Pro (051-334 4499) at weekends.
Green fees: weekdays £7.50 (£4 with member), weekends and Bank Holidays £9 (£4.50 with member).
Society meetings: catered for on Wed; early booking essential.
Catering: snacks available every day and lunches except Sun; meals by arrangement.
Hotels: Dibbinsdale, Dibbinsdale Rd, Bromborough; Thornton Hall, Thornton Houge, Wirral.

P8 Caldy

☎ 051-625 5660
Links Hey Rd, Caldy, Wirral, Merseyside L48 1NB
A540 from Chester turn left at Caldy crossroads.
Seaside/parkland course.
18 holes, 6665 yards, S.S.S.73
Course designed by James Braid.
Club founded in 1923.
Visitors: welcome on weekdays, except Tues mornings, and with member at weekends.
Green fees: £10 per day, £7.50 after 2 pm (with member £3.75).
Society meetings: catered for on weekdays except Wed.
Catering: lunches and snacks served every day; dinners by arrangement.
Hotels: Parkgate, Parkgate; Green Lodge, Hoylake; Leasowe Castle, Leasowe; Kings Gap Court, Hoylake.

P9 Childwall

☎ 051-487 0654
Naylor's Rd, Liverpool, Merseyside L27 2YB
Junction of M57 and M62, 2 miles on A5080 Huyton exit.
Parkland course.
18 holes, 6425 yards, S.S.S.71
Visitors: welcome on weekdays.
Green fees: weekdays £7.50 per day.
Society meetings: welcome weekdays.
Catering: meals served by arrangement.
Hotels: Gateacre Hall.

P10 Eastham Lodge

☎ 051-327 3008 Pro, 3003 Sec.
117 Ferry Rd, Eastham, Wirral L62 0AP
Off A41 to Eastham Country Park, 6 miles from Birkenhead.
Parkland course.
15 holes, 5826 yards, S.S.S.68
Course designed by Hawtree & Son.
Club founded in 1976.
Visitors: welcome on weekdays.
Green fees: weekdays £7 (£3.25 with member), weekends and Bank Holidays £3.75 with member.
Society meetings: catered for on Tues only by arrangement.
Catering: bar snacks available and meals if ordered in advance.
Hotels: Dresden, New Chester Rd, Bromborough; Woodhey, Berwick Rd, Little Sutton, S Wirral.

P11 **Formby**
☎ Formby (070 48) 72164
Golf Rd, Formby, Liverpool L37 1LQ
1 mile W of A565, adjacent to Freshfield station.
Links course.
18 holes, 6871 yards, S.S.S.74
Club founded in 1884.
Visitors: by arrangement, with letter of introduction, or handicap certificate
Green fees: weekdays £14, weekends and Bank Holidays £16.
Society meetings: by arrangement on weekdays except Wed.
Catering: lunches served except Mon.
Hotels: Tree Tops, Formby.

P12 **Formby Ladies'**
☎ Formby (070 48) 74127 club, 73493 Sec.
Golf Rd, Formby, Liverpool L37 1LQ
6 miles S of Southport off A565.
Seaside course.
18 holes, 5374 yards, S.S.S.71
Club founded in 1896.
Visitors: welcome, advisable to ring first.
Green fees: weekdays £10, weekends £12.
Society meetings: by arrangement.
Catering: bar snacks and salads.
Hotels: Prince of Wales, Lord St, Southport; Royal Clifton, The Promenade, Southport; Scarisbrick, Lord St, Southport; Bold, Lord St, Southport.

P13 **Grange Park**
☎ St Helens (0744) 26318
Prescot Rd, St Helens, Merseyside WA10 3AD
On A58 1 mile from town centre towards Prescot.
Parkland course.
18 holes, 6429 yards, S.S.S.71
Club founded in 1891.
Visitors: welcome on weekdays (Ladies Day Tues), by arrangement at weekends.
Green fees: weekdays £9, weekends and Bank Holidays £12.
Society meetings: by arrangement with special tariff on Mon.
Catering: bar snacks available, other

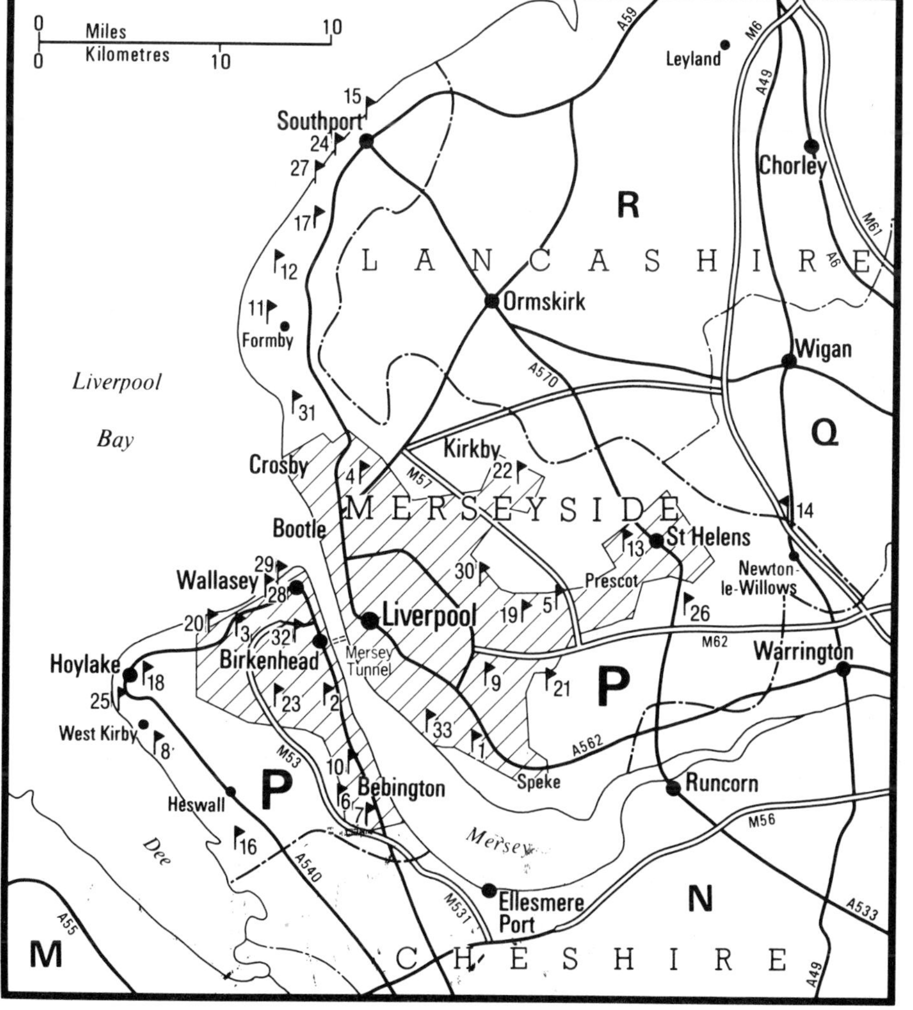

meals by arrangement.
Hotels: Fleece, Church St, St Helens.

P14 Haydock Park

☎ Newton-le-Willows (092 52) 4389
Golborne Park, Newton-le-Willows, Merseyside WA12 0HX
M6 to A580, then 1 mile E.
Parkland course.
18 holes, 6000 yards, S.S.S.69
Club founded in 1877.
Visitors: welcome on weekdays, except Tues, weekends with member only.
Green fees: £8 per day.
Society meetings: by arrangement.
Catering: meals served except Mon, by arrangement only on Mon.
Hotels: Post House, Haydock.

P15 Hesketh

☎ Southport (0704) 36897 Sec, 30050 Pro.
Cockle Dicks Lane, off Cambridge Rd, Southport, Merseyside PR9 9QQ
1 mile N of Southport town centre on the main Preston road, A565.
Links course.
Yellow 18 holes, 6160 yards, S.S.S.70
White 18 holes, 6478 yards, S.S.S.72
Club founded in 1885.
Visitors: welcome on weekdays and by prior arrangement with Pro on certain weekends.
Green fees: weekdays £10.50 per day, £7.50 per round; weekends and Bank Holidays £13 per day, £9 per round.
Society meetings: welcome by arrangement with Sec.
Catering: bar snacks available; meals by arrangement.
Hotels: Bold; Scarisbrick, Lord St; Metropole, King St.

P16 Heswall

☎ 051-342 1237
Cottage Lane, Heswall, Wirral, Merseyside L60 8PB
Leave M53, exit 4; at roundabout turn into Well Lane, leads into Cottage Lane.
Meadowland course.
18 holes, 6420 yards, S.S.S.72
Club founded in 1901.
Visitors: welcome.
Green fees: weekdays £9.50 (£3.50 with member), weekends £12.50 (£4.50 with member).
Society meetings: by arrangement.
Catering: bar snacks and light meals; full meals by arrangement.
Hotels: Victoria, Lower Village, Heswall.

P17 Hillside

☎ Southport (0704) 67169
Hastings Rd, Hillside, Southport PR8 2LU
Take A565 Southport to Liverpool road, turn right before Hillside railway station, club at end of Hastings Rd.
Parkland links course.
18 holes, 6850 yards, S.S.S.74
Course designed by Fred Hawtree.
Club founded in 1926.
Visitors: welcome by prior arrangement.
Green fees: £13 per day.
Society meetings: welcome by prior arrangement.
Catering: extensive restaurant service.
Hotels: numerous hotels in Southport.

P18 Hoylake

☎ 051-632 2956
Carr Lane, Hoylake, Merseyside
Off M53 10 miles SW of Liverpool, follow signs for Hoylake, 100 yards from Hoylake station.
Parkland course.
18 holes, 6312 yards, S.S.S.70
Course designed by James Braid.
Club founded in 1933.
Visitors: welcome.
Green fees: £2.60 per round.
Society meetings: catered for on weekdays and at weekends by arrangement.
Catering: by arrangement with Steward.
Hotels: Stanley; Green Lodge.

P19 Huyton & Prescot

☎ 051-489 3948
Hurst Park, Huyton Lane, Huyton, Liverpool L36 1UA
Approximately 10 miles from Liverpool city centre, just off M57.
Parkland course.
18 holes, 5738 yards, S.S.S.68
Club founded in 1905.
Visitors: welcome on weekdays.
Green fees: £9.50 per day, £7.25 per round; half-price with member.
Society meetings: catered for on Wed and Thurs only.
Catering: sandwiches and hot snacks available on weekdays.
Hotels: Hillcrest, Cronton; Crest, Knowsley; Rockland, Rainhill.

P20 Leasowe

☎ 051-677 5852
Leasowe Rd, Moreton, Wirral, L46 3RD
Take Wallasey turn off M53 1 mile after Queensway tunnel, 1 mile W of Wallasey village.
Seaside course.
18 holes, 5674 yards, S.S.S.71
Club founded in 1901.
Visitors: welcome except Sun.
Green fees: weekdays £6, Sat and Bank Holidays £8.
Society meetings: welcome by arrangement.
Catering: full catering facilities.
Hotels: Leasowe Castle.

P21 Lee Park

☎ 051-487 3882 Sec.
Childwall Valley Rd, Gateacre, Liverpool L27 3YA
On B5171 off A562, next to Netherley Comprehensive School.
Parkland course.
18 holes, 6024 yards, S.S.S.69
Course designed by Frank Pennink.
Club founded in 1950.
Visitors: welcome with reservation.
Green fees: weekdays £6.50, weekends £8.50; reduction with member.
Society meetings: by arrangement.
Catering: bar snacks served and meals by arrangement.
Hotels: Gateacre Hall, Halewood Rd.

P22 Liverpool Municipal

☎ 051-546 5435
Ingoe Lane, Kirkby, Liverpool L32 4SS
M57 exit B5192.
Meadowland course.
18 holes, 6588 yards, S.S.S.71
Club founded in 1965.
Visitors: welcome; booking system at weekends.
Green fees: £1.50.
Society meetings: by arrangement.
Catering: cafeteria facilities.

P23 Prenton

☎ 051-608 1053 or 1461
Golf Links Rd, Prenton, Birkenhead, Wirral L42 8LW
2 miles W of Birkenhead off A552, Junction 3 M53.
Flat parkland course.
18 holes, 6379 yards, S.S.S.71
Club founded in 1904.
Visitors: welcome on weekdays and Sun.
Green fees: weekdays £7 per day, Sun £12, 5 day (Mon to Fri) £25.
Society meetings: catered for on Wed.
Catering: full catering facilities.
Hotels: Bowler Hat, Oxton, Birkenhead; Leasowe Castle, Leasowe, Wirral.

P24 Royal Birkdale

☎ Southport (0704) 69903, 69928 or 67920 Sec.
Waterloo Rd, Birkdale, Southport,

Merseyside PR8 2LX
1½ miles S of Southport on A565.
Seaside course.
18 holes, 6711 yards, S.S.S.73
Course designed by Hawtree & Taylor.
Club founded in 1889.
Visitors: letter of introduction required from visitor's home club together with confirmation of handicap.
Society meetings: welcome on weekdays by arrangement.
Catering: light lunches and afternoon teas served, full lunches and dinners by arrangement.
Hotels: in Southport.

P25 Royal Liverpool

☎ 051-632 3101
Meols Drive, Hoylake, Wirral, Merseyside L47 4AL
A553 to Hoylake, 10 miles W of Liverpool.
Seaside links course.
18 holes, 6737 yards, S.S.S.74
Club founded in 1869.
Visitors: welcome on weekdays and weekends with letter of introduction from club or handicap certificate.
Green fees: weekdays £14 (£6 with member), weekends £16 (£8 with member).
Society meetings: welcome weekdays.
Catering: bar snacks available every day and lunches on Sun.
Hotels: Green Lodge, Hoylake; Bowler Hat, Talbot Rd, Birkenhead; Craxton Wood, Leasowe Castle, Leasowe Rd, Moreton, Wirral.

P26 Sherdley Park

☎ St Helens (0744) 813149
Elton Head Rd, St Helens, Merseyside.
2 miles from town centre on Warrington Rd.
Undulating parkland course.
18 holes, 5941 yards, S.S.S.69
Course designed by P.R. Parkinson.
Club founded in 1973.
Visitors: welcome.
Green fees: £2.
Society meetings: by arrangement.
Hotels: Fleece.

P27 Southport & Ainsdale

☎ Southport (0704) 78000
Bradshaws Lane, Ainsdale, Southport, Merseyside PR8 3LG
3 miles S of Southport on A565, ½ mile from Ainsdale railway station.
Championship links course.
18 holes, 6603 yards, S.S.S.73
Course designed by James Braid.
Club founded in 1907.
Visitors: welcome on weekdays, advance booking recommended.
Green fees: weekdays £12 per day or £9 per round.
Society meetings: welcome by advance booking.
Catering: full catering service to order.
Hotels: Tree Tops, Formby; Prince of Wales, Southport.

P28 Wallasey

☎ 051-639 3700 Sec, 3630 Clubhouse.
Bayswater Rd, Wallasey, Merseyside L45 8LA
Via M53 through Wirral or 15 minutes from Liverpool centre via Wallasey Tunnel.
Seaside course.
18 holes, 6607 yards, S.S.S.73
Club founded in 1891.
Visitors: welcome.
Green fees: weekdays £8 per day, weekends and Bank Holidays £10.
Society meetings: by arrangement.
Catering: full catering except Mon.
Hotels: Belvidere, Seabank Rd, Wallasey; Leasowe Castle, Leasowe Rd, Moreton, Wirral.

P29 Warren

☎ 051-639 5730
The Grange, Grove Rd, Wallasey, Merseyside.
500 yards up Grove Rd, beyond Grove Rd. station.
Municipal links course.
9 holes, 2700 yards, S.S.S.34 (68)
Club founded in 1911.
Visitors: welcome on weekdays; phone first at weekends.
Green fees: £2.60 for 18 holes.
Catering: lunches and teas at cafe in Clubhouse.
Hotels: Grove House.

P30 West Derby

☎ 051-228 3420 or 1540
Yew Tree Lane, West Derby, Liverpool L12 9HQ
4 miles E of Liverpool centre, 1 mile S of West Derby village.
Parkland course.
18 holes, 6333 yards, S.S.S.70
Club founded in 1896.
Visitors: welcome on weekdays.
Green fees: weekdays £6 per round, £8 per day; weekends and Bank Holidays £10 per day.
Society meetings: catered for on weekdays by arrangement.
Catering: lunches served daily.
Hotels: Alicia, Sefton Park, Liverpool.

P31 West Lancashire

☎ 051-924 1076
Hall Rd West, Blundellsands, Liverpool L23 8SZ
M57 to Aintree, A567 to Seaforth, then A565 to Crosby, follow signs to club, by Hall Rd station.
Seaside links course.
18 holes, 6756 yards, S.S.S.73
Course designed by C.K. Cotton.
Club founded in 1873.
Visitors: welcome.
Green fees: weekdays £10, weekends and Bank Holidays £13.
Society meetings: welcome weekdays.
Catering: lunches served except Mon.
Hotels: numerous hotels in Liverpool.

P32 Wirral Ladies'

☎ 051-652 1255
93 Budston Rd, Oxton, Birkenhead, Merseyside L43 6TS
On A41 adjacent to M53 Exit 3.
Moorland course.
18 holes, 4967 yards, S.S.S.70
Course designed by H. Hilton.
Club founded in 1894.
Visitors: welcome.
Green fees: £6 per round, £7.50 per day.
Society meetings: catered for on weekdays.
Catering: lunches and teas served.
Hotels: Bowler Hat Hotel, Talbot Rd, Birkenhead.

P33 Woolton

☎ 051-486 1601
Doe Park, Speke Rd, Woolton, Liverpool L25 7TZ
6 miles from City Centre.
Parkland course.
18 holes, 5706 yards, S.S.S.68
Visitors: welcome.
Green fees: weekdays £6.75, weekends £9.
Society meetings: by arrangement.
Catering: lunches served.
Hotels: in Liverpool.

Q Greater Manchester

Q1 Altrincham
☎ 061-928 0671
Stockport Rd, Timperley, Altrincham, Cheshire WA15
On A560 1 mile E of Altrincham.
Undulating parkland course.
18 holes, 6162 yards, S.S.S.69
Club founded in 1935.
Visitors: welcome.
Green fees: weekdays £2.20, weekends £3.45.
Society meetings: none.
Catering: meals available.
Hotels: Cresta Court, Church St, Altrincham; Woodlands, Wellington Rd, Timperley.

Q2 Ashton-in-Makerfield
☎ Ashton-in-Makerfield (0942) 727267
Garswood Park, Liverpool Rd, Ashton-in-Makerfield WN4 9LL
On A58, off M6, ½ mile to course.
Parkland course.
18 holes, 6160 yards, S.S.S.69
Course designed by F.W. Hawtree.
Club founded in 1902.
Visitors: welcome on weekdays, except Wed, and with member at weekends.
Green fees: weekdays £6 per day (£3 with member), weekends £4.
Society meetings: catered for on Tues.
Catering: meals available except Mon.
Hotels: Trust House Forte; Cranberry.

Q3 Ashton on Mersey
☎ 061-973 3220
Church Lane, Sale, Cheshire M33 5QQ
2 miles from Sale station.
Parkland course.
9 holes, 6202 yards, S.S.S.70
Club founded in 1897.
Visitors: welcome, except Tues after 3 (Ladies Day).
Green fees: £6 (£3 with member).
Society meetings: by arrangement.
Catering: snacks and lunches.
Hotels: Cresta Court.

Q4 Ashton-under-Lyne
☎ 061-330 1537
Kings Rd, Ashton-under-Lyne, Greater Manchester.
From Ashton take Mossley Rd, left at Queens Rd and right at Kings Rd.
Moorland course.
18 holes, 6157 yards, S.S.S.69
Club founded in 1913.
Visitors: welcome, only with member at weekends.
Green fees: weekdays £7 per day (£3 with member), weekends £7 with member.
Society meetings: welcome on weekdays by arrangement.
Catering: meals served except Mon.
Hotels: York House, York Place, Ashton; Birch Hall, Lees, Oldham.

Q5 Blackley
☎ 061-643 2980
Victoria Ave East, Blackley, Manchester M9 2HW
Parkland course.
18 holes, 6235 yards, S.S.S.70
Club founded in 1908.
Visitors: welcome.
Green fees: £7 per day.
Society meetings: catered for on Tues, Wed and Fri.
Catering: meals served except Mon.
Hotels: numerous hotels in Manchester.

Q6 Bolton
☎ Bolton (0204) 43067
Lostock Park, Chorley New Rd, Bolton BL6 4AJ
Leave M61 at Exit 6, off main road halfway between Bolton and Horwich.
Parkland course.
18 holes, 6215 yards, S.S.S.70
Club founded in 1912.
Visitors: welcome except on competition days.
Green fees: Mon, Tues, Thurs or Fri £9, Wed, Sat, Sun or Bank Holidays £11.
Society meetings: none.
Catering: full service except Sun.
Hotels: Pack; Last Drop; Swan; Crest.

Q7 Brackley
☎ 061-790 6076
Bullows Rd, Little Hulton, Worsley, Manchester.
9 miles from Manchester on A6, turn right at White Lion Hotel into Highfield Rd, left into Captain Fold Rd, left into Bullows Rd.
Parkland course.
9 holes, 3003 yards, S.S.S.69
Club founded in 1976.
Visitors: welcome.
Green fees: £1.65 per 9 holes.
Hotels: Crest, Bolton; Wendover, Morton.

Q8 Bramall Park
☎ 061-485 3119
20 Manor Rd, off Carrwood Rd, Bramhall Stockport SK7 3LY
8 miles S of Manchester, A6 to Bramhall Lane, then A5102 to Carrwood Rd.
Parkland course.
18 holes, 6214 yards, S.S.S.70
Club founded in 1894.
Visitors: welcome (no jeans to be worn and formal dress required after 2 pm).
Green fees: weekdays £9 per day or round, weekends and Bank Holidays £11.
Society meetings: catered for on Tues, up to 100, and Thurs up to 24.
Catering: full catering except Fri.
Hotels: Alma Lodge, Buxton Rd, Stockport; Ravenoak, Cheadle Hume; Queens Moat, Bramhall Lane, S Bramhall.

Q9 Bramhall
☎ 061-439 4057 or 6092 Sec.
Ladythorn Rd, Bramhall, Stockport, Ches SK7 2EY
Near Bramhall station, 8 miles S of Manchester on A5102.
Meadowland course.
18 holes, 6300 yards, S.S.S.70
Club founded in 1905.
Visitors: by arrangement with Pro if members of recognised golf club.
Green fees: weekdays £8, weekends and Bank Holidays £10.
Society meetings: catered for on Wed.
Catering: meals served, except Fri when only snacks available.
Hotels: Queens Moat House, Bramhall.

Q10 Breightmet
☎ Bolton (0204) 27381
Red Bridge, Ainsworth, Bolton, Lancs
From Bolton 3 miles on main road to Bury and turn left to Red Bridge.
Parkland course.
9 holes, 6407 yards, S.S.S.71
Course designed by Alliss & Thomas.
Club founded in 1912.
Visitors: welcome except on comp. days.
Green fees: weekdays £4 (£2 with member), weekends and Bank Holidays £6 (£3 with member).
Society meetings: by arrangement on weekdays.
Catering: meals available each day.
Hotels: Pack Horse, Bolton.

Q11 Brookdale
☎ 061-681 4534
Ashbridge, Woodhouses, Failsworth, Manchester N35 9WM
5 miles N of Manchester.
Parkland, meadowland course.

18 holes, 5878 yards, S.S.S.68
Club founded in 1961.
Visitors: welcome.
Green fees: weekdays £5.25 (£4 with member), weekends £6.25 (£5 with member).
Society meetings: by arrangement.
Catering: snacks, meals by arrangement.
Hotels: Belgrade, Oldham.

Q12 Bury

☎ 061-766 4897
Unsworth Hall, Blackford Bridge, Bury BL9 9TJ
On A56 7 miles N of Manchester.
Undulating moorland course.
18 holes, 5953 yards, S.S.S.69
Club founded in 1891.
Visitors: welcome on weekdays and weekends without competitions.
Green fees: weekdays £6.50, weekends £8.
Society meetings: catered for on weekdays only.
Catering: meals served except Mon.
Hotels: Woolfield, Bury; Hazeldine, Kersal; White Lion, Bury.

Q13 Castle Hawk

☎ Rochdale (0706) 40841
Heywood Rd, Castleton, Rochdale.
Leave Rochdale on Castleton road, in Castleton turn right directly before railway station, follow until reach Heywood Rd (dirt track).
Undulating parkland/meadowland course.
18 holes, 3158 yards, S.S.S.56
Course designed by T. Wilson.
Club founded in 1965.
Visitors: welcome.
Green fees: weekdays £2.50, weekends £3.
Society meetings: welcome.
Catering: snacks and lunches available; evening meals by arrangement.
Hotels: Norton Grange, Manchester Rd, Castleton.

Q14 Cheadle

☎ 061-428 2160
Cheadle, Cheshire SK8 1HW
1 mile S of Cheadle village, 1 mile N of Cheadle Hulme railway station.
Undulating parkland course.
9 holes, 2500 yards, S.S.S.65
Course designed by T. Renouf.
Club founded in 1885.
Visitors: welcome except Tues or Sat if member of golf club.
Green fees: weekdays £6, Sun £8.
Society meetings: by arrangement.
Catering: meals served.
Hotels: numerous good hotels in area.

Q15 Chorlton cum Hardy

☎ 061-881 3139 or 5830 Sec.
Barlow Hall Rd, Chorlton, Manchester M21 2JJ
3 miles from city centre, on A5103, near Southern Cemetery.
Meadowland course.
18 holes, 6004 yards, S.S.S.69
Club founded in 1905.
Visitors: welcome on weekdays and at weekends.
Green fees: weekdays £7, weekends and Bank Holidays £10; ½ price with member.
Society meetings: welcome weekdays.
Catering: meals served every day.
Hotels: Trust House, Northenden.

Q16 Crompton & Royton

☎ 061-624 2154
Highbarn, Royton, Oldham, Lancs OL2 6RW
Off A627 at Royton centre.
Moorland course.
18 holes, 6187 yards.
Club founded in c.1936.
Visitors: welcome.
Green fees: weekdays £6 (with member £4), weekends £8 (with member £6).
Society meetings: welcome by arrangement.
Hotels: Belgrade, Oldham.

Q17 Davyhulme Park

☎ 061-748 2856 Club, 2260 Office.
Gleneagles Rd, Davyhulme, Manchester M31 2SA
8 miles S of Manchester, adjacent to Park Hospital, Moorside Rd.
Parkland course.
18 holes, 6237 yards, S.S.S.70
Club founded in 1910.
Visitors: on weekdays except Wed.
Green fees: weekdays £8 per day, £7 per round (with member £4 per day, £3 per round); weekends and Bank Holidays £10 per day, £9 per round (with member £5 per day, £4 per round).
Society meetings: catered for on weekdays, except Wed.
Catering: lunches served except Mon; dinner by arrangement.
Hotels: numerous good hotels in Manchester.

Q18 Denton

☎ 051-336 3218
Manchester Rd, Denton, Manchester M34 2NU
A57, 5 miles SE of Manchester.
Parkland course.
18 holes, 6290 yards, S.S.S.70
Club founded in May 1909.
Visitors: welcome on weekdays and at weekends with member.
Green fees: weekdays £7 (with member £3.50), weekends and Bank Holidays with member £4.
Society meetings: catered for on Mon, Wed, Thurs and Fri.
Catering: lunches served except Mon.
Hotels: Old Rectory, Haughton Green, Denton, Manchester.

Q19 Didsbury

☎ 061-998 2743 or 2811 Pro
Ford Lane, Northenden, Manchester M22 4NQ
Off M63 at Junction 9, near Northenden Church, club sign on wall.
Parkland course.
18 holes, 6254 yards, S.S.S.70
Club founded in 1891.
Visitors: welcome.
Green fees: weekdays £7, weekends and Bank Holidays £9.
Society meetings: welcome.
Catering: full service available.
Hotels: The Post House, Palatine Rd.

Q20 Disley

☎ Disley (066 32) 2071
Stanley Hall Rd, Jackson's Edge, Disley, Stockport, Cheshire SK12 2AJ
A6, 6 miles from Stockport.
Moorland, meadowland course.
18 holes, 5977 yards, S.S.S.69
Course designed by James Braid.
Club founded in c.1888.
Visitors: welcome.
Green fees: £7 (£3.50 with member).
Society meetings: weekdays except Thurs.
Catering: meals served except Mon.
Hotels: Moorside.

Q21 Dunham Forest G & C C

☎ 061-928 2605
Oldfield Lane, Altrincham, Ches WA14 4TY
2 miles N of Junction 7 on M56, proceed in direction of Manchester, golf course is on left of main road.
Parkland course.
18 holes, 6800 yards, S.S.S.72
Club founded in 1961.
Visitors: welcome on weekdays.
Green fees: £10.
Society meetings: welcome.
Catering: full catering facilities.
Hotels: Cresta Court, Altrincham; George and Dragon, Altrincham; Swan, Bucklow Hill, Knutsford.

Q22 Dunscar
☎ Bolton (0204) 53321
Longworth Lane, Bromley Cross, Bolton BL7 9QY
N of Bolton about 2 miles off A666 Blackburn road, golf course signed to left at Dunscar Bridge.
Parkland/moorland course.
18 holes, 5995 yards, S.S.S.69
Club founded in 1908.
Visitors: welcome, advisable to contact Pro (Bolton 592992) for tee reservation.
Green fees: weekdays £7 (£3 with member), weekends and Bank Holidays £8.50 per day (£4 with member).
Society meetings: welcome, contact club for details.
Catering: daily, except Mon.
Hotels: Last Drop; Egerton House.

Q23 Ellesmere Port
☎ 051-339 7689 Clubhouse.
Chester Rd, Hooton, S Wirral, L66 1QH
Approximately 6 miles N of Chester, on main A41 road to Birkenhead, clubhouse at the rear of St Pauls Church, Hooton, opposite Burleydam Nurseries.
Parkland/meadowland course.
18 holes, 6436 yards, S.S.S.72
Course designed by Cotton, Pennink, Lawrie and Partners.
Club founded in 1971.
Visitors: welcome on weekdays and with reservation at weekends.
Green fees: weekdays £2.25 per round, weekends £2.75; reductions for Juniors, OAPs and unemployed on weekdays.
Society meetings: welcome on weekdays by arrangement with Pro.
Catering: full facilities available.
Hotels: Regency, Hooton, S Wirral; Wirral Mercury, Mollington, Chester; Woodhey, Berwick Rd, Little Sutton, S Wirral.

Q24 Fairfield G. & Sailing C.
☎ 061-370 1641
Booth Rd, Audenshaw, Manchester M34 5GA
A635, 6 miles from city centre.
Meadowland course.
18 holes, 5654 yards, S.S.S.68
Club founded in 1892.
Visitors: welcome on weekdays and with reservation at weekends, club competitions on Wed afternoon, Thurs and weekend mornings.
Green fees: weekdays £6 (with member £4), weekends and Bank Holidays £7 (with member £5).
Society meetings: by arrangement, preferably not on Wed and Thurs.
Catering: full catering facilities available by arrangement.
Hotels: Trough House.

Q25 Flixton
☎ 061-748 2116
Church Rd, Flixton, Urmston, Manchester.
½ mile from Flixton village.
Meadowland course.
9 holes, 6600 yards, S.S.S.71
Club founded in 1893.
Visitors: welcome except Wed.
Green fees: weekdays £6, weekends £7.
Society meetings: welcome except Wed.
Catering: bar snacks available; full meals by arrangement except Tues.
Hotels: hotels in Manchester.

Q26 Gathurst
☎ Appley Bridge (025 75) 2861
Miles Lane, Shevington, Wigan WN6 8EW
1 mile S of Junction 27 on M6.
Meadowland course.
9 holes, as 18 holes 6308 yards, S.S.S.70
Club founded in 1913.
Visitors: welcome on Mon, Tues, Thurs and Fri.
Green fees: £6.90 per round or per day.
Society meetings: by arrangement.
Catering: lunches except Mon and Tues.
Hotels: Lindley, Parbold; The Beeches, Standish.

Q27 Gatley
☎ 061-437 2091 or 436 2830 Pro.
Waterfall Farm, off Styal Rd, Heald Green, Cheadle, Ches SK8 3TW
Off Yew Tree Grove and Styal Rd 2m from Cheadle, 1m from Manchester Airport.
Parkland course.
9 holes, 5934 yards, S.S.S.68
Club founded in 1912.
Visitors: welcome weekdays except Tues.
Green fees: £6 (£3 introduced by member, £4 introduced by Cheshire Card).
Society meetings: welcome by arrangement with Sec on weekdays only.
Catering: full facilities; societies should book in advance.
Hotels: Excelsior, Manchester Airport; Post House, Northenden; Belfrey, Handforth.

Q28 Great Lever & Farnworth
☎ Bolton (0204) 62582
Lever Edge Lane, Bolton BL3 3EN
1½ miles from town centre.
Meadowland course.
18 holes, 5859 yards, S.S.S.69
Club founded in 1917.
Visitors: welcome by arrangement.
Green fees: weekdays £3.50, weekends and Bank Holidays £6.
Society meetings: by arrangement.
Catering: catering by arrangement with Stewardess; except Mon.
Hotels: numerous good hotels in Bolton.

Q29 Haigh Hall
☎ Wigan (0942) 831107
Haigh, Wigan.
Off B5238 or B5239, 6 miles NE of Wigan.
Parkland municipal course.
18 holes, 6423 yards, S.S.S.71
Club founded in 1973.
Visitors: welcome, book by phone on day.
Green fees: weekdays £2.80, weekends and Bank Holidays £3.
Society meetings: none.
Catering: snack bar facilities available.
Hotels: Victoria; Brockett Arms.

Q30 Hale
☎ 061-980 4225
Rappax Rd, Hale, Altrincham, Cheshire WA15 0NU
2 miles SE of Altrincham.
Undulating parkland course.
9 holes, 5241 yards, S.S.S.68
Club founded in 1903.
Visitors: welcome, weekends with member only.
Green fees: £8 per day (£2 with member).
Society meetings: by arrangement on weekdays.
Catering: meals served.
Hotels: Grand; Brockett Arms.

Q31 Heaton Moor
☎ 061-432 2134
Heaton Mersey, Stockport, Cheshire SK4 3NX
2 miles from Stockport.
Parkland course.
18 holes, 5876 yards, S.S.S.68
Visitors: welcome except Tues and Wed.
Green fees: weekdays £7.50, weekends £9 (less with member).
Society meetings: by arrangement.
Catering: meals served except Mon.
Hotels: in area.

Q32 Heaton Park
☎ 061-798 0295
Prestwich, Manchester.
Leave M62 at Exit 19, right at A576, 200 yards on right.
Undulating parkland course.
18 holes, 5849 yards, S.S.S.68
Course designed by C.H. Taylor.
Club founded in 1912.

Visitors: welcome, but book in advance.
Green fees: weekdays £2 per round, weekends and Bank Holidays £2.50 per round.
Society meetings: by arrangement.
Catering: none available.
Hotels: numerous good hotels in area.

Q33 Hindley Hall

☎ Wigan (0942) 55131 or 55991 Pro
Hall Lane, Hindley, Wigan, Lancs WN2 2SQ
Junction 6 off M61 into A6, take Dicconson Lane, then after 1 mile left at church into Hall Lane, club just after lake.
Moorland course.
18 holes, 5875 yards, S.S.S.68
Club founded in 1895.
Visitors: welcome if member of recognised golf club; advisable to check with Pro in advance.
Green fees: weekdays £6 per day, weekends and Bank Holidays £8 per day.
Society meetings: by arrangement.
Catering: meals served by arrangement, except Mon.
Hotels: Brockett Arms, Wigan.

Q34 Horwich

☎ Horwich (0204) 696980
Victoria Rd, Horwich, Bolton, Greater Manchester.
1½ miles from M61.
Parkland course.
9 holes, 2900 yards, S.S.S.67
Club founded in 1895.
Visitors: welcome with member only.
Green fees: £3 per day.
Society meetings: catered for on weekdays only by application.
Catering: bar snacks only available.
Hotels: Crest, Bolton.

Q35 Houldsworth

☎ 061-224 5055, 4571 or 8108
Wingate House, Higher Levenshulme, Manchester M19 3JW
M63 to Stockport finishing point, turn left onto A6 main Stockport to Manchester Road, right at lights at Barlow Rd.
Parkland course.
18 holes, 6078 yards, S.S.S.70
Course designed by T.G. Renouf.
Club founded in 1911.
Visitors: welcome any day but should check availability with Pro.
Green fees: weekdays £5, weekends and Bank Holidays £8; ½ price with member.
Society meetings: on written application.
Catering: full catering available.
Hotels: good hotels in Manchester.

Q36 Lobden

☎ Rochdale (0706) 343228
Lobden Moor, Whitworth, Rochdale.
A671 4 miles from Rochdale, ½ mile from centre of village.
Moorland course.
9 holes, 5750 yards, S.S.S.68
Club founded in 1888.
Visitors: welcome on weekdays and Sun.
Green fees: weekdays £4 (£2 with member), weekends and Bank Holidays £5.50 (£3 with member).
Society meetings: no.
Catering: by arrangement with Stewardess.
Hotels: hotels in area.

Q37 Lowes Park

☎ 061-764 1231
Hill Top, Walmersley, Bury, Lancs.
Take A56 Walmersley Road from Bury centre, after about 1½ miles turn right past Bury General Hospital into Lowes Rd, follow road until course signposted.
Moorland course.
9 holes, 6003 yards, S.S.S.69
Club founded in 1930.
Visitors: welcome on weekdays, except

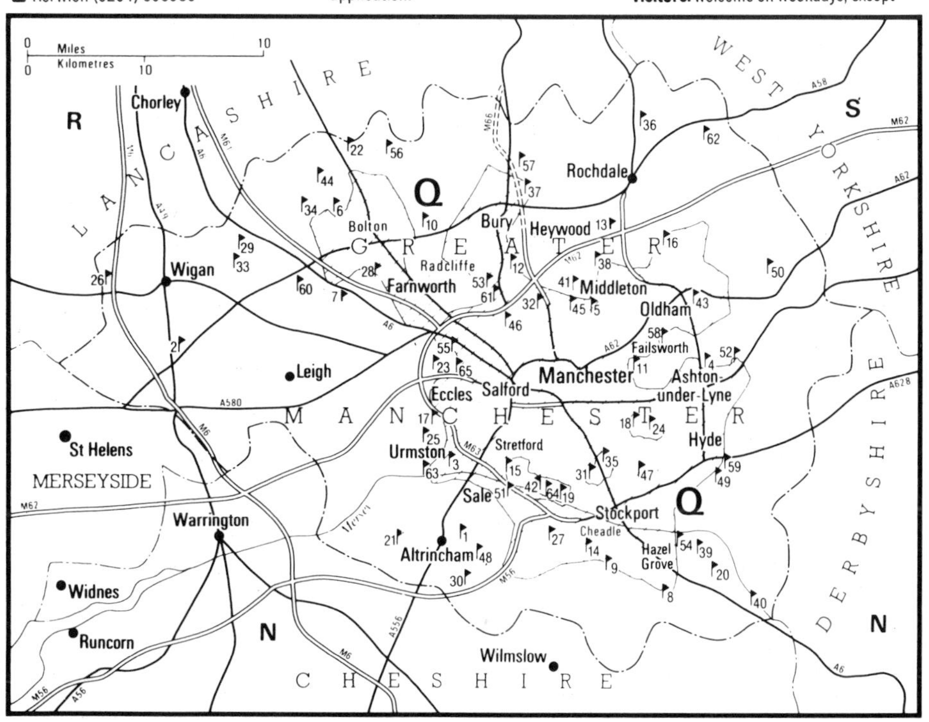

Wed (Ladies Day), and by invitation on Sun.
Green fees: weekdays £5 (with member £2.50), Sun £4; Juniors with member £1.50.
Society meetings: welcome on Mon, Tues or Thurs.
Catering: full catering except Mon.
Hotels: Woolfield House, Wash Lane.

Q38 Manchester

☎ 061-643 3202
Hopwood Cottage, Rochdale Rd, Middleton, Manchester M24 2QP
7 miles N of city on A664, 2 miles from Exits 19 and 20 off M62.
Undulating moorland course.
18 holes, 6554 yards, S.S.S.72
Course designed by H.S. Colt.
Club founded in 1882.
Visitors: welcome on weekdays and by arrangement at weekends.
Green fees: weekdays £8.50, weekends £10 (with member £4).
Society meetings: by prior arrangement with Sec.
Catering: full meal service.
Hotels: Norton Grange, Rochdale Rd, Castleton; Midway, Rochdale Rd, Castleton.

Q39 Marple

☎ 061-427 2311
Hawk Green, Marple, Stockport, Cheshire SK6 7EL
Off A6 at High Lane for 2 miles, left at Hawk Green.
Parkland/meadowland course.
18 holes, 5506 yards, S.S.S.69
Club founded in 1892.
Visitors: welcome on weekdays except Thurs after 5 pm, weekends with member only.
Green fees: £6 (with member £3).
Society meetings: by arrangement.
Catering: snacks served; meals by arrangement.
Hotels: West Towers.

Q40 Mellor & Townscliffe

☎ 061-427 2208
Tarden, Gibb Lane, Mellor, Stockport Ches.
Off A626 opposite Devonshire Arms on Longhurst Lane, Mellor.
Parkland/moorland course.
18 holes, 5925 yards, S.S.S.69
Club founded in 1894.
Visitors: welcome, except on Sat when must be with member.
Green fees: weekends and Bank Holidays £8 (with member £4), weekdays £6 (with member £3).
Society meetings: welcome, except Sat by arrangement.
Catering: full facilities, except Tues.
Hotels: West Towers, Marple.

Q41 New North Manchester

☎ 061-643 2941 Clubhouse, 9033 Sec, 7094 Pro Shop
Rhodes House, Manchester Old Rd, Middleton, Manchester M24 4PE
5 miles N of Manchester, Exit 18 off M62.
Moorland/parkland course.
18 holes, 6527 yards, S.S.S.72
Club founded in 1894.
Visitors: welcome on weekdays and by arrangement at weekends.
Green fees: on application.
Society meetings: welcome weekdays.
Catering: full service except Tues.
Hotels: Bower, Hollinwood Ave, Chadderton, Oldham; Birch, Manchester Rd, Heywood.

Q42 Northenden

☎ 061-998 4738 Sec, 998 2934 Steward and Members, 998 4079 or 945 3386 Pro.
Palatine Rd, Northenden, Manchester M22 4FZ
Exit 9 off M63, 1 mile into Northenden
Parkland course.
18 holes, 6435 yards, S.S.S.71
Club founded in 1914.
Visitors: by arrangement except Sat.
Green fees: weekdays £9 (with member £3.50), weekends £12 (with member £4.50).
Society meetings: catered for on Tues and Fri.
Catering: snacks every day, lunches and evening meals by arrangement.
Hotels: Trust House Forte, Northenden.

Q43 Oldham

☎ 061-624 4986
Lees New Rd, Oldham OL4 5EN
Just off minor road between Oldham and Ashton-under-Lyne or on A669 turn right at Lees.
Moorland/parkland course.
18 holes, 5045 yards, S.S.S.65
Club registered in 1891.
Visitors: welcome on weekdays or after 2 pm at weekends.
Green fees: weekdays £5, weekends and Bank Holidays £7.50.
Society meetings: catered for on weekdays except Tues.
Catering: luncheons or evening meals available except Mon.
Hotels: Birch Hall, Lees, Oldham.

Q44 Old Links

☎ Bolton (0204) 43089
Chorley Old Rd, Bolton BL1 5SU
On B6226 just N of A58.
Moorland course.
18 holes, 6406 yards, S.S.S.72
Club founded in 1892.
Visitors: welcome except Sat and competition days.
Green fees: weekdays £8 per day, weekends and Bank Holidays £10; half-price with member.
Society meetings: welcome, preferably on Wed, Thurs and Fri.
Catering: meals served except Mon.
Hotels: Crest, Beaumont Rd, Bolton; Pack Horse, Nelson Sq, Bolton; Last Drop, Turton, Bolton.

Q45 Pike Fold

☎ 061-740 1136
Cooper Lane, Victoria Ave, Blackley, Manchester M9 2QQ
4 miles N of city centre off Rochdale road.
Undulating meadowland course.
9 holes, 5789 yards, S.S.S.68
Club founded in 1909.
Visitors: welcome on weekdays.
Green fees: weekdays £4 per round or day, weekends and Bank Holidays £5.
Society meetings: available on request.
Catering: full meals except Thurs.
Hotels: many hotels in Manchester.

Q46 Prestwich

☎ 061-773 4578
Hilton Lane, Prestwich, Manchester M25 8SB
On A4066 ¼ mile W of junction with A56.
Parkland course.
18 holes, 4712 yards, S.S.S.63
Club founded in 1908.
Visitors: welcome.
Green fees: weekdays £5.50, weekends £7.
Society meetings: welcome except Tues (Ladies Day).
Catering: snacks and meals by arrangement with Steward except Mon.
Hotels: Village Squash, George St, Prestwich; Hazel Dean, Bury New Rd, Kersal, Salford.

Q47 Reddish Vale

☎ 061-480 2359
Southcliffe Rd, Reddish, Stockport, Cheshire SK5 7EE
1½ miles N of Stockport, off Reddish Rd.
Undulating course in valley.
18 holes, 6048 yards, S.S.S.69
Course designed by Dr A. Mackenzie.
Club founded in 1912.
Visitors: welcome on weekdays.

Green fees: £7.50 without member.
Society meetings: welcome on weekdays by arrangement.
Catering: meals served.
Hotels: Alma Lodge; Belgrade, Stockport.

Q48 Ringway
☎ 061-980 2630
Hale Mount, Hale Barns, Altrincham, Cheshire WA15 8SW
8 miles S of Manchester, off M56, Junction 6, follow sign for Hale, course is just through Hale Barns village.
Parkland course.
18 holes, 6494 yards, S.S.S.71
Club founded in 1909.
Visitors: welcome on Mon, Wed and at weekends.
Green fees: weekdays £10, weekends £14.
Society meetings: catered for on Thurs only from May to Sept.
Catering: full catering by arrangement with Stewardess (061-980 4468).
Hotels: Cresta Court, Altrincham; Four Seasons, Ringway, Hale.

Q49 Romiley
☎ 061-430 2392
Goosehouse Green, Romiley, Stockport SK6 4LJ
On B6104 off A560, ¾ mile from Romiley station.
Undulating parkland course.
18 holes, 6357 yards, S.S.S.70
Club founded in 1897.
Visitors: welcome except Thurs (Ladies Day).
Green fees: weekdays £8, weekends and Bank Holidays £10.
Society meetings: welcome on Tues and Wed by prior arrangement with Sec.
Catering: full catering service by prior arrangement with Steward, except Mon.
Hotels: West Towers, Church Lane, Marple, Stockport; Alma Lodge, 149 Buxton Rd, Stockport.

Q50 Saddleworth
☎ Saddleworth (045 77) 2059
Mountain Ash, Ladcastle Rd, Uppermill, Oldham
5 miles from Oldham, signposted off A670 Ashton to Huddersfield road at bend where road crosses railway bridge.
Moorland course.
18 holes, 5961 yards, S.S.S.69
Club founded in 1904.
Visitors: welcome; ring Pro (045 77 3653) to check availability.
Green fees: weekdays £6, £4 after 4 pm (£3 with member); weekends and Bank Holidays £8, £4.50 after 3 pm (£4.25 with member).
Society meetings: catered for on weekdays; small parties, 20 or under, on limited number of Sats.
Catering: catering available except Mon.
Hotels: Parkfield, Oldham; Belgrade, Oldham; Bower, Oldham; Birch Hall, Lees, Oldham.

Q51 Sale
☎ 061-973 3404 or 1638 Sec
Sale Lodge, Golf Rd, Sale, Ches M33 2LU
Boundary of Sale, 1 mile from Sale station.
Parkland course.
18 holes, 6351 yards, S.S.S.70
Club founded in 1913.
Visitors: welcome on weekdays.
Green fees: weekdays £8.50 (£3 with member), weekends and Bank Holidays £13.50 (£4 with member).
Society meetings: welcome weekdays.
Catering: full catering except Mon.
Hotels: Normanhurst, Brooklands Rd, Sale; Post House, Northenden, Manchester.

Q52 Stamford
☎ Mossley (045 75) 2126 or 4829 Pro
Oakfield House, Huddersfield Rd, Heyheads, Stalybridge, Ches SK15 3ET
On B6175 Huddersfield Rd, 3 miles from Ashton-under-Lyne.
Undulating moorland course.
18 holes, 5619 yards, S.S.S.67
Club founded in 1900.
Visitors: welcome on weekdays (Ladies Day Tues afternoons).
Green fees: weekdays £5 (with member £3), weekends and Bank Holidays £6.50 (with member £4).
Society meetings: catered for on weekdays except Mon and Tues.
Catering: meals served except Mon.
Hotels: York House, York Place, off Richmond St, Ashton-under-Lyne.

Q53 Stand
☎ 061-766 2388
The Dales, Ashbourne Grove, Whitefield, Manchester M25 7NL
1 mile N of M62, exit 17.
Undulating parkland course.
18 holes, 6411 yards, S.S.S.71
Club founded in 1904.
Visitors: welcome.
Green fees: £7 per day weekdays, £10 per day weekends.
Society meetings: by arrangement.
Catering: meals served.

Q54 Stockport
☎ 061-427 2001
Offerton Rd, Offerton, Stockport SK2 5HL
1 mile along A626 from Hazel Grove to Marple.
Parkland course.
18 holes, 6319 yards, S.S.S.71
Club founded in 1906.
Visitors: welcome most days except Tues morning.
Green fees: weekdays £9, weekends £10.
Society meetings: catered for on Wed and Thurs.
Catering: meals served except Mon.
Hotels: several good hotels in area.

Q55 Swinton Park
☎ 061-793 8077
East Lancashire Rd, Swinton, Manchester M27 1LX
On A580 Manchester to Liverpool road, about 4 miles from Manchester.
Parkland course.
18 holes, 6628 yards, S.S.S.72
Course designed by James Braid.
Club founded in 1926.
Visitors: welcome except on official club competition days.
Green fees: £8 per person.
Society meetings: welcome on Tues.
Catering: full catering, except Mon.
Hotels: many small hotels in area plus large hotels in Manchester.

Q56 Turton
☎ Bolton (0204) 852235
Wood End Farm, Chapeltown Rd, Bromley Cross, Bolton, Lancs BL7 9QH
3 miles N of Bolton on A676, adjacent to Last Drop Hotel.
Moorland course.
9 holes, 5805 yards, S.S.S.68
Club founded in 1908.
Visitors: welcome on weekdays without reservation.
Green fees: weekdays £4 (£2 with member), weekends and Bank Holidays £6 (£2 with member).
Society meetings: catered for on weekdays by arrangement.
Catering: by arrangement except Mon.
Hotels: Last Drop, Hospital Rd, Bromley Cross, Bolton.

Q57 Walmersley
☎ 061-764 1429 Steward, 0018 Sec
Garretts Close, Walmersley, Bury
On A56 about 2½ miles N of Bury.
Moorland course.
9 holes, 3057 yards, S.S.S.70
Club founded in 1906.
Visitors: welcome on Wed, Thurs and Fri.
Green fees: £5 per day.
Society meetings: by prior arrangement.
Catering: snack lunches and full catering available as required.
Hotels: Royal, Silver St, Bury; Old Mill, Ramsbottom, Bury; Normandie, Birtle, Bury.

Q58 Werneth (Oldham)

☎ 061-624 1190
Green Lane, Garden Suburb, Oldham, Lancs
5 miles from Manchester, take A62 to Hollinwood and then A6104.
Moorland course.
18 holes, 5363 yards, S.S.S.66
Club founded in 1904.
Visitors: welcome on weekdays.
Green fees: £5 plus VAT.
Society meetings: welcome w'kdays.
Catering: meals served except Mon.
Hotels: Belgrade.

Q59 Werneth Low

☎ 061-368 2503
Werneth Low Rd, Hyde, Ches SK14 3AF
2 miles from Hyde town centre via Gee Cross and Joel Lane.
Undulating course.
9 holes, 5734 yards, S.S.S.68
Club founded in 1918.
Visitors: welcome except Sun.
Green fees: weekdays £6.50 (£2.75 with member), Sat £9.50 (£3.50 with member).
Society meetings: welcome by arrangement.
Catering: daily, except Wed.
Hotels: numerous hotels in Stockport.

Q60 Westhoughton

☎ Westhoughton (0942) 811085
Long Island, Westhoughton, Bolton, Lancs.
4 miles SW of Bolton on A58.
Meadowland course.
9 holes, 5834 yards, S.S.S.68
Visitors: welcome weekdays, with member only at weekends.
Green fees: £4 weekdays (reduced with member).
Society meetings: by arrangement.
Catering: snacks and meals except Mon.
Hotels: Mercury.

Q61 Whitefield

☎ 061-766 2904
81/83 Higher Lane, Whitefield, Manchester M25 7EZ
Leave M62 at Exit 17 onto A56, club is 200 yards on left in Higher Lane.
Parkland course.
18 holes, 2580 yards, S.S.S.68
Club founded in 1932.
Visitors: welcome.
Green fees: on application.
Society meetings: welcome, special rates on application.
Catering: meals served.
Hotels: Bolton Crest, Beaumont Rd, Bolton; Hazeldean, 467 Bury New Rd, Salford.

Q62 Whittaker

☎ Littleborough (0706) 78310
Whittaker Lane, Littleborough, Lancs.
1½ miles from town centre.
Undulating moorland course.
9 holes, S.S.S.67
Club founded in 1906.
Visitors: welcome except Sun.
Green fees: on request.
Society meetings: arrangement with Sec.
Catering: none available.
Hotels: Sun; Dearnley Cottage.

Q63 William Wroe

☎ 061-748 8680
Penny Bridge Lane, Flixton, Manchester 31
M63, Exit 4, B5124, then B5158 to Flixton Rd.
Parkland course.
18 holes, 4395 yards, S.S.S.61
Visitors: welcome.
Green fees: weekdays £3.35, weekends £3.55.

Q64 Withington

☎ 061-445 9544
243 Palatine Rd, West Didsbury, Manchester M20 8UD
From Manchester S on A5103 then B5166 through Northenden.
Parkland course.
18 holes, 6411 yards, S.S.S.71
Club founded in 1892.
Visitors: welcome on weekdays.
Green fees: weekdays £7.50 (£3 with member), weekends and Bank Holidays £9.50 (£3 with member).
Society meetings: catered for on weekdays except Thurs.
Catering: full catering available (061-434 8716).
Hotels: Post House, Northenden; Britannia Ringway, Didsbury.

Q65 Worsley

☎ 061-789 4202
Stableford Ave, Monton, Eccles, Manchester M30 8AP
1 mile from junction of M62 and M63.
Parkland course.
18 holes, 6217 yards, S.S.S.70
Course designed by James Braid.
Club founded in 1894.
Visitors: welcome if member of golf club with official handicap.
Green fees: £9 per day.
Society meetings: catered for on Mon, Wed and Thurs.
Catering: service available from 12 noon.
Hotels: Wendover, Monton Rd, Morton.

R Lancashire, Isle of Man

Lancashire is renowned for the wonderful stretch of coastal courses; first of all, those between Liverpool and Southport and then the group in the Fylde area between Lytham and Blackpool.

There are enough championship links to satisfy the most avid golfers although not everyone should be tempted to try the championship tees even if permission is granted to do so. My own favourite is Formby. The dunes, pine and heather indicate easy walking on a sandy base and make an ideal combination of features. There is seclusion and beauty in so many of the holes and a variety in their challenge of which one never tires. Its first tee is almost on the platform of Freshfield Station, but first time travellers will have already spotted West Lancashire at Blundellsands; and Southport, Ainsdale and Hillside are the next stops up the line from Freshfield. There is a glimpse, too, of the clubhouse of Royal Birkdale set in an almost continuous avenue of dunes; Hesketh and Southport Municipal lie on the other side of Southport, journey's end for the train.

Another line, however, the one from Preston, provides a good view of Royal Lytham and St Annes which, if seaside in character, is hidden from the sea. It has been a regular home of the Open championship since 1926 and, more recently, has been fortunate in having such splendid qualifying courses as St Annes Old, Fairhaven, Lytham Green Drive and Blackpool North Shore.

From Blackpool, it is an easy hop to the Isle of Man which deserves the attention of golfers. Castletown wears the crown but Ramsey held the northern counties championship in 1985 while Douglas Municipal was designed by Alister Mackenzie and Peel, like Ramsey, by James Braid.

Lancashire's inland golfing attractions are bound to suffer but Manchester is surrounded by plenty of choice while Bolton boasts two fine courses, Bolton GC and Old Links.

R1 Accrington & District

☎ Accrington (0254) 32734
New Barn Farm, Devon Ave, West End, Oswaldtwistle, Accrington, Lancs BB5 4LR
On A679 5 miles from Blackburn.
Moorland course.
18 holes, 5954 yards, S.S.S.69
Visitors: welcome at any time.
Green fees: weekdays £4.70 (with member £2.75), weekends £6 (with member £4.40).
Society meetings: catered for at any time by arrangement.
Catering: full catering facilities.
Hotels: Kendal, Accrington; Moat House, Blackburn.

R2 Ashton & Lea

☎ Preston (0772) 726480
Tudor Ave, off Blackpool Rd, Lea, Preston PR4 0XA
3 miles from Preston centre on A584 Blackpool road, turn right opposite Pig and Whistle.
Parkland course.
18 holes, 6289 yards, S.S.S.70
Visitors: welcome.
Green fees: weekdays £7 (with member £3.50), weekends and Bank Holidays £8 (with member £4).
Society meetings: catered for on weekdays, preferred maximum 30.
Catering: bar snacks and meals.
Hotels: Crest, Preston; Tulketh, Ashton; Claremont, Ashton.

R3 Bacup

☎ Bacup (0706) 873170
Maden Rd, Bacup, Lancs OL13 8HM
Off A671, 7 miles N of Rochdale, ½ mile from Bacup centre.
Moorland course.
9 holes, 5652 yards, S.S.S.67
Club founded in 1911.
Visitors: welcome on weekdays, except Tues, and at weekends, after competitions.
Green fees: weekdays £5, weekends £6.
Society meetings: welcome on weekdays except Tues.
Catering: full catering facilities.
Hotels: Burwood, Bacup; Royal, Waterfoot.

R4 Beacon Park

☎ Up Holland (0695) 622700
Beacon Lane, Dalton, Up Holland, Wigan, Lancs WN8 7RU
Signposted from centre of Up Holland on A577 and from A5209 near Parbold, located on side of Ashurst Beacon Hill overlooking Skelmersdale.
Undulating/hilly parkland course.
18 holes, 5996 yards, S.S.S.69
Course designed by Donald Steel.
Club founded in 1982.
Visitors: welcome at any time.
Green fees: weekdays £1.90, weekends £2.30.
Society meetings: welcome during the week and by arrangement at weekends.
Catering: bar meals during bar hours; other meals by arrangement.
Hotels: Balcony Farm, Skelmersdale.

Castletown, Isle of Man

When the weather is fine, the greens holding and there is no wind, seaside links often present fewer problems than other types of course. In the 1980 Open championship, Muirfield suffered all sorts of indignities when its guard was lowered. Isao Aoki posted a 63 while Tom Watson and Horacio Carbonetti helped themselves to a 64; but the moment the wind stirred it was another matter.

Tales of the 1979 PGA Cup match at Castletown in the Isle of Man centred largely on days of sunshine, the ball running a mile and unanimous agreement that it was an idyllic spot. My baptism was a little more severe, a near gale springing up overnight and rain slanting in from the Irish Sea – all on the Longest Day of 1985, if you please. The clear outline of mountain peaks disappeared and there was a remoteness, almost a loneliness, on the little peninsula of land in the south-east corner of the island.

It was the sort of day when long par fives down the wind play shorter than modest par fours against it but the raw state is the true revealer of character and not even a princely soaking could dampen my enjoyment or admiration. Unless conditions blurred my judgement, its position as one of the great courses of the British Isles is undoubted.

Its modern version owes everything to Mackenzie Ross whose task of restoration after the war was similar to the miracle he wrought at Turnberry. To a greater degree than on most seaside links, good driving is essential. On such as the 7th and 8th, the fairway is the only place to be; yet the line from the championship tees involves quite a carry.

Castletown's hazards are entirely natural – gorse, bracken, rough, rocks and the beach which gives the course more coastal frontage than perhaps any other in the world. Apart from a clump of forlorn palms behind the 8th green, and some planting to mask the wall behind the 4th – a relic of a wartime firing range – there isn't a tree to be seen. Though the golfer has nothing to shield him, there is nothing to obscure the majestic panoply of views either; the sea, two great sweeps of bay, the small boats, the many landmarks including the castle which gave the place its name and, on a good day, the Cumbrian hills.

In days gone by, it was the residence of the Earl of Derby who, when Lord of Man (what an all embracing title), started the Derby at Castletown prior to taking it to Epsom. The 10th, nearly three furlongs in length, was the actual site, the hole not surprisingly assuming the name of 'Racecourse'. In this, Castletown has something in common with Hoylake and Torquay whose courses were originally homes of racing.

Castletown deserves the undivided attention of those who play it although the start is no indication of what lies ahead. The 1st is a short, uphill par four, one yard, in fact, over the par 3 limit, and the 2nd a somewhat plain two shotter. It is when you turn away down the long 5th, a dogleg round the corner of a stone wall, with a second shot (or third or fourth) between a large mound and an old pill box, that the course really begins.

The 5th, not quite such a good par five as the 3rd, sandwiches the 4th where the drive must be left to obtain the correct angle to negotiate the slope of the green and to miss the guardian bunkers on the right. Castletown's short holes make a wonderful set, the 6th, the shortest of them, providing an inviting shot even if the green is encircled by trouble. The same applies to the drive at the 7th and the second shot to a green typical of Mackenzie Ross's imaginative designs and shapes.

However, the 8th is no easier. The fairway may present a nice target at a lower level but it is also alarmingly narrow and the road is only a thin strip separating errant drives from the beach on which golf balls, pebbles and boulders are indistinguishable. This is Derbyhaven Bay with Derbyhaven village beckoning on the right of the 10th. But, before that is reached, the drive at the 9th must be aimed on the outline of King William's College, a solid fortress of Manx stone, although, having made what may have been the home turn in the first Derby down by the 10th green, Castletown Bay hoves in sight to further goad the golfer. There is no let-up.

At the delightful short 11th and the next two par fours, it is all too simple to let a tee shot drift to the right and, if the 14th is a shade less of a threat in this regard, the tee marker tells the bad news that it is 468 yards. On the 15th, a stone wall denotes out of bounds and the contouring of the greens foils those playing too safe to the left; but the best is yet to come – notably the 17th with its gaping gorge in front of the tee and resplendent rocks to the right introducing a touch of Cypress Point.

The 18th is a challenging finishing hole set against the square form of the welcoming Links Hotel which was purpose built in the last century. Those who originally spied out the land certainly knew what they were doing but a slight questioning word must be levelled at Manx folk lore and the island's emblem of the Three Legs of Man. It has as its motto 'whichever way you throw me, I shall stand' but did they ever experiment on the championship tee at the 17th with a gale off the sea?

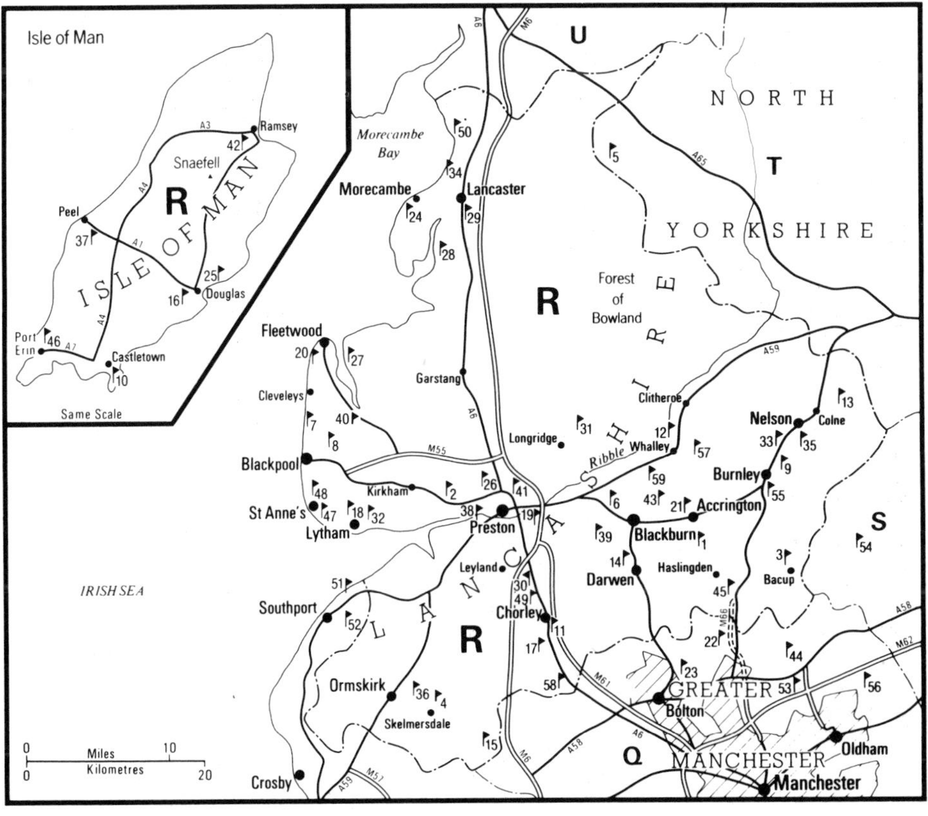

R5 Bentham
☎ Bentham (0468) 61018
Robin Lane, Bentham, Lancaster LA2 7LF
Halfway between Lancaster and Settle on B6480, 13 miles E of Junction 34 off M6.
Undulating meadowland course.
9 holes, 5752 yards, S.S.S.69
Club founded in 1922.
Visitors: welcome, check for competition weekends.
Green fees: weekdays £4 (£2.50 with member), weekends and Bank Holidays £5 (£3.50 with member).
Society meetings: welcome.
Catering: bar snacks available; meals by prior arrangement.
Hotels: Black Bull, Bentham; Melling Hall, Melling.

R6 Blackburn
☎ Blackburn (0254) 51122
Beardwood Brow, Blackburn, Lancs BB2 7AX
Situated in W end of town off Revidge Rd, from Moat House Hotel on A677 proceed to traffic lights and turn left, at Dog Hotel turn left to clubhouse.
Undulating meadowland course.
18 holes, 6099 yards, S.S.S.70
Club founded in 1894.
Visitors: welcome on weekdays and weekends if no competitions.
Green fees: weekdays £7, weekends and Bank Holidays £8.
Society meetings: catered for on weekdays, details on application.
Catering: meals every day except Mon.
Hotels: Moat House; Woodlands.

R7 Blackpool North Shore
☎ Blackpool (0253) 51017 or 52054 Sec
Devonshire Rd, Blackpool FY2 0RD
On A587 N of town centre behind North Promenade.
Undulating parkland course.
18 holes, 6442 yards, S.S.S.71
Club founded in 1904.
Visitors: welcome.
Green fees: weekdays £9, weekends and Bank Holidays £10.
Society meetings: welcome, details on application.
Catering: snacks, lunches and dinners available daily.
Hotels: many good hotels in area.

R8 Blackpool – Stanley Park
☎ Blackpool (0253) 33960
N.Park Drive, Blackpool, Lancs FY3 8LS
Ask for Stanley Park.
Parkland course.
18 holes, 6060 yards, S.S.S.69
Course designed by Dr Mackenzie.
Visitors: welcome any time.
Green fees: weekdays £3, weekends £4 per round.
Society meetings: by application.
Catering: for Societies by appointment except Tues.
Hotels: anywhere in Blackpool.

R9 Burnley
☎ Burnley (0282) 21045
Glen View, Burnley BB11 3RW
Off A56 to Glen View Rd, after 300 yards turn right.
Moorland/meadowland course.
18 holes, 5899 yards, S.S.S.69
Club founded in 1905.
Visitors: welcome on weekdays and most Suns.
Green fees: weekdays £5.75, weekends and Bank Holidays £7.50.
Society meetings: catered for on weekdays and Sun.
Catering: meals served except Mon.
Hotels: Rosehill House, Oaks, Kierby.

R10 Castletown
☎ Castletown (0624 82) 2125
Fort Island, Castletown, Isle of Man
1½ miles E of Castletown.
Seaside course.
18 holes, 6804 yards, S.S.S.73
Course designed by Mackenzie Ross.
Visitors: welcome.
Green fees: £6.
Society meetings: by arrangement.
Catering: snack lunches, evening meals.
Hotels: Castletown Golf Links.

R11 Chorley
☎ Adlington (0257) 480263
Hall o' th' Hill, Heath Charnock, Chorley, Lancs PR6 9HX
On A673 100 yards S of junction with A6 at Skew Bridge traffic lights.
Undulating course.
18 holes, 6277 yards, S.S.S.70
Course designed by J.A. Steer (1925).
Club founded in 1898.
Visitors: welcome on weekdays and by arrangement at weekends.
Green fees: £7.50.
Society meetings: welcome by arrangement on weekdays.
Catering: by arrangement with Steward.
Hotels: Harwood Hall; Pines, Clayton Green.

R12 Clitheroe
☎ Clitheroe (0200) 22618 Club, 22292 Sec, 24242 Pro.
Whalley Rd, Pendleton, Clitheroe BB7 1PP
Off A59 2 miles S of Clitheroe.
Undulating parkland course.
18 holes, 6311 yards, S.S.S.71
Course designed by James Braid.
Club founded in 1891.
Visitors: welcome subject to competition days on Sat and Thurs.
Green fees: weekdays £7, weekends and Bank Holidays £9.
Society meetings: welcome by arrangement, maximum 24 on Sun.
Catering: meals served.
Hotels: Roefield, Edisford Rd, Clitheroe; Swan and Royal, Castle St, Clitheroe; Fairway, King St, Clitheroe; Stirk House, Gisburn, Clitheroe.

R13 Colne
☎ Colne (0282) 863391
Law Farm, Skipton Old Rd, Colne, Lancs BB8 7EB
¾ mile off A56 at Colne Cricket Club.
Moorland course.
9 holes, 5961 yards, S.S.S.68
Club founded in 1901.
Visitors: welcome on weekdays and by arrangement at weekends.
Green fees: weekdays £5 per day, weekends and Bank Holidays £6 per day, reductions for parties of 12 or more.
Catering: meals served except Mon.
Hotels: many hotels in area.

R14 Darwen
☎ Darwen (0254) 71287
Winter Hill, Darwen, Lancs
1½ miles from Darwen town centre, off A666 Bolton to Blackburn road.
Moorland course.
18 holes, 5752 yards, S.S.S.68
Club founded in 1893.
Visitors: welcome on weekdays and with advance booking at weekends.
Green fees: weekdays £4.60 (introduced by member £2.30), weekends £5.75 (introduced by member £3.45).
Society meetings: catered for any day.
Catering: full, except Mon.
Hotels: Whitehall and Country Club.

R15 Dean Wood
☎ Up Holland (0695) 622219 Sec, 622980 Clubhouse
Lafford Lane, Up Holland, Skelmersdale, Lancs WN8 0QZ
Exit 26 from M6, 1½ miles on A577 to Up Holland.
Undulating parkland course.
18 holes, 6097 yards, S.S.S.70
Course designed by James Braid.
Club founded in 1922.

Visitors: members of golf club welcome on weekdays and with member at weekends.
Green fees: weekdays £7.50, weekends £9 (£3.50 with member).
Society meetings: welcome by arrangement on Mon or Fri, maximum 16, or on Thurs.
Catering: full catering available.
Hotels: Holland Hall.

R16 Douglas
☎ Douglas (0624) 75952
Pulrose Rd, Douglas, Isle of Man
1 mile from Douglas town centre, clubhouse situated near to large cooling tower for Electricity Dept Power Station.
Parkland municipal course.
18 holes, 6080 yards, Par 70, S.S.S. 69.
Course designed by Dr Mackenzie.
Club founded in 1927.
Visitors: welcome.,
Green fees: £3.70 per round, £4.50 per day, £12 per week.
Society meetings: welcome.
Catering: meals and snacks served from 11 am to 11 pm from May to end of Sept.
Hotels: numerous good hotels in Douglas.

R17 Duxbury Park
☎ Chorley (025 72) 65380
Duxbury Park, Chorley, Lancs
1½ miles S of Chorley, off A6, 200 yards along A5106 Chorley to Wigan road.
Parkland municipal course.
18 holes, 6390 yards, S.S.S.70
Visitors: welcome at all times.
Green fees: weekdays £2.40, weekends and Bank Holidays £3.60.
Catering: no catering facilities.
Hotels: The Pines, Clayton-le-Woods; Gladmar, Railway Rd, Adlington.

R18 Fairhaven
☎ Lytham (0256) 736741
Lytham Hall Park, Ansdell, Lytham-St Annes FY8 4JU
On B5261 2 miles from Lytham.
Semi links course.
18 holes, 6810 yards, S.S.S.73
Course designed by James Braid.
Club founded in 1895.
Visitors: welcome by arrangement.
Green fees: weekdays £8 per round, £11 per day; weekends and Bank Holidays £11 per round, £13 per day.
Society meetings: welcome by prior arrangement.
Catering: meals served except Mon when sandwiches are available from bar.
Hotels: Clifton Arms, Lytham; Grand, St Annes; Dalmeney, St Ives; Fearnlee, St Annes.

R19 Fishwick Hall
☎ Preston (0772) 798300
Glenluce Drive, Farringdon Park, Preston, Lancs PR1 5TB
Leave M6 at Samlesbury (Junction 31), take A59 towards Preston, past Tickled Trout Hotel, Glenluce Drive is first left at top of hill.
Undulating meadowland/parkland course.
18 holes, 6203 yards, S.S.S.70
Club founded in 1912.
Visitors: welcome.
Green fees: weekdays £4 (£2 with member), weekends and Bank Holidays £6.50 (£4 with member).
Society meetings: welcome on written application to Sec.
Catering: full catering facilities except Mon from Nov to March.
Hotels: Tickled Trout; Crest.

R20 Fleetwood
☎ Fleetwood (039 17) 3661
Princes Way, Fleetwood, Lancs FY7 8AF
On A587, 7 miles N of Blackpool.
Seaside links course.
18 holes, 6437 yards, S.S.S.71
Club founded in 1932.
Visitors: welcome without reservation.
Green fees: weekdays £7, weekends and Bank Holidays £8.
Society meetings: with reservation.
Catering: full catering except Thurs.
Hotels: North Euston, Promenade, Fleetwood; Boston, Promenade, Fleetwood.

R21 Green Haworth
☎ Accrington (0254) 37580
Green Haworth, Accrington, Lancs BB5 3SL
From Accrington town centre take main road to Blackburn, turn left on Willows Lane, follow road for 2 to 3 miles, sign just past Red Lion Hotel.
Moorland course.
9 holes, 5513 yards, S.S.S.67
Club founded in 1917.
Visitors: welcome on weekdays; ladies only after 5 pm on Wed.
Green fees: weekdays £4 per day, weekends £5 per day; ½ price with member.
Society meetings: welcome on weekdays by arrangement.
Catering: meals available at weekends and by arrangement on weekdays.
Hotels: Moat House, Blackburn.

R22 Greenmount
☎ Tottington (020 488) 3712
Greenhalgh Fold Farm, Greenmount, Bury BL8 4LA
Off M66 towards Ramsbottom on Bolton road, left at T-junction, club 1 mile on right.
Undulating parkland/moorland course.
9 holes, 4915 yards, S.S.S.64
Club founded in 1920.
Visitors: welcome on weekdays and with member at weekends.
Green fees: £5 (£3 with member).
Society meetings: catered for on weekdays except Tues.
Catering: full service except Mon.
Hotels: Old Mill, Ramsbottom.

R23 Harwood
☎ Bolton (0204) 22878
Springfirlys, Roaming Brook Rd, Harwood, Bolton, Lancs
On B6391 off A666 4 miles NE of Bolton town centre.
Undulating parkland course.
9 holes, 6028 yards, S.S.S.71
Club founded in 1927.
Visitors: welcome on weekdays and with member at weekends.
Green fees: £7.
Society meetings: none.
Catering: by arrangement.
Hotels: Last Drop, Bromley Cross; Pack Horse, Bolton.

R24 Heysham
☎ Lancaster (0524) 51011
Trumacar Park, Heysham, LA3 3JH
Drive S along Morecambe Promenade for 2½ miles and golf club is on right hand side on main road to Middleton.
Parkland course.
18 holes, 6234 yards, S.S.S.70
Club founded in 1884.
Visitors: welcome at all times; contact Pro for available starting time.
Green fees: weekdays £7.50 per day, £5 per round; weekends £9.50.
Society meetings: welcome anytime.
Catering: lunches served every day and high tea on Sun by arrangement.
Hotels: Post House, Lancaster; Midland, Morecambe.

R25 Howstrake
☎ Douglas (0624) 22086 Sec's Home No
Groudle Rd, Onchan, Isle of Man
On A11, 2 miles NE of Douglas.
Moorland/seaside course.
18 holes, 5243 yards, S.S.S.66
Club founded in 1914.
Visitors: welcome.
Green fees: weekdays and weekends £3.
Society meetings: on weekdays only.
Catering: none.
Hotels: Viliers; Septon; Palace; all in Douglas.

R26 Ingol G & Squash Club

☎ Preston (0772) 734556
Tanterton Hall Rd, Ingol, Preston, Lancs PR2 7BY
From A6 to Preston turn right down Lightfoot Lane, take second turn on left and first left again, signposted.
Parkland course.
18 holes, 6345 yards, S.S.S.71
Course designed by Cotton, Pennink, Lawrie & Partners.
Club founded in May 1981.
Visitors: welcome except on competition days, usually Sun.
Green fees: weekdays £5 (£3 with member), weekends and Bank Holidays £8 (£5 with member).
Society meetings: catered for every day.
Catering: meals available every day.
Hotels: Barton Grange, Garstang Rd, Preston; Broughton Park, Garstang Rd, Preston.

R27 Knott End

☎ Knott End (0253) 810576
Wyreside, Knott End on Sea, Blackpool FY6 0AA
Take A585 Fleetwood road off M55, and then B2588 to Knott End.
Meadowland course.
18 holes, 5852 yards, S.S.S.68
Course designed by James Braid.
Club founded in 1908.
Visitors: welcome on weekdays, not before 9.30 am or between 12.30 and 1.30.
Green fees: weekdays £8, weekends £10.
Society meetings: by arrangement.
Catering: full catering available.
Hotels: Bourne Arms, Knott End; Fernhill, Pilling.

R28 Lancaster

☎ Lancaster (0524) 751247
Ashton Hall, Ashton-with-Stodday, Lancaster LA2 0AJ
On A588 2½ miles SW of Lancaster.
Undulating parkland course.
18 holes, 6422 yards, S.S.S.72
Course designed by James Braid.
Visitors: welcome but restricted at weekends.
Green fees: £9 per day (£4 with member).
Society meetings: welcome by arrangement.
Catering: meals served.
Hotels: Post House, Lancaster.

R29 Lansil

☎ Lancaster (0524) 39269 Club
Caton Rd, Lancaster, Lancs LA1 3PE
2 miles E of Lancaster centre on A683.
Parkland/meadowland course.
9 holes, 5608 yards, S.S.S.67
Club founded in 1947.
Visitors: welcome on weekdays and after 1 pm at weekends.
Green fees: weekdays £4 (£2 with member), weekends and Bank Holidays £6 (£3 with member).
Society meetings: welcome weekdays.
Catering: lunches and bar snacks served all week with prior notice.
Hotels: Post House, Caton Rd, Lancaster; Castle, China St, Lancaster.

R30 Leyland

☎ Leyland (0772) 421359
Wigan Rd, Leyland, Lancs PR2 5UD
Off A49, ¼ mile from Exit 28 off M6.
Meadowland course.
18 holes, 6067 yards, S.S.S.69
Club founded in 1923.
Visitors: welcome on weekdays.
Green fees: weekdays £6 (with member £2.50), weekends and Bank Holidays £8 (with member £3.50): package deal £10 including catering.
Society meetings: welcome most weekdays.
Catering: full catering facilities.
Hotels: Ladbroke Mercury.

R31 Longridge

☎ Longridge (077 478) 3291
Fell Barn, Jeffrey Hill, Longridge, Preston, Lancs PR3 2TU
B6243 to B5269 to Longridge, climb through village, continue climbing for 1½m.
Moorland course.
18 holes, 5678 yards, S.S.S.68
Club founded in 1877.
Visitors: welcome at all times.
Green fees: weekdays £5 (£2.50 with member), weekends and Bank Holidays £7 (£4 with member).
Society meetings: by arrangement.
Catering: available except Mon.
Hotels: Shireburn Arms, Hurst Green, Blackburn; Gibbon Bridge, Chipping, Preston; Black Moss Guest House, Longridge, Preston.

R32 Lytham Green Drive

☎ Lytham (0253) 737390
Ballam Rd, Lytham, Lancs FY8 4LE
¾ miles from Lytham centre.
Parkland course.
18 holes, 6120 yards, S.S.S.69
Club founded in 1922.
Visitors: welcome on weekdays and by application at weekends with hand. cert.
Green fees: weekdays £7.50, weekends and Bank Holidays £8.50.
Society meetings: catered for on weekdays by prior arrangement.
Catering: full catering services daily.
Hotels: Clifton Arms, Lytham; Dalmeney, St Annes; Lancliffe, St Annes.

R33 Marsden Park

☎ Nelson 67525
Downhouse Rd, Nelson, Lancs BB9 8GD
Off A56, 8 miles N of Burnley.
Undulating meadowland course.
18 holes, 5806 yards, S.S.S.68
Course designed by C.K. Cotton & Partners.
Club founded in 1968.
Visitors: welcome.
Green fees: weekdays £2.50 (£1.25 juniors and OAPs), weekends £3.50.
Society meetings: by arrangement.
Catering: snacks in evenings, all day weekends.
Hotels: Great Marsden.

R34 Morecambe

☎ Morecambe (0524) 412841 Sec, 418050 Members, 415596 Pro.
Bare, Morecambe, Lancs LA4 6AJ
5 miles from M6 at Carnforth, follow signs to Morecambe.
Seaside/parkland course.
18 holes.
Course designed by Dr. Clegg.
Club founded in 1922.
Visitors: welcome by arrangement.
Green fees: weekdays £5.50, weekends and Bank Holidays £7.50 (with member £3).
Society meetings: welcome by arrangement with Sec, if members of recognised golf club.
Catering: full catering available except Mon when bar snacks only.
Hotels: Elms; Strathmore.

R35 Nelson

☎ Nelson (0282) 64583
King's Causeway, Brierfield, Nelson, Lancs BB9 0EU
Off A56 2 miles E of Brierfield
Moorland course.
18 holes, 5679 yards, S.S.S.69
Visitors: welcome on weekdays except Thurs afternoons; weekends and Bank Holidays by application.
Green fees: weekdays £6 (£3 with member), weekends and Bank Holidays £7 (£3.50 with member).
Society meetings: by arrangement.
Catering: lunches served except Mon, evening meals except Mon or Fri.
Hotels: Keirby, Burnley; Oaks, Reedley, Burnley.

R36 Ormskirk

☎ Ormskirk (0695) 72112
Cranes Lane, Lathom, Ormskirk, Lancs L40 5UV
2 miles E of Ormskirk.
Parkland course.
18 holes, 6333 yards, S.S.S.70
Club founded in 1899.
Visitors: welcome, prior booking

necessary.
Green fees: Mon, Tues, Thurs and Fri £10, Wed, Sat, Sun and Bank Holidays £12.
Society meetings: welcome, prior booking essential.
Catering: meals served except Mon.

R37 Peel
☎ Peel (0624) 84227 Steward, 843456 Sec.
Rheast Lane, Peel, Isle of Man
On A1, signposted on outskirts of Peel, coming from Douglas.
Moorland course.
18 holes, 5914 yards, S.S.S.68
Course designed by A. Herd.
Club founded in 1895.
Visitors: welcome, but not before 10.30 am at weekends.
Green fees: weekdays £5, after 4 pm £3; weekends £6 (with member £3).
Society meetings: by arrangement with Sec.
Catering: lunches and snacks available.
Hotels: Cherry Orchard, Port Erin; Sefton, Douglas; Villiers, Douglas.

R38 Penwortham
☎ Preston (0772) 744630
Blundell Lane, Penwortham, Preston, Lancs PR1 0AX
Off A5 at Penwortham traffic lights, 1 mile from Preston.
Parkland course.
18 holes, 5915 yards, S.S.S.68
Club founded in 1908.
Visitors: welcome on weekdays.
Green fees: £8 (£3.50 with member).
Society meetings: catered for on weekdays except Tues.
Catering: lunches and evening meals available except Mon.
Hotels: Crest, The Ringway, Preston.

R39 Pleasington
☎ Blackburn (0254) 22177
Pleasington, Blackburn, Lancs BB2 5JF
3 miles from Blackburn off A674.
Undulating parkland course.
18 holes, 6417 yards, S.S.S.71
Club founded in 1891.
Visitors: by arrangement.
Green fees: weekdays £10 per person, weekends and Bank Holidays £12 per person.
Society meetings: catered for on Mon, Wed and Fri.
Catering: by arrangement with Mrs V.C. Holliday (Blackburn 21028).
Hotels: Moat House, Preston New Rd, Blackburn; Tickled Trout, Preston New Rd, Samlesbury; Trafalgar, Preston New Rd, Samlesbury.

R40 Poulton-le-Fylde
☎ Poulton-le-Fylde (0253) 899357
Myrtle Farm, Breck Rd, Poulton-le-Fylde, Lancs
2 mins from Poulton town via Breck Rd.
Meadowland course.
9 holes.
Visitors: welcome.
Green fees: £2.
Society meetings: by arrangement.
Catering: meals served.
Hotels: River Wyre.

R41 Preston
☎ Preston (0772) 700011
Fulwood Hall Lane, Fulwood, Preston, Lancs PR2 4DD
N of Preston off Watling Street Rd.
Undulating course.
18 holes, 6249 yards, S.S.S.70
Course designed originally by James Braid.
Club founded in 1892.
Visitors: welcome.
Green fees: weekdays £8, weekends £10 (reduction with a member).
Society meetings: by arrangement.
Catering: meals (except Mon) by arrangement only.
Hotels: Barton Grange, Barton; Crest, Preston.

R42 Ramsey
☎ Ramsey (0624) 812244
Brookfield, Ramsey
12 miles N of Douglas, 5 minutes walk from town centre.
Parkland course.
18 holes, 6003 yards, S.S.S.69
Course designed by James Braid.
Club founded in 1890.
Visitors: welcome on weekdays and with booking at weekends.
Green fees: weekdays £5 per day, weekends £6 per day.
Society meetings: welcome.
Catering: lunches served except Thurs.
Hotels: Grand Island; Viking Apart; Beach.

R43 Rishton
☎ Blackburn (0254) 885498
Eachill Links, Rishton, Blackburn, Lancs BB1 4HG
Past Blackburn towards new M65, halfway to Accrington, turn off at roundabout near Red Lion Public House.
Undulating meadowland course.
9 holes, 6094 yards, S.S.S.69
Course designed by Alliss & Thomas.
Club founded in 1930.
Visitors: welcome on weekdays and with member at weekends.
Green fees: £3 (£1.50 with member).
Catering: by arrangement only.
Hotels: Dunkenhalgh.

R44 Rochdale
☎ Rochdale (0706) 43818 Sec, 46024 Club.
Edenfield Rd, Bagslate, Rochdale
3 miles from Exit 20 off M62 on A680.
Parkland course.
18 holes, 5981 yards, S.S.S.69
Club founded in 1888.
Visitors: welcome.
Green fees: weekdays £7, weekends £7.50.
Society meetings: catered for on Wed and Fri.
Catering: coffee, lunch and evening meals served except Mon.
Hotels: numerous hotels in area.

R45 Rossendale
☎ Rossendale (0706) 213056
Ewood Lane Head, Haslingden, Rossendale, Lancs BB4 6LH
16 miles from Manchester off A56.
Moorland/meadowland course.
18 holes, 6267 yards, S.S.S.70
Club founded in 1903.
Visitors: welcome except Sat.
Green fees: weekdays £6, Sun and Bank Holidays £8.
Society meetings: no.
Catering: meals served except Mon.
Hotels: Royal, Waterfoot; Queens Arms, Rawtenstall.

R46 Rowany
☎ Port Erin (0624) 834108
Rowany Drive, Port Erin, Isle of Man
Off Promenade.
Seaside course.
18 holes, 5813 yards, S.S.S.68
Visitors: welcome.
Green fees: weekdays £4.50 (men), £3 (ladies), £2 (juniors); weekends £6 (men), £5 (ladies), £3 (juniors).
Catering: full meals available.
Hotels: Cherry Orchard & Ocean Castle (free golf for residents); Towers.

R47 Royal Lytham & St Annes
☎ St Annes (0523) 724206 or 724207
Links Gate, St Annes on Sea, Lytham St Annes, Lancs FY8 3LQ.
1 mile from centre of St Annes on Sea.
Links course.
18 holes, 6673 yards, S.S.S.73

Club founded in 1886.
Visitors: welcome on weekdays only with letter of introduction.
Green fees: £12.50 per round, £17 per day.
Society meetings: by prior arrangement.
Catering: bar snacks, lunches and dinners available throughout day.
Hotels: Dormy House; many hotels in Lytham and St Annes.

R48 St Annes Old Links

☎ St Annes (0253) 723597
Highbury Rd, St Annes, Lytham St Annes, Lancs FY8 2LD
On A584 coast road towards St Annes turn right at traffic lights past holiday camp, club is 400 yards left of road.
Links course.
18 holes, 6616 yards, S.S.S.72
Club founded in 1901 and course in 1886.
Visitors: welcome on weekdays; limited numbers on Tues.
Green fees: weekdays £9 per day, weekends £12.
Society meetings: by prior arrangement with Sec.
Catering: bar, restaurant facilities.
Hotels: Dalmeny, South Promenade, St Annes; Chadwick, 113 South Promenade, St Annes; Harcourt Private, 21 Richmond Rd, St Annes.

R49 Shaw Hill G & C C

☎ Chorley (025 72) 69221
Whittle-le-Woods, Chorley, Lancs PR6 7PP
On A6 1½ miles N of Chorley.
Parkland course.
18 holes, 6467 yards, S.S.S.71
Club founded in 1925.
Visitors: welcome.
Green fees: £8 per round or day.
Society meetings: welcome, details on application.
Catering: full range of meals and snacks.
Hotels: Shaw Hill.

R50 Silverdale

☎ Carnforth (0524) 701300
Red Bridge Lane, Silverdale, Carnforth, Lancs
Off M6 at Carnforth, course opposite Silverdale railway station via Carnforth and Warton.
Hilly heathland course.
9 holes, 5262 yards, S.S.S.67
Club founded in 1906.
Visitors: welcome with restrictions on Wed and Sun.
Green fees: weekends and Bank Holidays £6 (with member £3), weekdays £3 (with member £2).
Society meetings: no.
Catering: lunchtime meals served on Mon, Wed and Fri or by arrangement with Club Sec (044 82 3782).
Hotels: Silverdale, Shore Rd, Silverdale; Wheatsheaf, Beetham, Milnthorpe.

R51 Southport Municipal

☎ Southport 35286
Park Rd, West, Southport, Merseyside
N end of Promenade.
Seaside course.
18 holes, 5939 yards, S.S.S.70
Visitors: welcome.
Green fees: weekdays £2.20 (£1.10 juniors), weekends £2.75.
Society meetings: by arrangement.
Catering: meals served.
Hotels: in Southport.

R52 Southport Old Links

☎ Southport (0704) 28207 Club, 24294 Sec.
Moss Lane, Southport, Merseyside PR9 7QS
From town centre take Lord St to roundabout at Law Courts, turn right into Manchester Rd, into Roe Lane and into Moss Lane.
Seaside course.
9 holes, 6486 yards, S.S.S.71
Club founded in 1926.
Visitors: welcome, but only after 4 pm on Wed, Sat, Sun and Bank Holidays.
Green fees: weekdays £4 (£2 with full member), weekends and Bank Holidays £6 (£3 with full member).
Society meetings: by arrangement.
Catering: full catering facilities.
Hotels: Nova, 85 Avondale Rd; Lincoln, Leicester St.

R53 Springfield Park/Marland course

☎ Rochdale (0706) 49801
Marland, Rochdale, Lancs
3 miles from M62.
Parkland course.
18 holes, 5981 yards, S.S.S.65
Club founded in 1928.
Visitors: welcome.
Green fees: £2.30 weekdays, £2.60 weekends.
Catering: none available.
Hotels: in area.

R54 Todmorden

☎ Todmorden (070 681) 2986
Rive Rocks, Cross Stone Rd, Todmorden, Lancs
Ascend Cross Stone Rd off A646 Halifax road, ¾ mile from town centre.
Moorland course.
9 holes, 5818 yards, S.S.S.68
Club founded in 1895.
Visitors: welcome except Mon.
Green fees: weekdays £4 (£2 with member), weekends £8 (£4 with member).
Society meetings: catered for on weekdays and Sun.
Catering: lunches, teas and evening meals served except Sun pm and Mon.
Hotels: Queens, Todmorden.

R55 Towneley

☎ Burnley (0282) 38473
Todmorden Rd, Burnley, Lancs BB11 3ED
Leaving Burnley town centre following Halifax and Todmorden signs, turn right at traffic lights near Burnley Football Ground, about 1 mile on left.
Parkland/meadowland course.
18 holes, 5812 yards, S.S.S.68
Course designed by Burnley Council (extended to 18 holes in 1967).
Club founded in 1932.
Visitors: welcome anytime.
Green fees: weekdays £2, weekends £2.80.
Society meetings: welcome by arrangement.
Catering: bar snacks at weekends.
Hotels: The Oaks, Reedley, Burnley; The Keirby, Burnley.

R56 Tunshill

☎ Rochdale (0706) 342095
Kiln Lane, Milnrow, Lancs
Follow Kiln Lane out of Milnrow town centre and continue along narrow lane to clubhouse.
Moorland course.
9 holes, 2902 yards, S.S.S.68
Club founded in 1943.
Visitors: welcome on weekdays except Tues evening and with special permission at weekends.
Green fees: weekdays £5 (£3 with member), weekends £5.50 (£3.50 with member).
Society meetings: welcome on weekdays.
Catering: by prior arrangement.
Hotels: Midway; Castleton; Rochdale.

R57 Whalley

☎ Whalley (025 482) 2236
Portfield Lane, Whalley, Blackburn, Lancs BB6 9DR
A59 to Whalley, course on left of road to

Accrington.
Parkland course.
9 holes, 5913 yards, S.S.S.69
Club founded in 1912.
Visitors: welcome.
Green fees: weekdays £5, weekends £6.50.
Society meetings: welcome, contact Sec.
Catering: lunches, dinners and snacks available.
Hotels: Moat House, Blackburn; Stirk House, Gisburn; Trafalgar, Blackburn.

R58 Wigan

☎ Standish (0257) 421360
Arley Hall, Haigh, Wigan WN1 2UH
On B5239 2 miles N of Wigan, through Standish, turn left at traffic lights on Canal Bridge, opposite Crawford Arms Public House.
Parkland course.
9 holes, 6058 yards, S.S.S.69
Club founded in 1898.
Visitors: welcome on weekdays except Tues (Ladies Day).
Green fees: weekdays £6 per day, weekends £8 per day.
Society meetings: applications considered.
Catering: snack lunches and evening meals available.
Hotels: Bellingham, Wigan Lane, Wigan; Brockett Arms, Mesnes Rd, Wigan.

R59 Wilpshire

☎ Blackburn (0254) 48260
72 Whalley Rd, Wilpshire, Blackburn, Lancs BB1 9LF
On A666 4 miles N of Blackburn.
Moorland course.
18 holes, 5911 yards, S.S.S.69
Club founded in 1898.
Visitors: welcome on weekdays.
Green fees: weekdays £6 (£3 with member), weekends £7.50 (£3.50 with member).
Society meetings: catered for on weekdays.
Catering: lunches daily, except Mon.
Hotels: Moat House, Blackburn; Trafalgar, Salmesbury, Blackburn.

S West & South Yorkshire

S1 Abbeydale
☎ Sheffield (0742) 360763
Twentywell Lane, Dore, Sheffield, S Yorks S17 4QA
Off A621 Sheffield to Baslow road at Dore and Totley station.
Parkland course.
18 holes, 6419 yards, S.S.S.71
Visitors: welcome any day by arrangement.
Green fees: weekdays £8.50 per round or day, weekends £10.50 per round or day.
Society meetings: catered for on Tues and Fri by arrangement with Sec.
Catering: bar snacks, lunches and dinners served every day except Mon.
Hotels: Grosvenor House; St George; Hallam Towers.

S2 Alwoodley
☎ Leeds (0532) 681680
Wigton Lane, Alwoodley, Leeds, W Yorks.
5 miles N of Leeds via A61.
Heathland course.
18 holes, 6301 yards, S.S.S.70
Course designed by Dr A Mackenzie.
Club founded in 1907.
Visitors: welcome by previous arrangement, restricted at weekends.
Green fees: weekdays £14, weekends and Bank Holidays £18.
Society meetings: by previous arrangement.
Catering: lunch and dinner served by previous arrangement.
Hotels: Post House, Bramhope, Leeds; Harewood Arms, Harewood.

S3 Austerfield Park
☎ (0302) 710841
Cross Lane, Austerfield, S Yorks
Off A614, 4 miles N of Bawtry.
Moorland course.
18 holes, 6824 yards, S.S.S.73
Course designed by E and M Baker Ltd.
Club founded in 1974.
Visitors: welcome.
Green fees: weekdays £6, weekends £8.
Society meetings: by arrangement.
Catering: snacks and restaurant daily.
Hotels: Mount Pleasant; Crown.

S4 Baildon
☎ Bradford (0274) 584266
Moorgate, Baildon, Shipley, W Yorks BD17 5PP
5 miles N of Bradford, A6037 to Shipley, ¾ mile NE on A6038, left at Junction Hotel.
Moorland course.
18 holes, 6178 yards, S.S.S.69
Club founded in 1896.
Visitors: welcome on weekdays and at weekends by arrangement.
Green fees: weekdays £4 (with member £2.45), weekends and Bank Holidays £6.60 (with member £4.50).
Society meetings: welcome.
Catering: lunches available except Mon.
Hotels: Bankfield, Cottingley.

S5 Barnsley
☎ Barnsley 382856
Wakefield Rd, Staincross, Nr Barnsley, S Yorks
On A61 3 miles from Barnsley.
Undulating meadowland course.
18 holes, 6048 yards, S.S.S.69
Visitors: welcome.
Green fees: weekdays £2.40, weekends £3.
Society meetings: by arrangement.
Catering: bar snacks.
Hotels: Royal; Ardsley House; Queens.

S6 Beauchief
☎ Sheffield (0742) 360648
Abbey Lane, Sheffield S8 0DB
5 miles from city centre, Abbeydale Rd is on A625 to Baslow.
Meadowland municipal course.
18 holes, 5423 yards, S.S.S.66
Club founded in 1925.
Visitors: welcome by arrangement.
Green fees: weekdays £2.50 per round, weekends £3.
Society meetings: welcome by arrangement.
Catering: meals served except Tues.
Hotels: many good hotels in Sheffield.

S7 Ben Rhydding
☎ Ilkley (0943) 608759
High Wood, Ben Rhydding, Ilkley, W Yorks LS29 8SB
Keep left after passing Wheatley Hotel to top of hill.
Moorland course.
9 holes, 4711 yards, S.S.S.64
Club founded in 1947.
Visitors: welcome except Sun morning.
Green fees: weekdays £3, weekends and Bank Holidays £5.
Society meetings: no.
Catering: no facilities.
Hotels: Wheatley, Ben Rhydding; Craiglands, Ilkley.

S8 Bingley St Ives
☎ Bradford (0274) 562506
St Ives Estate, Harden, Bingley, W Yorks BD16 1AT
Off B6429.
Wooded parkland/moorland course.
18 holes, 6480 yards, S.S.S.71
Club founded in 1931.
Visitors: welcome on weekdays.
Green fees: weekdays £3.80, weekends £6.50.
Catering: meals served except Mon.
Hotels: Bankfield, Bingley.

S9 Bradford
☎ Guiseley (0943) 75570 Sec, 73719 Pro
Hawksworth Lane, Guiseley, Leeds LS20 8NP
From Shipley 3½ miles NE of A6038, left to Hawksworth Lane.
Moorland/parkland course.
18 holes, 6259 yards, S.S.S.70
Club founded in 1891.
Visitors: welcome.
Green fees: weekdays £7.50 (£3.75 with member), weekends and Bank Holidays £10.50 (£5.25 with member).
Society meetings: catered for on weekdays by arrangement with Sec.
Catering: meals and snacks at all times.
Hotels: Craiglands, Ilkley; Cow and Calf, Ilkley; Bankfield, Bingley.

S10 Bradford Moor
☎ Bradford (0274) 638318
Scarr Hall, Pollard Lane, Bradford BD2 4RW
2 miles from Bradford.
Undulating meadowland course.
9 holes, S.S.S.68
Club founded in 1907.
Visitors: welcome.
Green fees: weekdays £4 (£2 with member), weekends £6.50 (£3 with member).
Catering: meals served.
Hotels: good hotels in area.

S11 Bradley Park
☎ Huddersfield (0484) 39988
Bradley Rd, Huddersfield, W Yorks HD2 1DZ
M62 runs along boundary of course between junction 24, Huddersfield and Junction 25, Huddersfield W; boundary borders on A6107 Bradley Rd, Huddersfield, entrance to course is signposted midway along Bradley Rd.
Hilly parkland course.
18 holes, 6100 yards, S.S.S.69
Course designed by Donald Steel.
Club founded in 1978.
Visitors: welcome.
Green fees: weekdays £2.50 per round, weekends £3.60 per round; £5 per day.
Society meetings: catered for on weekdays.

Catering: full catering facilities.
Hotels: Ladbroke Mercury; George, St Georges Sq, Huddersfield; Huddersfield, Rosemary Lane, Huddersfield.

S12 Branshaw

☎ Haworth (0535) 43235
Branshaw Moor, Keighley, W Yorks
B6143 2 miles SW of Keighley.
Moorland course.
18 holes, 5790 yards, S.S.S.68
Visitors: welcome.
Green fees: on request.
Society meetings: by arrangement.
Catering: lunches served.
Hotels: Black Bull, Haworth; Fleece Inn, Oakworth.

S13 City of Wakefield

☎ Wakefield (0924) 374316 or 376214 Sec
Lupset Park, Horbury Rd, Wakefield, W Yorks WF2 8QS
Approximately 2 miles from M1 Junctions 39 or 40, course situated on A642 Huddersfield road, turn at Empire Mail Order Stores.
Parkland course.
18 holes, 6405 yards, S.S.S.71
Club founded in 1936.
Visitors: welcome.
Green fees: weekdays £2.81, weekends and Bank Holidays £4.36.
Society meetings: by arrangement with Sec.
Catering: meals and snacks served; for groups arrange with Sec.
Hotels: Swallow, Wakefield; Post House; Cedar Court.

S14 Clayton

☎ Bradford (0274) 880047
Thornton View Rd, Clayton, Bradford, W Yorks BD14 6JX
On A647 from Bradford, then turn right and follow signs to Clayton.
Moorland course.
9 holes, 5527 yards, S.S.S.67
Club founded in 1906.
Visitors: welcome on weekdays.
Green fees: £2.30.
Society meetings: welcome on weekdays by arrangement.
Catering: by arrangement.
Hotels: Norfolk Gardens; Victoria.

S15 Cleckheaton & District

☎ Cleckheaton (0274) 877851
Bradford Rd, Cleckheaton, W Yorks BD19 6BU
Exit 26 from M62 onto A638 towards Bradford.
Parkland course.
18 holes, 6000 yards, S.S.S.69
Club founded in 1900.
Visitors: welcome.
Green fees: weekdays £7, weekends and Bank Holidays £9.
Society meetings: welcome weekdays.
Catering: full facilities available by arrangement with Catering Manager (jacket, collar and tie to be worn in dining room after 6.30 pm).
Hotels: Novotel, Merrydale Rd, Bradford.

S16 Concord Park

☎ Sheffield (0742) 613605 Sec
Shiregreen Lane, Sheffield S5

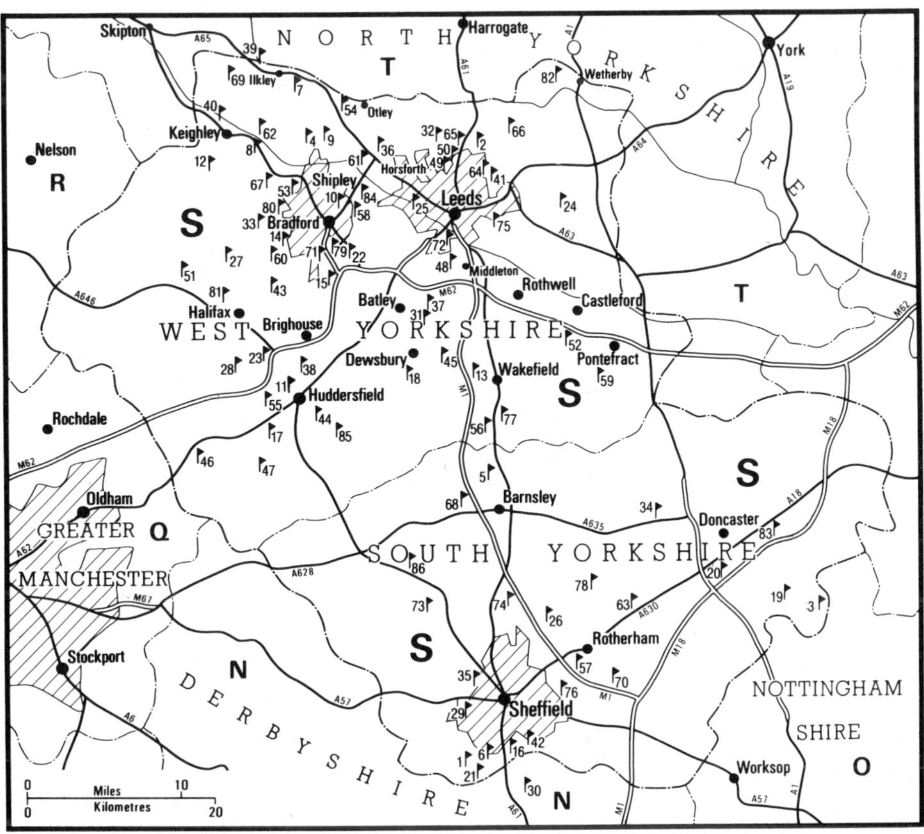

On A57 3½ miles N of Sheffield, next to Concord Sports Centre, Shiregreen.
Undulating parkland course.
18 holes, 4330 yards, S.S.S.61
Club founded in 1952.
Visitors: welcome.
Green fees: weekdays £1.50, weekends £2.50.
Society meetings: no.
Catering: snacks in sports centre.
Hotels: good hotels in Sheffield.

S17 Crosland Heath

☎ Huddersfield (0484) 653216
Felk Stile Rd, Crosland Heath, Huddersfield HD4 7AF
A62 Oldham road from Huddersfield (4m), follow signs for Goodalls Caravans.
Moorland course.
18 holes, 5962 yards, S.S.S.70
Visitors: welcome by arrangement.
Green fees: on application.
Society meetings: welcome except Tues and Sat, contact Sec.
Catering: full catering except Tues.
Hotels: Dryclough, Crosland Moor, Huddersfield; Durker Roods, Meltham, Huddersfield.

S18 Dewsbury District

☎ Mirfield (0924) 492399 or 496033 Pro
The Pinnacle, Sands Lane, Mirfield, W Yorks WF14 8HJ
Off A644, 2½ miles from Dewsbury, at Swan Hotel turn left into Steanard Lane, sign at Sands Lane.
Undulating meadowland/moorland course.
18 holes, 6266 yards, S.S.S.71
Course re-designed by Peter Alliss & Dave Thomas (1970).
Club founded in 1891.
Visitors: welcome on weekdays by prior arrangement, also on certain weekends.
Green fees: weekdays £5 (£3.50 with member), weekends £7 (£5.50 with member).
Society meetings: welcome weekdays.
Catering: full catering, except Mon.
Hotels: Little Chef, Cooper Bridge, Mirfield; The Cottage, Huddersfield Rd, Mirfield.

S19 Doncaster

☎ Doncaster (0302) 868316 Clubhouse, 868404 Pro
278 Bawtry Rd, Bessacarr, Doncaster, S Yorks DN4 7PD
Easy to locate between Doncaster and Bawtry on A638.
Undulating heathland course.
18 holes, 6015 yards, S.S.S.69
Club founded in 1894.
Visitors: welcome with or without member, on weekends.
Green fees: weekdays £7.50, weekends and Bank Holidays £9.
Society meetings: welcome on weekdays by prior arrangement with Sec.
Catering: main meals available by prior arrangement daily except Wed.
Hotels: Punch's, Bawtry Rd; Danum, High St, Doncaster.

S20 Doncaster Town Moor

☎ Doncaster (0302) 535286
Neatherds House, Belle Vue, Doncaster, S Yorks DN4 5HU
400 yds S of racecourse roundabout on A638 travelling towards Bawtry.
Parkland course.
18 holes, 6100 yards, S.S.S.69
Club founded in 1911.
Visitors: welcome except before 11.30 am on Sun.
Green fees: weekdays £5 per day (£2.50 with member), weekends and Bank Holidays £6 per day (£3 with member).
Society meetings: catered for by arrangement with Sec.
Catering: bar snacks available and evening meals by arrangement with Steward except Mon and Sun.
Hotels: Danum, High St, Doncaster; Earl of Doncaster, Bennetthorpe, Doncaster; Punches, Bawtry Rd, Bessacarr, Doncaster; Rockingham, Bennetthorpe, Doncaster.

S21 Dore & Totley

☎ Bradway (0742) 360492
Bradway Rd, Sheffield S17 4QR
Off A61 Sheffield to Chesterfield on Holmesfield road.
Parkland course.
18 holes, 6301 yards, S.S.S.70
Club founded in 1913.
Visitors: welcome on weekdays by prior arrangement.
Green fees: £6 per round, £8.50 per day.
Society meetings: welcome on weekdays only by prior arrangement.
Catering: full catering, except Mon.
Hotels: Roslyn Court; Hallam Tower.

S22 East Bierley

☎ Bradford (0274) 681023
South View Rd, Bierley, Bradford, W Yorks
3 miles SE of Bradford on Wakefield/Heckmondwike Rd.
9 holes, 5800 yards, S.S.S.63
Club founded in 1909.
Visitors: welcome except Sun mornings.
Green fees: weekdays £3.50 (£1.75 with member), weekends £5.75 (£3.50 with member).
Catering: snacks served, meals by arrangement.
Hotels: in Bradford.

S23 Elland

☎ Elland (0422) 72505
Hammerstones, Leach Lane, Elland, W Yorks HX5 0QP
Leave M62 at Junction 24, head for Blackley, golf club is 1 mile on left.
Parkland/meadowland course.
9 holes, 5526 yards, S.S.S.66
Club founded in 1912.
Visitors: welcome on weekdays and now, competition days.
Green fees: weekdays £4 (£2 with member), weekends and Bank Holidays £6 (£3 with member).
Society meetings: none.
Catering: bar snacks, except Mon.
Hotels: Ladbroke Mercury, Elland; The Rock, Holywell Green.

S24 Garforth

☎ Garforth (0532) 862021
Long Lane, Garforth, Leeds LS25 2DS
6½ miles E of Leeds on A63, then left onto A642.
Parkland course.
18 holes, 6296 yards, S.S.S.70
Club founded in 1913.
Visitors: welcome on weekdays.
Green fees: £8.
Society meetings: by arrangement with Sec (Garforth 863308).
Catering: full service available.
Hotels: Ladbroke Mercury, Garforth.

S25 Gott's Park

☎ Leeds (0532) 638232
Armley Ridge Rd, Leeds LS12 2QX
About 3 miles W of city centre.
Parkland course.
18 holes, 4449 yards, S.S.S.62
Visitors: welcome.
Green fees: weekdays £2.70, weekends £3.20; 80p for Juniors, unemployed, OAPs.
Society meetings: booked through Council.
Catering: meals served.
Hotels: Queens; Dragonara.

S26 Grange Park

☎ Rotherham (0709) 559497
Upper Wortley Rd, Rotherham S61 2SJ
2 miles W of town on A629.
Parkland municipal course.
18 holes, 6461 yards, S.S.S.71
Club founded in 1972.
Visitors: welcome.
Green fees: weekdays £1.90 per round, weekends £2.40 per round.
Society meetings: not catered for.
Catering: lunches and evening meals available except Mon.
Hotels: Brecon, 49 Moorgate Rd, Rotherham; Brentwood, Moorgate, Rotherham.

S27 **Halifax**
☎ Halifax (0422) 244171
Union Lane, Ogden, Halifax HX2 8XR
4 miles from town centre on A629 to Keighley.
Moorland course.
18 holes, 6030 yards, S.S.S.70
Club founded in 1900.
Visitors: welcome on weekdays and by prior appointment at weekends.
Green fees: weekdays £6 per day, weekends £9 per day.
Society meetings: welcome by prior arrangement with reduced party rates.
Catering: full range of catering services available at most times except Mon.
Hotels: Holdsworth House, Holmfield, Halifax; Princess, Princess St, Halifax.

S28 **Halifax Bradley Hall**
☎ Elland (0422) 74108
Stainland Rd, Holywell Green, Halifax
Halfway between Halifax and Huddersfield on B6112.
Moorland course.
18 holes, 6213 yards, S.S.S.70
Visitors: welcome.
Green fees: weekdays £5 per day, weekends £8 per day.
Society meetings: welcome.
Catering: full catering, except Tues.
Hotels: Old Golf House, Outlane, Huddersfield; hotels in Halifax or Huddersfield.

S29 **Hallamshire**
☎ Sheffield (0742) 302153
Sandygate, Sheffield S10 4LA
A57 from centre of Sheffield, left fork at Crosspool (3 miles from centre), 1 mile to course.
Moorland course.
18 holes, 6396 yards, S.S.S.71
Club founded in 1897.
Visitors: welcome with evidence of club membership.
Green fees: weekdays £10 per day, weekends £12 per day.
Society meetings: by arrangement.
Catering: full catering facilities.
Hotels: Hallam Towers; St George's; Rutland.

S30 **Hallowes**
☎ Dronfield (0246) 413734 Sec, 411196 Pro, 413149 Clubhouse.
Hallowes Lane, Dronfield, Sheffield S18 6UA
Take A61 Sheffield to Chesterfield road into Dronfield (do not take the by-pass), turn sharp right under railway bridge, club signposted.
Undulating moorland course.
18 holes, 6366 yards, S.S.S.71
Club founded in 1892.
Visitors: welcome on weekdays and with member at weekends or Bank Holidays; advisable to ring Pro or Sec in advance.
Green fees: £7 per round, £9 per day.
Society meetings: only 12 per year, arrange with Sec.
Catering: bar snacks available and full meals by arrangement, except Mon.
Hotels: many good hotels in Sheffield.

S31 **Hanging Heaton**
☎ Dewsbury (0924) 461606
White Cross Rd, Bennett Lane, Dewsbury, W Yorks WF12 7HJ
On A653 1 mile from Dewsbury town centre.
Parkland course.
9 holes, 5874 yards, S.S.S.68
Visitors: welcome on weekdays.
Green fees: weekdays £5 (£3 with member), weekends £7 (£4 with member).
Society meetings: welcome weekdays.
Catering: lunches served except Mon.
Hotels: numerous hotels in area.

S32 **Headingley**
☎ Leeds (0532) 679573
Back Church Lane, Adel, Leeds LS16 8DW
At roundabout on Leeds ring road take A660 towards Otley, turn right at traffic lights, course is just past Adel Church.
Undulating moorland course.
18 holes, 6238 yards, S.S.S.70
Club founded in 1892.
Visitors: welcome on weekdays.
Green fees: weekdays £10, weekends and Bank Hols £12 per round, £14 per day.
Society meetings: welcome weekdays.
Catering: lunches and evening meals available.
Hotels: Parkway, Otley Rd, Leeds; Post House, Bramhope, Otley Rd, Leeds.

S33 **Headley**
☎ Bradford (0274) 833348
Lower Kipping Lane, Thornton, Bradford, W Yorks BD13 3AJ
4 miles W of Bradford, on B6145 Thornton road, in village of Thornton.
Moorland course.
9 holes, 2457 yards, S.S.S.64
Club founded in 1907.
Visitors: welcome by prior arrangement.
Green fees: weekdays £3 (£1.50 with member), weekends £5 (£2.50 with member).
Society meetings: by arrangement.
Catering: by arrangement.
Hotels: Norfolk Gardens, Bradford.

S34 **Hickleton**
☎ Rotherham 892496
Hickleton, Doncaster, S Yorks
7 miles out of Doncaster on A635 to Barnsley.
Undulating meadowland course.
18 holes, 6361 yards, S.S.S.70
Course designed by Huggett, Coles & Dyer.
Club founded in 1909.
Visitors: welcome if members of recognised club.
Green fees: weekdays £4.50, weekends £6.
Society meetings: welcome weekdays.
Catering: by arrangement, except Mon.
Hotels: in Doncaster.

S35 **Hillsborough**
☎ Sheffield (0742) 343608
Worrall Rd, Sheffield S6 4BE
Moorland/parkland course.
18 holes, 6100 yards, S.S.S.70
Club founded in 1920.
Visitors: welcome on weekdays.
Green fees: £6.50 per round, £8.50 per day.
Society meetings: welcome weekdays.
Catering: lunches served except Fri; meals by arrangement.
Hotels: many hotels in Sheffield.

S36 **Horsforth**
☎ Leeds (0532) 585200
Layton Rd, Horsforth, Leeds, W Yorks LS18 5EX
On A65 Leeds to Ilkley road, Layton Rd is on right after crossing A6120 Leeds ring road, and after passing Rawdon Crematorium on left.
Undulating moorland course.
18 holes, 6243 yards, S.S.S.70
Club founded in 1907.
Visitors: welcome, advisable to check with Pro in advance.
Green fees: weekdays £8 per round or day, weekends and Bank Holidays £10 per round or day.
Society meetings: welcome by arrangement.
Catering: meals served except Mon.
Hotels: Post House, Otley Rd, Bramhope, Leeds; Parkway, Otley Rd, Adel, Leeds.

S37 **Howley Hall**
☎ Batley (0924) 472432 Club, 47385 Pro, 478417 Sec.
Scotchman Lane, Morley, Leeds LS27 0NX
From A650, main Bradford to Wakefield rd, take B6123, situated in Morley.
Parkland course.
18 holes, 6446 yards, S.S.S.71
Club founded in 1900.
Visitors: welcome on weekdays.
Green fees: weekdays £9 per day, £7 per round; weekends and Bank Holidays £10.
Society meetings: catered for on weekdays by arrangement with Sec.
Catering: meals daily, except Mon.
Hotels: Post House, Ossett.

S38 Huddersfield
☎ Huddersfield (0484) 26203 or 20110
Fixby Hall, Fixby, Huddersfield HD2 2EP
From M62 Exit 24 follow A643 to Clough House Inn then first right down Lightridge Road, clubhouse gates on right.
Parkland course.
18 holes, S.S.S.71
Club founded in 1891.
Visitors: welcome with recognised handicap.
Green fees: weekdays £10, weekends £12.50.
Society meetings: welcome by arrangement with Sec.
Catering: meals served.
Hotels: Ladbroke Motor; George, Huddersfield.

S39 Ilkley
☎ Ilkley (0943) 600214 or 607463 Pro
Myddleton, Ilkley, W Yorks LS29 0BE
On A65 18 miles NW of Leeds.
Parkland course.
18 holes, 5953 yards, S.S.S.70
Club founded in 1889.
Visitors: welcome on weekdays and at weekends by arangement.
Green fees: weekdays £10.50 per day or round, weekends and Bank Holidays £13.
Society meetings: by arrangement.
Catering: full catering facilities.
Hotels: Craiglands, Ilkley; Rombalds, Ilkley; Graystones, Ilkley.

S40 Keighley
☎ Keighley (0535) 604778 or 603179
Howden Park, Utley, Keighley, W Yorks BD20 6DA
1 mile W of Keighley on A650 Skipton road.
Parkland course.
18 holes, 6139 yards, S.S.S.70
Club founded in 1904.
Visitors: welcome.
Green fees: weekdays £7.50 per round or day, weekends and Bank Holidays £9.50 per round or day.
Society meetings: by prior arrangement.
Catering: bar snacks, lunches, high teas and evening meals served.
Hotels: The Beeches, Bradford Rd, Keighley; Bankfield, Cottingley, Bingley.

S41 Leeds
☎ Leeds (0532) 658775
Elmete Lane, Leeds LS8 2LJ
Off A58 4 miles from Leeds.
Parkland course.
18 holes, 6087 yards, S.S.S.69
Club founded in 1896.
Visitors: welcome on weekdays and with member at weekends.
Green fees: weekdays £9 per day, £6.50 per round.
Society meetings: welcome on weekdays by arrangement with Sec.
Catering: full catering except Mon.
Hotels: numerous good hotels in Leeds.

S42 Lees Hall
☎ Sheffield (0742) 554402 Club, 552900 Sec
Hemsworth Rd, Norton, Sheffield S8 8LL
3 miles S of Sheffield, A61 then A6054 towards Gleadless, first exit at roundabout, follow road to next roundabout passing water tower on left, take first exit, course 300 yds on right.
Parkland/meadowland course.
18 holes, 6137 yards, S.S.S.69
Visitors: welcome without reservation on weekdays.
Society meetings: by arrangement.
Catering: light snacks and meals served.
Hotels: any hotel in Sheffield.

S43 Lightcliffe
☎ (0422) 202459
Knowle Top Rd, Lightcliffe, Halifax
On A58 Leeds to Halifax road, on left entering Lightcliffe/Hipperholme village 4 miles from Halifax.
Parkland course.
9 holes, 5388 yards, S.S.S.68
Club founded in 1907.
Visitors: welcome apart from Wednesdays and Saturdays.
Green fees: weekdays £6, weekends £8.
Society meetings: catered for on weekdays except Wed.
Catering: lunch and evening meals except Thurs.

S44 Longley Park
☎ Huddersfield (0484) 22304
Maple St, off Somerset Rd, Huddersfield HD5 9AX
½ mile from town centre.
Parkland course.
9 holes, 5269 yards, S.S.S.65
Club founded in 1911.
Visitors: welcome.
Green fees: on application.
Society meetings: by arrangement on weekdays except Tues.
Catering: full catering or bar meals on application to Stewardess except Mon.
Hotels: various hotels of all categories within 1 mile.

S45 Low Laithes
☎ Ossett (0924) 273275
Parkmill Lane, Flushdyke, Ossett, W Yorks
Leave M1 at Exit 40, follow signs to Low Laithes and Flushdyke, about 1 mile.
Undulating course.
18 holes, 6450 yards, S.S.S.71
Course designed by Dr A. Mackenzie.
Club founded in 1925.
Visitors: welcome.
Green fees: weekdays £6 per round or day, weekends and Bank Holidays £8 per round or day.
Society meetings: welcome by arrangement on weekdays.
Catering: meals served every day except Thurs by arrangement with Stewardess.
Hotels: Post House; Swallow Inn, Wakefield.

S46 Marsden
☎ Huddersfield (0484) 844253
Mount Rd, Hemplow, Marsden, Huddersfield HD7 6NN
Off A62 8 miles out of Huddersfield towards Manchester.
Moorland course.
9 holes, 5702 yards, S.S.S.68
Club founded in 1921.
Visitors: welcome on Sat in summer.
Green fees: weekdays £2 (£1.50 with member), weekends and Bank Holidays £4.50 (£3 with member).
Society meetings: welcome.
Catering: full catering facilities.
Hotels: Durker Roods, Meltham; Hey Green, Marsden.

S47 Meltham
☎ Huddersfield (0484) 850227
Thickhollins Hall, Meltham, Huddersfield HD7 3DQ
5 miles from Huddersfield on B6108, in Meltham take B6107.
Moorland/parkland course.
18 holes, 6145 yards, S.S.S.70
Club founded in 1907.
Visitors: welcome on weekdays, and by arrangement at weekends.
Green fees: weekdays £4 (£2 with member), weekends £6 (£3 with member).
Society meetings: by appointment.
Catering: meals served except Tues.
Hotels: Durker Roods, Meltham.

S48 Middleton Park
☎ Leeds (0532) 700449
Middleton Park, Leeds
3 miles S of city centre.
Parkland course.
18 holes, 5233 yards, S.S.S.66
Club founded in 1933.
Visitors: welcome.
Green fees: £2.50.
Society meetings: welcome.
Catering: none.
Hotels: numerous good hotels in Leeds.

S49 Moor Allerton
☎ Leeds (0532) 661154 or 661155
Coal Rd, Wike, Leeds LS17 9NH
Take A61 Harrogate Road, about 1 mile past intersection with A6120 ring road

turn right onto Wigton Lane, at T-Junction take first left, first right then signposted.
Undulating parkland course.
1-9 holes, 3242 yards, 1-18 S.S.S.72
10-18 holes, 3138 yards, 1-9 19-27 S.S.S.73
19-27 holes, 3441 yards, 10-27 S.S.S.72
Course designed by Robert Trent Jones.
Club founded in 1923.
Visitors: welcome on weekdays and with reservation at weekends.
Green fees: weekdays £11 per round, from 8 Nov to March £6.50 after 4.00 pm; Sat £14 per round.
Society meetings: welcome.
Catering: meals available at lunchtimes and on weekdays in evening.
Hotels: Windmill, Seacroft, Leeds; Posthouse, Bramhope, Leeds.

S50 **Moortown**
☎ Leeds (0532) 681682
Harrogate Rd, Leeds LS17 7DB
On A61 main Leeds to Harrogate road.
Moorland course.
18 holes, 6503 yards, S.S.S.72
Course designed by Dr Mackenzie.
Club founded in 1909.
Visitors: welcome on weekdays and at weekends by arrangement with Sec and Pro.
Green fees: weekdays £12 per round, £14 per day.
Society meetings: welcome weekdays.
Catering: lunches served except Mon; other meals by arrangement.
Hotels: Harewood Arms, Harewood; Post House, Bramhope;

S51 **Mount Skip**
☎ Hebden Bridge (0422) 842896
Wadsworth, Hebden Bridge, W Yorks HX7 8PH
1m N of Hebden Bridge on Birchcliffe rd.
Moorland course.
9 holes, 5114 yards, S.S.S.66
Club founded in 1930.
Visitors: welcome.
Green fees: £4 (£2 with member).
Society meetings: welcome except Mon.
Catering: full service except Mon.
Hotels: White Lion, Hebden Bridge; Hebden Lodge, Hebden Bridge.

S52 **Normanton**
☎ Wakefield (0924) 892943
Syndale Rd, Normanton, Wakefield, W Yorks WF6 1PA
Off M62 at Junction 31 ½ mile from Normanton centre.
Flat meadowland course.
9 holes, 5284 yards, S.S.S.66
Club founded in 1903.
Visitors: welcome except Sun.
Green fees: weekdays £3, Sat and Bank Holidays £5.
Society meetings: on weekdays only.
Catering: snacks available and meals by arrangement.
Hotels: good hotels in area.

S53 **Northcliffe**
☎ Bradford (0274) 584085
High Bank Lane, Shipley, W Yorks BD18 4LJ
Take A650 Bradford to Keighley road to Saltaire roundabout, turn up Moorhead Lane, leading to High Bank Lane, club ½ mile on left.
Undulating parkland course.
18 holes, 6093 yards, S.S.S.69
Course designed by Sidney Weldon.
Club founded in 1920.
Visitors: welcome at all times.
Green fees: weekdays £7 (£3.50 with member), weekends and Bank Holidays £9 (£4.50 with member).
Society meetings: welcome weekdays.
Catering: full service at most times, except Mon.
Hotels: Bankfield, Bingley; Regency, Blenheim Mount, Manningham Lane, Bradford.

S54 **Otley**
☎ Otley (0943) 461015 Club, 465329 Sec, 463403 Pro
West Busk Lane, Otley, W Yorks LS21 3NG
On Otley to Bradford road 1½ miles from

Otley.
Meadowland course.
18 holes, 6229 yards, S.S.S.70
Club founded in 1905.
Visitors: welcome on weekdays and on Sun by arrangement.
Green fees: weekdays £9, after 5 pm £5.50; weekends and Bank Holidays £11.
Society meetings: welcome by prior arrangement.
Catering: full catering except Mon.
Hotels: Post House, Bramhope.

S55 Outlane
☎ Elland (0422) 74762
Slack Lane, Outlane, Huddersfield, W Yorks
Off A640 Rochdale road, 4 miles out of Huddersfield, through village of Outlane, turn left under motorway.
Moorland course.
18 holes, 5590 yards, S.S.S.67
Club founded in 1906.
Visitors: welcome.
Green fees: weekdays £4 (£2.50 with member), weekends £6 (£4 with member).
Society meetings: by prior arrangement.
Catering: meals daily except Tues.
Hotels: Old Golf House, Outlane, Huddersfield; Ladbroke Mercury, Ainley Top, Huddersfield.

S56 Painthorpe House
☎ Wakefield (0924) 255083
Painthorpe Lane, Crigglestone, Wakefield.
1 mile from Junction 39 off M1.
Meadowland course.
9 holes, 4100 yards, S.S.S.60
Club founded in 1961.
Visitors: welcome except Sun.
Green fees: £2 per day.
Catering: meals served.
Hotels: Cedar Court.

S57 Phoenix
☎ Rotherham (0709) 363864
Pavilion Lane, Brinsworth, Rotherham
1 mile along Bawtry turning from Tinsley roundabout on M1.
Undulating meadowland course.
18 holes, 6145 yards, S.S.S.69
Club founded in 1932.
Visitors: welcome from 9 am to noon and from 3 pm onwards.
Green fees: weekdays £6 per day, weekends and Bank Holidays £8 per day.
Catering: meals served.
Hotels: Carlton Park, Rotherham; Brecon, Rotherham.

S58 Phoenix Park
☎ Bradford (0274) 667178
Phoenix Park, Dick Lane, Thornbury, Bradford, W Yorks
From Bradford take Leeds road for 2½ miles to Thornbury roundabout, course situated at side of roundabout.
Undulating parkland course.
9 holes, 4776 yards, S.S.S.63
Visitors: welcome on weekdays only.
Green fees: weekdays £3, Bank Hols. £4.
Society meetings: by prior arrangement with Sec (Bradford 662369).
Catering: by arrangement with Steward prior to visit.
Hotels: many good hotels in Bradford.

S59 Pontefract & District
☎ Pontefract (0977) 792241
Park Lane, Pontefract, W Yorks WF8 4QS
Exit 32 on M62, situated on B6134.
Parkland course.
18 holes, 6227 yards, S.S.S.70
Club founded in 1900.
Visitors: welcome on weekdays.
Green fees: weekdays £7, weekends and Bank Holidays £8.50.
Society meetings: catered for weekdays except Wed.
Catering: daily, except Mon.
Hotels: Red Lion, Market Place, Pontefract; Wentbridge House, Wentbridge, Pontefract.

S60 Queensbury
☎ Bradford (0274) 882155
Brighouse Rd, Queensbury, Bradford, W Yorks BD13 1QF
4 miles from Bradford on A647.
Undulating parkland course.
9 holes, 5102 yards, S.S.S.65
Visitors: welcome.
Green fees: weekdays £4 (£2 with member), weekends £7 (£2 with member).
Society meetings: by arrangement.
Catering: meals served except Mon.
Hotels: Norfolk Gardens, Bradford; White Swan, Halifax.

S61 Rawdon
☎ (0532) 506040
Buckstone Drive, Rawdon, Leeds LS19 6BD
On A65 6 miles from Leeds.
Undulating parkland course.
9 holes, 5964 yards, S.S.S.69
Club founded in 1896.
Visitors: welcome on weekdays.
Green fees: £7.50 per day.
Society meetings: welcome on weekdays by arrangement.
Catering: lunches served except Mon.
Hotels: Peas Hill; Robin Hood, Yeadon.

S62 Riddlesden
☎ Keighley (0535) 602148
Howden Rough, Elam Wood Rd, Riddlesden, Keighley, W Yorks
A650 Keighley to Bradford road, left into Bar Lane, left into Scott Lane for 2 miles.
Moorland course.
18 holes, 4247 yards, S.S.S.61
Club founded in 1927.
Visitors: welcome.
Green fees: weekdays £3, weekends £4.
Society meetings: catered for.
Catering: bar snacks available.
Hotels: Beeches, Bradford Rd, Keighley.

S63 Rotherham
☎ Rotherham (0709) 850480 Pro, 850466 Steward, 850812 Sec
Thrybergh Park, Thrybergh, Rotherham S65 4NU
On main road from Doncaster to Rotherham, from A1M, 3m from M18 at Bramley, 7m from M1 at Junction35.
Parkland course.
18 holes, 6324 yards, S.S.S.70
Club founded in 1903.
Visitors: welcome by arrangement with Pro or Sec.
Green fees: weekdays £9 per day, weekends and Bank Holidays £11 per day.
Society meetings: welcome with restrictions.
Catering: full catering by prior arrangement, restricted on Wed; snacks generally available.
Hotels: Carlton Park, Rotherham; Brecon, Rotherham; Brentwood, Rotherham.

S64 Roundhay
☎ Leeds (0532) 662695
Park Lane, Leeds LS8 2EJ
A58 to Oakwood Clock, then Princes Ave, Street Lane, right at Park Lane, 4 miles from city centre.
Parkland municipal course.
9 holes, 5166 yards, S.S.S.65
Club founded in 1926.
Visitors: welcome.
Green fees: Mon to Sat £2.50, Sun £2.80.
Society meetings: by arrangement with Council Leisure Services.
Catering: snacks available at weekends; restaurant open in evenings.
Hotels: Beechwood, 26 Street Lane, Leeds; Clock, Roundhay Rd, Leeds.

S65 Sand Moor
☎ Leeds (0532) 685180 Members.
Alwoodley Lane, Leeds LS17 7DJ
A61 from Leeds centre 6 miles, turn left into Alwoodley Lane ½ mile on right.
Undulating parkland/moorland course.
18 holes, 6429 yards, S.S.S.71
Course designed by N. Barnes.
Club founded in 1926.
Visitors: welcome on weekdays except Tues and Thurs mornings.
Green fees: weekdays £8 per round, £10 per day; weekends and Bank Holidays £12.

Society meetings: welcome.
Catering: lunches and evening meals served except Mon.
Hotels: Harewood Arms, Harewood; Post House, Bramhope; Parkway, Bramhope; White Lodge, Harrogate Rd, Alwoodley.

S66 Scarcroft

☎ Thomer (0532) 892263
Syke Lane, Leeds LS14 3BQ
On A58 NE of Leeds, immediately after the New Inn on the left is Syke Lane.
Parkland course.
18 holes, 6426 yards, S.S.S.71
Club founded in 1937.
Visitors: welcome on weekdays.
Green fees: weekdays £9.50 per round or day, weekends and Bank Holidays £15 (£5 with member).
Society meetings: welcome on weekdays except Mon.
Catering: full catering except Mon.
Hotels: Post House, Bramhope, Parkway.

S67 Shipley

☎ Bradford (0274) 568652 Sec, 563212 Steward, 563674 Pro.
Beckfoot Lane, Cottingley Bridge, Bingley, W Yorks BD16 1LX
Situated off A650 Bradford to Keighley road at Cottingley Bridge, Bingley.
Parkland course.
18 holes, 6203 yards, S.S.S.70
Course designed by Colt, Alison & Morrison.
Club founded in 1896.
Visitors: welcome on weekdays.
Green fees: weekdays £8.50 per round, £9.50 per day; weekends and Bank Holidays £10 (£4 with member).
Society meetings: catered for by arrangement on weekdays.
Catering: lunches and dinners by arrangement except Mon.
Hotels: Bankfield, Bingley.

S68 Silkstone

☎ Barnsley (0226) 790328 or 205717 Hon Sec
Field Head, Silkstone, Barnsley, S Yorks
1 mile from M1 on A628 towards Manchester.
Undulating meadowland course.
18 holes, 6045 yards, S.S.S.70
Club founded in 1905.
Visitors: welcome on weekdays.
Green fees: £7 per day or round (£3.50 with member).
Society meetings: welcome by arrangement with Hon Sec.
Catering: full catering facilities by arrangement with Stewardess.
Hotels: Ardsley House, Doncaster Rd, Barnsley.

S69 Silsden

☎ Steeton (0535) 52998
High Brunthwaite, Silsden, Keighley BD20 0NH
A629, 4 miles from Keighley, on to A6034 to Silsden town centre, turn E at canal.
Moorland/meadowland course.
14 holes, 4870 yards, S.S.S.64
Club founded in 1913.
Visitors: welcome on weekdays and at weekends with restrictions on Sat afternoons and Sun mornings.
Green fees: weekdays £4 (£2 with member), weekends and Bank Holidays £6 (£3 with member).
Society meetings: no.
Catering: none.
Hotels: Steeton Hall, Station Rd, Steeton.

S70 Sitwell Park

☎ Rotherham (0709) 541046
Shrogswood Rd, Rotherham, S Yorks S60 4BY
Exit 33 M1 or Exit 1 M18, off A631, 2 miles

SE of Rotherham.
Undulating parkland course.
18 holes, 6203 yards, S.S.S.70
Course designed by Dr Mackenzie.
Club founded in 1913.
Visitors: welcome.
Green fees: weekdays £7 per day, weekends £8 per day.
Society meetings: welcome weekdays.
Catering: meals served except Tues.
Hotels: Moat House, Brecon, Brentwood.

S71 South Bradford

☎ Bradford (0274) 679195
Pearson Rd, Odsal, Bradford BD6 1BH
From Odsal roundabout take Stadium Rd (first rd left down Cleckheaton Rd) then Pearson Rd to club.
Undulating meadowland course.
9 holes, 6004 yards, S.S.S.69
Club founded in 1906.
Visitors: welcome on weekdays.
Green fees: weekdays £4.50 (with member £2.50), weekends and Bank Holidays £7 (with member £4).
Society meetings: welcome weekdays.
Catering: lunches and evening meals served except Mon.
Hotels: Novotel, Euroway Estate, Bradford.

S72 South Leeds

☎ Leeds (0532) 700479
Gipsy Lane, Beeston Ring Rd, Leeds
Take Leeds to Dewsbury road to traffic lights at Tommy Wass Hotel, follow ring road for 100 yards then left into Gipsy Lane, leading to clubhouse.
Parkland course.
18 holes, 5835 yards, S.S.S.68
Club founded in 1914.
Visitors: welcome at any time with member or by arrangement.
Green fees: £6 per day (with member £4).
Society meetings: welcome by application to Sec except Tues.
Catering: full catering except Tues.
Hotels: several hotels in Leeds city.

S73 Stocksbridge & District

☎ Stocksbridge (0742) 882003
30 Royd Lane, Townend, Deepcar, Sheffield S30 5RZ
On Sheffield to Manchester road, A616, 9 miles from Sheffield to Deepcar.
Moorland course.
15 holes, 5055 yards, S.S.S.65
Club founded in 1925.
Visitors: welcome any time.
Green fees: weekdays £5.50, weekends and Bank Holidays £6.50.
Society meetings: on request.
Catering: on request except Mon.
Hotels: Grosvenor, Sheffield; Hallam Towers, Sheffield.

S74 Tankersley Park

☎ Sheffield (0742) 468247
High Green, Sheffield S30 4LG
1 mile off A6135 N of Chapeltown.
Parkland course.
18 holes, 6241 yards, S.S.S.70
Visitors: welcome on weekdays, weekends with member only.
Green fees: £5.50 per round, £7.50 per day.
Society meetings: by arrangement.
Catering: lunches served except Mon.
Hotels: in area.

S75 Temple Newsam

☎ Leeds (0532) 645624
Temple Newsam Rd, Leeds LS15
On A63 Selby road, 5 miles from Leeds centre, follow signs for Temple Newsam House.
Undulating parkland course.
18 holes, 6448 yards, S.S.S.71
18 holes, 6029 yards, S.S.S.72
Club founded in 1923.
Visitors: welcome.
Green fees: weekdays £2.50, weekends £3.
Society meetings: welcome.
Catering: meals served at weekends.
Hotels: Windmill, Scarcroft, Leeds; Mercury, Garforth, Leeds.

S76 Tinsley Park

☎ Sheffield (0742) 442237
High Hazel Park, Darnall, Sheffield S9
Take A57 off M1 at Junction 33, at traffic lights turn right on Greenland Rd and right by bus depot.
Parkland course.
18 holes, 6045 yards, S.S.S.69
Club founded in 1921.
Visitors: welcome, no phone booking.
Green fees: weekdays £2.50 per round, weekends £3 per round.
Society meetings: not accepted.
Catering: meals served except Mon.
Hotels: in Sheffield.

S77 Wakefield

☎ Wakefield (0924) 255104
Woodthorpe Lane, Sandal, Wakefield WF2 6JH
3 miles S of Wakefield on A61, from M1 Exit 39.
Parkland course.
18 holes, 6626 yards, S.S.S.72
Club founded in 1891.
Visitors: welcome.
Green fees: weekdays £9 per round or day, weekends and Bank Holidays £10 per round or day.
Society meetings: by arrangement.
Catering: facilities available except Mon.
Hotels: Cedar Court, Denby Dale Rd, Wakefield; Swallow, Queen St, Wakefield.

S78 Wath

☎ Rotherham (0709) 878677
Abdy, Blackamoor, Rotherham, S Yorks S62 7SJ
Off A633 in Wath, 7 miles N of Rotherham.
Meadowland course.
9 holes, S.S.S.67
Visitors: welcome on weekdays, with member at weekends.
Green fees: on request.
Society meetings: welcome by arrangement.

S79 West Bowling

☎ Bradford (0274) 724449
Newall Hall, Rooley Lane, Bradford, W Yorks BD5 8LB
On Bradford inner ring road, 2 miles from town centre, adjacent to M606 and M62.
Parkland/meadowland course.
18 holes, 5800 yards, S.S.S.68
Club founded in 1896.
Visitors: welcome weekdays.
Green fees: weekdays £5 (£2 with member), weekends £8 (£3 with member).
Society meetings: welcome on weekdays.
Catering: lunches and dinners served except Mon.
Hotels: Novotel, Euroway Estate; Victoria, Bradford.

S80 West Bradford

☎ Bradford (0274) 427671
Chellow Grange, Haworth Rd, Bradford 9, W Yorks
B6144 4 miles from Bradford.
Meadowland course.
18 holes, 5752 yards, S.S.S.68
Club founded in 1908.
Visitors: welcome.
Green fees: weekdays £5.75 (£3.50 with member), weekends £7.50 (£5.75 with member).
Society meetings: welcome weekdays.
Catering: meals available except Mon.
Hotels: Bankfield, Bingley.

S81 West End

☎ Halifax (0422) 53608
Paddock Lane, Highroad Well, Halifax,

Yorkshire

Yorkshire, as the biggest county, has a lot to offer with much contrast, too. Its coastal courses are rather more of the cliff-top variety than embossed with great dunes but it possesses four of our very finest inland courses – Alwoodley, Ganton, Lindrick and Moortown.

To avoid accusations of partiality, I list them alphabetically as any attempt to grade them on merit would be extremely difficult. Alwoodley is perhaps the least well known because she used to guard her secrets jealously. It wasn't until 1965 that the Yorkshire championship was granted leave to be held there but it was the home course of Alister Mackenzie, the celebrated course architect, and its lovely moorland character undoubtedly left its mark on his thinking.

As it happened, Mackenzie was also responsible for Moortown which lies just across the Harrogate Road from Alwoodley and was part of the same moor until becoming more or less surrounded by housing developments, a course which used to rub shoulders with Moor Allerton and Sand Moor. For many years, Moortown was a suburb of Leeds rather than now, it seems, part of it. By contrast no setting could be more rurally splendid or scenically glorious than Ganton which lies in the Vale of Pickering between Malton and Scarborough. Everything about it bears such an air of elegance that nobody could fail to enjoy the challenge of the golf over a course that has housed countless national championships as well as the Ryder Cup of 1949. Moortown, Ganton and Lindrick have all, in fact, hosted the Ryder Cup. Lindrick followed the unforgettable scenes of the British victory in 1957 by staging the Curtis Cup of 1960.

Lindrick's delights, conveying the virtues of heath and common, extol the best of South Yorkshire, so far south, to be strictly accurate, that the river behind the famous 4th green forms the boundary with Nottinghamshire. From Lindrick, along the busy A57, it is a short journey to Sheffield where Hallamshire and Abbeydale are well worth a visit and, edging north and a little west, I have a soft spot for the Huddersfield Club at Fixby and for Woodsome Hall.

However, to complete the county of many acres and many courses, Ilkley, Otley and Bradford are equally pleasant; Harrogate is well served by Pannal, the Harrogate Club and Oakdale while travellers to the coast should never overlook Fulford at York or, moving further afield, some of the more isolated clubs out in the country.

W Yorks
Take A61 Burnley road from town centre, at traffic lights complex at King Cross, 1 mile from town, turn sharp right at sign to Warley and ascend Warley road to T-junction in ¾ mile, turn left to Highroad Well village then right at end of village, up Court Lane, signposted.
Moorland course.
18 holes, 5489 metres, S.S.S.69
Club founded in 1903.
Visitors: welcome.
Green fees: weekends £8 (with member £3), weekdays £6 (with member £2.50).
Society meetings: by arrangement.
Catering: meals served except Mon.
Hotels: Holdsworth House, Holmfield, Halifax; Princess, Princess St, Halifax.

S82 **Wetherby**
☎ Wetherby (0937) 62527 Clubhouse, 63375 Pro and Sec
Linton Lane, Wetherby, LS22 4JF
Off A1 at Wetherby.
Parkland course.
18 holes, 6244 yards, S.S.S.70
Club founded in 1910.
Visitors: welcome, but members have priority until 9.30 am, from 12 to 2 pm and after 4 pm.
Green fees: weekdays £10 per day, £6.50 per round; weekends £15 per day or round.
Society meetings: catered for on Wed, Thurs and Fri only.
Catering: lunches and dinners served except Mon.
Hotels: Ladbroke Mercury.

S83 **Wheatley**
☎ Doncaster (0302) 831655, 831203, or 834085
Armthorpe Rd, Doncaster, S Yorks DN2 5QB
Follow S ring road from old A1 E along boundary of St Leger racecourse to next crossroads, clubhouse is on right opposite large water tower.
Undulating parkland course.
18 holes, 6345 yards, S.S.S.70
Course designed by George Duncan (1933).
Club founded in 1913.
Visitors: welcome.
Green fees: weekdays £5.50 per round, £8 per day; weekends and Bank Holidays £8 per round, £10 per day.

Society meetings: welcome on weekdays, early booking advisable.
Catering: meals served.
Hotels: Danum, High St; Earl of Doncaster, Bennetthorpe; Balmoral, Thorne Rd.

S84 Woodhall Hills

☎ Leeds (0532) 564771
Woodhall Rd, Calverley, Rudsey, W Yorks
Adjacent to main Leeds to Bradford road, 6 miles from Leeds.
Undulating parkland course.
18 holes, 6102 yards, S.S.S.69
Club founded in 1905.
Visitors: welcome every day except Sat.
Green fees: weekdays £5 (£3 with member), Sun £7 (£4 with member).
Society meetings: catered for every day except Sat.
Catering: lunches served except Mon; other meals by arrangement.
Hotels: many good hotels in area.

S85 Woodsome Hall

☎ Huddersfield (0484) 602971
Fenay Bridge, Huddersfield, W Yorks HD8 0LQ
5 miles SE of Huddersfield on A629 Sheffield to Penistone road.
Parkland course.
18 holes, 6068 yards, S.S.S.69
Club founded in 1925.
Visitors: welcome on weekdays, except Tues afternoons.
Green fees: weekdays £9.50 (with member £4), weekends and Bank Holidays £12 (with member £5).
Society meetings: by arrangement.
Catering: bar snacks, lunches and evening meals available except Mon.
Hotels: George, Huddersfield; Ladbroke Mercury, Rinley Top, Huddersfield.

S86 Wortley

☎ Sheffield (0742) 885294
Hermit Hill Lane, Wortley, Sheffield S30 4DF
Off M1 at Junction 35, take A629 through Wortley village, course first right.
Undulating wooded parkland course.
18 holes, 5960 yards, S.S.S.69
Club founded in 1894.
Visitors: welcome.
Green fees: weekdays £7.50 per day or round, weekends and Bank Holidays £9.
Society meetings: by arrangement on Wed and Fri.
Catering: lunch and evening meals by prior arrangement except Mon.
Hotels: Middlewood Hall, Mowson Lane, Oughtibridge, Sheffield.

T North Yorkshire, Humberside

T1 Bedale
☎ Bedale (0677) 22568
Leyburn Rd, Bedale, N Yorks DL8 1EZ
On A684 ¼ mile N of Bedale.
Parkland course.
18 holes, 5746 yards, S.S.S.67
Visitors: welcome.
Green fees: weekdays £6 (£2 with member), weekends £7.50 (£2.50 with member).
Society meetings: welcome daily except Sun.
Catering: meals served except Mon.
Hotels: several in Bedale.

T2 Beverley & East Riding
☎ Beverley (0482) 868757 Sec, 867190 Club, 869519 Pro
Ante Mill, The Westwood, Beverley HU17 8RG
On Beverley to Walkington road.
Undulating course.
18 holes, 5414 yards, S.S.S.68
Club founded in 1889.
Visitors: welcome on weekdays.
Green fees: £4.50 per day.
Society meetings: catered for on weekdays except Wed.
Catering: lunches and dinners served except Wed.
Hotels: Beverley Arms, Beverley.

T3 Boothferry
☎ (0430) 30364
Spaldington, Howden, Goole DN14 7NG
A63 towards Howden then B1228 to Bubwith for 3 miles.
Meadowland course.
18 holes, 6651 yards, S.S.S.72
Course designed by Donald Steel.
Club founded in 1981.
Visitors: welcome at all times.
Green fees: weekdays £3 per round, £4 per day; weekends £4.20 per round, £5.70 per day.
Society meetings: welcome all times.
Catering: lunches and bar meals served every day, dinner only on Fri and Sat.
Hotels: Bowmans, Howden; Wellington, Howden.

T4 Bridlington
☎ Bridlington (0262) 672092
Belvedere Rd, Bridlington, N Humberside YO15 3NA
1½ miles S of Bridlington station, off A165 from Hull.
Seaside course.
18 holes, 6320 yards, S.S.S.70
Course designed by James Braid.
Club founded in 1907.
Visitors: welcome on weekdays and with restrictions at weekends.
Green fees: weekdays £3.75 per round, £6 per day; weekends and Bank Holidays £6 per round, £8.50 per day.
Society meetings: catered for by arrangement.
Catering: lunches served except Tues.

T5 Brough
☎ Hull (0482) 667374
Cave Rd, Brough, N Humberside HU15 1HB
10 miles W of Hull off A63.
Parkland course.
18 holes, 6012 yards, S.S.S.69
Club founded in 1891.
Visitors: welcome on weekdays except Wed.
Green fees: weekdays £8.
Society meetings: catered for on Tues and Fri.
Catering: full catering facilities.
Hotels: Cave Castle, South Cave; Crest, North Ferriby.

T6 Catterick Garrison
☎ Richmond (0748) 833268
Leyburn Rd, Catterick Garrison, N Yorks DL9 3QE
6 miles S of Scotch Corner, turn off A1 at Catterick Bridge, 2½ miles to Catterick Garrison.
Undulating moorland/parkland course.
18 holes, 6332 yards, S.S.S.70
Course designed by Arthur Day.
Club founded in 1930.
Visitors: welcome at any time.
Green fees: weekdays £6, weekends and Bank Holidays £9.
Society meetings: welcome by prior arrangement.
Catering: meals and snacks except Mon.
Hotels: Bridge House, Catterick Bridge, N Yorks; Kings Head, Market Place, Richmond, N Yorks.

T7 Cleethorpes
☎ Grimsby (0472) 812059 or 814060
Kings Rd, Cleethorpes, S Humberside DN35 0PN
Off A1031 1 mile S of Cleethorpes.
Meadowland course.
18 holes, 6015 yards, S.S.S.69
Course designed by Harry Vardon.
Club founded in 1896.
Visitors: welcome but must be member of a recognised club (Ladies only, Wed afternoon).
Green fees: weekdays £6, weekends and Bank Holidays £8.50.
Society meetings: only by arrangement
Catering: full catering available by arrangement with Steward.
Hotels: Kingsway, Kingsway, Cleethorpes; Wellow, Kings Rd, Cleethorpes; Blundell Park, Grimsby Rd, Cleethorpes.

T8 Driffield
☎ Driffield (0377) 43116
Sunderlandwick, Driffield, N Humberside
1 mile from Driffield town centre towards Hull on A164.
Parkland course.
9 holes, 6225 yards, S.S.S.70
Course due to be extended to 18 holes.
Club founded in 1935.
Visitors: welcome at all times.
Green fees: weekdays £6 (£3 with member), weekends £9 (£4 with member).
Society meetings: catered for weekdays.
Catering: lunches and evening meals available except Mon.
Hotels: Bell, Driffield.

T9 Easingwold
☎ Easingwold (0347) 21486 or 21964 Pro
Stillington Rd, Easingwold YO6 3ET
¾ mile off A19, entering Easingwold from York turn right immediately past garage.
Parkland course.
18 holes, 6222 yards, S.S.S.70
Club founded in 1930.
Visitors: welcome on weekdays, advance booking through Assistant Sec.
Green fees: weekdays £8 (£3 with member), weekends and Bank Holidays £11 (£4 with member).
Society meetings: welcome.
Catering: bar snacks and afternoon tea; evening meals if booked before play.
Hotels: George, Market Place, Easingwold.

T10 Elsham
☎ Barnetby (0652) 688382 or 680291
Barton Rd, Elsham, Brigg, S Humberside DN20 0LS
Situated on E side of Brigg to Barton road, B1206, 3 miles N of Brigg.
Parkland course.
18 holes, 6420 yards, S.S.S.71
Club founded in 1926.
Visitors: welcome on weekdays.
Green fees: weekdays £6.50 per day.

T11 Filey

☎ Filey (0723) 513293
West Ave, Filey, N Yorks YO14 9BQ
Private road off end of West Ave in S end of town.
Seaside course.
18 holes, 6030 yards, S.S.S.69
Club founded in 1898.
Visitors: only members of golf club welcome.
Green fees: weekdays £8 per round or day, weekends £10 per round or day.
Society meetings: welcome with written application.
Catering: meals served from April to Oct.
Hotels: White Lodge, The Crescent; Binton House, West Ave.

T12 Flamborough Head

☎ Flamborough (0262) 850333
Lighthouse Rd, Flamborough, Bridlington, N Humberside YO15 1AR
5 miles NE of Bridlington on B1255, near lighthouse on headland at Flamborough.
Undulating course.
18 holes, 5438 yards, S.S.S.66
Club founded in 1931.
Visitors: welcome at all times, but only after 11.30 am on Sun.
Green fees: weekdays £5.50, weekends and Bank Holidays £7.50, weekly (Mon to Fri) £22.
Society meetings: welcome at all times.
Catering: by arrangement with Steward.
Hotels: Flaneburg, N Marine Rd, Flamborough; Timoneer, Southsea Rd, Flamborough.

T13 Fulford

☎ York (0904) 412882 Visitors
Heslington Lane, Heslington, York YO1 5DY
Off A19 from York, follow signs to University.
Parkland course.
18 holes, 6779 yards, S.S.S.72
Course designed by Dr. A. Mackenzie.
Club founded in 1911.
Visitors: only by prior arrangement.
Society meetings: by prior arrangement on Tues and Thurs.
Catering: meals served.
Hotels: hotels in abundance in York.

T14 Ganstead Park

☎ Hull (0482) 811280 or 811121 Pro Shop
Longdales Lane, Coniston, Hull HU11 4LB
On A165 E of Hull, 2 miles from city boundary
Parkland course.
9 holes, 5769 yards, S.S.S.68
Club founded in 1968.
Visitors: welcome Mon to Sat.
Green fees: weekdays £4 (with member £3), weekends £8 (with member £6).
Society meetings: catered for Tues to Sat by arrangement.
Catering: full catering from Tues to Fri.
Hotels: many good hotels in area.

T15 Ganton

☎ Sherburn (0944) 70329
Ganton, Scarborough, N Yorks YO12 4PA
11 miles from Scarborough on A64.
18 holes, 6693 yards, S.S.S.73
Course designed by Dr A. Mackenzie & H.S. Colt.
Club founded in 1891.
Visitors: by prior arrangement.
Green fees: weekdays £14, weekends £18.
Society meetings: catered for regularly throughout summer.
Catering: full range of meals available.
Hotels: many good hotels in area.

T16 Ghyll

☎ Earby (0282) 842466
Thornton-in-Craven, N Yorks
Off A56, 1 miles from Barnoldswick.
Parkland course.
9 holes, 5738 yards, S.S.S.68
Club founded in c 1907.
Visitors: welcome.
Green fees: weekdays £5 per day, weekends and Bank Holidays £6 (£4 with member's introduction).
Society meetings: by arrangement.
Hotels: Stirk House.

T17 Grimsby

☎ Grimsby (0472) 42630 Sec, 42823 Clubhouse, 56981 Pro
Littlecoates Rd, Grimsby, S Humberside DN34 4LU
Turn left off A18 at first roundabout in Grimsby, ¾ mile on left, next to Humber Royal Hotel.
Undulating parkland course.
18 holes, 6058 yards, S.S.S.69
Club founded in 1923.
Visitors: only members of golf clubs welcome (Ladies Day Tues).
Green fees: weekdays £6, weekends £8.
Society meetings: Mon and Fri only.
Catering: bar snacks available, other meals by arrangement, except Wed.
Hotels: Humber Royal.

T18 Harrogate

☎ Harrogate (0423) 862999 Sec, 863158 Steward, 862547 Pro
Forest Lane Head, Starbeck, Harrogate, N Yorks HG2 7TF
About 1 mile from Knaresborough on Harrogate to Knaresborough road, A59.
Parkland course.
18 holes, 6204 yards, S.S.S.70
Course designed by Sandy Herd.
Club founded in March, 1892.

Visitors: welcome on weekdays.
Green fees: weekdays £9 per day or round (£4.50 with member), weekends and Bank Holidays £12.50 per day or round (£6.25 with member).
Society meetings: welcome on weekdays by prior arrangement.
Catering: lunches and evening meals served except Fri.
Hotels: Dower House, Knaresborough; Granby, Harrogate.

T19 Hessle

☎ Hull (0482) 650171
Westfield Rd, Cottingham, Hull, N Humberside HU16 5YL
3 miles SW of Cottingham, off A164.
Undulating meadowland course.
18 holes, 6638 yards, S.S.S.72
Course designed by Peter Alliss & Dave Thomas.
New course opened in June 1975.
Visitors: welcome with reservation except Tues 9.15 am to 1 pm.
Green fees: weekdays £6 per round, £8 per day; weekends and Bank Holidays £9 per round or day.
Society meetings: catered for subject to availability by prior arrangement.
Catering: full catering except Mon.
Hotels: good hotels in area.

T20 Heworth

☎ York (0904) 424618
Muncaster House, Muncastergate, York YO3 9JX
1½ miles from city centre, on A1036 York to Scarborough road.
Meadowland/parkland course.
11 holes, 6078 yards, S.S.S.69
Club founded in 1912.
Visitors: welcome except Sun mornings.
Green fees: weekdays £6 (with member £4), weekends £7 (with member £4).
Catering: full catering facilities.
Hotels: many good hotels in York.

T21 Holme Hall

☎ Scunthorpe (0724) 862078
Holme Lane, Bottesford, Scunthorpe DN16 3RF
2 miles SE of Scunthorpe near E exit of M180.
Parkland course.
18 holes, 6475 yards, S.S.S.71
Club founded in 1912.
Visitors: welcome on weekdays and with member at weekends.
Green fees: weekdays £6 per day.
Society meetings: catered for on weekdays by arrangement.
Catering: lunches served except Fri.
Hotels: Royal; Wortley; Beverley.

T22 Hornsea

☎ Hornsea (040 12) 2020
Rolston Rd, Hornsea, N Humberside HU18 1XG
Follow sign for Hornsea Pottery in Hornsea and clubhouse is approximately 600 yards past entrance to pottery on road to Withernsea.
Parkland/moorland course.
18 holes, 6470 yards, S.S.S.71
Course designed by Alexander Herd & Dr A. Mackenzie.
Club founded in 1898.
Visitors: welcome, with restrictions at weekends.
Green fees: weekdays £6 per round, £9 per day; weekends £9 per round, £11 per day.
Catering: meals daily except Fri.
Hotels: nearest large hotels are in Beverley and Bridlington.

T23 Hull

☎ Hull (0482) 658919
The Hall, 27 Packman Lane, Kirk Ella, Hull HU10 7TJ
5 miles W of Kingston-upon-Hull, off A164.
Parkland course.
18 holes, 6242 yards, S.S.S.70
Course designed by James Braid.
Club founded in 1904.

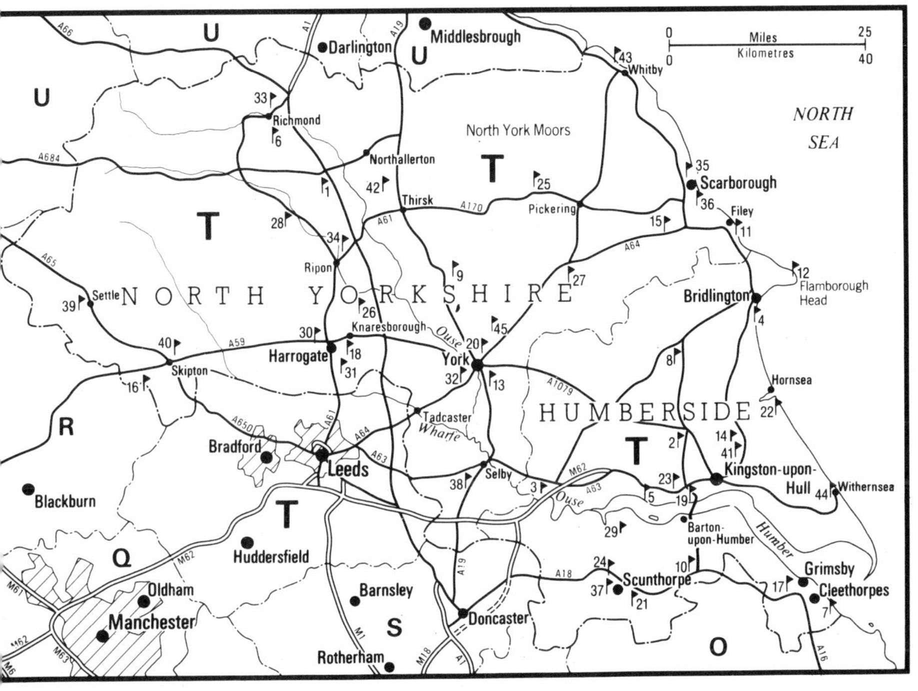

Visitors: welcome on weekdays.
Green fees: weekdays £8 per round or day (£4 with member).
Society meetings: catered for on Tues and Thurs by prior arrangement.
Catering: bar snacks available daily; full catering by prior arrangement.
Hotels: Willerby Manor, Well Lane, Willerby; Grange Park, Main St, Willerby.

T24 Kingsway
☎ Scunthorpe (0724) 840945
Kingsway, Scunthorpe, S Humberside
S of A18 between Berkeley and Queensway roundabouts.
Undulating, parkland course.
9 holes, 1915 yards, S.S.S.59
Club founded in 1971.
Visitors: welcome.
Green fees: weekdays £1.10, weekends £1.40.
Hotels: Royal; Priory; Wortley.

T25 Kirkbymoorside
☎ Kirkbymoorside (0751) 31525
Manor Vale, Kirkbymoorside, N Yorkshire YO6 6EQ
On A170 Thirsk to Scarborough road; Helmsley 7 miles, Pickering 7 miles.
Undulating moorland course.
18 holes, 5958 yards, S.S.S.68
Club founded in 1905.
Visitors: welcome at all times.
Green fees: weekdays £6 per day (£4 with member), weekends and Bank Holidays £7 per day.
Society meetings: special rates available by arrangement.
Catering: meals and snacks daily.
Hotels: George and Dragon, Kirkbymoorside; Feversham Arms, Helmsley; Feathers, Helmsley.

T26 Knaresborough
☎ Harrogate (0423) 863219
Boroughbridge Rd, Knaresborough HG5 0QQ
1½ miles N of Knaresborough off the main Boroughbridge road.
Parkland course.
18 holes, 6281 yards, S.S.S.70
Course designed by Hawtree & Son.
Club founded in Jan 1920.
Visitors: welcome.
Green fees: weekdays £7 per round, £8.50 per day; weekends and Bank Holidays £10.50 per round or day.
Society meetings: welcome.
Catering: meals served except Tues.
Hotels: Dower House, Knaresborough.

T27 Malton & Norton
☎ Malton (0653) 2959
Welham Park, Norton, Malton, N Yorks YO17 9QE
From Malton and Norton level crossing S on Welham road for ¾ mile, turn right.
Parkland course.
18 holes, 6421 yards, S.S.S.71
Course designed by F.W. Hawtree & Son.
Club founded in 1910.
Visitors: welcome on weekdays.
Green fees: weekdays £7 (£4 with member), weekends and Bank Holidays £9 (£5 with member).
Society meetings: welcome weekdays; bookings taken by Sec (Malton 7912).
Catering: full catering available.
Hotels: Leat House, Welham Rd; Talbot, Yorkersgate, Malton; Green Man, Market Square, Malton.

T28 Masham
☎ Ripon (0765) 89379
Swinton Rd, Masham, Ripon, Yorks
8 miles NW of Ripon on A6108.
Parkland course.
9 holes, 2269 yards, S.S.S.65
Club founded in 1900.
Visitors: welcome on weekdays.
Green fees: £5 per round or day.
Catering: none.
Hotels: Kings Head, Masham.

T29 Normanby Hall
☎ Scunthorpe (0724) 720226 Pro
Normanby Park, Normanby, Scunthorpe, S Humberside DN15 9HU
5 miles N of Scunthorpe adjacent to Normanby Hall.
Parkland course.
18 holes, 6398 yards, S.S.S.70
Club founded in 1978.
Visitors: welcome every day.
Green fees: £3 per round, £4.50 per day.
Society meetings: welcome during week (Scunthorpe 862141 Extn 444).
Catering: catering facilities available during normal licensing hours.
Hotels: Wortley, Scunthorpe; Sheffield Arms, Burton on Stather.

T30 Oakdale
☎ Harrogate (0423) 67162
Oakdale, Harrogate HG1 2LN
Off A61 from Harrogate at Kent Rd, about ¼ mile from Royal Hall.
Undulating parkland course.
18 holes, 6456 yards, S.S.S.71
Course designed by Dr Mackenzie.
Club founded in 1914.
Visitors: welcome but check with Sec.
Green fees: £9 per day.
Society meetings: welcome on weekdays and occasional Sun.
Catering: snacks and grills every day; evening meals by arrangement.
Hotels: Crown; Majestic; Granby; Old Swan; Cairn.

T31 Pannal
☎ Harrogate (0423) 871641 or 872628 Sec
Follifoot Rd, Pannal, Harrogate HG3 1ES
Just off A61 Leeds to Harrogate road at Pannal.
Parkland/moorland course.
18 holes, 6594 yards, S.S.S.71
Course designed by Sandy Herd.
Club founded in 1906.
Visitors: welcome on weekdays.
Green fees: £10 per round, £12 per day.
Society meetings: by arrangement with Sec on weekdays.
Catering: meals served every day.
Hotels: Majestic; Old Swan; Cairn; Granby.

T32 Pike Hills
☎ York (0904) 706566
Tadcaster Rd, Copmanthorpe, York
On A64 4 miles from York.
Parkland course.
18 holes, 6048 yards, S.S.S.69
Visitors: welcome on weekdays.
Green fees: weekdays £6.
Society meetings: weekdays.
Catering: light snacks available; full meals by arrangement.
Hotels: Post House, Tadcaster Rd, York; Chase, Tadcaster Rd, York.

T33 Richmond
☎ Richmond (0748) 2457
Bend Hagg, Richmond, N Yorks DL10 5EX
A6108 from Scotch Corner, turn right at traffic lights after 4 miles.
Parkland course.
18 holes, 5704 yards, S.S.S.68
Course designed by Frank Pennink.
Club founded in 1892.
Visitors: welcome every day (on Sun after 11 am).
Green fees: weekdays £5 per round, £6 per day; half-price with member; weekends £7.50.
Society meetings: welcome every day.
Catering: meals served except Mon; parties by arrangement.
Hotels: Frenchgate, Frenchgate, Richmond.

T34 Ripon City
☎ Ripon (0765) 3640 Clubhouse, 700411 Pro, 3992 Hon Sec
Palace Rd, Ripon, N Yorks HGA 3HH
1 mile N on A6108 towards Leyburn.
Undulating parkland course.
9 holes, 5752 yards, S.S.S.68
Club founded in 1904.
Visitors: welcome.
Green fees: weekdays £4 per day,

weekends £6 per day.
Society meetings: welcome weekdays.
Catering: available by prior arrangement for parties.
Hotels: Ripon Spa, Park St, Ripon; Unicorn, Market Place, Ripon.

T35 Scarborough North Cliff

☎ Scarborough (0723) 360786
North Cliff Ave, Burniston Rd, Scarborough YO12 6PP
2 miles N of town centre on coast road (Burniston Rd), turn right along North Cliff Ave.
Seaside/parkland course.
18 holes, 6425 yards, S.S.S.71
Course designed by James Braid.
Club founded in 1911.
Visitors: welcome, except during club competitions.
Green fees: weekdays £7.50, weekends and Bank Holidays £10.
Society meetings: catered for by arrangement.
Catering: snacks, lunches and evening meals available except Mon.
Hotels: Majestic; Clifton; Rivelin.

T36 Scarborough South Cliff

☎ Scarborough (0723) 374737
Deepdale Ave, Scarborough YO11 2UE
1m S of Scarborough on main Filey rd.
Parkland/seaside course.
18 holes, 6085 yards, S.S.S.69
Course designed by Dr Mackenzie.
Club founded in 1903.
Visitors: welcome.
Green fees: weekdays £6.90, weekends and Bank Holidays £9.20.
Society meetings: catered for on weekdays and at weekends.
Catering: full catering facilities.
Hotels: Royal; Crown; St Nicholas; Brooklands; Southlands; Holbeck Hall.

T37 Scunthorpe

☎ Scunthorpe (0724) 866561 or 842913
Burringham Rd, Scunthorpe, S Humberside DN17 2AB
On B1450, adjoining Mallard Hotel.
Parkland course.
18 holes, 6281 yards, S.S.S.71
Club founded in 1936.
Visitors: members of recognised golf clubs welcome except Sun.
Green fees: weekdays £5.50 (£4.50 with member), Sat £7.50 (£5.50 with member).
Society meetings: welcome on weekdays and limited number on Sat.
Catering: full catering every day except Fri, by arrangement only.
Hotels: Royal, Doncaster Rd, Scunthorpe; Wortley, Cottage Beck, Scunthorpe.

T38 Selby

☎ Selby (075 782) 622
Mill Lane, Brayton Barff, Selby, N Yorks YO8 9LD
From Leeds turn right off A63 at the Wheatsheaf in Hambleton, left at cemetery then right, next left to course.
Flat links course.
18 holes, 6246 yards, S.S.S.70
Club founded in 1907.
Visitors: welcome on weekdays.
Green fees: weekdays £8 per round, weekends £10 per round.
Society meetings: catered for on Wed, Thurs and Fri by arrangement.
Catering: coffee, lunch and evening meals available except Mon.
Hotels: Monk Fryston Hall, Monk Fryston; Selby Fork; Londesborough, Market Place, Selby.

T39 Settle

☎ Settle (072 92) 2617
Huntsworth, Buck Haw Brow, Giggleswick, Settle BD24 9BB
Main A65 Settle to Kendal road, opposite Giggleswick Quarry.
Parkland/moorland course.

9 holes, 4900 yards, S.S.S.62
Club founded in 1891.
Visitors: welcome on weekdays.
Green fees: £2 (with member £1), Juniors £1 (with member 50p).
Society meetings: none.
Catering: none.
Hotels: Black Horse, Giggleswick; Royal Oak, Settle; Falcon Manor, Settle.

T40 Skipton

☎ Skipton (0756) 3922 or 3257
Short Lea Lane, Grassington Rd, Skipton, N Yorks BD23 1LL
On N by-pass (A59 and A65) 1 mile from town centre.
Moorland course.
18 holes, 6100 yards, S.S.S.69
Visitors: welcome on weekdays and some weekends.
Green fees: on application.
Society meetings: welcome on weekdays and some weekends.
Catering: lunches served except Mon.
Hotels: Wilson Arms, Grassington; Stirk House, Sawley.

T41 Sutton Park

☎ Hull (0482) 74242
Saltshouse Rd, Holderness Rd, Hull, N Humberside HU8 9HF
4 miles E of city centre on A165 (B1237).
Parkland course.
18 holes, 6251 yards, S.S.S.70
Club founded in 1935.
Visitors: welcome on weekdays.
Green fees: £2 per round.
Society meetings: welcome weekdays.
Catering: bar meals always available; lunch and dinner by advance booking.
Hotels: many good hotels in Hull.

T42 Thirsk & Northallerton

☎ Thirsk (0845) 22170
Thornton-le-Street, Thirsk, N Yorks
2 miles N of Thirsk on A168, the Northallerton spur ½ mile from the dual carriageway A19.
Meadowland course.
9 holes, 6087 yards, S.S.S.70
Club founded in 1914.
Visitors: welcome on weekdays and Sat, but with member only on Sun.
Green fees: weekdays £5, Sat and Bank Holidays £7.
Society meetings: by arrangement for small parties, maximum 24.
Catering: snacks available and meals by arrangement, except Tues.
Hotels: in Thirsk and Northallerton.

T43 Whitby

☎ Whitby (0947) 602768 Club, 600660 Sec
Low Straggleton, Whitby, N Yorks YO21 3SR
On main coast road between Whitby and Sandsend.
Seaside course.
18 holes, 5710 yards, S.S.S.67
Club founded in 1892.
Visitors: welcome.
Green fees: weekdays £6.90 per day, weekends £8 per day.
Society meetings: welcome.
Catering: meals served.
Hotels: good hotels in Whitby.

T44 Withernsea

☎ Withernsea (096 42) 2258
Chestnut Ave, Withernsea, N Humberside HU19 2QD
S end of town.
Seaside course.
9 holes, 5112 yards, S.S.S.64
Club founded in 1909.
Visitors: welcome any time but with certain restrictions on some weekends.
Green fees: £3 per day or round, under 18 £1.50 per day or round.
Society meetings: by prior arrangement with Sec.
Catering: no catering at lunchtime, but meals served some evenings.
Hotels: Queen's, Queen St.

T45 York

☎ York (0904) 490304
Lords Moor Lane, Strensall, York YO3 5XF
6 miles N of York Minster, near Strensall Barracks and village.
Woodland course.
18 holes, 6225 yards, S.S.S.70
Course designed by J.H. Taylor (1904).
Club founded in 1890.
Visitors: always welcome but advisable to enquire in advance or ring.
Green fees: weekdays £9, weekends £11.
Society meetings: catered for on weekdays except Fri and on Sun.
Catering: meals served except Fri when bar snacks only.
Hotels: Worsley Arms, Hovingham; George, Easingwold; many others in York.

U Cumbria, Northumberland, Durham, Tyne & Wear, Cleveland

Mercifully golf has never betrayed the old county nomenclature; Cumberland and Westmorland sound so much nicer and more romantic than Cumbria and it has never occurred to me to regard Tyne and Wear as an acceptable division to anyone except the postal authorities.

Of the counties of the north-east and north-west, Northumberland has been the strongest in terms of golfing numbers which, in view of the area it covers, is hardly surprising. The thickest cluster surrounds Newcastle and includes the Northumberland club, City of Newcastle, Gosforth, Ponteland and Whitley Bay but there is much rewarding exploring to be done along the coast, taking in Dunstanburgh, Seahouses, Bamburgh, Alnmouth and ending up at the home of the Berwick-on-Tweed Club on Goswick which is most appealing.

Morpeth, Hexham and Arcot Hall are well worth a visit but the wise explorers moving north will have already tested the best of Durham. Seaton Carew is the pick but Hartlepool, Brancepeth Castle, Durham City and Eaglescliffe are worthy of a mention in despatches.

Apart from Carlisle, or City of Carlise, as it used to be known, Cumbria has many attractive outposts and none better than the championship reaches of Silloth on Solway which is an ideal retreat famous as the course on which Cecil Leitch was raised. Seascale is another treat and I hear good things of the Furness club in Barrow.

U1 Allendale

☎ (043 483) 412
Thornley Gate, Allendale, Hexham, Northumberland NE47 9LQ
10m SW of Hexham on Menthead rd.
Meadowland course.
9 holes, 2290 yards, S.S.S.63
Club founded in 1907.
Visitors: welcome except on Aug Bank Holiday Mon.
Green fees: weekdays £2.50 (with member £2), weekends and Bank Holidays £3.50 (£2.50 with member); Juniors pro rata.
Society meetings: welcome by arrangement.
Catering: no catering but tea-making facility.
Hotels: Ridings, Allendale; Hare and Hounds, Allendale; Golden Lion, Allendale.

U2 Alnmouth

☎ Alnmouth (0665) 830231, 830368 Sec, 830687 Stewardess
Foxton Hall, Alnmouth, Alnwick, Northumberland NE66 3BE
Take Alnmouth road from Alnwick, at Alnmouth turn right, Foxton 1 mile on right.
Seaside meadowland course.
18 holes, 6414 yards, S.S.S.71
Club founded in 1869.
Visitors: welcome.
Green fees: weekdays £6 per round, £8 per day (£3.50 with member); weekends £8 per round, £10 per day (£4.50 with member).
Society meetings: welcome by prior arrangement on weekdays except Fri.
Catering: full catering available.
Hotels: White Swan, Alnwick; Schooner, Alnmouth; Dormy House.

U3 Alnmouth Village

☎ Alnmouth (0665) 830370
Marine Rd, Alnmouth, Northumberland
From Alnwick on A1 to Alnmouth on A1068.
Undulating seaside course.
9 holes, 6078 yards, S.S.S.70
Club founded in 1869.
Visitors: welcome.
Green fees: weekdays £4, weekends £6, weekly £15.
Society meetings: no.
Catering: by arrangement.
Hotels: Marine, Marine Rd.

U4 Alnwick

☎ Alnwick (0665) 602632 or 602499 Sec
Swansfield Park, Alnwick, Northumberland
On entering Alnwick from S turn left at Aydon Guest House, follow Bridge St and Swansfield Park Rd to park gates, turn left and first right.
Parkland course.
9 holes, 5379 yards, S.S.S.66
Club founded in 1907.
Visitors: welcome except on comp. days.
Green fees: weekdays £3 (£1.50 with member), weekends and Bank Holidays £4 (£2 with member).
Society meetings: catered for on application to Committee.
Catering: limited catering service.
Hotels: White Swan.

U5 Alston Moor

☎ Alston (0498) 81675
The Hermitage, Alston, Cumbria CA9 3DB
1¾ miles from Alston on B6277.
Meadowland course.
9 holes, 4840 yards, S.S.S.64
Club founded in 1969.
Visitors: welcome.
Green fees: weekdays £3, weekends £4.
Society meetings: welcome anytime.
Catering: light snacks at weekends.
Hotels: Angel; Hillcrest; Low Byre; Lovelady Shield; Nenthall.

U6 Appleby
☎ Appleby (0930) 51432
Blackenber Moor, Appleby in Westmorland, Cumbria CA16 6LP
2 miles S of Appleby on A66.
Moorland course.
18 holes, 5895 yards, S.S.S.68
Club founded in 1902.
Visitors: welcome at any time.
Green fees: weekdays £4.50, weekends and Bank Holidays £6.
Society meetings: welcome at any time subject to prior arrangement.
Catering: by arrangement.
Hotels: Tufton Arms; Royal Oak; Appleby Manor.

U7 Arcot Hall
☎ Wideopen (0632) 362794
Dudley, Cramlington, Northumberland NE23 7QP
1 mile E of A1 on A1068.
Parkland course.
18 holes, 6389 yards, S.S.S.70
Course designed by James Braid.
Club founded in 1909.
Visitors: welcome on weekdays.
Green fees: weekdays £7.50 (£4 with member), weekends and Bank Holidays £9 (£5 with member).
Society meetings: welcome weekdays.
Catering: bar lunches and high teas served except Mon.
Hotels: Holiday Inn, Newcastle; Gosforth Park, Newcastle; Queens Moat House, Wallsend.

U8 Backworth
☎ Tyneside (091) 2681048
Backworth Welfare, The Hall, Backworth, Shiremoor, Tyne and Wear NE27 0AH
Off Tyne Tunnel link road at Holystone roundabout.
Parkland course.
9 holes, 5930 yards, S.S.S.69
Club founded in 1937.
Visitors: welcome with restrictions, ring for details.
Green fees: £5 (£3.75 with member), Bank Holidays £6.25.
Society meetings: no.
Catering: by arrangement with Steward.
Hotels: numerous good hotels in area.

U9 Bamburgh Castle
☎ Bamburgh (066 84) 378 Steward, 321 Sec
The Wynding, Bamburgh, Northumberland NE69 7DE
Turn off A1 between Alnwick and Berwick, on reaching village, turn left opposite Lord Crewe Arms, and travel along The Wynding.
Seaside course.
18 holes, 5465 yards, S.S.S.67
Club founded in 1904.
Visitors: welcome at all times, but advisable to phone in advance.
Green fees: weekdays £5 per day, weekends and Bank Holidays £9 per day, £6 per round.
Society meetings: by arrangement with Sec.
Catering: every day except Tues.
Hotels: Victoria; Sunningdale; Mizen Head; Lord Crewe Arms.

U10 Barnard Castle
☎ Barnard Castle (0833) 38355
Harmire Rd, Barnard Castle, Co Durham DL12 8QN
On N boundary of town on B6278 Barnard Castle to Eggleston road.
Undulating parkland course.
Visitors: welcome except on competition days.
Green fees: weekdays £6, weekends and Bank Holidays £8; weekly (Mon to Fri) £20.
Society meetings: welcome, max. 40.
Catering: meals and bar snacks served.
Hotels: King's Head, Barnard Castle; Rose and Crown, Romaldkirk.

U11 Barrow
☎ Barrow-in-Furness (0229) 25444
Bakesmoor Lane, Hawcoat, Barrow-in-Furness, Cumbria LA14 4QB
Turn right to Hawcoat off A590 on entering boundary of Barrow.
Undulating meadowland course.
18 holes, 6209 yards, S.S.S.70
Club founded in 1922.
Visitors: welcome.
Green fees: £5 per round or day (£4 with member).
Catering: meals served except on Mon or Tues when catering for parties only.
Hotels: Victoria Park, Barow; Michaelson House, Fairfield Lane, Barrow; Lisdoonie, Abbey Rd, Barrow.

U12 Beamish Park
☎ Durham (0632) 701133
Beamish, Stanley, Co Durham DH9 0RH
From Chester-le-Street follow signs for Beamish Open Air Museum.
Parkland course.
18 holes, 6205 yards, S.S.S.70
Course designed by Henry Cotton & W. Woodend.
Present course founded in 1950.
Visitors: welcome (no denim jeans to be worn).
Green fees: weekdays £5.75 (with member £3), weekends and Bank Holidays £8 (with member £4).
Society meetings: welcome weekdays.
Catering: bar meals or à la carte menu.
Hotels: Beamish.

U13 Bedlingtonshire
☎ Bedlington (0670) 822087 Pro, 822457 Sec, 822457 Steward.
Acorn Bank, Bedlington, Northumberland.
½ mile W of Bedlington on A1068.
Meadowland/parkland course.
18 holes, 6224 metres, S.S.S.73
Course designed by Frank Pennink.
Club founded in April 1972.
Visitors: welcome on weekdays from 9 am to sunset and at weekends from 9.30 am to sunset, except on competition days.
Green fees: weekdays £2.75 per round, weekends £3 per round.
Society meetings: on application.
Catering: on request.
Hotels: Holiday Inn, Seaton Burn; Red Lion, Bedlington; Ridge Farm, Bedlington; North Seaton, Ashington.

U14 Bellingham
☎ Bellingham (0660) 20530
Boggle Hole, Bellingham, Hexham, Northumberland NE48 2DT
Off B6320, 16 miles NE of Hexham, easy access from A68.
Undulating meadowland course.
9 holes, 5226 yards, S.S.S.66
Course designed by Edward Johnson.
Club founded in 1893.
Visitors: welcome; restrictions on Sun.
Green fees: weekdays £3.50 per day, Sat £4 per day, Sun £5 per day.
Society meetings: welcome.
Catering: Mrs. A. Teague, Burnside Cottage, Bellingham.
Hotels: Riverdale; Rose and Crown Inn.

U15 Berwick-upon-Tweed
☎ Ancroft (0289) 87256 or 87348 Sec
Goswick, Berwick-upon-Tweed TD15 2RW
4 miles S of Berwick-upon-Tweed E of A1, signposted on A1.
Seaside links course.
18 holes, 6399 yards, S.S.S.71
Club founded in 1892.
Visitors: welcome.
Green fees: weekdays £7 per day, £5 per round; weekends and Bank Holidays £10 per day, £8 per round.
Society meetings: catered for every day.
Catering: full catering daily except Mon, parties catered for on Mon by prior arrangement.
Hotels: Kings Arms, Berwick-upon-Tweed.

U16 Billingham

☎ Billingham (0642) 533816
Sandy Lane, Billingham, Cleveland TS22 5NA
E of A19 Billingham by pass, near town centre.
Undulating parkland course.
18 holes, 6430 yards, S.S.S.71
Course designed by Frank Pennink.
Club founded in 1968.
Visitors: welcome on weekdays only.
Green fees: £7 per day or round.
Society meetings: welcome, max. 50.
Catering: meals served except Mon.
Hotels: Billingham Arms.

U17 Birtley

☎ Tyneside (091) 4102207
Portobello Rd, Birtley, Co Durham
A6127 off A1, 6 miles S of Newcastle.
Parkland course.
9 holes, 5154 yards, S.S.S.67
Visitors: welcome weekdays.
Green fees: weekdays £3 (£2 with member), weekends £3 with members only.
Society meetings: by arrangement.
Catering: snacks and meals available.
Hotels: Post House, Washington; Coach and Horses, Birtley.

U18 Bishop Auckland

☎ Bishop Auckland (0388) 602198
High Plains, Durham Rd, Bishop Auckland, Co Durham DL14 8DL
Left side of road going N immediately out of town.
Parkland course.
18 holes, 6420 yards, S.S.S.71
Club founded in July 1894.
Visitors: welcome
Green fees: weekdays £7, weekends £9.
Catering: lunches and evening meals served daily except Mon.
Hotels: Park Head; Binchester; Drive Inn.

U19 Blackwell Grange

☎ Darlington (0325) 464464
Briar Close, Blackwell, Darlington, Co Durham DL3 8QX
1 mile S of Darlington, ¼ mile W off A66.
Undulating parkland course.

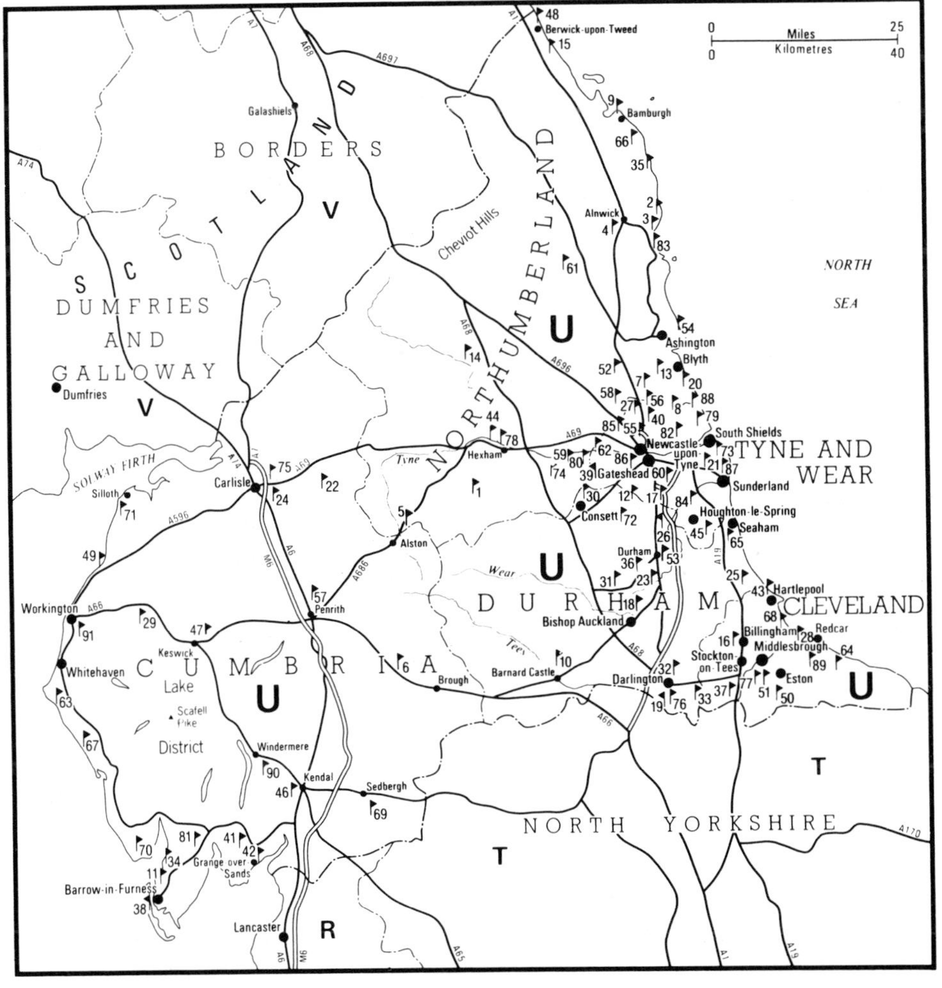

18 holes, 5587 yards, S.S.S.67
Course designed by Frank Pennink.
Club founded in 1930.
Visitors: welcome except Wed afternoon (Ladies Day).
Green fees: weekdays £7 per day, weekends and Bank Holidays £8 (half-price with member).
Society meetings: by arrangement on weekdays.
Catering: lunches served except Mon.
Hotels: Blackwell Grange Moat House.

U20 Blyth

☎ Blyth (0670) 367728
New Delaval, Blyth, Northumberland
14 miles N of Newcastle, 6 miles N of Whitley Bay.
18 holes, 6533 yards, S.S.S.71
Club founded in 1905.
Visitors: welcome on weekdays.
Green fees: £4 per round, £5 per day (£3 with member).
Society meetings: welcome on weekdays.
Catering: lunches served on weekdays.
Hotels: many good hotels in area.

U21 Boldon

☎ Boldon (0783) 364182
Dipe Lane, E Boldon, Tyne and Wear NE36 0PQ
On A184, 3 miles NW of Sunderland.
Meadowland course.
18 holes, 6319 yards, S.S.S.70
Club founded in 1925.
Visitors: welcome on weekdays, weekends restricted.
Green fees: £6 per day.
Society meetings: by arrangement.
Catering: meals served by arrangement.
Hotels: Sunderland; George Washington; Post House.

U22 Brampton

☎ Brampton (069 77) 2255
Brampton, Cumbria CA8 1HN
Club is 1¾ miles from centre of Brampton on B6413 Castle Carrock road.
Moorland course.
18 holes, 6426 yards, S.S.S.71
Course designed by James Braid.
Club founded in 1907.
Visitors: welcome.
Green fees: weekdays £5, weekends and Bank Holidays £7.
Society meetings: catered for on weekdays and limited number of weekends.
Catering: available daily except Mon and Fri; parties fully catered for on these days.
Hotels: Sands House, The Sands, Brampton; Weary Sportsman Inn, Castle Carrock, Brampton.

U23 Brancepeth Castle

☎ Durham (0385) 780075
Brancepeth Village, Durham DH7 8EA
4½ miles from Durham city on A690 to Crook.
Parkland course.
18 holes, 6300 yards, S.S.S.70
Course designed by H.S. Colt.
Club founded in 1924.
Visitors: welcome on weekdays and only by prior arrangement at weekends.
Green fees: weekdays £9 (£4 with member), weekends and Bank Holidays £10 (£5 with member).
Society meetings: welcome on weekdays and some Sat by prior arrangement.
Catering: snacks available; full meals by prior arrangement.
Hotels: Bridge, Croxdale, Durham.

U24 Carlisle

☎ Scotby (022 872) 303
Aglionby, Carlisle CA4 8AG
2 miles E of Carlisle, leave M6 at Exit 43 and take A69 for about ¾ mile.
Parkland course.
18 holes, 6278 yards, S.S.S.70
Course designed by Tom Simpson, McKenzie Ross & latterly by Frank Pennink.
Club founded in 1909.
Visitors: welcome, advisable to check availability.
Green fees: weekdays £7.50 per day (£3.75 with member), weekends £8.50.
Society meetings: catered for on Wed and Fri.
Catering: meals and snacks available except Mon.
Hotels: Queens Arms, Warwick; Brown, Wetheral; Kilorren, Wetheral.

U25 Castle Eden & Peterlee

☎ Wallfield (0429) 836510 or 836220
Castle Eden, Hartlepool, Cleveland TS27 4SS
Take Durham to Hartlepool road off A19, follow signs to Castle Eden, course is opposite to Whitbread Brewery.
Parkland course.
18 holes, 6297 yards, S.S.S.70
Second half of course designed by Henry Cotton.
Club founded in 1927.
Visitors: welcome.
Green fees: weekends £9, weekdays £8, half-price with member.
Society meetings: welcome on weekdays except Tues afternoon by arrangement with Sec.
Catering: meals served by arrangement with Steward.
Hotels: Castle Eden Inn, Castle Eden; Hardwicke Hall Manor, Blackhall, Hartlepool; Norseman, Peterlee, Co Durham; Crossways, Dunelm Rd, Thornley, Co Durham.

U26 Chester-le-Street

☎ Chester-le-Street (0385) 883218
Lumley Park, Chester-le-Street, Co Durham DH3 4NS
Leave A1(M) to Chester-le-Street, follow A167 signposted Durham, course ¼ mile E of Chester-le-Street, beside Lumley Castle.
Parkland course.
18 holes, 6245 yards, S.S.S.70
Club founded in 1909.
Visitors: welcome, but at weekends not before 10.30 am or between 12 and 2 pm.
Green fees: weekdays £6, weekends and Bank Holidays £8.
Society meetings: welcome weekdays.
Catering: meals by arrangement.
Hotels: Lumley Castle, Lumley Park, Chester-le-Street.

U27 City of Newcastle

☎ Tyneside (091) 2851775
Three Mile Bridge, Gosforth, Newcastle upon Tyne NE3 2DR
3 miles N of Newcastle city centre on left hand side of main A1 road heading N, opposite Three Mile Inn.
Parkland course.
18 holes, 6492 yards, S.S.S.71
Course designed by Harry Vardon.
Club founded in 1892.
Visitors: welcome.
Green fees: weekdays £7 (£3 with member), weekends and Bank Holidays £10 (£4 with member).
Society meetings: welcome, especially on Tues, Wed and Thurs.
Catering: bar snacks, lunches and evening meals available except Sun evenings and Mon.
Hotels: Gosforth Park, High Gosforth Park, Newcastle upon Tyne; Holiday Inn, Great North Rd, Seaton Burn, Newcastle upon Tyne.

U28 Cleveland

☎ Redcar 483693 Clubhouse, 471798 Sec
Queen St, Redcar, Cleveland TS10 1BT
From A174 to A1042 to Coatham.

Links championship course.
Club founded in 1887.
Visitors: as per brochure.
Green fees: weekdays £6.90, weekends and Bank Holidays £10.
Society meetings: As per brochure.
Catering: full catering facilities except Mon when limited service only.
Hotels: numerous good hotels in area.

U29 Cockermouth

☎ Bassenthwaite Lake (059 681) 223
Embleton, Cockermouth, Cumbria CA13 9SG
1 mile E of A66, 4 miles from Cockermouth.
Moorland course.
18 holes, 5496 yards, S.S.S.67
Club founded in 1896.
Visitors: welcome.
Green fees: weekdays £5 per day, weekends and Bank Holidays £6.
Catering: snacks and meals by arrangement with Stewardess.
Hotels: Castle Inn, Bassenthwaite; Pheasant Inn, Bassenthwaite; Globe, Cockermouth.

U30 Consett & District

☎ Consett (0207) 502186
Elmfield Rd, Consett, Co Durham DH8 5NN
Off A68 2 miles from Castleside or Allensford; 12 miles from Durham (A691) and Newcastle (A694).
Undulating parkland course.
18 holes, 6001 yards, S.S.S.69
Course designed by Harry Vardon.
Club founded in 1911.
Visitors: welcome except at weekends with competitions.
Green fees: weekdays £5 (£2.50 with member), weekends and Bank Holidays £8 (£6 with member).
Society meetings: welcome by arrangement on weekdays, maximum 40.
Catering: lunches and high teas available every day by arrangement.
Hotels: many good hotels in area.

U31 Crook

☎ Bishop Auckland (0388) 762429
Low Jobs Hill, Crook, Co Durham DL15 9AA
On A690 6 miles W of Durham city.
Moorland/parkland course.
18 holes, 6089 yards, S.S.S.69
Club founded in 1919.
Visitors: welcome.
Green fees: weekends £5, weekdays £4 (£3 with member).
Society meetings: catered for any time.
Catering: lunches and high teas served every day except Thurs.
Hotels: Uplands, Crook; Three Tuns, Durham.

U32 Darlington

☎ Darlington (0325) 463936
Haughton Grange, Darlington, Co Durham DL1 3JD
NE of town on A1150.
Parkland course.
18 holes, 6032 yards, S.S.S.70
Club founded in 1908.
Visitors: welcome on weekdays (Ladies Day Tues) and at weekends if no comp.
Green fees: £7 per day, £40 per week.
Society meetings: no.
Catering: full catering available.
Hotels: Kings Head, Priestgate, Darlington; White Horse, North Rd, Darlington; Devonport, Middleton-One-Row, Darlington.

U33 Dinsdale Spa

☎ Dinsdale (0325) 332297 Sec, 332515 Pro, 332222 Clubhouse
Middleton St George, Darlington, Co Durham DL2 1DW
From A66 or A19 follow signs for Teesside Airport until village of Middleton St George, clubhouse is 1½ miles from Middleton St George on Neasham road.
Parkland course.
18 holes, 6078 yards, S.S.S.69
Club founded in 1910.
Visitors: welcome on weekdays (Ladies Day Tues) and with member at weekends or Bank Holidays.
Green fees: £6.50 per round, £7.50 per day.
Society meetings: by prior arrangement with Sec.
Catering: meals and snacks available by arrangement except Mon.
Hotels: Devonport, Middleton-One-Row, Darlington; Newbus Arms, Hurworth Rd, Neasham, Darlington; Croft Spa, Croft, Darlington.

U34 Dunnerholme

☎ Dalton-in-Furness (0229) 62675
Duddon Rd, Askam in Furness, Cumbria LA16 7AW
A590 to Askam, over Askam railway crossing towards seashore, turn right over cattle grid.
Links course.
10 holes, 6105 yards, S.S.S.69
Club founded in 1905.
Visitors: welcome on weekdays and at weekends.
Green fees: weekdays £4 (£2 with member), weekends and Bank Hols £5.
Society meetings: welcome weekdays.
Catering: meals served at weekends.
Hotels: Clarence House, Dalton-in-Furness, Cumbria; Wellington, Dalton-in-Furness, Cumbria.

U35 Dunstanburgh

☎ Embleton 672
Embleton, Alnwick, Northumberland NE66 3XQ
Off A1, 8 miles NE of Alnwick.
Seaside course.
18 holes, 5817 metres, S.S.S.70
Visitors: welcome.
Green fees: weekdays £4.75, weekends £6.50.
Society meetings: by arrangement.
Catering: meals served by arrangement.
Hotels: Dunstanburgh Castle, Embleton.

U36 Durham City

☎ Durham (0385) 780069
Littleburn Farm, Langley Moor, Durham DH7 8HL
Off A690 2 miles SW of Durham City.
Meadowland course.
18 holes, 6118 yards, S.S.S.69
Course designed by C.C. Stanton.
Club founded in 1887.
Visitors: welcome.
Green fees: weekdays £5 (£2.50 with member), weekends and Bank Holidays £6 (£3 with member).
Society meetings: catered for on weekdays except Mon.
Catering: meals served except Mon.
Hotels: good hotels in Durham.

U37 Eaglescliffe

☎ Stockton on Tees (0642) 780238 or 780089
Yarm Rd, Eaglescliffe, Stockton on Tees, Cleveland TS16 0DQ
On the left of main road from Stockton on Tees to Yarm in Eaglescliffe.
Undulating parkland course.
18 holes, 6275 yards, S.S.S.70
Course designed by James Braid & Henry Cotton.
Club founded in 1914.
Visitors: welcome (Ladies Day Tues).
Green fees: weekdays £6.50 per day, weekends and Bank Holidays £9.
Society meetings: welcome weekdays.
Catering: full catering except Mon.
Hotels: Parkmore, Yarm Rd, Eaglescliffe; Swallow, Stockton on Tees.

U38 Furness

☎ Barrow (0229) 41232
Central Drive, Barrow-in-Furness, Cumbria LA14 3LN
A590 to Barrow, follow sign to Walney Island through town, straight ahead at the lights on bridge over channel.
Links course.
18 holes, 5832 metres, S.S.S.70
Club founded in 1872.
Visitors: welcome on weekdays.
Green fees: weekdays £5, weekends and Bank Holidays £6 (£4 with member), weekly ticket £20.
Society meetings: welcome weekdays.
Catering: meals served except Mon.
Hotels: Victoria Park; White House; Imperial.

U39 Garesfield

☎ Ebchester (0207) 561278 or 561309
Chopwell, Tyne and Wear NE17 7AP
A 694 Newcastle to Consett road to Rowlands Gill, take B6315 to High Spen, then take Chopwell road 1 mile on left.
Undulating parkland course.
18 holes, 6610 yards, S.S.S.72
Course designed by Charles McCue.
Club founded in 1922.
Visitors: welcome anytime.
Green fees: weekdays £5 per day, £4 per round (£3 with member); weekends and Bank Holidays £7 per day, £5 per round (£4 with member).
Society meetings: welcome on weekdays by arrangement.
Catering: bar snacks available and meals by prior arrangement with Mr. J. Machram, Caterer.
Hotels: Gibside Arms, Whickham; Beamish Park, Beamish; Crown and Crossed Swords, Shotley Bridge.

U40 Gosforth

☎ Tyneside (091) 285 3495
Broadway East, Gosforth, Newcastle upon Tyne NE3 5ER
3 miles N of city centre, turn right at first main roundabout after Regent Centre metro station.
Meadowland course.
18 holes, 6030 yards, S.S.S.69
Club founded in 1905.
Visitors: welcome on weekdays (Ladies Day Tues); contact Sec for confirmation.
Green fees: weekdays £6 per day (£3 with member), weekends and Bank Holidays £9.50 (£5 with member).
Society meetings: welcome on weekdays only, applications to Sec.
Catering: lunch and high tea served
Hotels: Gosforth Park.

U41 Grange Fell

☎ Grange-over-Sands (044 84) 2536
Fell Rd, Grange-over-Sands, Cumbria LA11 6HB
Situated on main road from Grange-over-Sands to Cartmel.
Hillside course.
9 holes, 5278 yards, S.S.S.66
Club founded in 1953.
Visitors: welcome at all times.
Green fees: weekdays £4, Sat £5, Sun and Bank Holidays £6.
Catering: no catering available.
Hotels: Greyrigg, Grange; Hardcragg, Grange; Netherwood, Grange; Aynsome Manor, Cartmel; Priory, Cartmel.

U42 Grange-over-Sands

☎ Grange-over-Sands (044 84) 3180
Meathop Rd, Grange-over-Sands, Cumbria LA11 6QX
Leave A590 at roundabout signposted Grange, course on left hand side just before entering Grange.
Flat parkland course.
18 holes, 5660 yards, S.S.S.68
Club founded in 1920.
Visitors: welcome at any time.
Green fees: weekdays £5, weekends and Bank Holidays £7 per day.
Society meetings: by arrangement.
Catering: full catering except Tues.
Hotels: Grand; Netherwood; Grange; Grayrigge.

U43 Hartlepool

☎ Hartlepool (0429) 67473
Hart Warren, Hartlepool, Cleveland TF24 9QE
King Oswy Dr, off A1086 at N end of town.
Seaside course.
18 holes, 6325 yards, S.S.S.70
Course designed by James Braid & others.
Club founded in c.1905.
Visitors: welcome if members of recognised clubs.
Green fees: weekdays £5, weekends £6.50.
Society meetings: by arrangement.
Catering: by arrangement except Mon.
Hotels: Grand, Hartlepool; Staincliffe, Seaton Carew.

U44 Hexham

☎ Hexham (0434) 603072
Spital Park, Hexham, Northumberland NE46 3RZ
On A69, 1 mile W of Hexham town centre.
Undulating parkland course.
18 holes, 6026 yards, S.S.S.68
Course designed by Harry Vardon.
Club founded in 1907.
Visitors: welcome.
Green fees: weekdays £6 per round, £8 per day; weekends £7 per round, £9 per day.
Society meetings: welcome except Sun.
Catering: snacks and meals served.
Hotels: Beaumont, Beaumont St; Royal, Priestpopple, Hexham.

U45 Houghton-le-Spring

☎ Houghton-le-Spring (0783) 841198
Copt Hill, Houghton-le-Spring DH5 8LU
On A1085 Houghton-le-Spring to Seaham Harbour road, 1½ miles from Houghton-le-Spring.
Undulating moorland course.
18 holes, 6248 yards, S.S.S.70
Club founded in 1934.
Visitors: welcome on Mon to Sat and with telephone booking on Sun.
Green fees: £4 per round, £6 per day.
Society meetings: by prior arrangement.
Catering: bar meals during bar hours; other catering by arrangement.
Hotels: White Lion, Houghton-le-Spring; Ramside Hall, Rainton; Barnes, Durham Rd, Sunderland.

U46 Kendal

☎ Kendal (0539) 24079
The Heights, Kendal, Cumbria
To Kendal on A6 signposted in town.
Moorland course.
18 holes, 5483 yards, S.S.S.67
Club founded in 1903.
Visitors: welcome any time but prior application suggested.
Green fees: £5.50 (£2.75 with member).
Society meetings: catered for anytime subject to availability.
Catering: full catering except Mon.
Hotels: County; Woolpack.

U47 Keswick

☎ Keswick (0596) 83324 or 72147
Threlkeld Hall, Keswick, Cumbria CA12 4HF
4 miles E of Keswick on A66.
Undulating moorland/parkland course.
18 holes, 6175 yards, S.S.S.70
Course designed by Eric Brown.
Club founded in 1977.
Visitors: welcome.
Green fees: £6 per day.
Society meetings: welcome by arrangement.
Catering: by arrangement.
Hotels: Lodore Swiss; Borrowdale.

U48 **Magdalene Fields**
☎ Berwick (0289) 306384
Berwick-upon-Tweed.
5 minutes walk from town centre.
Seaside course (parkland fairways).
18 holes, 6551 yards, S.S.S.71
Visitors: welcome.
Green fees: weekdays £3.75 per round, weekends £5.25 per round.
Society meetings: by arrangement.
Catering: meals during summer, at other times by arrangement.
Hotels: Kings Arms; Ravensholme Guest House, Berwick.

U49 **Maryport**
☎ Maryport (0900) 812605
Bank End, Maryport, Cumbria
N of Maryport, turn left off A596 onto B5300 (Silloth), course 1 mile.
Seaside links course.
11 holes, 6272 yards, S.S.S.71
Club founded in 1902.
Visitors: welcome.
Green fees: £5.
Society meetings: welcome.
Catering: by arrangement.
Hotels: Waverley, Curzon St, Maryport; Sandpiper, Allonby, Maryport.

U50 **Middlesbrough**
☎ Middlesbrough (0642) 311515 or 316430
Brass Castle Lane, Marton, Middlesbrough, Cleveland TS8 9EE
5 miles S of Middlesbrough, 1 mile W of A172.
Parkland course.
18 holes, 6106 yards, S.S.S.69
Course designed by James Braid.
Club founded in 1908.
Visitors: welcome on weekdays.
Green fees: weekdays £8 (with member £4), weekends and Bank Holidays £10 (with member £6).
Society meetings: catered for on Wed, Thurs and Fri.
Catering: full catering facilities except Mon.
Hotels: Marton, Marton; The Post House, Stainton; Blue Bell, Brookfield.

U51 **Middlesbrough Municipal**
☎ Middlesbrough (0642) 315533
Ladgate Lane, Middlesbrough, Cleveland TS5 7YZ
Access from A19 via A174 to Acklam.
Undulating parkland course.
18 holes, 6314 yards, S.S.S.70
Club founded in 1977.
Visitors: welcome.
Green fees: weekdays £3.25, weekends £4.25.
Society meetings: welcome weekdays.
Catering: snacks and meals served.
Hotels: Blue Bell, Acklam; Post House, Hemlington.

U52 **Morpeth**
☎ Morpeth (0670) 519980 Sec, 512065 Pro
The Common, Morpeth, NE61 2BT
On A197 1 mile S of Morpeth.
Parkland course.
18 holes, 6215 yards, S.S.S.70
Course designed by Harry Vardon (1922).
Club founded in 1906.
Visitors: welcome by arrangement.
Green fees: weekdays £6.50 per round, weekends and Bank Holidays £8 per round.
Society meetings: welcome by arrangement with Sec.
Catering: bar meals, snacks and teas available; catering for parties by arrangement with Steward.
Hotels: Queens Head, Morpeth.

U53 **Mount Oswald**
☎ Durham (0385) 67527
South Rd, Durham DH1 3TQ
Club is SW of Durham on A1050.
Parkland course.
18 holes, 6009 yards, S.S.S.69
Visitors: welcome.
Green fees: weekdays £3.50 per round, £6 per day; weekends £4.50 per round, £8 per day.
Society meetings: at weekends.
Catering: meals and snacks served.
Hotels: Royal County; Three Tuns.

U54 **Newbiggin-by-the-Sea**
☎ Ashington (0670) 817344
Newbiggin-by-the-Sea, Northumberland
On A197, 9 miles E of Morpeth
Seaside course.
18 holes, 6444 yards, S.S.S.71
Club founded in 1884.
Visitors: welcome.
Green fees: weekdays £4.50 (£2.50 with member), weekends £6 (£3.50 with member).
Society meetings: by arrangement.
Catering: meals daily by arrangement.
Hotels: In Newbiggin.

U55 **Newcastle United**
☎ Newcastle-upon-Tyne (0632) 864693
Ponteland Rd, Cowgate, Newcastle upon Tyne, Northumberland NE5 3GW
1 mile W of city centre.
Moorland course.
18 holes, 6498 yards, S.S.S.71
Club founded in 1890.
Visitors: welcome on weekdays.
Green fees: £4.50 per day (£3 with member).
Society meetings: by arrangement.
Catering: meals by arrangement.
Hotels: in Newcastle.

U56 **Northumberland**
☎ Wideopen (0632) 362009 Steward, 362498 Sec
High Gosforth Park, Newcastle upon Tyne NE3 5HT.
Situated off A1 4 miles N of Newcastle upon Tyne city centre.
Undulating parkland course.
18 holes, 6640 yards, S.S.S.72
Course designed by H.S. Colt & James Braid.
Club founded in 1898.
Visitors: welcome on weekdays by reservation with Sec and letter of introduction.
Green fees: £12.50 per round, £15 per day.
Society meetings: catered for on Tues, Thurs and Fri only.
Catering: luncheon served except Mon.
Hotels: Gosforth Park; Holiday Inn.

U57 **Penrith**
☎ Penrith (0768) 62217
Salkeld Rd, Penrith, Cumbria CA11 8SP
½ mile NE of Penrith.
Parkland course.
18 holes, 6026 yards, S.S.S.69
Club founded in 1890.
Visitors: members of golf club welcome with handicap.
Green fees: weekdays £6, weekends £7.
Society meetings: welcome by arrangement with Sec; must be members of golf club with handicap.
Catering: meals except Mon and Tues.
Hotels: numerous hotels and boarding houses in Penrith and surrounding area.

U58 **Ponteland**
☎ Ponteland (0661) 22689
53 Bell Villas, Ponteland, Newcastle upon Tyne NE20 9BD
On A696 road to Jedburgh, 2 miles N of Newcastle Airport.
Meadowland course.
18 holes, 6512 yards, S.S.S.71
Club founded in 1928.

Visitors: welcome on weekdays and with member at weekends.
Green fees: £6.50 per round, £7.50 per day (£3 with member).
Society meetings: catered for by arrangement on Tues and Thurs.
Catering: bar snacks available and meals by arrangement except Fri.
Hotels: Stakis Airport; Holiday Inn, Seaton Burn.

U59 Prudhoe
☎ Prudhoe (0661) 32466
Eastwood Park, Prudhoe, Northumberland NE42 5DX
12 miles W of Newcastle on A695.
Parkland course.
18 holes, 5812 yards, S.S.S.68
Club founded in 1930.
Visitors: welcome on weekdays.
Green fees: weekdays £4.50 per round, £5.50 per day; weekends £6.
Society meetings: welcome weekdays.
Catering: bar snacks and meals served.
Hotels: Broomhaugh, Riding Mill, Northumberland.

U60 Ravensworth
☎ Tyneside (091) 487 6014
Moss Heaps, Wrekenton, Gateshead, Tyne & Wear NE9 7UU
Off A1, 2 miles S of Gateshead.
Moorland/parkland course.
18 holes, 5872 yards, S.S.S.68
Club founded in 1906.
Visitors: welcome.
Green fees: weekdays £5 (£3.50 with member); weekends and Bank Holidays £6 (£4.50 with member); plus V.A.T.
Society meetings: by arrangement on weekdays.
Catering: by arrangement.
Hotels: Five Bridges, Gateshead; Springfield, Gateshead.

U61 Rothbury
☎ Rothbury (0669) 20718
Old Race Course, Rothbury, Morpeth, Northumberland NE65 7UB
Off A697, 15 miles NE of Morpeth.
Meadowland course.
9 holes, 5146 metres, S.S.S.67
Club founded in 1890.
Visitors: welcome on weekdays and most Sun.
Green fees: weekdays £1.50, weekends £3; half-price with member.
Society meetings: no.
Catering: no catering facilities.
Hotels: Coquetvale; Queens Head; Newcastle; all in Rothbury.

U62 Ryton
☎ Tyneside (091) 413 3737
Dr Stanners, Clara Vale, Ryton, Tyne & Wear NE40 3TD
Off A695 8 miles from Newcastle, follow signs from Ryton to Wylam then Clara Vale.
Moorland/parkland course.
18 holes, 6034 yards, S.S.S.69
Club founded in 1891.
Visitors: welcome on weekdays and by arrangement at weekends.
Green fees: weekdays £3.50 (£2 with member), weekends and Bank Holidays £6 (£5 with member).
Society meetings: welcome by written application.
Catering: meals and bar snacks served by prior arrangement with Steward.
Hotels: Ryton Country Club.

U63 St Bees School
☎ St Bees 695
Station Rd, St Bees
On B5345, 4 miles S of Whitehaven.
Seaside course.
9 holes, S.S.S.65
Club founded in 1942/43.
Visitors: welcome except on competition days in summer.
Green fees: Adults weekdays £3, weekends £4; Juniors weekdays £1.50, weekends £2.
Catering: none available.
Hotels: Seacote; Manor House.

U64 Saltburn-by-Sea
☎ Guisborough (0287) 22812
Guisborough Rd, Hob Hill, Saltburn-by-Sea, Cleveland TS12 1NJ
1 mile from centre of Saltburn on B1268.
Undulating meadowland course.
18 holes, 5803 yards, S.S.S.68
Visitors: welcome if members of recognised club.
Green fees: weekdays £6.60, weekends with reservation only.
Society meetings: by arrangement.
Catering: full catering except Mon.

U65 Seaham
☎ Seaham (0783) 812354
Dawdon, Seaham, Co Durham SR7 7RD
Off A19, 6 miles S of Sunderland, take road to Seaham.
Heathland course.
18 holes, 5972 yards, S.S.S.69
Course designed by Dr A. Mackenzie.
Club founded in May 1911.
Visitors: welcome on weekdays.
Green fees: weekends and Bank Holidays £7 (£6 with member), weekdays £6 (£5 with member); Juniors £3.
Society meetings: welcome weekdays.
Catering: lunches and evening meals.
Hotels: Harbour View, 18 North Terrace, Seaham Harbour, Seaham Hall, Seaham, Co Durham.

U66 Seahouses
☎ Seahouses (0661) 720794
Beadnell Rd, Seahouses, Northumberland NE68 7XT
Off A1 5 miles N of Alnwick.
Seaside course.
18 holes, 5399 yards, S.S.S.66
Visitors: welcome.
Green fees: weekdays £4.50, weekends and Bank Holidays £6.
Society meetings: catered for on weekdays and most weekends.
Catering: bar lunches except Mon.
Hotels: Bamburgh Castle, Seahouses; Beadnell Towers, Beadnell.

U67 Seascale
☎ Seascale (0940) 28202
The Banks, Seascale, Cumbria CA20 1QL
On coast to N of village.
Seaside links course.
18 holes, 6372 yards, S.S.S.70
Club founded in 1893.
Visitors: welcome.
Green fees: weekdays £6, weekends and Bank Holidays £7.
Society meetings: by arrangement with Sec.
Catering: meals served except Mon and Tues, when only limited catering available.
Hotels: Scawfell; Calder House; Wansfell; all in Seascale.

U68 Seaton Carew
☎ Hartlepool (0429) 66249
Tees Rd, Seaton Carew, Hartlepool TS25 1DE
Off A689 3 miles S of Hartlepool.
Links course.
Club founded in 1874.
Visitors: welcome.
Green fees: weekdays £9, weekends and Bank Holidays £11.
Society meetings: welcome by arrangement.
Catering: snacks and meals by arrangement with Manager.
Hotels: Grand, Swainson St, Hartlepool; Staincliffe, The Cliff, Seaton Carew; Marine, Seaton Carew.

U69 Sedbergh
☎ Sedbergh (0587) 20993
The Riggs, Millthrop, Sedbergh, Cumbria
1 mile from Sedbergh on Dent Rd, via hamlet of Millthrop.
Undulating fell land course.
9 holes, 4134 yards, S.S.S.61
Club founded in 1896.
Visitors: welcome by arrangement with Hon Sec.
Green fees: weekdays £1, Sun and Bank Holidays £1.50.
Society meetings: no suitable facilities.
Catering: no catering available.
Hotels: Bull, Sedbergh; Red Lion, Sedbergh.

U70 Silecroft
☎ Silecroft (0657) 4250
Silecroft, Cumbria LA18 4NX
On A5093 3 miles N of Millom, through Silecroft village towards shore.
Seaside course.
9 holes, 5627 yards, S.S.S.66
Club founded in 1903.
Visitors: welcome on weekdays and at weekends, with restrictions until 5.30 pm.
Green fees: weekdays £4, weekends £5.
Society meetings: no.
Catering: no catering facilities.
Hotels: Miners Arms, Silecroft; Bankfield Hotel, Kirksanton.

U71 Silloth on Solway
☎ Silloth (0965) 31179
Silloth on Solway, Carlisle, Cumbria CA5 4AT
B5302 off A596 at Wigton, 18 miles W of Carlisle.
Undulating seaside course.
18 holes, 6343 yards, S.S.S.70
Course designed by Dr Leach.
Club founded in 1892.
Visitors: welcome.
Green fees: weekdays £8, weekends £10, Mon - Fri £30.
Society meetings: by arrangement.
Catering: meals as required.
Hotels: Golf; Queens; Skinburness.

U72 South Moor
☎ Stanley (0207) 232848
The Middles, Craghead, Stanley, Co Durham DH9 6AG
2 miles from Stanley on B6313.
Moorland course.
18 holes, 6445 yards, S.S.S.71
Course designed by Dr Mackenzie.
Club founded in 1923.
Visitors: welcome.
Green fees: weekdays £5 (£3 with member), weekends and Bank Holidays £6 (£4 with member).
Society meetings: catered for all week.
Catering: lunches and evening meals served except Mon (summer) and Mon and Tues (winter).
Hotels: Post House, Washington; Lumley Castle, Chester le Street; Imperial, Stanley; Beamish Park.

U73 South Shields
☎ South Shields (0632) 560475 Club, 568942 Sec.
Cleadon Hills, South Shields, Tyne & Wear NE34 8EG
A19 turn off at Quarry Lane, near Cleadon Chimney.
Seaside course.
18 holes, 6264 yards, S.S.S.70
Club founded in 1893.
Visitors: welcome.
Green fees: weekdays £5, weekends and Bank Holidays £8.
Society meetings: on Thurs only.
Catering: full catering facilities.
Hotels: Sea; Ambassador; New Crown; Marsden Inn.

U74 Stocksfield
☎ Stocksfield (0661) 843041
New Ridley, Stocksfield, Northumberland NE43 7RE
On A68 between Corbridge and Prudhoe.
Parkland/wooded course.
18 holes, 6037 yards, S.S.S.70
Course designed by Frank Pennink.
Club founded in 1920.
Visitors: welcome.
Green fees: weekdays £6, weekends £8.
Society meetings: welcome by arrangement with Sec.
Catering: full catering facilities.
Hotels: Angel, Corbridge; Riding Mill.

U75 Stonyholme Municipal
☎ Carlisle (0228) 34856 Pro, 33208 Clubhouse
St Aidans Rd, Carlisle
Off A69, 1 mile E of M6, Junction 43.
Flat meadowland course.
18 holes, 5600 yards, S.S.S.68
Course designed by Frank Pennink.
Club founded in 1974.
Visitors: welcome.
Green fees: weekdays £2.50 per round, weekends £3 per round.
Society meetings: welcome.
Catering: meals served.
Hotels: many good hotels in Carlisle.

U76 Stressholme
☎ Darlington (0325) 461002 Pro, 463229 Steward
Snipe Lane, Darlington, Co Durham
About 8 miles N of Scotch Corner.
Parkland municipal course.
18 holes, 6511 yards, S.S.S.71
Visitors: welcome.
Green fees: weekdays £2.75, weekends and Bank Holidays £4.20.
Society meetings: welcome on weekdays.
Catering: meals by arrangement with Steward.
Hotels: Blackwell Grange, Darlington.

U77 Teesside
☎ Stockton (0642) 676249 or 616516 Sec.
Acklam Rd, Thornaby, Cleveland TS17 7JS
Off A19 take A1130 to Stockton, course is situated 1 mile from A19 on right.
Meadowland course.
18 holes, 6472 yards, S.S.S.71
Club founded in 1901.
Visitors: welcome on weekdays before 4.30 pm and at weekends after 11 am.
Green fees: weekdays £6 per day, weekends £10 per day, weekly (Mon – Fri) £20.
Society meetings: catered for on weekdays.
Catering: full catering except Mon.
Hotels: Golden Eagle, Thornaby; Swallow, Stockton; Post House, Thornaby.

U78 Tynedale
Tyne Green, Northumberland
½ mile from town centre in Tyne Green Country Park.
Parkland course.
9 holes, S.S.S.67
Visitors: welcome, but booking required on Sun.
Green fees: weekdays £2.50, weekends £3.50.
Society meetings: no.
Catering: no catering available.
Hotels: numerous hotels in Hexham.

U79 Tynemouth
☎ North Shields (0632) 573381 Sec, 574578 Clubhouse.
Spital Dene, Tynemouth, North Shields, Tyne & Wear NE30 2ER
On A695.
Parkland course.
18 holes, 6351 yards, S.S.S.70
Course designed by Willie Park.
Club founded in 1913.
Visitors: welcome on weekdays.

Green fees: weekdays £6 (£3 with member), weekends and Bank Holidays £8 (£4 with member).
Society meetings: welcome weekdays.
Catering: lunches, teas and snacks served except Mon.
Hotels: Newcastle Moat House, Coast Rd, Wallsend; Park Hotel, Tynemouth.

U80 Tyneside

☎ Tyneside (091) 413 2742 Sec, 2177 Clubhouse Westfield Lane, Ryton, Tyne & Wear NE40 3QE
7 miles W of Newcastle-upon-Tyne on S side of Tyne, on A695, turn N at Ryton Down to Old Ryton village, turn left, pass Cross Inn, and then right at end of row of old houses on right.
Parkland course.
18 holes, 6055 yards, S.S.S.69
Course designed by H.S. Colt (1910).
Club founded in 1897.
Visitors: welcome.
Green fees: weekdays £6 per round, £8 per day; weekends £9 per round.
Society meetings: welcome on weekdays by prior arrangement with Sec.
Catering: meals and snacks available from 8 am to 10 pm.
Hotels: Ryton Park Country Club, Holburn Lane, Ryton Park, Ryton.

U81 Ulverston

☎ Ulverston (0229) 52824
Bardsea Park, Ulverston, Cumbria LA12 92J
From Ulverston town centre to Bardsea on B5087.
Parkland course.
18 holes, 6126 yards, S.S.S.69
Course designed by W.H. Colt.
Club founded in 1895.
Visitors: welcome except on competition days.
Green fees: weekdays £7, weekends £8.50.
Society meetings: welcome, max. 40.
Catering: meals served except Mon.
Hotels: Eccle Riggs, Broughton; Farmers Arms, Lewick; Fishermans Arms.

U82 Wallsend

☎ Tyneside (091) 262 1973
Biggs Main, Wallsend-on-Tyne, NE28 8SX
From Newcastle E along Shields road, turn left at sign to Wallsend Sports Centre.
Parkland course.
18 holes, 6601 yards, S.S.S.72
Club founded in 1905.
Visitors: welcome.
Green fees: weekdays £3.05 per round, weekends £3.85.
Society meetings: on written request.
Catering: on request.
Hotels: good hotels in area.

U83 Warkworth

☎ Alnwick (0665) 711596
Warkworth, Northumberland
Off A1068 to Warkworth.
Seaside course.
9 holes, 5856 yards, S.S.S.68
Course designed by Tom Morris.
Club founded in 1891.
Visitors: welcome, but check for competition days (Ladies Day Tues).
Green fees: weekdays £4, weekends and Bank Holidays £6.
Society meetings: limited number catered for.
Catering: by arrangement.
Hotels: Warkworth House; Sun.

U84 Wearside

☎ Sunderland (0783) 342518
Coxgreen, Sunderland SR4 9JT
Take A185 Chester-le-Street road off A19, after 400 yds turn right at Coxgreen sign, left at small T-junction, follow road down hill to clubhouse.
Meadowland/parkland course.
18 holes, 6204 yards, S.S.S.70
Club founded in 1892.
Visitors: welcome.
Green fees: weekdays £6 per round, £8 per day; weekends £9 per day or round.
Society meetings: welcome on weekdays before 4 pm.
Catering: meals served except Mon.
Hotels: Sedburn; Roker; Washington Post House; Mowbray.

U85 Westerhope

☎ Newcastle (0632) 869125
Whorlton Grange, Westerhope, Newcastle upon Tyne NE5 1PP
5 miles W of Newcastle; Airport Rd for 3 miles then follow signs to Westerhope.
Parkland course.
18 holes, 6468 yards, S.S.S.71
Club founded in 1939.
Visitors: welcome weekdays.
Green fees: weekdays £5.50, weekends £7 (£3.50 with member).
Society meetings: by arrangement.
Catering: lunches and high teas served except Mon.
Hotels: Denton; Airport; Gosforth Park.

U86 Whickham

☎ Tyneside (091) 488 7309
Hollinside Park, Whickham, Newcastle upon Tyne NE16 5BA
5 miles W of Newcastle.
Undulating parkland course.
18 holes, 6129 yards, S.S.S.69
Club founded in 1911.
Visitors: welcome on weekdays.
Green fees: weekdays £5 per day, weekends and Bank Holidays £7.50.
Society meetings: welcome.
Catering: full catering facilities.
Hotels: Gibside, Whickham.

U87 Whitburn

☎ Whitburn (0783) 292144
Lizard Lane, South Shields, Tyne & Wear NE34 7AH
Halfway between Sunderland and SouthShields off coast road.
Parkland course.
18 holes, 6035 yards, S.S.S.69
Club founded in 1931.
Visitors: welcome but advisable to check at weekends.
Green fees: weekdays £4 per day or round; weekends and Bank Holidays £5.50 per round, £7 per day.
Society meetings: welcome on weekdays except Tues by prior arrangement with Sec.
Catering: meals served except Mon.
Hotels: Sea, South Shields; New Crown, South Shields; Seaburn, Sunderland.

U88 Whitley Bay

☎ Tyneside (091) 252 5688

Claremont Rd, Whitley Bay, Tyne & Wear NE26 3UF
On A183, 10 miles NE of Newcastle.
Undulating seaside course.
18 holes, 6712 yards, S.S.S.72
Visitors: weekdays only.
Green fees: weekdays £8 (£4 with member), weekends £4 with member only.
Society meetings: by arrangement.
Catering: meals served daily, snacks only on Mon.
Hotels: in Whitley.

U89 Wilton

☎ Eston Grange (0642) 454626 or 465265
Wilton Castle, Redcar, Cleveland TS10 4QY
Off A174, 4 miles W of Redcar, take road for Wilton village and castle.
Parkland course.
18 holes, 6104 yards, S.S.S.69
Club founded in 1952.
Visitors: welcome except on Sat or before 9.30 am Sun.

Green fees: weekdays £8, weekends and Bank Holidays £9 (£4 with member).
Society meetings: by arrangement with Committee through Sec.
Catering: full catering service except Sat and Sun evenings.
Hotels: York, Redcar.

U90 Windermere

☎ Windermere (096 62) 3123
Cleabarrow, Windermere, Cumbria
LA23 3NB
From M6 (junctions 36/37) this golf course is 9 miles NE of Kendal. Turn off A591 at Crooklands roundabout; join B5284.
Undulating parkland course.
18 holes, 5002 yards, S.S.S.65
Course designed by George Low.
Club founded in 1890.
Visitors: welcome.
Green fees: weekdays £6 per day, weekends £8 per day.
Society meetings: by arrangement with Sec, maximum 40.
Catering: bar snacks available, full meals by arrangement.
Hotels: Wild Boar, Crook; Royal, Bowness; Old England; Belsfield, Bowness.

U91 Workington

☎ Workington (0900) 3460
Branthwaite Rd, Workington, Cumbria
CA1 4NW
Off A595 2 miles SE of town centre.
Undulating meadowland course.
18 holes, 6202 yards, S.S.S.70
Course designed by James Braid.
Club founded in 1906.
Visitors: members of recognised clubs welcome.
Green fees: weekdays £7, weekends and Bank Holidays £9; reductions for Juniors, parties and during winter months.
Society meetings: by prior arrangement.
Catering: full catering facilities except Mon and Thurs evenings.
Hotels: Westlands, Workington; Washington Central, Workington; Clifton, Gt Clifton, Workington.

V Lothians, Borders, Dumfries and Galloway

Golfers visiting Scotland traditionally head for St Andrews, Dornoch, Gleneagles, Carnoustie or Muirfield, very often without any idea of what they may be missing elsewhere. So let me do my little bit of voluntary publicity for Southerness, one of the finest in Britain, and for the other courses of Dumfries and Galloway.

They form part of a convenient detour that highlights a lesser known part of a country famous for its golf, and if the subsidiary courses are not on quite the same scale as Southerness, they are highly enjoyable. Powfoot, amid the gorse and within easy reach of Dumfries, ranks nearest to it. Dumfries itself boasts Thornhill and Dumfries and County but, having explored the glories of Southerness, the charms of Portpatrick (Dunskey) and Stranraer are well worth an extra day – maybe en route for Turnberry.

The alternative to heading west from Carlisle along the northern shores of the Solway Firth is the road through the lovely Border country where, again, the scenic beauty makes up for any shortcomings in the golf. Kelso, Hirsel, Innerleithen, Jedburgh, Langholm, St Boswells and Melrose are only nine holes but Galashiels, Moffat, Peebles and Minto are 18 holes and a pleasant way of breaking yourself in for sterner things ahead in the Lothians.

Apart from a variety of courses around Edinburgh, the Lothians embrace the sterling stretch of golfing country from Longniddry through Kilspindie, Luffness, Gullane, Muirfield and North Berwick to Dunbar which is first class. The staging of the Boys championship and the Scottish strokeplay championship at Dunbar is testimony to its quality but travellers to Glasgow may well like to break their journey and play some of the West Lothian courses.

V1 Baberton
☎ 031-453 4911
Baberton Avenue, Juniper Green, Edinburgh EH14 3DU
On main Lanark rd from Edinburgh.
Parkland course.
18 holes, 6140 yards, S.S.S.69
Club founded in 1893.
Visitors: welcome if introduced by member.
Green fees: £6 per round, £8 per day.
Society meetings: welcome by arrangement.
Catering: meals served except Thurs.
Hotels: Glenburn; Marchbank; Johnsburn.

V2 Bathgate
☎ Bathgate (0506) 52232 Club, 630505 Sec, 630553 Pro
Edinburgh Rd, Bathgate, West Lothian
400 yds E from town centre.
Parkland course.
18 holes, 6326 yards, S.S.S.70
Club founded in 1892.
Visitors: welcome except on comp. days.
Green fees: weekdays £5, weekends £7 (£1 with member).
Catering: meals served.
Hotels: Golden Circle; Dreadnought; Kaim Park.

V3 Braids United
☎ 031-447 3327
Braids Hill Approach, Edinburgh EH10
A702 from city centre.
Hillside courses.
18 holes, 5731 yards, S.S.S.68
18 holes, 4832 yards, S.S.S.63
Visitors: welcome except Sun.
Green fees: on request.
Hotels: Braid Hills.

V4 Broomieknowe
☎ 031-663 9317
36 Golf Course Rd, Bonnyrigg, Midlothian EH19 2HZ
Take Bonnyrigg road at Eskbank (Dalkeith) roundabout 1 mile to Bonnyrigg.
Gently undulating parkland course.
18 holes, 6046 yards, S.S.S.69
Course designed by James Braid.
Club founded in 1906.
Visitors: welcome on weekdays.
Green fees: weekdays £6 per round, £7 for 2 rounds; weekends £7 per round.
Society meetings: welcome weekdays.
Catering: bar lunches available, and evening meals by arrangement with Steward, except Mon.
Hotels: Dalhousie Castle, Bonnyrigg.

V5 Bruntsfield Links
☎ 031-336 1479
32 Barnton Ave, Davidsons Mains, Edinburgh EH4 6JH
Off A90 in Davidsons Mains 2 to 3 miles W of Edinburgh city centre.
Parkland course.
18 holes, 6407 yards, S.S.S.71
Course designed by Willie Park.
Club founded in 1761.
Visitors: welcome with letter of

introduction.
Green fees: on application.
Catering: lunches served daily.
Hotels: Barnton.

V6 Carrickvale

☎ 031-337 1932
Glendevon Park, Edinburgh EH12 5VZ
Opposite the Post House Hotel, down Balgreen Rd.
Meadowland course.
18 holes, 6299 yards, S.S.S.70
Club founded in 1933.
Visitors: welcome.
Green fees: £2 per round.
Society meetings: by arrangement.
Catering: by arrangement with Sec.
Hotels: Post House.

V7 Castle Douglas

☎ Castle Douglas (0556) 2801
Abercromby Rd, Castle Douglas.
400 yds on Ayr road from town clock.
Parkland course.
9 holes, 5408 yards, S.S.S.66
Green fees: £4 per day or round.
Catering: bar facilities in evenings.
Hotels: many in town.

V8 Colvend

☎ Rockcliffe (055 663) 398
Sandyhills, by Dalbeattie, Kirkcudbrightshire DG5 4PY
6 miles from Dalbeattie on A710 Solway coast road.
Undulating meadowland course.
9 holes, 2103 yards, S.S.S.61
Club founded in 1908.
Visitors: welcome except on comp. days.
Green fees: £3 per day; half-price for children on weekdays.
Society meetings: welcome by arrangement.
Catering: none.
Hotels: Clonyard House, Colvend; Anchor, Kippford; Mariner, Kippford.

V9 Craigmillar Park

☎ 031-667 2837 Clubhouse, 0047 Office
1 Observatory Rd, Edinburgh EH9 3HG

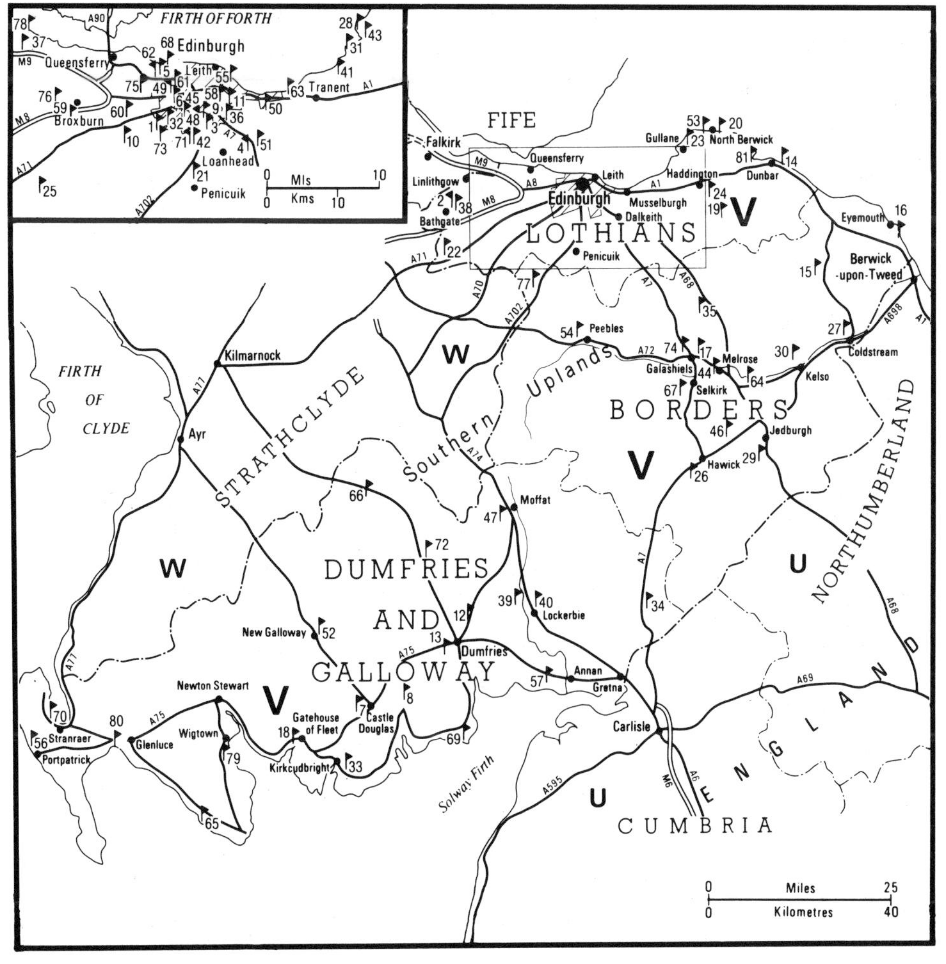

Approximately 3 miles from city centre close to Royal Observatory, Blackford Hill.
Parkland course.
18 holes, 5846 yards, S.S.S.68
Course designed by James Braid.
Club founded in 1895.
Visitors: welcome.
Green fees: weekdays £4.60 (£1.20 with member), weekends £7 (£1.20 with member).
Society meetings: welcome on weekdays only on written application to Sec.
Catering: lunches, high teas and dinners served every day except Mon.
Hotels: all hotels on S side of Edinburgh.

V10 Dalmahoy
☎ 031-333 2055
Dalmahoy, Kirknewton, Midlothian EH27 8EB
On A71 Edinburgh to Kilmarnock road.
Parkland courses.
East 18 holes, 6664 yards, S.S.S.72
West 18 holes, 5212 yards, S.S.S.66
Course designed by J. Braid.
Club founded in 1927.
Visitors: welcome.
Green fees: on application.
Society meetings: welcome.
Catering: full catering facilities available.
Hotels: Dalmahoy C.C.; Norton House.

V11 Duddingston
☎ 031-661 7688 or 4301 Pro
Duddingston Rd W, Edinburgh EH15 3QD
3 miles from city centre E on A1.
Parkland course.
18 holes, 6647 yards, S.S.S.72
Club founded in 1897.
Visitors: welcome.
Green fees: weekdays £6.90 per round, £8.05 per day; weekends £9.20 per round or day.
Society meetings: welcome on Tues and Thurs or by special arrangement.
Catering: full service except Mon.
Hotels: Lady Nairne; King's Manor; Duddingston Mansion House.

V12 Dumfries & County
☎ Dumfries (0387) 53585
Edinburgh Rd, Dumfries DG1 1JX
1m N of Dumfries town centre on A701.
Parkland course.
18 holes, 5914 yards, S.S.S.68
Course designed by Wilie Fernie.
Club founded in 1912.
Visitors: welcome except on comp. days.
Green fees: weekdays £6, weekends £7.50.
Society meetings: by arrangement.
Catering: lunches and high teas served.
Hotels: Station; Cairndale.

V13 Dumfries & Galloway
☎ Dumfries (0387) 3582
Laurieston Ave, Dumfries DG2 7NY
On A75 W of Dumfries.
Parkland course.
18 holes, 5782 yards, S.S.S.68
Club founded in 1880.
Visitors: welcome.
Green fees: on application.
Society meetings: welcome weekdays.
Catering: full catering except Mon.
Hotels: Cairndale; Dalston.

V14 Dunbar
☎ Dunbar (0368) 62317
East Links, Dunbar EH42 1LT
½ mile from Dunbar centre.
Seaside course.
18 holes, 6426 yards, S.S.S.71
Club founded in 1856.
Visitors: welcome.
Green fees: weekdays £7.50 per day, weekends £10 per day.
Society meetings: welcome.
Catering: meals served except Tues in winter.
Hotels: Bayswell, Dunbar.

V15 Duns
☎ Duns (03612) 83377
Hardens Rd, Duns, Berwickshire
1 mile W of Duns on A6105.
Undulating meadowland course.
9 holes, 5754 yards, S.S.S.68
Visitors: welcome except on Tues evenings.
Green fees: weekdays £3 per day, weekends £4 per day.
Catering: limited facilities available by arrangement.
Hotels: many good hotels in Duns.

V16 Eyemouth
☎ Eyemouth (0390) 50551 (only at weekends)
Gunsgreen House, Eyemouth TD14 5DW
2½ miles E of Burmouth, off A1, signposted on A1107.
Seaside course.
9 holes, 2723 yards, S.S.S.66
Club founded in 1880.
Visitors: welcome with restrictions on competition days.
Green fees: weekdays £3 (Juniors £1), weekends £4 (Juniors £2).
Hotels: Home Arms, Eyemouth; Contented Sole, Eyemouth.

V17 Galashiels
☎ Galashiels (0986) 3724
Ladhope Recreation Ground, Galashiels, Selkirkshire
¼ mile N of town off A7.
Hilly course.
18 holes, 5309 yards, S.S.S.67
Course designed by James Braid.
Club founded in 1884.
Visitors: welcome without reservation.
Green fees: £3.50 per day, Sun £4.
Catering: snacks only served.
Hotels: several hotels in area.

V18 Gatehouse
☎ Gatehouse (055 74) 654
Laurieston Rd, Gatehouse-of-Fleet
First right on entering Gatehouse-of-Fleet from E.
Undulating course.
9 holes, 2398 yards, S.S.S.63
Club founded in 1921.
Visitors: welcome.
Green fees: weekdays £3 per day, weekends £4 per day; Juniors half-price.
Hotels: Murray Arms; Bank of Fleet; Angel; Anwoth.

V19 Gifford
☎ Gifford (062 081) 267
c/o Sec, Cawdor Cottage, 11 Station Rd, Gifford, East Lothian EH41 4QL
4½ miles S of Haddington off A6137.
Meadowland/woodland course.
9 holes, 6138 yards, S.S.S.69
Club founded in 1904.
Visitors: welcome, except on Tues and Wed from 4 pm or Sun from 12 noon.
Green fees: weekdays £3 per day, weekends £3 for 18 holes.
Society meetings: catered for on weekdays by arrangement with Sec.
Catering: none.
Hotels: Goblin Ha', Gifford; Tweeddale Arms, Gifford.

V20 Glen
☎ North Berwick (0620) 2221
Tantallon Terrace, North Berwick, East Lothian EH39 4LE
22 miles NE of Edinburgh on A198, follow rd along E beach, clubhouse is last building on right.
Seaside/parkland course.
18 holes, 6086 yards, S.S.S.69

Club founded in 1906.
Visitors: welcome.
Green fees: weekends £7.25 per day, weekdays £5.50 per day.
Society meetings: welcome by arrangement with Clubmaster.
Catering: meals and snacks served.
Hotels: Marine, Strathearn Rd, North Berwick; Royal, Station Rd, North Berwick; Point Garry, West Bay Rd, North Berwick.

V21 Glencorse

☎ Pencuik (0968) 77177
Milton Bridge, Pencuik, Midlothian
On A701, 9 miles S of Edinburgh.
Parkland course.
18 holes, 5205 yards, S.S.S.66
Club founded in 1895.
Visitors: welcome on weekdays, weekends with reservation.
Green fees: weekdays £5 per round, £7 per day; weekends £7 per round.
Society meetings: by arrangement.
Catering: snacks, lunches and high teas served.
Hotels: in Edinburgh.

V22 Greenburn

☎ Fauldhouse (0501) 70292
Bridge St, Fauldhouse, W Lothian EH47 9HG
Midway between Glasgow and Edinburgh, turn off M8 at Whitburn, 3 miles.
Moorland course.
18 holes, 6210 yards, S.S.S.70
Club founded in 1933.
Visitors: welcome.
Green fees: weekdays £3.30 per round. £4.40 per day; weekends £4.40 per round, £6.60 per day.
Society meetings: by arrangement.
Catering: meals by arrangement.
Hotels: Whitedale, Whitburn.

V23 Gullane

☎ Gullane (0620) 842255
Gullane, East Lothian EH31 2BB
Off A1, on A198 to Gullane.
Links courses.
No. 1 18 holes, 6479 yards, S.S.S.71
No. 2 18 holes, 6127 yards, S.S.S.69
No. 3 18 holes, 5035 yards, S.S.S.64
Club founded in 1882.
Visitors: welcome on all courses except at weekends on No 1.
Green fees: on request.
Society meetings: catered for by arrangement.
Catering: catering facilities available except Mon by arrangement.
Hotels: many good hotels in area.

V24 Haddington

☎ Haddington (062 082) 3627 or 2727
Amisfield Course, Haddington, East Lothian.
17 miles E of Edinburgh on A1, cross Victoria Bridge on E edge of town, golf course is 500 yds on left.
Parkland course.
18 holes, 6280 yards, S.S.S.70
Club founded in 1865.
Visitors: welcome on weekdays and at weekends with restrictions.
Green fees: weekdays £3.60 per round, £5.50 per day; weekends £4.65 per round, £7.25 per day.
Catering: full catering facilities by arrangement.
Hotels: George; Railway; Mercat; Maitlandfield.

Four links in one

Whenever the question of a centre for a golfing holiday is raised, Gullane in East Lothian is always one of the first that comes to my mind. If anyone feels so inclined, and has the strength and fitness to match, he can play in delightful surroundings on seven different courses in one day.

More likely, however, he will prefer to take a more leisurely look at each or simply stay and sample those absolutely at his doorstep – Luffness New, and the three Gullanes which lie on the other side of Gullane Hill from Muirfield.

Everyone has courses for which he feels unreasoning affection, and Luffness and Gullane No. 1 are two of my favourites.

The incomparable stretch of country on which they stand was introduced to me by a kind uncle during my time at school in Edinburgh when a day at Luffness really was an escape from the problems of Plato and Pythagoras; and my earliest recollections are of gloriously smooth, fast putting greens, a blind short hole across a quarry – and a magnificent lunch.

The short hole, at the point where the main road curves sharply for North Berwick, has long since been given a more straightforward approach, but I was glad to see on my last visit that the course, the greens and the lunch had lost none of their appeal.

To my mind the best holes are those from the 8th onwards down nearer Aberlady Bay, where a sense of peace and beauty is complete and the golfer cannot fail to enjoy himself. On a calm day, the demands made upon him are not all that severe, but it is most important to keep straight.

From Luffness it is perfectly possible to hit a ball across the other two Gullane courses – neither of which suffers by comparison with its celebrated neighbour – to Gullane No. 1, and to a stranger the four ay at first be indistinguishable from each other. In character they have much in common but the starts at Gullane are a little more mountainous.

However, when the view is as magnificent as it is from the third tee, or even better from the seventh tee, on Gullane No. 1, it is worth enduring any climb.

It is one of the great sights in the whole world of golf and except in grey, wet and windswept conditions, the Firth of Forth and its golden sands, the distant outline of Edinburgh and the two Forth Bridges, the green fields of Fife and an assortment of boats slipping out to sea past the Bass Rock, can distract one's thoughts from the golf which at this stage is gaining in challenge.

The 7th, rather like the 8th at Luffness, offers an inviting drive down the hill; the 8th gives the chance of a three and the 9th is an engaging short hole where the eye wanders again across the popular beach to the less exposed setting of Muirfield; but then there are three very fine long holes with which to start the homeward half, the 11th and 12th being particularly satisfying to play well, if one can forget the view.

Another testing short hole in a crosswind follows, and two more long holes which can make or mar a medal round. These take us gradually back up the slope to the short 16th along the crest and, in sight of home, we prepare for the final descent to the clubhouse, outside which the legendary Babe Zaharias was once presented with the British Women's Championship Trophy.

That was over thirty years ago, but happily little has changed in the meantime; the starter's bell on the first tee is still a welcome sound; the little village street down which so many famous names have stepped has lost none of its charm, and golfers from all parts still converge upon Gullane, Luffness and the many other courses along that coast because they know the quality and fun of the golf never disappoint.

V25 **Harburn**
☎ Bo'ness (0506) 871256
West Calder, West Lothian EH55 8RS
Turn S at West Calder off A70 Lanark to Edinburgh road.
Parkland course.
18 holes, 5843 yards, S.S.S.68
Club founded in 1933.
Visitors: welcome.
Green fees: weekdays £5 per round, £7 per day; weekends £6.50 per round, £9 per day.
Society meetings: welcome by prior arrangement with Sec.
Catering: full catering facilities available by prior arrangement.
Hotels: Meadowhead, West Calder; Golden Circle, Bathgate.

V26 **Hawick**
☎ Hawick (0450) 72293
Vertish Hill, Hawick, Roxburghshire
SE of Edinburgh on A7.
Undulating course.
18 holes, 5929 yards, S.S.S.69
Club founded in 1877.
Visitors: welcome, except competition days.
Green fees: weekdays £3 per round, £5 per day; weekends £5 per day only.
Society meetings: welcome.
Catering: meals and snacks.
Hotels: Kirklands; Borthaugh; Mansfield House; Bucclidest.

V27 **Hirsel**
☎ Coldstream (0890) 2678
Woodlands, Coldstream, Berwickshire TS12 4LG
W end of Coldstream on A697, Edinburgh to Newcastle road.
Parkland course.
9 holes, 2828 yards, S.S.S.67
Club founded in 1964.
Visitors: welcome.
Green fees: weekdays £3 per day, weekends £4 per day.
Society meetings: by arrangement with Sec.
Catering: meals served in evening and at weekends.
Hotels: Majicado; Cornhill; Tillmouth Park.

V28 **Honourable Company of Edinburgh Golfers**
☎ Gullane (0620) 842123
Muirfield, Gullane, East Lothian EH31 2EG
Last road on left leaving Gullane for North Berwick on A198, approximately 18 miles from Edinburgh.
Links course.
Medal 18 holes, 6601 yards, S.S.S.73
Course designed by Tom Morris.
Club founded in 1744.
Visitors: welcome by arrangement with Sec on Tues, Thurs and Fri mornings.
Green fees: £16 per round, £26 per day.
Society meetings: welcome by prior arrangement with Sec on Tues, Thurs and Fri mornings.
Catering: lunches weekdays except Mon.
Hotels: Greywalls, Gullane; Open Arms, Dirleton; Marine, North Berwick.

V29 **Jedburgh**
☎ Jedburgh (0835) 63587 or 63770 Sec
Dunion Rd, Jedburgh
Leave town by way of Castlegate, clubhouse about ½ mile on right.
Undulating parkland course.
9 holes, 5522 yards, S.S.S.67
Club founded in 1890.
Visitors: welcome except on competition days.
Green fees: weekdays £4 per round or day, weekends £5 per round or day.
Society meetings: welcome except on competition days.
Catering: bar meals available at weekends from June to Sept; at other times by arrangement.
Hotels: Royal, Canongate, Jedburgh; Jedforest, Jedburgh.

V30 **Kelso**
☎ Kelso (0573) 23009
Racecourse Rd, Kelso, Roxburghshire TD5 7SL
1 mile to N of town centre within National Hunt Racecourse.
Flat parkland course.
18 holes, 6066 yards, S.S.S.69
Course designed by James Braid.
Club founded in 1887.
Visitors: welcome.
Green fees: weekdays £4 per round, £6 per day; weekends £5 per round, £8 per day; Juniors £1.50.
Society meetings: welcome by prior arrangement.
Catering: catering facilities available during opening hours except Mon and Tues; societies catered for on these days by prior arrangement.
Hotels: many good hotels in area.

V31 **Kilspindie**
☎ Aberlady (0875) 358 or 216
Aberlady, East Lothian EH32 0QD
Immediately E of Aberlady village, private road to left leading to club.
Seaside course.
18 holes, 5410 yards, S.S.S.66
Club founded in 1867.
Visitors: welcome on weekdays.
Green fees: weekdays £5.50 per round, £8 per day.
Society meetings: welcome weekdays.
Catering: lunches and high teas available except Fri.
Hotels: Kilspindie House, Aberlady; various hotels in Gullane and North Berwick.

V32 **Kingsknowe**
☎ 031-441 1144/45
326 Lanark Rd, Edinburgh EH14 2JD
W of Edinburgh on A71.
Parkland course.
18 holes, 5979 yards, S.S.S.69
Course designed by J.C. Stutt.
Club founded in 1908.
Visitors: welcome on weekdays.
Green fees: £4.50 per round, £6.50 per day.
Catering: lunches and high teas served except Mon.
Hotels: many good hotels in Edinburgh.

V33 **Kirkcudbright**
☎ Kirkcudbright (0557) 30542
Stirling Crescent, Kirkcudbright
Turn left off A75 into town from Castle Douglas.
Hilly parkland course.
18 holes, 5598 yards, S.S.S.67
Club founded in 1895.
Visitors: welcome except on competition days.
Green fees: £5 per day, £15 per week.
Society meetings: catered for on first Mon of each month.
Catering: none.
Hotels: Mayfield; Arden House; Royal; Selkirk; Gordon House.

V34 **Langholm**
Whitaside, Langholm, Dumfriesshire DG13 0JR
Between Carlisle and Hawick on A7, 400 metres from Market Place.
Hillside course.
9 holes, 5246 yards, S.S.S.66
Club founded in 1892.
Visitors: welcome.
Green fees: £3 per round or day.
Society meetings: enquiries welcomed.
Catering: none.
Hotels: Eskdale, Market Place, Langholm.

V35 **Lauder**
Galashiels Rd, Lauder
Off A68, ½ mile from Lauder.
Undulating course.
9 holes, 6002 yards, S.S.S.70
Club founded in 1896.
Visitors: welcome.
Green fees: weekdays £2.70, Sun £3.20; OAPs £1, Juniors £1.40.
Hotels: good hotels in Lauder.

V36 **Liberton**
☎ 031-664 8580
297 Gilmerton Rd, Edinburgh EH16 5UJ
S of Edinburgh on A7.
Parkland course.
18 holes, 5299 yards, S.S.S.66
Club founded in 1920.
Visitors: welcome except after 5 pm on Mon, Wed and Fri.
Green fees: £5 per round, £18 per day.
Society meetings: welcome weekdays.
Catering: full facilities available.
Hotels: Kildonan Lodge; Minto; Suffolk.

V37 **Linlithgow**
☎ Linlithgow (0506) 842585
Braehead, Linlithgow, West Lothian
M9 from Edinburgh, just SW of Linlithgow.
Undulating parkland course.
18 holes, 5858 yards, S.S.S.68
Club founded in 1913.
Visitors: welcome except on Wed and Sat.
Green fees: weekdays £4 per round, £6 per day; weekends £5.50 per round, £7.50 per day.
Society meetings: welcome except Wed and Sat.
Catering: bar snacks on weekdays and meals at weekends; societies catered for by arrangement.
Hotels: many good hotels in area.

V38 **Livingston G & C C**
☎ Livingston (0506) 38843
Carmondean, Livingston, West Lothian EH54 8PG
Leave M8 at Livingston interchange, follow signposts to Knightsridge, club signposted from there.
Meadowland course.
18 holes, 6636 yards, S.S.S.72
Club founded in 1978.
Course designed by Charles Lawrie.
Visitors: welcome.
Green fees: £5 per round, £9 per day.
Society meetings: welcome.
Catering: meals served.
Hotels: Houston House.

V39 **Lochmaben**
☎ Lochmaben (038 781) 552
Castlehill Gate, Lochmaben, Dumfriesshire DG11 1NT
On A709 between Dumfries and Lockerbie.
Undulating parkland course.
9 holes, 5304 yards, S.S.S.66
Course designed by James Braid.
Club founded in 1926.
Visitors: welcome except on comp. days.
Green fees: weekdays £4, weekends £6; Juniors half-price.
Society meetings: catered for on weekdays.
Catering: catering by arrangement for meetings.
Hotels: Balcastle, Lochmaben; Queens, Lockerbie.

V40 **Lockerbie**
☎ Lockerbie (057 62) 3363
Currie Rd, Lockerbie, Dumfriesshire DG11 2ND
A74 to Lockerbie, take road to Langholme and turn left at T-junction towards Corrie, club ½ mile on right.
Parkland course.
9 holes, 2614 yards, S.S.S.66
Course designed by James Braid.
Club founded in 1889.
Visitors: welcome on weekdays and on Sun from 12 noon to 3 pm.
Green fees: Mon to Sun £5 (£2.50 with member).
Society meetings: catered for by arrangement.
Catering: limited service available by arrangement.
Hotels: Lockerbie House; Blue Bell.

V41 **Longniddry**
☎ Longniddry (0875) 52141
Links Rd, Longniddry, E Lothian EH32 0NL
Take A1 from Edinburgh, at Wallyford roundabout take A198 to Longniddry, turn left at Longniddry Inn down Links Rd.
Parkland/seaside course.
18 holes, 6210 yards, S.S.S.70
Course designed by Harry Colt.
Club founded in 1921.
Visitors: welcome.
Green fees: weekdays £8 per round, £12 per day; weekends £16.
Society meetings: welcome from Mon to Thurs.
Catering: meals served except Fri; bar service with snacks or soup and sandwiches generally available.
Hotels: Marine, North Berwick; Golf Inn, Gullane; Kilspindie House, Aberlady; Greencraig, Longniddry.

V42 **Lothianburn**
☎ 031-445 2206 Clubhouse, 2288 Pro
106 Biggar Rd, Edinburgh EH10 7DU
S boundary of Edinburgh.
Hillside course.
18 holes, S.S.S.69
Course designed by James Braid.
Club founded in 1893.
Visitors: welcome on weekdays only.
Green fees: £4 per round, £6 per day.
Society meetings: welcome by arrangement with Sec on weekdays.
Catering: lunches, bar meals and high teas available.
Hotels: numerous hotels in Edinburgh.

V43 **Luffness New**
☎ Gullane (0620) 843114 or 843376 Clubmaster, 843336 Sec
Aberlady, East Lothian EH32 0QA
E of Edinburgh, follow trunk road A198 along coast, club lies between Aberlady and Gullane.
Undulating seaside course.
18 holes, 6085 yards, S.S.S.69
Club founded in 1892/93.
Visitors: welcome.
Green fees: £8 per round, £12 per day.
Society meetings: welcome by advance booking (usually in previous year); small parties by arrangement.
Catering: meals by arrangement except Mon when sandwiches are available.
Hotels: many good hotels in area.

V44 **Melrose**
☎ Melrose (089 682) 2855 or 2811 Sec
Dingleton, Melrose, Rox
½ mile S of Melrose at base of Eildon Hills.
Parkland course.
9 holes, 5464 yards, S.S.S.68
Club founded in 1880.
Visitors: welcome on weekdays and Sun by arrangement with Sec.
Green fees: weekdays £3 per day, weekends £4 per day.
Society meetings: by arrangement except Sat.
Catering: snacks available.
Hotels: numerous good hotels in Melrose.

V45 **Merchants of Edinburgh**
☎ 031-447 1219
10 Craighill Gardens, Edinburgh EH10 5PY
S side of Edinburgh off A701.
Hilly parkland course.
18 holes, 4889 yards, S.S.S.65
Club founded in 1907.
Visitors: welcome on introduction by member or on application to Sec.
Green fees: £6 per round, £8 per day.
Society meetings: welcome on weekdays by arrangement with Sec.
Catering: snacks available daily; meals by arrangement with Steward.
Hotels: Braid Hills.

V46 **Minto**
Minto Village, by Denholm, Hawick, Roxburghshire
5 miles NE of Hawick off A698, turn left in Denholm for Minto.
Parkland course.
18 holes, 5460 yards, S.S.S.68
Visitors: welcome.
Green fees: weekdays £5 per round or day (£2.50 with member), weekends and Bank Holidays £6 per round or day (£3 with member).
Society meetings: by arrangement with Treasurer, 19 Buccleuch St, Hawick.
Catering: lunches, high teas and bar meals available at clubhouse.
Hotels: Cross Keys, Main St, Denholm, Hawick; Kirklands, West Steward Pl, Hawick; Buccleuch, Trinity St, Hawick.

V47 **Moffat**
☎ Moffat (068 33) 20020
Coateshill, Moffat DG10 9SB
On A701/A74 between Beattock and Moffat.
Hillside course.
18 holes, 4771 yards, S.S.S.66
Course designed by Ben Sayers.
Club founded in 1884.
Visitors: welcome.
Green fees: weekdays £4 per round, £6 per day; weekends £7 per day; weekly ticket £24; 5 day ticket (Mon – Fri) £18.
Society meetings: catered for by arrangement.
Catering: by arrangement with Steward.
Hotels: several in Moffat.

V48 **Mortonhall**
☎ 031-447 2411
231 Braid Rd, Edinburgh EH10 6PB
2 miles S of city centre on A702, situated on S of Braid Hills.
Moorland course.
18 holes, 6557 yards, S.S.S.71
Course designed by James Braid & Fred Hawtree.
Club founded in 1892.
Visitors: welcome on weekdays.
Green fees: £9 per round, £11 per day.
Society meetings: welcome by arrangement on weekdays.
Catering: snacks and lunches served.
Hotels: Braid Hills.

V49 **Murrayfield**
☎ 031-337 3478
Murrayfield Rd, Edinburgh EH12 6EU
2 miles W of city centre.
Parkland course.
18 holes, 5727 yards, S.S.S.68
Club founded in 1896.
Visitors: welcome on weekdays with letter of introduction.
Green fees: £7 per round, £10 per day.
Society meetings: by arrangement.
Catering: meals served except Sun.
Hotels: Ellersly House; Murrayfield; Post House.

V50 **Musselburgh**
☎ 031-665 2005
Monktonhall, Musselburgh, Midlothian
1 mile S off A1 at Musselburgh.
Parkland course.
18 holes, 6620 yards, S.S.S.72
Course designed by James Braid.
Club founded in 1937.
Visitors: details by request.
Green fees: details by request.
Catering: every day except Tues.
Hotels: 5 miles Edinburgh.

V51 **Newbattle**
☎ 031-667 2123
Abbey Rd, Dalkeith, Midlothian
7 miles SW of Edinburgh on A7, take Newbattle exit at Esbank roundabout, go uphill opposite police station, club 300 yds on right.
Undulating parkland course.
18 holes, 6012 yards, S.S.S.69
Club founded in 1934.
Visitors: welcome weekdays before 4 pm.
Green fees: £5 per round, £7 per day.
Society meetings: welcome at restricted times on weekdays by arrangement with Sec.
Catering: full catering facilities available by arrangement.
Hotels: Lugton Inn, Bridgend, Dalkeith; Motel Derry, 29 Dalhousie Rd, Dalkeith; Stair Arms, Pathhead, Ford.

V52 **New Galloway**
☎ New Galloway (064 42) 239
Castle Douglas, Kirkcudbrightshire DG7 3RP
Easily located on way out of village on A762.
Hilly course.
9 holes, 2508 yards, S.S.S.64
Club founded in 1902.
Visitors: welcome.
Green fees: on application at clubhouse.
Society meetings: welcome by arrangement with Sec.
Catering: no facilities available.
Hotels: Kenmure Arms, New Galloway; Cross Keys, New Galloway; Ken Bridge, New Galloway.

V53 **North Berwick**
☎ North Berwick (0620) 2135
Beach Rd, North Berwick EH39 4BB
23 miles E of Edinburgh on A198.
Seaside course.
18 holes, 6317 yards, S.S.S.70
Club founded in 1832.
Visitors: welcome.
Green fees: weekdays £6.50 per round (March to Oct), £9 per day; weekends £9 per round (March to Oct), £13 per day.
Catering: full catering except Thurs.
Hotels: Marine, Cromwell Rd, North Berwick.

V54 **Peebles**
☎ Peebles (0721) 20197 Clubhouse, 20153 Reservations.
Kirkland St, Peebles EH45 8EU
NW of town off A72.
Undulating parkland course.
18 holes, S.S.S.69
Course designed by James Braid, with alterations by H.S. Colt.
Club founded in 1892.
Visitors: welcome on weekdays and at weekends but check for reservations at weekends.
Green fees: weekdays £4.50 per round, £6.50 per day; weekends £6.50 per round, £8.50 per day.
Society meetings: catered for on weekdays and weekends.
Catering: lunches, high teas and bar snacks available.
Hotels: Peebles Hydro; Park, Peebles; Tontine, Peebles.

V55 **Portobello**
☎ 031-669 4361
Stanley St, Portobello, Edinburgh EH15
E of Edinburgh on A1 to Milton Rd.
Parkland course.
9 holes, 2419 yards, S.S.S.32
Visitors: welcome except Sun.
Green fees: 85p per round, (OAPs & Juniors 20p per round).
Hotels: Kings Manor; Lady Nairne.

V56 **Portpatrick (Dunskey)**
☎ Portpatrick (0776) 81 273
Portpatrick, Stranraer, Wigtownshire DG9 8TB
A75 to Stranraer, follow signs to Portpatrick, fork right at War Memorial, 300 yds on right signpost to club.
Undulating meadowland/seaside course.
9 holes, 1442 yards, S.S.S.27
18 holes, 5644 yards, S.S.S.67
Club founded in 1901.
Visitors: welcome.
Green fees: weekdays £4.50 per round, £6 per day; weekends £5.50 per round, £7 per day (Juniors half-price); weekly £20, fortnightly £30; small course £3, under 18 £1.50.

Society meetings: welcome by arrangement except in July and Aug.
Catering: full facilities except Mon.
Hotels: Fernhill; Portpatrick; Roslin; Downshire; Crown; Mount Stewart; all in Portpatrick.

V57 Powfoot

☎ Annan (04612) 2866
Cummertrees, Annan, Dumfriesshire.
3 miles W of Annan, off B724.
Seaside course.
18 holes, 6283 yards, S.S.S.70
Course designed by James Braid.
Visitors: welcome on weekdays.
Green fees: weekdays £7, weekends £9.
Society meetings: welcome on weekdays only by arrangement.
Catering: lunches and teas by arrangement except Fri.
Hotels: Powfoot Golf; Richmond.

V58 Prestonfield

☎ 031-667 1273 or 9665
6 Priestfield Rd N, Edinburgh EH16 5SH
Near to Commonwealth Pool, Dalkeith Rd.
Parkland course.
18 holes, 6216 yards, S.S.S.70
Course designed by James Braid.
Club founded in 1920.
Visitors: welcome with letter of introduction; certain restrictions at weekends.
Green fees: weekdays £6 per round, £8 per day; weekends £7 per round, £9 per day.
Society meetings: weekdays only.
Catering: full catering by arrangement with Clubmaster except Mon.
Hotels: many good hotels in Edinburgh.

V59 Pumpherston

☎ Livingston (0506) 32869
Drumshoreland Rd, Pumpherston, Livingston EH53 0LF
1 mile S of Uphall off A89.
Undulating parkland course.
9 holes, 5154 yards, S.S.S.65
Visitors: welcome only if introduced by member.
Green fees: weekdays £3, weekends £4.50.
Society meetings: none.
Catering: snack meals available.
Hotels: Houston House, Uphall.

V60 Ratho Park

☎ 031-333 1752 Sec, 1252 Clubhouse
Ratho, Newbridge, Midlothian EH28 8NX
8 miles W of Edinburgh on A71 or A8.
Parkland course.
18 holes, 6028 yards, S.S.S.69
Course designed by James Braid.
Club founded in May 1929.
Visitors: by arrangement with Pro.
Green fees: weekdays £6 per round, £8 per day; weekends £10.
Society meetings: welcome on Tues, Wed and Thurs by arrangement with Sec.
Catering: meals served except Mon.
Hotels: Orwell Lodge, Polwarth Terrace, Edinburgh.

V61 Ravelston

☎ 031-332 3486
Ravelston Dykes Rd, Blackhall, Edinburgh EH4 3NZ
Off A90 Queensferry Rd, at Blackhall.
Parkland course.
9 holes, 5200 yards, S.S.S.66
Course designed by James Braid.
Club founded in 1912.
Visitors: with members preferred.
Green fees: weekdays £1 with member, weekends £1.50 with member.
Catering: light snacks served.
Hotels: Dragonara.

V62 Royal Burgess

☎ 031-339 2075
181 Whitehouse Rd, Edinburgh EH4 6BY
W side of Edinburgh on Queensferry Rd, 100 metres N of Barnton roundabout.
Parkland course.
18 holes, 6604 yards, S.S.S.72
Club founded in 1735.
Visitors: welcome on weekdays; ladies may only play in morning.
Green fees: on request.
Society meetings: welcome on Tues, Thurs and Fri only.
Catering: lunches and bar snacks
Hotels: Barnton; Royal Scot.

V63 Royal Musselburgh

☎ Prestonpans (0875) 810276
Prestongrange House, Prestonpans, East Lothian
7 miles E of Edinburgh, 1 mile from Wallyford roundabout on A1, take A198 North Berwick road.
Parkland course.
18 holes, 6204 yards, S.S.S.70
Course designed by James Braid.
Club founded in 1774.
Visitors: welcome on weekdays by arrangement and with member at weekends.
Green fees: weekdays £5.50 per round, £9.50 per day.
Catering: meals and bar lunches available except Tues.
Hotels: Ravelston, Musselburgh; Woodside, Musselburgh; Wallyford, Musselburgh.

V64 St Boswells

☎ St Boswells (0835) 22359
St Boswells, Roxburghshire TD6 0AT
¼ mile off A68 Newcastle to Edinburgh road, junction with B6404.
Meadowland course.
9 holes, 2527 yards, S.S.S.65
Course redesigned by John Slade.
Club founded in 1899.
Visitors: welcome.
Green fees: weekdays £2.50 per round or day, weekends £3 per round or day.
Society meetings: welcome by arrangement with Sec.
Catering: none.
Hotels: Dryburgh Abbey; Buccleuch Arms.

V65 St Medan

☎ Port William (098 87) 358
Monreith, Port William, Wigtownshire DG8 8NJ
3 miles S of Port William on A747.
Seaside course.
9 holes, 4554 yards, S.S.S.62
Club founded in 1905.
Visitors: welcome.
Green fees: £3 for 18 holes, £4 per day.
Society meetings: welcome by arrangement.
Catering: meals served from April to Sept except Tues.
Hotels: Eagle, Port William; Monreith Arms, Port William; Greenmantle, Mochrum; Corsemalzie House; Bruce, Queen St, Newton Stewart.

V66 Sanquhar

☎ Sanquhar (065 92) 577
Old Barr Rd, Sanquhar, Dumfriesshire DG4 6JZ
Off A76 ½ mile from Sanquhar.
Parkland course.
9 holes, 2572 yards, S.S.S.68
Club founded in 1894.
Visitors: welcome.
Green fees: weekdays £4, weekends £5.
Catering: by prior arrangement.
Hotels: Blackaddie House; Glendyne; Nithsdale; Mennock Lodge.

V67 Selkirk

☎ Selkirk (0750) 20621
The Hill, Selkirk
1 mile S of Selkirk on A7 to Hawick.
Moorland course.
9 holes, 5560 yards, S.S.S.67
Club founded in 1883.
Visitors: welcome on weekdays and some weekends.
Green fees: weekdays £4 per day, weekends £6 per day; half-price with member.
Society meetings: welcome weekdays.
Catering: catering for parties by prior arrangement.
Hotels: Woodburn House, Selkirk.

V68 **Silverknowes**
☎ 031-336 5359
Silverknowes, Parkway, Edinburgh EH4 5ET
W end of Edinburgh, off Cramond Foreshore.
Municipal course.
18 holes, 6210 yards, S.S.S.70
Club founded in 1958.
Visitors: welcome, with reservation only.
Green fees: £2 weekdays, £2.20 weekends.
Hotels: Commodore, adjacent to course.

V69 **Southerness**
☎ Kirkbean (038 788) 677
Southerness, Dumfries DG2 8AZ
16 miles SW of Dumfries off A710
Links course.
18 holes, 6548 yards, S.S.S.72
Course designed by Mackenzie Ross.
Club founded in 1947.
Visitors: welcome.
Green fees: weekdays £8 per day, weekends £10 per day.
Society meetings: welcome most days on application to Sec.
Catering: full catering facilities available except Wed.
Hotels: Baron's Craig, Rockcliffe, Dalbeattie; Station, Dumfries; Cairndale, 132-136 English St, Dumfries.

V70 **Stranraer**
☎ Stranraer (0776) 87245
Creachmore, Stranraer DG9 0LF
Take A718 from Stranraer towards Leswalt, golf club is well signposted on right.
Parkland course.
18 holes, 6300 yards, S.S.S.71
Course designed by James Braid.
Club founded in 1905.
Visitors: welcome on weekdays and at weekends by arrangement.
Green fees: weekdays £4.75 per round, £6.30 per day; weekends £6.30 per round, £9.50 per day.
Society meetings: catered for by arrangement with Sec.
Catering: meals available.
Hotels: North West Castle; George; Craignelder.

V71 **Swanston**
☎ 031-445 2239
111Swanston Rd, Edinburgh EH10
SE side of city.
Hillside course.
18 holes, 5024 yards, S.S.S.65
Course designed by Herbert More.
Club founded in 1927.
Visitors: welcome on weekdays and with restrictions at weekends.
Green fees: £3.45 per round, £5.75 per day.
Society meetings: by arrangement.
Catering: meals served except Tues.
Hotels: Pentland Hills.

V72 **Thornhill**
☎ (0387 95) 30546
Blacknest, Thornhill, Dumfries
14 miles N of Dumfries on A76 to Thornhill village, turn right at cross, 1 mile on right.
Moorland/parkland course.
18 holes, 6011 yards, S.S.S.69
Club founded in 1893.
Visitors: welcome.
Green fees: weekdays £4.50, weekends £6.50, weekly £20.
Society meetings: catered for by arrangement.
Catering: full facilities available.
Hotels: Buccleuch, Thornhill.

V73 **Torphin Hill**
☎ 031-441 1100
Torphin Rd, Colinton, Edinburgh EH13 0PG
SW of Colinton village.
Hillside course.
18 holes, 4850 yards, S.S.S.67
Club founded in 1895.
Visitors: welcome on weekdays and at most weekends.
Green fees: weekdays £7 per day, £6 per round; weekends £8 per day, £7 per round (£1 with member).
Society meetings: welcome weekdays.
Catering: meals served except Wed.
Hotels: many good hotels in Edinburgh.

V74 **Torwoodlee**
☎ Galashiels (0896) 2660
Galashiels, Selkirkshire
On A7 Galashiels to Edinburgh road, 1 mile from town centre.
Parkland course.
9 holes, 5800 yards, S.S.S.68
Course designed by James Braid.
Club founded in 1895.
Visitors: welcome with restrictions on Sat.
Green fees: £5 per day (£2 with member), Sun £7.
Society meetings: catered for on weekdays.
Catering: full facilities except on Tues.
Hotels: Burts, Melrose; George and Abbotsford, Melrose.

V75 **Turnhouse**
☎ 031-339 1014
154 Turnhouse Rd, Edinburgh EH12 0AD
W of city on A9080 near airport.
Parkland/heathland course.
18 holes, 6171 yards, S.S.S.69
Club founded in 1909.
Visitors: welcome by arrangement with Pro (031-339 7701) except at weekends and on competition days.
Green fees: £8 per day, £5 per round.
Catering: meals served except Mon.
Hotels: Royal Scot.

V76 **Uphall**
☎ Broxburn (0506) 856404
Uphall, W Lothian
Off M8, 14 miles W of Edinburgh.
Meadowland course.
18 holes, 6250 yards, S.S.S.68
Visitors: welcome.
Green fees: weekdays £5, weekends £9.
Society meetings: by arrangement.
Catering: bar snacks, meals by arrangement.
Hotels: Houston House, Uphall; Golden Circle, Bathgate.

V77 **West Linton**
☎ West Linton (0968) 60256 Pro, 60589 Clubmaster
West Linton, Peeblesshire
15 miles from Edinburgh on A702.
Moorland course.
18 holes, 5835 yards, S.S.S.68
Club founded in 1890.
Visitors: welcome, but generally busy at weekends.
Green fees: weekdays £5 per round, £7 per day; weekends £6 per round, £8.50 per day.
Catering: full facilities except Tues.
Hotels: Gordon Arms, West Linton; Linton, West Linton; Raemartin, West Linton.

V78 **West Lothian**
☎ Bo'ness (0506) 826030
Airngath Hill, Linlithgow, West Lothian
On hill separating Bo'ness and Linlithgow, marked by Hope Monument.
Undulating meadowland course.
18 holes, 6629 yards, S.S.S.72
Club founded in 1892.
Visitors: welcome except on comp. days.
Green fees: weekdays £4 per round, £6 per day; weekends £5 per round, £8 per day.
Society meetings: welcome except on competition days.
Catering: bar snacks available, full catering for societies.
Hotels: various hotels in Bo'ness and Linlithgow.

V79 **Wigtown & Bladnoch**
☎ Wigtown (098 84) 3354
Lightlands Ave, Wigtown, Wigtownshire
Turn right at town square, turn left at Agnew Crescent 400 yds on right.

Parkland course.
9 holes, 5462 yards, S.S.S.67
Club founded in 1960.
Visitors: welcome any day.
Green fees: weekdays £3.50 per day, weekends £4.50 per day.
Society meetings: welcome.
Catering: catering for competition days and society outings.
Hotels: Forobank, Wigtown.

V80 Wigtownshire County

☎ Glenluce (058 13) 420
Mains of Park, Glenluce, Newton Stewart, Wigtownshire DG8 0QN
8 miles E of Stranraer on A75, 2 miles W of Glenluce.
Links course.
9 holes, 5726 yards, S.S.S.68
Club founded in 1894.
Visitors: welcome.
Green fees: weekdays £3.50, weekends £4, weekly £15, fortnightly £25 (under 18 half-price).
Catering: meals served from April to Sept.
Hotels: Judges Keep; Auld Kings Arms; Kings Arms; Crown; Kelvin; Glenluce.

V81 Winterfield

☎ (0368) 62280
North Rd, Dunbar, E Lothian
W side of Dunbar.
Seaside course.
18 holes, 5035 yards, S.S.S.65
Club founded in 1935.
Visitors: welcome.
Green fees: weekdays £3.30 per round, £4.50 per day; weekends £4 per round, £6.50 per day; OAPs £1.50 per round.
Society meetings: welcome by arrangement with Pro.
Catering: meals served except Thurs.
Hotels: in Dunbar.

W Strathclyde

There are almost one hundred and thirty courses in the area of Strathclyde which includes Glasgow, Arran, the remoter courses of Islay and the Mull of Kintyre and a seemingly endless chain along the Firth of Clyde as far south as Girvan.

Foremost among them are the championship links of Prestwick, Royal Troon and Turnberry and serious disciples of the game would never dream of passing them by. Prestwick, the home of championship golf, is, in many ways, a reminder of the days of jiggers and Norfolk jackets but its place in the modern world is every bit as genuine. The Amateur championship is to return there in 1987, one of the greatest compliments that could be paid.

Royal Troon, with something for every golfing taste, has been on active Open service since 1923 while Turnberry is a place that, once seen, is never forgotten. On a fair day, it is impossible to beat but for golfing neighbourliness there is nothing to match the string of courses north of Troon that takes in Barassie, Glasgow Gailes, Irvine and Western Gailes, home of the 1972 Curtis Cup match.

Heading up into Glasgow, East Renfrewshire occupies a lonely spot on the moors long before the city boundary is reached. Another landmark is Whitecraigs but, for those making for the airport with time to spare, Renfrew and the delightful courses of Bridge of Weir lie within easy reach.

The city itself is well served but Strathclyde has its remote corners as well including the Isle of Arran which is such a central, scenic feature of the area. I confess that I still have not managed to get there but I learned early of the spell it casts over its admirers. A late lamented Scottish golf writer was recounting to me the tale of his annual holiday there when I made the innocent mistake of asking him if it was nice. "Nice", he spluttered. "Nice? It's paradise".

W1 Airdrie

☎ Airdrie (023 64) 62195
Rochsoles, Airdrie ML6 SDZ
From Airdrie Cross in centre of town travel N on Glebmavis Rd.
Parkland course.
18 holes, S.S.S.69
Course designed by James Braid.
Club founded in 1877.
Visitors: welcome with introduction from own Sec.
Catering: meals and snacks served; parties should contact Mrs Linde at club.
Hotels: Tudor, Alexander St, Airdrie; Kenilworth, Motherwell St, Airdrie.

W2 Alexandra

☎ 041-556 3711
Alexandra Park, Alexandra Parade, Glasgow G31 8SE
Parkland course.
9 holes, 5000 yards,
Course designed by Graham McArthur.
Club founded in 1818.
Visitors: welcome.
Green fees: adults 75p, Juniors 40p, OAPs 10p.
Society meetings: by arrangement.
Catering: catering facilities available.
Hotels: Holiday Inn, Glasgow Central; Trust House, Glasgow.

W3 Annanhill

☎ Kilmarnock (0563) 21644
Irvine Rd, Kilmarnock KA3 1DW
Off main Kilmarnock to Irvine road.
Parkland course.
18 holes, 6269 yards, S.S.S.70
Course designed by J. McLean.
Club founded in 1957.
Visitors: welcome weekdays, with reservation at weekends.
Green fees: weekdays £3, weekends £5.
Society meetings: by arrangement.
Catering: by prior arrangement.
Hotels: Ross; Howard Park.

W4 Ardeer

☎ Stevenston (0294) 64542
Greenhead, Stevenston, Ayrshire
Follow A78 (signs for Largs and Greenock), on High Rd by passing Stevenston, turn right into Kerelaw Rd and continue for 1 mile.
Parkland course.
18 holes, 6630 yards, S.S.S.72
Club founded in 1880.
Visitors: welcome except on Sat.
Green fees: weekdays £6, Sun £8.
Society meetings: welcome.
Catering: full catering facilities available except Thurs.
Hotels: Redburn, Kilwinning Rd, Irvine; High Tide, Parkhouse Rd, Ardrossan.

W5 Ayr Belleisle

☎ Alloway (0292) 41258
Belleisle Park, Doonfoot Rd, Ayr
1½ miles S of Ayr on A719.
Parkland course.
18 holes, 6540 yards, S.S.S.71
Course designed by James Braid & Stutt.
Course founded in 1927.
Visitors: welcome.
Green fees: weekdays £3.50 per round, £4.65 per day; weekends £4.35 per round, £7 per day.
Society meetings: apply to Course Administrator at address above.
Catering: meals and snacks available in hotel.
Hotels: Belleisle House; Balgarth, Dunure Rd, Ayr; Old Racecourse, Victoria Park, Ayr.

W6 Ayr Dalmilling

☎ Ayr (0292) 263893
Westwood Ave, Ayr, Strathclyde
1½ miles from town centre on NE boundary off A77.
Meadowland course.
18 holes, 5401 yards, S.S.S.66
Club founded in 1960.
Visitors: welcome.
Green fees: weekdays £3 per round, £3.85 per day; weekends £3.75 per round, £6 per day.
Society meetings: catered for.
Catering: meals and snacks available.
Hotels: Racers.

W7 Ayr Seafield

☎ Alloway (0292) 41258
Belleisle Park, Doonfoot Rd, Ayr
1½ miles S of Ayr on A719.
Parkland/seaside course.
18 holes, 5244 (or 4889) yards, S.S.S.66 (or 64)
Course founded in 1927.
Visitors: welcome.
Green fees: weekdays £2.45 per round, £3.20 per day; weekends £2.90 per round, £4.90 per day.
Society meetings: apply to Course Administrator at address above.
Catering: meals and snacks in hotel.
Hotels: Belleisle House; Balgarth, Dunur Rd, Ayr; Old Racecourse, Victoria Park, Ayr

W8 Ballochmyle

☎ Mauchline (0290) 50469
Ballochmyle, Mauchline, Ayrshire KA5 6RR
Adjoining A76(T) Kilmarnock to Dumfries rd, 1m S of Mauchline village.
Parkland course.
18 holes, 5952 yards, S.S.S.69
Club founded in 1937.
Visitors: welcome.
Green fees: weekdays £8.50 per day, weekends £10 per day.
Society meetings: welcome except on Wed and Sat by arrangement with Sec (groups of 8 or more).
Catering: meals and snacks served.
Hotels: Royal, Cumnock; Dalgarth, Dunur Rd, Ayr; Annfield, Maybole Rd, Ayr.

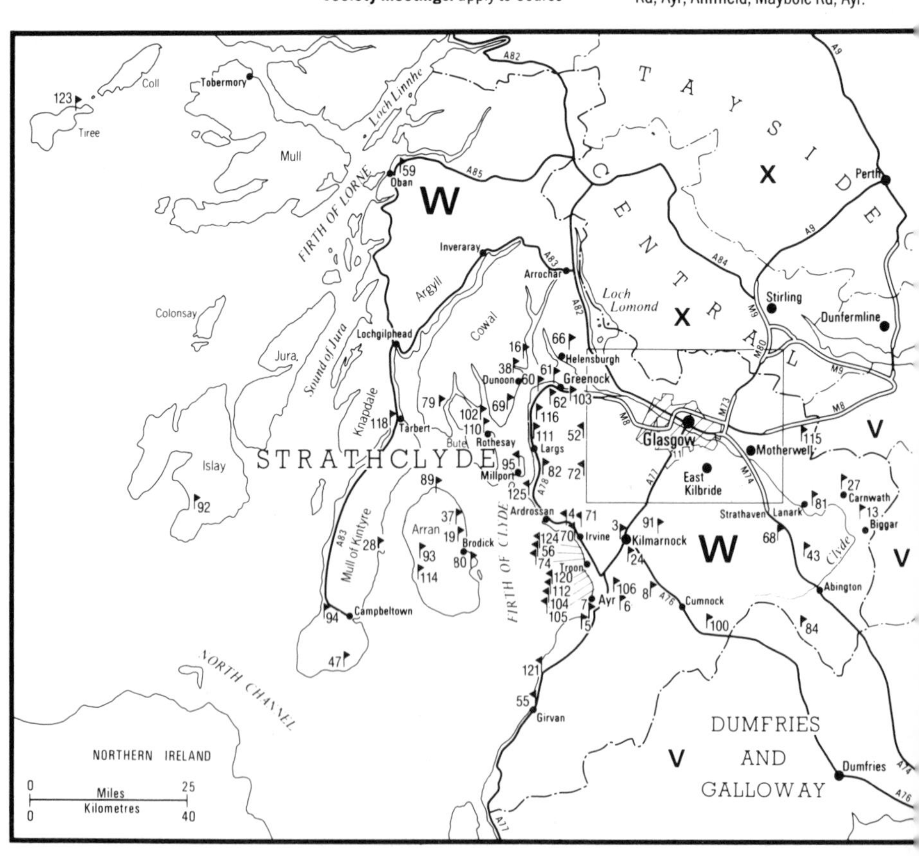

W9 Balmore

☎ Balmore (0360) 21240
Balmore, Torrance, Stirlingshire
2 miles N of Glasgow on A803 and then A807.
Parkland course.
18 holes, 5516 yards, S.S.S.67
Course designed by James Braid.
Club founded in 1906.
Visitors: welcome with introduction from member.
Green fees: £6.
Catering: full catering facilities.
Hotels: Black Bull, Milngavie.

W10 Barshaw

☎ 041-889 2908 or 884 2533 Sec
Barshaw Park, Glasgow Rd, Paisley, Renfrewshire
A737 from Glasgow W to Paisley, 1 mile before Paisley Cross.
Meadowland municipal course.
18 holes, 5703 yards, S.S.S.67
Club founded in 1927.
Visitors: welcome (bookings through Mr McAdam, Paisley Parks Dept).
Green fees: £1.70 per round.
Catering: none.
Hotels: Brabloch, Renfrew Rd, Paisley.

W11 Bearsden

☎ 041-942 2351
Thorn Rd, Bearsden, Glasgow
1 mile from Bearsden Cross on Thorn Rd.
Parkland course.
9 holes, 5977 yards, S.S.S.70
Club founded in 1892.
Visitors: welcome with introduction from member.
Green fees: weekdays £1 per round, weekends £2 per round.
Society meetings: none.
Catering: meals and snacks available.
Hotels: Burnbrae, Milngavie Rd, Bearsden, Glasgow.

W12 Beith

☎ Beith (050 55) 3166
Threepwood Rd, Bigholm, Beith
Situated about 1 mile E of Beith.
Hilly course.
9 holes, 5488 yards, S.S.S.67
Club founded in 1896.
Visitors: welcome on weekdays, after 5 pm on Sat and before 1 pm on Sun.
Green fees: £3.50 per day.
Society meetings: not catered for.
Catering: light lunches and bar snacks.
Hotels: Saracen; Anderson.

W13 Biggar

☎ Biggar (0899) 20319 Tee Reservation, 20618 Steward
The Park, Broughton Rd, Biggar, Lanarkshire
1 mile E of Biggar on Broughton Rd, opposite police station.
Parkland course.
18 holes, 5600 yards, S.S.S.66
Club founded in 1895.
Visitors: welcome; prior booking advised.
Green fees: weekdays £3, weekends £5.
Society meetings: welcome on weekdays and at weekends.
Catering: lunches and high teas served except Mon.
Hotels: several hotels nearby.

W14 Bishopbriggs

☎ 041-772 1810
Brackenbrae Rd, Bishopbriggs, Glasgow G64 1QX
4 miles N of Glasgow on A803, turn left 200 yds short of Bishopbriggs Cross.
Parkland course.
18 holes, 6041 yards, S.S.S.69
Club founded in 1906.
Visitors: welcome with member or by application to Committee.

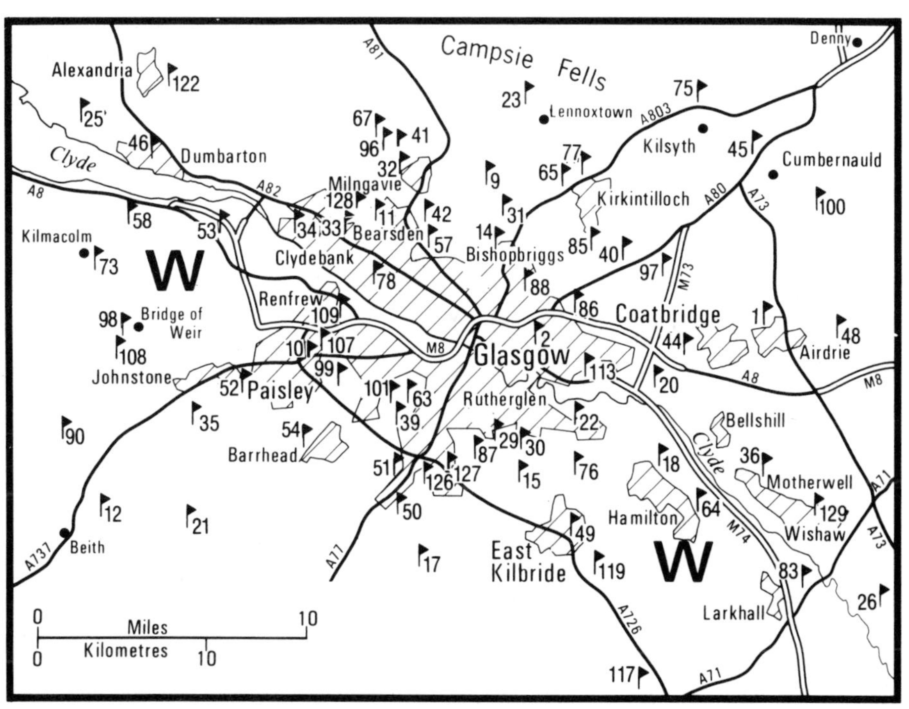

Green fees: £8.
Catering: meals and snacks served except Wed.
Hotels: many good hotels in Glasgow.

W15 Blairbeth

☎ 041-634 3355
Fernhill, Rutherglen, Glasgow
2 miles S of Rutherglen via Stonelaw Rd.
Parkland course.
18 holes, 5448 yards, S.S.S.67
Visitors: welcome with member.
Green fees: weekdays £1 per day, weekends £3.
Catering: by arrangement.
Hotels: Kings Park, Rutherglen.

W16 Blairmore & Strone

☎ Blairmore (036 984) 676
High Rd, Blairmore, Argyll.
¾ mile N of Strone on A880.
Undulating parkland/moorland course.
9 holes, 2112 yards, S.S.S.62
Club founded in 1895.
Visitors: welcome on weekdays, except Mon after 6 pm, and at weekends, except Sat between 1 pm and 4 pm.
Green fees: £2 per day (Juniors £1), weekly £10, fortnightly £15.
Catering: none at present.
Hotels: Blairmore House; Argyll; Kilmun.

W17 Bonnyton

☎ Eaglesham 2781
Eaglesham, Glasgow G76 0QA
City centre S to Eaglesham.
Moorland course.
18 holes, 6252 yards, S.S.S.71
Club founded in 1957.
Visitors: any day, by arrangement. Not Sat or Sun.
Green fees: £8 per day.
Society meetings: by arrangement.
Catering: weekdays full facilities by arrangement, not Sat or Sun.
Hotels: McDonald, Eastwood Toll, Giffnock, Glasgow ; Eglinton, Eaglesham, Glasgow

W18 Bothwell Castle

☎ Bothwell (0698) 853177
Blantyre Rd, Bothwell, Glasgow
On A74 3 miles N of Hamilton.
Meadowland course.
18 holes, 6432 yards, S.S.S.71
Club founded in 1922.
Visitors: welcome on weekdays from 8 am to 3.30 pm by arrangement with Pro, Willie Walker (Bothwell 852052).
Green fees: £5 per round, £7 per day.
Society meetings: welcome by arrangement with Committee.
Catering: meals and snacks served.
Hotels: Silvertrees, Silverwells Cres, Bothwell; Bothwell Bridge, Main St, Bothwell.

W19 Brodick

☎ Isle of Arran (0770) 2349
Brodick, Isle of Arran
½ mile from Brodick pier.
Seaside course.
18 holes, 4401 yards, S.S.S.62
Visitors: welcome.
Green fees: £4.50 per day.
Society meetings: welcome by arrangement with Sec, G.I. Jameson, Invercloy Hotel, Brodick, Isle of Arran (0770 2225).
Catering: snack lunches served; parties by arrangement with Club Steward.
Hotels: numerous good hotels in area.

W20 Calderbraes

☎ Uddingston (0698) 813425
57 Roundknowe Rd, Uddingston, Lanarkshire G71 7TS
Start of M74, 4 miles from Glasgow.
Parkland course.
9 holes, 5186 yards, S.S.S.67
Club founded in 1893.
Visitors: welcome with member only.
Green fees: weekdays £1, weekends £2.
Catering: meals and snacks available.
Hotels: Redstones, Uddingston; Golden Gates, Mount Vernon.

W21 Caldwell

☎ Uplawmoor (050 585) 329 Clubhouse, 616 Pro
Uplawmoor, Renfrewshire
Off A736 5 miles SW of Barrhead, 12 miles NE of Irvine.
Moorland course.
18 holes, 6102 yards, S.S.S.69
Club founded in 1903.
Visitors: welcome on weekdays but advisable to check in advance.
Green fees: £6 per round, £9 per day.
Society meetings: catered for on weekdays.
Catering: welcome weekdays.
Hotels: Uplawmoor, Uplawmoor; Dalmeny, Barrhead.

W22 Cambuslang

☎ 041-641 3130
30 Westburn Drive, Cambuslang, Glasgow
Off main Glasgow to Hamilton road at Cambuslang.
Parkland course.
9 holes, 6072 yards, S.S.S.69
Club founded in 1891.
Visitors: welcome on weekdays except Tues by arrangement with Sec.
Green fees: £5.
Society meetings: by arrangement.
Catering: full catering facilities.
Hotels: Cambus Court, Cambuslang.

W23 Campsie

☎ Lennoxtown (0360) 310244
Crow Rd, Lennoxtown, Glasgow G65 7HX
N of Lennoxtown on B822.
Hillside course.
18 holes, 5517 yards, S.S.S.67
Club founded in 1897.
Visitors: welcome on weekdays and by prior arrangement at weekends.
Green fees: £3.50 per round, £6 per day.
Society meetings: catered for by arrangement with Sec.
Catering: bar snacks available; meals served by prior arrangement.
Hotels: Glazertbank, Lennoxtown; Kincaid House.

W24 Caprington

☎ Kilmarnock (0563) 23702
Ayr Rd, Kilmarnock KA1 4UW
S of Kilmarnock on Ayr Rd.
Parkland course.
18 holes, S.S.S.68
Visitors: welcome.
Green fees: on request (municipal course).
Hotels: Golden Sheaf.

W25 Cardross

☎ Cardross (0389) 841213 Club, 841350 Pro Shop, 841754 Sec
Main Rd, Cardross, Dumbarton E82 5LB
Between Dumbarton and Helensburgh on A814.
Parkland course.
18 holes, 6466 yards, S.S.S.71
Course designed by Willie Fernie of Troon and James Braid.
Club founded in 1895.
Visitors: welcome on weekdays only.
Green fees: £6 per round, £9 per day.
Society meetings: welcome by arrangement with Sec.
Catering: bar snacks, lunches and high teas available except Mon.
Hotels: Dumbuck, Dumbarton; many hotels in area.

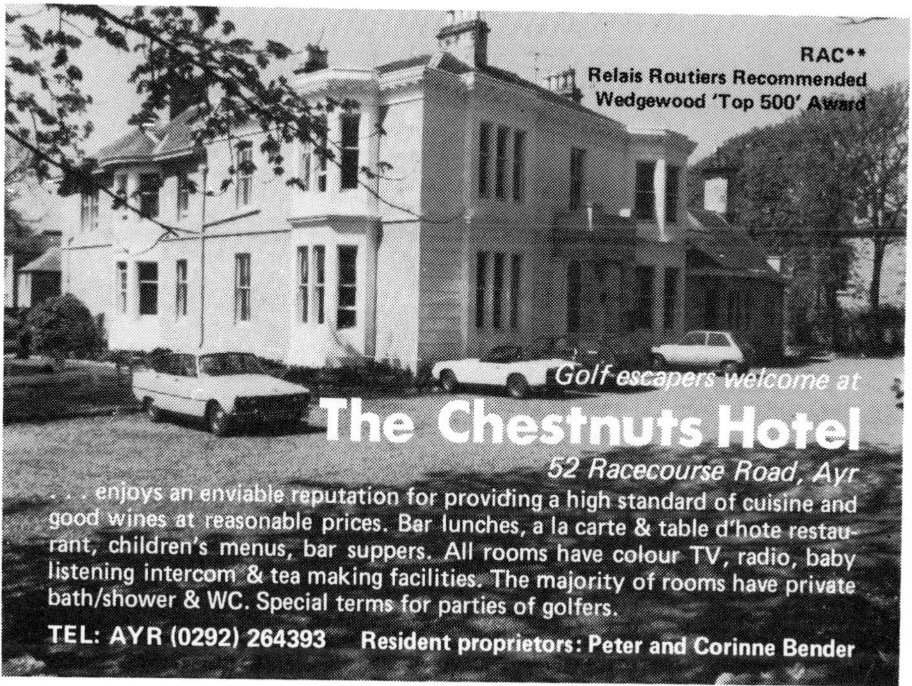

W26 Carluke

☎ Carluke (0555) 71070
Hallcraig, Mauldslie Rd, Carluke ML8 5HG
About 1½ miles from traffic lights at town centre on road to Hamilton and Larkhall.
Undulating parkland course.
18 holes, 5800 yards, S.S.S.68
Club founded in 1894.
Visitors: welcome on weekdays before 4.30 pm.
Green fees: £6 per day or round.
Society meetings: catered for by arrangement with Committee.
Catering: catering facilities available.
Hotels: Popinjay.

W27 Carnwath

☎ Carnwath (0555) 840251
1 Main St, Carnwath
5 miles NE of Lanark.
Undulating course.
18 holes, 5860 yards, S.S.S.68
Club founded in 1907.
Visitors: welcome on Mon, Wed, Fri and Sun.
Green fees: weekdays £5.50, Sun £7.50.
Society meetings: catered for.
Catering: meals served except Tues and Thurs.
Hotels: Tinto, Symington.

W28 Carradale

☎ Carradale (058 33) 624
Carradale, Campbeltown, Argyll PA28 6QX
Off B842 from Campbeltown to Carradale.
Undulating course.
9 holes, 2387 yards, S.S.S.32
Club founded in 1888.
Visitors: welcome.
Green fees: on application.
Catering: catering facilities in hotel.
Hotels: Carradale.

W29 Cathcart Castle

☎ 041-638 0082
Mearns Rd, Clarkston, Glasgow
On A77, 7 miles from Glasgow.
Undulating parkland course.
18 holes, 5832 yards, S.S.S.68
Club founded in 1895.
Visitors: welcome with member.
Green fees: on application to Sec.
Society meetings: by arrangement.
Catering: meals served.
Hotels: Redhurst, Giffnock; McDonald, Giffnock.

W30 Cathkin Braes

☎ 041-634 4007
Cathkin Rd, Rutherglen, Glasgow G73 4SE
SE of Glasgow off road to E Kilbride.
Moorland course.
18 holes, 6266 yards, S.S.S.71
Course designed by James Braid.
Club founded in 1888.
Visitors: welcome with introduction.
Green fees: £6 per round, £8 per day.
Catering: catering facilities available.
Hotels: Burnside; Busby; Stuart.

W31 Cawder
☎ 041-772 7101
Cadder Rd, Bishopbriggs, Glasgow G64 3QD
½ mile E of Bishopbriggs cross.
Parkland course.
Cawder 18 holes, 6229 yards, S.S.S.71
Keir 18 holes, 5877 yards, S.S.S.68
Course designed by Donald Steel (Cawder course), James Braid (Keir course).
Club founded in 1933.
Visitors: welcome on weekdays by arrangement with Sec.
Green fees: £9 per day.
Society meetings: welcome on weekdays by arrangement with Sec.
Catering: full catering facilities.
Hotels: Black Bull, Milngavie; Glazertbank, Lennoxtown.

W32 Clober
☎ 041-956 1685
Craigton Rd, Milngavie G62 7HP
7 miles NW of Glasgow.
Parkland course.
18 holes, 5068 yards, S.S.S.65
Club founded in 1951.
Visitors: welcome on weekdays before 4.30 pm and with member at weekends.
Green fees: £4 per round.
Society meetings: welcome weekdays.
Catering: meals available except Mon and Thurs.
Hotels: Black Bull, Milngavie.

W33 Clydebank & District
☎ Duntocher (0389) 73289
Hardgate, Clydebank, Dunbartonshire G81 5QY
8m NW of Glasgow via Great Western Rd.
Parkland course.
18 holes, 5825 yards, S.S.S.68
Club founded in 1905.
Visitors: welcome on weekdays; weekends with member only.
Green fees: £6 per day.
Society meetings: by arrangement.
Catering: meals served.
Hotels: Cameron House; Boulevard; Pine Trees.

W34 Clydebank Overtoun
☎ 041-952 6372 Pro Shop
Overtoun Rd, Clydebank, Dunbartonshire
5 minutes from Dalmuir station.
Parkland municipal course.
18 holes, 5359 yards, S.S.S.66
Visitors: welcome except on Sat between 11.30 am and 2.30 pm.
Green fees: weekdays £1.80, weekends £2.
Society meetings: welcome by arrangement with Pro.
Catering: café within complex.
Hotels: Boulevard, Great Western Rd; Radnor, Kilbowie Rd.

W35 Cochrane Castle
☎ Johnstone (0505) 20146
Craigston, Scott Ave, Johnstone PA5 0HF
¼ mile off Johnstone to Beith road to S of town, Bird in the Hand Hotel is good landmark near turning to club.
Undulating moorland course.
18 holes, 6226 yards, S.S.S.69
Course designed by Charles Hunter of Prestwick but altered by James Braid.
Club founded in 1895.
Visitors: welcome on weekdays and with member at weekends.
Green fees: £7 per day, £5 per round.
Society meetings: welcome on weekdays by arrangement with Sec.
Catering: full facilities except Mon.
Hotels: Lyndhurst, Park Rd, Johnstone; Watermill, Lonend, Paisley; Excelsior, Glasgow Airport, Paisley.

W36 Colville Park
☎ Motherwell (0698) 63017
Jerviston Estate, Motherwell, Strathclyde ML1 4UG
On left hand side of A723, 1 mile N of Motherwell town centre.
Parkland course.
18 holes, 6208 yards, S.S.S.70
Course designed by James Braid.
Club founded in 1924.
Visitors: welcome with introduction from member.
Green fees: weekdays £5 per day, £1 with introduction, weekends £2 with introduction.
Society meetings: welcome weekdays.
Catering: full facilities available.
Hotels: Garrion, Motherwell; Old Mill, Motherwell; Bentley, Motherwell.

W37 Corrie
☎ Corrie (077 081) 223
Sannox, Isle of Arran
By A84 coast road from Brodick.
Undulating course.
9 holes, 3896 yards, S.S.S.61
Club founded in 1892.
Visitors: welcome.
Green fees: £3 per day (Juniors £1.50).
Catering: light meals and snacks served.
Hotels: Corrie.

W38 Cowal
☎ Dunoon (0396) 5673 or 2216
Ardenslate Rd, Kirn, Dunoon, Argyll PA23 8LT
¼ mile from A815 at Kirn.
Moorland course.
18 holes, 5820 yards, S.S.S.70
Course designed by James Braid.
Club founded in 1890.
Visitors: welcome.
Green fees: weekdays £5.75 per round, £6.90 per day; weekends £8 per round, £10.35 per day.
Society meetings: welcome, with special package deal available.
Catering: meals and snacks available.
Hotels: Rosscairn; Slatefield; Cedars.

W39 Cowglen
☎ 041-632 0556
301 Barrhead Rd, Glasgow
S side of Glasgow, following signs to Burrell Collection, opposite Pollok golf club.
Undulating parkland course.
18 holes, 5976 yards, S.S.S.69
Club founded in 1906.
Visitors: welcome with member and for parties by arrangement with Sec.
Green fees: visiting party £7 per round, £10 per day.
Catering: catering and bar facilities available.
Hotels: Tinto Firs, Kilmarnock, Glasgow.

W40 Crow Wood
☎ 041-779 1943
Garnkirk Estate, Muirhead, Chryston, Glasgow G69 9JF
1 mile N of Stepps on A80.
Parkland course.
18 holes, 6209 yards, S.S.S.70
Course designed by James Braid.
Visitors: with member only.
Green fees: subject to review.
Society meetings: by arrangement.
Catering: meals served except Mon.
Hotels: Garfield, Crow Wood Road House.

W41 Dougalston
☎ 041-956 5750
Strathblane Rd, Milngavie, Glasgow
7 miles N of Glasgow city centre on A879 and A81.
Parkland course.
18 holes, 6683 yards, S.S.S.72
Course designed by John Harris.
Visitors: welcome.
Green fees: weekdays £4; weekends £6 per round, £8 per day.
Society meetings: welcome.
Catering: bar snacks and meals served.
Hotels: Burnbrae; Black Bull.

W42 Douglas Park
☎ 041-942 2220 (Sec 041-331 1837)
Hillfoot, Bearsden, Glasgow.
Next to Hillfoot Station.
18 holes, 5957 yards, S.S.S.68
Visitors: welcome with member only.
Green fees: on request.
Society meetings: by arrangement with Sec.
Catering: meals served by arrangement.

W43 Douglas Water
☎ Lanark (0555) 2295
Ayr Rd, Rigside, Lanark
7 miles SW of Lanark on A70, 2 miles E of A74, signposted Rigside.
Undulating parkland course.
9 holes, 5832 yards, S.S.S.69
Club founded in 1922.
Visitors: welcome except on Sat.
Green fees: Men – weekdays £1.50, weekends £2.50; Ladies – weekdays 75p, weekends £1.50.
Society meetings: none.
Catering: meals available by arrangement.
Hotels: good hotels in area.

W44 Drumpellier
☎ Coatbridge (0236) 24139 Pro, 28723 Clubmaster
Drumpellier Ave, Coatbridge ML5 1RX
8 miles E of Glasgow on A89, 1 mile from Coatbridge.
Parkland course.
18 holes, 6229 yards, S.S.S.70
Course designed by W. Fernie.
Club founded in 1894.
Visitors: welcome on weekdays by arrangement with Sec.
Green fees: £6 per round, £9 per day.
Society meetings: catered for on weekdays except for Bank Holidays.
Catering: meals served except Thurs.
Hotels: Coatbridge, Coatbridge Rd, Coatbridge; Georgian, Lefroy St, Coatbridge.

W45 Dullatur
☎ Cumbernauld (023 67) 23230
Dullatur, Glasgow
1½ miles from Cumbernauld village.
Undulating moorland course.
18 holes, 6195 yards, S.S.S.70
Club founded in 1897.
Visitors: welcome on weekdays by arrangement.
Green fees: £7.50 per day, £5 after 1 pm.
Society meetings: catered for on weekdays.
Catering: full facilities available.
Hotels: many hotels in Glasgow.

W46 Dumbarton
☎ Dumbarton (0389) 32830
Broadmeadows, Dumbarton, Dunbartonshire G82 2BQ
15 miles NW of Glasgow.
Meadowland course.
18 holes, 5913 yards, S.S.S.69
Club founded in 1888.
Visitors: welcome on weekdays.
Green fees: £8 per day.
Society meetings: by arrangement.
Catering: meals served.
Hotels: Dumbuck; Dumbarton.

W47 Dunaverty
Southend, Campbeltown, Argyll PA28 6RF
On B842, 10 miles S of Campbeltown.
Undulating seaside course.
18 holes, 4597 yards, S.S.S.63
Visitors: welcome.
Green fees: on request through Campbeltown Courier office.
Catering: snacks available.
Hotels: Keil.

W48 Easter Moffat
☎ Caldercruix 289
Mansion House, Plains, by Airdrie, Lanarkshire
Course is situated 2 miles E of Airdrie on the old Edinburgh to Glasgow road.
Moorland/parkland course.
18 holes, 6221 yards, S.S.S.70
Club founded in 1922.
Visitors: weekdays only.
Green fees: £5 per round, £7 per day.
Society meetings: welcome weekdays.
Catering: lunches, high teas, dinners, bar snacks except Thurs.
Hotels: Tudor, Airdrie.

W49 East Kilbride
☎ East Kilbride (0352) 20913, 47728 or 22192
Chapelside Rd, Nerston, East Kilbride
On Glasgow to East Kilbride road turn off at Nerston village by Borlands Cars.
Undulating meadowland course.
18 holes, 6419 yards, S.S.S.71
Course designed by Fred Hawtree.
Club founded in 1900.
Visitors: welcome with member.
Green fees: on application.
Society meetings: welcome by arrangement on Mon and Fri.
Catering: lunches and high teas served except Tues when snacks available.
Hotels: Stuart; Bruce.

W50 East Renfrewshire
☎ (03555) 206
Loganswell, Pilmuir, Newton Mearns, Glasgow
A77, 1 mile from Mearns Cross.
Moorland course.
18 holes, 6100 yards, S.S.S.70
Course designed by Tom Dobson.
Club founded in 1926.
Visitors: welcome with member.
Green fees: £7 per round, £10 per day.
Society meetings: by arrangement.
Catering: meals served.
Hotels: MacDonald's.

W51 Eastwood
☎ Loganswell (035 55) 261
Muirshield, Loganswell, Newton Mearns, Glasgow G77 6RX
On A77 from Glasgow, 3 miles S of Newton Mearns Cross at junction of Old Mearns Rd.
Moorland course.
18 holes, 5864 yards, S.S.S.68
Course designed by Moore.
Club founded in 1893.
Visitors: welcome with introduction from member.
Green fees: £9.50 per day, £6 per round.
Society meetings: by arrangement.
Catering: bar meals, high teas and dinners served except Mon.
Hotels: McDonald, Eastwood Toll; Fenwick, Fenwick.

W52 Elderslie
☎ Johnstone (0505) 22835 or 23956
63 Main Rd, Elderslie, Renfrewshire PA5 9AZ
On A737 between Paisley and Johnstone.
Undulating parkland course.
18 holes, 6004 yards, S.S.S.69
Club founded in 1909.
Visitors: welcome with member or with letter of introduction from own Sec.
Green fees: £6 per round, £8 per day.
Society meetings: catered for by arrangement.
Catering: full catering and bar facilities.
Hotels: Lyndhurst, Johnstone; Bird in the Hand, Johnstone.

W53 Erskine
☎ Bishopton (0505) 863327
Bishopton, Renfrewshire PA7 5PH
N of M8, leave Erskine Toll Bridge and turn left along B815 for 1½ miles.
Parkland course.
18 holes, 6287 yards, S.S.S.70
Club founded in 1903.
Visitors: welcome if introduced by or playing with a member.
Green fees: on application.
Society meetings: by arrangement.
Catering: meals served to members and guests only, or by arrangement.
Hotels: Bishopton; Crest.

W54 Fereneze
☎ 041-881 1519
Fereneze Ave, Barrhead, Glasgow G78 1HJ
9 miles SW of Glasgow.
Moorland course.
18 holes, 5821 yards, S.S.S.68
Club founded in 1904.
Visitors: welcome with member only.
Green fees: on application.
Society meetings: by arrangement.
Catering: lunches served except Mon.
Hotels: Dalmeny Park.

W55 Girvan
☎ 0465 4272
Girvan, Ayrshire KA26 9HW
Off A77.
Seaside/meadowland course.
18 holes, 5078 yards, S.S.S.65
Visitors: welcome.
Green fees: weekdays £3 per round, £3.85 per day; weekends £3.75 per round, £6 per day.
Society meetings: welcome by arrangement.
Catering: meals served by arrangement.
Hotels: in area.

W56 Glasgow (Ayr)
☎ 041-942 2011
Gailes, Irvine, Ayrshire
2 miles S of Irvine on road to Troon.
Links course.
18 holes, 6447 yards, S.S.S.71
Course designed by Willie Park Jr.
Club founded in 1787.
Visitors: by arrangement with Sec at Killermont, Bearsden, Glasgow.
Green fees: £12 per round or day.
Society meetings: welcome weekdays.
Catering: snacks, lunches and high teas available except Mon and Fri when only snacks provided.
Hotels: Hospitality Inn; Roseholm; Annick Water; Irvine.

W57 Glasgow
☎ 041-942 2011
Killermont, Bearsden, Glasgow G61 2TW
6 miles NW of Glasgow near Killermont Bridge.
Parkland course.
18 holes, 5968 yards, S.S.S.69
Course designed by Tom Morris Sen.
Club founded in 1787.
Visitors: welcome by introduction.
Green fees: £12 per round or day.
Society meetings: restricted availability.
Catering: snacks and lunches except Mon.
Hotels: Burnbrae, Bearsden; Black Bull, Milngavie.

W58 Gleddoch G. & C.C.
☎ Langbank (047 554) 304
Langbank, Renfrewshire PA14 6YE
M8 to Greenock, first turning to Langbank Houston.
Parkland/moorland course.
18 holes, 5661 yards, S.S.S.67
Course designed by Hamilton Stutt.
Club founded in 1975.
Visitors: welcome by arrangement with Pro, Keith Campbell (047 554 704).
Green fees: £7 per round, £10 per day; weekends £13.
Society meetings: welcome.
Catering: meals and snacks.
Hotels: Gleddoch House Hotel.

W59 Glencruitten
☎ Oban (0631) 62868
Glencruitten Rd, Oban
1 mile from town centre off A816.
Hilly parkland/moorland course.
18 holes, 4452 yards, S.S.S.63
Course designed by James Braid.
Club founded in 1908.
Visitors: welcome on weekdays, with restrictions on Thurs and Sat.
Green fees: weekdays £4.50 per round, £5.50 per day; weekends £5.50 per round, £6.50 per day.
Society meetings: limited number of societies accepted.
Catering: meals and snacks available.
Hotels: numerous good hotels in area.

W60 Gourock
☎ Gourock (0475) 31001
Cowal View, Gourock, Renfrewshire
2 miles SW from Gourock station via Victoria Rd, Golf Rd and Cowal View.
Moorland course.
18 holes, 6492 yards, S.S.S.71
Course designed by Henry Cotton.
Club founded in 1896.
Visitors: welcome on weekdays and with member at weekends.
Green fees: £9 per day.
Society meetings: apply in writing.
Catering: lunches and evening meals served except Mon and Thurs.
Hotels: Gantock, Cloch Rd, Gourock; Ashton, Albert Rd, Gourock; Queens, Ashburn Gardens, Gourock.

W61 Greenock
☎ Greenock (0475) 20793
Forsyth St, Greenock, Renfrewshire PA16 8RE
1m SW of town centre, main rd to Gourock away from River Clyde.
Moorland course.
27 holes, 5346 yards, S.S.S.68
Club founded in 1890.
Visitors: welcome except on Sat.
Green fees: weekdays £6.50 per round or day, weekends £8.25.
Catering: full service except Thurs.
Hotels: Tontine, 6 Ardgowan Square, Greenock.

W62 Greenock Whinhill
☎ 0475 24694
Beith Rd, Greenock, Renfrewshire
23 miles W of Glasgow via M8.
Moorland course.
18 holes, 5454 yards, S.S.S.68
Club founded in 1908.
Visitors: welcome.
Green fees: £2.80 per day.
Society meetings: by arrangement.
Catering: meals by arrangement.
Hotels: Tontine.

W63 Haggs Castle
☎ 041-427 0480 Club, 1157 Office
70 Dumbreck Rd, Glasgow GW1 4SN
SW of Glasgow near Ibrox Stadium and Bellahouston Park.
Parkland course.
18 holes, 6464 yards, S.S.S.71
Course re-designed by Peter Alliss & Dav- Thomas.
Club founded in 1910.
Visitors: welcome with member.
Green fees: £7 per round, £12 per day.
Society meetings: catered for on Wed.
Catering: full catering available.
Hotels: Bellahouston, 517 Paisley Rd West, Glasgow; Sherbrooke, 11 Sherbrooke Ave, Glasgow.

W64 Hamilton
☎ Hamilton (0698) 282872 (Sec 286131)
Riccarton, Ferniegair, Hamilton, Lanarkshire
Off A74 between Larkhill and Hamilton.
Parkland course.
18 holes, 6264 yards, S.S.S.70
Course designed by James Braid.
Visitors: welcome with member, others by arrangement.
Green fees: on request.
Society meetings: by arrangement with Sec.
Catering: snacks daily, meals served by arrangement.
Hotels: Royal, Hamilton; Avonbridge.

W65 Hayston
☎ 041-776 1244, 1390 or 775 0882 Pro
Campsie Rd, Kirkintilloch, Glasgow G66 1RN
NE from Glasgow via Bishopbriggs and Kirkintilloch, 1 mile N of Kirkintilloch.

Undulating course.
18 holes, 6042 yards, S.S.S.69
Course designed by James Braid.
Club founded in 1926.
Visitors: welcome on weekdays with introduction from own Sec and with member at weekends.
Green fees: weekdays £6 per round, £11 per day.
Society meetings: catered for on Tues and Thurs.
Catering: lunches, teas and snacks served; dinners available by arrangement.
Hotels: Black Bull, Milngavie; Burnbrae, Milngavie.

W66 Helensburgh
☎ Helensburgh (0436) 4173
25 Abercromby St, Helensburgh, Dunbartonshire
Abercromby St, off Sinclair St.
Moorland course.
18 holes, 5966 yards, S.S.S.69
Course designed by Tom Morris.
Club founded in 1894.
Visitors: welcome on weekdays, weekends with member only.
Green fees: £6 per round, £8 per day.
Society meetings: welcome by arrangement.
Catering: full catering facilities.
Hotels: Lomond Castle; Rosslea; Commodore.

W67 Hilton Park
☎ 041-956 4657
Stockiemuir Rd, Milngavie, Glasgow G62 9HB
8 miles N of Glasgow on A809.
Moorland courses.
Allander 18 holes, 5409 yards, S.S.S.67
Hilton 18 holes, 6021 yards, S.S.S.70
Club founded in 1927.
Visitors: welcome by arrangement with Sec.
Green fees: £6 per round, £9 per 2 rounds.
Society meetings: welcome by arrangement on weekdays except Fri.
Catering: full facilities available.
Hotels: Dormy House available.

W68 Hollandbush
☎ Lesmahagow (0555) 893484
Acretophead, Lesmahagow.
Off A74 between Lesmahagow and Coalburn.
Parkland/moorland course.
18 holes, 6110 yards, S.S.S.70
Course designed by Ken Pate.
Club founded in 1954.
Visitors: welcome.
Green fees: weekdays £2.20, weekends £5.
Catering: full catering facilities
Hotels: Station, Coalburn.

W69 Innellan
☎ Innellan (036 983) 242, 0369 5081 Sec
Knockamillie Rd, Innellan, Argyll
Directions at Innellan Pier.
Undulating parkland course.
9 holes, 2321 yards, S.S.S.63
Club founded in 1891.
Visitors: welcome at all times except Mon evenings.
Green fees: £2.50 per round, £4 per day.
Society meetings: by arrangement.
Catering: limited by arrangement.
Hotels: Osbourne, adjacent to Pier.

W70 Irvine
☎ Irvine (0294) 75979
Bogside, Irvine KA12 8SN
On road from Irvine to Kilwinning, turn left after Ravenspark Academy, and carry straight on for ½ mile over railway bridge.
Links course.
18 holes, 6454 yards, S.S.S.71
Course designed by James Braid.
Club founded in 1887.
Visitors: welcome on weekdays except Fri.
Green fees: £10 per round or day.
Catering: meals and snacks served.
Hotels: Hospitality Inn; Redburn; Eglinton Arms.

W71 Irvine Ravenspark
☎ Irvine (0294) 79550
Kidsneuk, Irvine, Ayrshire
On A78 midway between Irvine and Kilwinning.
Meadowland course.
18 holes, 6429 yards, S.S.S.71
Course designed by J. Walker.
Visitors: welcome.
Green fees: weekdays £2 per round, £3 per day, weekends £5 per day.
Catering: available except Tues and Thurs.
Hotels: Holiday Inn, Irvine; Redburn, Irvine Rd.

W72 Kilbirnie Place
☎ Kilbirnie (050 582) 683398
Largs Rd, Kilbirnie, Ayrshire
On outskirts of Kilbirnie on road to Largs.
Parkland course.
18 holes, 5479 yards, S.S.S.67
Club founded in 1922.
Visitors: welcome on weekdays and Sun.
Green fees: weekdays £4 per round, £5.50 per day; Sun £6 per round.
Catering: meals only at weekends.
Hotels: Milton, Kilbirnie.

W73 Kilmacolm
☎ Kilmacolm (050 587) 2978
Porterfield Rd, Kilmacolm
A740 to Linwood, then A761 to Bridge of Weir.
Moorland course.
18 holes, 5964 yards, S.S.S.68
Course designed by James Braid.
Club founded in 1891.
Visitors: welcome on weekdays except Fri and Mon.
Green fees: £8 per round, £10 per day.
Society meetings: welcome by arrangement.
Catering: full facilities available.
Hotels: Gryffe, Bridge of Weir.

W74 Kilmarnock (Barassie)
☎ Troon (0292) 313920 Sec, 311077 Clubhouse, 311322 Pro.
Hillhouse Rd, Barassie, Troon, Ayrshire K10 6SY
Off A78 2 miles N of Troon.
Seaside course.
18 holes, 6460 yards, S.S.S.71
Course designed by Matthew M Monie.
Club founded in 1887.
Visitors: welcome on weekdays, except Bank Holidays, by arrangement with Pro.
Green fees: £12 per day.
Society meetings: catered for by arrangement with Sec.
Catering: meals and snacks available.
Hotels: many good hotels in area.

W75 Kilsyth Lennox
☎ Kilsyth (0236) 822190
Tak-Ma-Doon Rd, Kilsyth, Glasgow G65 0HX
12 miles from Glasgow on A80.
Moorland/parkland course.
9 holes, 5944 yards, S.S.S.69
Club founded in 1907.
Visitors: welcome without introduction until 5 pm on weekdays, after 4 pm on Sat and after 2 pm on Sun.
Green fees: weekdays £4 per day, weekends £4 per round.
Society meetings: catered for on weekdays.
Catering: lunches served except Thurs; high teas served at weekends from June to Sept.
Hotels: Coachman, Kilsyth.

W76 Kirkhill
☎ 041-641 3083
Greenlees Rd, Cambuslang, Glasgow G72 8YN
Follow East Kilbride road from Burnside, take first turning on left past Cathkin by-pass roundabout.
Meadowland course.
18 holes, 5862 yards, S.S.S.69
Course designed by James Braid.
Club founded in 1910.
Visitors: welcome on weekdays by arrangement.
Green fees: £7 per day, £5 per round.
Society meetings: welcome by prior arrangement in writing.
Catering: bar snacks and full meals by arrangement with Club Steward.

Hotels: Kings Park, Mill St, Rutherglen; Burnside, East Kilbride Rd, Burnside.

W77 Kirkintilloch
☎ 041-776 1256
Todhill, Campsie Rd, Kirkintilloch, Glasgow G66 1RN
1 mile from Kirkintilloch on road from Kirkintilloch to Lennoxtown.
Meadowland course.
18 holes, 5269 yards, S.S.S.66
Course designed by James Braid.
Club founded in 1892.
Visitors: welcome with introduction from member.
Society meetings: catered for only if sponsored by member.
Catering: meals served from Wed to Sat; bar lunches available on Mon and Tues.
Hotels: Kincaid House; Milton of Campsie; Broadcroft, Kirkintilloch.

W78 Knightswood
☎ 041-959 2131
Lincoln Ave, Knightswood, Glasgow
Off Dumbarton Rd from city centre.
Parkland course.
9 holes, 2717 yards, S.S.S.64
Club founded in 1920s.
Visitors: welcome.
Green fees: weekdays 75p (Juniors and OAPs 40p), weekends £1.
Society meetings: welcome by arrangement.
Catering: none.
Hotels: Pond, Great Western Rd, Glasgow.

W79 Kyles of Bute
☎ Tighnabruaich (0700) 811 355
Tighnabruaich, Argyll
B836 from Dunoon or A886 from Strachur, then take A8003 to Tighnabruaich, through village to Kanes Cross, then B8000 to Millhouse, club entrance on left at top of first rise.
Undulating moorland course.
9 holes, 2379 yards, S.S.S.33
Club founded in 1907.
Visitors: welcome.
Green fees: £2.50 per day (Juniors £1.50 per day).
Society meetings: welcome by special arrangement only.
Catering: snacks served during summer season only.
Hotels: Royal; Tighnabruaich; Kyles of Bute; Kanes.

W80 Lamlash
☎ Lamlash (077 06) 296
Brodick Rd, Lamlash
3 miles S of Brodick on Lamlash to Whiting Bay road.
Undulating moorland course.
18 holes, 4681 yards, S.S.S.63
Club founded in 1902.
Visitors: welcome.
Green fees: £3.50 per day.
Society meetings: welcome.
Catering: snacks and light meals available.
Hotels: Marine; Bay.

W81 Lanark
☎ Lanark (0555) 3219
The Moor, Lanark ML11 7RX
Off A73 or A72, turn left in Lanark into Whitelees Rd, for ½ mile.
Moorland course.
18 holes, 6416 yards, S.S.S.71
Club founded in 1851.
Visitors: welcome on weekdays until 4.30 pm and with member at weekends.
Green fees: £7 per round, £10 per day.
Society meetings: catered for usually on Mon and Tues.
Catering: full facilities available.
Hotels: Cartland Bridge, Lanark.

W82 Largs
☎ Largs (0475) 673594
Irvine Rd, Largs, Ayrshire KA30 8EU
1 mile S of Largs on A78.
Parkland/seaside course.
18 holes, 6220 yards, S.S.S.70
Club founded in 1891.
Visitors: welcome.
Green fees: £9 per day, £6 per round.
Society meetings: catered for on weekdays except Wed.
Catering: full catering available.
Hotels: Hayzie; Springfield; Victoria.

W83 Larkhall
☎ Larkhall (0698) 881113
Burnhead Rd, Larkhall, Lanarkshire
SW on B7019.
9 holes, 6236 yards, S.S.S.70
Visitors: Municipal course, all welcome.
Green fees: season tickets £27 (men), £22 (women). £1.40 per round (70p OAPs, juniors and unemployed).
Society meetings: by arrangement.

W84 Leadhills
☎ Biggar (065 94) 222
Leadhills, Biggar, Lanarkshire ML12 6XR
6 miles from A74 Abington, course within village at rear of hotel.
Moorland course.
9 holes, 4062 yards, S.S.S.62
Club founded in 1935.
Visitors: welcome.
Green fees: weekdays £1.50 per day, weekends £2 per day.
Society meetings: welcome.
Catering: none.
Hotels: Hopetoun Arms, Leadhills; Glendyne, Sanquhar; Glenelvan, Elvanfoot.

W85 Lenzie
☎ 041-776 1535
19 Crosshill Rd, Lenzie, Glasgow G66 3DA
A80 to Stepps, Lenzie road turn left at traffic lights.
Moorland course.
18 holes, 5982 yards, S.S.S.69
Club founded in 1889.
Visitors: welcome with member.
Green fees: weekdays 60p, weekends and Bank Holidays £2.
Society meetings: welcome weekdays.
Catering: meals and snacks available except Mon.

W86 Lethamhill
☎ 041-770 6220
Cumbernauld Rd, Glasgow G33 1AH
On A80 adjacent to Hogganfield Loch.
Municipal course.
18 holes, 6073 yards, S.S.S.69
Visitors: welcome.
Green fees: weekdays £1.50 (75p concs, 40p OAPs), weekends £2 for all.
Catering: tea room at club April to Sept.

W87 Linn Park
☎ 041-637 5871
Simshill Rd, Glasgow
Off M74 S of Glasgow.
Parkland course.
18 holes, S.S.S.63
Visitors: welcome.
Green fees: weekdays £1.50 (75p concs, 40p OAPs), weekends £2.
Catering: snacks served 10 am to 4 pm.

W88 Littlehill
☎ 041-772 1916
Auchinairn Rd, Bishopbriggs, Glasgow
3 miles N of city centre.
Parkland course.
18 holes, 6199 yards, S.S.S.70
Visitors: welcome.
Green fees: £1.50 weekdays (75p concs, after 3.30 pm, 40p OAPs), weekends £2.
Catering: meals and snacks served.

W89 Lochranza
☎ Lochranza (077 083) 273
Brodick, Isle of Arran GA27 8HJ
Off "the road".
9 holes, 3580 yards, S.S.S.40
Visitors: welcome.
Green fees: £1.35 per round, £1.60 per day.
Society meetings: by arrangement.
Catering: cold snacks available.
Hotels: 3 in area.

W90 Lochwinnoch
☎ Lochwinnoch (0505) 842153
Burnfoot Rd, Lochwinnoch
On A760 about 10 miles S of Paisley, first on right after Struthers Garage, 400 yds along Burnfoot Rd.

Parkland course.
18 holes, 6241 yards, S.S.S.70
Club founded in 1897.
Visitors: welcome by arrangement.
Green fees: £5 per round, £7 per day.
Catering: full facilities available by arrangement with Clubmaster.
Hotels: Lyndhurst, Johnstone; Greenacres; Howwood.

W91 Loudoun
☎ Galston (0563) 821993 Sec, 820551 Clubhouse
Galston, Ayrshire KA4 8PA
A77 to Kilmarnock, take Edinburgh road, club lies on main road between Galston and Newmilns.
Parkland course.
18 holes, 5824 yards, S.S.S.68
Club founded in 1909.
Visitors: welcome on weekdays.
Green fees: £5 per round, £8 per day.
Society meetings: welcome.
Catering: catering facilities available.
Hotels: Broomhill, Kilmarnock; Foxbar, Kilmarnock.

W92 Machrie
☎ (0496) 2310
Machrie Hotel, Port Ellen, Isle of Islay, Argyll PA42 7AN
By plane from Glasgow or ferry from Kennacraig, on A846 S of Airfield.
Seaside links course.
18 holes, 6226 yards, S.S.S.71
Course designed by Willie Campbell, redesigned by Donald Steel.
Club founded in 1891.
Visitors: welcome.
Green fees: £5 per round, £9 per day, golf complimentary to hotel guests.
Society meetings: by arrangement.
Catering: meals at hotel.
Hotels: Machrie.

W93 Machrie Bay
☎ Machrie (077 084) 267
c/o Sec, Camus Ban, Machrie, by Brodick, Isle of Arran KA27 8DZ
Ferry to Brodick and via String Rd to Machrie.
Fairly flat seaside course.
9 holes, 2123 yards, S.S.S.32
Course designed by William Fernie.
Club founded in 1900.
Visitors: welcome.
Green fees: £1 per round, £1.50 per day; weekly £5, fortnightly £8.
Catering: snacks available in June, July and Aug.
Hotels: many good hotels on island.

W94 Machrihanish
☎ Machrihanish (0586) 81213
Machrihanish, Campbeltown, Argyll
5 miles W of Campbeltown on B843.
Links seaside course.
18 holes, 6228 yards, S.S.S.70
9 hole course.
Club founded in 1876.
Visitors: welcome
Green fees: under review for 1986.
Society meetings: catered for by arrangement with Club Steward.
Catering: full catering facilities available except Wed.
Hotels: Royal, Campbeltown; Ardshiel; Whitehart, Campbeltown; Ardell, Machrihanish.

W95 Millport
☎ Millport (0475) 530485/530311
Golf Rd, Millport, Isle of Cubrae KA28 0BA
Seaside/moorland course.
18 holes, 5831 yards, S.S.S.68
Club founded in 1888.
Visitors: welcome.
Green fees: weekdays £4 per round, £6 per day; weekends £4.50 per round, £6.50 per day.
Society meetings: welcome except at peak periods.
Catering: meals served.
Hotels: Royal George; Westbourne.

W96 Milngavie
☎ 041-956 1619
Laighpark, Milngavie, Glasgow G62 8EP
Off A809 NW of Glasgow.
Moorland course.
18 holes, 5818 yards, S.S.S.68
Club founded in 1895.
Visitors: welcome with introduction by member.
Green fees: £8.
Society meetings: welcome.
Catering: bar snacks and meals available by arrangement.
Hotels: Black Bull, Milngavie.

W97 Mount Ellen
☎ Glenboig (0236) 872277
Johnston House, Johnston Rd, Gartcosh, Glasgow
1 mile S of A80 Glasgow to Stirling road, between Muirhead village and Coatbridge.
Undulating meadowland course.
18 holes, 5525 yards, S.S.S.68
Club founded in 1905.
Visitors: welcome by arrangement on weekdays or with member at weekends.
Green fees: weekdays £5 (£1 with member).
Society meetings: welcome weekdays.
Catering: meals available except Thurs.
Hotels: Coatbridge, Coatbridge; Garfield, Stepps.

W98 Old Ranfurly
☎ Bridge of Weir (0505) 613612
Ranfurly Place, Bridge of Weir, Renfrewshire PA11 3DE
7 miles W of Paisley.
Moorland course.
18 holes, 6266 yards, S.S.S.70
Club founded in 1905.
Visitors: welcome on weekdays by introduction and weekends with member.
Green fees: on application.
Society meetings: catered for by special arrangement.
Catering: snack lunches and high teas available.
Hotels: Gryffe Arms, Bridge of Weir

W99 Paisley
☎ 041-884 2292
Braehead, Paisley PA2 8TZ
From Glasgow, A737 to Paisley, 3 miles S of Paisley centre.
Moorland course.
18 holes, 6424 yards, S.S.S.71
Club founded in 1895.
Visitors: welcome on weekdays, except Bank Holidays, by arrangement with Sec.
Green fees: £5 per round, £8 per day.
Society meetings: welcome on weekdays, except Bank Holidays, by prior arrangement with Sec.
Catering: full service available.
Hotels: Watermill, Paisley.

W100 Palacerigg
☎ Cumbernauld (023 67) 34969 Club, 21461 Starter
Palacerigg Country Park, Cumbernauld G67 3HU
Take A80 to Cumbernauld, follow signs to Country Park.
Parkland course.
18 holes, 6444 yards, S.S.S.71
Club founded in 1975.
Visitors: welcome by prior arrangement.
Green fees: £3.20 per day, weekends £3.80.
Society meetings: welcome on weekdays by arrangement.
Catering: meals available.
Hotels: Castlecary.

W101 Pollok
☎ 041-632 4351
90 Barrhead Rd, Glasgow G43 1BG
On A736, 4 miles S of city centre.
Parkland course.
18 holes, 6257 yards, S.S.S.70
Club founded in 1892.
Visitors: welcome with member or letter of introduction.
Green fees: £10 per round, £15 per day.
Society meetings: by arrangement.
Catering: meals served.
Hotels: Macdonald; Tinto Firs; Holiday Inn.

W102 Port Bannatyne
☎ Isle of Bute (0700) 2009

Machrie and Machrihanish

As their names suggest, Machrie and Machrihanish sound related and can, in fact, be described as close cousins, separated only by a few miles of sea. Machrihanish is on the mainland of Kintyre in Argyll, Machrie on the Isle of Islay, the southernmost of Scotland's charming outer isles.

The charm of both lies in their remote setting, a pace to life that is appealingly unhurried and, for the golfer, two courses in the finest traditions of British seaside links. Machrihanish, situated on the west coast of the Mull of Kintyre, a feature of the famous view from Turnberry, is marginally better known perhaps because it can be approached entirely on dry land.

In fact, it takes a long, circuitous drive from Glasgow which passes through Tarbert, the port from which the ferries depart for Islay, which makes the scheduled air service from Glasgow decidedly more convenient. You can chat to the pilot and improve your geography on a clear day by being able to see every inch of the journey. There are no interminable waits for your baggage and no stream of inaudible announcements from the tiny terminal buildings at the other end.

In the old days, your next door neighbour on the flight was quite likely to have been a box of kippers but the other great joy is that you can survey the golf courses as you land and be on the first tee within minutes. On Islay, it is a question of a quick flip down the Bowmore road and turn left into the Machrie Hotel whose rooms and adjacent cottages make a perfect base.

Those who haven't seen the course for ten years will notice significant changes, the land which used to house the 2nd, 3rd and 4th being replaced by some new holes out at the far end. The 1st, a gentle opener, has a raised tee from which the whole scenic panorama is apparent, but the new 2nd quickly gets down to the real golfing business, a par 5 doglegging sharply left along the path of a fast flowing stream.

The 5th is a fine short hole and the 6th typical of Machrie's natural blessings, a drive on the left providing the correct approach as well as a view of the green in a dell. In its early days in the last century, the drive at the 7th over a vast sandhill was rather more formidable than it is now. Its dimensions were similar to those of the Maiden at Sandwich but, once cleared, the golf follows the line of a glorious sandy beach. Unlike many other seaside courses, here is the opportunity of really seeing the sea.

The 10th tee is another wonderful lookout point although the mind has to concentrate on the task ahead, the introduction to the new golfing country and a scenic change to the hills and lonely peat moors. After a spell of stout hitting for four or five holes, the finish is not quite as severe but it immediately commands an affection both genuine and lasting.

Machrihanish is remembered with similar enthusiasm. From the moment that you tee up by the professional's shop, wondering just how much of the sandy bay you dare cut off, the prospects are invigorating. A notice for non-golfers proclaims "Danger. First tee above, please move further along the beach". Another might say, "Next stop to the west, Long Island" but after the Machrihanish Burn and the shot over the crest to the 2nd green have been negotiated, the true duneland character of a fine outward half is apparent.

This is the true heart land of Machrihanish, a course that has tested the Scottish Women and the Scottish Professionals in their championships a time or two but is essentially a holiday course with a combination of challenge and surroundings rare

The first shot at **MACHRIHANISH GOLF CLUB** is probably the most exhilarating opening drive in the whole of the British Isles. The Atlantic Ocean to be driven over - that's what awaits the visitor to these famous links.

Once they were the most remote of the championship courses in Britain but with improved roads and a 30-minute air link from Glasgow all can now enjoy golf at Machrihanish. The SSS and par of 70 provide an excellent test, with the prevailing south westerly winds always to be considered.

Visitors are made welcome, but we suggest they contact the club secretary or professional about tee times. Our steward and his wife will willingly cater for any parties and individuals, by arrangement.

Incidentally, among our life members is Henry Cotton. And finally, in the words of old Tom Morris, "Machrihanish was designed by the Almighty" for playing golf.

even in a country where spectacular golf abounds.

In common with many seaside links, Machrihanish, founded as the Kintyre Club and more than a century old, goes out and back but it follows the curve of the great bay just enough to make sure the wind isn't constantly facing or behind. The greens, generally large, are thoroughly in keeping with a course whose founders would still happily recognise it.

The one exception perhaps is the background to the 9th where the guide post is mixed up with the landing lights for the airfield which has the second longest runway in Europe; but the terrain for the homeward half, moving inland, heralds a change of character. The journey back to the row of houses by the clubhouse which looks out on the ever changing moods of the ocean is some contrast but there is nothing much wrong with the 10th and 12th, the two par fives. The 11th and 15th greens can be elusive targets. The 13th green is subtly raised and there is the unusual feature of successive short holes, the 15th and 16th. Cypress Point, West Sussex, Royal Jersey and Sandy Lodge are other examples, but if short holes, in theory, should help the score, the 17th strikes danger.

With out of bounds along the left, the fairway is alarmingly narrow but elsewhere there is plenty of opportunity to open the shoulders.

Bannatyne Mains Rd, Port Bannatyne, Isle of Bute
2 miles N of Rothesay on A845.
Hilly seaside course.
13 holes, 4654 yards, S.S.S.63
Course designed by James Braid.
Visitors: welcome.
Green fees: £2 per day, £7 per week.
Catering: available by arrangement for parties.
Hotels: Marine House, Marine Place, Rothesay.

W103 Port Glasgow
☎ Port Glasgow (0475) 704181
Devol Farm Industrial Estate, Port Glasgow, Renfrewshire
SW of Glasgow on M8 towards Greenock. In town of Port Glasgow.
Undulating course.
18 holes, 5712 yards, S.S.S.69
Visitors: weekdays only.
Green fees: £3 per round, £5 per day.
Catering: snacks every day, meals by arrangement.
Hotels: Clune Brae.

W104 Prestwick
☎ Prestwick (0292) 77404
2 Links Rd, Prestwick, Ayrshire KA9 1QG
1 mile from Prestwick Airport adjacent to Prestwick station.
Seaside links course.
18 holes, 6544 yards, S.S.S.72
Club founded in 1851.
Visitors: welcome on weekdays and with restrictions on Sun.
Green fees: before 3 pm £22, after 3 pm £13.
Society meetings: catered for by arrangement.
Catering: snacks and meals by arrangement.
Hotels: Links, Links Rd, Prestwick; Marine, Troon; Turnberry.

W105 Prestwick St Cuthbert
☎ Prestwick (0292) 77101
East Rd, Prestwick, Ayrshire KA9 2SX
Off main Ayr to Prestwick Rd at Bellevue Rd.
Parkland course.
18 holes, 6470 yards, S.S.S.71
Course designed by Stutt Ltd.
Club founded in 1899.
Visitors: welcome on weekdays, weekends with member only.
Green fees: £7 per round, £10 per day.
Society meetings: welcome by arrangement.
Catering: meals served except Thurs.
Hotels: St Nicholas; North Beach; Carlton.

W106 Prestwick St Nicholas
☎ Prestwick (0292) 77608
Grangemuir Rd, Prestwick, Ayrshire KA9 1SN
Off A79, from Main St turn into Grangemuir Rd which runs down to sea.
Links course.
18 holes, 5864 yards, S.S.S.68
Club founded in 1851.
Visitors: welcome on weekdays and with member at weekends; letter of introduction from own club required.
Green fees: £10 per day.
Society meetings: catered for on Tues and Thurs by prior arrangement with Sec.
Catering: meals and snacks available except Mon.
Hotels: Links, Prestwick; Balgarth, Ayr.

W107 Ralston
☎ 041-882 1349
Strathmore Ave, Ralston, Paisley, Renfrewshire PE1 3EP
Off main Paisley to Glasgow road.
Parkland course.
18 holes, 6100 yards, S.S.S.69
Visitors: organised parties only.
Green fees: by arrangement.
Catering: meals served.

W108 Ranfurly Castle
☎ Bridge of Weir (0505) 612609
Golf Rd, Bridge of Weir, Renfrewshire PA11 3HN
Off M8 at sign for Linwood.
Undulating moorland course.
18 holes, 6284 yards, S.S.S.70
Club founded in 1904.
Visitors: letter of introduction required.
Green fees: £8 per round, £10 per day.
Society meetings: by arrangement.
Catering: lunches by arrangement.
Hotels: Gryfe Arms.

W109 Renfrew
☎ 041-886 6692
Blythswood Estate, Inchinnan Rd, Renfrew
Off A8 at Normandy Hotel.
Parkland course.
18 holes, 6818 yards, 6406 yards, 5969 yards, S.S.S.73

Course designed by John Harris.
Club founded in 1894.
Visitors: welcome with introduction from member.
Green fees: £7 per round, £10 per day.
Society meetings: welcome by arrangement, maximum 30.
Catering: full facilities available.
Hotels: Normandy; Excelsior; Dean Park.

W110 Rothesay
☎ Rothesay (0700) 3554 Pro Shop, 2244 Clubhouse
Canada Hill, Rothesay, Isle of Bute
Undulating course.
18 holes, 5370 yards, S.S.S.67
Course designed by James Braid.
Club founded in 1892.
Visitors: welcome.
Green fees: weekdays £2.50 per day, weekends £6 per day.
Society meetings: welcome except in July and Aug.
Catering: full facilities available.
Hotels: Hillside; Royal.

W111 Routenburn
☎ Largs (0475) 673230 or 674289 Pro
Largs, Ayrshire KA30 9AH
1 mile N of Largs, first major left turn coming into Largs from Greenock.
Seaside hill course.
18 holes, 5650 yards, S.S.S.67
Club founded in 1914.
Visitors: welcome on weekdays.
Green fees: weekdays £2 per round, £3 per day; weekends £5.
Society meetings: welcome weekdays.
Catering: lunches, bar lunches and evening meals served except Thurs.
Hotels: Charleston, Largs.

W112 Royal Troon & Portland
☎ Troon (0292) 311555
Craigend Rd, Troon, Ayrshire KA10 6EP
3 miles from Prestwick Airport.
Seaside courses.
Portland 18 holes, 6274 yards, S.S.S.71
Old 18 holes, 6641 yards, S.S.S.73
Club founded in 1878.
Visitors: welcome on weekdays with letter of introduction, advance booking essential.
Green fees: £20 day ticket for one round on each course.
Society meetings: welcome on weekdays only, maximum 40.
Catering: meals and snacks available.
Hotels: Marine; Sun Court; Piersland; Craiglea.

W113 Sandyhills
☎ 041-778 1179
223 Sandyhills Rd, Glasgow G32 9NA
E side of Glasgow, from Tollcross Rd, left at Killin St and right into Sandyhills Rd.
Parkland course.
18 holes, 6253 yards, S.S.S.70
Visitors: welcome by arrangement.
Green fees: £6 per round, £9 per day.
Society meetings: welcome by arrangement.
Catering: full catering except Mon.
Hotels: good hotels in Glasgow.

W114 Shiskine
☎ Isle of Arran (077 086) 226
Blackwaterfoot, Isle of Arran KA27 8HA
300 yards off A841 in Blackwaterfoot.
Seaside course.
12 holes, 3000 yards, S.S.S.42
Club founded in 1896.
Visitors: welcome except on comp. days.
Green fees: £2.25 per round, £2.75 per day, £14 per week; reductions for Juniors.
Society meetings: by arrangement.
Catering: full catering facilities available from May to Sept only.
Hotels: Kinloch, Blackwaterfoot; Rock, Blackwaterfoot.

W115 Shotts
☎ Shotts (0501) 20431
Blairhead, Shotts ML7 5BJ
2 miles from M8 off Benhar Rd.
Moorland course.
18 holes, 6125 yards, S.S.S.70
Visitors: welcome except Sat.
Catering: full facilities available.
Hotels: Station, Dykehead; Stane, Stane

W116 Skelmorlie
☎ (0475) 520152
Skelmorlie, Ayrshire PA17 5ES
1 mile from Wemyss Bay station.
Parkland/moorland course.
13 holes, 5104 yards, S.S.S.65
Course designed by James Braid.
Club founded in 1891.
Visitors: welcome except Sat from Mar to Oct.
Green fees: weekdays £4 per day, weekends £6 per day.
Society meetings: welcome except Sat.
Catering: lunches, dinners and teas served.
Hotels: Manor Park; Heywood; Wemyss Bay; Redcliffe.

W117 Strathaven
☎ Strathaven (0357) 20421
Overton Ave, Glasgow Rd, Strathaven ML10 6NF
Situated on outskirts of town on A726.
Parkland course.
18 holes, 6226 yards, S.S.S.70
Course designed by William Fernie of Troon and extended to 18 holes by J.R. Stutt.
Club founded in 1908.
Visitors: welcome on weekdays until 4.30 pm except Bank Holidays.
Green fees: £6.50 per round, £10 per day.
Society meetings: welcome on Mon and Tues from May to Oct.
Catering: full facilities available.
Hotels: Springvale, Strathaven; Strathaven, Strathaven.

W118 Tarbert
☎ Tarbert (088 02) 565
Kilberry Rd, Tarbert, Argyll
1 mile on A83 to Campbeltown from Tarbert, turn right onto B8024 for ¼ mile.
Hilly seaside course.
9 holes, 2230 yards, S.S.S.64
Visitors: welcome on weekdays and with restrictions at weekends.
Green fees: £2 per round, £3 per day, £10 per week.
Society meetings: welcome by arrangement with Sec.
Catering: limited catering facilities available.
Hotels: Tarbert, Harbour St, Tarbert; Bruce, Harbour St, Tarbert; West Loch, Campbeltown Rd, Tarbert; Stonefield Castle, Tarbert.

W119 Torrance House
☎ E Kilbride (035 52) 33451
Strathaven Rd, E Kilbride, Glasgow G75 0QZ
On A726 on outskirts of E Kilbride.
Parkland course.
18 holes, 6640 yards, S.S.S.71
Course designed by Hawtree & Son.
Club founded in 1969.
Visitors: welcome by reservation.
Green fees: £4.40 per round.
Catering: meals served.
Hotels: Stuart; Bruce; Torrance; Crutherland.

W120 Troon Municipal
☎ Troon (0292) 312464
Harling Drive, Troon, Ayrshire KA10 6NE
100 yds from railway station.
Links course.
Lochgreen 18 holes, 6687 yards, S.S.S.72
Darley 18 holes, 6327 yards, S.S.S.70
Fullarton 18 holes, 4784 yards, S.S.S.63
Club founded in 1907.
Visitors: welcome on weekends.
Green fees: Lochgreen and Darley weekdays £3.75 per round, £5 per day; weekends £4.65 per round, £7.50 per day; Fullarton weekdays £2.60 per round, £3.40 per day; weekends £3.10 per round, £5.25 per day.
Society meetings: welcome weekdays.
Catering: lunches served.
Hotels: Ardneil; South Beach.

W121 **Turnberry Hotel**
☎ Turnberry (06553) 202
Turnberry Hotel, Turnberry, Ayrshire KA26 9LT
Off A77 from Glasgow just before Girvan.
Seaside courses.
Ailsa 18 holes, 6384 yards, S.S.S.69
Arran 18 holes, 6276 yards, S.S.S.69
Course designed by Mackenzie Ross.
Visitors: welcome.
Green fees: £20 per day.
Society meetings: welcome.
Catering: full facilities.
Hotels: Turnberry; Dormy House.

W122 **Vale of Leven**
☎ Alexandria (0389) 52351
Northfield Course, Bonfield, Alexandria, Dunbartonshire
Off A82 at Bonhill.
Moorland course.
18 holes, 5155 yards, S.S.S.65
Visitors: welcome April – Sept except Sat.
Green fees: on request.
Society meetings: welcome except Sat.
Catering: meals available.
Hotels: Griffen, Alexandria; Loch Lomond, Balloch.

W123 **Vaul**
☎ Scarinish (087 92) 566
Scarinish, Isle of Tiree, Argyll
Seaside course.
9 holes, 6246 yards, S.S.S.70
Club founded in 1920.
Visitors: welcome. No Sun golf.
Green fees: £3 per day, £10 per week.
Society meetings: by arrangement.
Hotels: Lodge; Scarinish.

W124 **Western Gailes**
☎ Irvine (0294) 311354
Gailes, by Irvine, Ayrshire KA11 5AE
5 miles N of Troon on A78.
Seaside course.
18 holes.
Club founded in 1897.
Visitors: welcome on weekdays except Thurs and Sat (no Lady visitors on Tues); advisable to book in advance.
Green fees: £12.50.
Society meetings: welcome by arrangement on weekdays except Thurs and Sat.
Catering: lunches and snacks available.
Hotels: many hotels in Troon and Ayr.

W125 **West Kilbride**
☎ West Kilbride (0294) 823128
Fullerton Drive, Seamill, West Kilbride, Ayrshire KA23 9HS
On main Ardrossan to Largs road at Seamill.
Seaside/links course.
18 holes, 6235 yards, S.S.S.70
Club founded in 1893.
Visitors: welcome on weekdays.
Green fees: £9 per day.
Society meetings: catered for on only Tues and Thurs; no bookings in June, July or Aug.
Catering: full facilities available.
Hotels: Seamill Hydro, Ardrossan Rd, Seamill; Ardenlee, Ardrossan Rd, Seamill; Galleon Inn, Ardrossan Rd, Seamill.

W126 **Whitecraigs**
☎ 041-639 4530
72 Ayr Rd, Giffnock, Glasgow G46 6SW
7 miles S of Glasgow on A77.
Parkland course.
18 holes, 6230 yards, S.S.S.70
Club founded in 1905.
Visitors: welcome with introduction.
Green fees: £9 per round (£1 with member).
Society meetings: catered for on Wed.
Catering: meals and snacks except Mon.
Hotels: MacDonald, Liffnock.

W127 **Williamwood**
☎ 041-637 1783
Clarkston Rd, Netherlee, Glasgow G44
5 miles S of Glasgow.
Wooded parkland course.
18 holes, 5808 yards, S.S.S.68
Course designed by James Braid.
Visitors: by introduction only, unless resident over 40 miles away.
Green fees: by arrangement.
Society meetings: weekdays, by arrangement.
Catering: lunches and evening meals served.
Hotels: MacDonald, Giffnock; Bedhurst, Clarkston.

W128 **Windyhill**
☎ 041-942 2349
Baljaffray Rd, Bearsden, Glasgow G61 4QQ
Take A739 from Glasgow, after 8 miles turn right onto A809, after 1 mile turn left onto A810, club 1 mile on right.
Undulating moorland course.
18 holes, 6254 yards, S.S.S.70
Club founded in 1908.
Visitors: welcome on weekdays.
Green fees: £7 per day.
Catering: full facilities available.
Hotels: Burnbrae, Bearsden; Black Bull, Milngavie.

W129 **Wishaw**
☎ Wishaw (0698) 372869
55 Cleland Rd, Wishaw, Lanarkshire MLT 7PH
15m SW of Glasgow, 5m From A74.
Parkland course.
18 holes, 6134 yards, S.S.S.69
Course designed by James Braid.
Club founded in 1896.
Visitors: welcome on weekdays before 4 pm, organized parties preferred Sun.
Green fees: £7 per day weekdays, £10 per day at weekends.
Society meetings: by arrangement.
Catering: normally meals served except Mon and Wed.
Hotels: Crown; Popinjay; Rosebank; Garrion, Motherwell.

X Tayside, Central Region, Fife

St Andrews may be the jewel in the crown but the central and eastern part of Scotland glitters with other rare delights. Carnoustie, Gleneagles and Blairgowrie feature on nearly all golfing itineraries and no form of recommendation is necessary by way of introduction. They are all now within easy reach of Edinburgh or Glasgow but that doesn't mean that they should be the subject of a flying visit.

Like Venice, St Andrews' secrets take a lifetime to untie and golfers should acknowledge the fact. Carnoustie is essentially a place to appreciate the golf, a place where in 1953 Ben Hogan prepared more meticulously for the Open than perhaps any other championship for which he entered. It is hallowed ground with the golfer cast more in the role of a pilgrim but the Americans are more inclined to swoon at the sight of Gleneagles with its hotel and five star scenery to match. This spectacular seam runs through the whole of the golf to the west and north of Perth, a city with an historical golfing gem in King James VI on the banks of the Tay.

Close by golf has probably been played on the North Inch since 1502 but the East of Scotland is full of clubs and courses with distinguished family trees and lengthy pedigrees. Monifieth and Montrose are cases in point and, between Dundee and Carnoustie, we must not forget Panmure at Barry. Moving inland, Downfield (modern by comparison), Edzell and Forfar all have their protagonists but so do the other Fife courses which have to live in the shadow of St Andrews.

Leven, Lundin Links and Ladybank more or less rub shoulders with each other, Scotscraig is another Open championship qualifying course while Elie and Crail are ancient reminders of the natural environment in which the game was founded and has always thrived.

X1 Aberdour

☎ Aberdour (0383) 860256
Seaside Place, Aberdour, Fife KY3 0TX
Parkland/seaside course.
18 holes, 5432 yards, S.S.S.66
Course designed by Peter Robertson & Joe Anderson.
Club founded in 1904.
Visitors: welcome on weekdays.
Green fees: £4.50 per round, £7.50 per day.
Society meetings: visiting clubs bookings by arrangement but not Sat.
Catering: by arrangement, meals served except Tues.
Hotels: Woodside; Fairways.

X2 Aberfeldy

☎ Aberfeldy (0887) 20535
Taybridge Rd, Aberfeldy, Perthshire PH15 2BH
10 miles off A9 at Ballinluig.
Parkland course.
9 holes, 2733 yards, S.S.S.67
Visitors: welcome.
Green fees: £5 per day, £16 per week, £25 for two weeks.
Society meetings: small society meetings could be arranged.
Catering: snacks available.
Hotels: Weem; Cruachan; Breadalbane; Ailean Chraggan; Station.

X3 Aberfoyle

☎ Aberfoyle (087 72) 493
Braeval, Aberfoyle, Stirling FK8 3RL
1 mile from Aberfoyle on A81 Stirling road.
Hillside course.
18 holes, 5205 yards, S.S.S.66
Club founded in 1890.
Visitors: welcome.
Green fees: £5 per day.
Society meetings: welcome by arrangement.
Catering: catering available at weekends or by arrangement on weekdays.
Hotels: Inverard, Lochard Rd, Aberfoyle.

X4 Alloa

☎ Alloa (0259) 722745
Schawpark, Sauchie, Clackmannanshire FK10 3AX
On A908 1 mile N of Alloa.
Parkland course.
18 holes, 6230 yards, S.S.S.70
Course designed by James Braid.
Club founded in 1936.
Visitors: welcome on weekdays.
Green fees: £5 per round, £7 per day.
Society meetings: welcome on weekdays.
Catering: full facilities available.
Hotels: Station; Dunmar; Royal Oak; Castle Craig.

X5 Alva

☎ Alva (0259) 60431
Beauclerc St, Alva, Clackmannanshire
On A91 3 miles N of Alloa.
Undulating course.
9 holes, 4574 yards, S.S.S.64
Club founded in 1900.
Visitors: welcome.
Green fees: weekdays £2, weekends £3.
Catering: none.
Hotels: Glen; Johnstone.

X6 Alyth
☎ Alyth (082 83) 2268
Pitcrocknie, Alyth, Perthshire
On B894 Alyth to Glenisla road about ½ mile from major roundabout on A926 Blairgowrie to Kirriemuir road.
Moorland course.
18 holes, 6226 yards, S.S.S.70
Course designed by James Braid.
Club founded in 1894.
Visitors: welcome.
Green fees: weekdays £7 per day, weekends £9 per day.
Society meetings: welcome by arrangement with Sec.
Catering: full catering facilities.
Hotels: Alyth, Commercial St, Alyth; Lands of Loyal, Loyal Rd, Alyth.

X7 Anstruther
☎ Anstruther (0333) 310224 Sec
Marsfield, Shore Rd, Anstruther, Fife KY10 3DZ
Turn S off main road at Craw's Nest Hotel.
Seaside course.
9 holes, 4120 yards, S.S.S.63
Club founded in 1890.
Visitors: welcome except on comp. days.
Green fees: weekdays £2.50 per day, weekends £4 per day (Juniors £1.50).
Catering: snacks and lunches served.
Hotels: Craws Nest; Royal; Smugglers Inn.

X8 Arbroath
☎ Arbroath 72272
Elliot, Arbroath, Angus
On A92, 2 miles S of Arbroath.
Seaside course.
18 holes, 6078 yards, S.S.S.69
Visitors: welcome.
Green fees: £5.25 weekdays, £7.50 weekends.
Society meetings: by arrangement.
Catering: snacks, meals by arrangement.
Hotels: in Arbroath.

X9 Auchterarder
☎ Auchterarder (076 46) 2804
Orchil Rd, Auchterarder, Perthshire
Off A9 to SW of town, about 400 yards up A824, hidden entrance to club.
Moorland course.
18 holes, 5741 yards, S.S.S.68
Course designed by Bernard Sayers.
Club founded in 1892.
Visitors: welcome on weekdays and most weekends.
Green fees: weekdays £5 per day (winter £2.50), weekends £6 per day (winter £3), weekly £25.
Society meetings: welcome by prior arrangement.
Catering: lunches, dinners and bar meals available.
Hotels: numerous good hotels in area.

X10 Auchterderran
Woodend Rd, Cardenden, Fife KY5 0NH
N of Auchterderran High School on Glenrothes to Cardenden road.
Undulating moorland/parkland course.
9 holes, 5250 yards, S.S.S.66
Club founded in 1906.
Visitors: welcome.
Green fees: weekdays £2 per round, weekends £3 per round.
Society meetings: welcome by advance

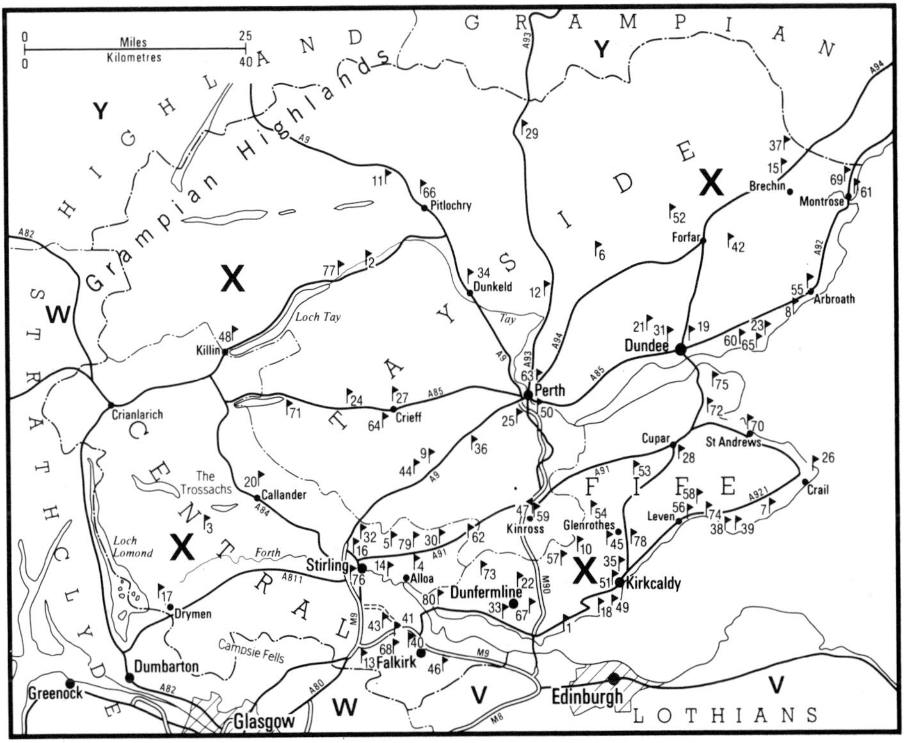

booking.
Catering: bar facilities available.
Hotels: Bowhill, Cardenden; Central, Cardenden.

X11 Blair Atholl
☎ Blair Atholl (0796) 81407
Blair Atholl, Perthshire
On A9 6 miles N of Pitlochry.
Flat parkland course.
9 holes, 2855 yards, S.S.S.69
Club founded in 1896.
Visitors: welcome.
Green fees: £4 per day, £20 per week; half-price if under 16.
Society meetings: catered for.
Catering: bar meals and snacks available.
Hotels: Tilt, Blair Atholl; Blair Castle Caravan Site; Atholl Arms, Blair Atholl.

X12 Blairgowrie
☎ Blairgowrie (0250) 2622
Rosemount, Blairgowrie, Perthshire PH10 6LG
A93 from Perth.
Moorland course.
18 holes, 6581 yards, S.S.S.72
18 holes, 6865 yards, S.S.S.73
Club founded in 1889.
Visitors: welcome on Wed and weekends.
Green fees: on application to Sec.
Society meetings: by arrangement.
Catering: meals served.
Hotels: in area.

X13 Bonnybridge
☎ Bonnybridge (0324) 812645
Larbert Rd, Bonnybridge, Stirlingshire
On B816, 3 miles W of Falkirk.
Undulating moorland course.
9 holes, 6060 yards, S.S.S.69
Club founded in 1925.
Visitors: welcome with member only.
Green fees: £1.50 weekdays, £2 weekends.
Society meetings: no.
Catering: meals served, limited in Winter.
Hotels: Norwood (adjacent to course).

X14 Braehead
☎ Alloa (0259) 722078
Cambus, by Alloa
On A907 on Stirling to Alloa road, about 1½ miles from Alloa.
18 holes, 6013 yards, S.S.S.69
Club founded on 29 May 1891.
Visitors: welcome, but advisable to telephone in advance.
Green fees: weekdays £4 per day; weekends £5 per round, £7 per day; weekly (Mon to Fri) £15.
Catering: meals served at weekends and in evening.
Hotels: Royal Oak, Alloa; Dunmar, Alloa.

X15 Brechin
☎ Brechin (035 62) 2383
Trinity, by Brechin, Angus DD9 7PD
Take B966 out of Brechin toward Aberdeen, course is 1 mile from Brechin and is clearly signposted.
Parkland/meadowland course.
18 holes, 5267 yards, S.S.S.66
Course designed by James Braid.
Club founded in 1893.
Visitors: welcome.
Green fees: weekdays £3.50 per round, £5 per day; weekends £4.50 per round, £7 per day.
Society meetings: competitions weekly.
Catering: snacks, lunches and high teas available.
Hotels: Northern, Brechin.

X16 Bridge of Allan
☎ Bridge of Allan (0786) 832332
Sunnlaw, Bridge of Allan, Stirling
3 miles N of Stirling, at bridge over River Allan turn up hill to golf course for 1 mile.
Undulating course.
9 holes, 4932 yards, S.S.S.65
Club founded in 1895.
Visitors: welcome on weekdays before 5.30 pm and on Sun.
Green fees: weekdays £3, Sun £4.
Catering: bar snacks available on weekday evenings and at weekends.
Hotels: Royal, Bridge of Allan; Old Manor, Bridge of Allan; Eagleton, Bridge of Allan.

X17 Buchanan Castle
☎ Drymen (0360) 60307
Drymen, Glasgow
Off A809, 17 miles NW of Glasgow.
Parkland course.
18 holes, 6032 yards, S.S.S.69
Course designed by James Braid.
Club founded in 1936.
Visitors: welcome with reservation.
Green fees: £10 per round, £15 per day.
Society meetings: limited days, by arrangement.
Catering: meals served by arrangement.
Hotels: Buchanan Arms, Winnock.

X18 Burntisland
☎ Burntisland (0592) 874093 Manager, 873247 Starter and Pro
Dodhead, Burntisland, Fife
On B923, ½ mile E of Burntisland.
Moorland course.
18 holes, S.S.S.68
Course redesigned by James Braid.
Club founded in 1897.
Visitors: welcome; contact Pro for starting time.
Green fees: weekdays £4 per round, £6 per day; weekends £6 per round, £9 per day.
Catering: snacks and meals served except Tues.
Hotels: many good hotels in area.

X19 Caird Park
☎ Dundee (0382) 453606
Mains Loan, Dundee, Tayside DD4 9BX
Via Kingsway to NE of town.
Parkland course.
18 holes, 6303 yards, S.S.S.70
Club founded in 1926.
Visitors: welcome.
Green fees: on application to General Manager of Parks, City of Dundee District Council, Parks Dept. 353, Clepington Rd, Dundee DD3 8PL (0382 23141 Extn 414).
Catering: by arrangement.
Hotels: many good hotels in area.

X20 Callander
☎ Callander (0877) 30090 Clubhouse, 30975 Pro
Aveland Rd, Callander, Perthshire FK17 8EN
A84 from Stirling, turn right at Roman Camp Hotel about ½ mile from Main St, car park and clubhouse signposted.
Parkland course.
18 holes, 5125 yards, S.S.S.66
Course designed by Tom Morris.
Club founded in 1890.
Visitors: welcome.
Green fees: weekdays £4.50 per round, £7 per day; weekends £5.50 per round, £8 per day.
Society meetings: welcome by arrangement with Sec, 5 Livingstone Ave, Callander, Perthshire FK17 8EP (0877 30931).
Catering: full catering and bar daily.
Hotels: Roman Camp; Dalgair House; Ancaster Arms; Dreadnought.

X21 Camperdown (Municipal)
☎ Dundee (0382) 645450
Camperdown Park, Dundee
Coupar Angus Rd at Kingsway junction.
Parkland course.
18 holes, 6561 yards, S.S.S.72
Club founded in 1960.
Visitors: welcome.
Green fees: £5 per day, Residents; £1.90

weekdays, £2.50 weekends; Season; 15p weekdays, 60p weekends.
Society meetings: no.
Catering: meals by arrangement except Tues.
Hotels: Park.

X22 Canmore

☎ Dunfermline (0383) 724969
Venturefair Ave, Dunfermline, Fife
On A823, 1 mile N of Dunfermline.
Undulating parkland course.
18 holes, 5474 yards, S.S.S.66
Club founded in 1897.
Visitors: welcome weekdays and Sat after 4 pm.
Green fees: £4 per round.
Society meetings: welcome by arrangement.
Catering: full catering.
Hotels: King Malcolm.

X23 Carnoustie

☎ Carnoustie (0241) 53249
Links Parade, Carnoustie, Angus DD7 6JE
On A630, 12 miles E of Dundee.
Seaside course.
Championship 18 holes, 6931 yards, S.S.S.74
Burnside 18 holes, 5935 yards, S.S.S.69
Buddon Links 18 holes, 6445 yards, S.S.S.71
Visitors: welcome with reservation.
Green fees: on application.
Society meetings: by arrangement.
Catering: available.
Hotels: Brax; Glencoe; Bruce; Station; Kinloch; Aran.

X24 Comrie

☎ c/o Sec, Donald G McGlashan, 10 Polinard, Comrie, Perthshire
On A85 6 miles W of Crieff.
Highland course.
9 holes, 2743 yards, S.S.S.69
Club founded in 1891.
Visitors: welcome.
Green fees: weekdays £3, weekends and Bank Holidays £4 (Juniors £1.50).
Society meetings: by arrangement with Sec.
Catering: snacks available during summer.
Hotels: Royal, Comrie; Ancaster, Comrie; Comrie.

X25 Craigie Hill

☎ Perth (0738) 22644 Sec, 24377 Clubhouse and Steward
Cherrybank, Perth PH2 0NE
About 1 mile W of Perth, easy access from Stirling to Perth road.
Hilly course.
18 holes, 5379 yards, S.S.S.66
Club founded in 1911.
Visitors: welcome.
Green fees: weekdays £3.50 per round, £5 per day; weekends £8 per day.
Society meetings: welcome except on Sat.
Catering: lunches and high teas available by arrangement with Steward.
Hotels: Lovat; City Mills; Station.

X26 Crail

☎ Crail (0333) 50278 Starter and Steward, 50686 Sec.
Balcomie Clubhouse, Fifeness, Crail KY10 3XN
2 miles E of Crail.
Links/parkland course.
18 holes, 5720 yards, S.S.S.68
Course designed by Tom Morris Sen.
Club founded in 1786.
Visitors: welcome.
Green fees: weekdays £5 per round, £7.50 per day; weekends £6.50 per round, £9.50 per day.
Society meetings: welcome.
Catering: full catering available in season.
Hotels: Marine, Crail; Golf, Crail; Craw's Nest, Anstruther.

X27 Crieff

☎ Crieff (0764) 2546 Sec, 2397 Clubhouse, 2909 Pro
Perth Rd, Crieff, Perthshire PH7 3LR
Take A85 Perth to Crieff road for 17½ miles, course is at 40 mile per hour limit entering Crieff.
Ferntower 18 holes, 6363 yards, S.S.S.70
Dornock 9 holes, 2386 yards, S.S.S.63
Club founded in 1891.
Visitors: welcome by prior arrangement with Pro.
Green fees: Ferntower – weekdays £6 per round, weekends £10, weekly £30; Dornock – weekdays £4 for 18 holes, weekends £5 for 18 holes.
Society meetings: catered for by arrangement with Pro.
Catering: meals and snacks available.
Hotels: Crieff Hydro; Murraypark, Crieff.

X28 Cupar

☎ Cupar (0334) 53549
Hilltarvit, Cupar
10 miles from St Andrews off A91
9 holes, 5300 yards, S.S.S.65
Club founded in 1855.
Visitors: welcome on weekdays.
Green fees: weekdays £3, weekends £4.
Society meetings: catered for on weekdays and Sun.
Catering: lunches and high teas by arrangement.
Hotels: many good hotels in area.

X29 Dalmunzie

☎ Glenshee (025 085) 226
Spittal o'Glensee, Blairgowrie, Perthshire PH10 7QE
On A93 Blairgowrie to Braemar road, 22 miles N of Blairgowrie, adjacent to Dalmunzie Hotel.
Undulating course.
9 holes, 2229 yards, S.S.S.64
Course designed by Alister Mackenzie in 1921.
Club founded in 1952.
Visitors: welcome.
Green fees: £2 per round, £3 per day (half-price for 10 – 14 year olds); £18 for 8 days, family ticket £36.
Society meetings: welcome by arrangement.
Catering: facilities in nearby hotels.
Hotels: Dalmunzie; Spittal; Dalmulzion; Blackwater Inn.

X30 Dollar

☎ Dollar (02594) 2400
Brewlands House, Dollar, Clackmannanshire
On A91, 13 miles E of Stirling.
Hillside course.
18 holes, 5144 yards, S.S.S.66
Club founded in 1896.
Visitors: welcome weekdays, with member only at weekends.
Green fees: weekdays £3.50 per round, £4.50 per day, £5.50 (for both) at weekends.
Society meetings: by arrangement.
Catering: meals served by arrangement.

X31 Downfield

☎ Dundee (0382) 825595
Turnberry Ave, Dundee DD2 3QP
Turn off Kingsway into A923, 100 yards from roundabout turn right into Harrison Rd, ½ mile to clubhouse.
Heathland course.
White 18 holes, 6899 yards, S.S.S.73
Yellow 18 holes, 6266 yards, S.S.S.70
Course designed by James Braid.
Club founded in 1932.
Visitors: welcome on weekdays from 9.30 to 11.48 am and from 2.18 to 3.48 pm.
Green fees: £13 per day, £8.50 per round.
Society meetings: catered for by arrangement with Committee, maximum 88 in morning and 60 for all day.
Catering: full facilities available.

Hotels: Swallow, Kingsway West, Invergowrie, Dundee; Park, 40 Coupar Angus Rd, Dundee.

X32 Dunblane New

☎ Dunblane (0786) 823711
Perth Rd, Dunblane, Perthshire FK15
On A9 6 miles N of Stirling.
Undulating parkland course.
18 holes, 5878 yards, S.S.S.68
Club founded in 1923.
Visitors: welcome on weekdays.
Green fees: £5 per round, £9 per day.
Society meetings: welcome by arrangement with Match Sec.
Catering: full catering facilities.
Hotels: Dunblane Hydro.

X33 Dunfermline

☎ Dunfermline (0383) 723534
Pitfirrane, Crossford, Dunfermline KY12 8QV
4 miles W of Dunfermline on road to Kincardine Bridge.
Parkland course.
18 holes, 6271 yards, S.S.S.70
Club founded in 1887.
Visitors: welcome by arrangement.
Green fees: £9.50 per day, £6.50 per round.
Society meetings: by arrangement.
Catering: snacks and lunches available.
Hotels: Pitfirrane Arms; Keavil House.

X34 Dunkeld & Birnam

☎ Dunkeld (035 02) 524
Fungarth, Dunkeld, Perthshire
1 mile N of Dunkeld on Blairgowrie road.
Heathland course.
9 holes, 5264 yards, S.S.S.66
Club founded in 1911.
Visitors: welcome.
Green fees: weekdays £3 per round, £4 per day; Sat £4.50, Sun £5.
Society meetings: welcome by arrangement with Club.
Catering: meals and snacks available.
Hotels: Atholl Arms; Birnam.

X35 Dunnikier Park

☎ Kirkcaldy (0592) 261599
Dunnikier Way, Kirkcaldy, Fife KY1 3LP
N boundary of town.
Parkland course.
18 holes, 6601 yards, S.S.S.72
Club founded in 1963.
Visitors: welcome.
Green fees: weekdays £2.20 per round, weekends £3.20 per round.
Society meetings: by prior arrangement with Sec.
Catering: full catering facilities available.
Hotels: Dunnikier House.

X36 Dunning

☎ Dunning (076 484) 398 (Treasurer)
Rollo Park, Dunning, Perth
Off A9, 9 miles SW of Perth.
Parkland course.
9 holes, 4836 yards, S.S.S.64
Visitors: welcome.
Green fees: £2 weekdays, £2.50 weekends.
Society meetings: by arrangement.
Catering: at Dunning Hotel.
Hotels: Dunning; Kirk Style; Thorntree.

X37 Edzell

☎ Edzell (035 64) 7283
High St, Edzell, by Brechin, Angus DD9 7TF
A94 Forfar to Aberdeen road, turn onto B966 at end of Brechin by-pass, golf course on left past arch at entrance to village.
Undulating heathland course.
18 holes, 6299 yards, S.S.S.70
Club founded in 1895.
Visitors: welcome with restrictions.
Green fees: weekdays £5.50 per round, £8 per day; weekends £9 per day or round; £25 per week.
Catering: full bar and catering facilities.
Hotels: Glenesk, Edzell; Central, Edzell; Panmure Arms, Edzell.

X38 Elie

☎ Elie (0333) 330301 Sec, 330327 Clubhouse
Golf House Club, Elie, Leven, Fife KY9 1AS
12 miles from St Andrews on A915, 6 miles from Leven on A917.
Links course.
18 holes, 6241 yards, S.S.S.70
Club founded in 1875.
Visitors: welcome except on competition days.
Green fees: weekdays £7 per round, £10 per day; weekends £8 per round, £12 per day.
Society meetings: by arrangement.
Catering: coffee, lunches and high teas served by arrangement with Steward.
Hotels: Golf, Elie; Craw's Nest, Anstruther; Old Manor, Lundin Links.

X39 Elie Sports Club

☎ Elie (0333) 330955
Elie, Fife KY9 1AG
10 miles S of St Andrews.
Seaside course.
9 holes, 5800 yards, S.S.S.66
Visitors: welcome.
Green fees: £3 per day.
Society meetings: by arrangement.
Catering: meals served.
Hotels: Golf, Elie; New Queens.

X40 Falkirk

☎ Falkirk (0324) 23457
Stirling Rd, Falkirk
1½ miles W of Falkirk town centre on A9.
Parkland course.
18 holes, 6090 yards, S.S.S.69
Club founded in 1922.
Visitors: welcome on Mon, Tues and Thurs until 2 pm and with member on Thurs, Fri and at weekends.
Green fees: £5 per round, £7 per day.
Society meetings: welcome by arrangement with Sec on Mon, Tues and Thurs.
Catering: snacks available from noon to 2 pm and meals by arrangement.
Hotels: Park, Camelon Rd, Falkirk; Hathkerley, Arnot Hill, Falkirk; Claohn, Temper Ave, Falkirk.

X41 Falkirk Tryst

☎ Larbert (032 456) 2415
86 Burnhead Rd, Larbert
4m from Falkirk, ¾m from Larbert stn.
Flat links course.
18 holes, 6053 yards, S.S.S.69
Club founded in 1885.
Visitors: welcome on weekdays.
Green fees: £4.50 per round, £6 per day (£1.25 with member).
Society meetings: catered for on weekdays except Wed.
Catering: full catering facilities.
Hotels: Plough, Stenhousemuir, Larbert.

X42 Forfar

☎ Forfar (0307) 62120
Cunninghill, Arbroath Rd, by Forfar, Angus DD8 2RL
1 mile from town on road to Arbroath.
Undulating moorland course.
18 holes, 6255 yards, S.S.S.69
Course designed by James Braid.
Club founded in 1871.
Visitors: welcome.
Green fees: weekdays £6.90, weekends £9.20.
Society meetings: welcome except Sat.
Catering: meals served.
Hotels: Royal; Benholm House.

X43 Glenbervie

☎ Larbert (0234) 562605
Stirling Rd, Larbert, Stirlingshire FK5 4SJ

On A9 between Falkirk and Stirling.
Parkland course.
18 holes, 6452 yards, S.S.S.71
Course designed by James Braid.
Club founded in 1932.
Visitors: welcome with introduction on weekdays and with member at weekends.
Green fees: £8 per round, £12 for 2 rounds.
Society meetings: catered for on Tues and Thurs.
Catering: meals and snacks served.
Hotels: Park, Falkirk.

X44 Gleneagles Hotel
☎ Auchterarder (076 46) 3543
Auchterarder, Perthshire PH3 1NF
Halfway between Perth and Stirling on A9.
Undulating moorland courses.
King's 18 holes, 6452 yards, S.S.S.71
Queen's 18 holes, 5964 yards, S.S.S.69
Glendevon 18 holes, 5719 yards, S.S.S.68
Prince's 18 holes, 4664 yards, S.S.S.64
King's and Queen's courses designed by James Braid.
Club founded in 1908.
Visitors: welcome with written application.
Green fees: on application to Golf Office.
Society meetings: welcome subject to availability of courses.
Catering: meals and snacks available.
Hotels: Gleneagles.

X45 Glenrothes
☎ (0592) 758686
Golf Course Rd, Glenrothes, Fife KY6 2LA
W end of town 8 miles from M90.
Undulating parkland course.
18 holes, 5449 yards, S.S.S.71
Course designed by J.R. Stutt.
Club founded in 1968.
Visitors: welcome by arrangement 24 hours in advance.
Green fees: weekdays £2.20 per round, weekends £3.20 per round.
Society meetings: catered for by arrangement with Sec one month in advance, minimum 15 and maximum 40.
Catering: lunches, teas and snacks served.
Hotels: Rescobbie, Leslie; Rothes Arms, Glenrothes; Albany, Glenrothes.

X46 Grangemouth Municipal
☎ Polmont (0324) 711500
Polmont, Falkirk, Stirlingshire
M9, junction 4, follow signpost at roundabout to Polmont Hill.
Parkland course.
18 holes, subject to alteration 1986.
Visitors: welcome.
Green fees: weekdays £4.50, weekends £5.50.
Society meetings: by arrangement.
Catering: meals by arrangement, 24 hours in advance.
Hotels: Inchrya Grange.

X47 Green Hotel
☎ Kinross (0577) 63467 Hotel, 62237 Club
Green Hotel, Kinross KY13 7AS
On M90 between Edinburgh and Perth.
Parkland course.
18 holes, 6339 yards, S.S.S.71
Visitors: welcome.
Green fees: weekdays £4.50 per round, £7 per day; weekends £7 per round, £11 per day.
Society meetings: by arrangement.
Catering: meals served.
Hotels: Green.

X48 Killin
☎ Killin (056 72) 312
Killin, Perthshire FK21
On outskirts of village on Aberfeldy road going E.
Parkland course.
9 holes, 2508 yards, S.S.S.65
Course designed by J. Anderson.
Club founded in 1913.
Visitors: welcome.
Green fees: weekdays £3.50, weekends £4.
Society meetings: catered for in April, May, Sept and Oct, maximum 24.
Catering: snacks available and meals by arrangement.
Hotels: Killin; Bridge of Lochay; Falls of Dochart.

X49 Kinghorn
☎ Kinghorn (0592) 890345
Macduff Cresc, Kinghorn, Fife
Off A92 3 miles W of Kirkcaldy.
Undulating links course.
18 holes, 5269 yards, S.S.S.67
Club founded in 1887.
Visitors: welcome.
Green fees: weekdays £2.20 per round, weekends £3.20.
Society meetings: by arrangement.
Catering: by arrangement.
Hotels: Kingswood, Burntisland; Kinghorn, Kinghorn; Cuinzie Neuk, Kinghorn.

X50 King James VI
☎ Perth (0738) 25170 and 32460
Moncreiffe Island, Perth PH2 8NR
On River Tay, in centre of city.
Inland course.
18 holes, 6037 yards, S.S.S.69
Club founded in 1858.
Visitors: welcome.
Green fees: weekdays £7.50, weekends £9.50.
Society meetings: by arrangement.
Catering: lunches served by arrangement.
Hotels: Salutation; Royal George.

X51 Kirkcaldy
☎ Kirkcaldy (0592) 260370
Balwearie Rd, Kirkcaldy, Fife KY2 5LT
On A92 at W end of town.
Parkland course.
18 holes, 6004 yards, S.S.S.70
Club founded in 1904.
Visitors: welcome on weekdays and Sun.
Green fees: weekdays £4 per round, £6 per day; weekends £5 per round, £7.50 per day.
Society meetings: welcome on weekdays and Sun.
Catering: full facilities available.
Hotels: Parkway; Abbotshall; Station.

X52 Kirriemuir
☎ Kirriemuir (0575) 72144 or 73317 Pro
23 Bank St, Kirriemuir, Angus DD8 4BE
1 mile N of town centre.
Moorland/parkland course.
18 holes, 5591 yards, S.S.S.67
Course designed by James Braid.
Club founded in 1907.
Visitors: weekdays welcome, weekends with member only.
Green fees: £6.50 per day, £20 per week.
Society meetings: welcome weekdays.
Catering: full catering facilities all week.
Hotels: Ogilvy Arms; Airlie Arms, Kirriemuir; Dykehead, Cortachy.

X53 Ladybank
☎ Ladybank (0337) 30814
Annsmuir, Ladybank, Fife KY7 7RA
6 miles W of Cupar on main Edinburgh to Dundee road.
Moorland course.
18 holes, 6617 yards, S.S.S.72
Course designed by Tom Morris.
Club founded in 1879.
Visitors: welcome except on Sat.
Green fees: weekdays £6.50 per round, £10 per day; weekends £8.50 per round, £12 per day.
Society meetings: catered for.
Catering: full facilities available.
Hotels: Fernie Castle, Letham; Bein Inn, Glenfarg.

X54 Leslie
Balsillie, Leslie, Fife
Undulating course.
9 holes, 4670 yards, S.S.S.63
Visitors: welcome.
Green fees: on request.
Society meetings: No Clubhouse.
Hotels: Rothes Oak; Station; Greenside.

X55 Letham Grange G & C C

☎ Gowanbank (0241) 89373
Letham Grange, Colliston, by Arbroath, Angus
1 mile E of Colliston village church; Colliston is 3 miles N of Arbroath on Brechin road.
Undulating parkland course.
Men 18 holes, 6290 yards, S.S.S.72
Ladies 18 holes, 5795 yards, S.S.S.72
Course designed by Donald Steel & G.K. Smith.
Club founded in 1985.
Course opens in June 1986.
Visitors: welcome.
Green fees: weekdays £6 per round, £9 per day; weekends £8 per round.
Society meetings: welcome.
Catering: lunches and evening meals served.
Hotels: Letham Grange, Colliston, by Arbroath.

X56 Leven

☎ Leven (0333) 26096
Links Rd, Leven, Fife KY8 4HS
Travel E along Promenade, turn left into Church Rd, turn right into Links Rd, clubhouse at end of road on right.
Seaside course.
18 holes, 6434 yards, S.S.S.71
Club founded in 1820.
Visitors: welcome except on Sat.
Green fees: weekdays £9 per day (with member £5.50), £5.50 per round (with member £2.75); Sun £10 per day (with member £5.50), £6.60 per round (with member £3.30).
Society meetings: by arrangement with Mr R Denholm, Clydesdale Bank Buildings, Dunin St, Leven.
Catering: full catering except Mon.
Hotels: Caledonian, Leven; Beach, Leven; Old Manor, Lundin Links.

X57 Lochgelly

☎ Lochgelly (0592) 480174
Cartmore Rd, Lochgelly, Fife
On A910 2 miles NE of Cowdenbeath.
Parkland course.
18 holes, 5768 yards, S.S.S.67
Club founded in 1911.
Visitors: welcome.
Green fees: weekdays £3.25 per round, £5.50 per day; weekends £4.50 per round, £7.50 per day.
Catering: catering facilities available.
Hotels: many good hotels in area.

X58 Lundin

☎ Lundin Links (0333) 320202
Golf Rd, Lundin Links, Fife KY8 6BA
On A915, 3 miles NE of Leven.
Seaside course.
18 holes, 5394 yards, S.S.S.71
Club founded in 1868.
Visitors: welcome, not on Sun.
Green fees: £7 per round (£2 with member), £10 per day (£3.25 with member).
Catering: Tues to Fri full facilities available.
Hotels: Old Manor; Lundin Links.

X59 Milnathort

☎ Milnathort (0577) 64069
South St, Milnathort KY13 2AW
Off M90 1½ miles N of Kinross.
Parkland course.
9 holes, 5411 yards, S.S.S.68
Club founded in 1890.
Visitors: welcome except on comp. days.
Green fees: weekdays £3, weekends £4; weekly £12 (Junior 50p).
Society meetings: welcome by prior arrangement with Hon Sec.
Catering: meals and snacks available.
Hotels: Royal, South St, Milnathort; Thistle, New Rd, Milnathort.

X60 Monifieth

☎ Monifieth (0382) 532767
c/o Sec, I.F. Baxter, 45 Ferry Rd, Monifieth DD5 4NG
6 miles N of Dundee between Broughty Ferry and Carnoustie.
Seaside courses.
Medal 18 holes, 6657 yards, S.S.S.72
Ashludie 18 holes, 5123 yards, S.S.S.66
Visitors: welcome by arrangement with Starter (0382 532767) except on Sat.
Green fees: Medal – weekdays £5 per round, £7 per day; Sun £6 per round, £8 per day; Ashludie – weekdays £3 per round, £5 per day; Sun £3.40 per round, £5 per day.
Society meetings: welcome by arrangement with Sec usually on weekdays.
Catering: catering facilities except Tues at one of four clubs.
Hotels: Palmure, Monifieth; Woodlands, Barnhill.

X61 Montrose Links Trust

☎ Montrose (0674) 72634
Starters Box, East Links, Trail Drive, Montrose, Angus DD10 8SW
Off A92 Dundee to Aberdeen road, 1 mile from town centre.
Seaside courses.
Medal 18 holes, 6451 yards, S.S.S.71
Broomfield 18 holes, 4815 yards, S.S.S.63
Club founded in 1810.
Visitors: welcome but advisable to book at weekends.
Green fees: Medal – weekdays £7 per day, £5 per round; weekends £7.50 per day, £5.50 per round; Broomfield – weekdays £4 per day, £3.25 per round, weekends £4.75 per day, £3.75 per round (Juniors half-price).
Society meetings: welcome by arrangement.
Catering: full catering and bar service at one of four clubs daily.
Hotels: Park, John St, Montrose; Links, Mid Links, Montrose; Corner House, High St, Montrose.

X62 Muckhart

☎ Muckhart (025 981) 423
Drumburn Rd, Muckhart, Dollar, Clackmannanshire FK14 7JH
Lies between A91 and A823 S of Muckhart, signposted off above roads.
Undulating moorland course.
18 holes, 6115 yards, S.S.S.70
Club founded in 1908.
Visitors: welcome on weekdays and with limitations at weekends, contact Pro (025 981 493).
Green fees: weekdays £3.50 per round, £5 per day; Sat £5 per round, £7 per day; Sun £7 per round.
Society meetings: catered for by arrangement with Clubmaster.
Catering: full catering facilities except Wed when only sandwiches available.
Hotels: Gartwhinzean, Powmill.

X63 Murrayshall

☎ Scone (0738) 52784
Murrayshall, by Scone, Perthshire PH2 7PH
A94 from Perth turning right before New Scone.
Undulating parkland course.
18 holes, 6416 yards, S.S.S.71
Course designed by J. Hamilton Stutt.
Club founded in 1981.
Visitors: welcome.
Green fees: weekdays £7 per round, £10 per day; weekends £8 per round, £15 per day.
Society meetings: welcome.
Catering: meals and snacks served.
Hotels: Murrayshall House, by Scone; Balcraig, by Scone.

X64 Muthill

☎ Crieff (0764) 3319 Sec
Peat Rd, Muthill, Crieff PH5 2AL
500 yards off Stirling to Crieff road A822, signposted at foot of road.
Parkland course.
9 holes, 2371 yards, S.S.S.63
Club founded in 1934.
Visitors: welcome except during club competitions.
Green fees: weekdays £2.50 per day, weekends £3 per day.
Society meetings: limited by

arrangement with Sec, W.H. Gordon, 62, Broich Tce, Crieff PH7 3BE
Catering: no catering at clubhouse.
Hotels: Drummond Arms, Willoughby St, Muthill.

X65 Panmure
☎ (0241) 53120
Barry, Angus DD7 7RT
Off A930, 2 miles W of Carnoustie.
Seaside course.
18 holes, 6301 yards, S.S.S.70
Club founded in 1845.
Visitors: welcome except Sat.
Green fees: weekdays £6 per round, £9 per day; weekends £7 per round, £10 per day.
Society meetings: by arrangement.
Catering: snacks served; meals except Mon.
Hotels: Bruce.

X66 Pitlochry
☎ Pitlochry (0796) 2792 Pro and Starter
Golf Course Rd, Pitlochry
A9 to Pilochry, then via Atholl Rd, Larchwood Rd, and Golf Course Rd.
Hill course.
18 holes, 5811 yards, S.S.S.68
Course designed by Willie Fernie of Troon and modernised by Major Cecil Hutchinson.
Club founded in 1908.
Visitors: welcome.
Green fees: weekdays £7 per day, weekends £9 per day.
Society meetings: welcome by arrangement with Estate Office (0796 2114).
Catering: meals and snacks served – breakfast and dinner by arrangement with Steward (0796 2334).
Hotels: many good hotels in area.

X67 Pitreavie (Dunfermline)
☎ Dunfermline (0383) 722591
Queensferry Rd, Dunfermline, Fife KY11 5PR
From A90(M) turn off for Dunfermline to join A823, course halfway between Rosyth and Dunfermline on E side of dual carriageway.
Undulating parkland course.
18 holes, 6086 yards, S.S.S.69
Club founded in 1922.
Visitors: welcome on weekdays.
Green fees: weekdays £4.50 per round, £6.50 per day; weekends £10 per day.
Society meetings: catered for by arrangement with Sec.
Catering: lunches and snacks served; meals available by advance booking.
Hotels: King Malcolm, Queensferry Rd, Dunfermline; Pitbauchlie, Aberdour Rd, Dunfermline.

X68 Polmont
☎ Polmont (0324) 711277
Manuelrigg, Maddiston, by Falkirk
4 miles S of Falkirk, first right after Central Region Fire Brigade HQ.
Undulating parkland course.
9 holes, 3044 yards, S.S.S.69
Club founded in 1904.
Visitors: welcome except on Sat morning.
Green fees: weekdays £2 per round (£1 with member), Sat £2.50 per round (£1 with member), Sun £3 per round (£1 with member).
Society meetings: catered for.
Catering: full catering facilities available on application to Sec or Bar Stewardess.
Hotels: Inchyra Grange, Polmont.

X69 Royal Albert
☎ Montrose (0674) 72376
Dorward Rd, Montrose, Angus
Seaside courses.
18 holes, 4863 yards, S.S.S.66
18 holes, 6442 yards, S.S.S.71
Visitors: welcome.
Green fees: on request.
Catering: lunches served.
Hotels: Park; Corner House.

X70(A) St Andrews Balgrove Course
☎ St Andrews (0334) 75757
St Andrews, Fife KY16 9JA
A91 to St Andrews.
Seaside course.
9 holes,
Club founded in 1974.
Visitors: welcome.
Green fees: £1.50 per round of 18 holes.
Society meetings: welcome in Links Room.
Catering: full facilities available.
Hotels: in St Andrews.

X70(B) St Andrews Eden Course
☎ St Andrews (0334) 75757
Golf Place, St Andrews, Fife KY16 9JA
A91 to St Andrews.
Seaside course.
18 holes, 5971 yards, S.S.S.69
Visitors: welcome.
Green fees: £6 per round.
Society meetings: welcome in Links Room.
Catering: full facilities available.
Hotels: in St Andrews.

X70(C) St Andrews Jubilee Course
☎ St Andrews (0334) 75757
St Andrews, Fife KY16 9JA
A91 to St Andrews.
Seaside course.
18 holes, 6284 yards, S.S.S.70
Visitors: welcome.
Green fees: £4 per round.
Society meetings: welcome in Links Room.
Catering: full facilities available.
Hotels: in St Andrews.

X70(D) St Andrews New Course
☎ St Andrews (0334) 75757
St Andrews, Fife KY16 9JA
A91 to St Andrews.
Seaside course.
18 holes, 6604 yards, S.S.S.72
Visitors: welcome.
Green fees: £7 per round.
Society meetings: welcome in Links Room.
Catering: full facilities available.
Hotels: in St Andrews.

X70(E) St Andrews Old Course
☎ St Andrews (0334) 75757
St Andrews, Fife KY16 9JA
A91 to St Andrews.
Seaside course.
18 holes, 6566 yards, S.S.S.72
Visitors: welcome (except Sun) only with letter of introduction or handicap certificate.
Green fees: £16.50 per round.
Society meetings: welcome in Links Room.
Catering: full facilities available.
Hotels: in St Andrews.

X71 St Fillans
☎ St Fillans (076 485) 312
St Fillans, Perthshire PH6 2NF
On A85 between Crieff and Lochearnhead, at E end of Loch Earn.
Parkland course.
9 holes, 2634 yards, S.S.S.66
Club founded in 1903.
Visitors: welcome.
Green fees: weekdays £3, weekends and Bank Holidays £4, weekly £15.
Society meetings: catered for on weekdays and at weekends during off peak periods.
Catering: snacks available.
Hotels: Achray House, St Fillans; Drummond Arms, St Fillans; Four Seasons, St Fillans.

X72 St Michaels
☎ Leuchars (033 483) 365
Leuchars, St Andrews, Fife
On A919 6 miles from St Andrews and Dundee at W end of Leuchars village turn

over rail bridge about 200 yards out of village.
Undulating meadowland course.
9 holes, 5510 yards, S.S.S.67
Club founded in 1903.
Visitors: welcome except on Sun mornings.
Green fees: weekdays £3 per round, £4.50 per day; weekends £3.50 per day; half-price for Juniors.
Society meetings: welcome by prior arrangement; for weekdays telephone Steward at Leuchars (033 483) 365, for weekends telephone Sec at Balmullo (0334) 870421 (evenings).
Catering: snacks always available and meals by arrangement with Steward.
Hotels: numerous good hotels in area.

X73 Saline
☎ Saline (0383) 852591
Kinneddar Hill, Saline, Fife KY12 9UN
4½ miles NW of Dunfermline, signposted off A907 Dunfermline to Stirling road.
Undulating course.
9 holes, 5302 yards, S.S.S.66
Club founded in 1912.
Visitors: welcome except Sat.
Green fees: £2 per day, Sun £3.
Society meetings: catered for by arrangement.
Catering: snacks available; catering by prior arrangement.
Hotels: Saline, Saline; Pitfirrane, Crossford.

X74 Scoonie
North Links, Leven, Fife
10 miles SW of St Andrews
Parkland course.
18 holes, 4931 metres, S.S.S.66
Club founded in 1951.
Visitors: welcome.
Green fees: weekdays £2.20, weekends £3.30.
Society meetings: welcome at weekends, minimum 15 and max. 30.
Catering: snacks available.
Hotels: Caledonian.

X75 Scotscraig
☎ Tayport (0382) 552515
Golf Rd, Tayport, Fife DD6 9DZ
On B946 3 miles from S end of Tay Road Bridge, turn left 3rd street past petrol station.
Links/seaside course.
18 holes, 6486 yards, S.S.S.71
Club founded in 1817.
Visitors: welcome on weekdays and by arrangement at weekends.
Green fees: weekdays £6 per round, £9 per day; weekends £7.50 per round, £10 per day.
Society meetings: welcome by arrangement.
Catering: meals served except Tues.
Hotels: Seymour, Newport on Tay; Pinewoods, St Michaels.

X76 Stirling
☎ Stirling (0786) 64098 Sec to book in advance, 71490 Pro to book on day.
Queens Rd, Stirling FK8 2QY
½ mile W of town centre on A811 on left hand side.
Parkland course.
18 holes, 5976 yards, S.S.S.69
Club founded in 1869.
Visitors: welcome on weekdays and Sun.
Green fees: weekdays £6 per round, £9 per day; weekends £11 per day.
Catering: lunches and high teas available by arrangement.
Hotels: Garfield; Kingsgate; Golden Lion; Station.

X77 Taymouth Castle
☎ Kenmore (088 73) 228
Kenmore, by Aberfeldy, Tayside PH15 2NT
6 miles W of Aberfeldy, large sign by castle gates on right of road.
Fairly flat parkland course.
18 holes, 6066 yards, S.S.S.69
Course designed by James Braid.
Club founded in 1923.
Visitors: welcome.
Green fees: weekdays £7 per round, £10 per day; weekends £9 per round, £13 per day.
Society meetings: welcome by arrangement.
Catering: full facilities available.
Hotels: Kenmore.

X78 Thornton
☎ Glenrothes (0592) 771111
Station Rd, Thornton, Fife KY1 4DW
1 mile E of A92 through Thornton.
Parkland course.
18 holes, 6177 yards, S.S.S.69
Club founded in 1921.
Visitors: welcome.
Green fees: weekdays £6 per day, £4 per round; weekends £9 per day, £6 per round.
Society meetings: catered for.
Catering: lunches, snacks and high teas
Hotels: Crown, Thornton; Albany, Glenrothes.

X79 Tillicoultry
☎ Tillicoultry (0259) 50741
Alva Rd, Tillicoultry
9 miles E of Stirling on A91.
Undulating meadowland course.
9 holes, 5266 yards, S.S.S.66
Club founded in 1899.
Visitors: welcome except on comp. days.
Green fees: weekdays £2.50 per day, weekends £5 per day.
Society meetings: welcome by arrangement with Sec.
Catering: catering facilities by prior arrangement.
Hotels: Royal Arms; Castle Craig; Crown; all in High St, Tillicoultry.

X80 Tulliallan
☎ Alloa (0259) 30396
Alloa Rd, Kincardine on Forth, by Alloa
1½ miles N of Kincardine Bridge on Alloa road, next to Police College.
Parkland course.
18 holes, 5982 yards, S.S.S.69
Club founded in 1902.
Visitors: welcome by arrangement with Pro.
Green fees: weekdays £5 per round, £7.50 per day; weekends £6 per round, £10 per day.
Society meetings: welcome by prior arrangement except on Sat; weekdays maximum 40, Sun maximum 30.
Catering: meals and snacks served.
Hotels: Powfoulis Manor, Airk; Grange Manor, Grangemouth.

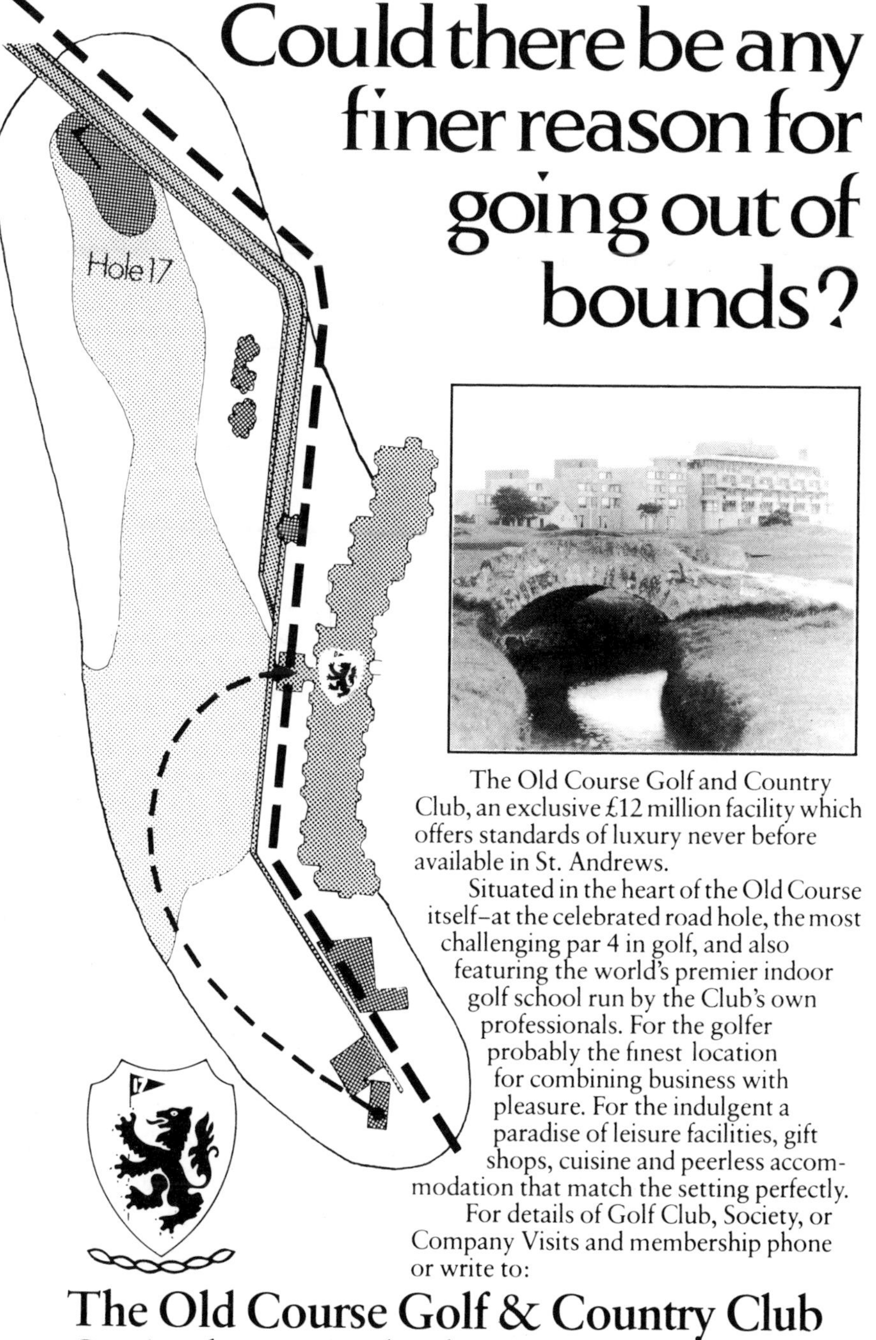
Could there be any finer reason for going out of bounds?
Hole 17
The Old Course Golf and Country Club, an exclusive £12 million facility which offers standards of luxury never before available in St. Andrews.
Situated in the heart of the Old Course itself–at the celebrated road hole, the most challenging par 4 in golf, and also featuring the world's premier indoor golf school run by the Club's own professionals. For the golfer probably the finest location for combining business with pleasure. For the indulgent a paradise of leisure facilities, gift shops, cuisine and peerless accommodation that match the setting perfectly.
For details of Golf Club, Society, or Company Visits and membership phone or write to:
The Old Course Golf & Country Club
St. Andrews. Telephone (0334) 74371.

Y Highlands, Grampian

The availability of golf courses has, for some time now, been one of the most important factors in deciding where to take a holiday. All over the Continent, particularly in Spain and Portugal, the number of courses has increased spectacularly – more often than not as the centre of elaborate development projects embracing villas, apartments and hotels.

These are designed to attract the tourist arriving by the Jumbo package load and there is no doubt such holidays are extremely popular but there is equally no doubt that there is nothing to beat golf in Britain for quality, variety or cheapness.

Nowhere in Britain have new roads opened up previously inaccessible parts more dramatically than in the north of Scotland. You can now drive from Edinburgh to Inverness almost exclusively on motorway and dual carriageway and the improvements don't stop there. New bridges across the Firths have brought Royal Dornoch ever nearer, a factor that undoubtedly led to its selection for the 1985 Amateur championship.

It is the jewel of the north although it was recognised years ago as a favourite holiday haunt of Roger and Joyce Wethered and Sir Ernest Holderness, another British champion. In the days before you could fly to Aberdeen or Inverness, or put your car on the train to Perth, this was the greatest possible compliment it could be paid and one which really put it on the golfing map.

Dornoch has become an important port of call for connoisseurs from all over the world and, not surprisingly, some of the region's other courses suffer a little by comparison; but Golspie and Brora, further north still, should not be missed. Green fee figures are incredibly reasonable and, in the long summer evenings, it is light enough to be playing until approaching midnight.

As the golfing crow flies, Nairn is no great distance although the journey south by road is by way of Inverness and Culloden Moor: Nairn, where David Blair played much of his golf, lies on the Moray Firth and is another ideal centre with several good hotels, notably the aptly named Golf View.

Nairn has been used for a number of Scottish championships and has its first few holes along the water's edge but a little further inland lies Boat of Garten, and further along the coast right round to Aberdeen can be found a succession of appealing places to play. On the road south from Inverness, Newtonmore and Kingussie are particularly recommended.

The nearest to matching Nairn on the coastal stretch is Lossiemouth which I first remember seeing as a town from a windswept hockey pitch at Gordonstoun School; while a few miles to the east can be found a sporting course at Spey Bay, the pleasantest memory I have of a week in an Army camp at Fochabers.

Rounding Kinnaird's Head, we come to Cruden Bay, a few miles from Old Meldrum, the birthplace of George Duncan; and finally to the delights of Aberdeen with Balgownie or Royal Aberdeen the pick. However, there is another easy drive along the banks of the Dee to Banchory, Aboyne, Ballater and Braemar.

Y1 Abernethy
☎ Nethybridge (047 982) 311 Sec
Nethybridge, Inverness-shire
On B970 Grantown on Spey to Coylum Bridge road, ¼ mile N of Nethybridge.
Undulating course.
9 holes, 2484 yards, S.S.S.66
Club founded in 1895.
Visitors: welcome.
Green fees: £3.50 per day, £17 per week, £35 per season.
Catering: meals served.
Hotels: Nethybridge; Mountview.

Y2 Aboyne
☎ Aboyne (0339) 2328
Formaston Park, Aboyne, Aberdeenshire AB3 5HD
Travelling W on A93 from Aberdeen, take first turning on right after entering village, signposted on A93.
Undulating parkland course.
18 holes, 5330 yards, S.S.S.66
Club founded in 1883.
Visitors: welcome.
Green fees: weekdays £5, weekends £8.
Society meetings: welcome except Sun.
Catering: full catering service available from April to Oct.
Hotels: Huntly Arms; Balnacoil House; Birse Lodge.

Y3 Alness
☎ Alness (0349) 883877
Royal Bank, Alness, Ross-shire
on A9 10 miles N of Dingwall.
9 holes, 4718 yards, S.S.S.63
Club founded in 1904.
Visitors: welcome.
Green fees: weekdays £2.50, weekends £4.
Hotels: Station, Alness; Novar Arms, Evanton.

Y4 Askernish
Askernish, South Uist, Western Isles
5 miles NW of Lochboisdale, ferry terminal from Oban.
Seaside course.
9 holes, 5312 yards, S.S.S.67
Course designed by Tom Morris.
Club founded in 1891.
Visitors: welcome.
Green fees: £2 per day, £10 per week.
Society meetings: welcome.
Catering: none.
Hotels: Borrodale, Daliburgh; Lochboisdale, Lochboisdale.

Y5 Auchenblae
☎ Auchenblae (05612) 407 Sec
Auchenblae, Laurencekirk, Kincardineshire
2 miles off A94 at Fardom.
Parkland course.
9 holes, 4158 yards, S.S.S.30
Visitors: welcome.
Green fees: £2 per day, £3 on Sun.
Catering: pubs in village – no catering on course.
Hotels: Drumtochty Arms.

Y6 Auchmill
☎ Aberdeen (0224) 714577
Auchmill, Aberdeen
5 miles N of Aberdeen
9 holes, S.S.S.35
Visitors: municipal course, all welcome.
Green fees: £1.20 per round (35p for juniors during week).
Hotels: in Aberdeen.

Y7 Ballater
☎ Ballater (0338) 55200/55567
Ballater, Aberdeenshire AB3 5QX
A93 on Deeside, 40 miles W of Aberdeen.
Flat, inland course.
18 holes, 6106 yards, S.S.S.69
Club founded in 1893.
Visitors: welcome.
Green fees: £5.50 per day weekdays, weekends £7 per day.
Society meetings: by arrangement.

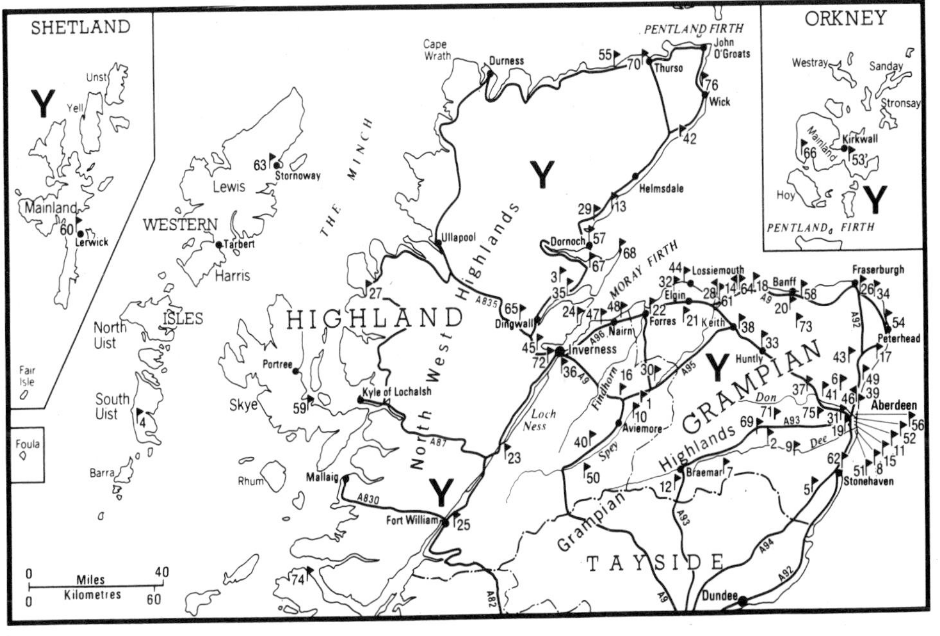

Brora

An integral part of the pleasures of golf at Brora is the drive to get there. From north or south, the road follows Sutherland's spectacular coastline overlooked by the brooding, heather-clad hills which echo to the call of rare birds. Dornoch is journey's end for most golfers to such distant parts but Golspie and Brora are only a few miles further on and both are authentic delights.

Brora is a seaside course without the dunes although few links get closer to the beach and the sea itself is always visible. There is a degree or two of latitude from the tee but there is urgent need for sound positional play in order to obtain the correct angle for the second shots and there is a definite spring in the turf.

As you might expect from the designing hand of James Braid, the greens are imaginatively shaped and contoured without being large targets and they complement the overall length which, with only one par five to bolster it, is still over 6,100 yards. With a wind from the north such as blew on the day that I stole away from Dornoch's first Amateur in 1985, it seemed altogether longer, many of the holes on the front nine being particularly demanding.

The 3rd and 5th, "Canal" and "Burn", 447 and 428 yards, left more than enough to do. The attractive 3rd green is guarded by bunkers left and right and the 5th possesses entirely natural defences. An inch the wrong side of a diagonally running sandy ridge on the green's approach and you are down the bank from where a daring chip is the only hope of rescuing par.

Brora is well in keeping with many of Britain's links which have the clubhouse at one end and the 9th green at the other but the 6th, turning at right angles inland, provides a welcome touch of variety as well as being an absolutely first class short hole. The options from the tee are to carry the bunkers on the left set into the slope or bring in a shot from the right.

Brora's one par 5 is the 8th which favours an approach down the left to a green lying adjacent to the beach although not quite as alarmingly close as at the short 9th. Here, the local rule reminding you to treat the beach as a lateral water hazard is specially relevant. Boulders are, in fact, the main hazard but there is an unusual local rule which urges players "to treat cow droppings as casual water".

Local residents have certain grazing rights making necessary the presence of small electric fences round the greens but neither animals nor fences struck me as any inconvenience or did anything to lessen the enjoyment.

My reservation as we turned for home was that the back nine, on the inland side, might suffer by comparison. Not so. The 10th, with its tee beside the railway line which sees only a handful of trains a week, immediately dispelled any doubt. It and the 11th, with its rippling apron to the green, are fine 4s and there follows another good two-shot hole along a gentle valley to a green backed by gorse.

The gorse is a hint of what to expect at the 13th, a short, short hole (125 yards) across a gentle stream, only a truly hit shot holding anywhere near the flat when it is situated at the front of the green. It is a reminder that a lack of length is no lack of quality and the same applies to a shortish par four like the 15th where the drive has to scale quite a slope to get a sight of the green.

The second shots at the 15th and 16th call for more judgement and precision but the 17th is the hole which will probably leave the most indelible memory. The prospect from the tee against a background of sea is superb and there is every inclination, and need, to flex your muscles on a drive to a fairway below. Another small, cleverly shaped green is no easy target and don't be fooled by ending with a short hole. It is another satisfying shot to try and master, invariably a long iron or wood.

In high summer, golf at Brora can also be a game for insomniacs as evening becomes twilight and twilight mingles with the dawn. The club has long been famous for its midnight competition in June but, whether you play four rounds a day or just one, Brora is emphatically worth the journey.

Catering: meals served.
Hotels: Westbank; Craigendarroch; Craigard; Glen Lui; Deeside.

Y8 Banchory

☎ Banchory (03302) 2365
Kinneskie, Banchory, Kincardineshire AB3 3TA
18m W of Aberdeenshire, on N Deeside Rd.
Parkland course.
18 holes, 5271 yards, S.S.S.66
Club founded in 1905.
Visitors: welcome.
Green fees: weekdays £6 per day, weekends £8 per day.
Society meetings: welcome by arrangement.
Catering: meals served.
Hotels: Tornacoil; Burnett Arms; Banchory Lodge.

Y9 Belnagask

☎ Aberdeen (0224) 76407
St Fittick's Rd, Aberdeen
2 miles SE of city centre.
Undulating seaside courses.
9 holes,
18 holes, S.S.S.69
Course designed by Hawtree & Son.
Visitors: welcome.
Green fees: £2.40 18 holes, £1.20 9 holes; Juniors £1.20 18 holes, 65p 9 holes.
Hotels: in Aberdeen.

Y10 Boat of Garten

☎ Boat of Garten (047 983) 282 Golf Shop, 351 Clubhouse
Boat of Garten, Inverness-shire PH24 3BQ
5 miles N of Aviemore on old A9 road, turn right onto B970.
Undulating parkland course.
18 holes, 5690 yards, S.S.S.68
Course designed by James Braid.
Club founded in 1898.
Visitors: welcome.
Green fees: weekdays £5, weekends £6; weekly £25, fortnightly £40.
Society meetings: catered for.
Catering: catering facilities from 10 am to 6 pm; bar facilities from 11 am to 11 pm.
Hotels: Craigard; Moorfield House; Boat.

Y11 Bon-Accord

☎ Aberdeen (0224) 633464
19 Golf Rd, Aberdeen AB2 1QB
Beside Pittodrie Stadium at beach.
Seaside course.
18 holes, 6384 yards, S.S.S.70

Boat of Garten

There is a wonderfully romantic ring about some of the more remote outposts of the British golfing empire. Westward Ho!, Machrihanish, Castletown and Lamlash, but most romantically named of all is Boat of Garten, named after the old ferry which used to carry passengers from the area around Loch Garten across the Spey.

In more recent times, publicity has centred more upon noble local efforts to save the osprey and it is against a background that varies from gentle greenness to rugged beauty that golfers enjoy a course that is almost as rare. The mountain heart of Scotland on the journey north from Pitlochry is one of the few parts of Britain where thoughts of golf are faraway and it is not until the road drops down from Drumochter into more fertile plains around Newtonmore and Kingussie that they are revived.

Even then, the relative sparseness of the population hardly matches the demand for the game that exists elsewhere, but Boat of Garten, lying about six miles east of Aviemore, has an army of admirers. It only needs the briefest introduction to understand why.

It is a joy to find a course where the emphasis is not on length. Small greens and even smaller landing areas make the par of 69 highly elusive, imposing the vital need for precise striking and clear judgement. The fairways, nicely undulating though never severely so, are none too wide and liberally fringed by a mixture of birch, heather and broom.

There has been a course of some sort at Boat of Garten for almost a hundred years but it was the handiwork of James Braid which, by extending it to eighteen holes, really put it on the map. It was always said of Braid, five times Open champion, that he drove with "divine fury". Yet that is far from the main requirement. Controlled accuracy is a rather more important quality than fury, divine or ungodly.

The 1st hole is no guide to what follows, the chief danger to an opening short hole taking the form of out of bounds on the right. The 2nd is a much truer indication of the general character and the short 3rd an example of the difficulty of negotiating a successful route to the green if the shot is not all carry; but at the 4th, where twin crests have to be cleared, the power has to be turned up a notch or two.

As the only par 5, it has distinct novelty value although its name, "Birches", could equally be applied to many other holes. If it is not apparent by now, the awareness quickly increases that the course was originally a birch wood, the 6th, "The Avenue", a clue in itself, weaving a narrow path between the trees on one of three par fours over 400 yards.

In contrast to the blind second at the 7th, the raised 8th green poses an inviting prospect from the tee, as does the 10th, 265 yards. Played simply as a four, there are no great problems, but the tiger's line really is a tiger's line.

On a clear day when the highland air sparkles, the distant views provide an extra dimension to the golf with, it is hoped, inspiring results; but the drive at the 14th has got to be nailed and it has to be straight if a long second over a sharp brow is to reach the green. Some respite is found at the next four holes, three of which, modest fours, help to explain the overall yardage of 5,690.

The 15th, something of an old-fashioned hole, and none the worse for that, derives the name "Gully" from the situation and shape of its green but the 16th is the only par three on the back nine and, to dispel any complacency, there is definite sting in the tail.

At the 18th, out of bounds lurks down the right; there is no great latitude to the

Western Isles Hotel

Tobermory, Isle of Mull, Scotland. Tel. Tobermory 2012

A welcoming and comfortable family hotel.
The hotel enjoys a superb position high above Tobermory Bay.
Our menu features local seafood and venison.
Free golf and free fishing for residents.

Hosts: Philip and Cathy Bird

The Machrie Hotel & Golf Course

MACHRIE ISLE OF ISLAY ARGYLL PA42 7AN TELEPHONE: 0496 2310

The original Machrie Golf Course, laid out by Willie Campbell in 1891 as a Championship Course, has recently been updated to conform to modern golfing requirements while remaining a stern test of any golfers ability. Hotel and Cottage Guests have the courtesy of the course during their visit.

- ★ Golf on our own 18 hole course.
- ★ Fish for brown trout on five lochs.
- ★ Ride at the local schools – novice or expert.
- ★ Wander the hill trails and paths.
- ★ Relax on uncrowded sandy beaches.
- ★ Sea angling.
- ★ Bird watching in an ornithologist's paradise.
- ★ Shooting and stalking arranged.
- ★ Visit the local distilleries.
- ★ Simply listen to the Peace.

For those who wish simply to relax or enjoy a game of bridge or backgammon, a tastefully furnished Resident's Lounge is available while separate Television Room and Billiards Room complete the extensive range of facilities available to residents at Machrie.

left and the second shot has to take account of a long incline and an even steeper slope to the green itself. A glance to the right shows the smart new bridge that replaced the old chain ferry and, beside the clubhouse, two all weather tennis courts are reminders of changing times. However, one thing that never changes is the grandeur of the setting and the infinite pleasure of the golf which is full of charm and subtle challenge.

Club founded in 1872.
Visitors: welcome.
Green fees: £3.60 per round.
Catering: meals served at weekends.
Hotels: Caledonian, Union Terrace.

Y12 Braemar
☎ Braemar (033 83) 618
Cluniebank Rd, Braemar, Aberdeenshire AB3 5YT
Signposted from village of Braemar, club lies approximately ½m from village centre.
Parkland/moorland course.
18 holes, 4562 yards, S.S.S.64
Club founded in 1904.
Visitors: welcome.
Green fees: weekdays £3 per round, £4 per day; weekends £4.50 per round, £7 per day.
Catering: full catering and bar facilities.
Hotels: Fife Arms, Braemar; Invercauld Arms, Braemar.

Y13 Brora
☎ Brora (0408) 21417
Golf Rd, Brora, Sutherland KW9 6QS
75 miles N of Inverness on A9, signpost in middle of village giving direction.
Seaside links course.
18 holes, 6110 yards, S.S.S.69
Course designed by James Braid.
Club founded in 1897.
Visitors: welcome except on tourn. days.
Green fees: £5 per round or per day, £20 per week, £30 for 2 weeks, £35 for 3 weeks, £40 per month.
Society meetings: welcome by prior arrangement.
Catering: meals served from May to Sept from 11.30 to 2.30 pm; societies by special arrangement.
Hotels: Links, Golf Rd; Royal Marine, Golf Rd; Bayview, Golf Rd; Sutherland Arms, Fountain Square; Braes, Fountain Square.

Y14 Buckpool
☎ Buckie (0542) 32236
Barhill Rd, Buckie, Banffshire AB5 1PH
Leave A98 towards Buckpool, 1 mile signposted Buckie, course at end of road.
Seaside course.
18 holes, 6275 yards, S.S.S.70
Visitors: welcome.
Green fees: weekdays £3 per day, weekends £5 per day (£3 per round after 15.30 hours); £15 per week.
Society meetings: catered for by prior arrangement.
Catering: full facilities available by prior arrangement.
Hotels: Cluny, Buckie; Commercial, Buckie; St Andrews, Buckpool.

Y15 Caledonian
☎ Aberdeen (0224) 632443
20 Golf Rd, Aberdeen
Adjacent to Pittodrie Stadium.
18 holes,
Visitors: welcome.
Green fees: on application.
Society meetings: by arrangement.
Catering: snacks available.
Hotels: in Aberdeen

Y16 Carrbridge
☎ Carrbridge (047 986) 674 Hon Sec
Carrbridge, Inverness-shire PH23 3AU
About 200 yards from village on A938.
Parkland/moorland course.
9 holes, 2625 yards, S.S.S.66
Club founded in 1980.
Visitors: welcome except during tournament (usually in Sept).
Green fees: £2.50 per day (Junior £1.50 per day), £12 per week.
Catering: none.
Hotels: Carrbridge; Struan House.

Y17 Cruden Bay
☎ Cruden Bay (0779) 812285
Aulton Rd, Cruden Bay, Peterhead AB4 7NN
23 miles N of Aberdeen on coastal route to Peterhead.
Seaside course.
9 holes, 4710 yards, S.S.S.62
18 holes, 6401 yards, S.S.S.71
Course designed by Tom Morris & Archie Simpson.
Club founded in 1899.
Visitors: welcome on weekdays, except Wed between 4.30 and 6.30 pm, and at weekends after 10.30 am, except between 12 and 2.30 pm.
Green fees: weekdays – 18 hole £6, 9 hole £3; weekends 18 hole £8, 9 hole £4.
Society meetings: welcome on weekdays.
Catering: restaurant and bar facilities.
Hotels: Kilmarnock Arms; Red House; St Olaf; all in Cruden Bay.

Y18 Cullen
☎ Cullen (0542) 40685
The Links, Cullen, Buckie, Banffshire
200 yards from A98 on W side of Cullen.
Seaside course.
18 holes, 4610 yards, S.S.S.62
Visitors: welcome.
Green fees: weekdays £3, weekends £3.50.
Society meetings: none.
Catering: lunches from May to Sept.
Hotels: Royal Oak, Cullen; Grant Arms, Cullen; Seafields Arms, Cullen.

Y19 Deeside
☎ Aberdeen (0224) 867697
Bieldside, Aberdeen
3 miles W of Aberdeen on A93 North Deeside road.
Parkland course.
18 holes, 5972 yards, S.S.S.69
Club founded in 1903.
Visitors: welcome if recognised members of golf clubs and with letter of introduction from Sec.
Green fees: weekdays £10 per day, weekends and Bank Holidays £12 per day, £40 per week.
Society meetings: welcome on Thurs only.
Catering: full facilities available.
Hotels: Cults, Cults, Aberdeen; Bieldside Inn, Bieldside, Aberdeen.

Y20 Duff House Royal
☎ Banff (026 12) 2062
Barnyards, Banff AB4 3SX
On A98 entering town from S.
Parkland course
18 holes, 6161 yards, S.S.S.69
Course designed by Dr A. Mackenzie.

Club founded in 1909.
Visitors: welcome.
Green fees: weekdays £4.50 per round, £6 per day; weekends £5.50 per round, £7 per day.
Society meetings: catered for by prior arrangement.
Catering: full catering during season.
Hotels: Banff Springs; County; Fife Arms, Macduff.

Y21 Elgin

☎ Elgin (0343) 2338 Sec, 2884 Pro
Hardhillock, Elgin, Morayshire IV30 3SX
From centre of Elgin take A941 Rothes road to S side of New Elgin, then left on to Birnie road for 1 mile to clubhouse, turning off A941 indicated at sign to golf course.
Undulating moorland/parkland course.
18 holes, 6401 yards, S.S.S.71
Club founded in 1906.
Visitors: welcome.
Green fees: weekdays £7 per day, weekends £8.50 per day; £4.50 per round.
Society meetings: by arrangement with Sec.
Catering: full catering available except Tues; parties by arrangement with Steward.
Hotels: Eight Acres, Elgin; Laich Moray, Elgin; Rothes Glen (summer only), Rothes.

Y22 Forres

☎ Forres (0309) 72949 Office, 72261 Public
Muiryshade, Forres IV36 0RD
1 mile S of clock tower in town centre, by St Leonards Rd and Edgehill Rd.
Undulating parkland course.
18 holes, 6141 yards, S.S.S.69
Course designed by James Braid.
Club founded in 1889.
Visitors: welcome except on comp. days.
Green fees: £4 per round, £5 per day.
Society meetings: catered for mainly on weekdays; parties up to 20 on certain weekends.
Catering: snacks and meals served, prior booking advisable.
Hotels: Parkmount House, St Leonards Rd; Park, Victoria Rd; Ramnee, Victoria Rd; Royal, Tytler St; Heather, Tytler St.

Y23 Fort Augustus

☎ Fort Augustus (0320) 6460
Markethill, Fort Augustus, Inverness-shire
Off A82, entrance beyond 30 mph restriction S of village.
9 holes, 5454 yards (18 holes), S.S.S.68
Course designed by Dr. Lane.
Club founded in 1925.
Visitors: welcome.
Green fees: £3 per day.
Society meetings: weekdays only.
Catering: no catering available.
Hotels: Lovat Arms; Brae.

Y24 Fortrose & Rosemarkie

☎ Fortrose (0381) 20529 or 20140
Ness Rd East, Fortrose, Ross-shire IV10 8SE
Fortrose is on Cromarty road branching off A9 out of Inverness, about 16 miles N of Inverness.
Seaside course.
18 holes, 5964 yards, S.S.S.69
Course re-designed by James Braid.
Club founded in 1888.
Visitors: welcome.
Green fees: Men £5.50 per day, Ladies £4.50 per day.
Society meetings: catered for if possible on written application.
Catering: meals available during summer months with reasonable notice.
Hotels: Marine, Rosemarkie; Royal, Fortrose.

Y25 Fort William

☎ Fort William (0397) 4464
North Rd, Torlundy, Fort William PH33 6RD
On A82 Fort William to Inverness road, 2 miles N of Fort William.
Moorland course.
18 holes.
Course designed by Hamilton Stutt.
Club founded in 1975.
Visitors: welcome.
Green fees: £4 per day (Juniors £2).
Catering: snacks from May to Sept.
Hotels: Milton; Motor Inn.

Y26 Fraserburgh

☎ Fraserburgh (0346) 28287
Philarth, Fraserburgh AB4 5TL
1 mile E of Fraserburgh, on A92 Aberdeen to Fraserburgh road, turn off right on road to Cairnbulg.
Undulating seaside course.
18 holes, 6217 yards, S.S.S.70
Course designed by James Braid.
Club founded in 1881.
Visitors: welcome.
Green fees: weekdays £4.30 per round or day, weekends £5.40 per round or day.
Society meetings: welcome by arrangement.
Catering: lunches available and dinners by arrangement.
Hotels: Royal, Broad St, Fraserburgh; Alexandra, High St, Fraserburgh; Station, Seaforth St, Fraserburgh.

Y27 Gairloch

☎ Gairloch (0445) 2407
Gairloch, Ross-shire IV21 2BE
On A832, 72 miles NW of Inverness.
Seaside course.
9 holes, 4186 yards, S.S.S.63
Visitors: welcome on weekdays.
Green fees: £2.50 per day, £10 per week.
Society meetings: none.
Catering: none.
Hotels: Gairloch, Gairloch; Creag Mor, Gairloch.

Y28 Garmouth & Kingston

☎ Spey Bay (034 387) 388
Garmouth, Fochabers, Moray IV32 7LU
Off A96 8 miles E of Elgin.
Seaside course.
18 holes, 5649 yards, S.S.S.67
Club founded in 1929.
Visitors: welcome.
Green fees: weekdays £3, weekends £4; weekly £16.
Society meetings: catered for.
Catering: by arrangement.
Hotels: Gordon Arms, Fochabers.

Y29 Golspie

☎ Golspie (040 83) 3266
Ferry Rd, Golspie, Sutherland
First right in Golspie off A9 from Inverness.
Seaside course.
18 holes, 5763 yards, S.S.S.68
Club founded in 1889.
Visitors: welcome.
Green fees: £5 per day, £25 per week, £35 per fortnight.
Society meetings: welcome subject to tee reservations for competitions and tournaments.
Catering: lunches served except Thurs; evening meals served from 5 to 7 pm except Thurs and Sun.
Hotels: Golf Links; Ben Bhraggie; Sutherland Arms.

Y30 Grantown-on-Spey

☎ Grantown-on-Spey (0479) 2079
Golf Course Rd, Grantown-on-Spey
Leave A9 at Aviemore, take A939 to Grantown, situated at end of town.
Moorland/parkland course.
18 holes, 5700 yards, S.S.S.67
Course designed by Willie Park.
Club founded in 1890.
Visitors: welcome.
Green fees: £5.50 per day.
Society meetings: catered for.
Catering: full catering available.
Hotels: Seafield Lodge; Strathspey; Ben Mhor.

Y31 Hazlehead
☎ Aberdeen (0224) 317336 Pro
Hazlehead Park, Aberdeen
4 miles NW of city centre.
Moorland courses.
18 holes, 6045 yards, S.S.S.68
18 holes, 6205 yards, S.S.S.70
Visitors: municipal course, all welcome.
Green fees: £1.85 (9 holes), £3.60 (18 holes).
Hotels: in Aberdeen.

Y32 Hopeman
☎ (0343) 830444
Hopeman, Moray IV30 2SS
8 miles N of Elgin.
Seaside course.
18 holes, 5439 yards, S.S.S.66
Visitors: welcome.
Green fees: weekdays £3, weekends £4, Juniors half fee.
Catering: bar snacks available, restricted Oct – March.
Hotels: Station; Neuk.

Y33 Huntly
☎ Huntly (0466) 2643
Cooper Park, Huntly, Aberdeenshire
On A96 ½ mile from town centre.
Parkland course.
18 holes, 5399 yards, S.S.S.66
Club founded in 1900.
Visitors: welcome except on Thurs and Wed.
Green fees: weekdays £4 per day, weekends £5 per day, weekly £20.
Society meetings: by arrangement with Sec.
Catering: facilities by arrangement.
Hotels: Castle, Huntly; Huntly, The Square; Gordon Arms, The Square.

Y34 Inverallochy
☎ Inverallochy (034 65) 2324
Inverallochy, Fraserburgh
3 miles S of Fraserburgh on B9033.
Seaside links course.
18 holes, 5137 yards, S.S.S.65
Visitors: welcome.
Green fees: £3 per day.
Society meetings: catered for by arrangement with limited facilities.
Catering: snacks served.

Y35 Invergordon
☎ Invergordon (0349) 852116
Cromlet Dr, Invergordon, Ross-shire IV18 0EU
Off High St, Invergordon.
Parkland course.
9 holes, 3014 yards, S.S.S.69
Course designed by Fraser Middleton.
Club founded in 1955.
Visitors: welcome.
Green fees: weekdays £2.50 per day, weekends £3 per day.
Society meetings: by arrangement.
Catering: snacks served.
Hotels: Marine; Viewfirth.

Y36 Inverness
☎ Inverness (0463) 239882 Sec, 231989 Pro
Culcabock Rd, Inverness IV2 3XQ
1 mile from town centre on S side of River Ness.
Parkland course.
18 holes, 6226 yards, S.S.S.70
Club founded 13 Nov 1883.
Visitors: welcome.
Green fees: weekdays £6, weekends and Bank Holidays £8; weekly £20, fortnightly £30.
Society meetings: welcome weekdays.
Catering: lunch and evening meals.
Hotels: Kingsmills, Culcabock Rd, Inverness; Craigmonie, Annfield Rd, Inverness.

Y37 Inverurie
☎ Inverurie (0467) 24080
Blackhall Rd, Inverurie, Aberdeenshire
On A96 Aberdeen to Inverness road.
Parkland/wooded course.
18 holes, 5703 yards, S.S.S.68
Course designed by George Smith, Lossiemouth.
Club founded in 1923.
Visitors: welcome; advisable to book (0467 20193).
Green fees: weekdays £4 per day, weekends £6 per day.
Society meetings: welcome by arrangement.
Catering: none.
Hotels: Kintore Arms, Inverurie; Gordon Arms, Inverurie; Thainstone House, Inverurie.

Y38 Keith
☎ Keith (054 22) 2469 (2831 Sec)
Fife-Keith, Keith, Banffshire
½ mile off A96 on Dufftown Rd.
Undulating parkland course.
18 holes, S.S.S.68
Club founded in 1965.
Visitors: welcome.
Green fees: weekdays £3, weekends £4 subject to review.
Society meetings: by arrangement.
Catering: by arrangement.
Hotels: Gordon Arms.

Y39 Kings Links
☎ Aberdeen (0224) 632269
Kings Links, Aberdeen
E of city centre.
Seaside course.
Visitors: municipal course, all welcome.
Green fees: £2.40 per round (Juniors £1.20).
Hotels: in Aberdeen.

Y40 Kingussie
☎ Kingussie (054 02) 3741 Clubhouse, 600 Sec
Gynack Rd, Kingussie, Inverness-shire PH21 1LR
Leave A9 at N end of village, drive into village, turn right at Duke of Gordon Hotel and continue to end of road.
Hill course.
18 holes, 5456 yards, S.S.S.67
Course designed by Harry Vardon.
Visitors: welcome.
Green fees: weekdays £4 per round, £5 per day; weekends £5 per round, £6 per day; Juniors £2.50.
Society meetings: welcome by arrangement.
Catering: catering for parties by arrangement.
Hotels: many good hotels in area.

Y41 Kintore
0467 32252
Kintore, Inverurie, Aberdeenshire
Off A96, 12 miles N of Aberdeen.
Parkland course.
9 holes, 5240 yards, S.S.S.66
Visitors: welcome.
Green fees: on application.
Society meetings: welcome weekdays.
Catering: meals served.
Hotels: Kintore Arms; Crown; Torryburn.

Y42 Lybster
Main St. Lybster, Caithness KW1 6BL
13 miles S of Wick on A9, turn down village main street, golf course entrance opposite football pitch.
Moorland course.
9 holes, 1838 yards, S.S.S.62
Club founded in 1926.
Visitors: welcome.
Green fees: £1.50 per day, £6 per week; (Children 50p per day).
Society meetings: welcome except Sat evening.
Catering: none.
Hotels: Portland Arms; Bayview; Commercial.

Y43 **McDonald**
☎ Ellon (0358) 20576
Hospital Rd, Ellon, Aberdeenshire AB4 9AW
Leave Ellon by A948 Auchnagatt road and take first turning on left.
Parkland course.
18 holes, 5986 yards, S.S.S.69
Club founded in 1927.
Visitors: welcome.
Green fees: Mon to Sat £4.50 per day, Sun £7 per day.
Society meetings: welcome.
Catering: full catering facilities daily.
Hotels: Buchan, Bridge St, Ellon; New Inn, Market St, Ellon.

Y44 **Moray**
☎ Lossiemouth (034 381) 2018
Stotfield Rd, Lossiemouth, Moray IV31 6QS
From Elgin on A96 Aberdeen to Inverness road, travel on A941 Elgin to Lossiemouth road.
Links courses.
New 18 holes, 6258 yards, S.S.S.71
Old 18 holes, 6643 yards, S.S.S.72
Club founded in 1887.
Visitors: welcome, report to Pro.
Green fees: Old course – weekdays £6 per day, weekends £8 per day; New course – £4 per day.
Catering: by arrangement.
Hotels: Stotfield, Lossiemouth; Huntly House, Lossiemouth; Laverock Bank, Lossiemouth.

Y45 **Muir of Ord**
☎ Muir of Ord (0463) 870825
Great Northern Rd, Muir of Ord
15 miles N of Inverness.
Moorland/parkland course.
18 holes, 5022 yards, S.S.S.65
Visitors: welcome.
Green fees: weekdays £4, weekends £5.
Society meetings: by arrangement.
Catering: snacks and light meals served by arrangement.
Hotels: Moorings; Ord Arms; Tarradale; Ord House; Station.

Y46 **Murcar**
☎ Aberdeen (0224) 704370 Pro, 704345 Steward, 704354 Sec
Bridge of Don, Aberdeen AB2 8BD
3 miles from Aberdeen on A92 Fraserburgh road.
Seaside course.
18 holes, 6252 yards, S.S.S.70
Course designed by Archie Simpson.
Club founded in 1911.
Visitors: welcome on weekdays, except Wed afternoons and on Sun after 10 am.
Green fees: weekdays £10 per day, £6 per round (before noon); Sun and Bank Holidays £12 per day.
Society meetings: catered for on Tues and Thurs only.
Catering: catering facilities available except on Tues.
Hotels: numerous hotels in Aberdeen.

Y47 **Nairn**
☎ Nairn (0667) 53208
Seabank Rd, Nairn IV12 4HB
1 mile N of A96, W of Nairn, turn off onto Seabank Rd at church.
Seaside links course.
18 holes, 6540 yards, S.S.S.71
Course designed by Andrew Simpson and extended by Tom Morris and James Braid.
Club founded in 1887.
Visitors: welcome.
Green fees: weekdays £8 per round, £10 per day; weekends £9 per round, £11 per day.
Society meetings: by arrangement with Sec.
Catering: full catering daily except Thurs; limited catering in winter months.
Hotels: Golf View; Newton; Altonburn; Windsor; Royal Marine.

Y48 **Nairn Dunbar**
☎ Nairn (0667) 52741
Lochloy Rd, Nairn IV12 5AE
On A96, ½ mile E of town.
Seaside course.
18 holes, 6431 yards, S.S.S.71
Club founded in 1899.
Visitors: welcome.
Green fees: weekdays £5, weekends £6.
Society meetings: welcome.
Catering: meals by arrangement.
Hotels: Royal Marine; Sunnybrae Guest House.

Y49 **Newburgh-on-Ythan**
☎ Newburgh (035 86) 389
c/o 1 Millend, Newburgh, Aberdeenshire AB4 0AW
14 miles N of Aberdeen on Peterhead road, on entering village of Newburgh turn right at Ythan Hotel.
Seaside links course.
9 holes, 6404 yards, S.S.S.71
Club founded in 1912.
Visitors: welcome except on Tues after 4 pm from May to Sept.
Green fees: weekdays £5 per day, weekends £6 per day.
Society meetings: on application to Sec.
Catering: no facilities at club.
Hotels: Ythan; Goveran House; Udny.

Y50 **Newtonmore**
☎ Newtonmore (054 03) 328
Golf Course Rd, Newtonmore, Inverness-shire PH20 1AP
Leave A9 2 miles S of Newtonmore, road to golf course in centre of village 150 yards away.
Moorland/parkland course.
18 holes, 5890 yards, S.S.S.68
Course designed by James Braid.
Club founded in 1896.
Visitors: welcome.
Green fees: £5 per day.
Society meetings: welcome.
Catering: meals and snacks served.
Hotels: Craigerne; Alvey; Balavil; Braeriach; Mains.

Y51 **Nigg Bay**
☎ Aberdeen (0224) 871286
St Fitticks Rd, Balnagask, Aberdeenshire
SE of city centre.
Seaside course.
18 holes, 5984 yards, S.S.S.69
Club founded in 1955.
Visitors: welcome.
Green fees: £3.60.
Society meetings: by arrangement.
Hotels: in Aberdeen

Y52 **Northern**
☎ Aberdeen (0224) 636440
Golf Rd, Kings Links, Aberdeen
E of city centre.
Seaside course.
18 holes, 6700 yards, S.S.S.69
Visitors: welcome (municipal course).
Green fees: £3.60.
Society meetings: by arrangement.
Catering: at weekends, by arrangement during week.
Hotels: in Aberdeen

Y53 **Orkney**
☎ Kirkwall (0856) 2457
Grainbank, Kirkwall, Orkney
½ mile W of Kirkwall.
Parkland course.
18 holes, 5406 yards, S.S.S.68
Club founded in 1884.
Visitors: welcome.
Green fees: £3 per day, £10 per week.
Society meetings: welcome by arrangement with Sec.
Catering: none.
Hotels: Kirkwall; Ayr; Royal; in Kirkwall.

Y54 **Peterhead**
☎ Peterhead (0779) 72149

A Perfect Highland Interlude

For many years the name of Dornoch meant no more to me than the fact that, in my early school days, I shared a desk with a boy who lived there. Like all good young Scotsmen he played golf, and often used to speak of his course, adding with a typical youthful boast that I ought to go and see it for myself.

I never took him very seriously because I knew from the atlas that Dornoch was 620 miles from home and there was no reason to justify a trip. But, as time passed, more and more people confirmed what he had said; and as I listened one day at St Andrews to an enthusiastic description by Billy Joe Patton of a recent visit he had made, on the firm recommendation of his Walker Cup captain, Dick Tufts, I decided that I must go after all at the first opportunity.

Shortly afterwards, ambition was at last fulfilled. It was a perfect Highland interlude, and for three days my partner and I were caught in Dornoch's enchanting spell, playing round after round with an eagerness that is rare on a new course. Here was a traditional links, set amid gentle dune country, never out of sight or sound of the sea, and untouched by the centuries.

According to local records, golf was played at Dornoch as early as 1616, which would make it, according to some authorities, the second oldest golfing nursery in the world after St Andrews. It was not until 1877 that the Royal Dornoch Golf Club was founded and old Tom Morris was commissioned to come up from St Andrews to lay out nine holes.

Another nine were added and, shortly after the turn of the century, they were transformed into a championship links by John Sutherland, who for over fifty years was club secretary.

Dornoch used not to be widely known as a championship test because its remoteness made it impractical for such occasions; but the 1980 Home Internationals were played there three years after the club's centenary and final recognition came with the staging of the 1985 Amateur championship, won by Garth McGimpsey. So the course held by men close to the heart of the game to be one of the finest in the world was well and truly on the map.

First impressions are often the best and I still remember my initial visit. I became more than ever convinced of Dornoch's unmistakable quality of greatness and, to be fair, that opinion has been amply confirmed subsequently. It would be hard to think of a course that ranks above it as a pure test of golf or one that is more enjoyable to play.

For the Amateur championship, the weather held no hint of June. A cold wind from the north or north-west made the outward half unduly severe; but more than twenty years before, we experienced unusual contrasts, each time the links proving itself fair, challenging and rewarding for every class of player.

For years, the holes stayed firmly in the memory and I can see again the long, gradual curve at two levels of the first eight moving out to the point towards Embo where the 9th fairway turns for home along the shore.

The thrill of the drive from the 3rd tee to a narrow fairway on a shelf below; the pitch to the pulpit green at the 5th; the splendour of four superb short holes and the succession of good shots that are demanded from the turn if a score is not to get out of hand – that is the essence of Dornoch.

The tees are angled and the course slightly crescent shaped, so that the wind is not constantly in the face or the back, and the greens are so guarded or raised as to ensure that the ill-judged and ill-conceived second or approach is unlikely to succeed even from turf where the lies are seldom less than good.

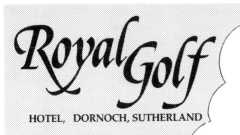

The 12th (500 yds) is a classic of its length and the 14th, "Foxy", an admirable illustration of a hole where bunkers need have no place, the second to a plateau green depending entirely on the placing of the drive.

These were one's special impressions, but when all thoughts of golf were forgotten, the matchless beauty of the setting remained. The massive, brooding hills of Sutherland, the golden stretch of sand that borders the huge sweep of the Dornoch Firth, and the lighthouse on its lonely distant point, give an added inspiration that make the world at large seem a thousand miles away.

Craigerran Links, Peterhead, Aberdeenshire
A92 and A975, 30 miles N of Aberdeen
Seaside course.
9 holes, S.S.S.34
18 holes, 6070 yards, S.S.S.69
Club founded in c.1850.
Visitors: welcome.
Green fees: weekdays £5, weekends £7.50.
Society meetings: by arrangement.
Catering: snacks, meals on request.
Hotels: Palace.

Y55 Reay
☎ Reay (084 781) 288
by Thurso, Caithness KW14 7RE
W from Thurso towards Bettyhill, 11 miles.
Undulating seaside course.
18 holes, 5876 yards, S.S.S.68
Club founded in 1886.
Visitors: welcome except during comps.
Green fees: £4 per day, £15 per week, £20 for a fortnight.
Catering: bar facilities available at normal hours; catering only for special events and open competitions.
Hotels: Bettyhill; many good hotels in Thurso.

Y56 Royal Aberdeen
☎ Aberdeen (0224) 702571
Balgownie, Bridge of Don, Aberdeen AB2 8AT
2 miles N of Aberdeen on A92, cross River Don, turn right at first set of traffic lights and then along Links Rd to course.
Links courses.
18 holes, 4033 yards, S.S.S.60
18 holes, 6372 yards, S.S.S.71
Course designed by Robert Simpson of Carnoustie.
Club founded in 1780.
Visitors: welcome with letter of introduction.
Green fees: weekdays £12 per day, £10 per round; weekends £14 per day, £12 per round.
Society meetings: welcome by arrangement with Sec.
Catering: full facilities available.
Hotels: Atholl, Kings Gate, Aberdeen; Caledonian, Elvan Terrace, Aberdeen; Holiday Inn, Dyce, Aberdeen.

Y57 Royal Dornoch
☎ Dornoch (0862) 810219
Golf Rd, Dornoch, Sutherland IV25 3LW
A9 from Inverness, take A949 for Dornoch, signposted in town.
Seaside course.
18 holes, 6577 yards, S.S.S.72
Course designed by Tom Morris and John Sutherland.
Club founded in 1877.
Visitors: welcome on weekdays and weekends; tee reservations in advance.
Society meetings: catered for except in July or Aug; early reservations required.
Catering: catering facilities available except on Mon.
Hotels: Burghfield House; Carling Bank; Dornoch Castle; Dornoch; Royal Golf.

Y58 Royal Tarlair
☎ Macduff (0261) 32897
Buchan St, Macduff AB4 1TA
On A98 48 miles from Aberdeen.
Undulating course.
18 holes, 5866 yards, S.S.S.68
Course designed by George Smith.
Club founded on 18 April 1923.
Visitors: welcome on weekdays and at weekends.
Green fees: weekdays £5, weekends £6.
Society meetings: catered for by arrangement.
Catering: lunches and snacks served.
Hotels: Fife Arms, Macduff; Deveron House, Macduff; Knowes, Macduff; Banff Springs, Banff.

Y59 Sconser
☎ Portree (0478) 2364
Sconser, Isle of Skye, Inverness
Between Broadford and Portree (on main road).
Seaside course.
9 holes, 4798 yards, S.S.S.63
Course designed by Dr Frank Deighton.
Club founded in 1964.
Visitors: welcome.
Green fees: £3 per day, Juniors £1 per day.
Hotels: Sconser Lodge.

Y60 Shetland
☎ Gott (059 584) 369
Dale, Shetland.
N road from Lerwick, 3 miles.
Undulating moorland course.
18 holes, 5900 yards, S.S.S.71
Course designed by Fraser Middleton.
Visitors: welcome.
Green fees: subject to review.
Society meetings: by arrangement.
Hotels: Lerwick; Grand; Queens.

Y61 Spey Bay
☎ Fochabers (0343) 820424
Spey Bay, Fochabers, Moray
Turn off A96 near Fochabers Bridge, follow B9104 Spey Bay road as far as coast.
Links course.
18 holes, 6059 yards, S.S.S.68
Visitors: welcome.
Green fees: £3.50.
Catering: meals served.
Hotels: Spey Bay.

Y62 Stonehaven
☎ Stonehaven (0569) 62124
Cowie, Stonehaven AB3 2RH
On A92 1 mile N of town, new roundabout at Commodore Hotel, take second exit on left, pass Leisure Centre on right.
Seaside/meadowland course.
18 holes, 5103 yards, S.S.S.65
Club founded in 1888.
Visitors: welcome with restrictions especially at weekends.
Green fees: weekdays £5, weekends £6.50.
Catering: full facilities available.
Hotels: Commodore; Royal; St Leonards; Heugh; Crown; Mill Inn; all in Stonehaven

Y63 Stornoway
☎ Stornoway (0851) 2240
Castle Grounds, Stornoway, Isle of Lewis

PA87 0XP
5 minutes walk from town centre, just within main entrance to castle grounds.
Parkland/moorland course.
18 holes, 5119 yards, S.S.S.66
Course designed by J. R. Stutt.
Club founded in 1890.
Visitors: welcome from Mon to Sat.
Green fees: £6 per day, £4 per round; £20 per week, £30 per fortnight.
Society meetings: catered for by arrangement.
Catering: catering facilities available by arrangement.
Hotels: Caberfeigh; County; Seaforth.

Y64 Strathlene
☎ Buckie (0542) 31798
Buckie, Banffshire AB5 2DJ
On A942, 2 miles E of Buckie Harbour, from main Banff to Inverness Rd, take turning to Strathlene 3 miles E of Buckie Rd sign.
Undulating seaside course.
18 holes, 5957 yards, S.S.S.69
Course designed by George E. Smith.
Club founded in 1877.
Visitors: welcome.
Green fees: weekdays £4 per day, weekends £5 per day.
Society meetings: welcome on weekdays, weekends by arrangement.
Catering: by arrangement.
Hotels: Commercial.

Y65 Strathpeffer Spa
☎ Strathpeffer (0997) 21219
Strathpeffer, Ross-shire IV14 9AS
5 miles W of Dingwall, ¼ mile N of village square (signposted).
Undulating course.
18 holes, 4813 yards, S.S.S.65
Club founded in 1888.
Visitors: welcome, but tee reserved at certain periods for club competitions.
Green fees: £4.50 per day, weekly (Mon to Fri) £18.
Society meetings: welcome by arrangement.
Catering: meals and snacks available except on Mon.
Hotels: Holly Lodge; Richmond; Brunstone Lodge; Ben Wyvis; Highland; all in Strathpeffer.

Y66 Stromness
☎ Stromness (0856) 850456
Ness, Stromness, Orkney K16 3DU
Adjacent to Point of Ness, S extremity of Stromness.
Seaside course.
18 holes.
Visitors: welcome.
Green fees: £3 per day.
Society meetings: Stromness open 36 hrs 1st Sat Aug.
Catering: evening bar facilities.
Hotels: many good hotels in area.

Y67 Tain
☎ Tain (0862) 2314
Tain, Ross-shire IV19 1PA
A9 N of Inverness, ½ mile from town centre.
Seaside/parkland course.
18 holes, 6222 yards, S.S.S.70/68
Course designed by Tom Morris.
Club founded in 1890.
Visitors: welcome.
Green fees: weekdays £6 per day, £4 per round; weekends £8 per day, £6 per round.
Society meetings: welcome.
Catering: by arrangement with Club Steward.
Hotels: Royal, Tain; Morangie, Tain; Mansfield, Tain.

Y68 Tarbat
☎ Portmahomack (086 287) 519
Portmahomack, Ross-shire IV20 1YQ
B9165 off A9, 7 miles E of Tain.
Seaside course.
9 holes, 4658 yards, S.S.S.63
Course designed by Tom Sutherland.
Club founded in 1909.
Visitors: welcome except on Sun.
Green fees: £2 per day.
Society meetings: by arrangement.
Catering: none at club, facilities at local hotels.
Hotels: Castle, Portmahomack; Caledonian, Portmahomack.

Y69 Tarland
☎ Tarland (033 981) 413
Tarland, Aboyne, Aberdeenshire AB3 4YL
On A974, 31 miles W of Aberdeen and 11 miles NE of Ballater.
Madowland course.
9 holes, 5812 yards, S.S.S.68
Course designed by Tom Morris.
Club founded in 1908.
Visitors: welcome.
Green fees: weekdays £3 per day, weekends £5 per day.
Society meetings: by arrangement.
Catering: snacks, lunches and teas.
Hotels: Commercial; Aberdeen Arms.

Y70 Thurso
☎ Thurso (0847) 63807
Newlands of Geise, Thurso, Caithness
2 miles SW from centre of Thurso on B870.
Parkland course.
18 holes, 5818 yards, S.S.S.69
Course designed by W. Stuart.
Club founded in 1894.
Visitors: welcome.
Green fees: weekdays £4, weekends £5.
Society meetings: catered for except during club competitions.
Catering: meals served at weekends and on Tues and Thurs evenings; snacks available.
Hotels: Pentland; St Clair; Royal.

Y71 Torphins
☎ Torphins (033 982) 493
Golf Rd, Torphins.
Mail to: 26, Beltie Rd, Torphins, Banchory AB3 4JT
6 miles W from Banchory on A980.
Undulating moorland course.
9 holes, 2300 yards, S.S.S.63
Club founded in 1895.
Visitors: welcome.
Green fees: weekdays £2 per day, weekends £3 per day.
Catering: none.
Hotels: Learney Arms, Torphins.

Y72 Torvean
☎ Inverness (0463) 237543 Starter, 225651 Clubhouse
Glenurquhart Rd, Inverness.
On A82 1 mile W of city centre, on W side of Caledonian Canal.
Parkland municipal course.
18 holes, 4308 yards, S.S.S.62
Club founded in 1962.
Visitors: welcome.
Green fees: on application to Inverness District Council.
Society meetings: by arrangement with Inverness District Council.
Catering: very limited facilities.
Hotels: Loch Ness House.

Y73 Turriff
☎ Turriff (0888) 62745
Rosehall, Turriff, Aberdeenshire AB5 7H
On Aberdeen side of town, about 1 mile up Huntly Rd on B9024.
Parkland course.
18 holes, 6105 yards, S.S.S.69
Club founded in 1895.
Visitors: welcome weekdays.
Green fees: weekdays £4 per round, £5 per day; weekends £4.50 per round, £6 per day.
Society meetings: welcome by arrangement with Sec.
Catering: meals served from April to Sept.

Y74 Western Isle
☎ Tobermory (0688) 2020
c/o Sec, Stronsaule, Tobermory, Isle of Mull PA75 6PR
A848 to Tobermory, course near Western Isles Hotel.
Hilly course.

9 holes, 4921 yards, S.S.S.64
Club founded in 1898.
Visitors: welcome.
Green fees: £3 per day.
Society meetings: welcome.
Catering: none.
Hotels: Western Isle, Tobermory.

Y75 Westhill

☎ Aberdeen (0224) 740159
Westhill Heights, Westhill, Skene, Aberdeenshire AB3 6TY
6 miles from Aberdeen on A944 Aberdeen to Alford road, course to N of town overlooking it.
Undulating parkland course.
18 holes, 5866 yards, S.S.S.68
Course designed by Charles Lawrie.
Club founded in 1977.
Visitors: welcome except on Sat and from 4.30 to 7 pm on weekdays.
Green fees: weekdays £4.50 per round, £6.50 per day; weekends and Bank Holidays £5.50 per round, £8.50 per day (£2 with member).
Society meetings: none at present.
Catering: meals available by arrangement; bar snacks on request at most times.
Hotels: Westhill Inn, Westhill Drive.

Y76 Wick

☎ Wick (0955) 2726
Reiss, Wick, Caithness KW1 4RW
2½ miles N of Wick on A9, turn right at signpost, ¾ mile to clubhouse.
Seaside links course.
18 holes, 5976 yards, S.S.S.69
Course designed by McCulloch.
Club founded in 1870.
Visitors: welcome, subject to club and open competitions.
Green fees: £4 per round or day, £15 per week, £24 per fortnight.
Society meetings: by arrangement.
Catering: none.
Hotels: Queens; Nethercliffe; Station; Mackays; Rosebank; Ladbroke Mercury; all in Wick.

Z Northern Ireland

Z1 Ardglass
☎ Ardglass (0396) 841219 or 841755
Castle Place, Ardglass
On B176 7 miles from Downpatrick.
Seaside course.
18 holes, 5215 metres, S.S.S.68
Club founded in 1896.
Visitors: welcome.
Green fees: weekdays £4, weekends £7.
Society meetings: welcome.
Catering: meals served except Mon.
Hotels: Abbey Lodge, Downpatrick; Arms, Ardglass.

Z2 Ballycastle.
☎ Ballycastle (026 57) 62536
Cushendall Rd, Ballycastle, Co Antrim BT54 6QP
About 50 miles along coast road, W of Larne Harbour.
Undulating seaside course.
18 holes, 5906 yards, S.S.S.68
Club founded in 1891.
Visitors: welcome.
Green fees: weekends and Bank Holidays £6, weekdays £4, weekly £20, monthly £45.
Society meetings: welcome by arrangement.
Catering: meals served by arrangement.
Hotels: Antrim Arms, The Diamond, Ballycastle; Hillsea, North St, Ballycastle; Mount Pleasant Guest House, Quay Rd, Ballycastle.

Z3 Ballyclare
☎ Ballyclare (09603) 22696
Springfield Rd, Ballyclare, Co Antrim
14 miles N of Belfast.
Parkland course.
9 holes, 6708 yards, S.S.S.71
Club founded in 1923.
Visitors: welcome.
Green fees: weekdays £4.50 (£3), weekends £7 (£4).
Society meetings: by prior arrangement.
Catering: meals served daily.
Hotels: Chimney Corner, Newtonabbey.

Z4 Ballymena
☎ Broughshane (0266) 861487
Broughshane Rd, Ballymena, Co Antrim
2½ miles E of town on A42 to Broughshane and Carnlough.
Parkland course.
18 holes, 5683 yards, S.S.S.67
Club founded in 1903.
Visitors: welcome.
Green fees: weekdays £5 (£3 with member), weekends £7.50 (£4 with member).
Society meetings: by arrangement.
Catering: every day except Mon.
Hotels: Adair Arms; Tullyglass House.

Z5 Balmoral
☎ Belfast (0232) 668514
518 Lisburn Rd, Belfast BT9 6GX
Clubhouse is immediately beside the King's Hall on Belfast's Lisburn Rd, and Balmoral Halt railway station is just on other side of road.
Parkland course.
18 holes, 5679 yards, S.S.S.70
Club founded in 1914.
Visitors: welcome on weekdays, except Fri (Ladies Day) and on Sun.
Green fees: weekdays Men £5.50 (£4 with member), Ladies £4 (£2.20 with member), Juveniles £2.20 (£1.30 with member).
Society meetings: catered for on weekdays, usually Mon and Thurs.
Catering: lunches and bar snacks served daily; à la carte menu available by arrangement with Caterer.
Hotels: Forum, Great Victoria St, Belfast; many other hotels in area.

Z6 Banbridge
☎ Banbridge (082 06) 22342
Huntly Rd, Banbridge, Co Down BT32 3UR
About ½ mile from town along Huntly Rd, River Bann on right all the way.
Parkland course.
12 holes, 5376 metres, S.S.S.68
Club founded in 1912.
Visitors: welcome (Ladies Day Tues).
Green fees: weekdays £3 (£2 with member), weekends £4 (£3 with member).
Society meetings: welcome by arrangement.
Catering: meals available by arrangement.
Hotels: Bannville House, Lurgan Rd, Banbridge; Downshire, Newry St, Banbridge; Belmont, Rathfriland St, Banbridge.

Z7 Bangor
☎ Bangor (0247) 3922
Broadway, Bangor, Co Down BT20 4RH
¾ mile from town centre.
Undulating parkland course.
18 holes, 5934 metres, S.S.S.71
Course designed by James Braid.
Club founded in 1903.
Visitors: welcome on weekdays.
Green fees: weekdays £6 (£4 with member), weekends and Bank Holidays £9 (£5 with member).
Society meetings: catered for on Mon, Wed and Fri.
Catering: full facilities except Sun p.m.
Hotels: Royal, Quay St; Sands, Seacliff Rd; Ballyholme, Seacliff Rd.

Z8 Belvoir Park
☎ Belfast (0232) 643693, 692817 or 641159
73 Church Rd, Newtownbreda, Belfast BT8 4AN
About 4 miles from centre of Belfast, off Ormean Rd which is main road to Saintfield and Newcastle.
Parkland course.
18 holes, 6276 yards, S.S.S.70
Course designed by H.S. Colt.
Club founded in 1927.
Visitors: welcome, except on Sat (Ladies Day Fri).
Green fees: Men – weekdays (except Wed) £6.50, weekends, Bank Holidays and Wed £8; Ladies – weekdays (except Wed) £5, weekends, Bank Holidays and Wed £5.50.
Society meetings: catered for on Mon, Tues and Thurs.
Catering: full facilities available.
Hotels: Drumreen.

Z9 Bushfoot
☎ Bushmills (026 57) 31317
50 Bushfoot Rd, Portballintrae, Bushmills, Co Antrim BT57 8RR
4 miles E of Portrush on coast.
Seaside course.
9 holes, 5572 yards, S.S.S.67
Club founded in 1890.
Visitors: welcome on weekdays and at weekends if no official club competitions.
Green fees: weekdays £4 (£3 with member), weekends and Bank Holidays £5 (£4 with member); under 18 – weekdays £2 (£1.50 with member), weekends and Bank Holidays £3 (£2 with member).
Society meetings: welcome by arrangement.
Catering: snacks served.
Hotels: Bayview; Beach; Causeway.

Z10 Cairndhu
☎ Ballygally (0574) 83324
192, Coast Rd, Ballygally, Larne BT40 2QC
On Antrim coast road, 3½ miles from Larne.
Parkland course.
18 holes, 6112 yards, S.S.S.69
Course designed by John S.F. Morrison.
Club founded in 1929.
Visitors: welcome except on Sat.

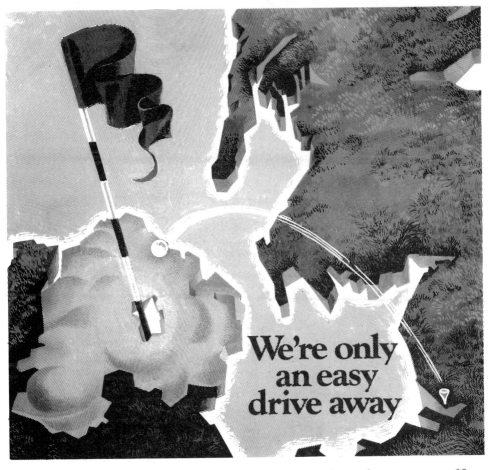

We're only an easy drive away

Drive over to Northern Ireland and you'll find you're welcome at over 60 uncrowded courses. If you're looking for a challenge you've got an internationally recognised talent-stretcher in the Royal County Down. If you like a little scenic grandeur with your golf you'll find magnificent landscapes come free with our very reasonable green fees. And that's not to mention the friendly hospitality you'll find at all our '19th holes'.

Belfast Car Ferries have a variety of attractive packages that can enable you to tee up in Northern Ireland for the golfing holiday of a lifetime. And as you'll find, we're just an easy drive away.

For further details call in or post the coupon to any of the addresses below:

northern ireland tourist board

I would like further information on golfing holidays.

Name...

Address..

....

BELFAST CAR FERRIES

River House, 48 High Street, Belfast BT1 2DS. 11 Berkeley Street, London W1X 6BU. 38 High Street, Sutton Coldfield, West Midlands B72 1UP.

Green fees: Men – weekdays £4.40, weekends and Bank Holidays £6.60; Ladies – weekdays £2.20, weekends and Bank Holidays £3.30.
Society meetings: welcome.
Catering: meals and snacks available on weekdays (8 pm to 10 pm), Sat (11.30 am to 6 pm) and Sun (2 pm to 9 pm); other meals available by arrangement.
Hotels: Ballygally Castle, Coast Rd, Ballygally; Halfway House, Coast Rd, Ballygally.

Z11 Carnalea
☎ Bangor (0247) 461368
Station Rd, Bangor, Co Down BT19 1EZ
Adjacent to Carnalea railway station, 1½ miles from Bangor.
Seaside meadowland course.
18 holes, 5513 yards, S.S.S.67
Club founded in 1927.
Visitors: welcome.
Green fees: weekdays £4 (£2.90 with member), weekends £6.75 (£4 with member).
Society meetings: welcome only on weekdays.
Catering: full facilities available.
Hotels: Crawfordsburn Inn, Crawfordsburn; Royal; Tedworthy, Bangor.

Z12 Carrickfergus
☎ Carrickfergus (09603) 63713
North Rd, Carrickfergus BT38 8LP
Off A2, 9 miles NE of Belfast.
Parkland/meadowland course.
18 holes, 5759 yards, S.S.S.68
Club founded in 1926.
Visitors: welcome on weekdays.
Green fees: £4.50 per round (£3 with member).
Society meetings: by arrangement.
Catering: meals served.
Hotels: Coast Road, Carrickfergus; Edenmore; Glenavna, Newtownabbey.

Z13 Castlerock
☎ Castlerock (0265) 848215
65 Circular Rd, Castlerock, Co Londonderry BT51 4TJ
On A2, 6 miles W of Coleraine.
Seaside course.
18 holes, 6515 yards, S.S.S.71
Course designed by Ben Sayers.
Club founded in 1900.
Visitors: welcome on weekdays.
Green fees: £5 (£3.50 with member).
Society meetings: welcome on weekdays except July and Aug.
Catering: snacks and high teas.
Hotels: Golf,

Z14 City of Derry
☎ Londonderry (0504) 46369
49 Victoria Rd, Londonderry BT47 2PU
On main Londonderry to Strabane Rd, 3 miles from Craigavon Bridge.
Parkland course.
Dunhugh 9 holes, 4708 yards, S.S.S.63
Prehen 18 holes, 6362 yards, S.S.S.71
Club founded in 1912.
Visitors: welcome on weekdays before 4.30 pm unless with member and at weekends by arrangement with Pro; Dunhugh course open at all times.
Green fees: weekdays £5 (£4 with member), weekends and Bank Holidays £6; Dunhugh – Adults £2.50, Children (under 18) £1.
Society meetings: catered for on weekdays and possibly at weekends.
Catering: full catering facilities available.
Hotels: Everglades, Prehen Rd, Londonderry; Broomhill House, Limavady Rd, Londonderry; White Horse Inn, Campsie Rd, Londonderry; Glen House, Eglinton, Londonderry.

Z15 Clandeboye
☎ Bangor (0247) 465767
Tower Rd, Conlig, Newtownards BT23 3TN
On main Bangor to Newtownards Rd, 2 miles from Bangor into Conlig village.
Ava: moorland/meadowland course.
Dufferin: parkland/woodland course.
Ava: 18 holes, 5634 yards, S.S.S.67
Dufferin: 18 holes, 6000-7000 yards, S.S.S.70-73
Course designed by W.R. Robinson, and Peter Alliss, Dave Thomas & Co.
Club founded in 1933.
Visitors: welcome.
Green fees: on application.
Society meetings: by arrangement.
Catering: meals served.
Hotels: Royal, Bangor; Culloden, Craigavad; Crawfordsburn Inn, Crawfordsburn; Strangford Arms, Newtownards.

Z16 Cliftonville
☎ Belfast (0232) 744158
44 Westland Rd, Belfast BT14 6NH
From centre of Belfast take Antrim road, about 2 miles from centre.
Meadowland course.
9 holes, 3120 yards, S.S.S.70
Club founded in 1922.
Visitors: welcome except Sat and Tues afternoons.
Green fees: £4.80 (£2.40 with member).
Society meetings: by arrangement with Council through Sec.
Catering: meals served by arrangement.
Hotels: Lansdowne Court, Antrim Rd, Belfast.

Z17 County Armagh
☎ Armagh (0861) 522501
Demesne, Newry Rd, Armagh, Co Armagh.
Off Newry Rd, ¼ mile from city centre.
Parkland course.
18 holes, 6147 yards, S.S.S.69
Club founded in 1893.
Visitors: welcome except between 12 and 2 pm on Sat and 12 and 3 pm on Sun.
Green fees: weekdays £2.50, weekends and Bank Holidays £5.
Society meetings: catered for except on Sat.
Catering: full facilities available.
Hotels: Charlemont Arms, Armagh; Drumsill House, Armagh.

Z18 Cushendall
☎ Cushendall (026 67) 71318
Shore Rd, Cushendall, Ballymena, Co Antrim BT44 0QQ
Turn right at Curfew Tower in village, proceed ¼ mile to Strand.
Seaside course.
9 holes, 2193 metres, S.S.S.63
Course designed by Daniel Delargy.
Club founded in 1937.
Visitors: welcome; avoid weekends if possible.
Green fees: weekdays £5, weekends £6; weekly (5 days) £20, monthly £45.
Society meetings: welcome on weekdays.
Catering: by arrangement.
Hotels: Thornlea; Londonderry Arms; Carnlough; Bay; Cushendall.

Z19 Donaghadee
☎ Donaghadee (0247) 883624 or 882519
Warren Rd, Donaghadee
On A2 18 miles E of Belfast.
Seaside/meadowland course.
18 holes, 5576 metres, S.S.S.68/69
Club founded in 1899.
Visitors: welcome except before 4 pm on Sat.
Green fees: weekdays – Men £5, Ladies £4; weekends and Bank Holidays £6.50 (£2.50 with member).
Society meetings: welcome on Mon, Wed and Thurs.
Catering: full facilities except Mon.
Hotels: Copeland.

Z20 Downpatrick
☎ Downpatrick (0396) 2773
Saul Rd, Downpatrick, Co Down BT30 6PA
A24 and A7 23 miles SE of Belfast.
Parkland course.
18 holes, 5823 yards, S.S.S.68
Visitors: welcome.
Green fees: weekdays £4 (less with member), weekends £6.
Society meetings: by arrangement.
Catering: full facilities, limited evenings.
Hotels: Denvir's; Abbey Lodge.

Z21 Dungannon

☎ Dungannon (08687) 22098
Dungannon, Co Tyrone
½ mile out of town on Donaghmore Rd.
Parkland course.
18 holes, 5818 yards, S.S.S.68
Visitors: welcome anytime.
Green fees: weekdays £3 (men), £2 (ladies); weekends £4 (men), £2.50 (ladies).
Society meetings: welcome by arrangement.
Catering: by arrangement.
Hotels: Dunowen; Inn on the Park.

Z22 Dunmurry

☎ Belfast (0232) 621402
91 Dunmurry Lane, Dunmurry, Belfast BT17 9JS
Situated between Dunmurry village and Upper Malone Rd, Belfast.
Parkland course.
18 holes, 5832 yards, S.S.S.68
Club founded in 1905.
Visitors: welcome with restrictions on weekdays and at weekends.
Green fees: weekdays £5, weekends and Bank Holidays £6.
Society meetings: welcome.
Catering: lunches, high teas and à la carte menu available except Mon.
Hotels: Conway, Dunmurry; Beechlawn, 4 Dunmurry Lane, Dunmurry; Woodlands, 3 Belfast Rd, Lisburn.

Z23 Enniskillen

☎ Enniskillen (0365) 25250
Castle Coole, Enniskillen, Co Fermanagh
1 mile from Enniskillen.
Parkland course.
9 holes, 5476 yards, S.S.S.70
Course designed by Dr Dixon & George Mawhinney.
Club founded in 1956.
Visitors: welcome.
Green fees: £4 per day.
Society meetings: by arrangement.
Catering: by arrangement.
Hotels: in area.

Z24 Fintona

☎ Fintona (0662) 841480
Ecclesville Demesne, Fintona, Co Tyrone
9 miles SW of Omagh.
Parkland course.
9 holes, 6251 yards, S.S.S.70
Club founded in 1896.
Visitors: welcome.
Green fees: weekdays £3, weekends £5.
Society meetings: catered for on weekdays.
Catering: available by prior arrangement.
Hotels: Royal Arms, Omagh; Silverbirch, Omagh; Valley, Fivemiletown.

Z25 Fortwilliam

☎ Belfast (0232) 771770
Downview Ave, Belfast B15 4EZ
On A2 3 miles N of Belfast.
Meadowland course.
18 holes, 5796 yards, S.S.S.67
Course designed by Mr Buchart.
Club founded in 1903.
Visitors: welcome except on Sat.
Green fees: weekdays £5 (£2.50 with member), weekends and Bank Holidays £7 (£4 with member).
Society meetings: welcome by arrangement except Sat.
Catering: full catering service available.
Hotels: Lansdowne Court, Antrim Rd, Belfast.

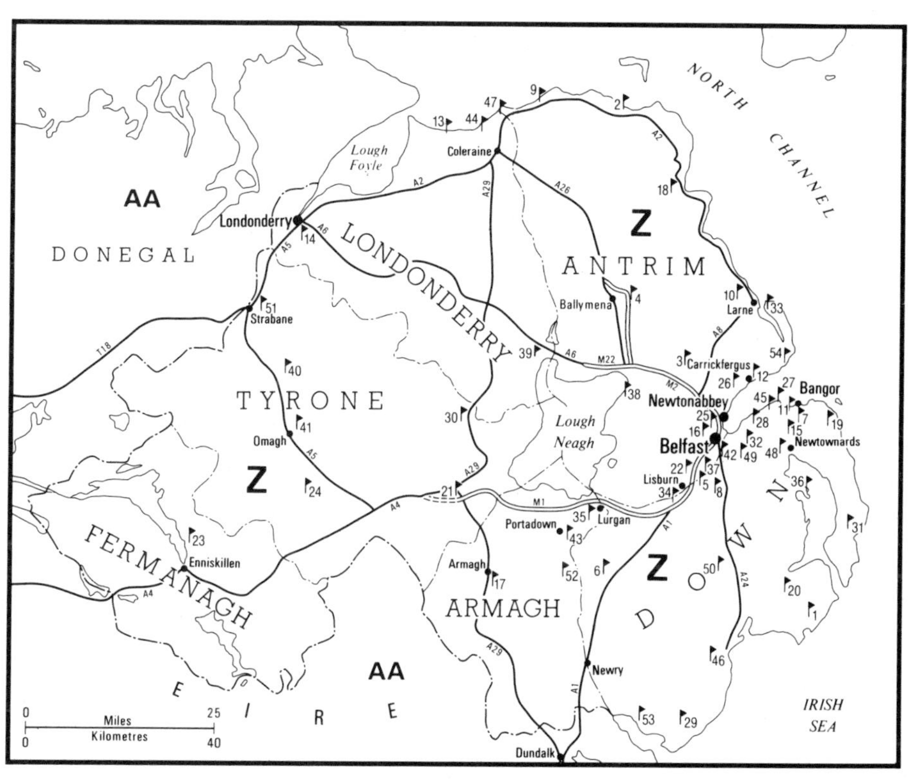

Z26 Greenisland
☎ Whiteabbey (0231) 62236
156 Upper Rd, Greenisland, Carrickfergus BT38 8RW
About 9 miles N of Belfast.
Meadowland course.
9 holes, 5951 yards, S.S.S.68
Course re-designed by H. Middleton.
Club founded in 1894.
Visitors: welcome, but not before 5 pm on Sat.
Green fees: weekdays £4, weekends and Bank Holidays £5.
Society meetings: welcome; 20% reduction in green fees if booked in advance.
Catering: lunches and high teas served, if booked before playing.
Hotels: Glenavna; Edenmore; both in Whiteabbey.

Z27 Helen's Bay
☎ Bangor (0247) 852601
Golf Rd, Helen's Bay, Bangor, Co Down BT19 1TL
Off A2, 9 miles E of Belfast.
9 holes, 5154 metres, S.S.S.67
Club founded in 1896.
Visitors: welcome, but with member only on Sat.
Green fees: weekdays £4.50 (£3 with member), Sun and Bank Holidays £5.50 (£4 with member).
Society meetings: catered for on Tues, Wed and Fri.
Catering: full catering facilities.

Z28 Holywood
☎ Holywood (023 17) 2138
Nuns Walk, Demesne Rd, Holywood, Co Down BT18 9DX
On A2 6 miles E of Belfast.
Undulating course.
18 holes, 5885 yards, S.S.S.69
Club founded in 1904.
Visitors: welcome except on comp. days.
Green fees: weekends £6.30, weekdays £4.80.
Society meetings: catered for on Mon, Tues and Wed.
Catering: catering facilities except Mon.
Hotels: Culloden; Cultra Holywood.

Z29 Kilkeel
☎ Kilkeel (069 37) 62 296
Mourne Park, Ballyardle, Newry, Co Down BT34 4LB
3 miles from Kilkeel on main road to Newry.
Parkland course.
9 holes, 5623 metres, S.S.S.69
Course designed by Lord Justice Babington.
Club founded in 1948.
Visitors: welcome on weekdays.
Green fees: weekends and Bank Holidays £5, weekdays £4; reduction with member.
Society meetings: catered for except Sat.
Catering: full à la carte menu available.
Hotels: Royal, Kilkeel; Cranfield House, Cranfield.

Z30 Killymoon
☎ Cookstown (064 87) 62254
200 Killymoon Rd, Cookstown, Co Tyrone BT80 8TW
Parkland course.
18 holes, 5498 metres, S.S.S.69
Club founded in 1889.
Visitors: welcome.
Green fees: weekdays £3, Sunday and Bank Holidays £4.
Society meetings: welcome except Sat.
Catering: meals available.
Hotels: Glenavon, 52 Drum Rd, Cookstown.

Z31 Kirkistown Castle
☎ Portavogie (024 77) 71233 or 71353
142 Main Rd, Cloughey, Newtownards, Co Down BT22 1HZ
A20 from Belfast to Kircubbin, follow signs to Newtownards and Portaferry, then B173 to Cloughey.
Links course.
18 holes, 6157 yards, S.S.S.70
Course designed by B. Polley.
Club founded in October 1902.
Visitors: welcome.
Green fees: Men– weekdays £4, weekends and Bank Holidays £6; Ladies £3, Juniors £1.
Society meetings: welcome on weekdays, except Bank Holidays.
Catering: full facilities available.
Hotels: The Roadhouse, 204 Main Rd, Cloughey.

Z32 The Knock
☎ Dundonald (023 18) 2249 or 3251 Sec
Summerfield, Upper Newtownards Rd, Dundonald, Belfast BT16 0QX
On A2 main Newtownards road to East Belfast (across Queens or Albert Bridges from Belfast city centre), 4 miles on left hand side just ½ mile beyond Stormont Houses of Parliament.
Parkland course.
Medal 18 holes, 6392 yards, S.S.S.71
Ladies 18 holes, 6392 yards, S.S.S.73
Club founded in 1895.
Visitors: welcome except on comp. days.
Green fees: Men – weekdays £6.50, weekends and Bank Holidays £8; Ladies – weekdays £4.75, weekends and Bank Holidays £6; Juveniles – weekdays £2.50, weekends and Bank Holidays £4; reduction with member.
Society meetings: welcome on Mon and Thurs, maximum 60.
Catering: meals and snacks except Sun.
Hotels: Stormont.

Z33 Larne
☎ Islandmagee (096 03) 82228
54 Ferris Bay Rd, Islandmagee, Larne BT40 3RT
From Belfast, N to Carrickfergus and 6 miles from Whitehead, from Larne S along coast road to Islandmagee.
Seaside course.
9 holes, 3033 yards, S.S.S.69
Course designed by G.L. Bailie.
Club founded in 1894.
Visitors: welcome on weekdays except Fri (Ladies Day).
Green fees: weekdays £2 (with member £1.50), weekends and Bank Holidays £5 (with member £2).
Society meetings: welcome on weekdays and Sun mornings.
Catering: snacks served daily and dinners at weekends.
Hotels: Magheramorne House.

Z34 Lisburn
☎ Lisburn (0846) 77216
68 Eglantine Rd, Lisburn, Co Antrim BT27 5RQ
3 miles S of Lisburn, 200 yards from BBC radio transmitter mast.
Meadowland/parkland course.
18 holes, 5708 metres, S.S.S.72
Course designed by Hawtree & Son.
Club founded in 1905.
Visitors: welcome but advisable to check in advance.
Green fees: weekdays £6, Sat (after 5.30 pm) £7.
Society meetings: catered for on Mon and Thurs.
Catering: meals served except Mon.
Hotels: Woodlands, Lisburn; White Gables, Hillsborough.

Z35 Lurgan
☎ Lurgan (076 22) 22087 or 5306
The Denesne, Lurgan, Co Armagh BT67 9BN
Centre of Lurgan to Windsor Ave and proceed past castle gates.
Parkland course.
5836 metres, S.S.S.70
Course designed by Cotton, Pennink, Lawrie & Partners Ltd.
Visitors: welcome except on Sat.
Green fees: weekdays £5, weekends £7.
Society meetings: catered for by arrangement.
Catering: meals available.
Hotels: Silverwood.

Z36 Mahee Island
☎ Killinchy (0727) 541234
Comber, Newtownards, Co Down
Killinchy Rd, signposted 6 miles from

The Courses of Ireland

Golfing tours of Ireland require a special kind of stamina. By that, I don't mean that every fairway is as soft as a peat bog or that the winds down Killarney way are any stronger than those that blow at Muirfield or Machrihanish. The locals may try to convince you they are but then the Irish are a persuasive race.

They also have an idiosyncratic logic. "You've a strong crosswind against you", I was once told, and Michael Bonallack had an Irish caddie who advised him that the putt facing him was "slightly straight". What I mean by special stamina is that you have to pace your day in the certain knowledge that what precedes and follows the golf will be more exhausting. I was initiated as to what to expect during a cricket tour long ago. Well after midnight, I enquired tentatively what time the bars closed, thinking (correctly) it would be the only way of breaking up the party. "About October, I think", came the reply.

It is not that the Irish don't take their golf seriously but simply, as I found at cricket, that they have no set hours of play. They ply you with Guinness, regale story after story about Carr, Bruen, Bradshaw and O'Connor and, by the time you leave, you will have sung every conceivable Irish ballad. However, in your few waking moments, you will also remember their courses. They more than live up to all the talk.

To summarise their delights in one short commentary is akin to devoting a single day to the historical wonders of Rome. Each area deserves a holiday in itself but the purpose of this exercise is to whet an appetite that may take a life time to satisfy fully.

However, the important thing is that the seeds are easy to sow and it matters not where you begin particularly as the North and South are united as one golfing country. Portrush, scene of Max Faulkner's victory in the 1951 Open championship, and Royal County Down at Newcastle are undoubtedly the pride of the North. Each claims an enchanting setting, Portrush not far from the Giant's Causeway and Newcastle watched over by the Mountains of Mourne.

As a combination of beauty and superb tests of golf, they have few equals; but it is a combination that tends to be applicable all over Ireland. A journey from Newcastle to Dublin must include County Louth at Baltray, the handiwork of Tom Simpson, a course whose praises are not sung as loudly as they should be.

Dublin is only about thirty miles by road where Portmarnock – the most widely used course for international occasions – is there to savour. Royal Dublin is a few steps nearer the centre of a city that is well served by courses. Cork has Little Island and Carlow, in its lovely old deer park, is an ideal stopping place on the way to the West, Eire's golfing pride.

Killarney, host to the 1973 European team championship, like Gleneagles, has a beautiful inland setting but the real flavour of Irish golf centres upon Ballybunion, Lahinch, County Sligo at Rosses Point, Waterville and, more recently, Tralee. All possess true greatness in the most wonderfully natural coastal settings.

Ballybunion now has a second course designed by Robert Trent Jones; Lahinch attracts a huge entry each year for the South of Ireland championship and is to be host to the Home Internationals in 1987 while Rosses Point, deep in the heart of the country made famous by the poetry of W.B. Yeats, is another delight.

Comber.
9 holes, 5108 metres, S.S.S.67
Club founded in 1929.
Visitors: welcome except Sat.
Green fees: weekdays £3.50, weekends £5.
Society meetings: by arrangement.
Catering: parties only by arrangement.
Hotels: La Mon (approx 10 miles).

Z37 Malone

☎ Belfast (0232) 612758
240 Upper Malone Rd, Dunmurry, Belfast BT17 9LB
5 miles from Belfast centre, take Upper Malone Rd.
Parkland course.
18 holes, 6433 yards, S.S.S.71
Course designed by Fred Hawtree.
Club founded in 1895.
Visitors: welcome except on Wed after 2 pm and on Sat before 5 pm.
Green fees: weekdays £8 (£3.50 with member), weekends and Bank Holidays £11 (£4.50 with member).
Society meetings: catered for on Mon and Thurs.
Catering: full catering facilities available except Sun after 2 pm.
Hotels: Conway, Dunmurry; Beechlawn, Dunmurry.

Z38 Massereene

☎ Antrim (084 94) 62096
Lough Rd, Antrim
1 mile S of town, 3½ miles from Aldergrove Airport.
Parkland course.
18 holes, 6614 yards, S.S.S.73
Club founded in 1895.
Visitors: welcome on weekdays.
Green fees: Men – weekdays £5 (£3 with member), weekends £7.50 (£5 with member); Ladies – weekdays £3.25 (£2 with member), weekends £4.50 (£2.50 with member); Juniors – weekdays £2.25 (£1.50 with member), weekends £4 (£2.50 with member).
Society meetings: welcome on some weekdays and on Sun from April to Sept by arrangement.
Catering: meals and snacks served (on Sun only from 3 pm to 8 pm).
Hotels: Deerpark.

Z39 Moyola Park

☎ Castledawson (0648) 68392/68468
Shanemullagh, Castledawson, Magherafelt, Co Londonderry BT45 8DG
Turn right ½ way through Castledawson village, along Curran Rd, entrance 400 yds on right, two to left of Corran Rd.
Parkland course.
18 holes, 6517 yards, S.S.S.71
Course designed by Don Patterson.
Society meetings: welcome at all times.
Catering: weekends all day, weekdays by arrangement with Steward.
Hotels: The Arches, Market St, Magherafelt; Moyola Lodge, Broagh Rd, Castledawson.

Z40 Newtownstewart

☎ Newtownstewart (066 26) 61466 or 61829
38 Golf Course Rd, Newtownstewart, Co Tyrone BT78 4HU
2 miles SW of Newtownstewart via B84 from Newtownstewart to Drumquin.
Undulating parkland course.
18 holes, 5448 metres, S.S.S.69
Course designed by Frank Pennink.
Club founded in 1914.
Visitors: welcome, but advance booking advisable.
Green fees: weekdays £4, weekends and Bank Holidays £5.
Society meetings: catered for by prior arrangement.
Catering: meals served by arrangement.
Hotels: Hunting Lodge, Letterbin, Baronscourt, Co Tyrone; Royal Arms, High St, Omagh; Silverbirch, Gortin Rd, Omagh; Fir Trees Lodge, Melmount Rd, Strabane.

Z41 Omagh

☎ Omagh (0662) 3160
Dublin Rd, Omagh, Co Tyrone BT78 1HX
On A5 in outskirts of Omagh.
Undulating parkland course.
18 holes, 5051 metres, S.S.S.67
Club founded in 1910.
Visitors: welcome except on Sat or major competition days.
Green fees: £3.
Society meetings: welcome weekdays.
Catering: catering available for societies.
Hotels: Royal Arms; Knock na Moe; Silver Birch.

Z42 Ormeau

☎ Belfast (0232) 641069
Ravenhill Rd, Belfast BT6 0BN
2 miles from city centre.
Parkland course.
9 holes, 2653 yards, S.S.S.65
Club founded in 1893.
Visitors: welcome on weekdays.
Green fees: weekdays £3 (£2 with member), Sat and Bank Holidays £4.
Society meetings: by arrangement.
Catering: none.
Hotels: Drumkeen, Newtownards, Belfast.

Z43 Portadown

☎ Portadown (0762) 335356 Sec, 332296 Clubhouse
Carrickblacker, Gilford Rd, Portadown, Co Armagh BT63 5LF
On A50 SE of Portadown, proceed for 2 miles and entrance to clubhouse is 400 yards beyond Metal Box factory on right.
Parkland course.
18 holes, 6200 yards, S.S.S.70
Club founded in 1905.
Visitors: welcome except on Sat (Ladies Day Tues).
Green fees: weekdays £4 per day (£3 with member), Sat (after 5 pm), Sun and Bank Holidays £6 (£4 with member); Juniors £1.
Society meetings: welcome except on Tues and Sat.
Catering: meals and snacks except Mon.
Hotels: Seagoe, Upper Church Lane, Portadown; Carn Grove, Seagoe, Portadown.

Z44 Portstewart

☎ Portstewart (026 583) 2015 or 3839
117 Strand Rd, Portstewart, Co Londonderry BT55 7PG
4 miles W of Portrush.
Links course.
18 holes, 6784 yards, S.S.S.72
Club founded in 1895.
Visitors: welcome on weekdays and by arrangement at weekends.
Green fees: weekdays £5.50 (£3.50 with member), weekends and Bank Holidays £7.50 (£5 with member).
Society meetings: catered for on weekdays by arrangement.
Catering: meals served.
Hotels: Strand; Edgewater; Carrig-na-Cule.

Z45 Royal Belfast

☎ Holywood (023 17) 2165
Station Rd, Craigavad, Holywood, Co Down BT18 0BT
E of Belfast on A2.
Parkland course.
18 holes, 5691 metres, S.S.S.70
Course designed by H.S. Colt.
Club founded in 1881.
Visitors: welcome with letter of introduction from home club or introduced by member, except Thurs and Sat.

Green fees: weekdays £7, Sun and Bank Holidays £10.
Society meetings: welcome on weekdays except Thurs by arrangement.
Catering: full facilities available.
Hotels: Culloden.

Z46 Royal County Down

☎ Newcastle (039 67) 23314
Newcastle, Co Down BT33 0AN
From Belfast take A24 to Carryduff, A7 to Ballynahinch and A2 to Newcastle, about 30 miles.
Links course.
18 holes, 6968 yards, S.S.S.74
Course designed by Tom Morris Sen.
Club founded in 1898.
Visitors: welcome on Mon, Tues and Fri.
Green fees: weekdays £10 per day, weekends and Bank Holidays £12 per day.
Society meetings: by arrangement only.
Catering: by arrangement only.
Hotels: Slieve Donard; Burrendale.

Z47 Royal Portrush

☎ Portrush (0265) 822311
Bushmills Rd, Portrush, Co Antrim BT56 8JQ
1 mile from Portrush town off A1.
Links course.
18 holes, 6680 yards, S.S.S.72
Club founded in 1888.
Visitors: welcome with prior reservation.
Green fees: Dunluce weekdays £8, weekends £12; Valley weekdays £5, weekends £7.
Society meetings: welcome by arrangement.
Catering: meals served.
Hotels: Bayview, Portballantrae; Edgewater, Portstewart.

Z48 Scrabo

☎ Newtownards (0247) 812355
233 Scrabo Rd, Newtownards, Co Down BT23 4SL
Off A20 10 miles E of Belfast.
Undulating course.
18 holes, 5699 metres, S.S.S.71
Club founded in 1907.
Visitors: welcome on weekdays (Ladies Day Wed) and Sun.
Green fees: weekdays £4, Sun and Bank Holidays £6.
Society meetings: welcome on weekdays except Wed.
Catering: meals served except Tues.
Hotels: Strangford Arms, Church St, Newtownards.

Z49 Shandon Park

☎ Belfast (0232) 793730
73 Shandon Park, Belfast BT5 6NY
3 miles from city centre via Knock dual carriageway.
Parkland course.
18 holes, 6252 yards, S.S.S.70
Club founded in 1926.
Visitors: welcome on w'kdays and on Sun.
Green fees: weekdays £6 (£4 with member), Sun and Bank Holidays £7.50 (£5 with member).
Society meetings: catered for by arrangement.
Catering: meals and snacks available.
Hotels: Stormont; Drumkeen.

Z50 Spa

☎ Ballynahinch (0238) 562365
20 Grove Rd, Ballynahinch, Co Down BT24 8PN
A24, Exit at sign for Spa or Dromara, 1 mile from Ballynahinch.
Parkland course.
9 holes, 5770 yards, S.S.S.70
Course designed by R.R. Bell & A Mathers.
Club founded in 1907.
Visitors: welcome weekdays.
Green fees: weekdays £4 (£3 with member), weekends and Bank Holidays £5 (£4 with member).
Society meetings: weekdays and some Sun.
Catering: meals available.
Hotels: Millbrook Lodge, Ballynahinch; White Horse.

Z51 Strabane

☎ Strabane (0504) 882271
Ballycolman, Strabane, Co Tyrone BT82 9PH
1 mile from Strabane on Dublin road beside church and three schools.
Parkland course.
18 holes, 5458 metres, S.S.S.69
Course designed by Eddie Hackett.
Club founded in 1909.
Visitors: welcome.
Green fees: weekdays £3 (£2 with member), weekends £4 (£3 with member).
Society meetings: by arrangement.
Catering: by arrangement with Club Sec.
Hotels: Fir Trees Lodge, Dublin Rd.

Z52 Tandragee

☎ Tandragee (0762) 840727/841272
Markethill Rd, Tandragee, Craigavon BT62 2ER
5 miles from Portadown on Newry Rd.
Parkland course.
18 holes, 6084 yards, S.S.S.69
Club founded in 1922.
Visitors: welcome.
Green fees: weekdays £3.50, weekends and Bank Holidays £6.
Society meetings: welcome except Sat.
Catering: full catering except Mon.
Hotels: Seagle, Portadown; Carngrove, Portadown; Gisford, Market Hill.

Z53 Warrenpoint

☎ Warrenpoint (069 37) 73695
Lower Dromore Rd, Warrenpoint, Co Down BT34 3LN
Situated on A2 Newry road, ½ mile W of Warrenpoint.
Parkland course.
18 holes, 5626 metres, S.S.S.70
Club founded in 1893.
Visitors: welcome except on Sat.
Green fees: weekdays £5, weekends £7.
Society meetings: catered for except on Sat.
Catering: full catering facilities.
Hotels: Osborne Hotel.

Z54 Whitehead

☎ Whitehead (096 03) 72792
Clubhouse, 78631 Sec
McCrae's Brae, Whitehead, Co Antrim BT38 9NZ
Take turning into Whitehead off main Carrickfergus to Larne road to Islandmagee road, signpost at bottom of McCrea's Brae to golf club.
Undulating parkland course.
18 holes, 6412 yards, S.S.S.71
Club founded in 1904.
Visitors: welcome except on Sat and on competition days.
Green fees: Men – weekdays £4.50, weekends and Bank Holidays £6; Ladies – weekdays £4, weekends and Bank Holidays £5.50.
Society meetings: by arrangement with Sec/Manager.
Catering: by arrangement with Steward.
Hotels: Dolphin Hotel, Marine Parade, Whitehead.

AA North Eire

AA1 Achill Island
☎ (098) 43202
Keel, Achill, Co Mayo.
Via Castlebar or Westport.
Seaside course.
9 holes, 5410 yards, S.S.S.67
Club founded in 1951.
Visitors: welcome.
Green fees: £2 per day.
Society meetings: welcome.
Catering: none.
Hotels: Slievemore; Atlantic; Wave Crest; Achill Sound; Dugort; Achill Head.

AA2 Ardee
☎ Ardee (041) 53227
Town Parks, Ardee, Co Louth.
¼ mile N of town.
Parkland course.
9 holes, 3057 yards, S.S.S.69
to be extended to 18 holes in April 1986.
Club founded in 1911.
Visitors: welcome except on Sun.
Green fees: weekdays £5, weekends £6.
Society meetings: welcome except on Sun.
Catering: meals served at weekends or by arrangement on weekdays.
Hotels: many good hotels in area.

AA3 Athenry
☎ (091) 94466
Palmerstown, Oranmore, Co Galway.
5 miles from Athenry on main road to Galway.
Parkland course.
9 holes, 5550 yards, S.S.S.67
Club founded in 1927.
Visitors: welcome except on Sun.
Green fees: weekdays £3, Sat £4.
Society meetings: welcome except on Sun.
Catering: light refreshments available.
Hotels: Western, Athenry; Hanberry's, Athenry.

AA4 Athlone
☎ Athlone (0902) 2073
Hodson Bay, Athlone.
3 miles from Athlone on Roscommon road on shores of Lough Ree.
Undulating parkland course.
18 holes, 6000 yards, S.S.S.70
Course designed by Fred Hawtree.
Club founded in 1892.
Visitors: welcome on weekdays and by arrangement on Sat.
Green fees: weekdays £4, weekends and Bank Holidays £5.
Society meetings: catered for on weekdays.
Catering: full catering facilities except Mon.
Hotels: Hodson Bay; Prince of Wales; Royal Hoey; Shamrock Lodge.

AA5 Balbriggan
☎ Dublin (01) 412173 or 412229
Sec/Manager
Blackhall, Balbriggan, Co Dublin.
½ mile S of town on main Belfast to Dublin road, 17 miles from Dublin.
Meadowland course.
18 holes, 6300 yards, S.S.S.70
Course designed by B. Browne (new 9 holes).
Club founded in 1945.
Visitors: welcome but advisable to check at weekends.
Green fees: weekdays £6, weekends and Bank Holidays £7 (£3 with member).
Society meetings: welcome by arrangement on Mon and Wed.
Catering: snacks available.
Hotels: Grand, Balbriggan.

AA6 Ballina
☎ (096) 21050
Mossgrove, Shanaghy, Ballina, Co Mayo.
On outskirts of town on road to Bonniconlon.
Undulating course.
9 holes, 5182 yards, S.S.S.66
Club founded in 1924.
Visitors: welcome except on Sun mornings and competition days.
Green fees: weekdays £3, weekends £4.
Society meetings: by arrangement with Sec.
Catering: meals served.
Hotels: Downhill; Bartra; American.

AA7 Ballinamore
☎ Ballinamore (078) 44346
Creevy, Ballinamore, Co Leitrim.
1 mile from town centre, sign at bridge.
Moorland course.
9 holes, 5680 yards, S.S.S.67
Club founded in 1923.
Visitors: welcome.
Green fees: £3 per day.
Society meetings: welcome.
Catering: soup and sandwiches available.
Hotels: Slieve-an-Iaraim; Commercial; McAllisters.

AA8 Ballinasloe
☎ Ballinasloe (0905) 42126
Ballinasloe, Co Galway.
2 miles from Ballinasloe on Ballinasloe to Portumna road.
Parkland/ meadowland course.
18 holes, 5850 yards, S.S.S.66
Course designed by Eddie Hackett.
Club founded in 1905.
Visitors: welcome.
Green fees: weekdays £4, weekends £5.
Society meetings: welcome.
Catering: snacks and bar facilities available.
Hotels: Haydens; East County.

AA9 Ballybofey & Stranorlar
☎ Ballybofey 93
Ballybofey, Co Donegal
14 miles from Strabane, club signposted on Strabane road.
Parkland course.
18 holes, 5819 yards, S.S.S.69
Club founded in 1958.
Visitors: welcome.
Green fees: weekdays £3, weekends £5.
Society meetings: welcome.
Catering: none.
Hotels: Kee's, Stranorlar; Jackson's, Ballybofey.

AA10 Ballyhawnis
☎ Ballyhawnis (0907) 30014
Coolnaha, Ballyhawnis, Co Mayo.
1 mile from Ballyhawnis on Sligo road.
Undulating course.
10 holes, 2866 yards, S.S.S.69
Club founded in 1929.
Visitors: welcome except on Sun.
Green fees: £4 (£3 with member).
Society meetings: catered for by Ladies Committee.
Hotels: Central, Ballyhawnis; Westway, Kiltimagh.

AA11 Ballyliffin
☎ Clonmany 13
Ballyliffin, Clonmany, Co Donegal
8 miles from Buncrana, 6 miles from Carndonagh.
Seaside links course.
18 holes, 6611 yards, S.S.S.71
18 holes, 6229 yards, S.S.S.69
Club founded in 1947.
Visitors: welcome.
Green fees: weekdays £2.50 (£2 with member), weekends and Bank Holidays £3 (£2.50 with member).
Society meetings: welcome.
Hotels: Strand; Ballyliffin.

AA12 Belmullet
☎ Belmullet (097) 81266
Belmullet, Co Mayo.
Turn right at Binghaustown Church.
Seaside links course.
9 holes, 2857 yards, S.S.S.67
Club founded around 1923.
Visitors: welcome.
Green fees: £2 per day.
Catering: none.
Hotels: Western Strands Hotel.

AA13 Belturbet
☎ Belturbet (049) 22287
Erne Hill, Belturbet, Co Cavan.
½ mile on Cavan Rd from Belturbet, on left.
Parkland course.
9 holes, 5180 yards, S.S.S.65
Club founded in 1950.
Visitors: always welcome.
Green fees: £3 per day.
Society meetings: welcome by arrangement.
Catering: by appointment.
Hotels: 7 Horse Shoes, Belturbet; also guest house accommodation.

AA14 Boyle
☎ (010 353) 7962594
Boyle, Co Roscommon.
1½ miles from Boyle on Roscommon Rd.
Parkland course.
9 holes, 5312 yards, S.S.S.66
Visitors: welcome.
Green fees: £3 per day.
Catering: not available.
Hotels: Royal; Forest Park.

AA15 Bundoran
☎ Bundoran (072) 41302
Bundoran, Co Donegal.
32 miles W of Enniskillen, 25 miles N of Sligo.
Undulating seaside course.
18 holes, 6328 yards, S.S.S.71
Course designed by Harry Vardon.
Club founded in 1894.
Visitors: welcome.
Green fees: weekdays £6, weekends £7.
Society meetings: welcome, but 3 weeks advance notice required.
Catering: snacks only available, meals at Great Northern Hotel on course.
Hotels: Great Northern; Holyrood; Maghery; Atlantic Apartotel.

AA16 Carrickmines
☎ Dublin (01) 895676
Carrickmines, Co Dublin.
T43, 7 miles S of Dublin, left at Sandyford.
9 holes, 6026 yards, S.S.S.69
Visitors: welcome on weekdays and with member on Sat and Bank Holidays.
Green fees: on request.

AA17 Carrick-on-Shannon
☎ Carrick-on-Shannon (078) 20157
Woodbrook, Carrick-on-Shannon, Co Leitrim.
Between Carrick-on-Shannon and Blyle, on Dublin to Sligo road, 3 miles from station.
Undulating parkland course.
9 holes, 6000 yards, S.S.S.68
Club founded in 1910.
Visitors: welcome.
Green fees: £4 per day, £15 per week.
Society meetings: welcome.
Catering: snacks available.
Hotels: good hotels in Boyle and Carrick-on-Shannon.

AA18 Castle
☎ Dublin (01) 904207
Woodside Drive, Rathfarnham, Dublin 14.
From city turn left after Terenure and second right.
Parkland course.
18 holes, 6240 yards, S.S.S.69
Course designed by H.S. Colt.
Club founded in 1913.
Visitors: welcome on weekdays.
Green fees: £10 per round.
Society meetings: applications considered.
Catering: full lunch and dinner served.
Hotels: Orwell Lodge, Rathgar, Dublin 6.

AA19 Castlebar
☎ Castlebar (094) 21649
Rocklands, Castlebar, Co Mayo.
1¼ miles from town centre.
Parkland course.
18 holes, 6109 yards, S.S.S.69
Club founded in 1910.
Visitors: welcome on weekdays.
Green fees: £5 per day.
Society meetings: welcome.
Catering: catering available with 3 hours notice.
Hotels: Welcome Inn; Breaffy House; Travellers Friend; Imperial.

AA20 Castlerea
☎ Castlerea (0907) 20068
Clonalis, Castlerea, Co Roscommon.
On main Dublin to Castlebar road, course just outside town on Castlebar side.
Parkland course.
9 holes, 4974 yards, S.S.S.67
Club founded in 1905.
Visitors: welcome except on Sun if competition day.
Green fees: weekdays £3 per day, weekends £5 per day.
Society meetings: welcome by arrangement.
Catering: catering available by arrangement for societies.
Hotels: Don Arms; Tulleys.

AA21 Claremorris
☎ Claremorris (094) 71527
Rushbrook, Castlemaggaret, Claremorris, Co Mayo.
On Galway road coming from Claremorris town, 1½ miles from town.
Parkland course.
9 holes, 5898 yards, S.S.S.69
Club founded in 1927.
Visitors: welcome.
Green fees: £3 per day.
Society meetings: catered for on weekdays.
Catering: catering facilities available by arrangement.
Hotels: Western; Imperial; Central; all in Claremorris.

AA22 Clones
☎ Scotshouse (047) 56017
Hilton Park, Clones, Co Monaghan.
3 miles S of Clones towards Scotshouse.
Parkland course.
9 holes, 5570 yards, S.S.S.67
Club founded in 1913.
Visitors: welcome.
Green fees: weekdays £3, weekends £4.
Society meetings: welcome.
Catering: meals served except Mon.
Hotels: Creighton, Clones; Hibernian, Clones; Lennard Arms, Clones; White Horse, Cootehill.

AA23 Clontarf
☎ Dublin (01) 315085
Donnycarney House, Malahide Rd, Dublin 3.
NE of city centre, 3 miles on main road to Malahide.
Parkland course.
18 holes, 5447 metres, S.S.S.67
Club founded in 1912.
Visitors: welcome on weekdays (Ladies Day Mon) and with member at weekends.
Green fees: weekdays £8.
Society meetings: welcome on Tues and Fri by prior arrangement.
Catering: full catering facilities available.
Hotels: St Lawrence, Howth; Sheiling, Howth Rd.

AA24 Connemara
☎ (095) 21153
Ballyconneely, Co Galway.
4 miles from Ballyconneely.
Undulating seaside links course.
Championship 18 holes, 6604 metres, S.S.S.73
Medal 18 holes, 6186 metres, S.S.S.71
Course designed by Eddie Hackett.
Club founded in 1972.
Visitors: welcome.

Green fees: £8 per day.
Society meetings: welcome.
Catering: meals served.
Hotels: Allbeyglen Castle, Clifden; Rockglen, Clifden; Eadiseask, Ballyconneely; Clifden Bay, Clifden.

AA25 Corballis

☎ Dublin (01) 450583
Donabate, Co Dublin.
TI N from Dublin, right down L91, 2 miles beyond Swords.
Seaside course.
18 holes, 4898 yards, S.S.S.64
Visitors: welcome by arrangement.
Green fees: weekdays £3.50, weekends £4.50, OAPs and UB40s £2.
Society meetings: welcome by arrangement except Sat afternoon and Sun.
Catering: by arrangement.
Hotels: many good hotels in area.

AA26 County Cavan

☎ Cavan (049) 31283
Arnmore House, Drumelis, Cavan.
Located within 1 mile from Cavan town on Killeshandra road.
Parkland course.
18 holes, 6100 yards, S.S.S.69
Club founded in 1896.
Visitors: welcome any day but with restrictions on Wed and Sun.
Green fees: £5.
Society meetings: welcome.
Catering: full catering facilities available.
Hotels: Kilmore, Cavan; Farnham Arms, Cavan.

AA27 County Longford

☎ (43) 46310
Glack, Longford.
Off Dublin to Sligo Rd (N4) E of town, signposted.
Undulating course.
18 holes, 6028 yards, S.S.S.68
Course designed by E. Hackett.
Club founded in 1894.
Visitors: welcome.
Green fees: £5.
Society meetings: welcome by arrangement.
Catering: meals served.
Hotels: Annally; Longford Arms.

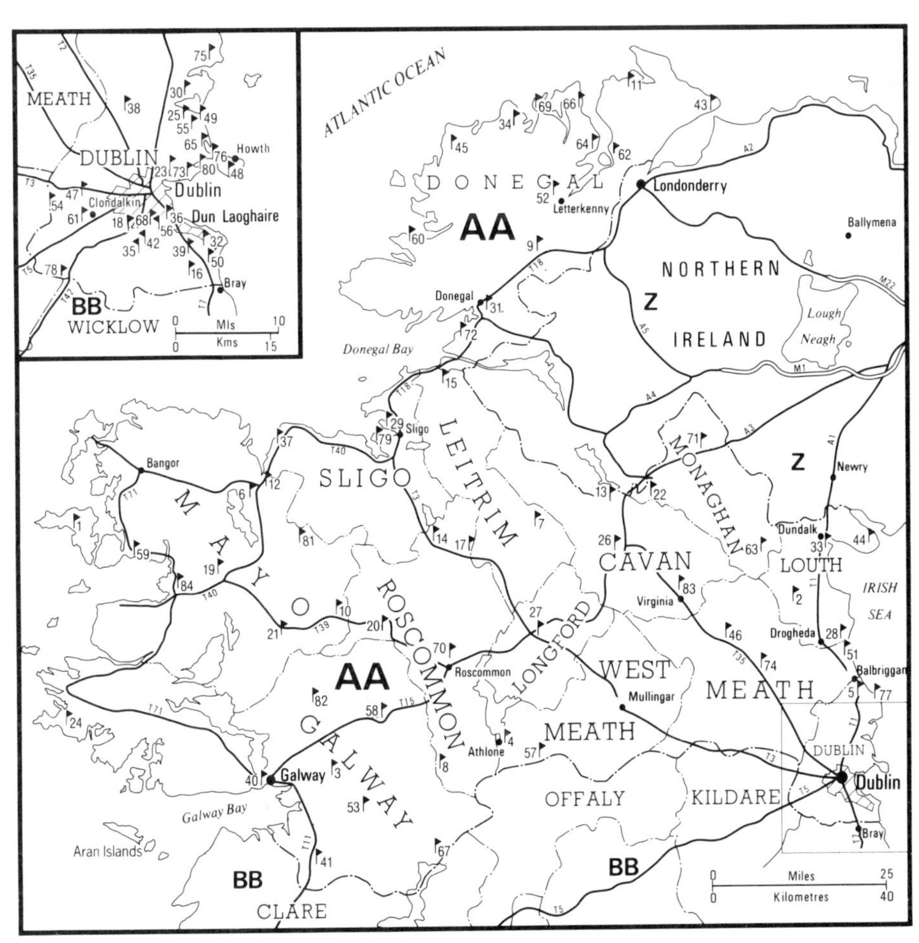

AA28 County Louth

☎ Drogheda (041) 22327 or 22329 Sec.
Baltray, Drogheda, Co Louth.
5 miles E of Drogheda, take road along N bank of River Boyne to Baltray village.
Championship links course.
18 holes, 6800 yards, S.S.S.73
Course designed by Tom Simpson.
Club founded in 1892.
Visitors: welcome by arrangement.
Green fees: on application.
Society meetings: welcome by arrangement on weekdays and on Sat from April to Oct.
Catering: full catering facilities.
Hotels: County Louth.

AA29 County Sligo

☎ Sligo (071) 77186
Rosses Point, Co Sligo.
5 miles from Sligo.
Seaside links course.
18 holes, 6646 yards, S.S.S.71
Course designed by Colt & Alison.
Club founded in 1894.
Visitors: welcome every day, wise to check before arrival.
Green fees: £10 per day.
Society meetings: welcome by arrangement with Sec/Manager.
Catering: snacks during day, à la carte after 6 pm. Dining closed Thurs. Other catering by arrangement.
Hotels: Yeats Country Ryan, Rosses Point, Co Sligo; Ballincar House, Ballincar, Sligo.

AA30 Donabate

☎ Dublin (01) 45035
Donabate, Balcarrick, Co Dublin.
1st right 1 mile N of Swords on Dublin to Belfast road.
Parkland course.
18 holes, 5679 metres, S.S.S.69
Visitors: welcome.
Green fees: £8.
Society meetings: welcome by arrangement.
Catering: meals served.
Hotels: Crofton Airport.

AA31 Donegal

☎ Ballintra (073) 34054
Murvagh, Laghey PO, Co Donegal.
About 1 mile off main Ballyshannon to Donegal Town road, half-way between towns.
Seaside links course.
Championship 18 holes, 7271 metres, 6648 yards, S.S.S.75
Medal 18 holes, 6844 metres, 6243 yards, S.S.S.73
Course designed by E. Hackett.
Club founded in 1960.
Visitors: welcome.
Green fees: weekdays £5 per day, weekends and Bank Holidays £6.
Society meetings: welcome by arrangement with Hon Sec.
Catering: full catering facilities.
Hotels: Abbey and Central, Donegal Town; Sandhouse, Rossnowlagh; Ernan Park.

AA32 Dundalk

☎ (042) 32731
Blackrock, Dundalk, Co Louth.
Off T1 3 miles S of Dundalk on Dundalk Bay.
Parkland course.
18 holes, 6740 yards, S.S.S.72
Course designed by Tom Shannon.
Club founded in 1905.
Visitors: welcome except on Sun (Tues Ladies Day).
Green fees: weekdays £7, weekends £9.
Society meetings: welcome by arrangement on weekdays except Tues.
Catering: full catering facilities
Hotels: Fairways; Imperial; Ballymascanlon; Derryhale.

County Louth

There are certain courses throughout Britain and Ireland where a sense of expectancy reaches a peak at a specific point near journey's end, when turning off the main road at Wadebridge for St Enodoc, for instance, or when a long drive nears its end along the only road to Southerness, a superb links on the Solway Firth, which in 1985 hosted the Scottish Amateur for the first time.

A similar sense of anticipation accompanies the last lap to Brancaster which takes you past the church and down through the marsh lined by tall rushes; and there is a less glamorous approach beyond the level crossing to the Royal Cinque Ports Golf Club at Deal. The twisty conclusion to the journey to Rye is another example. But there are a few sights as thrilling as the links of County Louth at Baltray at last coming into view.

It is a fine, challenging course in the traditional mould of dunes, undoubtedly one of my favourites and one whose rating within Ireland is not as high as it should be. It is worthy of the best, full of variety and contrast with always the magnificence of its distant views.

Although there have been modifications, one or two made necessary by moving the clubhouse some years ago, there is still an authentic touch of Tom Simpson about it that bears the unmistakable mark of quality. If I had to exemplify it, I would point to the long 3rd which, after a reasonably straightforward drive, reveals hidden talents once the brow of dunes has been scaled. Beautifully natural humps and hollows make careful placing of the second shot essential and, for those attempting to get home in two, there is only a narrow path between salvation and ruin. An attractive small green is not easy to hit.

The curving 1st and testing 2nd make a nice introduction but the 4th, a short par 4, offers some relief before the first of four first class short holes. The 5th and 7th, sandwiched around another fine par 5, demand well-controlled, truly hit iron shots while the 8th and 9th are no easy 4s.

A sense of space becomes more apparent on the second half which, having begun with a hole alongside the clubhouse, works its way towards the sea by means of the dogleg par 5 11th. It is then that a special character is lent by the 12th, 13th and 14th which, from a combination of factors, comprise a notable trio. They emphasise the merit of great par 4s, not perhaps daunting in terms of yardage but rewarding in the satisfaction they give by being played properly, as they must be if they are to yield a par or a birdie.

Changes to the course have resulted in two short holes in the last four but the 16th is appealing and the 18th the last of five par 5s. Baltray, as the course is more conveniently called after the local fishing village, has a championship cloak without a doubt and it has its less forbidding side which makes it so popular for a day out.

Harry Bradshaw's winning aggregate of 291 in the 1947 Irish Professional championship tells a tale or two about its full-blown potential. It is also rare among Irish clubs in having two legendary Irish women golfers as members. Val Reddan, as Clarrie Tiernan, won the Irish title twice and was also the first Irish woman to play in the Curtis Cup. After the war, she was confronted by her new local rival Philomena Garvey in the final of the Irish; not, as would have been most appropriate, at Baltray, but at Lahinch. After the longest final, Garvey won at the 39th, the first of her 15 victories.

Continuing the feminine influence, Mrs Josephine Connolly founded the East of Ireland men's championship played annually at Baltray, an event by which Irish golfers set great store. It can claim father and son winners in Joe and Roddy Carr, but when you speak of the course you speak of distinction. Its list of champions is no more than it deserves.

AA33 Dunfanaghy
Dunfanaghy, Co Donegal.
Off main road ¼ mile E of Dunfanaghy.
Seaside course.
18 holes, 4977 metres, S.S.S.66
Visitors: welcome.
Green fees: weekdays £3.50 per day, weekends £4.50.
Catering: none.
Hotels: Arnold's; Carrig Rua; Port na Blagh; Shandon.

AA34 Dun Laoghaire
☎ Dublin (01) 803916
Eglinton Park, Dun Laoghaire, Co Dublin.
7 miles from Dublin, ½ mile from Dun Laoghaire town centre and ferry port.
Parkland course.
18 holes, 5463 metres, S.S.S.69
Club founded in 1910.
Visitors: welcome on weekdays and by arrangement at weekends.
Green fees: weekdays £8 per day (£3 with member), weekends and Bank Holidays £10 (£9 with member).
Society meetings: catered for on Mon, Tues or Fri.
Catering: snacks available and evening meals from April to Sept.
Hotels: Royal Marine, Dun Laoghaire; Fitzpatricks Castle, Killiney, Co Dublin.

AA35 Edmondstown
☎ Dublin (01) 932461 Club, 931082 Sec.
Edmondstown, Rathfarnham, Dublin 16.
T42 S of Dublin, Rathfarnham, 1 mile.
Parkland course.
18 holes, 6177 yards, S.S.S.69
Course designed by E. Hackett.
Club founded in 1944.
Visitors: welcome on weekdays and Sun after 3 pm.
Green fees: weekdays £8 (£4 with member), weekends £10 (with member £5).

AA36 Elm Park
☎ Dublin (01) 693438, 693014 or 694505
Nutley Lane, Donnybrook, Dublin 4.
2 miles from city centre beside Montrose television studios and St Vincents Hospital.
Parkland course.
18 holes, 5485 yards, S.S.S.68
Course designed by Fred Davies.
Club founded in 1927.
Visitors: welcome but phone in advance.
Green fees: weekdays £10 (with member £4), weekends and Bank Holidays £14 (with member £4.50).
Society meetings: catered for on Tues only.
Catering: full catering facilities available.
Hotels: many good hotels in area.

AA37 Enniscrone
☎ (096) 36297
Enniscrone, Co Sligo.
8 miles N of Ballina, ½ mile from Enniscrone.
Seaside course.
18 holes, 6511 yards, S.S.S.72
Course designed by E. Hackett.
Club founded in 1931.
Visitors: welcome except on Sun mornings.
Green fees: £6 per day.
Catering: lunches served, advance booking necessary.
Hotels: Atlantic; Benbulben; Killala Bay; Alpine; Castle Arms.

AA38 Forrest Little
☎ Dublin (01) 401763 or 401183
Forrest Little, Cloghran, Co Dublin
½ mile beyond Dublin Airport on Dublin to Belfast road, take first turn left.
Parkland course.
18 holes, 5844 metres, S.S.S.70
Course designed by Fred Hawtree.
Club founded in 1940.
Visitors: welcome on weekdays.
Green fees: £8 per day (£3 with member).
Society meetings: catered for on Mon and Thurs afternoons.
Catering: snacks always available; à la carte menu from 5 pm daily.
Hotels: Dublin Airport; Hawthorn.

AA39 Foxrock
☎ Dublin (01) 893992 or 895668
Torquary Rd, Dublin 18.
Club is situated about 6 miles from Dublin, turn right off T7 just past Stillergan on to Leopardstown Rd, then left into Torquary Rd.
Parkland course.
9 holes, 5439 metres, S.S.S.69
Club founded in 1893.
Visitors: welcome on weekdays except Tues and with member on Sun.
Green fees: £8.50 per day.
Society meetings: by arrangement with Sec.
Catering: snacks available and meals by arrangement for societies.
Hotels: Killiney Castle; Jurys; Burlington; Montrose.

AA40 Galway
☎ Galway (091) 22169 Sec/Manager, 23038 Pro, 21827 Kitchen.
Blackrock, Salthill, Galway.
On L100 2 miles W of Galway.
Seaside course.
18 holes, 6192 yards, S.S.S.70
Club founded in 1895.
Visitors: welcome on weekdays.
Green fees: £9 (with member £5).
Society meetings: welcome on weekdays.
Catering: snacks and meals served.
Hotels: Salthill, Ardilaun; Bamba, Anto Santo.

AA41 Gort
☎ Gort (091) 31336
Laughty Shaughnessy, Gort, Co Galway.
24 miles S of Galway on County Road No 363 Gort to Tubber.
Parkland course.
9 holes, 5688 yards, S.S.S.67
Course designed by Matt Hackett.
Club founded in 1924.
Visitors: welcome.
Green fees: £4 per person.
Society meetings: welcome.
Catering: snacks available.
Hotels: O'Sullivan's Royal, Gort; Glymis, Gort.

AA42 Grange
☎ Dublin (01) 932832 or 932889
Grange Rd, Rathfarnham, Dublin 16.
7 miles S from city centre, near Rathfarnham village.
Parkland course.
18 holes, 5517 yards, S.S.S.69
Course designed by James Braid.
Club founded in 1910.
Visitors: welcome on weekdays except Tues and Wed afternoons.
Green fees: weekdays £8.
Society meetings: welcome Mon and Thurs.
Catering: full catering facilities available.
Hotels: Marlay, Rathfarnham, Dublin 14.

AA43 Greencastle
☎ Greencastle 13.
Greencastle, via Lifford, Co Donegal.
On L85 23 miles NE of Londonderry through Moville.
Seaside course.
9 holes, 5386 yards, S.S.S.66
Club founded in 1892.
Visitors: welcome.
Green fees: weekends £5, weekdays £3.
Society meetings: welcome.
Catering: meals served.
Hotels: Fort, Greencastle; McNamara's, Morville; Foyle, Morville.

AA44 Greenore
☎ (42) 73212
Greenore, Co Louth
15 miles N of Dundalk on Carlingford Rd.

Seaside course.
18 holes, 5614 metres, S.S.S.69
Course designed by E. Hackett.
Club founded in 1897.
Visitors: welcome.
Green fees: weekdays £5, weekends £7.
Society meetings: welcome.
Catering: lunches served except Tues.
Hotels: Village; Fairways.

AA45 Gweedore

☎ Gweedore (0075) 31140
Derrybeg, Letterkenny, Co Donegal.
L82 from Letterkenny or T72 from Donegal.
Seaside course.
9 holes, 2700 yards, S.S.S.66
Visitors: welcome.
Green fees: on request.
Catering: lunches served.
Hotels: Derrybeg; Seaview; Gweedove.

AA46 Headfort

☎ (046) 40146
Kells, Co Meath.
¼ mile from Kells on main Kells to Dublin road.
Parkland course.
18 holes, 6393 yards, S.S.S.70
Club founded in 1930.
Visitors: welcome.
Green fees: weekdays £6, weekends and Bank Holidays £7.
Society meetings: catered for except on Sun.
Catering: snacks available and meals by arrangement for societies.
Hotels: Headfort Arms, Kells.

AA47 Hermitage

☎ Dublin (01) 265049 or 268491
Lucan, Co Dublin.
T3 W from Dublin.
Championship 18 holes, 5942 metres, S.S.S.71
Medal 18 holes, 5668 metres, S.S.S.70
Green Pegs 18 holes, 5470 yards, S.S.S.69
Club founded in 1905.
Visitors: welcome by arrangement.
Green fees: weekdays £10, weekends £15.
Society meetings: by arrangement.
Catering: meals served.
Hotels: Ashling; West County; Lucan County.

AA48 Howth

☎ Dublin (01) 323055
Carrickbrack Rd, Sutton, Dublin.
9½ miles NE of city centre, 1½ miles from Sutton Cross towards Howth summit.
Moorland course.
18 holes, 6168 yards, S.S.S.69
Course designed by James Braid.
Club founded in 1916.
Visitors: welcome on weekdays except Wed.
Green fees: £8.
Society meetings: catered for by arrangement on weekdays except Wed.
Catering: snacks and teas available.
Hotels: Marine, Sutton; Sutton Castle, Sutton; Howth Lodge, Howth; Lawrence.

AA49 Island

☎ Dublin (01) 45095 Clubhouse, 452205 Sec.
Corballis, Donabate, Co Dublin.
From Dublin leave T1 approx 1 mile beyond Swords, then L91 for 3 miles and turn right.
Seaside course.
18 holes, 6203 yards, S.S.S.70
Course designed by Fred Hawtree & Eddie Hackett.
Club founded in 1890.
Visitors: welcome on weekdays, weekends by arrangement.
Green fees: weekdays £7, weekends £9.
Society meetings: by arrangement.
Catering: lunches served.
Hotels: Grand, Malahig.

AA50 Killiney

☎ Dublin (01) 851983
Killiney, Co Dublin.
3 miles from Dun Laoghaire town centre.
Parkland course.
9 holes, 3046 yards, S.S.S.69
Visitors: welcome on weekdays except Thurs.
Green fees: £8.
Society meetings: no.
Catering: snacks available.
Hotels: Fitzpatrick Castle, Killiney; Court, Killiney Bay.

AA51 Laytown & Bettystown

☎ Drogheda (041) 27170 or 27563.
Bettystown, Co Meath
On L125 off T1, 25 miles N of Dublin, 4 miles from Drogheda.
Seaside links course.
18 holes, 6200 yards, S.S.S.69
Club founded in 1909.
Visitors: welcome on weekdays.
Green fees: weekdays £7 (£4 with member), weekends £10 (£5 with member).
Society meetings: catered for on weekdays; bookable 1 year in advance.
Catering: meals and snacks served.
Hotels: Neptune, Bettystown; Boyne Valley, Stameen, Drogheda; Rosnaree, Dublin Rd, Drogheda; Mosney Holiday Centre, Mosney.

AA52 Letterkenny

☎ Letterkenny 144.
Barnhill, Letterkenny, Co Donegal.
On T72, 2 miles N of Letterkenny.
18 holes, 6299 yards, S.S.S.69
Course designed by E. Hackett.
Visitors: welcome.
Green fees: on request.
Society meetings: welcome.
Catering: snacks served, meals by arrangement.
Hotels: Ballymaine; Three Ways; Gallagher's; McCawy's.

AA53 Loughrea

☎ (010 35391) 41049
Loughrea, Co Galway.
On L11, 1 mile N of Loughrea.
Meadowland course.
9 holes, 5798 yards, S.S.S.68
Visitors: welcome.
Green fees: on request.
Society meetings: Mon – Sat by arrangement.
Catering: by arrangement.
Hotels: in area.

AA54 Lucan

☎ Dublin (01) 280246 or 282106
Celbridge Rd, Lucan, Co Dublin.
Take Galway road from Dublin, turn left at traffic lights after passing through village of Lucan, club is on left of road ½ mile towards Celbridge.
Meadowland course.
9 holes, 6287 yards, S.S.S.69
Club founded in 1902.
Visitors: welcome on weekdays except Thurs.
Green fees: £7 per day (£6 with member).
Society meetings: catered for on Mon, Tues and Fri with prior Committee approval.
Catering: full range of meals and snacks.
Hotels: Spa, Lucan; Springfield, Lucan; West County, Falmerstown, Co Dublin.

AA55 Malahide

☎ Dublin (01) 450248
Coast Rd, Malahide, Co Dublin.
8 miles S of Dublin, follow Malahide road.
Parkland course.
9 holes, 2674 yards, S.S.S.67
Course designed by Nathaniel Hone.
Club founded in 1892.
Visitors: welcome except on Sun and Wed.

Green fees: weekdays £5, weekends £6; reduction with member.
Catering: simple meals available.
Hotels: Grand, Malahide; Stuart, Malahide; Grove.

AA56 Milltown
☎ Dublin (01) 976090
Lower Churchtown Rd, Dublin 14.
3 miles S of city centre, via Ranelagh village.
Parkland course.
18 holes, 5703 metres, S.S.S.70
Club founded in 1907.
Visitors: welcome except Tues and Wed p.m.
Green fees: weekdays £10 (with member £5), weekends £12 (with member £7).
Society meetings: by arrangement.
Catering: lunch and dinner served.
Hotels: Orwell Lodge, Orwell Rd, Dublin 6.

AA57 Moate
☎ (0902) 31271
Moate, Co Westmeath.
On T4, 8 miles E of Athlone.
Parkland course.
9 holes, 5348 yards, S.S.S.65
Visitors: welcome.
Green fees: on application.
Society meetings: welcome.
Catering: meals by arrangement.
Hotels: Hayden's, Ballinsloe; Imperial, Tuam.

AA58 Mountbellew
☎ (0905) 79259
Shankhill, Mountbellew, Co Galway.
On T4, 28 miles E of Galway.
Parkland course.
9 holes, 5650 yards, S.S.S.67
Club founded in 1929.
Visitors: welcome.
Green fees: £3 per day, £15 per week.
Society meetings: welcome.
Catering: teas, soup, sandwiches, full meals on notification.
Hotels: Guest houses, hotels in Ballinasloe, 16 miles, and Tuam, 16 miles.

AA59 Mulrany
☎ Mulrany 3
Mulrany, Westport, Co Mayo.
N59, 10 miles from Newport.
Undulating seaside course.
9 holes, 6380 yards, S.S.S.70
Visitors: welcome.
Green fees: £3 per day.
Society meetings: welcome.
Catering: none.
Hotels: Newport House, Newport; Moynish House.

AA60 Narin & Portnoo
☎ Clooney 21.
Portnoo, Co Donegal.
8 miles W of Glenties via T72 and L81.
Seaside course.
18 holes, 5700 yards, S.S.S.68
Visitors: welcome.
Green fees: on request.
Society meetings: by arrangement.
Hotels: Lake House, Portnoo; Nesbitt Arms; Highlands.

AA61 Newlands
☎ Dublin (01) 593157
Clondalkin, Co Dublin.
6 miles from city centre on main southern Cork road.
Parkland course.
18 holes, 5705 metres, S.S.S.70
Course designed by James Braid.
Club founded in 1926.
Visitors: welcome by arrangement.
Green fees: £8.
Society meetings: by arrangement.
Catering: full catering.
Hotels: Green Isle.

AA62 North West
☎ Buncrana 12
Lisfannon, Fahan, Co Donegal.
12 miles from Derry on main Buncrana road.
Seaside course.
18 holes, 5928 yards, S.S.S.67
Visitors: welcome.
Green fees: on request.
Society meetings: welcome weekdays, by arrangement at weekends.
Catering: by arrangement.
Hotels: Roneragh House, Fahan; White Strand Motor Inn, Buncrana.

AA63 Nuremore
☎ (042) 61438
Carrickmacross, Co Monaghan.
On main Dublin to Derry road about 1 mile from Carrickmacross on Dublin side.
Parkland course.
9 holes, 5466 metres, S.S.S.69
Course designed by Eddie Dunne.
Club founded in 1964.
Visitors: welcome.
Green fees: £4 per day.
Society meetings: catered for by prior arrangement through hotel.
Catering: meals and snacks served at hotel.
Hotels: Nuremore.

AA64 Otway
Rathmullan, Co Donegal.
On W shore of Loch Swilly.
Seaside course.
9 holes, 4134 yards, S.S.S.60
Visitors: welcome.
Hotels: Fort Royal; Rathmullan House; Pier.

AA65 Portmarnock
☎ Dublin (01) 323082
Portmarnock, Co Dublin.
From Dublin along coast road to Baldoyle, on to Portmarnock, turn right at Jet Garage, 1 mile up private road.
Green 18 holes, 6064 yards, S.S.S.73
White 18 holes, 6276 yards, S.S.S.74
Yellow 18 holes, 6489 yards, S.S.S.75
Course designed by W.C. Pickeman & George Ross.
Club founded in 1894.
Visitors: welcome (no Ladies at weekends or Bank Holidays).
Green fees: Men – weekdays £15, weekends and Bank Holidays £17; Ladies – weekdays £5.
Society meetings: by arrangement, max 50.
Catering: snacks and meals served.
Hotels: Grand, Malihide.

AA66 Portsalon
☎ Portsalon 11
Portsalon, Co Donegal.
L78 from Letterkenny.
Seaside course.
18 holes, 5522 yards, S.S.S.67
Visitors: welcome.
Green fees: on request.
Hotels: Portsalon.

AA67 Portumna
☎ Portumna (0509) 41059
Portumna, Co Galway.
1½ miles from Portumna on Woodford road.
Woodland/parkland course.
9 holes, 5566 yards, S.S.S.68
Course designed by P. O'Brien.
Club founded in 1913.
Visitors: welcome.
Green fees: £3 per day.
Society meetings: welcome.
Catering: by arrangement only.
Hotels: Westpark, Portumna; Clonwyn House, Portumna; Portland House, Portumna.

AA68 Rathfarnham
☎ Dublin (01) 931201
Newtown, Rathfarnham, Dublin 16.
2 miles from Rathfarnham village.

LAYTOWN AND BETTYSTOWN GOLF CLUB, CO. MEATH

This 18-hole seaside course is 30 miles south of Dublin. Very popular for holidays, it caters for all the family and over the years it has been foremost in promoting juvenile golf.

Best days for visiting groups are mid-week. Catering facilities include a bar, snacks and lunch. Resident professional is Bobby Browne and the club's playing pro is Des Smyth, a Ryder cup player.

Club phone number is

041 27534

Meadowland course.
9 holes, 5833 metres, S.S.S.70
Club founded in 1896.
Visitors: welcome on weekdays except Tues and on Sun.
Green fees: £8 (£6 with member).
Society meetings: catered for on weekdays by arrangement.
Catering: by arrangement only.
Hotels: Marley Park, Grange Rd, Rathfarnham, Dublin 16.

AA69 Rosapenna

☎ (074) 55301
Downings, Letterkenny, Co Donegal.
22 miles from Letterkenny via Milford and Carrigart.
Seaside course.
18 holes, 6254 yards, S.S.S.71
Course designed by Tom Mitchell (1893) and re-designed by James Braid & Harry Vardon (1906).
Visitors: welcome.
Green fees: weekdays £5 per day, weekends and Bank Holidays £6 per day; £30 per week.
Catering: at Rosapenna Hotel.
Hotels: Rosapenna; Carrigart.

AA70 Roscommon

☎ (0903) 6283
Mote Park, Roscommon, Co Roscommon.
On T15, 96 miles W of Dublin.
Meadowland course.
9 holes, 6340 yards, S.S.S.70
Visitors: welcome.
Green fees: on application.
Society meetings: by arrangement.
Hotels: Abbey; Royal.

AA71 Rossmore

☎ (047) 81316
Rossmore Park, Monaghan.
About 2 miles from Monaghan on Monaghan to Cootehill road.
Undulating parkland course.
9 holes, 5859 yards, S.S.S.68
Club founded in 1920.
Visitors: welcome.
Green fees: weekdays £3, weekends and Bank Holidays £4.
Society meetings: catered for.
Catering: available by arrangement.
Hotels: Hillgrove; Four Seasons; Westenra.

AA72 Rossnowlagh

☎ Bundoran (072) 65343
Sand House Hotel, Rossnowlagh, Co Donegal.
Seaside course.
9 holes,
Visitors: welcome only during holiday season.
Green fees: on request.
Catering: lunches served.
Hotels: Sand House.

AA73 Royal Dublin

☎ Dublin (01) 336346 or 331262
Bull Island, Dollymount, Dublin 3.
4 miles NE of city centre on coast road to Howth.
Seaside links course.
18 holes, 6810 yards, S.S.S.73
Course designed by H.S. Colt.
Club founded in 1885.
Visitors: welcome on weekdays and by arrangement on Sun.
Green fees: weekdays £14 (£7 with member), Sun £16 (£8 with member).
Society meetings: by arrangement with Sec/Manager
Catering: full catering facilities available.
Hotels: Grand, Malahide; Howth Lodge, Howth; Marine, Sutton Cross.

AA74 Royal Tara

☎ Navan (046) 25244
Bellinter, Navan, Co Meath.
30 miles N of Dublin.
Parkland course.
18 holes, S.S.S.70
Club founded in 1923.
Visitors: welcome by arrangement.
Green fees: weekdays £6, weekends £7.
Society meetings: welcome by arrangement.
Catering: full catering facilities available.
Hotels: good hotels in area.

AA75 Rush

☎ Dublin (01) 438177
Rush, Co Dublin.
Dublin to Belfast road, turn right at Blakes Cross.
Seaside course.
9 holes, 5598 metres, S.S.S.69
Club founded in 1943.
Visitors: welcome except on Sun.
Green fees: £7.
Catering: on request.
Hotels: Pier House, Skerries; Argyle Lodge, Rush.

AA76 St Annes

☎ Dublin (01) 332797 (Sec 336471)
Bull Island, Clontarf, Dublin 5.
4 miles NE of Dublin.
Seaside course.
9 holes, 6104 yards, S.S.S.67
Visitors: welcome weekdays.
Green fees: £8 per day (£4 with member).
Society meetings: by arrangement.
Catering: full facilities.
Hotels: in Dublin.

AA77 Skerries

☎ Dublin (01) 491567 or 491204
Hacketstown, Skerries, Co Dublin
Take Belfast road N out of Dublin, past Airport and Swords, fork right for Lusk and Skerries after end of Swords by-pass.
Undulating parkland course.
18 holes, 5852 metres, S.S.S.70
Club founded in 1906.
Visitors: welcome.
Green fees: weekdays £8 (£3 with member), weekends £12 (£4.50 with member).
Society meetings: catered for on Mon, Thurs and Fri.
Catering: full catering facilities available.
Hotels: Pier House, Harbour Rd, Skerries; Anna Villa, Convent Lane, Skerries.

AA78 Slade Valley

☎ Dublin (01) 582207 or 582183
Lynch Park, Brittas, Co Dublin
Off N1 Dublin to Naas road.
Undulating course.
Championship 18 holes, 5462 metres, S.S.S.69
18 holes, 5337 metres, S.S.S.68
Course designed by W.D. Sullivan & D. O'Brien.
Club founded in 1971.
Visitors: welcome by arrangement with Sec.
Green fees: weekdays £5 before noon, £7 after noon; weekends £8.
Society meetings: by arrangement with Sec.
Catering: meals available at weekends and also on Tues and Wed during summer.
Hotels: Green Isle; Downshire House, Blessington.

AA79 Strandhill

☎ Sligo (071) 68188
Strandhill, Co Sligo.
5 miles W of Sligo city, course is situated in resort of Strandhill and is well signposted.
Seaside links course.
18 holes, 5950 yards, S.S.S.69
Club founded in 1931.
Visitors: welcome on weekdays and most weekends.
Green fees: weekdays £5, weekends and Bank Holidays £6.
Society meetings: welcome.
Catering: snacks available and meals by arrangement.

Hotels: Ocean View, Strandhill; The Southern, Sligo; Silver Swan, Sligo.

AA80 Sutton

☎ Dublin (01) 323013
Cush Point, Sutton, Dublin 13.
7 miles NE of city centre.
Seaside links course.
9 holes, 5522 yards, S.S.S.67
Club founded in 1890.
Visitors: welcome except on Tues and Sat.
Green fees: weekdays £8, weekends and Bank Holidays £10.
Society meetings: catered for by prior agreement.
Catering: bar facilities and snacks available.
Hotels: Marine, Sutton Cross; Howth Lodge, Claremont, Howth, Co Dublin.

AA81 Swinford

☎ (094) 51378
Brabazon Park, Swinford, Co Mayo.
Beside town, opposite Western Health Board complex.
Parkland course.
9 holes, 2725 yards, S.S.S.67
Club founded in 1922.
Visitors: welcome.
Green fees: £3 per day, £10 per week, £20 per month.
Society meetings: enquiries welcome.
Catering: catering facilities available by arrangement.
Hotels: O'Connors, Swinford; Westway, Kiltinagh.

AA82 Tuam

☎ Tuam (093) 24354
Barnacurragh, Tuam, Co Galway.
$1\frac{1}{2}$ miles from town on the Athenry road which is off Dublin road.
Parkland course.
18 holes, 6321 yards, S.S.S.70
Club founded around 1910.
Visitors: welcome on weekdays.
Green fees: £5 per person.
Society meetings: catered for on weekdays and Sat by arrangement.
Catering: snacks available.
Hotels: Imperial, Tuam; Hermitage, Tuam.

AA83 Virginia

Virginia, Co Cavan.
50 miles N of Dublin on main Cavan to Dublin road, within Park Hotel, by Lough Ramor.
Meadowland course.
9 holes, 4083 metres, S.S.S.62
Club founded in 1946.
Visitors: welcome.
Green fees: weekdays £3, weekends and Bank Holidays £4.
Catering: meals and snacks available in hotel.
Hotels: Park.

AA84 Westport

☎ Westport 547
Carrowholly, Westport, Co Mayo.
2 miles from Westport.
Parkland course.
18 holes, 6706 yards, S.S.S.71
Course designed by Hawtree & Son.
Visitors: welcome.
Green fees: on request.
Society meetings: welcome.
Catering: snacks and meals served.
Hotels: Clew Bay; Castlecourt; Westport.

BB South Eire

BB1 Abbeyleix
☎ (0502) 31450
Abbeyleix, Co Laois.
Within ½ mile of Main St on Stradbally Rd.
Parkland course.
9 holes, S.S.S.68
Visitors: welcome.
Green fees: weekdays £3, weekends £5.
Society meetings: catered for usually on Sat.
Catering: catering by arrangement for societies.
Hotels: Hibernian, Abbeyleix; Killeshin, Porthoise; Montague, Porthoise.

BB2 Adare Manor
☎ (061) 86204
Adane, Co Limerick.
10 miles from Limerick city on main Killarney road.
Parkland course.
9 holes, 5530 yards, S.S.S.67
Club founded in 1880.
Visitors: welcome on weekdays.
Green fees: weekdays £7 (£3 with member).
Society meetings: by prior arrangement with Sec.
Catering: light snacks served.
Hotels: Dunraven Arms; Woodlands.

BB3 Arklow
☎ Arklow (0402) 2492
Abbeylands, Arklow, Co Wicklow.
½ mile from Arklow.
Seaside course, 18 holes, 5963 yards, S.S.S.68
Course designed by Hawtree & Taylor.
Visitors: welcome except Sun.
Green fees: on request.
Society meetings: welcome except Sun.
Catering: by arrangement.
Hotels: Arklow Bay; Royal; Bridge.

BB4 Athy
☎ Athy 21455
Geraldine, Athy, Co Kildare.
On T6, 2 miles N of Athy.
Undulating grassland course.
9 holes, 6200 yards, S.S.S.68
Visitors: welcome.
Society meetings: by arrangement.
Catering: by arrangement for groups only.
Hotels: Leinster Arms, Athy; Kilkea Castle, Castledemont.

BB5 Ballybunion
☎ Ballybunion (068) 2714
Sandhill Rd, Ballybunion, Co Kerry.
Seaside course.
Old 18 holes, 6542 yards, S.S.S.72
New 18 holes, 6477 yards, S.S.S.72
Club founded in 1896.
Visitors: welcome.
Green fees: £15 per day, weekly and monthly tickets available.
Society meetings: welcome.
Catering: snacks and meals served.
Hotels: Ambassador; Marine.

BB6 Baltinglass
☎ (0508) 81350
Baltinglass, Co Wicklow.
40 miles S of Dublin.
Parkland course.
9 holes, 6070 yards, S.S.S.69
Course designed by Dr. W.G. Lyons, Hugh Dark and Col. Mitchell.
Club founded in 1928.
Visitors: welcome.
Green fees: weekdays £4, weekends and Bank Holidays £6.
Society meetings: 3 outings allowed per month.
Catering: meals by arrangement.
Hotels: good hotels in area.

BB7 Bandon
☎ Bandon (023) 41111
Castlebernard, Bandon, Co Cork
1½ miles W of Bandon town.
Parkland course.
18 holes, 5663 metres, S.S.S.69
Club founded in 1909.
Visitors: welcome on weekdays.
Green fees: weekdays £5 per day, (£4 with member), weekends and Bank Holidays £6.
Society meetings: catered for except on Sun with one week's notice.
Catering: meals, snacks and bar facilities.
Hotels: Munster Arms, Bandon, Co Cork.

BB8 Berehaven
☎ Castletown Bear 24
Berehaven, Castletown Bear, Co Cork
9 holes, 4950 yards, S.S.S.64
Green fees: on request.
No other facilities.

BB9 Birr
☎ Birr (0509) 20082
Glenns, Birr, Co Offaly.
2 miles from Birr on road to Banager.
Undulating parkland course.
18 holes, 6262 yards, S.S.S.70
Club founded in 1896.
Visitors: welcome, but should check on Sun.
Green fees: £6 per day (£4 with member).
Society meetings: catered for every day except Sun.
Catering: catering available by arrangement except Tues.
Hotels: County Arms, Birr; Doolys, Birr; Shannon, Banagher.

BB10 Blainroe
☎ Wicklow (0404) 3168
Blainroe, Co Wicklow.
3 miles S of Wicklow town on coast road.
Seaside course.
18 holes, 6681 yards, S.S.S.72
Course designed by Hawtree & Son.
Club founded in 1978.
Visitors: welcome.
Green fees: weekdays £7, weekends and Bank Holidays £10, weekly £35, monthly £75.
Society meetings: catered for on weekdays and at weekends.
Catering: full catering facilities available.
Hotels: Grand, Wicklow Town; Tinakilly House; Old Rectory.

BB11 Borris
☎ Carlow (0503) 73143
Deer Park, Borris, Co Carlow.
Drive S from Carlow via Begenalstown; drive E from Kilkenny via Gowran and Goresbridge.
Parkland course.
10 holes, 6041 yards, S.S.S.69
Visitors: welcome on weekdays and with member on Sun.
Green fees: weekdays £5, Sun £6; half-price with member.
Society meetings: catered for on weekdays and Sat mornings between 10 and 12.
Catering: catering available for societies by arrangement.
Hotels: Newport, Kilkenny; Springhill, Kilkenny; Clubhouse, Kilkenny; Rose Hill, Kilkenny; Royal, Carlow; Seven Oaks, Carlow.

BB12 Bray
☎ Bray 862484 Sec, 862092 Public
Ravenswell Rd, Bray, Co Wicklow.
L29 from Dublin, turn left at bridge entering town.
Parkland course.
9 holes, 2866 metres, S.S.S.70
Club founded in 1897.
Visitors: welcome on weekdays except Mon.
Green fees: £6 per day.

Society meetings: societies affiliated to Golfing Union catered for.
Catering: limited catering available.
Hotels: many good hotels in area.

BB13 Cahir Park

☎ (052) 41474
Kilcommon, Cahir, Co Tipperary
1 mile out of Cahir on Clogheen road.
Parkland course.
9 holes, 5696 metres, S.S.S.69
Course designed by Eddie Hackett.
Club founded in 1968.
Visitors: welcome.
Green fees: weekdays £3, weekends £4.
Society meetings: catered for except on Sun.
Catering: snacks available.
Hotels: Cahir House; Galtee, Cahir; The Wishing Well, Cahir.

BB14 Callan

☎ Callan (056) 25136
Geraldine, Callan, Co Kilkenny.
From Kilkenny to Callan, 1 mile from Callan to course.
Meadowland course.
9 holes, 5444 yards, S.S.S.68
Club founded on 30th April 1929.
Visitors: welcome.
Green fees: £4 per day.
Society meetings: welcome except on Sun.
Catering: by prior arrangement only.
Hotels: many good hotels in area.

BB15 Carlow

☎ Carlow (0503) 31695 or 42599
Deerpark, Dublin Rd, Carlow, Co Carlow.
1 mile from Carlow station, take Naas road from Dublin.
Parkland course.
18 holes, 5806 metres, S.S.S.71
Course designed by Tom Simpson.
Club founded in 1899.
Visitors: welcome except Sun.
Green fees: weekdays £6, weekends £9.
Society meetings: catered for on weekdays or Sat mornings.
Catering: full catering available.
Hotels: Seven Oaks, Athy Rd, Carlow; Royal, Dublin St, Carlow.

BB16 Carrick-on-Suir

☎ Carrick-on-Suir (051) 40047
Garravoone, Co Tipperary.
Course is situated approx 2 miles from town of Carrick-on-Suir, on main Carrick-on-Suir to Dungarvan road; there is a signpost on right side of road.
Undulating meadowland course.
9 holes, 5948 yards, S.S.S.68
Course designed by Eddie Hackett.
Club founded in 1939.
Visitors: welcome except on Sun.
Green fees: £3.
Society meetings: catered for except on Sun.
Catering: meals available by arrangement for groups except on Sun.
Hotels: Tinvane, Carrick-on-Suir; Clonmel Arms, Clonmel; Tower, Waterford.

BB17 Castlecomer

☎ (056) 41139
Drumgoole, Castlecomer, Co Kilkenny.
On N7 10 miles from Kilkenny.
Parkland course.
9 holes, 6300 yards, S.S.S.71
Course designed by Pat Ruddy.
Club founded in 1935.
Visitors: welcome on weekdays.
Green fees: weekdays £3, weekends and Bank Holidays £4 (with member £2).
Society meetings: welcome except on Sun.
Catering: lunches served for societies.
Hotels: Avalon Inn, Castlecomer; Newpark, Kilkenny.

BB18 Castletroy

☎ Limerick (061) 335753 Sec, 335261 Members
Castletroy, Limerick.
3 miles from Limerick city on Dublin road, turn at signpost in Castletroy, course 300 yards on left.
Parkland course.
18 holes, 6001 metres. S.S.S.70

Club founded in 1937.
Visitors: welcome on weekdays and with member at weekends; advisable to check course availability in advance.
Green fees: £7 per day (£5 with member).
Society meetings: welcome on Mon, Wed and Fri.
Catering: full catering facilities available; please order before playing.
Hotels: Cruises; Royal George; Jurys; Glentworth; Two Mile Inn; Limerick Inn; Limerick Ryan.

BB19 Charleville

☎ Charleville (063) 257
Ardmore, Charleville, Co Cork.
About 35 miles from Cork and 25 miles from Limerick.
Parkland course.
18 holes, 6380 yards, S.S.S.70
Club founded in 1947.
Visitors: welcome on weekdays.
Green fees: £5.
Society meetings: catered for at weekends.
Catering: meals served by arrangement.
Hotels: Deerpark.

BB20 Cill Dara

☎ Kildare (045) 21433
Kildare, Co Kildare.
1 mile E of Kildare.
Moorland course.
9 holes, 6196 yards, S.S.S.66
Visitors: welcome.
Catering: meals served by arrangement.
Hotels: Derby House, Kildare; Kaedeen, Newbridge.

BB21 Clonmel

☎ Clonmel (052) 21138 Bar, 24050 Sec/Manager.
Lyranearla, Clonmel, Co Tipperary.
On mountain road on way to Comeragh mountains, 3 miles SE of Clonmel.
Parkland course.
18 holes, 6365 yards, S.S.S.70
Course designed by Eddie Hackett.
Club founded in 1910.
Visitors: welcome.
Green fees: weekdays £5, weekends and Bank Holidays £6.
Society meetings: welcome.
Catering: full catering facilities available.
Hotels: Clonmel Arms; Hearns; Minella.

BB22 Cork

☎ Cork (021) 353451, 353037 or 353263
Little Island, Co Cork.
5m due E of Cork city, ½m off Cork to Rosslare rd at Little Island railway stn.
Undulating parkland course.
Course designed by Dr. Alexander Mackenzie.
Club founded in 1888.
Visitors: welcome.
Green fees: weekdays £9 per day, weekends £10 (with member £5).
Society meetings: welcome except on competition days and Thurs.
Catering: full catering facilities.
Hotels: Silver Springs, Tivoli, Cork; Ashbourne House, Glounthaune; John Barleycorn, Riverstown; Commodore, Cosh, Co Cork

BB23 Courtown

☎ Gorey (055) 25166
Kiltennel, Gorey, Co Wexford.
3m from Gorey on Dublin to Rosslare rd.
Parkland course.
18 holes, 6398 yards, S.S.S.70
Course designed by Harris & Associates.
Club founded in 1936.
Visitors: welcome except on major competition days.
Green fees: weekdays £5, weekends and Bank Holidays £7.
Society meetings: catered for on weekdays and at weekends Sept to May.
Catering: meals and snacks served.
Hotels: Courtown; Bayview; Taravie; Dunamarra; all in Courtown Harbour; Marlfield House, Gorey.

BB24 Curragh

☎ Curragh (045) 41238
Curragh, Co Kildare.
28 miles from Dublin, signposted from Newbridge, Co Kildare.
Parkland course.
18 holes, 6565 yards, S.S.S.71
Course designed by David Ritchie (1852).
Club founded in 1883.
Visitors: welcome.
Green fees: weekdays £5, weekends and Bank Holidays £7.
Society meetings: welcome from 1 Jan to mid-Oct by prior arrangement.
Catering: lunches and snacks served.
Hotels: Keadeen; Derby; Lumville.

BB25 Delgany

☎ Dublin (01) 874536
Delgany, Co Wicklow.
Adjacent to village of Delgany off main road to Wexford.
Parkland course.
18 holes, 5454 metres, S.S.S.69
Club founded in 1908.
Visitors: welcome except on competition days.
Green fees: weekdays £7.50, weekends £9.
Society meetings: welcome.
Catering: full catering facilities
Hotels: Wicklow Arms; Glenview.

BB26 Doneraile

☎ Doneraile (022) 24137
Doneraile.
Off T11, 28 miles N of Cork, 9 miles from Mallow.
Parkland course.
9 holes, 5528 yards, S.S.S.66
Visitors: welcome.
Society meetings: welcome.
Catering: meals served.
Hotels: Central; Hibernian; Mallow.

BB27 Dooks

☎ (066) 68205
Glenbeigh, Co Kerry.
Off T66, 8 miles W of Killonglin, at bridge between Killonglin and Glenbeigh.
Seaside course.
18 holes, 5098 metres, S.S.S.68
Course designed by Eddie Hackett.
Club founded in 1889.
Visitors: welcome.
Green fees: £5 per day, £20 per week (Mon to Sun).
Society meetings: welcome.
Catering: snacks only available.
Hotels: Bianconi Inn, Killonglin; Towers, Glenbeigh; Glenbeigh, Glenbeigh.

BB28 Douglas

☎ Cork (021) 291086
Douglas, Co Cork.
Within 3 miles of Cork city, ½ mile beyond Douglas village.
Parkland course.
18 holes, 5294 metres, S.S.S.68
Club founded in 1910.
Visitors: welcome with reservation at weekends.
Green fees: weekdays £8, weekends £9.
Society meetings: catered for by arrangement before start of season.
Catering: snacks and meals served.
Hotels: several hotels within 3 miles of course.

BB29 Dromoland Castle

☎ (061) 71144 extn 618
Newmarket-on-Fergus, Co Clare.
On main Limerick to Galway road, 1½ miles through Newmarket-on-Fergus.
Parkland course.
9 holes, 3280 yards, S.S.S.35.
Course designed by Whittaker (USA).
Club founded in 1963.
Visitors: welcome.
Green fees: £5 per day.
Society meetings: welcome.
Catering: none; hotels below, both in grounds of course for meals.
Hotels: Dromoland Castle; Clare Inn.

BB30 Dungarvan

☎ (058) 41605
Ballinacourty, Dungarvan, Co Waterford

GALWAY
Galway
AA
WEST MEATH
MEATH
Dublin
Dun Laoghaire
OFFALY
KILDARE
Galway Bay
ATLANTIC
OCEAN
CLARE
LAOIS
Port Laoise
WICKLOW
Wicklow
BB
CARLOW
Kilkenny
KILKENNY
Limerick
Shannon
TIPPERARY
LIMERICK
Enniscorthy
WEXFORD
Wexford
Tralee
Clonmel
KERRY
BB
Waterford
Mallow
WATERFORD
Dingle Bay
Killarney
CORK
Dungarvan
Cork
Bantry
ST GEORGE'S CHANNEL
0 Miles 25
0 Kilometres 40

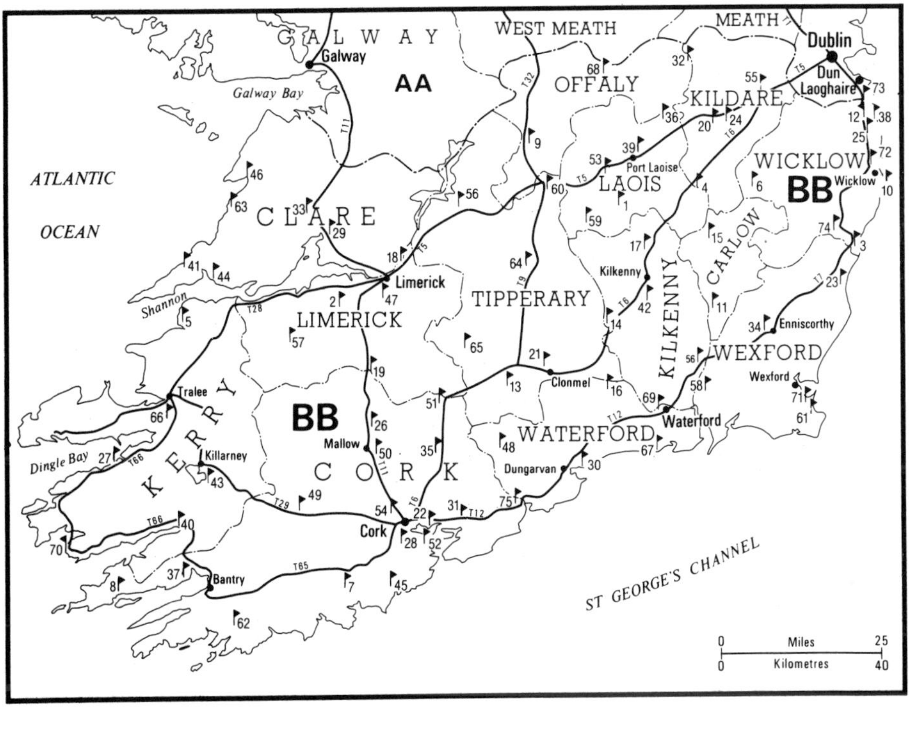

About 3 miles E of Dungarvan, from Dungarvan take course road to Tramore, first right turn leads to club.
Meadowland course.
9 holes, 6282 yards, S.S.S.69
Club founded in 1924.
Visitors: members of recognised golf club welcome.
Green fees: £5 per day.
Society meetings: welcome on weekdays from 1 May to 30 Sept.
Catering: snacks available; meals served at Gold Coast Leisure Centre.
Hotels: Gold Coast Leisure Centre; Glomea Strand.

BB31 East Cork
☎ Cork (021) 631687
Goatacrue, Midleton, Co Cork.
On main Cork to Waterford road 10 miles E of Cork city, turn left at roundabout in Midleton, signposted from same roundabout about 1½ miles.
Yellow 18 holes, 4874 yards, S.S.S.65
Ladies Red 18 holes, 4510 yards, S.S.S.69
Blue 18 holes, 5207 yards, S.S.S.67
Course designed by E. Hackett & R. Barry.
Club founded in 1969.
Visitors: welcome.
Green fees: £5.
Society meetings: welcome; phone clubhouse for details.
Catering: snacks served.
Hotels: Commodore; Garryvoe; Bayview; Kilcrone House.

BB32 Edenderry
☎ Edenderry (0405) 31072
Edenderry, Co Offaly.
¾ mile outside town.
Parkland/moorland course.
9 holes, 5900 yards, S.S.S.67
Course designed by Havers.
Club founded in 1947.
Visitors: welcome.
Green fees: weekdays £4, weekends £5.
Society meetings: welcome on Sat.
Catering: catering only on special occasions and for societies.

BB33 Ennis
☎ Ennis (065) 21070
Dumbiggle, Ennis, Co Clare.
1 mile W of Ennis.
Parkland course.
18 holes, 5890 yards, S.S.S.66
Visitors: welcome.
Green fees: on application.
Society meetings: by arrangement.
Catering: snacks served, meals by arrangement.
Hotels: Queens; West Country Inn; Old Ground.

BB34 Enniscorthy
☎ Enniscorthy (054) 33670
Knockmarshal, Enniscorthy, Co Wexford.
1½ miles from town on New Rose Rd.
Parkland course.
9 holes, 6220 yards, S.S.S.70
Club founded in 1908.
Visitors: welcome on weekdays and at special times at weekends.
Green fees: weekdays £3.50, weekends £5.
Society meetings: welcome by arrangement except on Sun.
Catering: full catering facilities.
Hotels: Murphy-Floods, Enniscorlhy.

BB35 Fermoy
☎ (025) 31472
Fermoy, Co Cork.
2m from Fermoy off Cork to Dublin rd.
Undulating course.
18 holes.
Course designed by Commander Harris.
Club founded in 1887.
Visitors: welcome at any time.
Green fees: £5 (£4 with member).
Society meetings: catered for on weekdays and Sat.
Catering: none.
Hotels: Royal, Fermoy; Grand, Fermoy.

BB36 Garryhinch
☎ Portarlington (0502) 23115
Portarlington, Co Offaly.
6 miles from Monasterevin.
Parkland course.
9 holes, 5598 yards, S.S.S.66
Visitors: welcome.
Green fees: on application.
Society meetings: welcome except Sun.
Catering: meals by prior arrangement.
Hotels: Hazel, Monasterevin; Montague, Portlaoise.

BB37 Glengarriff
☎ (027) 63150
Glengarriff, Co Cork.
On T65, 55 miles W of Cork.
Seaside course.
9 holes, 2042 metres, S.S.S.62
Club founded in 1936.
Visitors: welcome.
Green fees: on request.
Society meetings: special rates for societies.
Hotels: six hotels within 1 mile.

BB38 Greystones
☎ Dublin (01) 874614 or 874136
Greystones, Co Wicklow.
25 miles S of Dublin.
Parkland course.
18 holes, 5387 metres, S.S.S.68
Club founded in 1895.
Visitors: welcome on weekdays.
Green fees: £7.
Catering: by prior arrangement only.
Hotels: La Touche, Greystones.

BB39 Heath
☎ Portlaoise (0502) 26533
The Heath, Portlaoise, Co Laois.
5 miles NE of Portlaoise, just off main Dublin, Cork and Limerick road.
Heathland course.
18 holes, 5766 metres, S.S.S.70
Club founded in 1930.
Visitors: welcome on weekdays and by arrangement with Hon Sec at weekends.
Green fees: weekdays £4 per day, weekends and Bank Holidays £6.
Society meetings: welcome by arrangement.
Catering: full catering facilities available by arrangement with Steward.
Hotels: Killeshin, Portlaoise; Montague, Emo.

BB40 Kenmare
☎ (064) 41291
Kenmare, Co Kerry.
On T65, 20 miles S of Killarney, 100 yds out of town.
Seaside course.
9 holes, S.S.S.62
Club founded in 1908.
Visitors: welcome.
Green fees: £4 per day.
Society meetings: welcome.
Catering: bar and snacks available.
Hotels: Kenmare Bay; Park; Riversdale House.

BB41 Kilkee
☎ Kilkee 48
East End, Kilkee, Co Clare.
Within 400 metres of town.
Meadowland course.
9 holes.
Course designea by McAllister.
Club founded in 1892.
Visitors: welcome.
Green fees: £5 per day, £20 per week.
Society meetings: catered for in May, June and from Mid Aug to end of Sept.
Catering: snacks always available; meals for societies available by arrangement.
Hotels: Strand; Victoria; Thomond.

BB42 Kilkenny
☎ Kilkenny (056) 22024
Glendine, Kilkenny.

Lahinch

Tom Morris and Tom Dunn were the most modest and self-effacing of all golf course architects, dismissing their skills by claiming, "God obviously intended this for a golf course". Of Lahinch, which borders great beaches lashed by Atlantic rollers, Morris said the same thing in a different way, "the links is as fine a natural course as it has ever been my good fortune to play over".

After his extensive reconstruction in 1927, Dr Alister Mackenzie maintained that "Lahinch will make the finest and most popular course that I, or, I believe, anyone else, ever constructed". Divine intention could no longer be given all the credit although Mackenzie did pay tribute to the great number of natural hazards with which he had to work. One of the main contributions Mackenzie made to a profession he adopted after forsaking his medical practice was in the design, shaping and angling of greens.

In the early days, greens were simply regarded as hollows or artificial platforms on which to place the pin, but Colt, Fowler, Mackenzie and Ross believed that greens should be a study in themselves.

Mackenzie could make a dull piece of ground interesting just by his greens but nobody could label the land at Lahinch as anything other than full of variety. In places you might call it eccentric, if being critical, or highly individual, if being kind. The short 6th hole, the Dell, is unique, the green, unseen from the tee, nestling between two giant sandhills. Lahinch without the Dell would be like Pisa without the Leaning Tower. However the course, which is to house the Home Internationals in 1987, has other glories by which to be judged.

Its popularity, measured by the army of visitors that necessitated a second course being built, is centred upon its unmistakable seaside character which is felt and appreciated from the opening, uphill drive towards a green silhouetted against the skyline to the par 5 18th which climaxes a finish over the last seven holes which has recently been significantly lengthened.

The direction of the drive at the 1st is more crucial than may initially be apparent and the same applies at the 2nd which offers an inviting second shot as the fairway plunges down to a flatter approach. Next comes a classic short hole followed by a challenging tee shot at the 4th where a large dune waits to be carried. The 5th, Klondyke, is another hole that is peculiarly Lahinch.

The one reassuring piece of news is that, like the 2nd, it is a par 5 but, with a wind off the sea, the 7th is a mighty two-shotter whatever the card might say. On calmer days, it has picture book qualities, the view from the crest of the fairway embracing a green far below set against a backcloth of ocean. There are thoughts of modifications to the 8th but a new tee has added a cubit or two to the stature of the 9th although one of Lahinch's best holes, the short 11th, is one that it would be a travesty to alter.

It is proof that short holes don't need to be a long iron or wood to be difficult; here it is more touch and skill that are required to hold a beautiful example of Mackenzie's green designing. A contrasting prospect greets players on the 12th which follows the line of the river estuary; but the old green has been restored and the hole is now a stern four. It is a modification that has led to the lengthening of the 13th as well, a change, combined with the others, that has made Lahinch perhaps a couple of strokes harder.

The last five holes lack the scenic beauty of some of the others but they command attention and have decided many a match in the South of Ireland championship, Lahinch's famous annual festival. The finish comprises two par fives, the 14th and 18th, two long par fours and the last of the short holes, the 16th. There are times when they seem quite a haul but there is nothing overbearing about Lahinch whatever the weather; and if you want advice about that, the club goats, which make up its emblem, are held to be the most reliable indicators. The danger signs are when they surround the clubhouse. On my first visit, on a day when it was unfit even for hardy goats, I was greeted with the sight of four intrepid souls, drenched to the skin, putting out in the dark on the 18th green. They must have got their weather forecast from the radio or they may have felt, if you will pardon the expression, that the goats were kidding.

2 miles N of town off Castlecomer Rd.
Parkland course.
18 holes, 5824 metres, S.S.S.70
Club founded in 1891.
Visitors: welcome except on competition days (usually at weekends).
Green fees: weekends and Bank Holidays £6, weekdays £5.
Society meetings: welcome.
Catering: meals and snacks served.
Hotels: Newpark; Clubhouse; Springhill; Kilkenny.

BB43 Killarney
☎ (064) 31034
Mahonys' Point, Killarney, Co Kerry.
3 miles W of town off Killarney to Killonglin Rd.
Undulating parkland course.
Kileen 18 holes, 6909 yards, S.S.S.73
Mahonys Point 18 holes, 6734 yards, S.S.S.71
Kileen course designed by Fred Hawtree and Mahonys course designed by Sir Guy Campbell.
Club founded in 1891.
Visitors: welcome.
Green fees: £10 per day, £45 per week.
Society meetings: catered for every day.
Catering: meals and snacks served.
Hotels: Castlerosse; Aghadoe; Europe.

BB44 Kilrush
☎ Kilrush 138
Parknamoney, Kilrush, Co Clare.
On main road into town from Ennis, Co Clare.
Parkland course.
9 holes, 2739 yards, S.S.S.67
Club founded in 1934.
Visitors: welcome.
Green fees: £4 per day.
Society meetings: catered for by arrangement.
Catering: bar facilities only.
Hotels: Orchard, Kilrush.

BB45 Kinsale
☎ Cork (021) 772197
Ringenane, Belgooly, Co Cork.
On main Cork to Kinsale road, 2 miles short of Kinsale and 10 miles from Cork Airport.
Moorland course.
9 holes, 5700 yards, S.S.S.68
Club founded in 1912.
Visitors: welcome.
Green fees: £5 (£3 with member).
Society meetings: welcome.
Catering: meals available.
Hotels: Actons; Blue Haven; Trident.

BB46 Lahinch
☎ (065) 81003
Lahinch, Co Clare.
34 miles from Shannon Airport.
Seaside courses.
Old 18 holes, 5923 yards, S.S.S.72
Castle 18 holes, 4864 yards, S.S.S.67
Course designed by Tom Morris & revised by Dr. A, Mackenzie.
Club founded in 1893.
Visitors: welcome.
Green fees: Old course £10, Castle course £6.
Society meetings: welcome on weekdays and on Sat out of season.
Catering: full catering facilities.
Hotels: Aberdeen Arms; Liscannor Golf.

BB47 Limerick
☎ (061) 44083
Ballyclough, Limerick.
Turn left off Limerick to Cork road at Punches Cross.
Parkland course.
18 holes, 5767 metres, S.S.S.70
Club founded in 1891.
Visitors: welcome on Mon, Wed, Thurs and Fri until 5 pm.
Green fees: £7 per round.
Society meetings: welcome with booking.
Catering: full catering facilities.
Hotels: Royal George; Glentworth.

BB48 Lismore
☎ Lismore (058) 54184
Lismore, Co Waterford.
½ mile from Lismore on Killarney road.
Parkland course.
9 holes, 5127 metres, S.S.S.67
Course designed by Eddie Hackett.
Club founded in 1965.
Visitors: welcome on weekdays and Sat.
Green fees: £4 per day.
Society meetings: welcome on weekdays.
Catering: bar, soup and sandwiches available.
Hotels: Lismore; Ballyrafter House.

BB49 Macroom
☎ (026) 41072
Lackaduve, Macroom, Co Cork.
On T29, 25 miles W of Cork.
Parkland course.
9 holes, 5439 metres, S.S.S.68
Club founded in 1924.
Visitors: welcome.
Green fees: £4 per day.
Society meetings: welcome by arrangement.
Catering: full catering available.
Hotels: Castle (adjacent with free golf for residents).

BB50 Mallow
☎ Mallow (022) 21145
Ballyellis, Mallow, Co Cork.
1 mile E of N20 at Mallow Bridge, 20 miles N of Cork city.
Parkland course.
18 holes, 6600 yards, S.S.S.71
Course designed by J.D. Harris and altered by Eddie Hackett.

Club founded in 1947.
Visitors: welcome except on major competition days.
Green fees: £5 (£3 with member).
Society meetings: catered for by arrangement with Hon Sec.
Catering: snacks available daily, lunches served except Sat and dinners by arrangement.
Hotels: Central & Hibernian, Main St, Mallow; Longuville House.

BB51 Mitchelstown

☎ (025) 24072
Mitchelstown, Co Cork.
1m from Mitchelstown off N1 Dublin to Cork rd.
Parkland course.
9 holes, 5057 metres, S.S.S.67
Course designed by Eddie Hackett.
Club founded in 1908.
Visitors: welcome.
Green fees: weekdays £4, weekends and Bank Holidays £5.
Society meetings: welcome except Sun.
Catering: full catering facilities available for societies by arrangement.
Hotels: Clongibbon House, New Square, Mitchelstown; Firgrove, Mitchelstown.

BB52 Monkstown

☎ Cork (021) 841225
Parkgariffe, Monkstown, Co Cork.
On L68 7 miles S of Cork.
Parkland course.
18 holes, 5642 yards, S.S.S.69
Club founded in 1908.
Visitors: welcome.
Green fees: weekdays £7, weekends £8.
Society meetings: welcome.
Catering: meals served.
Hotels: many good hotels in area.

BB53 Mountrath

Mountrath, Co Laois.
8 miles from Portlaoise on main Dublin to Limerick road.
9 holes, 5196 yards, S.S.S.65
Visitors: welcome.
Hotels: Pathe, Roscrea; Killeshin.

BB54 Muskerry

☎ Cork (021) 85104 Pro, 85297 Sec.
Carrickrohane, Co Cork.
7 miles W of city centre, near Blarney village.
Parkland course.
18 holes, 5786 metres, S.S.S.70
Club founded in 1897.
Visitors: welcome on weekdays except Wed afternoons and Thurs mornings before 12.30.
Green fees: Men £7, Ladies £6.
Catering: snacks available; meals by arrangement before play.
Hotels: Blarney.

BB55 Naas

☎ (045) 97509
Kardiffstown, Salins, Naas, Co Kildare.
Leave dual carriageway at Johnstown Village, and take link road N of carriageway to Salins.
18 holes, 6233 yards, S.S.S.68
Visitors: welcome.
Green fees: on request.
Society meetings: welcome Mon, Wed and Fri.
Hotels: Lawlor's; Osbertown House; Cill Dara; Town House.

BB56 Nenagh

☎ (067) 31476
Beechwood, Nenagh, Co Tipperary
4 miles from Nenagh Tam, well signposted.
Inland course.
18 holes, 5483 metres, S.S.S.68
Club founded in 1917.
Visitors: welcome.
Green fees: weekdays £5, weekends £6.
Society meetings: welcome by arrangement except on Sun.
Catering: meals and snacks served.
Hotels: Motor Inn; Beechwood House; O'Mearas; Ormond.

BB57 Newcastle West

☎ Newcastle West 76
Newcastle West, Co Limerick.
1 mile from town on Cork road.
Meadowland course.
9 holes, 5400 yards, S.S.S.65
Visitors: welcome.
Green fees: on application.
Society meetings: by arrangement.
Hotels: Central; Devon; River Room.

BB58 New Ross

☎ New Ross (051) 21433
Tinneanny, New Ross, Co Wexford
From town centre take Waterford Rd, turn right at Albatros factory, about 1 mile.
Parkland course.
9 holes, 6133 yards, S.S.S.69
Club founded in 1904.
Visitors: welcome except on Sun if there is a competition.
Green fees: £4.
Society meetings: by arrangement.
Catering: snacks always available; meals by arrangement.
Hotels: Five Counties; Royal.

BB59 Rathdowney

☎ (0505) 46170
Rathdowney, Portlaoise.
Take N7 to Abbeyleix, turn left for town of Rathdowney, follow signposts from square in Rathdowney, Co Laois.
Meadowland course.
9 holes, S.S.S.66
Course designed by Eddie Hackett.
Club founded in 1931.
Visitors: welcome.
Green fees: £2.
Society meetings: by arrangement.
Catering: by arrangement with Hon Sec giving one week notice.
Hotels: Central, Rathdowney; Leix Co, Borris in Ossory, Co Laois.

BB60 Roscrea

☎ (0505) 21130
Derry Vale, Dublin Rd, Roscrea, Co Tipperary
2 miles from Roscrea on Dublin side of town, beside main road on right hand side before railway bridge.
Parkland course.
9 holes, 6059 yards, S.S.S.69
Club founded in 1911.
Visitors: welcome.
Green fees: £4 per day.
Society meetings: catered for by arrangement with Sec.
Catering: catering only for societies.
Hotels: Rackett Hall, Rackett Hall, Roscrea.

BB61 Rosslare

☎ (053) 32113 bar.
Rosslare, Co Wexford
Links seaside course.
18 holes, 6502 yards, S.S.S.71
Club founded in 1908.
Visitors: welcome.
Green fees: weekdays £7, weekends £8.
Society meetings: welcome.
Catering: meals served.
Hotels: Kelly's Strand; Golf; Cedars; Iona.

BB62 Skibbereen

☎ Skibbereen (028) 21227
Skibbereen, Co Cork
Off T65, 47 miles SW of Cork
Moorland course.
9 holes, 5890 yards, S.S.S.67
Visitors: welcome.
Green fees: on request.
Society meetings: welcome.
Hotels: Eldon; West Cork; Lissard House.

BB63 Spanish Point

☎ (065) 84198
Spanish Point, Miltown Malbay, Co Clare

9 miles from Lahinch Golf Club, 2 miles from Miltown Malbay on seafront.
Seaside course.
9 holes, 6171 metres, S.S.S.54
Club founded in 1940.
Visitors: welcome.
Green fees: £3.50.
Society meetings: welcome except on Sun.
Catering: only on special occasions.
Hotels: Central, Miltown Malbay, Co Clare.

BB64 Thurles

☎ Thurles (0504) 21983
Turtulla, Thurles, Co Tipperary
1 mile S of Thurles on Cork road.
Parkland course.
18 holes, 6300 yards, S.S.S.70
Club founded in 1911.
Visitors: welcome except on Sun.
Green fees: £6.
Society meetings: catered for on weekdays and Sat.
Catering: full catering available.
Hotels: Hayes, Thurles; Munster, Thurles.

BB65 Tipperary

☎ (062) 51119
Rathanny, Tipperary
1 mile from town.
Parkland course.
9 holes, 6054 yards, S.S.S.68
Visitors: welcome except Mon.
Green fees: on application.
Society meetings: by arrangement.
Hotels: Glen; Royal; Aherlow House; Tipperary.

BB66 Tralee

☎ (066) 36379 or 38355
West Barrow, Ardfert, Co Kerry
From Tralee through villages of Spa and Churchill to Barrow, narrow roads.
Links course.
18 holes, 6800 yards, S.S.S.71
Course designed by Arnold Palmer Design Co.
Club founded in 1984.
Visitors: welcome, advisable to phone in advance at weekends.
Green fees: £8 per day.
Society meetings: welcome except on Sun.
Catering: lunches served by arrangement except Mon.
Hotels: Mount Brandon; Earl of Desmond; Banna Beach.

BB67 Tramore

☎ (051) 81247
Newtown Hill, Tramore, Co Waterford
Via Waterford, 1 mile beyond Tramore.
Parkland course.
18 holes, 6408 yards, S.S.S.70
Course designed by Tibbett (1936/7).
Visitors: welcome.
Green fees: on request.
Society meetings: by arrangement.
Catering: meals served except Mon.
Hotels: Majestic; Grand; Sea View.

BB68 Tullamore

☎ (0506) 21439
Brookfield, Tullamore, Co Offaly.
2½ miles from town centre on Birr road.
Parkland course.
18 holes, 6314 yards, S.S.S.71
Course designed by James Braid.
Club founded in 1896.
Visitors: welcome except during club competitions on Sun.
Green fees: weekdays £5, weekends £7.
Society meetings: catered for on weekdays and Sat.
Catering: by prior arrangement.
Hotels: Phoenix Arms.

BB69 Waterford

☎ Waterford (051) 76748 or 74182
New Rath, Waterford
¼ mile from city centre.
Parkland course.
18 holes, 6237 yards, S.S.S.69
Course designed by Cecil Barcroft and

Willie Park.
Club founded in 1912.
Visitors: welcome on weekdays.
Green fees: weekdays £6, weekends £9.
Society meetings: catered for on weekdays.
Catering: full catering facilities available.
Hotels: Ardree; Bridge; Granville; Dooleys; Tower.

BB70 **Waterville**
☎ Waterville (0667) 4102
Waterville, Co Kerry
N70 to Waterville, then coastal rd for 1 mile W of town.
Seaside links course.
18 holes, 7160 yards, S.S.S.73
Course designed by Eddie Hackett.
Club founded in 1970.
Visitors: welcome.
Green fees: £10.
Society meetings: welcome.
Catering: lunches and dinners served from April to Oct.
Hotels: Waterville Lake, Waterville, Co Kerry.

BB71 **Wexford**
☎ Wexford (053) 42238
Mulganon, Wexford.
Within ½ mile from town.
Parkland course.
18 holes, 6038 yards, S.S.S.69
Course designed by J. Hamilton Stutt & Co.
Club founded in 1961.
Visitors: welcome.
Green fees: £5 per day.
Society meetings: welcome.
Hotels: Talbot; Whites; Wexford; Kelly's Strand, Rosslare; Cedars, Rosslare.

BB72 **Wicklow**
☎ (0404) 2361
Dunbur Rd, Wicklow, Co Wicklow.
On L29 32 miles from Dublin
Seaside course.
9 holes, 2633 yards, S.S.S.67
Club founded in 1904.
Visitors: welcome on weekdays.
Green fees: weekdays £5 (£2.50 with member).
Catering: meals served except Tues.
Hotels: many good hotels in area.

BB73 **Woodbrook**
☎ Dublin (01) 824799
Bray, Co Wicklow.
From Dublin on main road to Bray, 1 mile outside Bray.
Parkland course.
18 holes, 6541 yards, S.S.S.71
Club founded in 1927.
Visitors: welcome on weekdays.
Green fees: £12.
Society meetings: catered for on weekdays.
Catering: bar snacks and full meals served.
Hotels: Royal, Bray; Victor, Dun Laoghaire; Killiney Castle, Killiney.

BB74 **Woodenbridge**
☎ Arklow (0402) 5202
Woodenbridge, Avoca, Co Wicklow
50 miles S of Dublin on route N11 to Arklow; town club 4 miles from Arklow
Parkland course
9 holes, 6104 yards, S.S.S.68
Club founded in 1884.
Visitors: welcome on weekdays and most Sun.
Green fees: weekdays £6, Sun £8.
Society meetings: welcome on weekdays by arrangement.
Catering: lunches and evening meals available except Mon.
Hotels: Woodenbridge, Woodenbridge, Co Wicklow; Valley, Woodenbridge; Vale View, Avoca.

BB75 **Youghal**
☎ (024) 92787
Knockaverry, Youghal, Co Cork
Overlooking Youghal town and bay.
Meadowland course.
18 holes, 6206 yards, S.S.S.69
Course designed by Commander Harris.
Club founded in 1911.
Visitors: welcome.
Green fees: Men £5, Ladies £4.
Society meetings: welcome.
Catering: coffee and sandwiches available at present; new clubhouse under construction.
Hotels: Hilltop; Devonshire Arms.

The GOLF COURSE Guide TO THE BRITISH ISLES

INDEX

B

C

G

H

I

J

K

L

M

N

O

P

Q

R

S

T

U

V

W